MW00619413

TESTIMONIES

FOR

THE CHURCH

VOLUME ONE

Comprising Testimonies Numbers 1 to 14
With a Biographical Sketch of the Author

by

ELLEN G. WHITE

PACIFIC PRESS® PUBLISHING ASSOCIATION
Nampa, Idaho
Oshawa, Ontario, Canada

Printed in United States of America

01 02 03 04 05

PREFACE TO FOURTH EDITION

The many printing impressions necessary to meet the continual and ever-widening distribution of the *Testimonies for the Church* have worn out the printing plates. To meet the demand for these volumes so vital to the welfare of the church, it has been necessary to reset the type. This and succeeding printings will be made from the new plates.

The paging of this, the fourth edition, conforms to that of the preceding edition in use for so many years. The reader will welcome the Scripture Index and the enlarged General Index which appear in each volume. These have been expanded to harmonize with the general *Index to the Writings of Mrs. Ellen G. White*.

Many years have passed since these messages were penned. As a knowledge of the circumstances and issues often aid to a better understanding of the messages to the church, the reader will find in each volume a brief statement of the background of the times spanned by the volume. A few appendix notes will also be of service to the reader who may be unfamiliar with the circumstances which called for counsel from the Lord. These statements were prepared by the Trustees of the Ellen G. White Publications.

The messages in this new reset edition are reproduced without change or editing, except for such slight adjustments as were necessary to make the new printing conform to current forms of spelling, grammar, and punctuation. There have been no additions or deletions.

That the testimony counsels which have blessed, guided, and guarded the church may continue in this God-appointed service in this new edition is the sincere wish of the publishers and—

THE TRUSTEES OF THE
ELLEN G. WHITE PUBLICATIONS.

Washington, D. C.
May 1, 1947.

CONTENTS

TESTIMONY 4 (1857)

TESTIMONY 5 (1859)

TESTIMONY 6 (1861)

TESTIMONY 7 (1862)

TESTIMONY 13 (1867)

TESTIMONY 14 (1868)

THE BACKGROUND OF VOLUME ONE

The nine volumes of *Testimonies for the Church,* aggregating 4,738 pages of text, consist of articles and letters written by Ellen G. White, containing instruction to, and pertaining to the welfare of, the Seventh-day Adventist Church. A sixteen-page pamphlet, issued in December of 1855, marked the beginning of the series of such counsels which from time to time appeared in consecutively numbered pamphlets and books. These messages naturally dealt with issues that were current, but in most cases we are today confronted by the same same problems, perils, and opportunities which faced the church in earlier years.

The earliest numbered *Testimonies* were published only about seven years after the memorable "Sabbath conferences" of 1848, when Adventist believers in the newly revived Sabbath and sanctuary truths laid the foundations of the distinctive doctrines held by the Seventh-day Adventist denomination. During these few years the cause had advanced in a marked manner. At the beginning there were only three or four preachers, or "messengers" as they then styled themselves, all of them dependent upon what they earned by physical labor and the freewill offerings of the few believers, who also were poor in this world's goods. These beginnings were limited in area almost entirely to the New England States.

By 1855, the year of issuance of the first *Testimony* pamphlet, there were about a score of preachers of the Sabbath and advent message. The number of believers had grown from less than one hundred to well into the second thousand.

The publishing work, begun by Elder White in the summer of 1849 at Middletown, Connecticut, had been conducted in various places under adverse circumstances. Now in 1855 it was established in its own building in Battle Creek, Michigan.

The time covered by the first fourteen *Testimonies* now found in volume 1 was thirteen years. We note a few of the experiences and developments covered by the messages given during this period of 1855 to 1868.

The first defection, the apostasy and opposition of some of the former brethren in the ministry, known as the *Messenger* party because of their publication, the *Messenger of Truth,* brought sorrow and perplexity. Early counsels speak of this movement and predict its speedy ending in confusion.

Fanatical movements, tending to attract conscientious souls because of unfounded hope of "sanctification," appeared in various places, notably in some of the Eastern States and in Wisconsin. In some instances these teachings were accompanied by manifestation of the supposed "gift of tongues." But clear instruction was given to the church which saved the cause from such deceptions of the enemy.

The lapse of time and the apparent delay of the second advent, with the accession to the church of many who had not been in the 1844 movement, with its deep spiritual consecration, had resulted in the loss of that first love. It was a time of speculation in lands and homesteads as the Western States were opening up to settlers, among whom were a number of believers from the crowded Eastern States. Most earnest warnings and appeals were given regarding the prevailing dangers of conformity to the world, calling the church to deeper consecration.

In the latter part of 1856 attention was called to the "Laodicean" message of Revelation 3. Formerly this counsel was understood to apply to the advent believers who had not followed in the advancing light of the third angel and who had organized themselves into another church, bitterly opposing the Sabbath truth. Now they saw themselves as "lukewarm" and in need of heeding the counsel of the True Witness. For two years or more the believers were mightily stirred by this message, expecting that it would lead them directly into the loud cry of the third angel. The earnest messages in the *Testimonies* relating to this movement can better be understood with a knowledge of this background.

It was an age of discussion and debates. Many of our ministers were challenged to discuss the Sabbath and other truths, and some were even taking the aggressive in such debates. This called for counsel from heaven. One of our prominent ministers, Moses Hull, engaged in debates with spiritualists, at first at their challenge, later at his. As a result of this daring move he was swept into the mazes of spiritualism. Then it was that Mrs. White published her "Communications to Elder Hull," making public letters that had been written to him during past years that if heeded would have saved him from making shipwreck of his faith.

Those were the years when steps were being taken in organization. Against this move were the fears of some who had passed through the experiences of the second angel's message, that church organization was a mark of "Babylon." The issues of organization as they were met and discussed among the brethren are manifest in many of the communications given to the church through Mrs. White. And when in 1860 the publishing work was organized, and when, after much discussion and some questions, the name Seventh-day Adventist was adopted, the move and the name itself were shown to be in harmony with the divine will.

Immediately following the final steps in church order marked by the organization of the General Conference in May, 1863, came the memorable vision in Otsego in June, when Mrs. White was given a view of the principles of what was termed "health reform," with a revelation of the relation between obedience to the laws of health and the attainment of character necessary to fit the members of the church for translation. Closely associated with this was a reform in dress.

Two years later, counsel was given that "we should have a health home of our own," which led to the establishment of the Health Reform Institute, to which and regarding which much counsel was given. As the light was followed, this institution grew until it was one of the best of its kind in the world. During the period covered in this volume, the governing principles which led to its success were clearly laid down. The problems of the Civil War were also met in this period as Seventh-day Adventists faced the necessity of defining their relationship to civil government in time of war.

The importance of the home in the building of Christian character, and the responsibility of parents, were stressed, and many solemn messages, imparted especially for the youth, were also given emphasis in these pages.

Besides the specific issues that were closely tied into the movements of the time, there was much counsel and admonition of a general nature on church discipline and preparation for translation. This was an important period in the development of the remnant church, and the *Testimony* counsels exerted a large molding influence.

THE TRUSTEES OF THE
ELLEN G. WHITE PUBLICATIONS.

BIOGRAPHICAL SKETCH

CHAPTER I

MY CHILDHOOD

I was born at Gorham, Maine, November 26, 1827. My parents, Robert and Eunice Harmon, were for many years residents of this state. In early life they became earnest and devoted members of the Methodist Episcopal Church. In that church they held prominent connection, and labored for the conversion of sinners, and to build up the cause of God, for a period of forty years. During this time they had the joy of seeing their children, eight in number, all converted and gathered into the fold of Christ. Their decided second advent views, however, led to the separation of the family from the Methodist Church in the year 1843.

While I was but a child, my parents removed from Gorham to Portland, Maine. Here, at the age of nine years, an accident happened to me which was to affect my whole life. In company with my twin sister and one of our schoolmates, I was crossing a common in the city of Portland, when a girl about thirteen years of age, becoming angry at some trifle, followed us, threatening to strike us. Our parents had taught us never to contend with anyone, but if we were in danger of being abused or injured, to hasten home at once. We were doing this with all speed, but the girl followed us as rapidly, with a stone in her hand. I turned my head to see how far she was behind me, and as I did so, she threw the stone, and it hit me on the nose. I was stunned by the blow and fell senseless to the ground.

When consciousness returned, I found myself in a merchant's store; my garments were covered with blood, which was pouring from my nose and streaming over the floor. A kind stranger offered to take me home in his carriage, but I, not realizing my weakness, told him that I preferred to walk home rather than soil his carriage with blood. Those present were not aware that my injury was so serious, and allowed me to do as I wished; but after walking only a few rods, I grew faint and dizzy. My twin sister and my schoolmate carried me home.

I have no recollection of anything further for some time after the accident. My mother said that I noticed nothing, but lay in a stupor for three weeks. No one but herself thought it possible for me to recover; but for some reason she felt that I would live. A kind neighbor, who had been very much interested in my behalf, at one time thought me to be dying. She wished to purchase a burial robe for me, but my mother said, Not yet; for something told her that I would not die.

When I again aroused to consciousness, it seemed to me that I had been asleep. I did not remember the accident, and was ignorant of the cause of my illness. As I began to gain a little strength, my curiosity was aroused by overhearing those who came to visit me say: "What a pity!" "I should not have known her," etc. I asked for a looking glass, and upon gazing into it, was shocked at the change in my appearance. Every feature of my face seemed changed. The bones of my nose had been broken, which caused this disfigurement.

The thought of carrying my misfortune through life was insupportable. I could see no pleasure in my existence. I did not wish to live, and yet feared to die, for I was unprepared. Friends who visited us looked with pity upon me, and advised my parents to prosecute the father of the girl who had, as they said, ruined me. But my mother was for peace; she said that if such a course would bring me back my health and natural looks, there would be something gained; but as this was impossible, it was best not to make enemies by following such advice.

Physicians thought that a silver wire might be put in my nose to hold it in shape. This would have been very painful, and they feared it would be of little use, as I had lost so much blood and sustained such a nervous shock, that my recovery was very doubtful. Even if I revived, it was their opinion that I could live but a short time. I was reduced almost to a skeleton.

At this time I began to pray the Lord to prepare me for death. When Christian friends visited the family, they would ask my mother if she had talked to me about dying. I overheard this, and it roused me. I desired to become a Christian, and prayed earnestly for the forgiveness of my sins. I felt a peace of mind resulting, and loved everyone, feeling desirous that all should have their sins forgiven and love Jesus as I did.

I well remember one night in winter when the snow was on the ground, the heavens were lighted up, the sky looked red and angry, and seemed to open and shut, while the snow looked like blood. The neighbors were very much frightened. Mother took me out of bed in her arms and carried me to the window. I was happy; I thought Jesus was coming, and I longed to see Him. My heart was full; I clapped my hands for joy, and thought my sufferings were ended. But I was disappointed; the singular appearance faded away from the heavens, and the next morning the sun rose the same as usual.

I gained strength very slowly. As I became able to join in play with my young friends, I was forced to learn the bitter lesson that our personal appearance often makes a difference in the treatment we receive from our companions. At the time of my misfortune my father was absent in Georgia. When he returned, he embraced my brother and sisters, and then inquired for me. I, timidly shrinking back, was pointed out by my mother, but my own father did not recognize me. It was hard for him to believe that I was his little Ellen, whom he had left only a few months before a healthy, happy child. This cut my feelings deeply, but I tried to appear cheerful, though my heart seemed breaking.

Many times in those childhood days I was made to feel my misfortune keenly. My feelings were unusually sensitive and caused me great unhappiness. Often with wounded pride, mortified and wretched in spirit, I sought a lonely place and gloomily pondered over the trials I was doomed daily to bear.

The relief of tears was denied me. I could not weep readily, as could my twin sister; though my heart was heavy, and ached as if it were breaking, I could not shed a tear. I often felt that it would greatly relieve me to weep away my sorrow. Sometimes the kindly sympathy of friends banished my gloom and removed, for a time, the leaden weight that oppressed my heart. How vain and empty seemed the pleasures of earth to me then! how changeable the friendships of my young companions! Yet these little schoolmates were not unlike a majority of the great world's people. A pretty face, a handsome dress, attracts them; but let misfortune take these away, and the fragile friendship grows cold or is broken. But when I turned to my Saviour, He comforted me. I sought the Lord earnestly in my trouble, and received consolation. I felt assured that Jesus loved even me.

My health seemed to be hopelessly impaired. For two years I could not breathe through my nose, and was able to attend school but little. It seemed impossible for me to study and to retain what I learned. The same girl who was the cause of my misfortune was appointed monitor by our teacher, and it was among her duties to assist me in my writing and other lessons. She always seemed sincerely sorry for the great injury she had done me, although I was careful not to remind her of it. She was tender and patient with me, and seemed sad and thoughtful as she saw me laboring under serious disadvantages to get an education.

My nervous system was prostrated, and my hand trembled so that I made but little progress in writing, and could get no further than the simple copies in coarse hand. As I endeavored to bend my mind to my studies, the letters on the page would run together, great drops of perspiration would stand upon my brow, and a faintness and dizziness would seize me. I had a bad cough, and my whole system seemed debilitated. My teachers advised me to leave school and not pursue my studies further till my health should improve. It was the hardest struggle of my young life to yield to my feebleness and decide that I must leave my studies and give up the hope of gaining an education.

Three years later I made another trial to obtain an education. But when I attempted to resume my studies, my health rapidly failed, and it became apparent that if I remained in school, it would be at the expense of my life. I did not attend school after I was twelve years old.

My ambition to become a scholar had been very great, and when I pondered over my disappointed hopes, and the thought that I was to be an invalid for life, I was unreconciled to my lot and at times murmured against the providence of God in thus afflicting me. Had I opened my mind to my mother, she might have instructed, soothed, and encouraged me; but I concealed my troubled feelings from my family and friends, fearing that they could not understand me. The happy confidence in my Saviour's love that I had enjoyed during my illness was gone. My prospect of worldly enjoyment was blighted, and heaven seemed closed against me.

CHAPTER II

MY CONVERSION

In March, 1840, William Miller visited Portland, Maine, and gave his first course of lectures on the second coming of Christ. These lectures produced a great sensation, and the Christian church on Casco Street, occupied by Mr. Miller, was crowded day and night. No wild excitement attended these meetings, but a deep solemnity pervaded the minds of those who heard his discourses. Not only was there manifested a great interest in the city, but the country people flocked in day after day, bringing their lunch baskets, and remaining from morning until the close of the evening meeting.

In company with my friends I attended these meetings and listened to the startling announcement that Christ was coming in 1843, only a few short years in the future. Mr. Miller traced down the prophecies with an exactness that struck conviction to the hearts of his hearers. He dwelt upon the prophetic periods, and brought many proofs to strengthen his position. Then his solemn and powerful appeals and admonitions to those who were unprepared, held the crowds as if spellbound.

Special meetings were appointed where sinners might have an opportunity to seek their Saviour and prepare for the fearful events soon to take place. Terror and conviction spread through the entire city. Prayer meetings were established, and there was a general awakening among the various denominations, for they all felt more or less the influence that proceeded from the teaching of the near coming of Christ.

When sinners were invited forward to the anxious seat, hundreds responded to the call, and I, among the rest, pressed through the crowd and took my place with the seekers. But there was in my heart a feeling that I could never become worthy to be called a child of God. A lack of confidence in myself, and a conviction that it would be impossible to make anyone understand my feelings, prevented me from seeking advice and aid from my Christian friends. Thus I wandered needlessly in darkness and despair, while they, not penetrating my reserve, were entirely ignorant of my true state.

One evening my brother Robert and myself were returning home from a meeting where we had listened to a most impressive discourse on the approaching reign of Christ upon the earth, followed by an earnest and solemn appeal to Christians and sinners, urging them to prepare for the judgment and the coming of the Lord. My soul had been stirred within me by what I had heard. And so deep was the sense of conviction in my heart, that I feared the Lord would not spare me to reach home.

These words kept ringing in my ears: "The great day of the Lord is at hand! Who shall be able to stand when He appeareth!" The language of my heart was: "Spare me, O Lord, through the night! Take me not away in my sins, pity me, save me!" For the first time I tried to explain my feelings to my brother Robert, who was two years older than myself; I told him that I dared not rest nor sleep until I knew that God had pardoned my sins.

My brother made no immediate reply, but the cause of his silence was soon apparent to me; he was weeping in sympathy with my distress. This encouraged me to confide in him still more, to tell him that I had coveted death in the days when life seemed so heavy a burden for me to bear; but now the thought that I might die in my present sinful state and be eternally lost, filled me with terror. I asked him if he thought God would spare my life through that one night, if I spent it agonizing in prayer to Him. He answered: "I think He will if you ask Him with faith, and I will pray for you and for myself. Ellen, we must never forget the words we have heard this night."

Arriving at home, I spent most of the long hours of darkness in prayer and tears. One reason that led me to conceal my feelings from my friends was the dread of hearing a word of discouragement. My hope was so small, and my faith so weak, that I feared if another took a similar view of my condition, it would plunge me into despair. Yet I longed for someone to tell me what I should do to be saved, what steps to take to meet my Saviour and give myself entirely up to the Lord. I regarded it a great thing to be a Christian, and felt that it required some peculiar effort on my part.

My mind remained in this condition for months. I had usually attended the Methodist meetings with my parents; but since becoming interested in the soon appearing of Christ, I had attended the meetings on Casco Street. The following summer my parents went to the Methodist camp meeting at Buxton, Maine, taking me with them. I was fully resolved to seek the Lord in earnest there, and obtain, if possible, the pardon of my sins. There was a great longing in my heart for the Christian's hope and the peace that comes of believing.

I was much encouraged while listening to a discourse from the words, I will "go in unto the king," "and if I perish, I perish." In his remarks the speaker referred to those who were wavering between hope and fear, longing to be saved from their sins and receive the pardoning love of Christ, yet held in doubt and bondage by timidity and fear of failure. He counseled such ones to surrender themselves to God, and venture upon His mercy without delay. They would find a gracious Saviour ready to present to them the scepter of mercy, even as Ahasuerus offered to Esther the signal of his favor. All that was required of the sinner, trembling in the presence of his Lord, was to put forth the hand of faith and touch the scepter of His grace. That touch ensured pardon and peace.

Those who were waiting to make themselves more worthy

of divine favor before they venture to claim the promises of God, were making a fatal mistake. Jesus alone cleanses from sin; He only can forgive our transgressions. He has pledged Himself to listen to the petition and grant the prayer of those who come to Him in faith. Many had a vague idea that they must make some wonderful effort in order to gain the favor of God. But all self-dependence is vain. It is only by connecting with Jesus through faith that the sinner becomes a hopeful, believing child of God. These words comforted me and gave me a view of what I must do to be saved.

I now began to see my way more clearly, and the darkness began to pass away. I earnestly sought the pardon of my sins, and strove to give myself entirely to the Lord. But my mind was often in great distress because I did not experience the spiritual ecstasy that I considered would be the evidence of my acceptance with God, and I dared not believe myself converted without it. How much I needed instruction concerning the simplicity of it!

While bowed at the altar with others who were seeking the Lord, all the language of my heart was: "Help, Jesus, save me or I perish! I will never cease to entreat till my prayer is heard and my sins forgiven!" I felt my needy, helpless condition as never before. As I knelt and prayed, suddenly my burden left me, and my heart was light. At first a feeling of alarm came over me, and I tried to resume my load of distress. It seemed to me that I had no right to feel joyous and happy. But Jesus seemed very near to me; I felt able to come to Him with all my griefs, misfortunes, and trials, even as the needy ones came to Him for relief when He was upon earth. There was a surety in my heart that He understood my peculiar trials and sympathized with me. I can never forget this precious assurance of the pitying tenderness of Jesus toward one so unworthy of His notice. I learned more of the divine character of Christ in that short period when bowed among the praying ones than ever before.

One of the mothers in Israel came to me and said: "Dear child, have you found Jesus?" I was about to answer, "Yes," when she exclaimed: "Indeed you have, His peace is with you, I see it in your face!" Again and again I said to myself: "Can this be religion? Am I not mistaken?" It seemed too much for me to claim, too exalted a privilege. Though too timid to openly confess it, I felt that the Saviour had blessed me and pardoned my sins.

Soon after this the meeting closed, and we started for home. My mind was full of the sermons, exhortations, and prayers we had heard. Everything in nature seemed changed. During the meeting, clouds and rain prevailed a greater part of the time, and my feelings had been in harmony with the weather. Now the sun shone bright and clear, and flooded the earth with light and warmth. The trees and grass were a fresher green, the sky a deeper blue. The earth seemed to smile under the peace of God. So the rays of the Sun of Righteousness had penetrated the clouds and darkness of my mind, and dispelled its gloom.

It seemed to me that everyone must be at peace with God and animated by His Spirit. Everything that my eyes rested upon seemed to have undergone a change. The trees were more beautiful and the birds sang more sweetly than ever before; they seemed to be praising the Creator in their songs. I did not care to talk, for fear this happiness might pass away, and I should lose the precious evidence of Jesus' love for me.

As we neared our home in Portland, we passed men at work upon the street. They were conversing with one another upon ordinary topics, but my ears were deaf to everything but the praise of God, and their words came to me as grateful thanks and glad hosannas. Turning to my mother, I said: "Why, these men are all praising God, and *they* haven't been to the camp meeting." I did not then understand why the tears gathered in my mother's eyes, and a tender smile lit up her face, as she listened to my simple words that recalled a similar experience of her own.

My mother was a lover of flowers and took much pleasure in cultivating them and thus making her home attractive and pleasant for her children. But our garden had never before looked so lovely to me as upon the day of our return. I recognized an expression of the love of Jesus in every shrub, bud, and flower. These things of beauty seemed to speak in mute language of the love of God.

There was a beautiful pink flower in the garden called the rose of Sharon. I remember approaching it and touching the delicate petals reverently; they seemed to possess a sacredness in my eyes. My heart overflowed with tenderness and love for these beautiful creations of God. I could see divine perfection in the flowers that adorned the earth. God tended them, and His all-seeing eye was upon them. He had made them and called them good.

"Ah," thought I, "if He so loves and cares for the flowers that He has decked with beauty, how much more tenderly will He guard the children who are formed in His image." I repeated softly to myself: "I am a child of God, His loving care is around me. I will be obedient and in no way displease Him, but will praise His dear name and love Him always."

My life appeared to me in a different light. The affliction that had darkened my childhood seemed to have been dealt me in mercy for my good, to turn my heart away from the world and its unsatisfying pleasures, and incline it toward the enduring attractions of heaven.

Soon after our return from the camp meeting, I, with several others, was taken into the church on probation. My mind was very much exercised on the subject of baptism. Young as I was, I could see but one mode of baptism authorized by the Scriptures, and that was immersion. Some of my Methodist sisters tried in vain to convince me that sprinkling was Bible baptism. The Methodist minister consented to immerse the candidates if they conscientiously preferred that method, although he intimated that sprinkling would be equally acceptable with God.

Finally the time was appointed for us to receive this solemn ordinance. It was a windy day when we, twelve in number, went down into the sea to be baptized. The waves ran high and dashed upon the shore; but as I took up this heavy cross, my peace was like a river. When I arose from the water, my strength was nearly gone, for the power of the Lord rested upon me. I felt that henceforth I was not of this world, but had risen from the watery grave into a newness of life.

The same day in the afternoon I was received into the church in full membership. A young woman stood by my side who was also a candidate for admission to the church. My mind was peaceful and happy till I noticed the gold rings glittering upon this sister's fingers, and the large, showy earrings in her ears. I then observed that her bonnet was adorned with artificial flowers, and trimmed with costly ribbons arranged in bows and puffs. My joy was dampened by this display of vanity in one who professed to be a follower of the meek and lowly Jesus.

I expected that the minister would give some whispered reproof or advice to this sister; but he was apparently regardless of her showy apparel, and no rebuke was administered. We both received the right hand of fellowship. The hand decorated with jewels was clasped by the representative of Christ, and both our names were registered upon the church book.

This circumstance caused me no little perplexity and trial as I remembered the apostle's words: "In like manner also, that women adorn themselves in modest apparel, with shamefacedness and sobriety; not with broided hair, or gold, or pearls, or costly array; but (which becometh women professing godliness) with good works." The teaching of this scripture seemed to be openly disregarded by those whom I looked upon as devoted Christians, and who were much older in experience than myself. If it was indeed as sinful as I supposed, to imitate the extravagant dress of worldlings, surely these Christians would understand it and would conform to the Bible standard. Yet for myself I determined to follow my convictions of duty. I could but feel that it was contrary to the spirit of the gospel to devote God-given time and means to the decoration of our persons—that humility and self-denial would be more befitting those whose sins had cost the infinite sacrifice of the Son of God.

CHAPTER III

FEELINGS OF DESPAIR

In June, 1842, Mr. Miller gave his second course of lectures in Portland. I felt it a great privilege to attend these lectures, for I had fallen under discouragements and did not feel prepared to meet my Saviour. This second course created much more excitement in the city than the first. With few exceptions the different denominations closed the doors of their churches against Mr. Miller. Many discourses from the various pulpits sought to expose the alleged fanatical errors of the lecturer; but crowds of anxious listeners attended his meetings, while many were unable to enter the house.

The congregations were unusually quiet and attentive. His manner of preaching was not flowery or oratorical, but he dealt in plain and startling facts that roused his hearers from their careless indifference. He supported his statements and theories by Scripture proof as he progressed. A convincing power attended his words that seemed to stamp them as the language of truth.

He was courteous and sympathetic. When every seat in

the house was full, and the platform and places about the pulpit seemed crowded, I have seen him leave the desk and walk down the aisle, and take some feeble old man or woman by the hand and find a seat for them, then return and resume his discourse. He was indeed rightly called Father Miller, for he had a watchful care over those who came under his ministrations, was affectionate in his manner, of a genial disposition and tender heart.

He was an interesting speaker, and his exhortations, both to professed Christians and the impenitent, were appropriate and powerful. Sometimes a solemnity so marked as to be painful, pervaded his meetings. Many yielded to the conviction of the Spirit of God. Gray-haired men and aged women with trembling steps sought the anxious seats. Those in the strength of maturity, the youth and children, were deeply stirred. Groans and the voice of weeping and of praise to God were mingled at the altar of prayer.

I believed the solemn words spoken by the servant of God, and my heart was pained when they were opposed or made the subject of jest. I frequently attended the meetings, and believed that Jesus was soon to come in the clouds of heaven; but my great anxiety was to be ready to meet Him. My mind constantly dwelt upon the subject of holiness of heart. I longed above all things to obtain this great blessing and feel that I was entirely accepted of God.

Among the Methodists I had heard much in regard to sanctification. I had seen persons lose their physical strength under the influence of strong mental excitement, and had heard this pronounced the evidence of sanctification. But I could not comprehend what was necessary in order to be fully consecrated to God. My Christian friends said to me: "Believe in Jesus *now!* Believe that He accepts you *now!*" This I tried to do, but found it impossible to believe that I had received a blessing which, it seemed to me, should electrify my whole being. I wondered at my own hardness of heart in being unable to experience the exaltation of spirit that others manifested. It seemed to me that I was different from them and forever shut out from the perfect joy of holiness of heart.

My ideas concerning justification and sanctification were confused. These two states were presented to my mind as separate and distinct from each other; yet I failed to comprehend the difference or understand the meaning of the terms, and all the explanations of the preachers increased my difficulties. I was unable to claim the blessing for myself, and wondered if it was to be found only among the Methodists, and if, in attending the advent meetings, I was not shutting myself away from that which I desired above all else, the sanctifying Spirit of God.

Still, I observed that some of those who claimed to be sanctified, manifested a bitter spirit when the subject of the soon coming of Christ was introduced; this did not seem to me a manifestation of the holiness which they professed. I could not understand why ministers from the pulpit should so oppose the doctrine that Christ's second coming was near. Reformation had followed the preaching of this belief, and many of the most devoted ministers and laymen had received it as the truth. It seemed to me that those who sincerely loved Jesus would be ready to accept the tidings of His coming and rejoice that it was at hand.

I felt that I could claim only what they called justification. In the word of God I read that without holiness no man should see God. Then there was some higher attainment that I must reach before I could be sure of eternal life. I studied over the subject continually; for I believed that Christ was soon to come, and feared He would find me unprepared to meet Him. Words of condemnation rang in my ears day and night, and my constant cry to God was, What shall I do to to be saved?

In my mind the justice of God eclipsed His mercy and

love. I had been taught to believe in an eternally burning hell and the horrifying thought was ever before me that my sins were too great to be forgiven, and that I should be forever lost. The frightful descriptions that I had heard of souls in perdition sank deep into my mind. Ministers in the pulpit drew vivid pictures of the condition of the lost. They taught that God proposed to save none but the sanctified. The eye of God was upon us always; every sin was registered and would meet its just punishment. God Himself was keeping the books with the exactness of infinite wisdom, and every sin we commited was faithfully recorded against us.

Satan was represented as eager to seize upon his prey and bear us to the lowest depths of anguish, there to exult over our sufferings in the horrors of an eternally burning hell, where, after the tortures of thousands upon thousands of years, the fiery billows would roll to the surface the writhing victims, who would shriek: "How long, O Lord, how long?" Then the answer would thunder down the abyss: "Through all eternity!" Again the molten waves would engulf the lost, carrying them down into the depths of an ever-restless sea of fire.

While listening to these terrible descriptions, my imagination would be so wrought upon that the perspiration would start, and it was difficult to suppress a cry of anguish, for I seemed to already feel the pains of perdition. Then the minister would dwell upon the uncertainty of life. One moment we might be here, and the next in hell, or one moment on earth, and the next in heaven. Would we choose the lake of fire and the company of demons, or the bliss of heaven with angels for our companions? Would we hear the voice of wailing and the cursing of lost souls through all eternity, or sing the songs of Jesus before the throne?

Our heavenly Father was presented before my mind as a tyrant, who delighted in the agonies of the condemned; not the tender, pitying Friend of sinners, who loves His creatures with a love past all understanding and desires them to be saved in His kingdom.

My feelings were very sensitive. I dreaded giving pain to any living creature. When I saw animals ill-treated, my heart ached for them. Perhaps my sympathies were more easily excited by suffering because I myself had been the victim of thoughtless cruelty, resulting in the injury that had darkened my childhood. But when the thought took possession of my mind that God delighted in the torture of His creatures, who were formed in His image, a wall of darkness seemed to separate me from Him. When I reflected that the Creator of the universe would plunge the wicked into hell, there to burn through the ceaseless rounds of eternity, my heart sank with fear, and I despaired that so cruel and tyrannical a being would ever condescend to save me from the doom of sin.

I thought that the fate of the condemned sinner would be mine, to endure the flames of hell forever, even as long as God Himself existed. This impression deepened upon my mind until I feared that I would lose my reason. I would look upon the dumb beasts with envy, because they had no soul to be punished after death. Many times the wish arose that I had never been born.

Total darkness settled upon me, and there seemed no way out of the shadows. Could the truth have been presented to me as I now understand it, much perplexity and sorrow would have been spared me. If the love of God had been dwelt upon more, and His stern justice less, the beauty and glory of His character would have inspired me with a deep and earnest love for my Creator.

I have since thought that many inmates of insane asylums were brought there by experiences similar to my own. Their consciences were stricken with a sense of sin, and their trembling faith dared not claim the promised pardon of God. They listened to descriptions of the orthodox hell until it seemed to curdle the very blood in their veins, and burned an impression upon the tablets of their memory. Waking or sleeping, the frightful picture was ever before them, until reality became lost in imagination, and they saw only the wreathing flames of a fabulous hell, and heard only the shrieking of the doomed. Reason became dethroned, and the brain was filled with the wild phantasy of a terrible dream. Those who teach the doctrine of an eternal hell would do well to look more closely after their authority for so cruel a belief.

I had never prayed in public and had only spoken a few timid words in prayer meeting. It was now impressed upon me that I should seek God in prayer at our small social meetings. This I dared not do, fearful of becoming confused and failing to express my thoughts. But the duty was impressed upon my mind so forcibly that when I attempted to pray in secret I seemed to be mocking God because I had failed to obey His will. Despair overwhelmed me, and for three long weeks no ray of light pierced the gloom that encompassed me.

My sufferings of mind were intense. Sometimes for a whole night I would not dare to close my eyes, but would wait until my twin sister was fast asleep, then quietly leave my bed and kneel upon the floor, praying silently with a dumb agony that cannot be described. The horrors of an eternally burning hell were ever before me. I knew that it was impossible for me to live long in this state, and I dared not die and meet the terrible fate of the sinner. With what envy did I regard those who realized their acceptance with God! How precious did the Christian's hope seem to my agonized soul!

I frequently remained bowed in prayer nearly all night, groaning and trembling with inexpressible anguish and a hopelessness that passes all description. Lord, have mercy! was my plea, and, like the poor publican, I dared not lift my eyes to heaven, but bowed my face upon the floor. I became very much reduced in flesh and strength, yet kept my suffering and despair to myself.

While in this state of despondency I had a dream that made a deep impression upon my mind. I dreamed of seeing a temple, to which many persons were flocking. Only those who took refuge in that temple would be saved when time should close. All who remained outside would be forever lost. The multitudes without who were going about their various ways, derided and ridiculed those who were entering the temple, and told them that this plan of safety was a cunning deception, that in fact there was no danger whatever to avoid. They even laid hold of some to prevent them from hastening within the walls.

Fearing to be ridiculed, I thought best to wait until the multitude dispersed, or until I could enter unobserved by them. But the numbers increased instead of diminishing, and fearful of being too late, I hastily left my home and pressed through the crowd. In my anxiety to reach the temple I did not notice or care for the throng that surrounded me. On entering the building, I saw that the vast temple was supported by one immense pillar, and to this was tied a lamb all mangled and bleeding. We who were present seemed to know that this lamb had been torn and bruised on our account. All who entered the temple must come before it and confess their sins.

Just before the lamb were elevated seats, upon which sat a company looking very happy. The light of heaven seemed to shine upon their faces, and they praised God and sang songs of glad thanksgiving that seemed like the music of the angels. These were they who had come before the lamb, confessed their sins, received pardon, and were now waiting in glad expectation of some joyful event.

Even after I had entered the building, a fear came over me, and a sense of shame that I must humble myself before these people. But I seemed compelled to move forward, and was slowly making my way around the pillar in order to face the lamb, when a trumpet sounded, the temple shook, shouts of triumph arose from the assembled saints, an awful brightness illuminated the building, then all was intense darkness. The happy people had all disappeared with the brightness, and I was left alone in the silent horror of night. I awoke in agony of mind and could hardly convince myself that I had been dreaming. It seemed to me that my doom was fixed, that the Spirit of the Lord had left me, never to return.

Soon after this I had another dream. I seemed to be sitting in abject despair with my face in my hands, reflecting like this: If Jesus were upon earth, I would go to Him, throw myself at His feet, and tell Him all my sufferings. He would not turn away from me, He would have mercy upon me, and I would love and serve Him always. Just then the door opened, and a person of beautiful form and countenance entered. He looked upon me pitifully and said: "Do you wish to see Jesus? He is here, and you can see Him if you desire it. Take everything you possess and follow me."

I heard this with unspeakable joy, and gladly gathered up all my little possessions, every treasured trinket, and followed my guide. He led me to a steep and apparently frail stairway. As I commenced to ascend the steps, he cautioned me to keep my eyes fixed upward, lest I should grow dizzy and fall. Many others who were climbing the steep ascent fell before gaining the top.

Finally we reached the last step, and stood before a door. Here my guide directed me to leave all the things that I had brought with me. I cheerfully laid them down; he then opened the door and bade me enter. In a moment I stood before Jesus. There was no mistaking that beautiful countenance. That expression of benevolence and majesty could belong to no other. As His gaze rested upon me, I knew at once that He was acquainted with every circumstance of my life and all my inner thoughts and feelings.

I tried to shield myself from His gaze, feeling unable to endure His searching eyes, but He drew near with a smile, and, laying His hand upon my head, said: "Fear not." The sound of His sweet voice thrilled my heart with a happiness it had never before experienced. I was too joyful to utter a word, but, overcome with emotion, sank prostrate at His feet. While I was lying helpless there, scenes of beauty and glory passed before me, and I seemed to have reached the safety and peace of heaven. At length my strength returned, and I arose. The loving eyes of Jesus were still upon me, and His smile filled my soul with gladness. His presence filled me with a holy reverence and an inexpressible love.

My guide now opened the door, and we both passed out. He bade me take up again all the things I had left without. This done, he handed me a green cord coiled up closely. This he directed me to place next my heart, and when I wished to see Jesus, take it from my bosom and stretch it to the utmost. He cautioned me not to let it remain coiled for any length of time, lest it should become knotted and difficult to straighten. I placed the cord near my heart and joyfully descended the narrow stairs, praising the Lord and telling all whom I met where they could find Jesus. This dream gave me hope. The green cord represented faith to my mind, and the beauty and simplicity of trusting in God began to dawn upon my soul.

I now confided all my sorrows and perplexities to my mother. She tenderly sympathized with and encouraged me, advising me to go for counsel to Elder Stockman, who then preached the advent doctrine in Portland. I had great confidence in him, for he was a devoted servant of Christ. Upon hearing my story, he placed his hand affectionately upon my head, saying with tears in his eyes: "Ellen, you are only a child. Yours is a most singular experience for one of your tender age. Jesus must be preparing you for some special work."

He then told me that even if I were a person of mature years and thus harassed by doubt and despair, he should tell me that he *knew* there was hope for me through the love of Jesus. The very agony of mind I had suffered was positive evidence that the Spirit of the Lord was striving with me. He said that when the sinner becomes hardened in guilt, he does not realize the enormity of his transgression, but flatters himself that he is about right and in no particular danger. The Spirit of the Lord leaves him, and he becomes careless and indifferent or recklessly defiant. This good man told me of the love of God for His erring children, that instead of rejoicing in their destruction, He longed to draw them to Himself in simple faith and trust. He dwelt upon the great love of Christ and the plan of redemption.

He spoke of my early misfortune and said it was indeed a grievous affliction, but he bade me believe that the hand of a loving Father had not been withdrawn from me; that in the future life, when the mist that then darkened my mind had vanished, I would discern the wisdom of the providence which had seemed so cruel and mysterious. Jesus said to His disciples: "What I do thou knowest not now; but thou shalt know hereafter." In the great future we should no longer see as through a glass darkly, but come face to face with the mysteries of divine love.

"Go free, Ellen," said he; "return to your home trusting in Jesus, for He will not withhold His love from any true seeker." He then prayed earnestly for me, and it seemed that God would certainly regard the prayer of His saint, even if my humble petitions were unheard. I left his presence comforted and encouraged.

During the few minutes in which I received instruction from Elder Stockman, I had obtained more knowledge on the subject of God's love and pitying tenderness than from all the sermons and exhortations to which I had ever listened. I returned home and again went before the Lord, promising to do and suffer anything He might require of me, if only the smiles of Jesus might cheer my heart. The same duty was presented to me that had troubled my mind before—to take up my cross among the assembled people of God. An opportunity was not long wanting; there was a prayer meeting that evening, which I attended.

I bowed trembling during the prayers that were offered. After a few had prayed, I lifted up my voice in prayer before I was aware of it. The promises of God appeared to me like so many precious pearls that were to be received only for the asking. As I prayed, the burden and agony of soul that I had so long endured left me, and the blessing of the Lord descended upon me like the gentle dew. I praised God from the depths of my heart. Everything seemed shut out from me but Jesus and His glory, and I lost consciousness of what was passing around me.

The Spirit of God rested upon me with such power that I was unable to go home that night. When I did return, on the following day, a great change had taken place in my mind. It seemed to me that I could hardly be the same person that left my father's house the previous evening. This passage was continually in my thoughts: "The Lord is my shepherd; I shall not want." My heart was full of happiness as I softly repeated these words.

My views of the Father were changed. I now looked upon Him as a kind and tender parent, rather than a stern tyrant compelling men to a blind obedience. My heart went out toward Him in a deep and fervent love. Obedience to His will seemed a joy; it was a pleasure to be in His service. No shadow clouded the light that revealed to me the perfect will of God. I felt the assurance of an indwelling Saviour, and realized the truth of what Christ had said: "He that followeth Me shall not walk in darkness, but shall have the light of life."

My peace and happiness was in such marked contrast with my former gloom and anguish that it seemed to me as if I had been rescued from hell and transported to heaven. I could even praise God for the misfortune that had been the trial of my life, for it had been the means of fixing my thoughts upon eternity. Naturally proud and ambitious, I might not have been inclined to give my heart to Jesus had it not been for the sore affliction that had cut me off, in a manner, from the triumphs and vanities of the world.

For six months not a shadow clouded my mind, nor did I neglect one known duty. My whole endeavor was to do the will of God and keep Jesus and heaven continually in mind. I was surprised and enraptured with the clear views now presented to me of the atonement and the work of Christ. I will not attempt to further explain the exercises of my mind; suffice it to say that old things had passed away, all things had become new. There was not a cloud to mar my perfect bliss. I longed to tell the story of Jesus' love, but felt no disposition to engage in common conversation with anyone. My heart was so filled with love to God and the peace that passeth understanding that I loved to meditate and to pray.

The night after receiving so great a blessing, I attended the advent meeting. When the time came for the followers of Christ to speak in His favor, I could not remain silent, but rose and related my experience. Not a thought had entered my mind of what I should say; but the simple story of Jesus' love to me fell from my lips with perfect freedom, and my heart was so happy to be liberated from its bondage of dark despair that I lost sight of the people about me and seemed to be alone with God. I found no difficulty in expressing my peace and happiness, except for the tears of gratitude that choked my utterance as I told of the wondrous love that Jesus had shown for me.

Elder Stockman was present. He had recently seen me in deep despair, and the remarkable change in my appearance and feelings touched his heart; he wept out of rejoicing with me and praising God for this proof of His tender mercy and loving-kindness.

Not long after receiving this great blessing, I attended a conference meeting at the Christian church, where Elder Brown was pastor. I was invited to relate my experience, and I felt not only great freedom of expression, but happiness, in telling my simple story of the love of Jesus and the joy of being accepted of God. As I spoke, with subdued heart and tearful eyes, my soul seemed drawn toward heaven in thanksgiving. The melting power of the Lord came upon the assembled people. Many were weeping and others praising God.

Sinners were invited to arise for prayers, and many responded to the call. My heart was so thankful to God for the blessing He had given me that I longed to have others participate in this sacred joy. My mind was deeply interested for those who might be suffering under a sense of the Lord's displeasure and the burden of sin. While relating my experience, I felt that no one could resist the evidence of God's pardoning love that had wrought so wonderful a change in me. The reality of true conversion seemed so plain to me that I felt like helping my young friends into the light, and at every opportunity exerted my influence toward this end.

I arranged meetings with my young friends, some of whom were considerably older than myself, and a few were married persons. A number of them were vain and thoughtless; my experience sounded to them like an idle tale, and they did not heed my entreaties. But I determined that my efforts should never cease till these dear souls, for whom I had so great an interest, yielded to God. Several entire nights were spent by me in earnest prayer for those whom I had sought out and brought together for the purpose of laboring and praying with them.

Some of these had met with us from curiosity to hear what I had to say; others thought me beside myself to be so persistent in my efforts, especially when they manifested no concern on their own part. But at every one of our little meetings I continued to exhort and pray for each one separately, until every one had yielded to Jesus, acknowledging the merits of His pardoning love. Every one was converted to God.

Night after night in my dreams I seemed to be laboring for the salvation of souls. At such times special cases were presented to my mind; these I afterward sought out and prayed with. In every instance but one these persons yielded themselves to the Lord. Some of our more formal brethren feared that I was too zealous for the conversion of souls, but time seemed to me so short that it behooved all who had a hope of a blessed immortality and looked for the soon coming of Christ, to labor without ceasing for those who were still in their sins and standing on the awful brink of ruin.

Though I was very young, the plan of salvation was so clear to my mind, and my personal experience had been so marked, that, upon considering the matter, I knew it was my duty to continue my efforts for the salvation of precious souls and to pray and confess Christ at every opportunity. My entire being was offered to the service of my Master. Let come what would, I determined to please God, and live as one who expected the Saviour to come and reward the faithful. I felt like a little child coming to God as to my father, and asking Him what He would have me to do. Then as my duty was made plain to me, it was my greatest happiness to perform it. Peculiar trials sometimes beset me. Those older in experience than myself endeavored to hold me back and cool the ardor of my faith; but with the smiles of Jesus brightening my life, and the love of God in my heart, I went on my way with a joyful spirit.

As often as I recall the experience of my early life, my brother, the confidant of my hopes and fears, the earnest sympathizer with me in my Christian experience, comes to my mind with a flood of tender memories. He was one of those to whom sin presents but few temptations. Naturally devotional, he never sought the society of the young and gay, but chose rather the company of Christians whose conversation would instruct him in the way of life. His manner was serious beyond his years; he was gentle and peaceful, and his mind was almost constantly filled with religious thoughts. His life was pointed to, by those who knew him, as a pattern to the youth, a living example of the grace and beauty of true Christianity.

CHAPTER IV

LEAVING THE METHODIST CHURCH

My father's family still occasionally attended the Methodist church, and also the class meetings held in private houses. One evening my brother Robert and myself went to class meeting. The presiding elder was present. When it came my brother's turn, he spoke with great humility, yet with clearness, of the necessity for a complete fitness to meet our Saviour, when He should come in the clouds of heaven with power and great glory. While my brother was speaking, a heavenly light glowed upon his usually pale countenance. He seemed to be carried in spirit above present surroundings, and spoke as if in the presence of Jesus. When I was called upon to speak, I arose, free in spirit, with a heart full of love and peace. I told the story of my great suffering under the conviction of sin, how I had at length received the blessing so long sought, an entire conformity to the will of God, and expressed my joy in the tidings of the soon coming of my Redeemer to take His children home.

In my simplicity I expected that my Methodist brethren and sisters would understand my feelings and rejoice with me. But I was disappointed; several sisters groaned and moved their chairs noisily, turning their backs upon me. I could not think what had been said to offend them, and spoke very briefly, feeling the chilling influence of their disapprobation. When I had ceased speaking, Elder B. asked me if it would not be more pleasant to live a long life of usefulness, doing others good, than to have Jesus come speedily and destroy poor sinners. I replied that I longed for the coming of Jesus. Then sin would have an end, and we would enjoy sanctification forever, with no devil to tempt and lead us astray.

He then inquired if I would not rather die peacefully upon my bed than to pass through the pain of being changed, while living, from mortality to immortality. My answer was that I wished for Jesus to come and take His children; that I was willing to live or die as God willed, and could easily endure all the pain that could be borne in a moment, in the twinkling of an eye; that I desired the wheels of time to roll swiftly round, and bring the welcome day when these vile bodies should be changed, and fashioned like unto Christ's most glorious body. I also stated that when I lived nearest to the Lord, then I most earnestly longed for His appearing. Here some present seemed to be greatly displeased.

When the presiding elder addressed others in the class, he expressed great joy in anticipating the temporal millennium, when the earth should be filled with the knowledge of the Lord as the waters cover the sea. He longed to see this glorious period ushered in. After the meeting closed, I was conscious of being treated with marked coldness by those who had formerly been kind and friendly to me. My brother and I returned home feeling sad that we should be so misunderstood by our brethren, and that the subject of the near coming of Jesus should awaken such bitter opposition in their breasts. Yet we were thankful that we could discern the precious light and rejoice in looking for the coming of the Lord.

Not long after this we again attended the class meeting.

We wanted an opportunity to speak of the precious love of God that animated our souls. I particularly wished to tell of the Lord's goodness and mercy to me. So great a change had been wrought in me that it seemed my duty to improve every opportunity of testifying to the love of my Saviour.

When my turn came to speak, I stated the evidences I enjoyed of Jesus' love, and that I looked forward with the glad expectation of meeting my Redeemer soon. The belief that Christ's coming was near had stirred my soul to seek more earnestly for the sanctification of the Spirit of God. Here the class leader interrupted me, saying: "You received sanctification through Methodism, through *Methodism,* sister, not through an erroneous theory." I felt compelled to confess the truth, that it was not through Methodism that my heart had received its new blessing, but by the stirring truths concerning the personal appearing of Jesus. Through them I had found peace, joy, and perfect love. Thus my testimony closed, the last that I was to bear in class with my Methodist brethren.

Robert then spoke in his meek way, yet in so clear and touching a manner that some wept and were much moved; but others coughed dissentingly and seemed quite uneasy. After leaving the class room, we again talked over our faith, and marveled that our Christian brethren and sisters could so ill endure to have a word spoken in reference to our Saviour's coming. We thought if they loved Jesus as they should, it would not be so great an annoyance to hear of His second advent, but, on the contrary, they would hail the news with joy.

We were convinced that we ought no longer to attend the class meeting. The hope of the glorious appearing of Christ filled our souls and would find expression when we rose to speak. This seemed to kindle the ire of those present against the two humble children who dared, in the face of opposition, to speak of the faith that had filled their hearts with peace and happiness. It was evident that we could have no freedom in the class meeting, for our testimony provoked sneers and taunts that reached our ears at the close of the meeting, from brethren and sisters whom we had respected and loved.

The Adventists held meetings at this time in Beethoven Hall. My father, with his family, attended them quite regularly. The period of the second advent was thought to be in the year 1843. The time seemed so short in which souls could be saved that I resolved to do all that was in my power to lead sinners into the light of truth. But it seemed impossible for one so young, and in feeble health, to do much in the great work.

I had two sisters at home, Sarah, who was several years older, and my twin sister, Elizabeth. We talked the matter over among ourselves, and decided to earn what money we could, and spend it in buying books and tracts to be distributed gratuitously. This was the best we could do, and we did this little gladly. I could earn only twenty-five cents a day; but my dress was plain, nothing was spent for needless ornaments, for vain display appeared sinful in my eyes; so I had ever a little fund in store with which to purchase suitable books. These were placed in the hands of experienced persons to send abroad.

Every leaf of this printed matter seemed precious in my eyes, for it was as a messenger of light to the world, bidding them prepare for the great event near at hand. Day after day I sat in bed propped up with pillows, performing my allotted task with trembling fingers. How carefully would I lay aside the precious bits of silver taken in return, which were to be expended for reading matter to enlighten and arouse those who were in darkness. I had no temptation to spend my earnings for my own personal gratification; the salvation of souls was the burden of my mind, and my heart ached for those who flattered themselves that they were living in security, while the message of warning was being given to the world.

One day I listened to a conversation between my mother and a sister, in reference to a discourse which they had recently heard, to the effect that the soul had not natural immortality. Some of the minister's proof texts were repeated. Among them I remember these impressed me very forcibly: "The soul that sinneth, it shall die." "The living know that they shall die: but the dead know not anything." "Which in His times He shall show, who is the blessed and only Potentate, the King of kings, and Lord of lords; who *only* hath immortality." "To them who by patient continuance in well-doing seek for glory and honor and immortality, eternal life." "Why," said my mother, after quoting the foregoing passage, "should they seek for what they already have?"

I listened to these new ideas with an intense and painful interest. When alone with my mother, I inquired if she really believed that the soul was not immortal. Her reply was that she feared we had been in error on that subject as well as upon some others.

"But, mother," said I, "do you really believe that the soul sleeps in the grave until the resurrection? Do you think that the Christian, when he dies, does not go immediately to heaven, nor the sinner to hell?"

She answered: "The Bible gives us no proof that there is an eternally burning hell. If there is such a place, it should be mentioned in the Sacred Book."

"Why, mother!" cried I, in astonishment, "this is strange talk for you! If you believe this strange theory, do not let anyone know of it; for I fear that sinners would gather security from this belief, and never desire to seek the Lord."

"If this is sound Bible truth," she replied, "instead of preventing the salvation of sinners, it will be the means of winning them to Christ. If the love of God will not induce the rebel to yield, the terrors of an eternal hell will not drive him to repentance. Besides, it does not seem a proper way to win souls to Jesus, by appealing to one of the lowest attributes of the mind, abject fear. The love of Jesus attracts; it will subdue the hardest heart."

It was some months after this conversation before I heard anything further concerning this doctrine; but during this time my mind had been much exercised upon the subject. When I heard it preached, I believed it to be the truth. From the time that light in regard to the sleep of the dead dawned upon my mind, the mystery that had enshrouded the resurrection vanished, and the great event itself assumed a new and sublime importance. My mind had often been disturbed by its efforts to reconcile the immediate reward or punishment of the dead with the undoubted fact of a future resurrection and judgment. If at death the soul entered upon eternal happiness or misery, where was the need of a resurrection of the poor moldering body?

But this new and beautiful faith taught me the reason why inspired writers had dwelt so much upon the resurrection of the body; it was because the entire being was slumbering in the grave. I could now clearly perceive the fallacy of our former position on this question. The confusion and uselessness of a final judgment, after the souls of the departed had already been judged once and appointed to their lot, was very plain to me now. I saw that the hope of the bereaved is in looking forward to the glorious day when the Life-giver shall break the fetters of the tomb, and the righteous dead shall arise and leave their prison house to be clothed with glorious immortal life.

Our family were all interested in the doctrine of the Lord's soon coming. My father had long been considered one of the pillars of the Methodist church where he lived, and the whole family had been active members; but we made no secret of our new belief, although we did not urge it upon others on inappropriate occasions, or manifest any unfriendliness toward our church. However, the Methodist minister made us a special visit and took the occasion to inform us that our faith and Methodism could not agree. He did not inquire our reasons for believing as we did, nor make any reference to the Bible in order to convince us of our error; but he stated that we had adopted a new and strange belief that the Methodist Church could not accept.

My father replied that he must be mistaken in calling this a new and strange doctrine, that Christ Himself, in His teachings to His disciples, had preached His second advent. He had said: "In My Father's house are many mansions: if it were not so, I would have told you. I go to prepare a place for you. And if I go and prepare a place for you, I will come again, and receive you unto Myself; that where I am, there ye may be also." When He was taken up to heaven before their eyes and a cloud received Him out of their sight, as His faithful followers stood gazing after their vanishing Lord, "behold, two men stood by them in white apparel; which also said, Ye men of Galilee, why stand ye gazing up into heaven? this same Jesus, which is taken up from you into heaven, shall so come in like manner as ye have seen Him go into heaven."

"And," said my father, warming with his subject, "the inspired Paul wrote a letter to encourage his brethren in Thessalonica, saying: 'And to you who are troubled rest with us, when the Lord Jesus shall be revealed from heaven with His mighty angels, in flaming fire taking vengeance on them that know not God, and that obey not the gospel of our Lord Jesus Christ: who shall be punished with everlasting destruction from the presence of the Lord, and from the glory of His power; when He shall come to be glorified in His saints, and to be admired in all them that believe . . . in that day.' 'For the Lord Himself shall descend from heaven with a shout, with the voice of the Archangel, and with the trump of God: and the dead in Christ shall rise first: then we which are alive and remain shall be caught up together with them in the clouds, to meet the Lord in the air: and so shall we ever be with the Lord. Wherefore comfort one another with these words.'

"This is high authority for our faith. Jesus and His apostles dwell upon the event of the second advent with joy and triumph; and the holy angels proclaim that Christ, who ascended to heaven, shall come again. This is our offense, believing the word of Jesus and His disciples. This is a very old doctrine, and bears no taint of heresy."

The minister did not attempt to refer to a single text that would prove us in error, but excused himself on the plea of a want of time. He advised us to quietly withdraw from the church and avoid the publicity of a trial. We were aware that others of our brethren were meeting with similar treatment for a like cause, and we did not wish it understood that we were ashamed to acknowledge our faith, or were unable to sustain it by Scripture, so my parents insisted that they should be acquainted with the reasons for this request.

The only answer to this was an evasive declaration that we had walked contrary to the rules of the church, and the best course would be to voluntarily withdraw from it to save a trial. We answered that we preferred a regular trial, and demanded to know what sin was charged to us, as we were conscious of no wrong in looking for and loving the appearing of the Saviour.

Not long after, we were notified to be present at a meeting to be held in the vestry of the church. There were but few present. The influence of my father and his family was such that our opposers had no desire to present our case before a larger number of the congregation. The single charge preferred was that we had walked contrary to their rules. Upon our asking what rules we had violated, it was stated, after a little hesitation, that we had attended other meetings, and had neglected to meet regularly with our class. We stated that a portion of the family had been in the country for some time past, that none who remained in the city had been absent from class meeting more than a few weeks, and they were morally compelled to remain away because the testimonies they bore met with such marked disapprobation. We also reminded them that certain persons who had not attended class meeting for a year were yet held in good standing.

It was asked if we would confess that we had departed from their rules, and if we would also agree to conform to them in the future. We answered that we dared not yield our faith or deny the sacred truth of God; that we could not forego the hope of the soon coming of our Redeemer; that after the manner which they called heresy we must continue to worship the Lord. My father in his defense received the blessing of God, and we all left the vestry with free spirits, happy in the consciousness of right and the approving smile of Jesus.

The next Sunday, at the commencement of the love feast, the presiding elder read off our names, seven in number, as discontinued from the church. He stated that we were not expelled on account of any wrong or immoral conduct, that we were of unblemished character and enviable reputation but we had been guilty of walking contrary to the rules of the Methodist Church. He also declared that a door was now open, and all who were guilty of a similar breach of the rules would be dealt with in like manner.

There were many in the church who waited for the appearing of the Saviour, and this threat was made for the purpose of frightening them into subjection. In some cases this policy brought about the desired result, and the favor of God was sold for a place in the church. Many believed, but dared not confess their faith, lest they should be turned out of the synagogue. But some left soon afterward and joined the company of those who were looking for the Saviour.

At this time the words of the prophet were exceedingly

precious: "Your brethren that hated you, that cast you out for My name's sake, said, Let the Lord be glorified: but He shall appear to your joy, and they shall be ashamed."

CHAPTER V

OPPOSITION OF FORMAL BRETHREN

For six months not a cloud intervened between me and my Saviour. Whenever there was a proper opportunity, I bore my testimony, and was greatly blessed. At times the Spirit of the Lord rested upon me with such power that my strength was taken from me. This was a trial to some who had come out from the formal churches, and remarks were often made that grieved me much. Many could not believe that one could be so overpowered by the Spirit of God as to lose all strength. My position was exceedingly painful. I began to reason with myself whether I was not justified in withholding my testimony in meeting, and thus restraining my feelings, when there was such an opposition in the hearts of some who were older in years and experience than myself.

I adopted this plan of silence for a time, trying to convince myself that to repress my testimony would not hinder me from faithfully living out my religion. I often felt strongly impressed that it was my duty to speak in meeting, but refrained from doing so, and was sensible of having thereby grieved the Spirit of God. I even remained away from meetings sometimes because they were to be attended by those whom my testimony annoyed. I shrank from offending my brethren, and in this allowed the fear of man to break up that uninterrupted communion with God which had blessed my heart for so many months.

We had appointed evening prayer meetings in different localities of the city to accommodate all who wished to attend them. The family that had been most forward in opposing me attended one of these. Upon this occasion, while those assembled were engaged in prayer, the Spirit of the Lord came upon the meeting, and one of the members of this family was prostrated as one dead. His relatives stood weeping around him, rubbing his hands and applying restoratives. At length he gained sufficient strength to praise God, and quieted their tears by shouting with triumph over the marked evidence he had received of the power of the Lord upon him. The young man was unable to return home that night.

This was believed by the family to be a manifestation of the Spirit of God, but did not convince them that it was the same divine power that had rested upon me at times, robbing me of my natural strength and filling my soul with the peace and love of Jesus. They were free to say that my sincerity and perfect honesty could not be doubted, but they considered me self-deceived in taking that for the power of the Lord which was only the result of my own overwrought feelings.

My mind was in great perplexity in consequence of this opposition, and as the time drew near for our regular meeting, I was in doubt whether or not it was best for me to attend it. For some days previous I had been in great distress on account of the feeling manifested toward me. Finally I decided to remain at home, and thus escape the criticism of my brethren. In trying to pray I repeated these words again and again: "Lord, what wilt Thou have me to do?" The answer that came to my heart seemed to bid me trust in my heavenly Father and wait patiently to know His will. I yielded myself to the Lord with the simple trust of a little child, remembering He had promised that those who follow Him shall not walk in darkness.

A sense of duty impelled me to go to the meeting, and I went with the full assurance in my mind that all would be well. While we were bowed before the Lord, my heart was drawn out in prayer and filled with a peace that only Christ can give. My soul rejoiced in the love of the Saviour, and physical strength left me. With childlike faith I could only say: "Heaven is my home, and Christ my Redeemer."

One of the family before mentioned as being opposed to the manifestations of the power of God upon me, on this occasion stated his belief that I was under an excitement which he thought it my duty to resist, but instead of doing so, he thought I encouraged it as a mark of God's favor. His doubts and opposition did not affect me at this time, for I seemed shut in with the Lord, and lifted above all outward influence; but he had scarcely stopped speaking when a strong man, a devoted and humble Christian, was struck down before his eyes by the power of God, and the room was filled with the Holy Spirit.

Upon recovering, I was very happy in bearing my testimony for Jesus and in telling of His love for me. I confessed my lack of faith in the promises of God and my error in checking the promptings of His Spirit from fear of men, and acknowledged that, notwithstanding my distrust. He had bestowed upon me unlooked-for evidence of His love and sustaining grace. The brother who had opposed me then rose, and with tears confessed that his feelings in regard to me had been all wrong. He humbly asked my forgiveness, and said: "Sister Ellen, I will never again lay a straw in your way. God has shown me the coldness and stubbornness of my heart, which He has broken by the evidence of His power. I have been very wrong."

Then, turning to the people, he said: "When Sister Ellen seemed so happy, I would think, Why do I not feel like that? Why doesn't Brother R. receive some such evidence? for I was convinced that he was a devoted Christian, yet no such power had fallen upon him. I offered a silent prayer, that, if this was the holy influence of God, Brother R. might experience it this evening.

"Almost as the desire went up from my heart, Brother R.

fell, prostrated by the power of God, crying: 'Let the Lord work!' My heart is convinced that I have been warring against the Holy Spirit, but I will grieve it no more by stubborn unbelief. Welcome, light! Welcome, Jesus! I have been backslidden and hardened, feeling offended if anyone praised God and manifested a fullness of joy in His love; but now my feelings are changed, my opposition is at an end, Jesus has opened my eyes, and I may yet shout His praises myself. I have said bitter and cutting things of Sister Ellen that I sorrow over now, and I pray for her forgiveness and that of all others who are present."

Brother R. then bore his testimony. His face was lighted with the glory of heaven as he praised the Lord for the wonders He had wrought that night. Said he: "This place is awfully solemn because of the presence of the Most High. Sister Ellen, in future you will have our help and sustaining sympathies, instead of the cruel opposition that has been shown you. We have been blind to the manifestations of God's Holy Spirit."

All the opposers were now brought to see their mistake and to confess that the work was indeed of the Lord. In a prayer meeting soon after, the brother who had confessed that he was wrong in his opposition, experienced the power of God in so great a degree that his countenance shone with a heavenly light, and he fell helpless to the floor. When his strength returned, he again acknowledged that he had been ignorantly warring against the Spirit of the Lord in cherishing the feeling he had against me. In another prayer meeting still another member of the same family was exercised in a similar manner and bore the same testimony. A few weeks after, while the large family of Brother P. were engaged in prayer at their own house, the Spirit of God swept through the room and prostrated the kneeling suppliants. My father came in soon after, and found them all, both parents and children, helpless under the power of the Lord.

Cold formality began to melt before the mighty influence of the Most High. All who had opposed me confessed that they had grieved the Holy Spirit by so doing, and they united in sympathy with me and in love for the Saviour. My heart was glad that divine mercy had smoothed the path for my feet to tread, and rewarded my faith and trust so bounteously. Unity and peace now dwelt among our people who were looking for the coming of the Lord.

CHAPTER VI

ADVENT EXPERIENCE

With carefulness and trembling we approached the time* when our Saviour was expected to appear. With solemn earnestness we sought, as a people, to purify our lives that we might be ready to meet Him at His coming. Notwithstanding the opposition of ministers and churches, Beethoven Hall, in the city of Portland, was nightly crowded; especially was there a large congregation on Sundays. Elder Stockman was a man of deep piety. He was in feeble health; yet when he stood before the people he seemed to be lifted above physical infirmity, and his face was lighted with the consciousness that he was teaching the sacred truth of God.

There was a solemn, searching power in his words that struck home to many hearts. He sometimes expressed a fervent desire to live until he should welcome the Saviour coming in the clouds of heaven. Under his ministration the Spirit of God convicted many sinners and brought them into the fold of Christ. Meetings were still held at private houses in different parts of the city with the best results. Believers

*The year 1843, Jewish time, was believed to reach from March 21, 1843, to March 21, 1844. Those who received the advent faith looked for the coming of Christ during that year.

were encouraged to work for their friends and relatives, and conversions were multiplying day by day.

All classes flocked to the meetings at Beethoven Hall. Rich and poor, high and low, ministers and laymen, were all, from various causes, anxious to hear for themselves the doctrine of the second advent. Many came, who, finding no room to stand, went away disappointed. The order of the meetings was simple. A short and pointed discourse was usually given, then liberty was granted for general exhortation. There was, as a rule, the most perfect stillness possible for so large a crowd. The Lord held the spirit of opposition in check while His servants explained the reasons of their faith. Sometimes the instrument was feeble, but the Spirit of God gave weight and power to His truth. The presence of the holy angels was felt in the assembly, and numbers were daily added to the little band of believers.

On one occasion, while Elder Stockman was preaching, Elder Brown, a Christian Baptist minister, whose name has been mentioned before in this narrative, was sitting in the desk listening to the sermon with intense interest. He became deeply moved, and suddenly his countenance grew pale as the dead, he reeled in his chair, and Elder Stockman caught him in his arms just as he was falling to the floor and laid him on the sofa behind the desk, where he lay powerless until the discourse was finished.

He then arose, his face still pale, but shining with light from the Sun of Righteousness and gave a very impressive testimony. He seemed to receive holy unction from above. He was usually slow of speech, with an earnest manner, entirely free from excitement. On this occasion his solemn, measured words carried with them a new power as he warned sinners and his brother ministers to put away unbelief, prejudice, and cold formality, and, like the noble Bereans, search the sacred writings, comparing scripture with scripture, to ascertain if these things were not true. He entreated the ministers present not to feel themselves injured by the direct and searching manner in which Elder Stockman had presented the solemn subject that interested all minds.

Said he, "We want to reach the people; we want sinners to be convicted and become truly repentant before it is too late for them to be saved, lest they shall take up the lamentation, 'The harvest is past, the summer is ended, and we are not saved.' Brethren in the ministry say that our arrows hit them; will they please stand aside from between us and the people, and let us reach the hearts of sinners? If they make themselves a target for our aim, they have no reason to complain of the wounds they receive. Stand aside, brethren, and you will not get hit!"

He related his own experience with such simplicity and candor that many who had been greatly prejudiced were affected to tears. The Spirit of God was felt in his words and seen upon his countenance. With a holy exaltation he boldly declared that he had taken the word of God as his counselor, that his doubts had been swept away and his faith confirmed. With earnestness he invited his brother ministers, church members, sinners, and infidels to examine the Bible for themselves, and charged them to let no man turn them from the purpose of ascertaining what was the truth.

Elder Brown neither then nor afterward severed his connection with the Christian Baptist Church, but was looked upon with great respect by his people. When he had finished speaking, those who desired the prayers of the people of God were invited to rise. Hundreds responded to the call. The Holy Spirit rested upon the assembly. Heaven and earth seemed to approach each other. The meeting lasted until a late hour of the night. The power of the Lord was felt upon young, old, and middle-aged.

As we returned to our homes by various ways, a voice praising God would reach us from one direction, and, as if in response, voices from another and still another quarter shouted:

"Glory to God, the Lord reigneth!" Men sought their homes with praises upon their lips, and the glad sound rang out upon the still night air. No one who attended these meetings can ever forget those scenes of deepest interest.

Those who sincerely love Jesus can appreciate the feelings of those who watched with the most intense longing for the coming of their Saviour. The point of expectation was nearing. The time when we hoped to meet Him was close at hand. We approached this hour with a calm solemnity. The true believers rested in a sweet communion with God—an earnest of the peace that was to be theirs in the bright hereafter. None who experienced this hope and trust can ever forget those precious hours of waiting.

Worldly business was for the most part laid aside for a few weeks. We carefully examined every thought and emotion of our hearts, as if upon our deathbeds and in a few hours to close our eyes forever upon earthly scenes. There was no making of "ascension robes" for the great event; we felt the need of internal evidence that we were prepared to meet Christ, and our white robes were purity of soul, character cleansed from sin by the atoning blood of our Saviour.

But the time of expectation passed. This was the first close test brought to bear upon those who believed and hoped that Jesus would come in the clouds of heaven. The disappointment of God's waiting people was great. The scoffers were triumphant and won the weak and cowardly to their ranks. Some who had appeared to possess true faith seemed to have been influenced only by fear; and now their courage returned with the passing of the time, and they boldly united with the scoffers, declaring they had never been duped to really believe the doctrine of Miller, who was a mad fanatic. Others, naturally yielding or vacillating, quietly deserted the cause. I thought, If Christ had surely come, what would have become of those weak and changing ones? They professed to love and long for the coming of Jesus; but when He failed to appear, they seemed greatly relieved, and went back to a state of carelessness and disregard of true religion.

We were perplexed and disappointed, yet did not renounce our faith. Many still clung to the hope that Jesus would not long delay His coming; the word of the Lord was sure, it could not fail. We felt that we had done our duty, we had lived up to our precious faith; we were disappointed, but not discouraged. The signs of the times denoted that the end of all things was at hand; we must watch and hold ourselves in readiness for the coming of the Master at any time. We must wait with hope and trust, not neglecting the assembling of ourselves together for instruction, encouragement, and comfort, that our light might shine forth into the darkness of the world.

Calculation of the time was so simple and plain that even children could understand it. From the date of the decree of the king of Persia, found in Ezra 7, which was given in 457 before Christ, the 2300 years of Daniel 8:14 must terminate with 1843. Accordingly we looked to the end of this year for the coming of the Lord. We were sadly disappointed when the year entirely passed away and the Saviour had not come.

It was not at first perceived that if the decree did not go forth at the beginning of the year 457 B.C., the 2300 years would not be completed at the close of 1843. But it was ascertained that the decree was given near the close of the year 457 B.C., and therefore the prophetic period must reach to the fall of the year 1844. Therefore the vision of time did not tarry, though it had seemed to do so. We learned to rest upon the language of the prophet. "For the vision is yet for an appointed time, but at the end it shall speak, and not lie: though it tarry, wait for it; because it will surely come, it will not tarry."

God tested and proved His people by the passing of the time in 1843. The mistake made in reckoning the prophetic periods was not at once discovered even by learned men who opposed the views of those who were looking for Christ's coming. Scholars declared that Mr. Miller was right in his calculation of the time, though they disputed him in regard to the event that would crown that period. But they, and the waiting people of God, were in a common error on the question of time.

We fully believe that God, in His wisdom, designed that His people should meet with a disappointment, which was well calculated to reveal hearts and develop the true characters of those who had professed to look for and rejoice in the coming of the Lord. Those who embraced the first angel's message (see Revelation 14:6, 7) through fear of the wrath of God's judgments, not because they loved the truth and desired an inheritance in the kingdom of heaven, now appeared in their true light. They were among the first to ridicule the disappointed ones who sincerely longed for and loved the appearing of Jesus.

Those who had been disappointed were not long left in darkness; for in searching the prophetic periods with earnest prayer, the error was discovered, and the tracing of the prophetic pencil down through the tarrying time. In the joyful expectation of the coming of Christ the apparant tarrying of the vision had not been taken into account, and was a sad and unlooked-for surprise. Yet this very trial was necessary to develop and strengthen the sincere believers in the truth.

Our hopes now centered on the coming of the Lord in 1844. This was also the time for the message of the second angel, who, flying through the midst of heaven, cried: "Babylon is fallen, is fallen, that great city." That message was first proclaimed by the servants of God in the summer of 1844. As a result, many left the fallen churches. In connection with this message the midnight cry* was given: "Behold, the

*See Matthew 25:1-13.

Bridegroom cometh; go ye out to meet Him." In every part of the land, light was given concerning this message, and the cry aroused thousands. It went from city to city, from village to village, and into the remote country regions. It reached the learned and talented, as well as the obscure and humble.

This was the happiest year of my life. My heart was full of glad expectation, but I felt great pity and anxiety for those who were in discouragement and had no hope in Jesus. We united, as a people, in earnest prayer for a true experience and the unmistakable evidence of our acceptance with God.

We needed great patience, for the scoffers were many. We were frequently greeted by scornful references to our former disappointment. "You have not gone up yet; when do you expect to go up?" and similar taunts were often vented upon us by our worldly acquaintances, and even by some professed Christians who accepted the Bible, yet failed to learn its great and important truths. Their blinded eyes seemed to see but a vague and distant meaning in the solemn warning, God "hath appointed a day, in the which He will judge the world," and in the assurance that the saints will be caught up together to meet the Lord in the air.

The orthodox churches used every means to prevent the belief in Christ's soon coming from spreading. No liberty was granted in their meetings to those who dared mention a hope of the soon coming of Christ. Professed lovers of Jesus scornfully rejected the tidings that He whom they claimed as their best friend was soon to visit them. They were excited and angered against those who proclaimed the news of His coming, and who rejoiced that they should speedily behold Him in His glory.

Every moment seemed to me of the utmost importance. I felt that we were doing work for eternity and that the careless and uninterested were in the greatest peril. My faith was unclouded, and I appropriated to myself the precious promises of Jesus. He had said to His disciples: "Ask, and ye shall receive." I firmly believed that whatever I asked in accordance with the will of God would certainly be granted to me. I sank in humility at the feet of Jesus, with my heart in harmony with His will.

I often visited families and engaged in earnest prayer with those who were oppressed by fears and despondency. My faith was so strong that I never doubted for a moment that God would answer my prayers, and without a single exception the blessing and peace of Jesus rested upon us in answer to our humble petitions, and the hearts of the despairing ones were made joyful by light and hope.

With diligent searching of heart and humble confessions we came prayerfully up to the time of expectation. Every morning we felt that it was our first work to secure the evidence that our lives were right before God. Our interest for one another increased; we prayed much with and for one another. We assembled in the orchards and groves to commune with God and to offer up our petitions to Him, feeling more fully in His presence when surrounded by His natural works. The joys of salvation were more necessary to us than our food and drink. If clouds obscured our minds, we dared not rest or sleep till they were swept away by the consciousness of our acceptance with the Lord.

My health was very poor, my lungs were seriously affected, and my voice failed. The Spirit of God often rested upon me with great power, and my frail body could scarcely endure the glory that flooded my soul. I seemed to breathe in the atmosphere of heaven and rejoiced in the prospect of soon meeting my Redeemer and living forever in the light of His countenance.

The waiting people of God approached the hour when they fondly hoped their joys would be complete in the coming of the Saviour. But the time again passed unmarked by the advent of Jesus. It was hard to take up the cares of life that we thought had been laid down forever. It was a bitter disappointment that fell upon the little flock whose faith had been so strong and whose hope had been so high. But we were surprised that we felt so free in the Lord and were so strongly sustained by His strength and grace.

The experience of the former year was, however, repeated to a greater extent. A large class renounced their faith. Some, who had been very confident, were so deeply wounded in their pride that they felt like fleeing from the world. Like Jonah, they complained of God, and chose death rather than life. Those who had built their faith upon the evidence of others, and not upon the word of God, were now as ready to again change their views. The hypocrites, who had hoped to deceive the Lord as well as themselves with their counterfeit penitence and devotion, now felt relieved from impending danger and openly opposed the cause they had lately professed to love.

The weak and the wicked united in declaring that there could be no more fears or expectations now. The time had passed, the Lord had not come, and the world would remain the same for thousands of years. This second great test revealed a mass of worthless drift that had been drawn into the strong current of the advent faith, and been borne along for a time with the true believers and earnest workers.

We were disappointed, but not disheartened. We resolved to submit patiently to the process of purifying that God deemed needful for us, and to wait with patient hope for the Saviour to redeem His tried and faithful ones.

We were firm in the belief that the preaching of definite time was of God. It was this that led men to search the Bible diligently, discovering truths they had not before perceived. Jonah was sent of God to proclaim in the streets of Nineveh that within forty days the city would be overthrown; but God accepted the humiliation of the Ninevites and extended their period of probation. Yet the message that Jonah brought was sent of God, and Nineveh was tested according to His will. The world looked upon our hope as a delusion, and our disappointment as its consequent failure.

The words of the Saviour in the parable of the wicked servant apply very forcibly to those who ridicule the near coming of the Son of man: "But and if that evil servant shall say in his heart, My Lord delayeth His coming; and shall begin to smite his fellow servants, and to eat and drink with the drunken; the Lord of that servant shall come in a day when he looketh not for Him, and in an hour that he is not aware of, and shall cut him asunder, and appoint him his portion with the hypocrites."

We found everywhere the scoffers whom Peter said should come in the last days, walking after their own lusts, and saying: "Where is the promise of His coming? for since the fathers fell asleep, all things continue as they were from the beginning of the creation." But those who had looked for the coming of the Lord were not without comfort. They had obtained valuable knowledge in the searching of the word. The plan of salvation was plainer to their understanding. Every day they discovered new beauties in the sacred pages, and a wonderful harmony running through all, one scripture explaining another, and no word used in vain.

Our disappointment was not so great as that of the disciples. When the Son of man rode triumphantly into Jerusalem, they expected Him to be crowned king. The people flocked from all the regions about and cried: "Hosanna to the Son of David." And when the priests and elders besought Jesus to still the multitude, He declared that if they should hold their peace even the stones would cry out, for prophecy must be fulfilled. Yet in a few days these very disciples saw their beloved Master, whom they believed would reign on David's throne, stretched upon the cruel cross above the mocking, taunting Pharisees. Their high hopes were disappointed, and the darkness of death closed about them.

Yet Christ was true to His promises. Sweet was the consolation He gave His people, rich the reward of the true and faithful.

Mr. Miller and those who were in union with him supposed that the cleansing of the sanctuary spoken of in Daniel 8:14 meant the purifying of the earth by fire prior to its becoming the abode of the saints. This was to take place at the advent of Christ; therefore we looked for that event at the end of the 2300 days, or years. But after our disappointment the Scriptures were carefully searched with prayer and earnest thought, and after a period of suspense, light poured in upon our darkness; doubt and uncertainty were swept away.

Instead of the prophecy of Daniel 8:14 referring to the purifying of the earth, it was now plain that it pointed to the closing work of our High Priest in heaven, the finishing of the atonement, and the preparing of the people to abide the day of His coming.

CHAPTER VII

MY FIRST VISION

It was not long after the passing of the time in 1844 that my first vision was given me. I was visiting a dear sister in Christ, whose heart was knit with mine; five of us, all women, were kneeling quietly at the family altar. While we were praying, the power of God came upon me as I had never felt it before. I seemed to be surrounded with light, and to be rising higher and higher from the earth. I turned to look for the advent people in the world, but could not find them, when a voice said to me: "Look again, and look a little higher." At this I raised my eyes and saw a straight and narrow path, cast up high above the world. On this path the advent people were traveling toward the city. Behind them, at the beginning of the path, was a bright light which an angel told me was the midnight cry. This light shone all along the path, that their feet might not stumble. Jesus Himself went just before His people to lead them forward, and as long as they kept their eyes fixed on Him, they were safe. But soon some grew weary, and said the city was a great way off, and they expected to have entered it before. Then Jesus would encourage them by raising His glorious right arm, from which came a light that waved over the advent band; and they shouted: "Alleluia!" Others rashly denied the light behind them, and said it was not God that had led them out so far. The light behind them went out, leaving their feet in perfect darkness, and they stumbled and lost sight of the mark and of Jesus, and fell off the path down into the dark and wicked world below.

Soon we heard the voice of God like many waters, which gave us the day and hour of Jesus' coming. The living saints, 144,000 in number, knew and understood the voice, while the wicked thought it was thunder and an earthquake. When God spake the time, He poured upon us the Holy Spirit, and our faces began to light up and shine with the glory of God, as Moses' did when he came down from Mount Sinai.

The 144,000 were all sealed and perfectly united. On their foreheads were the words God, New Jerusalem, and a glorious star containing Jesus' new name. At our happy, holy state the wicked were enraged, and would rush violently up to lay hands on us to thrust us into prison, when we would stretch forth the hand in the name of the Lord, and they would fall helpless to the ground. Then it was that the synagogue of Satan knew that God had loved us, who could wash one another's feet, and salute the brethren with a holy kiss, and they worshiped at our feet.

Soon our eyes were drawn to the east, for a small black cloud had appeared, about half as large as a man's hand, which we all knew was the sign of the Son of man. In solemn silence we all gazed on the cloud as it drew nearer, and became lighter, glorious, and still more glorious, till it was a great white cloud. The bottom appeared like fire; a rainbow was over the cloud, while around it were ten thousand angels, singing a most lovely song; and upon it sat the Son of man. His hair was white and curly and lay on His shoulders, and upon His head were many crowns. His feet had the appearance of fire; in His right hand was a sharp sickle, in His left a silver trumpet. His eyes were as a flame of fire, which searched His children through and through.

Then all faces gathered paleness, and those that God had rejected gathered blackness. Then we all cried out: "Who shall be able to stand? Is my robe spotless?" The angels ceased to sing, and there was a time of awful silence, when Jesus spoke: "Those who have clean hands and pure hearts shall be able to stand; My grace is sufficient for you." At this, our faces lighted up, and joy filled every heart. And the angels struck a note higher and sang again, while the cloud drew still nearer the earth. Then Jesus' silver trumpet sounded, as He descended on the cloud, wrapped in flames of fire. He gazed on the graves of the sleeping saints, then raised His eyes and hands to heaven, and cried: "Awake! Awake! Awake! ye that sleep in the dust, and arise." Then there was a mighty earthquake. The graves opened, and the dead came up clothed with immortality. The 144,000 shouted, "Alleluia!" as they recognized their friends who had been torn from them by death, and in the same moment we were changed, and caught up together with them to meet the Lord in the air.

We all entered the cloud together, and were seven days ascending to the sea of glass, when Jesus brought the crowns, and with His own right hand placed them on our heads. He gave us harps of gold and palms of victory. Here on the sea of glass the 144,000 stood in a perfect square. Some had very bright crowns, others not so bright. Some crowns appeared heavy with stars, while others had but few. All were perfectly satisfied with their crowns. And they were all clothed with a glorious white mantle from their shoulders to their feet. Angels were all about us as we marched over the sea of glass to the gate of the city. Jesus raised His mighty, glorious arm, laid hold of the pearly gate, swung it back on its glittering hinges, and said to us: "You have washed your robes in My blood, stood stiffly for My truth, enter in." We all marched in and felt we had a perfect right there.

Within the city we saw the tree of life and the throne of God. Out of the throne came a pure river of water, and on either side of the river was the tree of life. On one side of the river was a trunk of a tree, and a trunk on the other side of the river, both of pure, transparent gold. At first I thought I saw two trees; I looked again, and saw that they were united at the top in one tree. So it was the tree of life on either side of the river of life. Its branches bowed to the place where we stood; and the fruit was glorious, which looked like gold mixed with silver.

We all went under the tree, and sat down to look at the glory of the place, when Brethren Fitch and Stockman, who had preached the gospel of the kingdom, and whom God had laid in the grave to save them, came up to us, and asked us what we had passed through while they were sleeping. We tried to call up our greatest trials, but they looked so small compared with the far more exceeding and eternal weight of glory that surrounded us, that we could not speak them out, and we all cried out, "Alleluia! Heaven is cheap enough," and we touched our golden harps and made heaven's arches ring.

CHAPTER VIII

CALL TO TRAVEL

I related this vision to the believers in Portland, who had full confidence that it was from God. The Spirit of the Lord attended the testimony, and the solemnity of eternity rested upon us. An unspeakable awe filled me, that I, so young and feeble, should be chosen as the instrument by which God would give light to His people. While under the power of the Lord I was filled with joy, seeming to be surrounded by holy angels in the glorious courts of heaven, where all is peace and gladness, and it was a sad and bitter change to wake up to the realities of mortal life.

In a second vision, which soon followed the first, I was shown the trials through which I must pass, and that it was my duty to go and relate to others what God had revealed to me. It was shown me that my labors would meet with great opposition, and that my heart would be rent with anguish, but that the grace of God would be sufficient to sustain me through all. The teaching of this vision troubled me exceedingly, for it pointed out my duty to go out among the people and present the truth.

My health was so poor that I was in constant bodily suffering, and, to all appearance, had but a short time to live. I was but seventeen years of age, small and frail, unused to society, and naturally so timid and retiring that it was painful for me to meet strangers. I prayed earnestly for several days, and far into the night, that this burden might be removed from me and laid upon someone more capable of bearing it. But the light of duty did not change, and the words of the angel sounded continually in my ears: "Make known to others what I have revealed to you."

I was unreconciled to going out into the world, and dreaded to meet its sneers and opposition. I had little self-confidence. Hitherto when the Spirit of God had urged me to duty, I had risen above myself, forgetting all fear and timidity in the thought of Jesus' love and the wonderful work He had done for me. The constant assurance that I was fulfilling my duty and obeying the will of the Lord gave me a confidence that surprised me. At such times I felt willing to do or suffer anything in order to help others into the light and peace of Jesus.

But it seemed impossible for me to perform this work that was presented before me; to attempt it seemed certain failure. The trials attending it appeared more than I could endure. How could I, a child in years, go forth from place to place, unfolding to the people the holy truths of God? My heart shrank in terror from the thought. My brother Robert, but two years older than myself, could not accompany me, for he was feeble in health and his timidity greater than mine; nothing could have induced him to take such a step. My father had a family to support, and could not leave his business; but he assured me that if God had called me to labor in other places, He would not fail to open the way for me. But these words of encouragement brought little comfort to my desponding heart; the path before me seemed hedged in with difficulties that I was unable to overcome.

I coveted death as a release from the responsibilities that were crowding upon me. At length the sweet peace I had so long enjoyed left me, and despair again pressed upon my soul. My prayers all seemed vain, and my faith was gone. Words of comfort, reproof, or encouragement were alike to me; for it seemed that no one could understand me but God, and He had forsaken me. The company of believers in Portland were ignorant concerning the exercises of my mind that had brought me into this state of despondency; but they knew that for some reason my mind had become depressed, and they felt that this was sinful on my part, considering the gracious manner in which the Lord had manifested Himself to me.

I feared that God had taken His favor from me forever. As I thought of the light that had formerly blessed my soul, it seemed doubly precious in contrast with the darkness that now enveloped me. Meetings were held at my father's house, but my distress of mind was so great that I did not attend them for some time. My burden grew heavier until the agony of my spirit seemed more than I could bear.

At length I was induced to be present at one of the meetings in my own home. The church made my case a special subject of prayer. Father Pearson, who in my earlier experience had opposed the manifestations of the power of God upon me, now prayed earnestly for me, and counseled me to surrender my will to the will of the Lord. Like a tender father he tried to encourage and comfort me, bidding me believe I was not forsaken by the Friend of sinners.

I felt too weak and despondent to make any special effort for myself, but my heart united with the petitions of my friends. I cared little now for the opposition of the world, and felt willing to make every sacrifice if only the favor of God might be restored to me. While prayer was offered for me, the thick darkness that had encompassed me rolled back, and a sudden light came upon me. My strength was taken away. I seemed to be in the presence of the angels. One of these holy beings again repeated the words: "Make known to others what I have revealed to you."

One great fear that oppressed me was that if I obeyed the call of duty, and went out declaring myself to be one favored of the Most High with visions and revelations for the people, I might yield to sinful exaltation and be lifted above the station that was right for me to occupy, bring upon myself the displeasure of God, and lose my own soul. I had before me several cases such as I have here described, and my heart shrank from the trying ordeal.

I now entreated that if I must go and relate what the Lord had shown me, I should be preserved from undue exaltation. Said the angel: "Your prayers are heard and shall be answered. If this evil that you dread threatens you, the hand of God will be stretched out to save you; by affliction He will draw you to Himself and preserve your humility. Deliver the message faithfully. Endure unto the end, and you shall eat the fruit of the tree of life and drink of the water of life."

After recovering consciousness of earthly things, I committed myself to the Lord, ready to do His bidding whatever that might be. Providentially, the way opened for me to go with my brother-in-law to my sisters in Poland, thirty miles from my home. I there had an opportunity to bear my testimony.

For three months my throat and lungs had been so diseased that I could talk but little, and that in a low and husky tone. On this occasion I stood up in meeting and commenced speaking in a whisper. I continued thus for about five minutes, when the soreness and obstruction left my throat and lungs, my voice became clear and strong, and I spoke with perfect ease and freedom for nearly two hours. When my message was ended, my voice was gone until I again stood before the people, when the same singular restoration was repeated. I felt a constant assurance that I was doing the will of God, and saw marked results attending my efforts.

The way providentially opened for me to go to the eastern part of Maine. Brother William Jordan was going on business to Orrington, accompanied by his sister, and I was urged to go with them. As I had promised the Lord to walk in the path He opened before me, I dared not refuse. At Orrington I met Elder James White. He was acquainted with my friends, and was himself engaged in the work of salvation.

The Spirit of God attended the message I bore; hearts were made glad in the truth, and the desponding ones were cheered and encouraged to renew their faith. At Garland a large number collected from different quarters to hear my message. But my heart was very heavy; I had just received a letter from my mother begging me to return home, for false reports were circulating concerning me. This was an unexpected blow. My name had always been free from the shadow of reproach, and my reputation was very dear to me. I also felt grieved that my mother should suffer on my account; her heart was bound up in her children, and she was very sensitive in regard to them. If there had been an opportunity, I should have set out for home immediately; but this was impossible.

My sorrow was so great that I felt too depressed to speak that night. My friends urged me to trust in the Lord; and at length the brethren engaged in prayer for me. The blessing of the Lord soon rested upon me, and I bore my testimony that evening with great freedom. There seemed to be an angel standing by my side to strengthen me. Shouts of glory and victory went up from that house, and the presence of Jesus was felt among us.

In my labors I was called to oppose the course of some who by their fanaticism were bringing reproach upon the cause of God. These fanatical ones seemed to think that religion consisted in great excitement and noise. They would talk in a manner that would irritate unbelievers, and cause them to hate them and the doctrines they taught; then they would rejoice that they suffered persecution. Unbelievers could see no consistency in their course. The brethren in some places were prevented from assembling for meetings. The innocent suffered with the guilty. I carried a sad and heavy heart much of the time. It seemed cruel that the cause of Christ should be injured by the course of these injudicious men. They were not only ruining their own souls, but placing upon the cause a stigma not easily removed. And Satan loved to have it so. It suited him well to see the truth handled by unsanctified men; to have it mixed with error, and then all together trampled in the dust. He looked with triumph upon the confused, scattered state of God's children.

One of these fanatical persons labored with some success to turn my friends and even my relatives against me. Because I had faithfully related that which was shown me respecting his unchristian course, he circulated falsehoods to destroy my influence and to justify himself. My lot seemed hard. Discouragements pressed heavily upon me; and the condition of God's people so filled me with anguish that for two weeks I was prostrated with sickness. My friends thought I could not live; but brethren and sisters who sympathized with me in this affliction met to pray for me. I soon realized that earnest, effectual prayer was offered in my behalf. Prayer prevailed. The power of the strong foe was broken, and I was released, and immediately taken off in vision. In this view I saw that if I felt a human influence affecting my testimony no matter where I might be, I had only to cry to God, and an angel would be sent to my rescue. I already had one guardian angel attending me continually, but when necessary, the Lord would send another to raise me above the power of every earthly influence.

CHAPTER IX

VISION OF THE NEW EARTH*

With Jesus at our head, we all descended from the city down to this earth, on a great and mighty mountain, which could not bear Jesus up, and it parted asunder, and there

*This vision describes events to take place at the close of the one thousand years after Christ's second advent. Revelation 20; 21; 22; Zechariah 14:4.

was a mighty plain. Then we looked up and saw the great city, with twelve foundations, and twelve gates, three on each side, and an angel at each gate. We all cried out: "The city, the great city, it's coming, it's coming down from God out of heaven," and it came and settled on the place where we stood. Then we began to look at the glorious things outside of the city. There I saw most beautiful houses, that had the appearance of silver, supported by four pillars set with pearls, most glorious to behold, which were to be inhabited by the saints, and in which was a golden shelf. I saw many of the saints go into the houses, take off their glittering crowns and lay them on the shelf, then go out into the field by the houses to do something with the earth; not as we have to do with the earth here; no, no. A glorious light shone all about their heads, and they were continually offering praise to God.

And I saw another field full of all kinds of flowers, and as I plucked them, I cried out: "They will never fade." Next I saw a field of tall grass, most glorious to behold; it was living green, and had a reflection of silver and gold, as it waved proudly to the glory of King Jesus. Then we entered a field full of all kinds of beasts—the lion, the lamb, the leopard, and the wolf, all together in perfect union. We passed through the midst of them, and they followed on peaceably after. Then we entered a wood, not like the dark woods we have here; no, no; but light, and all over glorious; the branches of the trees waved to and fro, and we all cried out: "We will dwell safely in the wilderness and sleep in the woods." We passed through the woods, for we were on our way to Mount Zion.

As we were traveling along, we met a company who were also gazing at the glories of the place. I noticed red as a border on their garments; their crowns were brilliant; their robes were pure white. As we greeted them, I asked Jesus who they were. He said they were martyrs that had been slain for Him. With them was an innumerable company of little ones; they had a hem of red on their garments also. Mount Zion was just before us, and on the mount was a glorious temple, and about it were seven other mountains, on which grew roses and lilies. And I saw the little ones climb, or, if they chose, use their little wings and fly to the top of the mountains, and pluck the never-fading flowers. There were all kinds of trees around the temple to beautify the place—the box, the pine, the fir, the oil, the myrtle, the pomegranate, and the fig tree bowed down with the weight of its timely figs; these made the place all over glorious. And as we were about to enter the temple, Jesus raised His lovely voice and said, "Only the 144,000 enter this place," and we shouted, "Alleluia!"

This temple was supported by seven pillars, all of transparent gold, set with pearls most glorious. The wonderful things I there saw, I cannot describe. Oh, that I could talk in the language of Canaan, then could I tell a little of the glory of the better world. I saw there tables of stone in which the names of the 144,000 were engraved in letters of gold.

After beholding the glory of the temple, we went out, and Jesus left us and went to the city. Soon we heard His lovely voice again, saying: "Come, My people, you have come out of great tribulation, and done My will, suffered for Me, come in to supper; for I will gird Myself and serve you." We shouted, "Alleluia, glory," and entered the city. Here I saw a table of pure silver; it was many miles in length, yet our eyes could extend over it. I saw the fruit of the tree of life, the manna, almonds, figs, pomegranates, grapes, and many other kinds of fruit. I asked Jesus to let me eat of the fruit. He said: "Not now. Those who eat of the fruit of this land, go back to earth no more. But in a little while, if faithful, you shall both eat of the fruit of the tree of life and drink of the water of the fountain. And," said He, "you must go back to the earth again, and relate to others what I have revealed to you." Then an angel bore me gently down to this dark world. Sometimes I think I can stay here no longer, all things of earth look so dreary. I feel very lonely here, for I have seen a better land. Oh that I had wings like a dove, then would I fly away and be at rest.

Brother Hyde, who was present during this vision, composed the following verses, which have gone the rounds of the religious papers, and have found a place in several hymn-books. Those who have published, read, and sung them have little thought that they originated from a vision of a girl persecuted for her humble testimony.

We have heard from the bright, the holy land;
We have heard, and our hearts are glad;
For we were a lonely pilgrim band,
And weary, and worn, and sad.
They tell us the saints have a dwelling there—
No longer are homeless ones;
And we know that the goodly land is fair,
Where life's pure river runs.

They say green fields are waving there,
That never a blight shall know;
And the deserts wild are blooming fair,
And the roses of Sharon grow.
There are lovely birds in the bowers green,
Their songs are blithe and sweet;
And their warblings, gushing ever new,
The angels' harpings greet.

We have heard of the palms, the robes, the crowns,
And the silvery band in white;
Of the city fair, with pearly gates,
All radiant with light.
We have heard of the angels there, and saints,
With their harps of gold, how they sing;
Of the mount, with the fruitful tree of life,
Of the leaves that healing bring.

The King of that country, He is fair,
He's the joy and light of the place;
In His beauty we shall behold Him there,
And bask in His smiling face.

We'll be there, we'll be there in a little while,
We'll join the pure and the blest;
We'll have the palm, the robe, the crown,
And forever be at rest.

CHAPTER X

WITHHOLDING REPROOF

About this time I was subjected to a severe trial. If the Spirit of God rested upon anyone in meeting, and he glorified God by praising Him, some raised the cry of mesmerism; and if it pleased the Lord to give me a vision in meeting, some would say that it was the effect of excitement and mesmerism. Grieved and desponding, I often went alone to some retired place to pour out my soul before Him who invites the weary and heavy-laden to come and find rest. As my faith claimed the promises, Jesus would seem very near. The sweet light of heaven would shine around me, and I would seem to be encircled by the arms of my Saviour, and would there be taken off in vision. But when I would relate what God had revealed to me alone, where no earthly influence could affect me, I was grieved and astonished to hear some intimate that those who lived nearest to God were most liable to be deceived by Satan.

According to this teaching, our only safety from delusion would be to remain at a distance from God, in a backslidden state. Oh, thought I, has it come to this, that those who honestly go to God alone to plead His promises, and to claim His salvation, are to be charged with being under the foul influence of mesmerism? Do we ask our kind Father in heaven for bread, only to receive a stone or a scorpion? These things wounded my spirit, and wrung my soul with keen anguish, well nigh to despair. Many would have me believe that there was no Holy Spirit, and that all the exercises that holy men of God experienced were only the effect of mesmerism or the deception of Satan.

Some had taken extreme views of certain texts of scripture, refraining wholly from labor, and rejecting all those who would not receive their ideas on this and other points pertaining to religious duty. God revealed these errors to me in vision, and sent me to instruct His erring children; but many of them wholly rejected the message, and charged me with conforming to the world. On the other hand, the nominal Adventists charged me with fanaticism, and I was falsely represented as the leader of the fanaticism which I was laboring constantly to arrest.

Different times were set for the Lord to come, and were urged upon the brethren. But the Lord showed me that they would pass by, for the time of trouble must take place before the coming of Christ, and that every time that was set, and passed, would weaken the faith of God's people. For this I was charged with being the evil servant that said: "My Lord delayeth His coming."

These statements relative to time setting were printed about thirty years ago, and the books containing them have been circulated everywhere; yet some ministers claiming to be well acquainted with me, state that I have set time after time for the Lord to come, and those times have passed, therefore my visions are false. No doubt these false statements are received by many as truth; but none who are acquainted with me or with my labors can in candor make such report. This is the testimony I have ever borne since the passing of the time in 1844: "Time after time will be set by different ones, and will pass by; and the influence of this time setting will tend to destroy the faith of God's people." If I had in vision seen definite time, and had borne my testimony to it, I could not have written and published, in the face of this testimony, that all times that should be set would pass, for the time of trouble must come before the coming of Christ. Certainly for the last thirty years, that is, since the publication of this statement, I would not be inclined to set time for Christ to come, and thus place myself under the same condemnation with those whom I was reproving. And I had no vision until 1845, which was after the passing of the time of general expectation in 1844. I was then shown what I have here stated.

And has not this testimony been fulfilled in every particular? The First-day Adventists have set time after time, and notwithstanding the repeated failures, they have gathered courage to set new times. God has not led them in this. Many of them have rejected the true prophetic time, and ignored the fulfillment of prophecy, because the time passed in 1844, and did not bring the expected event. They rejected the truth, and the enemy has had power to bring strong delusions upon them that they should believe a lie. The great test on time was in 1843 and 1844; and all who have set time since then have been deceiving themselves and deceiving others.

Up to the time of my first vision I could not write; my trembling hand was unable to hold my pen steadily. While in vision, I was commanded by an angel to write the vision. I obeyed, and wrote readily. My nerves were strengthened, and my hand became steady.

It was a great cross for me to relate to the erring what had been shown me concerning them. It caused me great distress to see others troubled or grieved. And when obliged to declare the messages, I would often soften them down, and make them appear as favorable for the individual as I could, and then would go by myself and weep in agony of spirit. I looked upon those who had only their own souls to care for, and thought if I were in their condition I would not murmur. It was hard to relate the plain, cutting testimonies given me of God. I anxiously watched the result, and if the persons reproved rose up against the reproof, and afterward opposed the truth, these queries would arise in my mind: Did I deliver the message just as I should? Could there not have been some way to save them? And then such distress pressed upon my soul that I often felt that death would be a welcome messenger, and the grave a sweet resting place.

I did not realize the danger and sin of such a course, until in vision I was taken into the presence of Jesus. He looked upon me with a frown, and turned His face from me. It is not possible to describe the terror and agony I then felt. I fell upon my face before Him, but had no power to utter a word. Oh, how I longed to be covered and hid from that dreadful frown! Then could I realize, in some degree, what the feelings of the lost will be when they cry: "Mountains and rocks, fall on us, and hide us from the face of Him that sitteth on the throne, and from the wrath of the Lamb."

Presently an angel bade me rise, and the sight that met my eyes can hardly be described. Before me was a company whose hair and garments were torn, and whose countenances were the very picture of despair and horror. They came close to me, and rubbed their garments upon mine. As I looked at my garments, I saw that they were stained with blood. Again I fell like one dead at the feet of my accompanying angel. I could not plead one excuse, and longed to be away from that holy place. The angel raised me to my feet, and said: "This is not your case now, but this scene has passed before you to let you know what your situation must be if you neglect to declare to others what the Lord has revealed to you. But if you are faithful to the end, you shall eat of the tree of life, and shall drink of the river of the water of life. You will have to suffer much, but the grace of God is sufficient." I then felt willing to do all that the Lord might require me to do, that I might have His approbation, and not feel His dreadful frown.

CHAPTER XI

MARRIAGE AND SUBSEQUENT LABORS

August 30, 1846, I was united in marriage to Elder James White. Elder White had enjoyed a deep experience in the advent movement, and his labors in proclaiming the truth had been blessed of God. Our hearts were united in the great work, and together we traveled and labored for the salvation of souls.

We entered upon our work penniless, with few friends, and broken in health. My husband had inherited a powerful constitution, but his health had been seriously impaired by close application to study at school, and in lecturing. I had suffered ill-health from a child, as I have related. In this condition, without means, with very few who sympathized with us in our views, without a paper, and without books, we entered upon our work. We had no houses of worship at that time. And the idea of using a tent had not then occurred to us. Most of our meetings were held in private houses. Our congregation was small. It was seldom that any came into our meetings excepting Adventists, unless they were attracted by curiosity to hear a woman speak.

At first I moved out timidly in the work of public speaking. If I had confidence, it was given me by the Holy Spirit. If I spoke with freedom and power, it was given me of God. Our meetings were usually conducted in such a manner that both of us took part. My husband would give a doctrinal discourse, then I would follow with an exhortation of considerable length, melting my way into the feelings of the congregation. Thus my husband sowed and I watered the seed of truth, and God did give the increase.

In the autumn of 1846 we began to observe the Bible Sabbath, and to teach and defend it. My attention was first called to the Sabbath while I was on a visit to New Bedford, Massachusetts, earlier in the same year. I there became acquainted with Elder Joseph Bates, who had early embraced the advent faith, and was an active laborer in the cause. Elder B. was keeping the Sabbath, and urged its importance. I did not feel its importance, and thought that Elder B. erred in dwelling upon the fourth commandment more than upon the other nine. But the Lord gave me a view of the heavenly sanctuary. The temple of God was opened in heaven, and I was shown the ark of God covered with the mercy seat. Two angels stood, one at each end of the ark, with their wings spread over the mercy seat, and their faces turned toward it. My accompanying angel informed me that these represented all the heavenly host looking with reverential awe toward the holy law which had been written by the finger of God. Jesus raised the cover of the ark, and I beheld the tables of stone on which the Ten Commandments were written. I was amazed as I saw the fourth commandment in the very center of the ten precepts, with a soft halo of light encircling it. Said the angel: "It is the only one of the ten which defines the living God who created the heavens and the earth and all things that are therein. When the foundations of the earth were laid, then was laid the foundation of the Sabbath also."

I was shown that if the true Sabbath had always been kept, there would never have been an infidel or an atheist. The observance of the Sabbath would have preserved the world from idolatry. The fourth commandment has been trampled upon; therefore we are called upon to repair the breach in the law, and plead for the downtrodden Sabbath. The man of sin who exalted himself above God, and thought to change times and laws, brought about the change of the Sabbath from the seventh to the first day of the week. In doing this, he made a breach in the law of God. Just prior to the great day of God, a message is sent forth to warn the people to come back to their allegiance to the law of God which antichrist has broken down. By precept and example, attention must be called to the breach in the law. I was shown that the third angel, proclaiming the commandments of God and the faith of Jesus, represents the people who receive this message and raise the voice of warning to the world, to keep the commandments of God as the apple of the eye, and that in response to this warning many would embrace the Sabbath of the Lord.

When we received the light upon the fourth commandment, there were about twenty-five Adventists in Maine who observed the Sabbath; but these were so diverse in sentiment upon other points of doctrine, and so scattered in location, that their influence was very small. There was about the same number, in similar condition, in other parts of New England. It seemed to be our duty to visit these frequently at their homes, and strengthen them in the Lord and in His truth, and as they were so much scattered, it was necessary for us to be on the road much of the time. For want of means we took the cheapest private conveyance, second-class cars, and lower-deck passage on steamers. In my feeble condition I found traveling by private conveyance most comfortable. When on second-class cars, we were usually enveloped in tobacco smoke from the effects, of which I often fainted. When on steamers, on lower deck, we suffered the same from the smoke of tobacco, besides the swearing and vulgar conversation of the ship hands and the baser portion of the traveling public. At night we lay down to sleep on the hard floor, dry goods boxes, or sacks of grain, with carpetbags for pillows, and overcoats and shawls for covering. If suffering from the winter's cold, we would walk the deck to keep warm. When oppressed by the heat of summer, we would go upon the upper deck to secure the cool night air. This was fatiguing to me, especially when traveling with an infant in my arms. This manner of life was by no means one of our choosing. God called us in our poverty, and led us through the furnace of affliction, to give us an experience which should be of great worth to us, and an example to others who should afterward join us in labor.

Our Master was a man of sorrows; He was acquainted with grief, and those who suffer with Him will reign with Him. When the Lord appeared to Saul in his conversion, He did not purpose to show him how much good he should enjoy, but what great things he should suffer for His name. Suffering has been the portion of the people of God from the days of the martyr Abel. The patriarchs suffered for being true to God and obedient to His commandments. The great Head of the church suffered for our sake; His first apostles and the primitive church suffered; the millions of martyrs suffered, and the Reformers suffered. And why should we, who have the blessed hope of immortality, to be consummated at the soon appearing of Christ, shrink from a life of suffering? Were it possible to reach the tree of life in the midst of the Paradise of God without suffering, we would not enjoy so rich a reward for which we had not suffered. We would shrink back from the glory; shame would seize us in the presence of those who had fought the good fight, had run the race with patience, and had laid hold on eternal life. But none will be there who have not, like Moses, chosen to suffer affliction with the people of God. The prophet John saw the multitude of the redeemed, and inquired who they were. The prompt answer came: "These are they which came out of great tribulation, and have washed their robes and made them white in the blood of the Lamb."

When we began to present the light on the Sabbath question, we had no clearly defined idea of the third angel's message of Revelation 14:9-12. The burden of our testimony as we came before the people was that the great second advent movement was of God, that the first and second messages had gone forth, and that the third was to be given. We saw that the third message closed with the words: "Here is the patience of the saints: here are they that keep the commandments of God, and the faith of Jesus." And we as clearly saw as we now see that these prophetic words suggested a Sabbath reform; but as to what the worship of the beast mentioned in the message was, or what the image and the mark of the beast were, we had no defined position.

God by His Holy Spirit let light shine forth upon His servants, and the subject gradually opened to their minds. It required much study and anxious care to search it out, link after link. By care, anxiety, and incessant labor has the work moved on until the great truths of our message, a clear, connected, perfect whole, have been given to the world.

I have already spoken of my acquaintance with Elder Bates. I found him to be a true Christian gentleman, courteous and kind. He treated me as tenderly as though I were his own child. The first time he heard me speak, he manifested deep interest. After I had ceased speaking, he arose and said: " I am a doubting Thomas. I do not believe in visions. But if I could believe that the testimony the sister has related tonight was indeed the voice of God to us, I should be the happiest man alive. My heart is deeply moved. I believe the speaker to be sincere, but cannot explain in regard to her being shown the wonderful things she has related to us."

A few months after my marriage, I attended, with my husband, a Conference at Topsham, Maine, at which Elder Bates was present. He did not then fully believe that my visions were of God. That meeting was a season of much interest. The Spirit of God rested upon me; I was wrapped in a vision of God's glory, and for the first time had a view of other planets. After I came out of vision, I related what I had seen. Elder B. then asked if I had studied astronomy. I told him I had no recollection of ever looking into an astronomy. Said he: "This is of the Lord." I never before saw him so free and happy. His countenance shone with the light of heaven, and he exhorted the church with power.

From the Conference I returned with my husband to Gorham, where my parents were then living. Here I was taken very sick, and suffered extremely. My parents, husband, and sisters united in prayer for me, but I suffered on for three weeks. I often fainted like one dead, but in answer to prayer revived again. My agony was so great that I pleaded with those around me not to pray for me; for I thought their prayers were protracting my sufferings. Our neighbors gave me up to die. For a time it pleased the Lord to try our faith. At length, as my friends again united in prayer for me, a brother who was present seemed much burdened, and with the power of God resting upon him, rose from his knees, came across the room, and laid his hands upon my head, saying: "Sister Ellen, Jesus Christ maketh thee whole," and fell back, prostrated by the power of God. I believed that the work was of God, and the pain lcft me. My soul was filled with gratitude and peace. The language of my heart was: "There is no help for us but in God. We can be in peace only as we rest in Him and wait for His salvation."

The next day there was a severe storm, and none of the neighbors came to our house. I was able to be up in the sitting room; and as some saw the windows of my room raised, they supposed that I was dead. They knew not that the Great Physician had graciously entered the dwelling, rebuked the disease, and set me free. The next day we rode thirty-eight miles to Topsham. Inquiries were made of my father, at what time the funeral would be. Father asked: "What funeral?" "The funeral of your daughter," was the reply. Father answered: "She has been healed by the prayer of faith, and is on her way to Topsham."

A few weeks after this, on our way to Boston we took the steamer at Portland. A violent storm came up, and we were in great peril. The boat rolled fearfully, and the waves dashed into the cabin windows. There was great fear in the ladies' cabin. Many were confessing their sins, and crying to God for mercy. Some were calling upon the Virgin Mary to keep them, while others were making solemn vows to God that if they reached land they would devote their lives to His service. It was a scene of terror and confusion. As the boat rocked, a lady turned to me and said: "Are you not terrified? I suppose it is a fact that we may never reach land." I told her that I had made Christ my refuge, and if my work was done, I might as well lie in the bottom of the ocean as in any other place; but if my work was not done, all the waters of the ocean could not drown me. My trust was in God; He would bring us safe to land if it was for His glory.

At this time I prized the Christian's hope. The scene before me brought vividly to my mind the day of the Lord's fierce anger, when the storm of His wrath will come upon the poor sinner. Then there will be bitter cries and tears, confession of sin, and pleading for mercy, when it will be too late. "Because I have called, and ye refused; I have stretched out My hand, and no man regarded; but ye have set at nought all My counsel, and would none of My reproof: I also will laugh at your calamity; I will mock when your fear cometh."

Through the mercy of God we were all landed safe. But some of the passengers who manifested much fear in the storm made no reference to it, only to make light of their fears. One who had solemnly promised that if she were preserved to see land she would be a Christian, mockingly cried out as she left the boat: "Glory to God, I am glad to step on land again!" I asked her to go back a few hours, and remember her vows to God. She turned from me with a sneer.

I was forcibly reminded of deathbed repentance. Some serve themselves and Satan all their lives, and then as sickness subdues them, and a fearful uncertainty is before them, they manifest some sorrow for sin, and perhaps say they are willing to die, and their friends make themselves believe that they have been truly converted and fitted for heaven. But if these should recover, they would be as rebellious as ever. I am reminded of Proverbs 1:27, 28: "When your fear cometh as desolation, and your destruction cometh as a whirlwind, when distress and anguish cometh upon you. Then shall they call upon Me, but I will not answer; they shall seek Me early, but they shall not find Me."

At Gorham, Maine, August 26, 1847, our eldest son, Henry Nichols White, was born. In October, Brother and Sister Howland of Topsham kindly offered us a part of their dwelling, which we gladly accepted, and commenced housekeeping with borrowed furniture. We were poor, and saw close times. We had resolved not to be dependent, but to support ourselves, and have something with which to help others. But we were not prospered. My husband worked very hard hauling stone on the railroad, but could not get what was due him for his labor. Brother and Sister H. freely divided with us whenever they could, but they were in close circumstances. They fully believed the first and second messages, and had generously imparted of their substance to forward the work, until they were dependent on their daily labor.

My husband left the railroad, and with his ax went into the woods to chop cordwood. With a continual pain in his side, he worked from early morning till dark to earn about fifty cents a day. He was prevented from sleeping nights by severe pain. We endeavored to keep up good courage, and trust in the Lord. I did not murmur. In the morning I felt grateful to God that He had preserved us through another night, and at night I was thankful that He had kept us through another day. One day when our provisions were gone, my husband went to his employer to get money or provisions. It was a stormy day, and he walked three miles and back in the rain. He brought home on his back a bag of provisions tied in different compartments, having in this manner passed through the village of Brunswick, where he had often lectured. As he entered the house, very weary, my heart sank within me. My first feelings were that God had forsaken us. I said to my husband: "Have we come to this? Has the Lord left us?" I could not restrain my tears and wept aloud for hours until I fainted. Prayer was offered in my behalf. When I breathed again, I felt the cheering influence of the Spirit of God, and regretted that I had sunk under discouragement. We desire to follow Christ and to be like Him, but we sometimes faint beneath trials, and remain at a distance from Him. Sufferings and trials bring us near to Jesus. The furnace consumes the dross and brightens the gold.

At this time I was shown that the Lord had been trying us for our good, and to prepare us to labor for others; that He had been stirring up our nest, lest we should settle down at ease. Our work was to labor for souls; if we had been prospered, home would be so pleasant that we would be unwilling to leave it; trials had been permitted to come upon us to prepare us for the still greater conflicts that we would meet in our travels. We soon received letters from brethren in different states inviting us to visit them; but we had no means to take us out of the state. Our reply was that the way was not open before us. I thought that it would be impossible for me to travel with my child. We did not wish to be dependent, and were careful to live within our means. We were resolved to suffer rather than get in debt. I allowed myself and child one pint of milk each day. One morning before my husband went to his work, he left me nine cents to buy milk for three mornings. It was a study with me whether to buy the milk for myself and babe or get an apron for him. I gave up the milk, and purchased the cloth for an apron to cover the bare arms of my child.

Little Henry was soon taken very sick, and grew worse so fast that we were much alarmed. He lay in a stupid state; his breathing was quick and heavy. We gave remedies with no success. We then called in a person of experience in sickness, who said that his recovery was doubtful. We had prayed for him, but there was no change. We had made the child an excuse for not traveling and laboring for the good of others, and we feared the Lord was about to remove him. Once more we went before the Lord, praying that He would have compassion upon us, and spare the life of the child, and solemnly pledging ourselves to go forth, trusting in God, wherever He might send us.

Our petitions were fervent and agonizing. By faith we claimed the promises of God, and we believed that He listened to our cries. Light from heaven was breaking through the clouds and shining upon us. Our prayers were graciously answered. From that hour the child began to recover.

While at Topsham we received a letter from Brother Chamberlain of Connecticut, urging us to attend a Conference in that state in April, 1848. We decided to go if we could obtain means. My husband settled with his employer, and found that there was ten dollars due him. With five of this I purchased articles of clothing which we much needed, and then patched my husband's overcoat, even piecing the patches, making it difficult to tell the original cloth in the sleeves. We had five dollars left to take us to Dorchester, Massachusetts. Our trunk contained nearly everything we possessed on earth; but we enjoyed peace of mind and a clear conscience, and this we prized above earthly comforts. In Dorchester we called at the house of Brother Nichols, and as we left, Sister N. handed my husband five dollars, which paid our fare to Middletown, Connecticut. We were strangers in that city, and had never seen one of the brethren in the state. We had but fifty cents left. My husband did not dare to use that to hire a carriage, so he threw the trunk up on a pile of boards, and we walked on in search of someone of like faith. We soon found Brother C., who took us to his house.

The Conference was held at Rocky Hill, in the large, unfinished chamber of Brother Belden's house. The brethren came in until we numbered about fifty; but these were not all fully in the truth. Our meeting was interesting. Brother Bates presented the commandments in a clear light, and their importance was urged home by powerful testimonies. The word had effect to establish those already in the truth, and to awaken those who were not fully decided.

We were invited to meet with the brethren in the State of New York the following summer. The believers were poor, and could not promise to do much toward defraying our expenses. We had no means with which to travel. My husband's health was poor, but the way opened for him to work in the hayfield, and he decided to make the effort. It seemed then that we must live by faith. When we arose in the morning, we bowed at our bedside and asked God to give us strength to labor through the day. We would not be satisfied unless we had the assurance that the Lord heard us pray. My husband then went forth to swing the scythe, not in his own strength, but in the strength of the Lord. At night, when he came home, we would again plead with God for strength to earn means to spread His truth. We were often greatly blessed. In a letter to Brother Howland, July, 1848, my husband wrote: "God gives me strength to labor hard all day. Praise His name! I hope to get a few dollars to use in His cause. We have suffered from labor, fatigue, pain, hunger, cold, and heat, while endeavoring to do our brethren and sisters good, and we hold ourselves ready to suffer more if God requires. I rejoice today that ease, pleasure, and comfort in this life are a sacrifice on the altar of my faith and hope. If our happiness consists in making others happy, we are happy indeed. The true disciple will not live to gratify beloved self, but for Christ, and for the good of His little ones. He is to sacrifice his ease, his pleasure, his comfort, his convenience, his will, and his own selfish wishes for Christ's cause, or never reign with Him on His throne."

The means earned in the hayfield was sufficient to supply our present wants, and also pay our expenses to go to western New York and return.

Our first Conference in New York was held at Volney, in a brother's barn. About thirty-five were present—all that could be collected in that part of the state. But of this number, hardly two were agreed. Some were holding serious errors, and each strenuously urged his own views, declaring that they were according to the Scriptures.

These strange differences of opinion brought a heavy weight upon me, as it seemed to me that God was dishonored; and I fainted under the burden. Some feared that I was dying; but the Lord heard the prayers of His servants, and I revived. The light of heaven rested upon me, and I was soon lost to earthly things. My accompanying angel presented before me some of the errors of those present, and also the truth in contrast with their errors. These discordant views which they claimed to be according to the Bible were only according to their opinion of the Bible, and they must yield their errors and unite upon the third angel's message. Our meeting closed triumphantly. Truth gained the victory. The brethren renounced their errors, and united upon the third angel's message, and God greatly blessed them and added to their numbers.

From Volney we went to Port Gibson to attend a meeting in Brother Edson's barn. There were those present who loved the truth, but were listening to and cherishing error. The Lord wrought for us in power before the close of that meeting. I was again shown in vision the importance of the brethren in western New York laying aside their differences, and uniting upon Bible truth.

We returned to Middletown, where we had left our child

during our western journey. And now a painful duty presented itself. For the good of souls we felt that we must sacrifice the company of our little Henry, that we might give ourselves unreservedly to the work. My health was poor, and he would necessarily occupy a great share of my time. It was a severe trial, yet I dared not let the child stand in the way of my duty. I believed that the Lord had spared him to us when he was very sick, and that if I should let him hinder me from doing my duty, God would remove him from me. Alone before the Lord, with most painful feelings and many tears, I made the sacrifice and gave up my only child, then one year old, for another to exercise a mother's feelings toward him, and to act a mother's part. We left him in Brother Howland's family, in whom we had the utmost confidence. They were willing to bear burdens to leave us as free as possible to labor in the cause of God. We knew that they could take better care of Henry than we could while journeying, and that it was for his good to have a steady home and good discipline. It was hard parting with my child. His sad little face, as I left him, was before me night and day; yet in the strength of the Lord I put him out of my mind, and sought to do others good. Brother Howland's family had the whole charge of Henry for five years.

CHAPTER XII

PUBLISHING AND TRAVELING

In June, 1849, the way was opened for us to make our home for a time at Rocky Hill, Connecticut. Here, on the 28th of July, our second child, James Edson, was born.

While we were living at this place, my husband was impressed that it was his duty to write and publish the present truth. He was greatly encouraged and blessed as he decided thus to do. But again he would be in doubt and perplexity, as he was penniless. There were brethren who had means, but they chose to keep it. He at length gave up in discouragement, and decided to look for a field of grass to mow. As he left the house, a burden was rolled upon me, and I fainted. Prayer was offered for me, and I was blessed, and taken off in vision. I saw that the Lord had blessed and strengthened my husband to labor in the field one year before; that he had made a right use of the means there earned; and that he would have a hundredfold in his life, and, if faithful, a rich reward in the kingdom of God; but that the Lord would not now give him strength to labor in the field, for He had another work for him; that he must walk out by faith, and write and publish the present truth. He immediately commenced to write, and when he came to some difficult passage, we would call upon the Lord to give us the true meaning of His word.

About the same time he began to publish a small sheet entitled, *The Present Truth.* The office of publication was at Middletown, eight miles from Rocky Hill, and he often walked this distance and back again, although he was then lame. When he brought the first number from the printing office we all bowed around it, asking the Lord, with humble hearts and many tears, to let His blessing rest upon the feeble efforts of His servant. He then directed the papers to all he thought would read them, and carried them to the post office in a carpetbag. Every number was taken from Middletown to Rocky Hill, and always before preparing them for the post office, we spread them before the Lord, and with earnest prayers mingled with tears, entreated that His blessing might attend the silent messengers. Very soon letters came bringing means to publish the paper, and the good news of many souls embracing the truth.

With the beginning of this work of publishing, we did not cease our labors in preaching the truth, but traveled from place to place, proclaiming the doctrines which had brought so great light and joy to us, encouraging the believers, correcting errors, and setting things in order in the church. In order to carry forward the publishing enterprise, and at the same time continue our labors in different parts of the field, the paper was from time to time moved to different places.

In 1850 it was issued at Paris, Maine. Here it was enlarged, and its name changed to that which it now bears, *The Advent Review and Sabbath Herald*. The friends of the cause were few in numbers and poor in worldly wealth, and we were still compelled to struggle with poverty and great discouragement. Excessive labor, care, and anxiety, a lack of proper and nourishing food, and exposure to cold in our long winter journeys, were too much for my husband, and he sank under the burden. He became so weak that he could scarcely walk to the printing office. Our faith was tried to the utmost. We had willingly endured privation, toil, and suffering; yet our motives were misinterpreted, and we were regarded with distrust and jealousy. Few of those for whose good we had suffered, seemed to appreciate our efforts. We were too much troubled to sleep or rest. The hours in which we should have been refreshed with sleep, were often spent in answering long communications occasioned by envy; and many hours while others were sleeping we spent in agonizing tears, and mourning before the Lord. At length my husband said: "Wife it is of no use to try to struggle on any longer. These things are crushing me, and will soon carry me to the grave. I cannot go any farther. I have written a note for the paper stating that I shall publish no more." As he stepped out of the door to carry it to the printing office, I fainted. He came back and prayed for me; his prayer was answered, and I was relieved.

The next morning, while at family prayer, I was taken off in vision, and was shown concerning these matters. I saw that my husband must not give up the paper, for such a step was just what Satan was trying to drive him to take, and he was working through agents to do this. I was shown that we must continue to publish, and that the Lord would sustain us; that those who had been guilty of casting upon us such burdens would have to see the extent of their cruel course, and come back confessing their injustice, or the frown of God would be upon them; that it was not against us merely that they had spoken and acted, but against Him who had called us to fill the place He wished us to occupy; and that all their suspicion, jealousy, and secret influence was faithfully chronicled in heaven, and would not be blotted out until everyone who had taken a part in it should see the extent of his wrong course, and retrace every step.

The second volume of the *Review* was published at Saratoga Springs, New York. In April, 1852, we moved to Rochester, New York. At every step we were obliged to move out by faith. We were still crippled by poverty, and compelled to exercise the most rigid economy and self-denial. I will give a brief extract from a letter to Brother Howland's family, dated April 16, 1852: "We are just getting settled in Rochester. We have rented an old house for one hundred and seventy-five dollars a year. We have the press in the house. Were it not for this, we should have to pay fifty dollars a year for office room. You would smile could you look in upon us and see our furniture. We have bought two old bedsteads for twenty-five cents each. My husband brought me home six old chairs, no two of them alike, for which he paid one dollar, and soon he presented me with four more old chairs without seating, for which he paid sixty-two cents. The frames are strong, and I have been seating them with drilling. Butter is so high that we do not purchase it, neither can we afford potatoes. We use sauce in the place of butter, and turnips for potatoes. Our first meals were taken on a fireboard placed upon two empty flour barrels. We are willing to endure privations if the work of God can be advanced. We believe the Lord's hand was in our coming to this place. There is a large field for labor, and but few laborers. Last Sabbath our meeting was excellent. The Lord refreshed us with His presence."

From time to time we went out to attend Conferences in different parts of the field. My husband preached, sold books, and labored to extend the circulation of the paper. We traveled by private conveyance, and stopped at noon to feed our horse by the roadside, and to eat our lunch. Then with paper and pencil, on the cover of our dinner box or the top of his hat, my husband wrote articles for the *Review* and *Instructor.* The Lord greatly blessed our labors, and the truth affected many hearts.

In the summer of 1853, we made our first journey to the State of Michigan. After publishing our appointments, my husband was prostrated with fever. We united in prayer for him, but though relieved, he still remained very weak. We were in great perplexity. Must we be driven from the work by bodily infirmities? Would Satan be permitted to exercise his power upon us, and contend for our usefulness and lives as long as we should remain in the world? We knew that God could limit the power of Satan. He might suffer us to be tried in the furnace, but would bring us forth purified and better fitted for His work.

Alone I poured out my soul before God in prayer that He would rebuke the disease and strengthen my husband to endure the journey. The case was urgent, and my faith firmly grasped the promises of God. I there obtained the evidence that if we should proceed on our journey to Michigan, the angel of God would go with us. When I related to my husband the exercise of my mind, he said that his own mind had been exercised in a similar manner, and we decided to go, trusting in the Lord. Every mile we traveled he felt strengthened. The Lord sustained him. And while he was preaching the word, I felt assured that angels of God were standing by his side to sustain him in his labors.

On this journey my husband's mind was much exercised upon the subject of spiritualism, and soon after our return he engaged in writing the book entitled, *Signs of the Times*. He was still feeble, and could sleep but little, but the Lord was his support. When his mind was in a confused, suffering state, we would bow before God, and in our distress cry unto Him. He heard our earnest prayers, and often blessed my husband so that with refreshed spirits he went on with the work. Many times in the day did we thus go before the Lord in earnest prayer. That book was not written in his own strength.

In the winter and spring I suffered much from heart disease. It was difficult for me to breathe while lying down, and I could not sleep unless raised in nearly a sitting posture. My breath often stopped, and I often fainted. I had upon my left eyelid a swelling which appeared to be a cancer. It had been increasing gradually for more than a year, until it had become quite painful, and affected my sight. When reading or writing, I was forced to bandage the afflicted eye. I feared that it was to be destroyed by a cancer. I looked back to the days and nights spent in reading proof sheets, which had strained my eyes, and thought: "If I lose my eye and my life, they will be sacrificed to the cause of God."

About this time a celebrated physician who gave counsel free visited Rochester, and I decided to have him examine my eye. He thought the swelling would prove to be a cancer. But upon feeling my pulse, he said: "You are much diseased, and will die of apoplexy before that swelling shall break out. You are in a dangerous condition with disease of the heart." This did not startle me, for I had been aware that without speedy relief I must go down to the grave. Two other women who had come for counsel were suffering with the same disease. The physician said that I was in a more dangerous condition than either of them, and it could not be more than three weeks before I would be afflicted with paralysis. I asked if he thought his medicine would cure me. He did not give me much encouragement. I tried the remedies which he prescribed, but received no benefit.

In about three weeks I fainted and fell to the floor, and remained nearly unconscious about thirty-six hours. It was feared that I could not live, but in answer to prayer I again revived. One week later I received a shock upon my left side. I had a strange sensation of coldness and numbness in my head, and severe pain in my temples. My tongue seemed heavy and numb; I could not speak plainly. My left arm and side were helpless. I thought I was dying, and my great anxiety was to have the evidence in my sufferings that the Lord loved me. For months I had suffered continual pain in my heart, and my spirits were constantly depressed. I had tried to serve God from principle without feeling, but I now thirsted for the salvation of God, I longed to realize His blessing notwithstanding my physical suffering.

The brethren and sisters came together to make my case a special subject of prayer. My desire was granted, I received the blessing of God, and had the assurance that He loved me. But the pain continued, and I grew more feeble every hour. Again the brethren and sisters assembled to present my case to the Lord. I was so weak that I could not pray vocally. My appearance seemed to weaken the faith of those around me. Then the promises of God were arrayed before me as I had never viewed them before. It seemed to me that Satan was striving to tear me from my husband and children and lay me in the grave, and these questions were suggested to my mind: Can you believe the naked promise of God? Can you walk out by faith, let the appearance be what it may? Faith revived. I whispered to my husband: "I believe that I shall recover." He answered: "I wish I could believe it." I retired that night without relief yet relying with firm confidence upon the promises of God. I could not sleep, but continued my silent prayer. Just before day I fell asleep.

I awoke at sunrise perfectly free from pain. The pressure upon my heart was gone, and I was very happy. Oh, what a change! It seemed to me that an angel of God had touched me while I was sleeping. I was filled with gratitude. The praise of God was upon my lips. I awoke my husband, and related to him the wonderful work that the Lord had wrought for me. He could scarcely comprehend it at first; but when I arose and dressed and walked around the house, he could praise God with me. My afflicted eye was free from pain. In a few days the swelling disappeared, and my eyesight was fully restored. The work was complete.

Again I visited the physician, and as soon as he felt my pulse, he said: "Madam, an entire change has taken place in your system, but the two women who visited me for counsel when you were last here are dead." I stated to him that his medicine had not cured me, as I could take none of it. After I left, the doctor said to a friend of mine: "Her case is a mystery. I do not understand it."

We soon visited Michigan again, and I endured long and wearisome journeys over the rough logways, and through mud sloughs, and my strength failed not. We felt that the Lord would have us visit Wisconsin, and arranged to take the cars at Jackson at ten in the evening.

As we were preparing to take the train, we felt very solemn, and proposed a season of prayer. And as we there committed ourselves to God, we could not refrain from weeping. We went to the depot with feelings of deep solemnity. On boarding the train, we went into a forward car, which had seats with high backs, hoping that we might sleep some that night. The car was full, and we passed back into the next, and there found seats. I did not, as usual when traveling in the night, lay off my bonnet, but held my carpetbag in my hand, as if waiting for something. We both spoke of our singular feelings.

The train had run about three miles from Jackson when its motion became very violent, jerking backward and forward, and finally stopping. I opened the window, and saw one car raised nearly upon end. I heard agonizing groans, and there was great confusion. The engine had been thrown from the track; but the car we were in was on the track, and was separated about one hundred feet from those before it. The baggage car was not much damaged, and our large trunk of books was uninjured. The second-class car was crushed, and the pieces, with the passengers, were thrown on both sides of the track. The car in which we tried to get a seat was much broken, and one end was raised upon the heap of ruins. The coupling did not break, but the car we were in was unfastened from the one before it, as if an angel had separated them. Four were killed or mortally wounded, and many were much injured. We could but feel that God had sent an angel to preserve our lives.

We returned to Jackson, and the next day took the train for Wisconsin. Our visit to that state was blessed of God. Souls were converted as the result of our efforts. The Lord strengthened me to endure the tedious journey.

August 29, 1854, another responsibility was added to our family in the birth of Willie. About this time the first number of the paper falsely called *The Messenger of Truth* was received. Those who slandered us through that paper had been reproved for their faults and errors. They would not bear reproof, and in a secret manner at first, afterward more openly, used their influence against us. This we could have borne, but some of those who should have stood by us were influenced by these wicked persons. Some whom we had trusted, and who had acknowledged that our labors had been signally blessed of God, withdrew their sympathy from us, and bestowed it upon comparative strangers.

The Lord had shown me the character and final come-out of that party; that His frown was upon those connected with that paper, and His hand was against them. And although they might appear to prosper for a time, and some honest ones be deceived, yet truth would eventually triumph, and every honest soul would break away from the deception which had held him, and come out clear from the influence of those wicked men; as God's hand was against them, they must go down.

Again my husband's health became very poor. He was troubled with cough and soreness of lungs, and his nervous system was prostrated. His anxiety of mind, the burdens which he bore in Rochester, his labor in the office, sickness and deaths in the family, the lack of sympathy from those who should have shared his labors, together with his traveling and preaching, were too much for his strength, and he seemed to be fast going down to a consumptive's grave. That was a time of gloom and darkness. A few rays of light occasionally parted the heavy clouds, giving us a little hope, or we should have sunk in despair. It seemed at times that God had forsaken us.

The *Messenger* party framed all manner of falsehoods concerning us. These words of the psalmist were often brought forcibly to my mind: "Fret not thyself because of evildoers, neither be thou envious against the workers of iniquity. For they shall soon be cut down like the grass, and wither as the green herb." Some of the writers of that sheet even triumphed over the feebleness of my husband, saying that God would take care of him, and remove him out of the way. When he read this as he lay sick, faith revived, and he exclaimed: "I shall not die, but live and declare the works of the Lord, and may yet preach at their funeral."

The darkest clouds seemed to shut down over us. Wicked men professing godliness, under the command of Satan were hurried on to forge falsehoods, and to bring the strength of their forces against us. If the cause of God had been ours alone, we might have trembled; but it was in the hands of Him who could say: "No one is able to pluck it out of My hands." We knew that Jesus lived and reigned. We could say before the Lord: The cause is Thine, and Thou knowest that it has not been our own choice, but by Thy command, that we have acted the part we have in it.

CHAPTER XIII

REMOVAL TO MICHIGAN

In 1855 the brethren in Michigan opened the way for the office of publication to be removed to Battle Creek. At that time my husband was owing between two and three thousand dollars, and all he had besides the books on hand was accounts for books, and some of these were doubtful. The cause had apparently come to a halt, orders for publications were very few and small, and he feared that he would die in debt. Brethren in Michigan assisted us in obtaining a lot and building a house. The deed was made in my name, so that I could dispose of it at pleasure after the death of my husband.

Those were days of sadness. I looked upon my three little boys, soon, as I feared, to be left fatherless, and thoughts like these forced themselves upon me: My husband dies of overwork in the cause of present truth; and who realizes what he has suffered, the burdens he has for years borne, the extreme care which has crushed his spirits and ruined his health, bringing him to an untimely grave, leaving his family destitute and dependent? I have often asked the question, Does God have no care for these things? Does He pass them by unnoticed? I was comforted to know that there is One who judgeth righteously, and that every sacrifice, every self-denial, and every pang of anguish endured for His sake, is faithfully chronicled in heaven, and will bring its reward. The day of the Lord will declare and bring to light things that are not yet made manifest.

I was shown that God designed to raise my husband up gradually; that we must exercise strong faith, for in every effort we should be fiercely buffeted by Satan; that we must look away from outward appearance, and believe. Three times a day we went alone before God, and engaged in earnest prayer for the recovery of his health. Frequently one of us would be prostrated by the power of God. The Lord graciously heard our earnest cries, and my husband began to recover. For many months our prayers ascended to heaven three times a day for health to do the will of God. These seasons of prayer were very precious. We were brought into a sacred nearness to God, and had sweet communion with Him. I cannot better state my feelings at this time than they are expressed in the following extracts from a letter I wrote to Sister Howland:

"I feel thankful that I can now have my children with me, under my own watchcare, and can better train them in the right way. For weeks I have felt a hungering and thirsting for salvation, and we have enjoyed almost uninterrupted communion with God. Why do we stay away from the fountain, when we can come and drink? Why do we die for bread, when there is a storehouse full? It is rich and free. O my soul, feast upon it, and daily drink in heavenly joys. I will not hold my peace. The praise of God is in my heart and upon my lips. We can rejoice in the fullness of our Saviour's love. We can feast upon His excellent glory. My soul testifies to this. My gloom has been dispersed by this precious light, and I can never forget it. Lord, help me to keep it in lively remembrance. Awake, all the energies of my soul! Awake, and adore thy Redeemer for His wondrous love!

"Souls around us must be aroused and saved, or they perish. Not a moment have we to lose. We all have an influence that tells for the truth or against it. I desire to carry with me unmistakable evidences that I am one of Christ's disciples. We want something besides Sabbath religion. We need the living principle, and to daily feel individual responsitility. This is shunned by many, and the fruit is carelessness, indifference, a lack of watchfulness and spirituality. Where is the spirituality of the church? Where are men and women full of faith and the Holy Spirit? My prayer is: Purify Thy church, O God. For months I have enjoyed freedom, and I am determined to order my conversation and all my ways aright before the Lord.

"Our enemies may triumph. They may speak bitter words, and their tongue frame slander, deceit, and falsehood, yet will we not be moved. We know in whom we have believed. We have not run in vain, neither labored in vain. A reckoning day is coming, when all will be judged according to the deeds done in the body. It is true the world is dark. Opposition may wax strong. The trifler and the scorner may grow bold in their iniquity. Yet for all this we will not be moved, but lean upon the arm of the Mighty One for strength.

"God is sifting His people. He will have a clean and holy church. We cannot read the heart of man. But the Lord has provided means to keep the church pure. A corrupt people has arisen who could not live with the people of God. They despised reproof, and would not be corrected. They had an opportunity to know that theirs was an unrighteous warfare. They had time to repent of their wrongs; but self was too dear to die. They nourished it, and it grew strong, and they separated from the trusting people of God, whom He is purifying unto Himself. We all have reason to thank God that a way has been opened to save the church; for the wrath of God must have come upon us if these corrupt pretenders had remained with us.

"Every honest soul that may be deceived by these disaffected ones, will have the true light in regard to them, if every angel from heaven has to visit them, to enlighten their minds. We have nothing to fear in this matter. As we near the judgment, all will manifest their true character, and it will be made plain to what company they belong. The sieve is moving. Let us not say: Stay Thy hand, O God. The church must be purged, and it will be. God reigns; let the people praise Him. I have not the most distant thought of sinking down. I mean to be right and do right. The judgment is to set, the books are to be opened, and we are to be judged according to our deeds. All the falsehoods that may be framed against me will not make me any worse, nor any better unless they have a tendency to drive me nearer my Redeemer."

From the time we moved to Battle Creek, the Lord began to turn our captivity. We found sympathizing friends in Michigan, who were ready to share our burdens and supply our wants. Old, tried friends in central New York and New England, especially in Vermont sympathized with us in our afflictions, and were ready to assist us in time of distress. At the Conference at Battle Creek in November, 1856, God wrought for us. The minds of His servants were exercised as to the gifts of the church. If God's frown had been brought upon His people because the gifts had been slighted and neglected, there was a pleasing prospect that His smiles would again be upon us, that He would graciously revive the gifts, and they would live in the church to encourage the fainting soul, and to correct and reprove the erring. New life was given to the cause, and success attended the labors of our preachers.

The publications were called for, and proved to be just what the cause demanded. *The Messenger of Truth* soon went down, and the discordant spirits who had spoken through it were scattered. My husband was enabled to pay all his debts. His cough ceased, the pain and soreness left his lungs and throat, and he was gradually restored to health, so that he could preach three times on the Sabbath and on first day with ease. This wonderful work in his restoration was of God, and He should have all the glory.

When my husband became so feeble, before our removal from Rochester, he desired to free himself from the responsibility of the publishing work. He proposed that the church take charge of the work, and that it be managed by a publishing committee whom they should appoint, and that no one connected with the office derive any financial benefit therefrom beyond the wages received for his labor.

Though the matter was repeatedly urged upon their attention, our brethren took no action in regard to it until 1861. Up to this time my husband had been the legal proprietor of the publishing house, and sole manager of the work. He enjoyed the confidence of the active friends of the cause, who trusted to his care the means which they donated from time to time, as the growing cause demanded, to build up the publishing enterprise. But although the statement was frequently repeated through the *Review,* that the publishing house was virtually the property of the church, yet as he was the only legal manager, our enemies took advantage of the situation, and under the cry of speculation, did all in their power to injure him, and to retard the progress of the cause. Under these circumstances he introduced the matter of organization, which resulted in the incorporation of the Seventh-day Adventist Publishing Association, according to the laws of Michigan, in the spring of 1861.

Although the cares that came upon us in connection with the publishing work and other branches of the cause involved much perplexity, the greatest sacrifice I was called to make in connection with the work was to leave my children to the care of others.

Henry had been from us five years, and Edson had received but little of our care. For years our family was very large, and our home like a hotel, and we from that home much of the time. I had felt the deepest anxiety that my children should be brought up free from evil habits, and I was often grieved as I thought of the contrast between my situation and that of others who would not take burdens and cares, who could ever be with their children, to counsel and instruct them, and who spent their time almost exclusively in their own families. And I have inquired: Does God require so much of us, and leave others without burdens? Is this equality? Are we to be thus hurried on from one care to another, one part of the work to another, and have but little time to bring up our children? Many nights, while others were sleeping, have been spent by me in bitter weeping.

I would plan some course more favorable for my children, then objections would arise which would sweep away these plans. I was keenly sensitive to faults in my children, and every wrong they committed brought on me such heartache as to affect my health. I have wished that some mothers could be circumstanced for a short time as I have been for years; then they would prize the blessings they enjoy, and could better sympathize with me in my privations. We prayed and labored for our children, and restrained them. We did not neglect the rod, but before using it we first labored to have them see their faults, and then prayed with them. We sought to have our children understand that we would merit the displeasure of God if we excused them in sin. And our efforts were blessed to their good. Their greatest pleasure was to please us. They were not free from faults, but we believed that they would yet be lambs of Christ's fold.

In 1860 death stepped over our threshold, and broke the youngest branch of our family tree. Little Herbert, born

September 20, 1860, died December 14 of the same year. When that tender branch was broken, how our hearts did bleed none may know but those who have followed their little ones of promise to the grave.

But oh, when our noble Henry died,* at the age of sixteen; when our sweet singer was borne to the grave, and we no more heard his early song, ours was a lonely home. Both parents and the two remaining sons felt the blow most keenly. But God comforted us in our bereavements, and with faith and courage we pressed forward in the work He had given us, in bright hope of meeting our children who had been torn from us by death, in that world where sickness and death will never come.

In August, 1865, my husband was suddenly stricken down by paralysis. This was a heavy blow, not only to myself and my children, but to the cause of God. The churches were deprived both of my husband's labors and of my own. Satan triumphed as he saw the work of truth thus hindered. But, thank God! he was not permitted to destroy us. After being cut off from all active labor for fifteen months, we ventured out once more together to work among the churches.

Having become fully satisfied that my husband would not recover from his protracted sickness while remaining inactive, and that the time had fully come for me to go forth and bear my testimony to the people, I decided to make a tour in northern Michigan, with my husband in his extremely feeble condition, in the severest cold of winter. It required no small degree of moral courage and faith in God to bring my mind to the decision to risk so much; but I knew that I had a work to do, and it seemed to me that Satan was determined to keep me from it. I had waited long for our captivity to be turned, and feared that precious

*The death of Henry N. White occurred at Topsham, Maine, December 8, 1863.

souls would be lost by the delay. To remain longer from the field seemed to me worse than death, and should we move out we could but perish. So, on the 19th of December, 1866, we left Battle Creek in a snowstorm for Wright, Michigan. My husband stood the journey of ninety miles much better than I feared, and seemed quite as well when we reached our destination as when we left Battle Creek.

Here commenced our first effective labors since his sickness. Here he began labor as in former years, though in much weakness. He would speak thirty or forty minutes in the forenoon of the Sabbath and on first day, while I would occupy the rest of the time, and then speak in the afternoon of each day, about an hour and a half each time. We were listened to with the greatest attention. I saw that my husband was growing stronger, clearer, and more connected in his subjects. And when on one occasion he spoke one hour with clearness and power, with the burden of the work upon him as before his sickness, my feelings of gratitude were beyond expression. I arose in the congregation, and for nearly half an hour tried with weeping to give utterance to them. The congregation was deeply moved. I felt assured that this was the dawn of better days for us.

The hand of God in his restoration was most apparent. Probably no other one upon whom such a blow has fallen ever recovered. Yet a severe shock of paralysis, seriously affecting the brain, was by the good hand of God removed from His servant, and new strength granted him both in body and mind.

During the years that followed the recovery of my husband, the Lord opened before us a vast field of labor. Though I took the stand as a speaker timidly at first, yet as the providence of God opened the way before me, I had confidence to stand before large audiences. Together we attended our camp meetings and other large gatherings, from Maine to Dakota, from Michigan to Texas and California.

The work begun in feebleness and obscurity has continued to increase and strengthen. Publishing houses in Michigan and in California, and missions in England, Norway, and Switzerland, attest its growth. In place of the edition of our first paper carried to the office in a carpetbag, about one hundred and forty thousand copies of our various periodicals are now sent out monthly from the offices of publication. The hand of God has been with His work to prosper and build it up.

The later history of my life would involve the history of the various enterprises which have arisen among us, and with which my lifework has been closely intermingled. For the upbuilding of these institutions, my husband and myself labored with pen and voice. To notice, even briefly, the experience of these active and busy years, would far exceed the limits of this sketch. Satan's efforts to hinder the work and to destroy the workmen have not ceased; but God has had a care for His servants and for His work.

CHAPTER XIV

THE DEATH OF MY HUSBAND

Notwithstanding the labors, cares, and responsibilities with which my husband's life had been crowded, his sixtieth year found him active and vigorous in mind and body. Three times had he fallen under a stroke of paralysis; yet by the blessing of God, a naturally strong constitution, and strict attention to the laws of health, he had been enabled to rally. Again he traveled, preached, and wrote with his wonted zeal and energy. Side by side we had labored in the cause of Christ for thirty-six years; and we hoped that we might stand together to witness the triumphant close. But such was not the will of God. The chosen protector of my youth, the companion of my life, the sharer of my labors and afflictions, has been taken from my side, and I am left to finish my work and to fight the battle alone.

The spring and early summer of 1881 we spent together at our home in Battle Creek. My husband hoped to arrange his business so that we could go to the Pacific Coast and devote ourselves to writing. He felt that we had made a mistake in allowing the apparent wants of the cause and the entreaties of our brethren to urge us into active labor in preaching when we should have been writing. My husband desired to present more fully the glorious subject of redemption, and I had long contemplated the preparation of important books. We both felt that while our mental powers were unimpaired we should complete these works—that it was a duty which we owed to ourselves and to the cause of God to rest from the heat of battle, and give to our people the precious light of truth which God had opened to our minds.

Some weeks before the death of my husband, I urged upon him the importance of seeking a field of labor where we would be released from the burdens necessarily coming upon us at Battle Creek. In reply he spoke of various matters which required attention before we could leave—duties which someone must do. Then with deep feeling he inquired: "Where are the men to do this work? Where are those who will have an unselfish interest in our institutions, and who will stand for the right, unaffected by any influence with which they may come in contact?"

With tears he expressed his anxiety for our institutions at Battle Creek. Said he: "My life has been given to the upbuilding of these institutions. It seems like death to leave them. They are as my children, and I cannot separate my interest from them. These institutions are the Lord's instrumentalities to do a specific work. Satan seeks to hinder and defeat every means by which the Lord is working for the salvation of men. If the great adversary can mold these institutions according to the world's standard, his object is gained. It is my greatest anxiety to have the right man in the right place. If those who stand in responsible positions are weak in moral power, and vacillating in principle, inclined to lead toward the world, there are enough who will be led. Evil influences must not prevail. I would rather die than live to see these institutions mismanaged, or turned aside from the purpose for which they were brought into existence.

"In my relations to this cause I have been longest and most closely connected with the publishing work. Three times have I fallen, stricken with paralysis, through my devotion to this branch of the cause. Now that God has given me renewed physical and mental strength, I feel that I can serve His cause as I have never been able to serve it before. I must see the publishing work prosper. It is interwoven with my very existence. If I forget the interests of this work, let my right hand forget her cunning."

We had an appointment to attend a tent meeting at Charlotte, Sabbath and Sunday, July 23 and 24. As I was in feeble health, we decided to travel by private conveyance. On the way, my husband seemed cheerful, yet a feeling of solemnity rested upon him. He repeatedly praised the Lord for mercies and blessings received, and freely expressed his own feelings concerning the past and future: "The Lord is good, and greatly to be praised. He is a present help in time of need. The future seems cloudy and uncertain, but the Lord would not have us distressed over these things. When trouble comes, He will give us grace to endure it. What the Lord has been to us, and what He has done for us, should make us so grateful that we would never murmur or complain. Our labors, burdens, and sacrifices will never be fully appreciated by all. I see that I have lost my peace of mind and the blessing of God by permitting myself to be troubled by these things.

"It has seemed hard to me that my motives should be misjudged, and that my best efforts to help, encourage, and strengthen my brethren should again and again be turned against me. But I should have remembered Jesus and His disappointments. His soul was grieved that He was not appreciated by those He came to bless. I should have dwelt upon the mercy and loving-kindness of God, praising Him more and complaining less of the ingratitude of my brethren. Had I ever left all my perplexities with the Lord, thinking less of what others said and did against me, I should have had more peace and joy. I will now seek first to guard myself that I offend not in word or deed, and then to help my brethren make straight paths for their feet. I will not stop to mourn over any wrong done to me. I have expected more of men than I ought. I love God and His work, and I love my brethren also."

Little did I think, as we traveled on, that this was the last journey we would ever make together. The weather changed suddenly from oppressive heat to chilling cold. My husband took cold, but thought his health so good that he would receive no permanent injury. He labored in the meetings at Charlotte, presenting the truth with great clearness and power. He spoke of the pleasure he felt in addressing a people who manifested so deep an interest in the subjects most dear to him. "The Lord has indeed refreshed my soul," he said, "while I have been breaking to others the bread of life. All over Michigan the people are calling eagerly for help. How I long to comfort, encourage, and strengthen them with the precious truths applicable to this time!"

On our return home, my husband complained of slight indisposition, yet he engaged in his work as usual. Every morning we visited the grove near our home, and united in prayer. We were anxious to know our duty. Letters were continually coming in from different places, urging us to attend the camp meetings. Notwithstanding our determination to devote ourselves to writing, it was hard to refuse to meet with our brethren in these important gatherings. We earnestly pleaded for wisdom to know the right course.

Sabbath morning, as usual, we went to the grove together, and my husband prayed most fervently three times. He seemed reluctant to cease pleading with God for special guidance and blessing. His prayers were heard, and peace and light came to our hearts. He praised the Lord, and said: "Now I give it all up to Jesus. I feel a sweet, heavenly peace, an assurance that the Lord will show us our duty; for we desire to do His will." He accompanied me to the Tabernacle, and opened the services with singing and prayer. It was the last time he was ever to stand by my side in the pulpit.

On the following Monday he had a severe chill, and the next day I, too, was attacked. Together we were taken to the sanitarium for treatment. On Friday my symptoms became more favorable. The doctor then informed me that my husband was inclined to sleep, and that danger was apprehended. I was immediately taken to his room, and as soon as I looked upon his countenance I knew that he was dying. I tried to arouse him. He understood all that was said to him, and responded to all questions that could be answered by Yes or No, but seemed unable to say more. When I told him I thought he was dying he manifested no surprise. I asked if Jesus was precious to him. He said: "Yes, oh, yes." "Have you no desire to live?" I inquired. He answered: "No."

We then knelt by his bedside, and I prayed for him. A peaceful expression rested upon his countenance. I said to him: "Jesus loves you. The everlasting arms are beneath you." He responded: "Yes, yes."

Brother Smith and other brethren then prayed around his bedside, and retired to spend much of the night in prayer. My husband said he felt no pain but he was evidently failing fast. Dr. Kellogg and his helpers did all that was in their power to hold him back from death. He slowly revived, but continued very weak.

The next morning he seemed slightly to revive, but about noon he had a chill, which left him unconscious. At 5 p.m., Sabbath, August 6, 1881, he quietly breathed his life away, without a struggle or a groan.

The shock of my husband's death—so sudden, so unexpected—fell upon me with crushing weight. In my feeble condition I had summoned strength to remain at his bedside to the last, but when I saw his eyes closed in death, exhausted nature gave way, and I was completely prostrated. For some time I seemed balancing between life and death. The vital flame burned so low that a breath might extinguish it. At night my pulse would grow feeble, and my breathing fainter and fainter till it seemed about to cease. Only by the blessing of God and the unremitting care and watchfulness of physician and attendants was my life preserved.

Though I had not risen from my sickbed after my husband's death, I was borne to the Tabernacle on the following Sabbath to attend his funeral. At the close of the sermon I felt it a duty to testify to the value of the Christian's hope in the hour of sorrow and bereavement. As I arose, strength was given me, and I spoke about ten minutes, exalting the mercy and love of God in the presence of that crowded assembly. At the close of the services I followed my husband to Oak Hill Cemetery, where he was laid to rest until the morning of the resurrection.

My physical strength had been prostrated by the blow, yet the power of divine grace sustained me in my great bereavement. When I saw my husband breathe his last, I felt that Jesus was more precious to me then than He ever had been in any previous hour of my life. When I stood by my first-born, and closed his eyes in death, I could say: "The Lord gave, and the Lord hath taken away; blessed be the name of the Lord." And I felt then that I had a comforter in Jesus.

And when my latest born was torn from my arms, and I could no longer see its little head upon the pillow by my side, then I could say: "The Lord gave, and the Lord hath taken away; blessed be the name of the Lord." And when he upon whose large affections I had leaned, with whom I had labored for thirty-six years, was taken away, I could lay my hands upon his eyes, and say: I commit my treasure to Thee until the morning of the resurrection.

When I saw him passing away, and saw the many friends sympathizing with me, I thought: What a contrast to the death of Jesus as He hung upon the cross! What a contrast! In the hour of His agony, the revilers were mocking and deriding Him. But He died, and He passed through the tomb to brighten it, and to lighten it, that we might have joy and hope even in the event of death; that we might say, as we lay our friends away to rest in Jesus: We shall meet them again.

At times I felt that I could not have my husband die. But these words seemed to be impressed on my mind: "Be still, and know that I am God." I keenly feel my loss, but dare not give myself up to useless grief. This would not bring back the dead. And I am not so selfish as to wish, if I could, to bring him from his peaceful slumber to engage again in the battles of life. Like a tired warrior, he has lain down to sleep. I will look with pleasure upon his resting place. The best way in which I and my children can honor the memory of him who has fallen, is to take the work where he left it, and in the strength of Jesus carry it forward to completion. We will be thankful for the years of usefulness that were granted to him; and for his sake, and for Christ's sake, we will learn from his death a lesson which we shall never forget. We will let this bereavement make us more kind and gentle, more forbearing, patient, and thoughtful toward the living.

I take up my lifework alone, in full confidence that my Redeemer will be with me. We have only a little while to wage the warfare; then Christ will come, and this scene of conflict will close. Then our last efforts will have been made to work with Christ, and advance His kingdom. Some who have stood in the forefront of the battle, zealously resisting incoming evil, fall at the post of duty; the living gaze sorrowfully at the fallen heroes, but there is no time to cease work. They must close up the ranks; seize the banner from the hand palsied by death, and with renewed energy vindicate the truth and the honor of Christ. As never before, resistance must be made against sin—against the powers of darkness. The time demands energetic and determined activity on the part of those who believe present truth. If the time seems long to wait for our Deliverer to come; if bowed by affliction and worn with toil, we feel impatient to receive an honorable release from the warfare, let us remember—and let the remembrance check every murmur—that we are left on earth to encounter storms and conflicts, to perfect Christian character, to become better acquainted with God our Father, and Christ our Elder Brother, and to do work for the Master in winning many souls to Christ. "They that be wise shall shine as the brightness of the firmament; and they that turn many to righteousness as the stars for ever and ever."

NUMBER ONE

TESTIMONY FOR THE CHURCH

THY BROTHER'S KEEPER

November 20, 1855, while in prayer, the Spirit of the Lord came suddenly and powerfully upon me, and I was taken off in vision.

I saw that the Spirit of the Lord has been dying away from the church. The servants of the Lord have trusted too much to the strength of argument, and have not had that firm reliance upon God which they should have. I saw that the mere argument of the truth will not move souls to take a stand with the remnant; for the truth is unpopular. The servants of God must have the truth in the soul. Said the angel: "They must get it warm from glory, carry it in their bosoms, and pour it out in the warmth and earnestness of the soul to those that hear." A few that are conscientious are ready to decide from the weight of evidence; but it is impossible to move many with a mere theory of the truth. There must be a power to attend the truth, a living testimony to move them.

I saw that the enemy is busy to destroy souls. Exaltation has come into the ranks; there must be more humility. There is too much of an independence of spirit indulged in among the messengers. This must be laid aside, and there must be a drawing together of the servants of God. There has been too much of a spirit to ask, "Am I my brother's keeper?" Said the angel: "Yea, *thou art* thy brother's keeper. Thou shouldest have a watchful care for thy brother, be interested for his welfare, and cherish a kind, loving spirit toward him. Press together, press together." God designed that man should be openhearted and honest, without affectation, meek, humble, with simplicity. This is the principle of heaven; God ordered it so. But poor, frail man has sought out something different—to follow his own way, and carefully attend to his own self-interest.

I asked the angel why simplicity had been shut out from the church, and pride and exaltation had come in. I saw that this is the reason why we have almost been delivered into the hand of the enemy. Said the angel: "Look ye, and ye shall see that this feeling prevails: Am I my brother's keeper?" Again said the angel: "Thou art thy brother's keeper. Thy profession, thy faith, requires thee to deny thyself and sacrifice to God, or thou wilt be unworthy of eternal life; for it was purchased for thee dearly, even by the agony, the sufferings, and blood of the beloved Son of God."

I saw that many in different places, East and West, were adding farm to farm, and land to land, and house to house, and they make the cause of God their excuse, saying they do this that they may help the cause. They shackle themselves so that they can be of but little benefit to the cause. Some buy a piece of land, and labor with all their might to pay for it. Their time is so occupied that they can spare but little time to pray, and serve God, and gain strength from Him to overcome their besetments. They are in debt, and when the cause needs their help they cannot assist, for they must get free from debt first. But as soon as they are free from debt they are farther from helping the cause than before; for they again involve themselves by adding to their property. They flatter themselves that this course is right, that they will use the avails in the cause, when they are actually laying up treasure here. They love the truth in word, but not in work.

They love the cause just as much as their works show. They love the world more and the cause of God less; the attraction to earth grows stronger and the attraction to heaven weaker. Their heart is with their treasure. By their example they say to those around them that they are intending to stay here, that this world is their home. Said the angel: "Thou art thy brother's keeper."

Many have indulged in needless expense, merely to gratify the feelings, the taste, and the eye, when the cause needed the very means thus used, and when some of the servants of God were poorly clothed and were crippled in their labor for lack of means. Said the angel: "Their time to do will soon be past. Their works show that self is their idol, and to it they sacrifice." Self must first be gratified; their feeling is: "Am I my brother's keeper?" Warning after warning many have received, but heeded not. Self is the main object, and to it everything must bow.

I saw that the church has nearly lost the spirit of self-denial and sacrifice; they make self and self-interest first, and then they do for the cause what they think they can as well as not. Such a sacrifice, I saw, is lame, and not accepted of God. All should be interested to do their utmost to advance the cause. I saw that those who have no property, but have strength of body, are accountable to God for their strength. They should be diligent in business and fervent in spirit; they should not leave those that have possessions to do all the sacrificing. I saw that they can sacrifice, and that it is their duty to do so as well as those who have property. But often those that have no possessions do not realize that they can deny themselves in many ways, can lay out less upon their bodies, and to gratify their tastes and appetites, and find much to spare for the cause, and thus lay up a treasure in heaven. I saw that there is loveliness and beauty in the truth; but take away the power of God, and it is powerless.

TIME TO BEGIN THE SABBATH*

I saw that it is even so: "From even unto even, shall ye celebrate your Sabbath." Said the angel: "Take the word of God, read it, understand, and ye cannot err. Read carefully, and ye shall there find *what* even is, and *when* it is." I asked the angel if the frown of God had been upon His people for commencing the Sabbath as they had. I was directed back to the first rise of the Sabbath, and followed the people of God up to this time, but did not see that the Lord was displeased, or frowned upon them. I inquired why it had been thus, that at this late day we must change the time of commencing the Sabbath. Said the angel: "Ye shall understand, but not yet, not yet." Said the angel: "If light come, and that light is set aside or rejected, then comes condemnation and the frown of God; but before the light comes, there is no sin, for there is no light for them to reject." I saw that it was in the minds of some that the Lord had shown that the Sabbath commenced at six o'clock, when I had only seen that it commenced at "even," and it was inferred that even was at six. I saw that the servants of God must draw together, press together.

OPPOSERS OF THE TRUTH*

I was shown the case of Stephenson and Hall of Wisconsin. I saw that while we were in Wisconsin, in June, 1854, they were convicted that the visions were of God; but they examined them and compared them with their views of the age to come, and because the visions did not agree with these, they sacrificed the visions for the Age-to-Come. And while on their journey East, last spring, they both were wrong and designing. They have stumbled over the Age-to-Come, and they

*See Appendix.

are ready to take any course to injure the *Review;* its friends must be awake and do what they can to save the children of God from deception. These men are uniting with a lying and corrupt people. They have had evidence of this. And while they were professing sympathy and union with my husband, they (especially Stephenson) were biting like an adder behind his back. While their words were smooth with him, they were inflaming Wisconsin against the *Review* and its conductors. Especially was Stephenson active in this matter. Their object has been to have the *Review* publish the Age-to-Come theory, or to destroy its influence. And while my husband was openhearted and unsuspecting, seeking ways to remove their jealousy, and frankly opening to them the affairs of the office, and trying to help them, they were watching for evil, and observing everything with a jealous eye. Said the angel as I beheld them: "Think ye, feeble man, that ye can stay the work of God? Feeble man, one touch of His finger can lay thee prostrate. He will suffer thee but a little while."

I was pointed back to the rise of the advent doctrine, and even before that time, and saw that there had not been a parallel to the deception, misrepresentation, and falsehood that has been practiced by the *Messenger* party, or such an association of corrupt hearts under a cloak of religion. Some honest hearts have been influenced by them, concluding that they must have at least some cause for their statements, thinking them incapable of uttering so glaring falsehoods. I saw that such will have evidence of the truth of these matters. The church of God should move straight along, as though there were not such a people in the world.

I saw that decided efforts should be made to show those who are unchristian in life their wrongs, and if they do not reform, they should be separated from the precious and holy, that God may have a clean and pure people that He can delight in. Dishonor Him not by linking or uniting the clean with the unclean.

I was shown some coming from the East to the West. I saw that it should not be the object of those who leave the East for the West to get rich, but to win souls to the truth. Said the angel: "Let your works show that it is not for honor, or to lay up a treasure on earth, that ye have moved West, but to hold up and exalt the standard of truth." I saw that those who move West should be like men waiting for their Lord. Said the angel: "Be a living example to those in the West. Let your works show that you are God's peculiar people, and that you have a peculiar work, to give the last message of mercy to the world. Let your works show to those around you that this world is not your home." I saw that those who have entangled themselves should break the snare of the enemy and go free. Lay not up treasures upon earth, but show by your lives that you are laying up treasure in heaven. If God has called you West, He has a work, an exalted work, for you to do. Let your faith and experience help those who have not a living experience. Let not the attraction be to this poor, dark speck of a world, but let it be upward to God, glory, and heaven. Let not the care and perplexity of farms here engross your mind, but you can safely be wrapped up in contemplating Abraham's farm. We are heirs to that immortal inheritance. Wean your affections from earth, and dwell upon heavenly things.

PARENTAL RESPONSIBILITY

I saw that great responsibility rests upon parents. They must not be led by their children, but must lead them. I was referred to Abraham. He was faithful in his house. He commanded his household after him, and it was remembered of God.

I was then referred to the case of Eli. He restrained not his children, and they became wicked and vile, and by their wickedness led Israel astray. When God had made known to Samuel their sins, and the heavy curse that was to follow because Eli restrained them not, He said that their sins should not be purged with sacrifice nor offering forever. When told by Samuel what the Lord had shown him, Eli submitted, saying: "It is the Lord: let Him do what seemeth Him good." The curse of God soon followed. Those wicked priests were slain, and thirty thousand of Israel were also slain, and the ark of God was taken by their enemies. And when Eli heard that the ark of God was taken, he fell backward and died. All this evil resulted from Eli's neglect to restrain his sons. I saw that if God was so particular as to notice such things anciently, He will be no less particular in these last days.

Parents must govern their children, correct their passions, and subdue them, or God will surely destroy the children in the day of His fierce anger, and the parents who have not controlled their children will not be blameless. Especially should the servants of God govern their own families and have them in good subjection. I saw that they are not prepared to judge or decide in matters of the church, unless they can rule well their own house. They must first have order at home, and then their judgment and influence will tell in the church.

I saw that the reason why visions have not been more frequent of late, is, they have not been appreciated by the church. The church have nearly lost their spirituality and faith, and the reproofs and warnings have had but little effect upon them. Many of those who have professed faith in them have not heeded them.

Some have taken an injudicious course; when they have talked their faith to unbelievers, and the proof has been asked for, they have read a vision, instead of going to the Bible for proof. I saw that this course was inconsistent, and prejudiced unbelievers against the truth. The visions can have no weight with those who have never seen them and know nothing of their spirit. They should not be referred to in such cases.

FAITH IN GOD

When at Battle Creek, Michigan, May 5, 1855, I saw that there was a great lack of faith with the servants of God, as well as with the church.

They were too easily discouraged, too ready to doubt God, too willing to believe that they had a hard lot and that God had forsaken them. I saw that this was cruel. God so loved them as to give His dearly beloved Son to die for them, and all heaven was interested in their salvation; yet after all that had been done for them, it was hard to believe and trust so kind and good a Father. He has said that He is more willing to give the Holy Spirit to them that ask Him, than earthly parents are to give good gifts to their children. I saw that the servants of God and the church were too easily discouraged. When they asked their Father in heaven for things which they thought they needed, and these did not immediately come, their faith wavered, their courage fled, and a murmuring feeling took possession of them. This, I saw, displeased God.

Every saint who comes to God with a true heart, and sends his honest petitions to Him in faith, will have his prayers answered. Your faith must not let go of the promises of God, if you do not see or feel the immediate answer to your prayers. Be not afraid to trust God. Rely upon His sure promise: "Ask, and ye shall receive." God is too wise to err, and too good to withhold any good thing from His saints that walk uprightly. Man is erring, and although his petitions are sent up from an honest heart, he does not always ask for the things that are good for himself, or that will glorify God. When this is so, our wise and good Father hears our prayers, and will answer, sometimes immediately; but He gives us the things that are for our best good and His own glory. God gives us blessings; if we could look into His plan, we would clearly see that He knows what is best for us and that our prayers are answered. Nothing hurtful is given, but the blessing we need, in the place of something we asked for that would not be good for us, but to our hurt.

I saw that if we do not feel immediate answers to our prayers, we should hold fast our faith, not allowing distrust to come in, for that will separate us from God. If our faith wavers, we shall receive nothing from Him. Our confidence in God should be strong; and when we need it most, the blessing will fall upon us like a shower of rain.

When the servants of God pray for His Spirit and blessing, it sometimes comes immediately; but it is not always then bestowed. At such times, faint not. Let your faith hold fast the promise that it will come. Let your trust be fully in God, and often that blessing will come when you need it most, and you will unexpectedly receive help from God when you are presenting the truth to unbelievers, and will be enabled to speak the word with clearness and power.

It was represented to me like children asking a blessing of their earthly parents who love them. They ask something that the parent knows will hurt them; the parent gives them the things that will be good and healthful for them, in the place of that which they desired. I saw that every prayer which is sent up in faith from an honest heart will be heard of God and answered, and the one that sent up the petition will have the blessing when he needs it most, and it will often exceed his expectations. Not a prayer of a true saint is lost if sent up in faith from an honest heart.

THE "MESSENGER" PARTY*

When at Oswego, New York, June, 1855, I was shown that God's people have been weighed down with clogs; that there have been Achans in the camp. The work of God has progressed but little, and many of His servants have been discouraged because the truth has taken no more effect in New York, and there have been no more added to the church. The *Messenger* party has arisen, and we shall suffer some from their lying tongues and misrepresentations, yet we should bear it all patiently; for they will not injure the cause of God, now they have left us, as much as they would have injured it by their influence had they remained with us.

God's frown has been brought upon the church on account of individuals with corrupt hearts being in it. They have wanted to be foremost, when neither God nor their brethren placed them there. Selfishness and exaltation have marked their course. A place is now open for all such where they can go and find pasture with those of their kind. And we should praise God that in mercy He has rid the church of them. God has given many of these persons up to their own ways to be filled with their own doings. An excitement and sympathy now leads them, which will deceive some; but every honest one will be enlightened as to the true state of this company, and will remain with God's peculiar people, hold fast the truth, and follow in the humble path, unaffected by the influence of those who have been given up of God to their own ways, to be filled with their own doings. I saw that God had given these persons opportunity to reform, He had enlightened them as to their love for self and their other sins; but they would not heed it. They would not be reformed, and He mercifully relieved the church of them. The truth will take effect if the servants of God and the church will devote themselves to Him and His cause.

---

*See Appendix

I saw that the people of God must arouse and put on the armor. Christ is coming, and the great work of the last message of mercy is of too much importance for us to leave it and come down to answer such falsehoods, misrepresentations, and slanders as the *Messenger* party have fed upon and have scattered abroad. Truth, present truth, we must dwell upon it. We are doing a great work, and cannot come down. Satan is in all this, to divert our minds from the present truth and the coming of Christ. Said the angel: "Jesus knows it all." In a little from this their day is coming. All will be judged according to the deeds done in the body. The lying tongue will be stopped. The sinners in Zion will be afraid, and fearfulness will surprise the hypocrites.

PREPARE TO MEET THE LORD

I saw that we should not put off the coming of the Lord. Said the angel: "Prepare, prepare, for what is coming upon the earth. Let your works correspond with your faith." I saw that the mind must be stayed upon God, and that our influence should tell for God and His truth. We cannot honor the Lord when we are careless and indifferent. We cannot glorify Him when we are desponding. We must be in earnest to secure our own soul's salvation, and to save others. All importance should be attached to this, and everything besides should come in secondary.

I saw the beauty of heaven. I heard the angels sing their rapturous songs, ascribing praise, honor, and glory to Jesus. I could then realize something of the wondrous love of the Son of God. He left all the glory, all the honor which He had in heaven, and was so interested for our salvation that He patiently and meekly bore every indignity and slight which man could heap upon Him. He was wounded, smitten, and bruised; He was stretched on Calvary's cross and suffered the most agonizing death to save us from death, that we might be washed in His blood and be raised up to live with Him in the mansions He is preparing for us, to enjoy the light and glory of heaven, to hear the angels sing, and to sing with them.

I saw that all heaven is interested in our salvation; and shall we be indifferent? Shall we be careless, as though it were a small matter whether we are saved or lost? Shall we slight the sacrifice that has been made for us? Some have done this. They have trifled with offered mercy, and the frown of God is upon them. God's Spirit will not always be grieved. It will depart if grieved a little longer. After all has been done that God could do to save men, if they show by their lives that they slight Jesus' offered mercy, death will be their portion, and it will be dearly purchased. It will be a dreadful death; for they will have to feel the agony that Christ felt upon the cross to purchase for them the redemption which they have refused. And they will then realize what they have lost—eternal life and the immortal inheritance. The great sacrifice that has been made to save souls shows us their worth. When the precious soul is once lost, it is lost forever.

I have seen an angel standing with scales in his hands weighing the thoughts and interest of the people of God, especially the young. In one scale were the thoughts and interest tending heavenward; in the other were the thoughts and interest tending to earth. And in this scale were thrown all the reading of storybooks, thoughts of dress and show, vanity, pride, etc. Oh, what a solemn moment! the angels of God standing with scales, weighing the thoughts of His professed children—those who claim to be dead to the world and alive to God. The scale filled with thoughts of earth, vanity, and pride quickly went down, notwithstanding weight after weight rolled from the scale. The one with the thoughts and interest tending to heaven went quickly up as the other went down, and oh, how light it was! I can relate this as I saw it; but never can I give the solemn and vivid impression stamped upon my mind, as I saw the angel with the scales weighing the thoughts and interest of the people of God. Said the angel: "Can such enter heaven? No, no, never. Tell them the hope they now possess is vain, and unless they speedily repent, and obtain salvation, they must perish."

A form of godliness will not save any. All must have a deep and living experience. This alone will save them in the time of trouble. Then their work will be tried of what sort it is; and if it is gold, silver, and precious stones, they will be hid as in the secret of the Lord's pavilion. But if their work is wood, hay, and stubble, nothing can shield them from the fierceness of Jehovah's wrath.

The young, as well as those who are older, will be required to give a reason for their hope. But the mind, designed by God for better things, formed to serve Him perfectly, has dwelt upon foolish things, instead of eternal interests. That mind which is left to wander here and there is just as well able to understand the truth, the evidence from the word of God for keeping the Sabbath, and the true foundation of the Christian's hope, as to study the appearance, the manners, the dress, etc. And those who give up the mind to be diverted with foolish stories and idle tales, have the imagination fed, but the brilliancy of God's word is eclipsed to them. The mind is led directly from God. The interest in His precious word is destroyed.

A book has been given us to guide our feet through the perils of this dark world to heaven. It tells us how we can escape the wrath of God, and also tells of the sufferings of Christ for us, the great sacrifice that has been made that we might be saved and enjoy the presence of God forever. And if any come short at last, having heard the truth as they have in this land of light, it will be their own fault; they will be without excuse. The word of God tells us how we may become perfect Christians and escape the seven last plagues. But they took no interest to find this out. Other things diverted the mind, idols were cherished by them, and God's Holy Word was neglected and slighted. God has been trifled with by professed Christians, and when His Holy Word shall judge them in the last day, they will be found wanting. That word which they have neglected for foolish storybooks, tries their lives. That is the standard; their motives, words, works, and the manner in which they use their time are all compared with the written word of God; and if they come short then, their cases are decided forever.

I saw that many measure themselves among themselves, and compare their lives with the lives of others. This should not be. No one but Christ is given us as an example. He is our true Pattern, and each should strive to excel in imitating Him. We are co-workers with Christ, or co-workers with the enemy. We either gather with Christ or scatter abroad. We are decided, wholehearted Christians, or none at all. Says Christ: "I would thou wert cold or hot. So then because thou art lukewarm, and neither cold nor hot, I will spew thee out of My mouth."

I saw that some hardly know as yet what self-denial or sacrifice is, or what it is to suffer for the truth's sake. But none will enter heaven without making a sacrifice A spirit of self-denial and sacrifice should be cherished. Some have not sacrificed themselves, their own bodies, on the altar of God. They indulge in hasty, fitful temper, gratify their appetites, and attend to their own self-interest, regardless of the cause of God. Those who are willing to make any sacrifice for eternal life, will have it, and it will be worth suffering for, worth crucifying self for, and sacrificing every idol for. The far more exceeding and eternal weight of glory swallows up everything and eclipses every earthly pleasure.

NUMBER TWO

TESTIMONY FOR THE CHURCH

THE TWO WAYS

At the Conference at Battle Creek, May 27, 1856, I was shown in vision some things that concern the church generally. The glory and majesty of God were made to pass before me. Said the angel: "He is terrible in His majesty, yet ye realize it not; terrible in His anger, yet ye offend Him daily. 'Strive to enter in at the strait gate;' 'for wide is the gate, and broad is the way, that leadeth to destruction, and many there be which go in thereat: because strait is the gate, and narrow is the way, which leadeth unto life, and few there be that find it.' " These roads are distinct, separate, in opposite directions. One leads to eternal life, the other to eternal death. I saw the distinction between these roads, also the distinction between the companies traveling them. The roads are opposite; one is broad and smooth, the other narrow and rugged. So the parties that travel them are opposite in character, in life, in dress, and in conversation.

Those who travel in the narrow way are talking of the joy and happiness they will have at the end of the journey. Their countenances are often sad, yet often beam with holy, sacred joy. They do not dress like the company in the broad road, nor talk like them, nor act like them. A pattern has been given them. A man of sorrows and acquainted with grief opened that road for them, and traveled it Himself. His followers see His footsteps, and are comforted and cheered. He went through safely; so can they, if they follow in His footsteps.

In the broad road all are occupied with their persons, their dress, and the pleasures in the way. They indulge freely in hilarity and glee, and think not of their journey's end, of the certain destruction at the end of the path. Every day they approach nearer their destruction; yet they madly rush on faster and faster. Oh, how dreadful this looked to me!

I saw many traveling in this broad road who had the words written upon them: "Dead to the world. The end of all things is at hand. Be ye also ready." They looked just like all the vain ones around them, except a shade of sadness which I noticed upon their countenances. Their conversation was just like that of the gay, thoughtless ones around them; but they would occasionally point with great satisfaction to the letters on their garments, calling for the others to have the same upon theirs. They were in the broad way, yet they professed to be of the number who were traveling the narrow way. Those around them would say: "There is no distinction between us. We are alike, we dress, and talk, and act alike."

Then I was pointed back to the years 1843 and 1844. There was a spirit of consecration then that there is not now. What has come over the professed peculiar people of God? I saw the conformity to the world, the unwillingness to suffer for the truth's sake. I saw a great lack of submission to the will of God. I was pointed back to the children of Israel after they left Egypt. God in mercy called them out from the Egyptians, that they might worship Him without hindrance or restraint. He wrought for them in the way by miracles, He proved and tried them by bringing them into strait places. After the wonderful dealings of God with them, and their deliverance so many times, they murmured when tried or proved by Him. Their language was: "Would to God we had died by the hand of the Lord in the land of Egypt." They lusted for the leeks and onions there.

I saw that many who profess to believe the truth for these last days think it strange that the children of Israel murmured as they journeyed; that after the wonderful dealings of God with them, they should be so ungrateful as to forget what He had done for them. Said the angel: "Ye have done worse than they." I saw that God has given His servants the truth so clear, so plain, that it cannot be resisted. Wherever they go, they have certain victory. Their enemies cannot get round the convincing truth. Light has been shed so clear that the servants of God can stand up anywhere and let truth, clear and connected, bear away the victory. This great blessing has not been prized, or even realized. If any trial arises, some begin to look back and think they have a hard time. Some of the professed servants of God do not know what purifying trials are. They sometimes make trials for themselves, imagine trials, and are so easily discouraged, so easily hurt, self-dignity is so quick to feel, that they injure themselves, injure others, and injure the cause. Satan magnifies their trials and puts thoughts into their minds that if given way to, will destroy their influence and usefulness.

Some have felt tempted to take themselves from the work, to labor with their hands. I saw that if the hand of God should be taken from them, and they be left subject to disease and death, then they would know what trouble is. It is a fearful thing to murmur against God. They do not bear in mind that the way which they are traveling is a rugged, self-denying, self-crucifying way, and they must not expect everything to move on as smoothly as though they were traveling in the broad road.

I saw that some of the servants of God, even ministers, are so easily discouraged, self is so quickly hurt, that they imagine themselves slighted and injured when it is not so.

They think their lot hard. Such realize not how they would feel should the sustaining hand of God be withdrawn, and they pass through anguish of soul. They would then find their lot tenfold harder than it was before, while they were employed in the work of God, suffering trials and privations, yet withal having the Lord's approbation. Some that are laboring in the cause of God know not when they do have an easy time. They have had so few privations and know so little of want or wearing labor or burden of soul that when they have an easy time, when they are favored of God and almost entirely free from anguish of spirit, they know it not and think their trials great. I saw that unless such have a spirit of self-sacrifice, and are ready to labor cheerfully, not sparing themselves, God will release them. He will not acknowledge them as His self-sacrificing servants, but will raise up those who will labor, not slothfully, but in earnest, and will know when they have an easy time. God's servants must feel the burden of souls and weep between the porch and the altar, crying: "Spare Thy people, O Lord."

Some of the servants of God have given up their lives to spend and be spent for the cause of God, until their constitutions are broken down, and they are almost worn out with mental labor, incessant care, toil, and privations. Others have not had and would not take the burden upon them. Yet just such ones think they have a hard time, because they have never experienced hardships. They never have been baptized into the suffering part, and never will be as long as they manifest so much weakness and so little fortitude, and love their ease so well. From what God has shown me, there needs to be a scourging among the ministers, that the slothful, dilatory, and self-caring ones may be scourged out, and there remain a pure, faithful, and self-sacrificing company who will not study their ease, but will minister faithfully in word and doctrine, willing to suffer and endure all things for

Christ's sake, and to save those for whom He died. Let these servants feel the woe upon them if they preach not the gospel, and it will be enough; but all do not feel this.

CONFORMITY TO THE WORLD

I was shown the conformity of some professed Sabbath-keepers to the world. Oh, I saw that it is a disgrace to their profession, a disgrace to the cause of God. They give the lie to their profession. They think they are not like the world, but they are so near like them in dress, in conversation, and actions, that there is no distinction. I saw them decorating their poor, mortal bodies, which are liable at any moment to be touched by the finger of God and laid upon a bed of anguish. Oh, then, as they approach their last change, mortal anguish racks their frames, and the great inquiry is: "Am I prepared to die? prepared to appear before God in judgment, and pass the grand review?" Ask them then how they feel about decorating their bodies, and if they have any sense of what it is to be prepared to appear before God, they will tell you that if they could take back and live over the past, they would correct their lives, shun the follies of the world, its vanity and pride, and would adorn the body with modest apparel, and set an example to all around them. They would live to the glory of God.

Why is it so hard to lead a self-denying, humble life? Because professed Christians are not dead to the world. It is easy living after we are dead. But many are longing for the leeks and onions of Egypt. They have a disposition to dress and act as much like the world as possible and yet go to heaven. Such climb up some other way. They do not enter through the strait gate and narrow way.

I was shown the company present at the Conference. Said

the angel: "Some food for worms,* some subjects of the seven last plagues, some will be alive and remain upon the earth to be translated at the coming of Jesus."

Solemn words were these, spoken by the angel. I asked the angel why so few were interested in their eternal welfare, so few preparing for their last change. Said he: "Earth attracts them, its treasures seem of worth to them." They find enough to engross the mind, and have no time to prepare for heaven. Satan is ever ready to plunge them deeper and deeper into difficulty; as soon as one perplexity and trouble is off the mind, he begets within them an unholy desire for more of the things of earth; and thus their time passes, and, when it is too late, they see that they have gained nothing substantial. They have grasped at shadows and lost eternal life. Such will have no excuse.

Many dress like the world, to have an influence. But here they make a sad and fatal mistake. If they would have a true and saving influence, let them live out their profession, show their faith by their righteous works, and make the distinction great between the Christian and the world. I saw that the words, the dress, and actions should tell for God. Then a holy influence will be shed upon all, and all will take knowledge of them that they have been with Jesus. Unbelievers will see that the truth we profess has a holy influence and that faith in Christ's coming affects the character of the man or woman. If any wish to have their influence tell in favor of the truth, let them live it out and thus imitate the humble Pattern.

I saw that God hates pride, and that all the proud and all that do wickedly shall be stubble, and the day that cometh shall burn them up. I saw that the third angel's message

*Sister Clarissa M. Bonfoey, who fell asleep in Jesus only three days after this vision was given, was present in usual health and was deeply impressed that she was one who would go into the grave, and stated her convictions to others.

must yet work like leaven upon many hearts that profess to believe it, and purge away their pride, selfishness, covetousness, and love of the world.

Jesus is coming; and will He find a people conformed to the world? and will He acknowledge these as His people that He has purified unto Himself? Oh, no. None but the pure and holy will He acknowledge as His. Those who have been purified and made white through suffering, and have kept themselves separate, unspotted from the world, He will own as His.

As I saw the dreadful fact that God's people were conformed to the world, with no distinction, except in name, between many of the professed disciples of the meek and lowly Jesus and unbelievers, my soul felt deep anguish. I saw that Jesus was wounded and put to an open shame. Said the angel, as with sorrow he saw the professed people of God loving the world, partaking of its spirit, and following its fashions: "Cut loose! Cut loose! lest He appoint you your portion with hypocrites and unbelievers outside the city. Your profession will only cause you greater anguish, and your punishment will be greater because ye knew His will, but did it not."

Those who profess to believe the third angel's message often wound the cause of God by lightness, joking, and trifling. I was shown that this evil was all through our ranks. There should be a humbling before the Lord; the Israel of God should rend the heart, and not the garment. Childlike simplicity is rarely seen; the approbation of man is more thought of than the displeasure of God. Said the angel: "Set your heart in order, lest He visit you in judgment, and the brittle thread of life be cut, and ye lie down in the grave unsheltered, unprepared for the judgment. Or if ye do not make your bed in the grave, unless ye soon make your peace with God, and tear yourselves from the world, your hearts will grow harder, and ye will lean upon a false prop, a supposed preparation, and find out your mistake too late to secure a well-grounded hope."

I saw that some professed Sabbathkeepers spend hours that are worse than thrown away, in studying this or that fashion to decorate the poor, mortal body. While you make yourselves appear like the world, and as beautiful as you can, remember that the same body may in a few days be food for worms. And while you adorn it to your taste, to please the eye, you are dying spiritually. God hates your vain, wicked pride, and He looks upon you as a whited sepulcher, full of corruption and uncleanness within.

Mothers set the example of pride for their children, and, by so doing, sow seed that will spring up and bear fruit. The harvest will be plenteous and sure. That which they sow, they shall reap. There will be no failure in the crop. I saw, parents, that it is easier for you to teach your children a lesson of pride, than a lesson of humility. Satan and his angels stand right by your side to make the act of yours, or the word that you speak to them, effectual to encourage them to dress, and in their pride to mingle with society that is not holy. O parents, you plant in your own bosoms a thorn that you will often feel in anguish. When you would counteract the sad lesson you have taught your children, you will find it a hard thing. It is impossible for you to do this. You may deny them things that would gratify their pride, yet it still lives in the heart, longing to be satisfied; and nothing can kill this pride but the quick and powerful Spirit of God. When this finds its way to the heart, it will work like leaven there and root it out.

I saw that young and old neglect the Bible. They do not make that book their study and their rule of life as they should. Especially are the young guilty of this neglect. Most of them are ready, and find plenty of time, to read almost any other book. But the word that points to life, eternal life, is not perused and daily studied. That precious, important book that is to judge them in the last day is scarcely studied at all. Idle stories have been attentively read, while the Bible has been passed by neglected. A day is coming, a day of clouds and thick darkness when all will wish to be thoroughly furnished by the plain, simple truths of the word of God, that they may meekly, yet decidely, give a reason of their hope. This reason of their hope, I saw, they must have to strengthen their own souls for the the fierce conflict. Without this they are wanting, and cannot have firmness and decision.

Parents would better burn the idle tales of the day and the novels as they come into their houses. It would be a mercy to the children. Encourage the reading of these storybooks, and it is like enchantment. It bewilders and poisons the mind. Parents, I saw that unless you awake to the eternal interest of your children, they will surely be lost through your neglect. And the possibility that unfaithfull parents will be saved themselves is very small. Parents should be exemplary. They should exert a holy influence in their families. They should let their dress be modest, different from the world around them. As they value the eternal interest of their children, they should rebuke pride in them, faithfully rebuke it, and encourage it not in word or deed. Oh, the pride that was shown me of God's professed people! It has increased every year, until it is now impossible to to designate professed advent Sabbathkeepers from all the world around them. I saw that this pride must be torn out of our families.

Much has been expended for ribbons and laces for the bonnets, for collars* and other needless articles to decorate

*The question has often been asked me if I believed it wrong to wear plain linen collars. My answer has always been No. Some have taken the extreme meaning of what I have written about collars, and have maintained that it is wrong to wear one of any description. I was shown expensively wrought collars, and expensive and unnecessary ribbons and laces, which some Sabbathkeepers have

the body, while Jesus the King of glory, who gave His life to redeem us, wore a crown of thorns. This was the way our Master's sacred head was decorated. He was "a man of sorrows, and acquainted with grief." "He was wounded for our transgressions, He was bruised for our iniquities: the chastisement of our peace was upon Him; and with His stripes we are healed." Yet the very ones that profess to be washed by the blood of Jesus, spilled for them, can dress up and decorate their poor, mortal bodies, and dare profess to be followers of the holy, self-denying, humble Pattern. Oh, that all could see this as God sees it and showed it to me! It seemed too much for me to bear, to feel the the anguish of soul that I felt as I beheld it. Said the angel: "God's people are *peculiar*; such He is purifying unto Himself." I saw that the outside appearance is an index to the heart. When the exterior is hung with ribbons, collars, and needless things, it plainly shows that the love for all this is in the heart; unless such persons are cleansed from their corruption, they can never see God, for only the pure in heart will see Him.

I saw that the ax must be laid at the root of the tree. Such pride should not be suffered in the church. It is these things that separate God from His people, that shut the ark away from them. Israel have been asleep to the pride, and fashion, and conformity to the world, in the very midst of them. They advance every month in pride, covetousness, selfishness, and love of the world. When their hearts are affected by the truth, it will cause a death to the world, and they will lay aside the ribbbons, laces, and collars; and, if they are dead, the laugh, the jeer, and scorn of unbelievers will not move them. They will feel anxious desire to be separate from

---

worn, and still wear for the sake of show and fashion. In mentioning collars, I did not design to be understood that nothing like a collar should be worn, or in mentioning ribbons that no ribbons at all should be worn. E. G. W., *note to second edition*.

the world, like their Master. They will not imitate its pride, fashions, or customs. The noble object will be ever before them, to glorify God and gain the immortal inheritance. This prospect will swallow up all beside of an earthly nature. God will have a people separate and distinct from the world. And as soon as any have a desire to imitate the fashions of the world, that they do not immediately subdue, just so soon God ceases to acknowledge them as His children. They are the children of the world and of darkness. They lust for the leeks and onions of Egypt, that is, desire to be as much like the world as possible; by so doing, those that profess to have put on Christ virtually put Him off, and show that they are strangers to grace and strangers to the meek and lowly Jesus. If they had acquainted themselves with Him, they would walk worthy of Him.

WIVES OF MINISTERS

I saw the wives of the ministers. Some of them are no help to their husbands, yet they profess the third angel's message. They think more of studying their own wishes and pleasure than the will of God, or how they can hold up the hands of their husbands by their faithful prayers and careful walk. I saw that some of them take so willful and selfish a course that Satan makes them his instruments and works through them to destroy the influence and usefulness of their husbands. They feel at liberty to complain and murmur if they are brought through any strait places. They forget the sufferings of the ancient Christians for the truth's sake and think that they must have their wishes and way, and follow their own will. They forget the suffering of Jesus, their Master. They forget the Man of Sorrows, who was acquainted with grief—He who had not where to lay His head. They do not care to remember that holy brow, pierced with a crown of thorns. They forget Him, who, bearing His own cross to Calvary, fainted beneath its burden. Not merely the burden of the wooden cross, but the heavy burden of the sins of the world, was upon Him. They forget the cruel nails driven through His tender hands and feet, and His expiring, agonizing cries: "My God, My God, why hast Thou forsaken Me?" After all this suffering endured for them, they feel a strong unwillingness to suffer for Christ's sake.

These persons, I saw, are deceiving themselves. They have no part nor lot in the matter. They have hold of the truth; but the truth has not hold of them. When the truth, the solemn, important truth, gets hold of them, self will die; then the language will not be, "I will go there, I will not stay here;" but the earnest inquiry will be, "Where does God want me to be? Where can I best glorify Him, and where can our united labors do the most good?" Their will should be swallowed up in the will of God. The willfulness and lack of consecration that some of the ministers' wives manifest will stand in the way of sinners; the blood of souls will be upon their garments. Some of the ministers have borne a strong testimony in regard to the duty and the wrongs of the church; but it has not had its designed effect, for their own companions needed all the straight testimony that had been borne, and the reproof came back upon themselves with great weight. They let their companions affect them and drag them down, prejudicing their minds, and their usefulness and influence are lost; they feel desponding and disheartened, and realize not the true source of the injury. It is close at home.

These sisters are closely connected with the work of God if He has called their husbands to preach the present truth. These servants, if truly called of God, will feel the importance of the truth. They are standing between the living and the dead, and must watch for souls as they that must give an account. Solemn is their calling, and their companions can be a great blessing or a great curse to them. They can cheer them when desponding, comfort them when cast down, and encourage them to look up and trust fully in God when their faith fails. Or they can take an opposite course, look upon the dark side, think they have a hard time, exercise no faith in God, talk their trials and unbelief to their companions, indulge a complaining, murmuring spirit, and be a dead weight and even a curse to them.

I saw that the wives of the ministers should help their husbands in their labors and be exact and careful what influence they exert, for they are watched, and more is expected of them than of others. Their dress should be an example. Their lives and conversation should be an example, savoring of life rather than of death. I saw that they should take a humble, meek, yet exalted stand, not having their conversation upon things that do not tend to direct the mind heavenward. The great inquiry should be: "How can I save my own soul, and be the means of saving others?" I saw that no half-hearted work in this matter is accepted of God. He wants the whole heart and interest, or He will have none. Their influence tells, decidedly, unmistakably, in favor of the truth or against it. They gather with Jesus, or scatter abroad. An unsanctified wife is the greatest curse that a minister can have. Those servants of God that have been and are still so unhappily situated as to have this withering influence at home, should double their prayers and their watchfulness, take a firm, decided stand, and let not this darkness press them down. They should cleave closer to God, be firm and decided, rule well their own house, and live so that they can have the approbation of God and the watchcare of the angels. But if they yield to the wishes of their unconsecrated companions, the frown of God is brought upon the dwelling. The ark of God cannot abide in the house, because they countenance and uphold them in their wrongs.

Our God is a jealous God. It is a fearful thing to trifle with Him. Anciently, Achan coveted a golden wedge and a Babylonish garment, and secreted them, and all Israel suffered; they were driven before their enemies. And when Joshua inquired the cause, the Lord said: "Up, sanctify the people, and say, Sanctify yourselves against tomorrow: for thus saith the Lord God of Israel, There is an accursed thing in the midst of thee, O Israel: thou canst not stand before thine enemies, until ye take away the accursed thing from among you." Achan had sinned, and God destroyed him and all his household, with all they possessed, and wiped the curse from Israel.

I saw that the Israel of God must arise and renew their strength in God by renewing and keeping their covenant with Him. Covetousness, selfishness, love of money, and love of the world, are all through the ranks of Sabbathkeepers. These evils are destroying the spirit of sacrifice among God's people. Those that have this covetousness in their hearts are not aware of it. It has gained upon them imperceptibly, and unless it is rooted out, their destruction will be as sure as was Achan's. Many have taken the sacrifice from God's altar. They love the world, love its gain and increase, and, unless there is an entire change in them, they will perish with the world. God has lent them means; it is not their own, but God has made them His stewards. And because of this, they call it their own and hoard it up. But, oh, how quick, when the prospering hand of God is removed from them, it is all snatched away in a moment! There must be a sacrificing for God, a denying of self for the truth's sake. Oh, how weak and frail is man! How puny his arm! I saw that soon the loftiness of man is to be brought down, and the pride of man humbled. Kings and nobles, rich and poor, alike shall bow, and the withering plagues of God shall fall upon them.

NUMBER THREE

TESTIMONY FOR THE CHURCH

BE ZEALOUS AND REPENT

Dear Brethren and Sisters: The Lord has shown me in vision some things concerning the church in its present lukewarm state, which I will relate to you. The church was presented before me in vision. Said the angel to the church: "Jesus speaks to thee, 'Be zealous and repent.' " This work, I saw, should be taken hold of in earnest. There is something to repent of. Worldly-mindedness, selfishness, and covetousness have been eating out the spirituality and life of God's people.

The danger of God's people for a few years past has been the love of the world. Out of this have sprung the sins of selfishness and covetousness. The more they get of this world, the more they set their affections on it; and still they reach out for more. Said the angel: "It is easier for a camel to go through a needle's eye, than for a rich man to enter into the kingdom of God." Yet many who profess to believe that we are having the last note of warning to the world, are striving with all their energies to place themselves in a position where it is easier for a camel to go through a needle's eye than for them to enter the kingdom.

These earthly treasures are blessings when rightly used. Those who have them should realize that they are lent them of God and should cheerfully spend their means to advance His cause. They will not lose their reward here. They will be kindly regarded by the angels of God and will also lay up a treasure in heaven.

I saw that Satan watches the peculiar, selfish, covetous temperament of some who profess the truth, and he will tempt them by throwing prosperity in their path, offering them the riches of earth. He knows that if they do not overcome their natural temperament, they will stumble and fall by loving mammon, worshiping their idol. Satan's object is often accomplished. The strong love of the world overcomes, or swallows up, the love of the truth. The kingdoms of the world are offered them, and they eagerly grasp their treasure and think they are wonderfully prospered. Satan triumphs because his plan has succeeded. They have given up the love of God for the love of the world.

I saw that those who are thus prospered can thwart the design of Satan if they will overcome their selfish covetousness by laying all their possessions upon the altar of God. And when they see where means are needed to advance the cause of truth and to help the widow, the fatherless, and afflicted, they should give cheerfully and thus lay up treasure in heaven.

Heed the counsel of the True Witness. Buy gold tried in the fire, that thou mayest be rich, white raiment that thou mayest be clothed, and eyesalve that thou mayest see. Make some effort. These precious treasures will not drop upon us without some exertion on our part. We must buy—"be zealous and repent" of our lukewarm state. We must be awake to see our wrongs, to search for our sins, and to zealously repent of them.

I saw that the brethren who have possessions have a work to do to tear away from these earthly treasures and to overcome their love of the world. Many of them love this world, love their treasure, but are not willing to see it. They must be zealous and repent of their selfish covetousness, that the love of the truth may swallow up everything else. I saw that many of those who have riches will fail to buy the gold, white raiment, and eyesalve. Their zeal does not possess intensity and earnestness proportionate to the value of the object of which they are in pursuit.

I saw these men while striving for the possessions of earth; what zeal they manifested, what earnestness, what energy to obtain an earthly treasure that must soon pass away! What cool calculations they made! They plan and toil early and late, and sacrifice their ease and comfort for earthly treasure. A corresponding zeal on their part to obtain the gold, white raiment, and eyesalve will bring them in possession of these desirable treasures and life, everlasting life, in the kingdom of God. I saw that if any need eyesalve, it is those who have earthly possessions. Many of them are blind to their own state, blind to their firm grasp upon this world. Oh, that they may see!

"Behold, I stand at the door, and knock: if any man hear My voice, and open the door, I will come in to him, and will sup with him, and he with Me." I saw that many have so much rubbish piled up at the door of their heart that they cannot get the door open. Some have difficulties between themselves and their brethren to remove. Others have evil tempers, selfish covetousness, to remove before they can open the door. Others have rolled the world before the door of their heart, which bars the door. All this rubbish must be taken away, and then they can open the door and welcome the Saviour in.

Oh, how precious was this promise, as it was shown to me in vision! "I will come in to him, and will sup with him, and he with Me." Oh, the love, the wondrous love of God! After all our lukewarmness and sins He says: "Return unto Me, and I will return unto thee, and will heal all thy backslidings." This was repeated by the angel a number of times. "Return unto Me, and I will return unto thee, and will heal all thy backslidings."

Some, I saw, would gladly return. Others will not let this message to the Laodicean church have its weight upon them. They will glide along, much after the same manner as before, and will be spewed out of the mouth of the Lord. Those only who zealously repent will have favor with God.

"To him that overcometh will I grant to sit with Me in My throne, even as I also overcame, and am set down with My Father in His throne." We can overcome. Yes; fully, entirely. Jesus died to make a way of escape for us, that we might overcome every evil temper, every sin, every temptation, and sit down at last with Him.

It is our privilege to have faith and salvation. The power of God has not decreased. His power, I saw, would be just as freely bestowed now as formerly. It is the church of God that have lost their faith to claim, their energy to wrestle, as did Jacob, crying: "I will not let Thee go, except Thou bless me." Enduring faith has been dying away. It must be revived in the hearts of God's people. There must be a claiming of the blessing of God. Faith, living faith, always bears upward to God and glory; unbelief, downward to darkness and death.

I saw that the minds of some of the church have not run in the right channel. There have been some peculiar temperaments that have had their notions by which to measure their brethren. And if any did not exactly agree with them, there was trouble in the camp at once. Some have strained at a gnat and swallowed a camel.

These set notions have been humored and indulged altogether too long. There has been a picking at straws. And when there were no real difficulties in the church, trials have been manufactured. The minds of the church and the servants of the Lord are called from God, truth, and heaven to dwell upon darkness. Satan delights to have such things go on; it feasts him. But these are none of the trials which are to purify the church and that will in the end increase the strength of God's people.

I saw that some are withering spiritually. They have lived some time watching to keep their brethren straight—watching for every fault to make trouble with them. And while doing this, their minds are not on God, nor on heaven, nor on the truth; but just where Satan wants them—on someone else. Their souls are neglected; they seldom see or feel their own faults, for they have had enough to do to watch the faults of others without so much as looking to their own souls or searching their own hearts. A person's dress, bonnet, or apron takes their attention. They must talk to this one or that one, and it is sufficient to dwell upon for weeks. I saw that all the religion a few poor souls have consists in watching the garments and acts of others, and finding fault with them. Unless they reform, there will be no place in heaven for them, for they would find fault with the Lord Himself.

Said the angel: "It is an individual work to be right with God." The work is between God and our own souls. But when persons have so much care of others' faults, they take no care of themselves. These notional, faultfinding ones would often cure themselves of the habit if they would go directly to the individual they think is wrong. It would be so crossing that they would give up their notions rather than go. But it is easy to let the tongue run freely about this one or that one when the accused is not present.

Some think it is wrong to try to observe order in the worship of God. But I have seen that it is not dangerous to observe order in the church of God. I have seen that confusion is displeasing to the Lord, and that there should be order in praying and also in singing. We should not come to the house of God to pray for our families unless deep feeling shall lead us while the Spirit of God is convicting them. Generally, the proper place to pray for our families is at the family altar. When the subjects of our prayers are at a distance, the closet is the proper place to plead with God for them. When in the house of God, we should pray for a present blessing and should expect God to hear and answer our prayers. Such meetings will be lively and interesting.

I saw that all should sing with the spirit and with the understanding also. God is not pleased with jargon and discord. Right is always more pleasing to Him than wrong. And the nearer the people of God can approach to correct, harmonious singing, the more is He glorified, the church benefited, and unbelievers favorably affected.

I have been shown the order, the perfect order, of heaven, and have been enraptured as I listened to the perfect music there. After coming out of vision, the singing here has sounded very harsh and discordant. I have seen companies of angels, who stood in a hollow square, everyone having a harp of gold. At the end of the harp was an instrument to turn to set the harp or change the tunes. Their fingers did not sweep over the strings carelessly, but they touched different strings to produce different sounds. There is one angel who always leads, who first touches the harp and strikes the note, then all join in the rich, perfect music of heaven. It cannot be described. It is melody, heavenly, divine, while from every countenance beams the image of Jesus, shining with glory unspeakable.

THE EAST AND THE WEST

Dear Brethren: The Lord has shown me in vision some things in regard to the East and the West which I feel it my duty to set before you. I saw that God has been opening the way for the spread of present truth in the West. It requires much more power to move the people in the East than in the

West, and at present but very little can be accomplished in the East. Special efforts should be made at the present time where most good will result.

The people in the East have heard the proclamation of the second coming of Christ, and have seen much of the display of the power of God, and have fallen back into a state of indifference and security where it is almost impossible to reach them at present. After uncommon efforts are made in the East, with the best gifts, but very little is accomplished.

I saw that the people in the West could be moved much more easily than those in the East. They have not had the light of the truth, and have not rejected it, and their hearts are more tender and susceptible to the truth and the Spirit of God. The hearts of many in the West are already prepared to eagerly receive the truth; and as the servants of God go out to labor for the salvation of precious souls, they have much to encourage them in their arduous work. As the people are anxious to hear, and many embrace the truth, the gift which God has given His servants is called out and strengthened. They see that their efforts are crowned with success.

I saw that tenfold more has been accomplished in the West than in the East with the same effort, and that the way is opening for still greater success. I have seen that much can be done at present in Wisconsin, and still more in Illinois, and that efforts to spread the truth must be made in Minnesota and Iowa. It will take effect in many hearts there. There was a large, very large, field of labor spread out before me in vision, which has not yet been entered; but there is not self-sacrificing help enough to fill half the places where the people are all ready to hear the truth, and many to receive it.

New fields of labor, entirely new, must be visited; many will have to go a warfare at their own charges, enter such fields with the expectation of bearing their own expenses. Here, I saw, is a good opportunity for the stewards of the Lord to act their part and support those who carry the truth to these places. It should be a great privilege for these stewards to render to God that which belongs to Him. By so doing they will discharge a Scriptural duty and free themselves of a portion of their earthly treasure, which is now a burden to many who have an abundance. It will also add to their treasure in heaven.

I saw that the Eastern tent should not be carried over and over the same ground. If need be those who accompany the tent should go a warfare at their own charges, they should pitch the tent where the truth has not been presented, and the tent when thus pitched should be well supplied with laborers.

I saw that there had been a failure in going over the same old ground, year after year, with almost exactly the same gifts. If possible, the most acceptable gifts should be obtained. It would be better, and accomplish more good, if there were fewer tent meetings, and a stronger force, or company, with different gifts to labor. Then there should be a longer tarry in a place where an interest is awakened. There has been too much haste in taking down the tent. Some begin to be favorably impressed, and there is need that persevering efforts be put forth till their minds become settled and they commit themselves on the truth. In many places where the tent has been pitched, the ministers stay till the prejudice begins to wear away, and some would then listen with minds free from prejudice; but just then the tent is taken down and sent on its way to another place. The rounds are gone over, time and means spent, and the servants of God can see but very little accomplished through the tent season. But few are brought to acknowledge the truth, and God's servants, having seen but very little to cheer and encourage them, and call out the gift within them, lose instead of gaining in strength, spirituality, and power.

I saw that special efforts should be made in the West with tents; for the angels of God are preparing minds there to receive the truth. This is why God has moved on some in the East to move to the West. Their gifts can accomplish more in the West than in the East. The burden of the work is in the West, and it is of the greatest importance that the servants of God should move in His opening providence.

I saw that when the message shall increase greatly in power, then the providence of God will open and prepare the way in the East for much more to be accomplished than can be at the present time. God will then send some of His servants in power to visit places where little or nothing can now be done, and some who are now indifferent will be aroused and will take hold of the truth.*

I saw that God has warned those who have moved from the East to the West. He has shown them their duty, that it must not be their object to get rich, but to do good to souls, to live out their faith, and tell those around them that this world is not their home.

The warning was sufficient, if it had been heeded; but many failed to consider what God had shown. They rushed on and on, and became drunk with the spirit of the world. "Look back," said the angel, "and weigh all that God has shown in regard to those moving from the East to the West." Have you obeyed it? I saw that you had gone entirely contrary to God's teachings, purchased largely, and instead of your works saying to those around you that you are seeking a better country, they have plainly declared that your home and treasure were here. Your works have denied your faith.

Nor is this all. The love that should exist between brethren has been lacking. "Am I my brother's keeper?" has been manifest; a selfish, covetous spirit has been in the hearts of the brethren. Instead of looking out for the interests of the brethren and caring for them, there has been manifested in deal a close, selfish spirit that God despises. Those who make

---

*The remainder of this article is from a vision given at Round Grove, Illinois, December 9, 1856.

so high a profession, and who number themselves among the peculiar people of God, saying by their profession that they are zealous of good works, should be noble and generous, and should ever manifest a disposition to favor their brethren instead of themselves, and should give their brethren the best chance. Generosity begets generosity. Selfishness begets selfishness.

I saw that through the past summer the prevailing spirit has been to grasp as much of this world as possible. The commandments of God have not been kept. With the mind we serve the law of God; but the minds of many have been serving the world. And while their minds were all occupied with things of earth and serving themselves, they could not serve the law of God. The Sabbath has not been kept. By some the work of six days has been carried into the seventh. One hour, and even more, has often been taken from the commencement and close of the Sabbath.

Some of the Sabbathkeepers who say to the world that they are looking for Jesus' coming, and that they believe we are having the last message of mercy, give way to their natural feelings, and barter, and trade, and are a proverb among unbelievers for their keenness in trade, for being sharp, and always getting the best end of a bargain. Such would better lose a little and exert a better influence in the world, and a happier influence among brethren, and show that this world is not their god.

I saw that brethren should feel interested for one another. Especially should those who are blessed with health have a kind regard and care for those who have not good health. They should favor them. They should remember the lesson taught by Jesus of the good Samaritan.

Said Jesus: "Love one another, as I have loved you." How much? His love cannot be told. He left the glory that He had with the Father before the world was. "He was wounded for our transgressions, He was bruised for our iniquities; the chastisement of our peace was upon Him; and with His stripes we are healed." He patiently bore every indignity and scorn. Behold His agony in the garden, when He prayed that the cup might pass from Him! Behold His sufferings on Calvary! All this for guilty, lost man. And Jesus says: "Love one another, as I have loved you." How much? Well enough to give your life for a brother. But has it come to this, that self must be gratified, and the word of God neglected? The world is their god. They serve it, they love it, and the love of God has departed. If ye love the world, the love of the Father is not in you.

The word of God has been neglected. In that are the warnings to God's people which point out their dangers. But they have had so many cares and perplexities that they hardly allow themselves time to pray. There has been a mere empty form without the power. Jesus prayed, and, oh, how earnest were His prayers. And yet He was the beloved Son of God!

If Jesus manifested so much earnestness, so much energy and agony, how much more need for those whom He has called to be heirs of salvation, dependent upon God for all their strength, to have their whole souls stirred to wrestle with God and say: "I will not let Thee go, except Thou bless me." But I saw that hearts have been overcharged with the cares of this life, and that God and His word have been neglected.

I saw that it is easier for a camel to go through the eye of a needle, than for a rich man to enter the kingdom. "Lay not up for yourselves treasures upon earth, where moth and rust doth corrupt, and where thieves break through and steal: but lay up for yourselves treasures in heaven, where neither moth nor rust doth corrupt, and where thieves do not break through nor steal: for where your treasure is, there will your heart be also."

I saw that when the truth is presented, it should be in the power and Spirit. Bring the people to the point to decide. Show them the importance of the truth—it is life or death. With becoming zeal, pull souls out of the fire. But, oh, the blighting influence that has been cast by men professing to be waiting for their Lord, and yet possessing large and attractive lands! The farms have preached louder, yes, much louder, than words can, that this world is their home. The evil day is put off. Peace and safety reign. Oh, the withering, blighting influence! God hates such worldly-mindedness. "Cut loose, cut loose," were the words of the angel.

I was shown that all should have an eye single to the glory of God. Those who have possessions have been too willing to excuse themselves on account of wife and children. But I saw that God would not be trifled with. When He speaks, He must be obeyed. If wife or children stand in the way and hold back, they should say as Jesus said to Peter: "Get thee behind Me, Satan." Why tempt ye me to withhold from God what justly belongs to Him, and ruin my own soul? Have an eye single to the glory of God.

I saw that many would have to learn what it is to be a Christian—that it is not in name, but it is having the mind of Christ, submitting to the will of God in all things. Especially will the young who have never known what privations or hardships are, who have a set will, and do not bend that will to the glory of God, have a great work to do. They go along very smoothly until their will is crossed, and then they have no control over themselves. They have not the will of God before them. They do not study how they can best glorify God, or advance His cause, or do good to others. But it is self, self, how can it be gratified? Such religion is not worth a straw. Those who possess it will be weighed in the balance and found wanting.

The true Christian will love to wait and watch for the teachings of God and the leadings of His Spirit. But with many, religion is merely a form. Vital godliness is lacking. Many dare to say, I will do this, or that, or I will not do this; and the fear of offending God is scarcely thought of. Those thus described, I saw, could not enter heaven as they are. They may flatter themselves that they will be saved, but God has no pleasure in them. Their lives do not please Him. Their prayers are an offense to Him.

Christ now calls them: "Be zealous and repent." He kindly and faithfully admonishes them to buy gold, white raiment, and eyesalve. They can choose either to be zealous, and partake largely of salvation, or be spewed out of the mouth of the Lord as disgusting, and be thrust from Him. God will not bear always. He is of tender pity, yet His Spirit will be grieved away for the last time. Mercy's sweet voice will be no more heard. Its last precious notes will have died away, and those described will be left to their own ways, to be filled with their own doings.

I saw that those who profess to be looking for the coming of the Lord should not have a close, penurious spirit. Some of those who have been called to talk the truth, and to watch for souls as they that must give an account, have wasted much precious time for the sake of saving a little, when their time was worth a great deal more than that which they gained. This displeases God. It is right that economy should be used, but it has by some been stretched into meanness with no other object than to add to their treasures, which will shortly eat their flesh like fire, unless they as faithful stewards make a right disposal of their Lord's goods.

NUMBER FOUR

TESTIMONY FOR THE CHURCH

YOUNG SABBATHKEEPERS

August 22, 1857, at the house of prayer in Monterey, Michigan, I was shown that many have not yet heard the voice of Jesus, and the saving message has not taken hold of the soul and worked a reformation in the life. Many of the young have not the spirit of Jesus. The love of God is not in their hearts, therefore all the natural besetments hold the victory instead of the Spirit of God and salvation.

Those who really possess the religion of Jesus will not be ashamed nor afraid to bear the cross before those who have more experience than they. They will, if they earnestly long to be right, desire all the help they can get from older Christians. Gladly will they be helped by them; hearts that are warmed by love to God will not be hindered by trifles in the Christian course. They will talk out what the Spirit of God works in. They will sing it out, pray it out. It is the lack of religion, lack of holy living, that makes the young backward. Their life condemns them. They know they do not live as Christians should, therefore they have not confidence toward God, or before the church.

Why the young feel more liberty when the older ones are absent is: They are with those of their kind. Each thinks he is as good as the other. All fail of the mark, but measure themselves by themselves, and compare themselves among themselves, and neglect the only perfect and true standard. Jesus is the true Pattern. His self-sacrificing life is our example.

I saw how little the Pattern was studied, how little exalted before them. How little do the young suffer, or deny self, for their religion! To sacrifice is scarcely thought of among them. They entirely fail of imitating the Pattern in this respect. I saw that the language of their lives is: Self must be gratified, pride must be indulged. They forget the Man of Sorrows, who was acquainted with grief. The sufferings of Jesus in Gethsemane, His sweating as it were great drops of blood in the garden, the platted crown of thorns that pierced His holy brow, do not move them. They have become benumbed. Their sensibilities are blunted, and they have lost all sense of the great sacrifice made for them. They can sit and listen to the story of the cross, hear how the cruel nails were driven through the hands and feet of the Son of God, and it does not stir the depths of the soul.

Said the angel: "If such should be ushered into the city of God, and told that all its rich beauty and glory was theirs to enjoy eternally, they would have no sense of how dearly that inheritance was purchased for them. They would never realize the matchless depths of a Saviour's love. They have not drunk of the cup, nor been baptized with the baptism. Heaven would be marred if such should dwell there. Those only who have partaken of the sufferings of the Son of God, and have come up through great tribulation, and have washed their robes and made them white in the blood of the Lamb, can enjoy the indescribable glory and unsurpassed beauty of heaven."

The want of this necessary preparation will shut out the greater portion of young professors, for they will not labor earnestly and zealously enough to obtain that rest that remains for the people of God. They will not honestly confess their sins, that they may be pardoned and blotted out. These sins in a short time will be revealed in just their enormity. God's eye does not slumber. He knows every sin that is hidden from mortal eye. The guilty know just what sins to confess that their souls may be clean before God. Jesus is now giving them opportunity to confess, to repent in deep humility, and purify their lives by obeying and living out the truth. Now is the time for wrongs to be righted and sins to be confessed, or they will appear before the sinner in the day of God's wrath.

Parents generally put too much confidence in their children; for often when the parents are confiding in them, they are in concealed iniquity. Parents, watch your children with a jealous care. Exhort, reprove, counsel them when you rise up and when you sit down, when you go out and when you come in, line upon line, precept upon precept, here a little, and there a little. Subdue your children when they are young. With many parents this is sadly neglected. They do not take as firm and decided a stand as they should in regard to their children. They suffer them to be like the world, to love dress, and associate with those who hate the truth and whose influence is poisonous. By so doing they encourage in their children a worldly disposition.

I saw that there should always be a fixed principle with Christian parents to be united in the government of their children. There is a fault in this respect with some parents—a lack of union. The fault is sometimes with the father, but oftener with the mother. The fond mother pets and indulges her children. The father's labor calls him from home often, and from the society of his children. The mother's influence tells. Her example does much toward forming the character of the children.

Some fond mothers suffer wrongs in their children which should not be allowed in them for a moment. The wrongs of the children are sometimes concealed from the father. Articles of dress or some other indulgence is granted by the mother with the understanding that the father is to know nothing about it, for he would reprove for these things.

Here a lesson of deception is effectually taught the children. Then if the father discovers these wrongs, excuses are made and but half the truth told. The mother is not openhearted. She does not consider as she should that the father has the same interest in the children as herself, and that he should not be kept ignorant of the wrongs or besetments that ought to be corrected in them while young. Things have been covered. The children know the lack of union in their parents, and it has its effect. The children begin young to deceive, cover up, tell things in a different light from what they are to their mother, as well as their father. Exaggeration becomes habit, and blunt falsehoods come to be told with but little conviction or reproof of conscience.

These wrongs commenced by the mother's concealing things from the father, who has an equal interest with her in the character their children are forming. The father should have been consulted freely. All should have been laid open to him. But the opposite course, taken to conceal the wrongs of the children, encourages in them a disposition to deceive, a lack of truthfulness and honesty.

The only hope of these children, whether they profess religion or not, is to be thoroughly converted. Their whole character must be changed. Thoughtless mother, do you know, as you teach your children, that their whole religious experience is affected by their teaching when young? Subdue them young; teach them to submit to you, and the more readily will they learn to yield obedience to the requirements of God. Encourage in them a truthful, honest disposition. Let them never have occasion to doubt your sincerity and exact truthfulness.

I saw that the young profess, but do not enjoy, the saving power of God. They lack religion, lack salvation. And, oh, the idle, unprofitable words they speak! There is a faithful, fearful record kept of them, and mortals will be judged according to the deeds done in the body. Young friends, your deeds and your idle words are written in the book. Your conversation has not been on eternal things, but upon this, that, and the other—common, worldly conversation that Christians should not engage in. It is all written in the book.

I saw that unless there is an entire change in the young, a thorough conversion, they may despair of heaven. From what has been shown me, there are not more than half of the young who profess religion and the truth who have been truly converted. If they had been converted they would bear fruit to the glory of God. Many are leaning upon a supposed hope without a true foundation. The fountain is not cleansed, therefore the streams proceeding from that fountain are not pure. Cleanse the fountain, and the streams will be pure. If the heart is right, your words, your dress, your acts will all be right. True godliness is lacking. I would not dishonor my Master so much as to admit that a careless, trifling, prayerless person is a Christian. No; a Christian has victory over his besetments, over his passions. There is a remedy for the sin-sick soul. That remedy is in Jesus. Precious Saviour! His grace is sufficient for the weakest; and the strongest must also have His grace or perish.

I saw how this grace could be obtained. Go to your closet, and there alone plead with God: "Create in me a clean heart, O God; and renew a right spirit within me." Be in earnest, be sincere. Fervent prayer availeth much. Jacoblike, wrestle in prayer. Agonize. Jesus, in the garden, sweat great drops of blood; you must make an effort. Do not leave your closet until you feel strong in God; then watch, and just as long as you watch and pray you can keep these evil besetments under, and the grace of God can and will appear in you.

God forbid that I should cease to warn you. Young

friends, seek the Lord with all your heart. Come with zeal, and when you sincerely feel that without the help of God you perish, when you pant after Him as the hart panteth after the water brooks, then will the Lord strengthen you speedily. Then will your peace pass all understanding. If you expect salvation, you must pray. Take time. Be not hurried and careless in your prayers. Beg of God to work in you a thorough reformation, that the fruits of His Spirit may dwell in you, and you shine as lights in the world. Be not a hindrance or curse to the cause of God; you can be a help, a blessing. Does Satan tell you that you cannot enjoy salvation, full and free? Believe him not.

I saw that it is the privilege of every Christian to enjoy the deep movings of the Spirit of God. A sweet, heavenly peace will pervade the mind, and you will love to meditate upon God and heaven. You will feast upon the glorious promises of His word. But know first that you have begun the Christian course. Know that the first steps are taken in the road to everlasting life. Be not deceived. I fear, yea, I know, that many of you know not what religion is. You have felt some excitement, some emotion, but have never seen sin in its enormity. You have never felt your undone condition and turned from your evil ways with bitter sorrow. You have never died to the world. You still love its pleasures; you love to engage in conversation on worldly matters. But when the truth of God is introduced, you have nothing to say. Why so silent? Why so talkative upon worldly things, and so silent upon the subject that should most concern you—a subject that should engage your whole soul? The truth of God does not dwell in you.

I saw that many are fair in their profession, while within is corruption. Deceive not yourselves, falsehearted professors. God looks at the heart. "Out of the abundance of the heart the mouth speaketh." The world, I saw, is in the heart of such, but the religion of Jesus is not there. If professed Christians love Jesus better than the world, they will love to speak of Him, their best Friend, in whom their highest affections are centered. He came to their aid when they felt their lost and perishing condition. When weary and heavy-laden with sin, they turned unto Him. He removed their burden of guilt and sin, took away their sorrow and mourning, and turned the whole current of their affections. The things they once loved, they now hate; and the things they hated, they now love.

Has this great change taken place in you? Be not deceived. I would never name the name of Christ, or I would give Him my whole heart, my undivided affections. We should feel the deepest gratitude that Jesus will accept this offering. He demands all. When we are brought to yield to His claims, and give up all, then, and not till then, will He throw around us His arms of mercy. But what do we give when we give all? A sin-polluted soul for Jesus to purify, to cleanse by His mercy, and to save from death by His matchless love. And yet I saw that some thought it hard to give up all. I am ashamed to hear it spoken of, ashamed to write it.

Do you talk about self-denial? What did Christ give for us? When you think it hard that Christ requires all, go to Calvary, and weep there over such a thought. Behold the hands and feet of your Deliverer torn by the cruel nails that you may be washed from sin by His own blood!

Those who feel the constraining love of God do not ask how little may be given in order to obtain the heavenly reward; they ask not for the lowest standard, but aim at a perfect conformity to the will of their Redeemer. With ardent desire they yield *all,* and manifest zeal proportionate to the value of the object of which they are in pursuit. What is the object? Immortality, eternal life.

Young friends, many of you are sadly deceived. You have

been satisfied with something short of pure and undefiled religion. I want to arouse you. The angels of God are trying to arouse you. Oh, that the important truths of the word of God may arouse you to a sense of your danger, and lead you to a thorough examination of yourselves! Your hearts are yet carnal. They are not subject to the law of God, neither indeed can be. These carnal hearts must be changed, and you see such beauty in holiness that you will pant after it as the hart panteth after the water brooks. Then you will love God and love His law. Then the yoke of Christ will be easy and His burden light. Although you will have trials, yet these trials, well borne, only make the way more precious. The immortal inheritance is for the self-denying Christian.

I saw that the Christian should not set too high a value, or depend too much, upon a happy flight of feeling. These feelings are not always true guides. It should be the study of every Christian to serve God from principle, and not be ruled by feeling. By so doing, faith will be brought into exercise, and will increase. I was shown that if the Christian lives a humble, self-sacrificing life, peace and joy in the Lord will be the result. But the greatest happiness experienced will be in doing others good, in making others happy. Such happiness will be lasting.

Many of the young have not a fixed principle to serve God. They do not exercise faith. They sink under every cloud. They have no power of endurance. They do not grow in grace. They appear to keep the commandments of God. They make now and then a formal prayer and are called Christians. Their parents are so anxious for them that they accept anything which appears favorable, and do not labor with them, and teach them that the carnal mind must die. They encourage them to come along and act a part; but they fail to lead them to search their own hearts diligently, to examine themselves, and to count the cost of what it is to be a

Christian. The result is, the young profess to be Christians without sufficiently trying their motives.

Says the True Witness: "I would thou wert cold or hot. So then because thou art lukewarm, and neither cold nor hot, I will spew thee out of My mouth." Satan is willing that you should be Christians in name, for you can suit his purpose better. If you have a form and not true godliness, he can use you to decoy others into the same self-deceived way. Some poor souls will look to you, instead of looking to the Bible standard, and will come up no higher. They are as good as you, and are satisfied.

The young are often urged to do duty, to speak or pray in meeting; urged to die to pride. Every step they are urged. Such religion is worth nothing. Let the carnal heart be changed, and it will not be such drudgery, ye coldhearted professors, to serve God. All that love of dress and pride of appearance will be gone. The time that you spend standing before the glass preparing the hair to please the eye, should be devoted to prayer and searching of heart. There will be no place for outward adornment in the sanctified heart; but there will be an earnest, anxious seeking for the inward adorning the Christian graces—the fruits of the Spirit of God.

Says the apostle: "Whose adorning let it not be that outward adorning of plaiting the hair, and of wearing of gold, or of putting on of apparel; but let it be the hidden man of the heart, in that which is not corruptible, even the ornament of a meek and quiet spirit, which is in the sight of God of great price."

Subdue the carnal mind, reform the life, and the poor mortal frame will not be so idolized. If the heart is reformed, it will be seen in the outward appearance. If Christ be in us the hope of glory, we shall discover such matchless charms in Him that the soul will be enamored. It will cleave to Him, choose to love Him, and in admiration of Him, self will be forgotten. Jesus will be magnified and adored, and self abased and humbled. But a profession, without this deep love, is mere talk, dry formality, and heavy drudgery. Many of you may retain a notion of religion in the head, an outside religion, when the heart is not cleansed. God looks at the heart; "all things are naked and opened unto the eyes of Him with whom we have to do." Will He be satisfied with anything but truth in the inward parts? Every truly converted soul will carry the unmistakable marks that the carnal mind is subdued.

I speak plainly. I do not think this will discourage a true Christian; and I do not want any of you to come up to the time of trouble without a well-grounded hope in your Redeemer. Determine to know the worst of your case. Ascertain if you have an inheritance on high. Deal truly with your own soul. Remember that a church without spot, or wrinkle, or any such thing, will Jesus present to His Father.

How are you to know that you are accepted of God? Study His word prayerfully. Lay it not aside for any other book. This Book convinces of sin. It plainly reveals the way of salvation. It brings to view a bright and glorious reward. It reveals to you a complete Saviour, and teaches you that through His boundless mercy alone can you expect salvation.

Do not neglect secret prayer, for it is the soul of religion. With earnest, fervent prayer, plead for purity of soul. Plead as earnestly, as eagerly, as you would for your mortal life, were it at stake. Remain before God until unutterable longings are begotten within you for salvation, and the sweet evidence is obtained of pardoned sin.

The hope of eternal life is not to be received upon slight grounds. It is a subject to be settled between God and your own soul—settled for eternity. A supposed hope, and nothing more, will prove your ruin. Since you are to stand or fall by the word of God, it is to that word you must look for testimony in your case. There you can see what is required of you to become a Christian. Do not lay off your armor, or leave the battlefield until you have obtained the victory, and triumph in your Redeemer.

CHURCH TRIALS

The following view was given at Ulysses, Pennsylvania, July 6, 1857. It relates to things as they have existed in ________ and other places in New York.

There have been so many church trials among the brethren in the State of New York, that God has not had the least to do with, that the church have lost their strength, and they know not how to regain it. Love for one another has disappeared, and a faultfinding, accusing spirit has prevailed. It has been considered a virtue to hunt up everything about one another that looked wrong, and make it appear fully as bad as it really was. The bowels of compassion that yearn in love and pity toward brethren, have not existed. The religion of some has consisted in faultfinding, picking at everything bearing the appearance of wrong, until the noble feelings of the soul are withered. The mind should be elevated to dwell upon eternal scenes, heaven, its treasures, its glories, and should take sweet and holy satisfaction in the truths of the Bible. It should love to feed upon the precious promises that God's word affords, draw comfort from them, and be lifted above trifles to weighty, eternal things.

But, oh, how differently has the mind been employed! Picking at straws! Church meetings, as they have been held, have been a living curse to many in New York. These manufactured trials have given full liberty to evil surmising. Jealousy has been fed. Hatred has existed, but they knew it not. A wrong idea has been in the minds of some, to reprove without love, hold others to their idea of what is right, and spare not, but bear down with crushing weight.

I saw that many in New York have had so much care for their brethren, to keep them straight, that they have neglected their own hearts. They are so fearful that their brethren will not be zealous and repent, that they forget that they have wrongs that must be righted. With their own hearts unsanctified, they try to right their brethren. Now the only way the brethren and sisters in New York can rise is for each to attend to his own individual case, and set his own heart in order. If sin is plain in a brother, breathe it not to another, but with love for the brother's soul, with a heart full of compassion, with bowels of mercy, tell him the wrong, then leave the matter with him and the Lord. You have discharged your duty. You are not to pass sentence.

It has been made too light an affair to rein up a brother, to condemn him, and hold him under condemnation. There has been a zeal for God, but not according to knowledge. If each would set his own heart in order, when the brethren meet together their testimony would be ready and come from a full soul, and the people around that believe not the truth would be moved. The manifestation of the Spirit of God would tell to their hearts that you are the children of God. Our love for one another should be visible to all. Then it will tell. It will have an influence.

I saw that the church in New York might rise. Take hold of the work individually, be zealous and repent; and after all known wrongs are righted, then believe that God accepts you. Go not mourning, but take God at His word. Seek Him diligently, and believe that He receives you. A part of the work is to believe He is faithful who has promised. Climb up by faith.

The brethren can rise in New York as well as in other places; and they can drink of the salvation of God. They can move understandingly, and each have an experience for himself in this message of the True Witness to the Laodiceans. The church feel that they are down, but know not how to rise. The intentions of some may be very good; they may confess; yet I saw that they are watched with suspicion, and are made offenders for a word, until they have no liberty, no salvation. They dare not act out the simple feelings of the heart, because they are watched. It is God's pleasure that His people should fear Him, and have confidence before one another.

I saw that many have taken advantage of what God has shown in regard to the sins and wrongs of others. They have taken the extreme meaning of what has been shown in vision, and then have pressed it until it has had a tendency to weaken the faith of many in what God has shown, and also to discourage and dishearten the church. With tender compassion should brother deal with brother. Delicately should he deal with feelings. It is the nicest and most important work that ever yet was done to touch the wrongs of another. With the deepest humility should a brother do this, considering his own weakness, lest he also should be tempted.

I have seen the great sacrifice which Jesus made to redeem man. He did not consider His own life too dear to sacrifice. Said Jesus: "Love one another, as I have loved you." Do you feel, when a brother errs, that you could give your life to save him? If you feel thus, you can approach him and affect his heart; you are just the one to visit that brother. But it is a lamentable fact that many who profess to be brethren, are not willing to sacrifice any of their opinions or their judgment to save a brother. There is but little love for one another. A selfish spirit is manifested.

Discouragement has come upon the church. They have been loving the world, loving their farms, their cattle, etc. Now Jesus calls them to cut loose, to lay up treasure in heaven, to buy gold, white raiment, and eyesalve. Precious treasures are these. They will obtain for the possessor an entrance into the kingdom of God.

The people of God must move understandingly. They should not be satisfied until every known sin is confessed; then it is their privilege and duty to believe that Jesus accepts them. They must not wait for others to press through the darkness and obtain the victory for them to enjoy. Such enjoyment will last only till the meeting closes. But God must be served from principle instead of from feeling. Morning and night obtain the victory for yourselves in your own family. Let not your daily labor keep you from this. Take time to pray, and as you pray, believe that God hears you. Have faith mixed with your prayers. You may not at all times feel the immediate answer; but then it is that faith is tried. You are proved to see whether you will trust in God, whether you have living, abiding faith. "Faithful is He that calleth you, who also will do it." Walk the narrow plank of faith. Trust all on the promises of the Lord. Trust God in darkness. That is the time to have faith. But you often let feeling govern you. You look for worthiness in yourselves when you do not feel comforted by the Spirit of God, and despair because you cannot find it. You do not trust enough in Jesus, precious Jesus. You do not make His worthiness to be all, all. The very best you can do will not merit the favor of God. It is Jesus' worthiness that will save you, His blood that will cleanse you. But you have efforts to make. You must do what you can on your part. Be zealous and repent, then believe.

Confound not faith and feeling together. They are distinct. Faith is ours to exercise. This faith we must keep in exercise. Believe, believe. Let your faith take hold of the blessing, and it is yours. Your feelings have nothing to do with this faith. When faith brings the blessing to your heart, and you rejoice in the blessing, it is no more faith, but feeling.

The people of God in New York must steadily rise, and come out of darkness, and let their light shine. They are standing right in the way of the work of God. They must let the message of the third angel do its work upon their hearts. Brethren, God is dishonored by your long, faithless prayers. Look away from the unworthiness of self, and exalt Jesus. Talk of faith, of light, and of heaven, and you will have faith, light, and love, and peace and joy in the Holy Ghost.

"TAKE HEED"

The following was addressed to two brethren at ______; but being applicable to many, it is here given for the benefit of the church:

Dear Brethren: In the vision given at your place, I was shown something concerning you both. The angel pointed to you, and repeated these words: "Take heed to yourselves lest at anytime your hearts be overcharged with surfeiting, and drunkenness, and cares of this life, and so that day come upon you unawares."

I saw that you both have a great conflict before you; you will have a constant warfare to keep this world out of your hearts, for you love it. The great study with you now must be how to love Jesus and His service better than the world. If you love the world most, your works will testify to the fact. If you love Jesus and His service most, your works will testify to that fact also. I saw that the gaze of many in this world is upon you. Many would exult in your downfall, others rejoice in your advancement. Satan and evil angels will present to you the glory of the kingdoms of this world. If you will worship him, or worship a worldly treasure, he will hold it up in every light to attract and lead you to love and worship.

Jesus and your guardian angels are pointing you above your farms, your cattle, and your earthly treasure, to the kingdom of heaven, to an immortal inheritance, an eternal substance in the kingdom of glory. Said the angel: "You must die to this world." "Love not the world, neither the things that are in the world. If any man love the world, the love of the Father is not in him."

I saw that if, in the providence of God, wealth has been acquired, there is no sin in possessing it; and if no opportunities present themselves to use this means to advance the cause of God, there is no sin in still possessing it. But if opportunities are presented to the brethren to use their property to the glory of God and the advancement of His cause, and they withhold it, it will be a cause of stumbling to them. In the day of trouble that which was their hoarded treasure will be an offense unto them. Then all opportunities will be past for using their substance to the glory of God, and in anguish of spirit they will cast it from them to the moles and to the bats. Their gold and their silver cannot save them in that day. It falls upon them with crushing weight, that an account must be given of their stewardship, what use they have made of their Lord's money. Self-love made them believe that it was all their own, and that they might want it all; but they then feel, bitterly feel and understand, that their means was only lent them of God, to be freely returned by being used to advance His cause. Their riches deceived them. They felt poor and lived for themselves, and at last they will find that the portion they might have used for God's cause is a terrible burden.

Said the angel of God: "Lay all upon the altar, a living, consuming sacrifice. Bind it with cords, if you cannot keep it there. Give yourselves to prayer. Live at the altar. Strengthen your purposes by the promises of God." "Sell that ye have, and give alms; provide yourselves bags which wax not old, a treasure in the heavens that faileth not, where no thief approacheth, neither moth corrupteth." "Lay not up for yourselves treasures upon earth, where moth and rust doth corrupt, and where thieves break through and steal: but lay up for yourselves treasures in heaven."

I saw that if God had given you wealth above the plainest and poorest, it should humble you, for it lays you under greater obligations. Where much is given, even of a worldly substance, much will be required. Upon this principle you are bound to possess noble, generous dispositions. Seek for opportunities to do good with what you have. "Lay up for yourselves treasures in heaven."

I saw that the least that has been required of Christians in past days, is to possess a spirit of liberality, and to consecrate to the Lord a portion of all their increase. Every true Christian has considered this a privilege, but some who have borne the name only, have considered it a task; the grace and love of God had never wrought in them the good work, or they would gladly have advanced the cause of their Redeemer. But Christians who are living in the last days, and who are waiting for their Lord, are required to do even more than this. God requires them to sacrifice.

Said the angel: "Jesus left a bright track for you to follow. Tread closely in His footsteps. Share His life of self-denial, His self-sacrificing life, and inherit with Him the crown of glory."

THE RICH YOUNG MAN

At Monterey, Michigan, October 8, 1857, I was shown in vision that the condition of many Sabbathkeepers was like that of the young man who came to Jesus to know what he should do to inherit eternal life.

"And, behold, one came and said unto Him, Good Master, what good thing shall I do, that I may have eternal life? And He said unto him, Why callest thou Me good? there is none good but One, that is, God: but if thou wilt enter into life, keep the commandments. He saith unto Him, Which? Jesus said, Thou shalt do no murder, Thou shalt not commit adultery, Thou shalt not steal, Thou shalt not bear false witness, Honor thy father and thy mother: and, Thou shalt love thy neighbor as thyself. The young man saith unto Him, All these things have I kept from my youth up: what lack I yet? Jesus said unto him, If thou wilt be perfect, go and sell that thou hast, and give to the poor, and thou shalt have treasure in heaven: and come and follow Me. But when the young man heard that saying, he went away sorrowful: for he had great possessions.

"Then said Jesus unto His disciples, Verily I say unto you, That a rich man shall hardly enter into the kingdom of heaven. And again I say unto you, It is easier for a camel to go through the eye of a needle, than for a rich man to enter into the kingdom of God. When His disciples heard it, they were exceedingly amazed, saying, Who then can be saved? But Jesus beheld them, and said unto them, With men this is impossible; but with God all things are possible." Matthew 19:16-26.

Jesus quoted five of the last six commandments to the young man, also the second great commandment, on which the last six commandments hang. Those mentioned he thought he had kept. Jesus did not mention the first four commandments, containing our duty to God. In answer to the inquiry of the young man, "What lack I yet?" Jesus said unto him: "If thou wilt be perfect, go and sell that thou hast, and give to the poor, and thou shalt have treasure in heaven."

Here was his lack. He failed to keep the first four commandments, also the last six. He failed to love his neighbor as himself. Said Jesus: "Give to the poor." Jesus touched his possessions. "Sell that thou hast, and give to the poor." In this direct reference He pointed out his idol. His love of riches was supreme; therefore it was impossible for him to love God with all his heart, with all his soul, with all his mind. And this supreme love for his riches shut his eyes to the wants of his fellow men. He did not love his neighbor as himself, therefore he failed to keep the last six commandments. His heart was on his treasure. It was swallowed up in his earthly possessions. He loved his possessions better than God, better than the heavenly treasure. He heard the conditions from the mouth of Jesus. If he would sell and give to the poor, he should have treasure in heaven. Here was a test of how much higher he prized eternal life than riches. Did he eagerly lay hold of the prospect of eternal life? Did he earnestly strive to remove the obstacle that was in his way of having a treasure in heaven? Oh, no; "he went away sorrowful: for he had great possessions."

I was pointed to these words: "It is easier for a camel to go through the eye of a needle, than for a rich man to enter into the kingdom of God." Said Jesus: "With men this is impossible; but with God all things are possible." Said the angel: "Will God permit the rich men to keep their riches, and yet enter into the kingdom of God?" Another angel answered: "No, never."

I saw that it is God's plan that these riches should be used properly, distributed to bless the needy, and to advance the work of God. If men love their riches better than they love their fellow men, better than they love God or the truths of His word, if their hearts are on their riches, they cannot have eternal life. They would rather yield the truth than sell and give to the poor. Here they are proved to see how much they love God, how much they love the truth; and, like the young man in the Bible, many go away sorrowful because they cannot have their riches and a treasure in heaven, too. They cannot have both; and they venture to risk their chance of eternal life for a worldly possession.

"It is easier for a camel to go through the eye of a needle, than for a rich man to enter into the kingdom of God." With

God all things are possible. Truth, set home to the heart by the Spirit of God, will crowd out the love of riches. The love of Jesus and of riches cannot dwell in the same heart. The love of God so far surpasses the love of riches that the possessor breaks away from his riches and transfers his affections to God. Through love he is then led to minister to the wants of God's cause. It is his highest pleasure to make a right disposition of his Lord's goods. Love to God and his fellow men predominates, and he holds all that he has as not his own, and faithfully discharges his duty as God's steward. Then can he keep both the great commandments of the law: "Thou shalt love the Lord thy God with all thy heart, and with all thy soul, and with all thy mind." "Thou shalt love thy neighbor as thyself." In this way it is possible for a rich man to enter the kingdom of God. "And everyone that hath forsaken houses, or brethren, or sisters, or father, or mother, or wife, or children, or lands, for My name's sake, shall receive an hundredfold, and shall inherit everlasting life. But many that are first shall be last; and the last shall be first."

Here is the reward for those who sacrifice for God. They receive a hundredfold in this life, and shall inherit everlasting life. "But many that are first shall be last; and the last shall be first." I was shown those who receive the truth, but do not live it. They cling to their possessions, and are not willing to distribute of their substance to advance the cause of God. They have not faith to venture and trust God. Their love of this world swallows up their faith. God calls for a portion of their substance, but they heed it not. They reason that they have labored hard to obtain what they have, and they cannot lend it to the Lord, for they may come to want. "O ye of little faith." That God who cared for Elijah in the time of famine, will not pass by one of His self-sacrificing children. He who has numbered the hairs of their head, will care for them, and in days of famine they will be satisfied. While the wicked are perishing all around them for want of bread, their bread and water will be sure. Those who still cling to their earthly treasure, and will not make a right disposition of that which is lent them of God, will lose their treasure in heaven, lose everlasting life.

God in His providence has moved upon the hearts of some of those who have riches, and has converted them to the truth, that they with their substance may assist to keep His work moving. And if those who are wealthy will not do this, if they do not fulfill the purpose of God, He will pass them by, and raise up others to fill their place who will fulfill His purpose, and with their possessions gladly distribute to meet the necessities of the cause of God. In this they will be first. God will have those in His cause who will do this.

He could send means from heaven to carry on His work; but this is out of His order. He has ordained that men should be His instruments, that as a great sacrifice was made to redeem them, they should act a part in this work of salvation, by making a sacrifice for one another, and by thus doing show how highly they prize the sacrifice that has been made for them.

I was directed to James 5:1-3: "Go to now, ye rich men, weep and howl for your miseries that shall come upon you. Your riches are corrupted, and your garments are moth-eaten. Your gold and silver is cankered; and the rust of them shall be a witness against you, and shall eat your flesh as it were fire. Ye have heaped treasure together for the last days."

I saw that these fearful words apply particularly to the wealthy who profess to believe the present truth. The Lord calls them to use their means to advance His cause. Opportunities are presented to them, but they shut their eyes to the wants of the cause, and cling fast to their earthly treasure. Their love for the world is greater than their love for the truth, their love for their fellow men, or their love for God.

He calls for their substance, but they selfishly, covetously, retain what they have. They give a little now and then to ease their conscience, but have not overcome their love for this world. They do not sacrifice for God. The Lord has raised up others that prize eternal life, and that can feel and realize something of the value of the soul, and they have freely bestowed their means to advance the cause of God. The work is closing; and soon the means of those who have kept their riches, their large farms, their cattle, etc., will not be wanted. I saw the Lord turn to such in anger, in wrath, and repeat these words: "Go to now, ye rich men." He has called, but you would not hear. Love of this world has drowned His voice. Now He has no use for you, and lets you go, bidding you: "Go to now, ye rich men."

Oh, I saw it was an awful thing to be thus forsaken by the Lord—a fearful thing to hold onto a perishable substance here, when He has said that if we will sell and give alms, we can lay up treasure in heaven. I was shown that as the work is closing up, and the truth is going forth in mighty power, these rich men will bring their means and lay it at the feet of the servants of God, begging them to accept it. The answer from the servants of God will be: "Go to now, ye rich men. Your means is not needed. Ye withheld it when ye could do good with it in advancing the cause of God. The needy have suffered; they have not been blessed by your means. God will not accept your riches now. Go to now, ye rich men."

Then I was directed to these words: "Behold, the hire of the laborers who have reaped down your fields, which is of you kept back by fraud, crieth: and the cries of them which have reaped are entered into the ears of the Lord of Sabaoth." I saw that God is not in all the riches that are obtained. Satan often has much more to do with acquiring property than God. Much of it is obtained by oppressing the hireling in his wages. The naturally covetous rich man obtains his riches by grinding down the hireling, and taking advantage of individuals wherever he can, thereby adding to a treasure that will eat his flesh as it were fire.

A strictly honest, honorable course has not been taken by some. Such must take a very different course and work fast to redeem the time. Many Sabbathkeepers are at fault here. Advantage is taken even of their poor brethren, and those who have an abundance exact more than the real worth of things, more than they would pay for the same things, while these same brethren are embarrassed and distressed for want of means. God knows all these things. Every selfish act, every covetous extortion, will bring its reward.

I saw that it is cruel and unjust to have no consideration for a brother's situation. If he is distressed, or poor, yet doing the best he can, allowance should be made for him, and even the full value of things he may purchase of the wealthy should not be exacted; but they should have bowels of compassion for him. God will approve of such kindly acts, and the doer will not lose his reward. But a fearful account stands against many Sabbathkeepers for close, covetous acts.

I was pointed back to a time when there were but few who listened to and embraced the truth. They had not much of this world's goods. The wants of the cause were divided among a very few. Then it was necessary for some to sell their houses and lands, and obtain cheaper to serve them as a shelter, or home, while their means were freely and generously lent to the Lord, to publish the truth, and to otherwise aid in advancing the cause of God. As I beheld these self-sacrificing ones, I saw that they had endured privation for the benefit of the cause. I saw an angel standing by them, pointing them upward, and saying: "Ye have bags in heaven! Ye have bags in heaven that wax not old! Endure unto the end, and great will be your reward."

God has been moving upon many hearts. The truth for

which a few sacrificed so much, in order to get it before others, has triumphed, and multitudes have laid hold of it. God in His providence has moved upon those who have means, and has brought them into the truth, that as His work increases, the wants of the cause may be met. Much means has been brought into the ranks of Sabbathkeepers, and I saw that at present God does not call for the houses His people need to live in, unless expensive houses are exchanged for cheaper ones. But if those who have an abundance do not hear His voice, cut loose from the world, and dispose of a portion of their property and lands, and sacrifice for God, He will pass them by, and call for those who are willing to do anything for Jesus, even to sell their homes to meet the wants of the cause. God will have freewill offerings. Those who give must esteem it a privilege to do so.

Some give of their abundance, but yet they feel no lack. They do not particularly deny themselves of anything for the cause of Christ. They still have all that heart can wish. They give liberally and heartily. God regards it, and the action and motive are known and strictly marked by Him. They will not lose their reward. You who cannot bestow so liberally must not excuse yourselves because you cannot do as much as some others. Do what you can. Deny yourselves of some article that you can get along without, and sacrifice for the cause of God. Like the widow, cast in your two mites. You will actually give more than all those who give of their abundance; and you will know how sweet it is to deny self, to give to the needy, to sacrifice for the truth, and to lay up treasure in heaven.

I was shown that the young, especially young men, who profess the truth, have yet a lesson of self-denial to learn. If these made more sacrifice for the truth, they would esteem it more highly. It would affect their hearts, and purify their lives, and they would hold it more dear and sacred.

The young do not take the burden of the cause of God, or feel any responsibility in regard to it. Is it because God has excused them? Oh, no; they excuse themselves! They are eased, and others are burdened. They do not realize that they are not their own. Their strength, their time, is not their own. They are bought with a price. A dear sacrifice was made for them, and unless they possess the spirit of self-denial and sacrifice, they can never possess the immortal inheritance.

THE PRIVILEGE AND DUTY OF THE CHURCH

The following relates to the Battle Creek church, but describes the condition and privileges of brethren and sisters scattered abroad:

I saw that a thick cloud enveloped them, but that a few rays of light from Jesus pierced this cloud. I looked to see those who received this light, and saw individuals earnestly praying for victory. It was their study to serve God. Their persevering faith brought them returns. The light of heaven was shed upon them; but the cloud of darkness over the church in general was thick. They were stupid and sluggish. My agony of soul was great. I asked the angel if that darkness was necessary. Said he: "Look ye!" I then saw the church begin to rise, and earnestly plead with God, and rays of light began to penetrate this darkness, and the cloud was removed. The pure light of heaven shone upon them, and with holy confidence their attention was attracted upward. Said the angel: "This is their privilege and duty."

Satan has come down in great power, knowing that his time is short. His angels are busy, and a great share of the people of God suffer themselves to be lulled to sleep by him. The cloud again passed over, and settled upon the church. I saw that it would be only by earnest effort and persevering prayer that this spell would be broken.

The alarming truths of the word of God had stirred the people of God a little. Now and then they would make feeble efforts to overcome, but they soon tired and sank back into the same lukewarm state. I saw that they did not have perseverance and fixed determination. Let the seeker for the salvation of God possess the same energy and earnestness that he would have for a worldly treasure, and the object would be gained. I saw that the church may just as well drink of a full cup, as to hold an empty one in the hand or at the mouth.

It is not the plan of God to have some eased and others burdened. Some feel the weight and responsibility of the cause, and the necessity of their acting that they may gather with Christ and not scatter abroad. Others go on free from any responsibility, acting as though they had no influence. Such scatter abroad. God is not partial. All who are made partakers of His salvation here, and who hope to share the glories of the kingdom hereafter, must gather with Christ. Each must feel that he is responsible for his own case, and for the influence he exerts over others. If these maintain their Christian walk, Jesus will be in them the hope of glory, and they will love to speak forth His praise that they may be refreshed. The cause of their Master will be near and dear to them. It will be their study to advance His cause and to honor it by holy living. Said the angel: "Every talent God will require with usury." Every Christian must go on from strength to strength, and employ all his powers in the cause of God.

THE SHAKING

November 20, 1857, I was shown the people of God, and saw them mightily shaken. Some, with strong faith and agonizing cries, were pleading with God. Their countenances were pale, and marked with deep anxiety, expressive of their internal struggle. Firmness and great earnestness were expressed in their countenances, while large drops of perspiration fell from their foreheads. Now and then their faces would light up with the marks of God's approbation, and again the same solemn, earnest, anxious look would settle upon them.*

Evil angels crowded around them, pressing their darkness upon them, to shut out Jesus from their view, that their eyes might be drawn to the darkness that surrounded them, and they distrust God and next murmur against Him. Their only safety was in keeping their eyes directed upward. Angels of God had charge over His people, and as the poisonous atmosphere from the evil angels was pressed around these anxious ones, the heavenly angels were continually wafting their wings over them, to scatter the thick darkness.

Some, I saw, did not participate in this work of agonizing and pleading. They seemed indifferent and careless. They were not resisting the darkness around them, and it shut

---

*"Blow the trumpet in Zion, sanctify a fast, call a solemn assembly: gather the people, sanctify the congregation, assemble the elders. . . . Let the priests, the ministers of the Lord, weep between the porch and the altar and let them say, Spare Thy people, O Lord, and give not Thine heritage to reproach, that the heathen should rule over them: wherefore should they say among the people, Where is their God?" Joel 2:15-17.

"Submit yourselves therefore to God. Resist the devil, and he will flee from you. Draw nigh to God, and He will draw nigh to you. Cleanse your hands, ye sinners; and purify your hearts, ye double-minded. Be afflicted, and mourn, and weep: let your laughter be turned to mourning, and your joy to heaviness. Humble yourselves in the sight of the Lord, and He shall lift you up." James 4:7-10.

"Gather yourselves together, yea, gather together, O nation not desired; before the decree bring forth, before the day pass as the chaff, before the fierce anger of the Lord come upon you, before the day of the Lord's anger come upon you. Seek ye the Lord, all ye meek of the earth, which have wrought His judgment; seek righteousness, seek meekness: it may be ye shall be hid in the day of the Lord's anger." Zephaniah 2:1-3.

them in like a thick cloud. The angels of God left these, and I saw them hastening to the assistance of those who were struggling with all their energies to resist the evil angels, and trying to help themselves by calling upon God with perseverance. But the angels left those who made no effort to help themselves, and I lost sight of them. As the praying ones continued their earnest cries, a ray of light from Jesus would at times come to them, to encourage their hearts, and light up their countenances.

I asked the meaning of the shaking I had seen, and was shown that it would be caused by the straight testimony called forth by the counsel of the True Witness to the Laodiceans. This will have its effect upon the heart of the receiver, and will lead him to exalt the standard and pour forth the straight truth. Some will not bear this straight testimony. They will rise up against it, and this will cause a shaking among God's people.

The testimony of the True Witness has not been half heeded. The solemn testimony upon which the destiny of the church hangs has been lightly esteemed, if not entirely disregarded. This testimony must work deep repentance, and all that truly receive it will obey it and be purified.

Said the angel: "List ye." Soon I heard a voice that sounded like many musical instruments, all in perfect strains, sweet and harmonious. It surpassed any music I had ever heard. It seemed to be so full of mercy, compassion, and elevating, holy joy. It thrilled through my whole being. Said the angel: "Look ye!" My attention was then turned to the company I had seen, who were mightily shaken. I was shown those whom I had before seen weeping and praying with agony of spirit. The company of guardian angels around them had been doubled, and they were clothed with an armor from their head to their feet. They moved in exact order, firmly, like a company of soldiers. Their countenances expressed the severe conflict which they had endured, the agonizing struggle they had passed through. Yet their features, marked with severe internal anguish, now shone with the light and glory of heaven. They had obtained the victory, and it called forth from them the deepest gratitude, and holy, sacred joy.

The numbers of this company had lessened. Some had been shaken out, and left by the way.* The careless and indifferent, who did not join with those who prized victory and salvation enough to perseveringly plead and agonize for it, did not obtain it, and they were left behind in darkness, but their numbers were immediately made up by others taking hold of the truth and coming into the ranks. Still the evil angels pressed around them, but they could have no power over them. **

I heard those clothed with the armor speak forth the truth in great power. It had effect. I saw those who had been bound; some wives had been bound by their husbands, and some children had been bound by their parents. The honest

---

*"I know thy works, that thou art neither cold nor hot: I would thou wert cold or hot. So then because thou art lukewarm, and neither cold nor hot, I will spew thee out of my mouth. Because thou sayest, I am rich, and increased with goods, and have need of nothing, and knowest not that thou art wretched, and miserable, and poor, and blind, and naked." Revelation 3:15-17.

** "For we wrestle not against flesh and blood, but against principalities, against powers, against the rulers of the darkness of this world, against spiritual wickedness in high places. [Or, "wicked spirits in heavenly places," as in the margin.] Wherefore take unto you the whole armor of God, that ye may be able to withstand in the evil day, and having done all, to stand. Stand therefore, having your loins girt about with truth, and having on the breastplate of righteousness; and your feet shod with the preparation of the gospel of peace; above all, taking the shield of faith, wherewith ye shall be able to quench all the fiery darts of the wicked. And take the helmet of salvation, and the sword of the Spirit, which is the word of God; praying always with all prayer and supplication in the Spirit, and watching thereunto with all perseverance and supplication for all saints." Ephesians 6:12-18.

who had been held or prevented from hearing the truth, now eagerly laid hold of it. All fear of their relatives was gone. The truth alone was exalted to them. It was dearer and more precious than life. They had been hungering and thirsting for truth. I asked what had made this great change. An angel answered: "It is the latter rain, the refreshing from the presence of the Lord, the loud cry of the third angel."

Great power was with these chosen ones. Said the angel: "Look ye!" My attention was turned to the wicked, or unbelievers. They were all astir. The zeal and power with the people of God had aroused and enraged them. Confusion, confusion was on every side. I saw measures taken against this company, who had the power and light of God. Darkness thickened around them, yet there they stood, approved of God, and trusting in Him. I saw them perplexed. Next I heard them crying unto God earnestly. Through the day and night their cry ceased not. *I heard these words: "Thy will, O God, be done! If it can glorify Thy name, make a way of escape for Thy people! Deliver us from the heathen round about us! They have appointed us unto death; but Thine arm can bring salvation." These are all the words that I can bring to mind. All seemed to have a deep sense of their unworthiness, and manifested entire submission to the will of God. Yet like Jacob, every one, without an exception, was earnestly pleading and wrestling for deliverance.

Soon after they had commenced their earnest cry, the angels, in sympathy, would have gone to their deliverance. But a tall, commanding angel suffered them not. Said he: "The will of God is not yet fulfilled. They must drink of the cup. They must be baptized with the baptism."

---

*"And shall not God avenge His own elect, which cry day and night unto Him, though He bear long with them? I tell you that He will avenge them speedily. Nevertheless when the Son of man cometh, shall He find faith on the earth?" Luke 18:7, 8. See also Revelation 14:14, 15.

Soon I heard the voice of God which shook the heavens and the earth.* There was a mighty earthquake. Buildings were shaken down, and fell on every side. I then heard a triumphant shout of victory, loud, musical, and clear. I looked upon this company, who, a short time before, were in such distress and bondage. Their captivity was turned. A glorious light shone upon them. How beautiful they then looked! All weariness and marks of care were gone; health and beauty were seen in every countenance. Their enemies, the heathen around them, fell like dead men. They could not endure the light that shone upon the delivered, holy ones. This light and glory remained upon them until Jesus was seen in the clouds of heaven, and the faithful, tried company were changed in a moment, in the twinkling of an eye, from glory to glory. The graves were opened and the saints came forth, clothed with immortality, crying: "Victory over death and the grave!" and together with the living saints they were caught up to meet their Lord in the air, while rich, musical shouts of glory and victory proceeded from every immortal tongue.

*"The Lord also shall roar out of Zion, and utter His voice from Jerusalem; and the heavens and the earth shall shake: but the Lord will be the hope of His people, and the strength of the children of Israel." Joel 3:16. See also Hebrews 12:26; Revelation 16:17.

NUMBER FIVE

TESTIMONY FOR THE CHURCH

THE LAODICEAN CHURCH

Dear Brethren and Sisters: The Lord has again visited me in much mercy. I have been greatly afflicted for a few months past. Disease has pressed heavily upon me. For years I have been afflicted with dropsy and disease of the heart, which has had a tendency to depress my spirits and destroy my faith and courage. The message to the Laodiceans has not accomplished that zealous repentance among God's people which I expected to see, and my perplexity of mind has been great. Disease seemed to make continual progress upon me, and I thought that I must lie down in the grave. I had no desire to live, therefore I could not take hold of faith and pray for my recovery. Often when I retired to rest at night I realized that I was in danger of losing my breath before morning. In this state I fainted at midnight. Brethren Andrews and Loughborough were sent for, and earnest petitions were offered to God on my behalf. The depression, the heavy weight, was lifted from my aching heart, and I was taken off in vision, and shown the things which I now present before you.

I saw that Satan had been trying to drive me to discouragement and dispair, to make me desire death rather than life. I was shown that it was not God's will that I should cease from the work and lie down in the grave; for then the enemies of our faith would triumph, and the hearts of God's children would be made sad. I saw that I should often feel anguish of spirit, and should suffer much; yet I had the promise that those around me would encourage and help me, that my courage and strength might not fail while I was so fiercely buffeted by the devil.

I was shown that the testimony to the Laodiceans applies to God's people at the present time, and the reason it has not accomplished a greater work is because of the hardness of their hearts. But God has given the message time to do its work. The heart must be purified from sins which have so long shut out Jesus. This fearful message will do its work. When it was first presented, it led to close examination of heart. Sins were confessed, and the people of God were stirred everywhere. Nearly all believed that this message would end in the loud cry of the third angel. But as they failed to see the powerful work accomplished in a short time, many lost the effect of the message. I saw that this message would not accomplish its work in a few short months. It is designed to arouse the people of God, to discover to them their backslidings, and to lead to zealous repentance, that they may be favored with the presence of Jesus, and be fitted for the loud cry of the third angel. As this message affected the heart, it led to deep humility before God. Angels were sent in every direction to prepare unbelieving hearts for the truth. The cause of God began to rise, and His people were acquainted with their position. If the counsel of the True Witness had been fully heeded, God would have wrought for His people in greater power. Yet the efforts made since the message has been given, have been blessed of God, and many souls have been brought from error and darkness to rejoice in the truth.

God will prove His people. Jesus bears patiently with them, and does not spew them out of His mouth in a moment. Said the angel: "God is weighing His people." If the message had been of as short duration as many of us supposed, there would have been no time for them to develop character. Many moved from feeling, not from principle and faith, and this solemn, fearful message stirred them. It wrought upon their feelings, and excited their fears, but did not accomplish the work which God designed that it should. God reads the heart. Lest His people should be deceived in regard to themselves, He gives them time for the excitement to wear off, and then proves them to see if they will obey the counsel of the True Witness.

God leads His people on, step by step. He brings them up to different points calculated to manifest what is in the heart. Some endure at one point, but fall off at the next. At every advanced point the heart is tested and tried a little closer. If the professed people of God find their hearts opposed to this straight work, it should convince them that they have a work to do to overcome, if they would not be spewed out of the mouth of the Lord. Said the angel: "God will bring His work closer and closer to test and prove every one of His people." Some are willing to receive one point; but when God brings them to another testing point, they shrink from it and stand back, because they find that it strikes directly at some cherished idol. Here they have opportunity to see what is in their hearts that shuts out Jesus. They prize something higher than the truth, and their hearts are not prepared to receive Jesus. Individuals are tested and proved a length of time to see if they will sacrifice their idols and heed the counsel of the True Witness. If any will not be purified through obeying the truth, and overcome their selfishness, their pride, and evil passions, the angels of God have the charge: "They are joined to their idols, let them alone," and they pass on to their work, leaving these with their sinful traits unsubdued, to the control of evil angels. Those who come up to every point, and stand every test, and overcome, be the price what it may, have heeded the counsel of the True Witness, and they will receive the latter rain, and thus be fitted for translation.

God proves His people in this world. This is the fitting-up place to appear in His presence. Here, in this world, in these last days, persons will show what power affects their hearts and controls their actions. If it is the power of divine truth, it will lead to good works. It will elevate the receiver, and make him noblehearted and generous, like his divine Lord. But if evil angels control the heart, it will be seen in various ways. The fruit will be selfishness, covetousness, pride, and evil passions.

The heart is deceitful above all things, and desperately wicked. Professors of religion are not willing to closely examine themselves to see whether they are in the faith; and it is a fearful fact that many are leaning on a false hope. Some lean upon an old experience which they had years ago; but when brought down to this heart-searching time, when all should have a daily experience, they have nothing to relate. They seem to think that a profession of the truth will save them. When they subdue those sins which God hates, Jesus will come in and sup with them and they with Him. They will then draw divine strength from Jesus, and will grow up in Him, and be able with holy triumph to say: "Thanks be to God, which giveth us the victory through our Lord Jesus Christ." It would be more pleasing to the Lord if lukewarm professors of religion had never named His name. They are a continual weight to those who would be faithful followers of Jesus. They are a stumbling block to unbelievers, and evil angels exult over them, and taunt the angels of God with their crooked course. Such are a curse to the cause at home or abroad. They draw nigh to God with their lips, while their heart is far from Him.

I was shown that the people of God should not imitate the fashions of the world. Some have done this, and are fast losing the peculiar, holy character which should distinguish them as God's people. I was pointed back to God's ancient people, and was led to compare their apparel with the mode of dress in these last days. What a difference! what a change! Then the women were not so bold as now. When they went in public, they covered their faces with a veil. In these last days, fashions are shameful and immodest. They are noticed in prophecy. They were first brought in by a class over whom Satan has entire control, who, "being past feeling [without any conviction of the Spirit of God] have given themselves over unto lasciviousness, to work all uncleanness with greediness." If God's professed people had not greatly departed from Him, there would now be a marked difference between their dress and that of the world. The small bonnets, exposing the face and head, show a lack of modesty. The hoops are a shame. The inhabitants of earth are growing more and more corrupt, and the line of distinction between them and the Israel of God must be more plain, or the curse which falls upon worldlings will fall on God's professed people.

I was directed to the following scriptures. Said the angel: "They are to instruct God's people." 1 Timothy 2:9, 10: "In like manner also, that women adorn themselves in modest apparel, with shamefacedness and sobriety; not with broided hair, or gold, or pearls, or costly array; but (which becometh women professing godliness) with good works." 1 Peter 3:3-5: "Whose adorning let it not be that outward adorning of plaiting the hair, and of wearing of gold, or of putting on of apparel; but let it be the hidden man of the heart, in that which is not corruptible, even the ornament of a meek and quiet spirit, which is in the sight of God of great price. For after this manner in the old time the holy women also, who trusted in God, adorned themselves."

Young and old, God is now testing you. You are deciding your own eternal destiny. Your pride, your love to follow the fashions of the world, your vain and empty conversation, your selfishness, are all put in the scale, and the weight of evil is fearfully against you. You are poor, and miserable, and blind, and naked. While evil is increasing and taking deep root, it is choking the good seed which has been sown in the heart; and soon the word that was given concerning Eli's house will be spoken to the angels of God concerning you: Your sins "shall not be purged with sacrifice nor offering forever." Many, I saw, were flattering themselves that they were good Christians, who have not a single ray of light from Jesus. They know not what it is to be renewed by the grace of God. They have no living experience for themselves in the things of God. And I saw that the Lord was whetting His sword in heaven to cut them down. Oh, that every lukewarm professor could realize the clean work that God is about to make among His professed people! Dear friends, do not deceive yourselves concerning your condition. You cannot deceive God. Says the True Witness: "I know thy works." The third angel is leading up a people, step by step, higher and higher. At every step they will be tested.

The plan of systematic benevolence* is pleasing to God. I was pointed back to the days of the apostles, and saw that God laid the plan by the descent of His Holy Spirit, and that by the gift of prophecy He counseled His people in regard to a system of benevolence. All were to share in this work of imparting of their carnal things to those who ministered unto them in spiritual things. They were also taught that the widows and fatherless had a claim upon their charity. Pure and undefiled religion is defined, To visit the widows and fatherless in their affliction, and to keep unspotted from the world. I saw that this was not merely to sympathize with them by comforting words in their affliction, but to aid them, if needy, with our substance. Young men and women to whom God has given health can obtain a great blessing by aiding the widow and the fatherless in their affliction. I saw that God requires young men to sacrifice more for the good

*See Appendix

of others. He claims more of them than they are willing to perform. If they keep themselves unspotted from the world, cease to follow its fashions, and lay by that which the lovers of pleasure spend in useless articles to gratify pride, and give it to the worthy afflicted ones, and to sustain the cause, they will have the approval of Him who says, "I know thy works."

There is order in heaven, and God is well pleased with the efforts of His people in trying to move with system and order in His work on earth. I saw that there should be order in the church of God, and that system is needed in carrying forward successfully the last great message of mercy to the world. God is leading His people in the plan of systematic benevolence, and this is one of the very points to which God is bringing up His people which will cut the closest with some. With them this cuts off the right arm, and plucks out the right eye, while to others it is a great relief. To noble, generous souls the demands upon them seem very small, and they cannot be content to do so little. Some have large possessions, and if they lay by them in store for charitable purposes as God has prospered them, the offering seems to them like a large sum. The selfish heart clings as closely to a small offering as to a larger one, and makes a small sum look very large.

I was pointed back to the commencement of this last work. Then some who loved the truth could consistently talk of sacrificing. They devoted much to the cause of God, to send the truth to others. They have sent their treasure beforehand to heaven. Brethren, you who have received the truth at a later period, and who have large possessions, God has called you into the field, not merely that you may enjoy the truth, but that you may aid with your substance in carrying forward this great work. And if you have an interest in this work, you will venture out and invest something in it, that others may be saved by your efforts, and you reap with them the final reward. Great sacrifices have been made and privations endured to place the truth in a clear light before you. Now God calls upon you, in your turn, to make great efforts and to sacrifice in order to place the truth before those who are in darkness. God requires this. You profess to believe the truth; let your works testify to the fact. Unless your faith works, it is dead. Nothing but a living faith will save you in the fearful scenes which are just before you.

I saw that it is time for those who have large possessions to begin to work fast. It is time that they were not only laying by them to store as God *is now* prospering them, but as He *has* prospered them. In the days of the apostles, plans were especially laid that some should not be eased and others burdened. Arrangements were made that all should share equally in the burdens of the church of God according to their several abilities. Said the angel: "The ax must be laid at the root of the tree." Those who, like Judas, have set their hearts upon earthly treasure will complain as he did. His heart coveted the costly ointment poured upon Jesus, and he sought to hide his selfishness under a pious, conscientious regard for the poor: "Why was not this ointment sold for three hundred pence, and given to the poor?" He wished that he had the ointment in his possession; it would not thus be lavished upon the Saviour. He would apply it to his own use; sell it for money. He prized his Lord just enough to sell Him to wicked men for a few pieces of silver. As Judas brought up the poor as an excuse for his selfishness, so professed Christians, whose hearts are covetous, will seem to hide their selfishness under a put-on conscientiousness. Oh, they fear that in adopting systematic benevolence we are becoming like the nominal churches! "Let not thy left hand know what thy right hand doeth." They seem to have a conscientious desire to follow exactly the Bible as they understand it in this matter; but they entirely neglect the plain admonition of Christ: "Sell that ye have, and give alms."

"Take heed that ye do not your alms before men, to be seen of them." Some think this text teaches that they must be secret in their works of charity. And they do but very little, excusing themselves because they do not know just how to give. But Jesus explained it to His disciples as follows: "Therefore when thou doest thine alms, do not sound a trumpet before thee, as the hypocrites do in the synagogues and in the streets, that they may have glory of men. Verily I say unto you, they have their reward." They gave to be regarded noble and generous by men. They received praise of men, and Jesus taught His disciples that this was all the reward they would have. With many, the left hand does not know what the right hand does, for the right hand does nothing worthy of the notice of the left hand. This lesson of Jesus to His disciples was to rebuke those who wished to receive glory of men. They performed their almsgiving at some very public gathering; and before doing this, a public proclamation was made heralding their generosity before the people; and many gave large sums merely to have their name exalted by men. And the means given in this manner was often extorted from others, by oppressing the hireling in his wages, and grinding the face of the poor.

I was shown that this scripture does not apply to those who have the cause of God at heart, and use their means humbly to advance it. I was directed to these texts: "Let your light so shine before men, that they may see your good works, and glorify your Father which is in heaven." "By their fruits ye shall know them." I was shown that Scripture testimony will harmonize when it is rightly understood. The good works of the children of God are the most effectual preaching that the unbeliever has. He thinks that there must be strong motives that actuate the Christian to deny self, and use his possessions in trying to save his fellow men. It is unlike the spirit of the world. Such fruits testify that the possessors are genuine Christians. They seem to be constantly reaching upward to a treasure that is imperishable.

With every gift and offering there should be a suitable object before the giver, not to uphold any in idleness, not to be seen of men or to get a great name, but to glorify God by advancing His cause. Some make large donations to the cause of God while their brother who is poor, may be suffering close by them, and they do nothing to relieve him. Little acts of kindness performed for their brother in a secret manner would bind their hearts together, and would be noticed in heaven. I saw that in their prices and wages the rich should make a difference in favor of the afflicted and widows and the worthy poor among them. But it is too often the case that the rich take advantage of the poor, reaping every benefit that is to be gained, and exacting the last penny for every favor. It is all written in heaven. "I know thy works."

The greatest sin which now exists in the church is covetousness. God frowns upon His professed people for their selfishness. His servants have sacrificed their time and strength to carry them the word of life, and many have shown by their works that they prize it but lightly. If they can help the servant of God just as well as not, they sometimes do it; but they often let him pass on, and do but little for him. If they employ a day laborer, he must be paid full wages. But not so with the self-sacrificing servant of God. He labors for them in word and doctrine; he carries the heavy burden of the work on his soul; he patiently shows from the word of God the dangerous errors which are hurtful to the soul; he enforces the necessity of immediately tearing up the weeds which choke the good seed sown; he brings out of the storehouse of God's word things new and old to feed the flock of God. All acknowledge that they have been benefited; but the poisonous weed, covetousness, is so deeply rooted that they let the servant of God leave them without ministering to him of their temporal things. They have prized his wearing labor just as highly as their acts show. Says the True Witness: "I know thy works."

I saw that God's servants are not placed beyond the temptations of Satan. They are often fearfully beset by the enemy, and have a hard battle to fight. If they could be released from their commission, they would gladly labor with their hands. Their labor is called for by their brethren; but when they see it so lightly prized, they are depressed. True, they look to the final settlement for their reward, and this bears them up; but their families must have food and clothing. Their time belongs to the church of God; it is not at their own disposal. They sacrifice the society of their families to benefit others; and yet some who are benefited by their labors are indifferent to their wants. I saw that it is doing injustice to such to let them pass on and deceive themselves. They think they are approved of God, when He despises their selfishness. Not only will these selfish ones be called to render an account to God for the use they have made of their Lord's money, but all the depression and heartache which they have brought upon God's chosen servants, and which have crippled their efforts, will be set to the account of the unfaithful stewards.

The True Witness declares: "I know thy works." The selfish, covetous heart will be tested. Some are not willing to devote to God a very small portion of the increase of their earthly treasure. They would start back with horror if you should speak of the principal. What have they sacrificed for God? Nothing. They profess to believe that Jesus is coming; but their works deny their faith. Every person will live out all the faith he has. Falsehearted professor, Jesus knows thy works. He hates your stinted offerings, your lame sacrifices.

HOUSES OF WORSHIP

I saw that many to whom God has entrusted means feel at liberty to use it freely for their own convenience in fitting up pleasant homes here; but when they build a house in which to worship the great God who inhabiteth eternity, they cannot afford to let Him have the use of the means which He has lent them. Each is not striving to excel the other in showing his gratitude to God for the truth by doing all he can to prepare a suitable place of worship; but some are trying to do just as little as possible; and they feel that the means is as good as lost which they spend in preparing a place for the Most High to visit them. Such an offering is lame, and not acceptable to God. I saw that it would be much more pleasing to God if His people would show as much wisdom in preparing a house for Him, as they do in their own dwellings.

The sacrifices and offerings of the children of Israel were commanded to be without blemish or spot, the best of the flock, and every one of the people was required to share in this work. The work of God for this time will be extensive. If you build a house for the Lord, do not offend and limit Him by casting in your lame offerings. Put the very best offering into a house built for God. Let it be the very best you have; show an interest to make it convenient and comfortable. Some think that this is of no consequence because time is so short. Then carry out the same in your dwellings, and in all your worldly arrangements.

I saw that God could carry on His work without any of man's help; but this is not His plan. The present world is designed as a scene of probation for man. He is here to form a character which will pass with him into the eternal world. Good and evil are placed before him, and his future state depends upon the choice he makes. Christ came to change the current of his thoughts and affections. His heart must be removed from his earthly treasure, and placed upon the heavenly. By his self-denial, God can be glorified. The great sacrifice has been made for man, and now he will be tested and proved to see if he will follow the example of Jesus, and make a sacrifice for his fellow man. Satan and his angels are combined against the people of God; but Jesus is seeking to purify them unto Himself. He requires them to advance His work. God has deposited with His people in this world enough to carry forward His work without embarrassment, and it is His plan that the means which He has entrusted to them be used judiciously. "Sell that ye have, and give alms," is a part of God's sacred word. The servants of God must arise, cry aloud, and spare not, "show My people their transgression, and the house of Jacob their sins." The work of God is to become more extensive, and if His people follow His counsel, there will not be much means in their possession to be consumed in the final conflagration. All will have laid up their treasure where moth and rust cannot corrupt; and the heart will not have a cord to bind it to earth.

LESSONS FROM THE PARABLES

I was shown that the parable of the talents has not been fully understood. This important lesson was given to the disciples for the benefit of Christians living in the last days. And these talents do not represent merely the ability to preach and instruct from the word of God. The parable applies to the temporal means which God has entrusted to His people. Those to whom the five and the two talents were given, traded and doubled that which was committed to their trust. God requires those who have possessions here, to put their money out to usury for Him—to put it into the cause to spread the truth. And if the truth lives in the heart of the receiver, he also will aid with his substance in sending it to others; and through his efforts, his influence, and his means, other souls will embrace the truth, and begin also to work for God. I saw that some of God's professed people are like the man who hid his talent in the earth. They keep their possessions from doing good in the cause of God. They claim that these are their own, and that they have a right to do what they please with their own; and souls are not saved by judicious efforts made by them with their Lord's money. Angels keep a faithful record of every man's work, and as judgment passes upon the house of God, the sentence of each is recorded by his name, and the angel is commissioned to spare not the unfaithful servants, but to cut them down at the time of slaughter. And that which was committed to their trust is taken from them. Their earthly treasure is then swept away, and they have lost all. And the crowns they might have worn, had they been faithful, are put upon the heads of those saved by the faithful servants whose means was constantly in use for God. And everyone they have been the means of saving, adds stars to their crown in glory, and increases their eternal reward.

I was also shown that the parable of the unjust steward was to teach us a lesson. "Make to yourselves friends of the mammon of unrighteousness; that, when ye fail, they may receive you into everlasting habitations." If we use our means to God's glory here, we lay up a treasure in heaven; and when earthly possessions are all gone, the faithful steward has Jesus and angels for his friends, to receive him home to everlasting habitations.

"He that is faithful in that which is least is faithful also in much." He that is faithful in his earthly possessions, which are least, making a judicious use of what God has lent him here, will be true to his profession. "He that is unjust in the least is unjust also in much." He that will withhold from God that which He has lent him, will be unfaithful in the things of God in every respect. "If therefore ye have not been faithful in the unrighteous mammon, who will commit to your trust the true riches?" If we prove unfaithful in the management of what God lends us here, He will never give us the immortal inheritance. "And if ye have not been faithful in that which is another man's, who shall give you that which is your own?" Jesus has purchased redemption for us. It is ours; but we are placed here on probation to see if we will prove worthy of eternal life. God proves us by trusting us with earthly possessions. If we are faithful to impart freely of what He has lent us, to advance His cause, God can entrust to us the immortal inheritance. "Ye cannot serve God and mammon." "If any man love the world, the love of the Father is not in him."

God is displeased with the slack, loose manner in which many of His professed people conduct their worldly business. They seem to have lost all sense of the fact that the property they are using belongs to God, and that they must render to Him an account of their stewardship. Some leave their worldly business in perfect confusion. Satan has his eye on it all, and he strikes at a favorable opportunity, and by his management takes much means out of the ranks of Sabbath-keepers. And this means goes into his ranks. Some who are aged are unwilling to make any settlement of their worldly business, and in an unexpected moment they sicken and die. Their children who have no interest in the truth, take the property. Satan has managed it as suited him. "If therefore ye have not been faithful in the unrighteous mammon, who will commit to your trust the true riches? And if ye have not been faithful in that which is another man's, who shall give you that which is your own?"

I was shown the awful fact that Satan and his angels have had more to do with the management of the property of God's professed people than the Lord has. Stewards of the last days are unwise. They suffer Satan to control their business matters, and get into his ranks what belongs to, and should be in, the cause of God. God takes notice of you, unfaithful stewards; He will call you to account. I saw that the stewards of God can by faithful, judicious management keep their business in this world square, exact, and straight. And it is especially the privilege and duty of the aged, the feeble, and those who have no children, to place their means where it can be used in the cause of God if they should be suddenly taken away. But I saw that Satan and his angels exult over their success in this matter. And those who should be wise heirs of salvation almost willingly let their Lord's money slip out of their hands into the enemy's ranks. In this way they strengthen Satan's kingdom, and seem to feel very easy about it!

SURETY FOR UNBELIEVERS

I saw that God was displeased with His people for becoming surety for unbelievers. I was directed to these texts: Proverbs 22:26: "Be not thou one of them that strike hands, or of them that are sureties for debts." Proverbs 11:15: "He that is surety for a stranger shall smart for it: and he that hateth suretyship is sure." Unfaithful stewards! They pledge that which belongs to another,—their heavenly Father,—and Satan stands ready to aid his children to wrench it out of their hands. Sabbathkeepers should not be in partnership with unbelievers. God's people trust too much to the words of strangers, and ask their advice and counsel when they should not. The enemy makes them his agents, and works through them to perplex and take from God's people.

Some have no tact at wise management of worldly matters. They lack the necessary qualifications, and Satan takes advantage of them. When this is the case, such should not remain in ignorance of their task. They should be humble enough to counsel with their brethren, in whose judgment they can have confidence, before they carry out plans. I was directed to this text: "Bear ye one another's burdens." Some are not humble enough to let those who have judgment calculate for them until they have followed their own plans, and have involved themselves in difficulties. Then they see the necessity of having the counsel and judgment of their brethren; but how much heavier the burden then than at first. Brethren should not go to law if it can be possibly avoided; for they thus give the enemy great advantage to entangle and perplex them. It would be better to make a settlement at some loss.

OATH TAKING

I saw that some of God's children have made a mistake in regard to oath taking, and Satan has taken advantage of this to oppress them, and take from them their Lord's money. I saw that the words of our Lord, "Swear not at all," do not touch the judicial oath. "Let your communication be, Yea, yea; Nay, nay: for whatsoever is more than these cometh of evil." This refers to common conversation. Some exaggerate in their language. Some swear by their own life; others swear by their head—as sure as they live; as sure as they have a head. Some take heaven and earth to witness that such things are so. Some hope that God will strike them out of existence if what they are saying is not true. It is this kind of common swearing against which Jesus warns His disciples.

We have men placed over us for rulers, and laws to govern the people. Were it not for these laws, the condition of the world would be worse than it is now. Some of these laws are good, others are bad. The bad have been increasing, and we are yet to be brought into strait places. But God will sustain His people in being firm and living up to the principles of His word. When the laws of men conflict with the word and law of God, we are to obey the latter, whatever the consequences may be. The law of our land requiring us to deliver a slave to his master, we are not to obey, and we must abide the consequences of violating this law. The slave is not the property of any man. God is his rightful master, and man has no right to take God's workmanship into his hands, and claim him as his own.

I saw that the Lord still has something to do with the laws of the land. While Jesus is in the sanctuary, God's restraining Spirit is felt by rulers and people. But Satan controls to a great extent the mass of the world, and were it not for the laws of the land, we should experience much suffering. I was shown that when it is actually necessary, and they are called upon to testify in a lawful manner, it is no violation of God's word for His children to solemnly take God to witness that what they say is the truth, and nothing but the truth.

Man is so corrupt that laws are made to throw the responsibility upon his own head. Some men do not fear to lie to their fellow man; but they have been taught, and the restraining Spirit of God has impressed them, that it is a fearful thing to lie to God. The case of Ananias and Sapphira his wife is given for an example. The matter is carried from man to God, so that if one bears false witness, it is not to man, but to the great God, who reads the heart, and knows the exact truth in every case. Our laws make it a high crime to take a false oath. God has often visited judgment upon the false swearer, and even while the oath was on his lips, the destroying angel has cut him down. This was to prove a terror to evildoers.

I saw that if there is anyone on earth who can consistently testify under oath, it is the Christian. He lives in the light of God's countenance. He grows strong in His strength. And when matters of importance must be decided by law, there is no one who can so well appeal to God as the Christian. I was bidden by the angel to notice that God swears by

Himself. Genesis 22:16; Hebrews 6:13, 17. He swore to Abraham (Genesis 26:3), to Isaac (Psalm 105:9; Jeremiah 11:5), and to David (Psalm 132:11; Acts 2:30). God required of the children of Israel an oath between man and man. Exodus 22:10, 11. Jesus submitted to the oath in the hour of His trial. The high priest said unto Him: "I adjure Thee by the living God, that Thou tell us whether Thou be the Christ, the Son of God." Jesus said unto him: "Thou hast said." If Jesus in His teachings to His disciples referred to the judicial oath, He would have reproved the high priest, and there enforced His teachings, for the good of His followers present. Satan has been pleased that some have viewed oath taking in a wrong light; for it has given him opportunity to oppress them and take from them their Lord's money. The stewards of God must be more wise, lay their plans, and prepare themselves to withstand Satan's devices; for he is to make greater efforts than ever before.

Some, I saw, have a prejudice against our rulers and laws, but if it were not for law, this world would be in an awful condition. God restrains our rulers; for the hearts of all are in His hands. Bounds are set, beyond which they cannot go. Many of the rulers are those whom Satan controls; but I saw that God has His agents, even among the rulers. And some of them will yet be converted to the truth. They are now acting the part that God would have them. When Satan works through his agents, propositions are made, that, if carried out, would impede the work of God and produce great evil. The good angels move upon these agents of God to oppose such propositions with strong reasons, which Satan's agents cannot resist. A few of God's agents will have power to bear down a great mass of evil. Thus the work will go on until the third message has done its work, and at the loud cry of the third angel, these agents will have an opportunity to receive the truth, and some of them will be converted, and endure with the saints through the time of trouble. When Jesus leaves the most holy, His restraining Spirit is withdrawn from rulers and people. They are left to the control of evil angels. Then such laws will be made by the counsel and direction of Satan, that unless time should be very short, no flesh could be saved.

ERRORS IN DIET

Dear Brother and Sister A: The Lord has seen fit in His goodness to give me a vision at this place; and among the different things shown were some relating to you. I saw that all was not right with you. The enemy has been seeking your destruction, and endeavoring to influence others through you. I saw that you both take an exalted position that God has never assigned you, and that you both consider yourselves far in advance of the people of God. I saw you looking to Battle Creek with jealousy and suspicion. You would place your hands in there, and mold their acts and doings to what you consider would be right. You are noticing little things that you do not understand, that you have not the least to do with, and that in no way concern you. God has committed His work at B.C. to chosen servants. He has laid the burden of the work upon them. Angels of God are commissioned to have oversight of the work; and if it does not move right, those who are at the head of the work will be corrected, and things will move in God's order without interference of this or that individual.

I saw that God wants you to turn your attention to yourselves. Try your motives. You are deceived in regard to yourselves. You have an appearance of humility, and this has influence with others, and leads them to think that you are far advanced in the Christian life; but when your peculiar notions are touched, self rises at once, and you manifest a willful, stubborn spirit. This is a sure evidence that you do not possess true humility.

I saw that you had mistaken notions about afflicting your bodies, depriving yourselves of nourishing food. These things lead some of the church to think that God is surely with you, or you would not deny self, and sacrifice thus. But I saw that none of these things will make you more holy. The heathen do all this, but receive no reward for it. A broken and contrite spirit before God is in His sight of great price. I saw that your views concerning these things are erroneous, and that you are looking at the church and watching them, noticing little things, when your attention should be turned to your own soul's interest. God has not laid the burden of His flock upon you. You think that the church is upon the background, because they cannot see things as you do, and because they do not follow the same rigid course which you think you are required to pursue. I saw that you are deceived in regard to your own duty and the duty of others. Some have gone to extremes in regard to diet. They have taken a rigid course, and lived so very plain that their health has suffered, disease has strengthened in the system, and the temple of God has been weakened.

I was referred back to our experience in Rochester, New York. I saw that when we lived there we did not eat nourishing food as we should, and disease nearly carried us to the grave. I saw that as God gives His beloved sleep, He is willing to grant them suitable food to nourish the strength. The motive we had was pure. It was to save means, that the paper might be sustained. We were poor. I saw that the fault then was in the church. Those who had means were covetous and selfish. If these had done their part, the burden upon us would have been lightened; but as some did not do their part, we were burdened and others eased. I saw that God does not require anyone to take a course of such rigid economy as to weaken or injure the temple of God. There are duties and requirements in His word to humble the church and cause them to afflict their souls, and there is no need of making crosses and manufacturing duties to distress the body in order to cause humility. All this is outside of the word of God.

The time of trouble is just before us; and then stern necessity will require the people of God to deny self, and to eat merely enough to sustain life; but God will prepare us for that time. In that fearful hour our necessity will be God's opportunity to impart His strengthening power, and to sustain His people. But now God requires them to labor with their hands, the thing that is good, and lay by them in store as He has prospered them, and do their part in sustaining the cause of truth. This is a duty enjoined upon all who are not especially called to labor in word and doctrine, to devote their time to proclaiming to others the way of life and salvation.

Those who labor with their hands must nourish their strength to perform this labor, and those also who labor in word and doctrine must nourish their strength; for Satan and his evil angels are warring against them to tear down their strength. They should seek rest of body and mind from wearing labor when they can, and should eat of nourishing, strengthening food to build up their strength; for they will be obliged to exercise all the strength they have. I saw that it does not glorify God in the least for any of His people to make a time of trouble for themselves. There is a time of trouble just before God's people, and He will prepare them for that fearful conflict.

I saw that your views concerning swine's flesh* would prove no injury if you have them to yourselves; but in your judgment and opinion you have made this question a test,

---

*This remarkable testimony was written October 21, 1858, nearly five years before the great vision of 1863, in which the light upon health reform was given. When the right time came, the subject was given in a manner to move all our people. How wonderful are the wisdom and goodness of God! It might be as wrong to crowd the milk, salt, and sugar question now, as the pork question in 1858. J.W., *note to second edition.*

and your actions have plainly shown your faith in this matter. If God requires His people to abstain from swine's flesh, He will convict them on the matter. He is just as willing to show His honest children their duty, as to show their duty to individuals upon whom He has not laid the burden of His work. If it is the duty of the church to abstain from swine's flesh, God will discover it to more than two or three. He will teach His *church* their duty.

God is leading out a people, not a few separate individuals here and there, one believing this thing, another that. Angels of God are doing the work committed to their trust. The third angel is leading out and purifying a people, and they should move with him unitedly. Some run ahead of the angels that are leading His people; but they have to retrace every step, and meekly follow no faster than the angels lead. I saw that the angels of God would lead His people no faster than they could receive and act upon the important truths that are communicated to them. But some restless spirits do not more than half do up their work. As the angel leads them, they get in haste for something new, and rush on without divine guidance, and thus bring confusion and discord into the ranks. They do not speak or act in harmony with the body. I saw that you both must speedily be brought where you are willing to be led, instead of desiring to lead, or Satan will step in and lead you in his way, to follow his counsel. Some look at your set notions, and consider them an evidence of humility. They are deceived. You both are making work for repentance.

Brother A, you are naturally close and covetous. You tithe mint and rue, but neglect the weightier matters. When the young man came to Jesus, and asked what he should do to have eternal life, Jesus told him to keep the commandments. He declared that he had done so. Said Jesus: Yet lackest thou one thing. Go sell that thou hast, and give to the poor, and thou shalt have treasure in heaven. The result was the young man went away sorrowful, for he had great possessions. I saw that you had wrong ideas. God requires economy of His people, but some have stretched their economy into meanness. I wish that you could see your case as it is. The true spirit of sacrifice, which is acceptable to God, you do not possess. You look at others, and watch them, and if they do not bring themselves to the same rigid course that you follow, you can do nothing for them. Your souls are withering beneath the blighting influence of your own errors. A fanatical spirit is with you, that you take to be God's Spirit. You are deceived. You cannot bear the plain, cutting testimony. You would have a smooth testimony borne to you; but when anyone reproves your wrongs, how quick self rises. Your spirits are not humbled. You have a work to do. . . . Such acts, such a spirit, I saw, was the fruit of your errors, and the fruit of setting up your judgment and notions as a rule for others, and against those whom God has called into the field. You have both overreached the mark.

I saw that you had thought this one and that one were called to labor in the field, when you know nothing of the matter. You cannot read the heart. If you had drunk deep of the truth of the third angel's message, you would not be so free to tell who were called of God, and who were not. The fact that one can pray and talk well is no evidence that God has called him. Everyone has an influence, and that influence should tell for God; but the question whether this one or that one should devote his time to labor for souls, is of the deepest importance, and none but God can decide who shall engage in the solemn work. There were good men in the apostles' days, men who could pray with power and talk to the point; yet the apostles, who had power over unclean spirits and could heal the sick, dared not with merely their wisdom set one apart for the holy work of being mouthpiece for God. They waited unmistakable evidence of the manifestation of the Holy Spirit. I saw that God had laid upon His chosen ministers the duty of deciding who was fit for the holy work; and in union with the church and the manifest tokens of the Holy Spirit, they were to decide who should go and who were unfit to go. I saw that if it should be left to a few individuals here and there to decide who was sufficient for this great work, confusion and distraction everywhere would be the fruit.

God has repeatedly shown that persons should not be encouraged into the field without unmistakable evidence that He has called them. The Lord will not entrust the burden for His flock to unqualified individuals. Those whom God calls must be men of deep experience, tried and proved men of sound judgment, men who will dare to reprove sin in the spirit of meekness, men who understand how to feed the flock. God knows the heart, and He knows whom to select. Brother and Sister A may decide in this matter, and be all wrong. Your judgment is imperfect, and can be no evidence in this matter. I saw that you were drawing off from the church, and if you continue to do so, you will have enough of it; for God will let you go, to suffer by following your own way.

Now God invites you to get right, to try your motives, and to press into harmony with His people.

Mannsville, New York, October 21, 1858.

NUMBER SIX

TESTIMONY FOR THE CHURCH

SLACKNESS REPROVED*

Dear Brethren and Sisters: The Lord has again visited me in mercy, in a time of bereavement and great affliction. December 23, 1860, I was taken off in vision, and was shown the wrongs of individuals which have affected the cause. I dare not withhold the testimony from the church to spare the feelings of individuals.

I was shown the low state of God's people; that God had not departed from them, but that they had departed from Him, and had become lukewarm. They possess the theory of the truth, but lack its saving power. As we near the close of time, Satan comes down with great power, knowing that his time is short. Especially will his power be exercised upon the remnant. He will war against them, and seek to divide and scatter them, that they may grow weak and be overthrown. The people of God should move understandingly, and should be united in their efforts. They should be of the same mind, of the same judgment; then their efforts will not be scattered, but will tell forcibly in the upbuilding of the cause of present truth. Order must be observed, and there must be union in maintaining order, or Satan will take the advantage.

I saw that the enemy would come in every way possible to dishearten the people of God and perplex and trouble

*See Appendix

them, and that they should move understandingly, and prepare themselves for the attacks of Satan. Matters pertaining to the church should not be left in an unsettled condition. Steps should be taken to secure church property for the cause of God, that the work may not be retarded in its progress, and that the means which persons wish to dedicate to God's cause may not slip into the enemy's ranks. I saw that God's people should act wisely, and leave nothing undone on their part to place the business of the church in a secure state. Then after all is done that they can do, they should trust the Lord to overrule these things for them, that Satan take no advantage of God's remnant people. It is Satan's time to work. A stormy future is before us; and the church should be awake to make an advance move that they may stand securely against his plans. It is time that something was done. God is not pleased to have His people leave the matters of the church at loose ends, and suffer the enemy to have the whole advantage and control affairs as best pleases him.

I was shown the wrong stand taken by Brother B in the *Review* in regard to organization, and the distracting influence he exerted. He did not sufficiently weigh the matter. His articles were perfectly calculated to have a scattering influence, to lead minds to wrong conclusions, and to encourage many in their slack ideas of managing matters relating to the cause of God. Those who do not feel the weight of this cause upon them do not feel the necessity of anything being done to establish church order. Those who have long borne the burden look to the future and weigh matters. They are convinced that steps must be taken to place the matters of the church in a more secure position, where Satan cannot come in and take advantage. Brother B's articles caused those who fear order to look with suspicion upon the suggestions of those who by the special providence of God move out in the important matters of the church. And when he saw that his position would not bear, he failed to frankly acknowledge his error, and labor to efface the wrong impression he had made.

I saw that in temporal matters Brother B was too easy and negligent. He has lacked energy, considering it a virtue to leave to the Lord that which the Lord has left to him. It is only in cases of great emergency that the Lord interposes for us. We have a work to do, burdens and responsibilities to bear, and in thus doing we obtain an experience. Brother B manifests the same character in spiritual matters as in his temporal affairs. There is a lack of zeal and earnestness to make thorough work. All should act with more discretion and wisdom in regard to the things of God than they manifest in temporal things to secure an earthly possession.

But while God's people are justified in securing church property in a lawful manner, they should be careful to maintain their peculiar and holy character. I saw that unconsecrated persons would take advantage of the position which the church has recently taken, and would overstep the bounds, carry matters to extremes, and wound the cause of God. Some will move without wisdom or judgment, engage in lawsuits that might be avoided, mingle with the world, partake of its spirit, and influence others to follow their example. One professed Christian who moves unadvisedly does much harm to the cause of present truth. Evil takes root much more readily than good, and flourishes when good and right languish unless carefully nourished.

I was pointed back, and saw that in every important move, every decision made or point gained by God's people, some have arisen to carry matters to extremes, and to move in an extravagant manner, which has disgusted unbelievers, distressed God's people, and brought the cause of God into disrepute. The people whom God is leading out in these last days, will be troubled with just such things. But much evil will be avoided if the ministers of Christ will be of one mind, united in their plans of action, and united in effort. If they will stand together, sustain one another, and faithfully reprove and rebuke wrong, they will soon cause it to wither. But Satan has controlled these matters very much. Private members and even preachers have sympathized with disaffected ones who have been reproved for their wrongs, and division of feeling has been the result. The one who has ventured out and discharged his disagreeable duty by faithfully meeting error and wrong, is grieved and wounded that he receives not the fullest sympathy of his preaching brethren. He becomes discouraged in discharging these painful duties, lays down the cross, and withholds the pointed testimony. His soul is shut up in darkness, and the church suffer for the lack of the very testimony which God designed should live among His people. Satan's object is gained when the faithful testimony is suppressed. Those who so readily sympathize with the wrong consider it a virtue; but they realize not that they are exerting a scattering influence, and that they themselves help to carry out Satan's plans.

I saw that many souls have been destroyed by their brethren unwisely sympathizing with them, when their only hope was to be left to see and realize the full extent of their wrongs. But as they eagerly accept the sympathy of unwise brethren, they receive the idea that they are abused; and if they attempt to retrace their steps, they make halfhearted work. They divide the matter to suit their natural feelings, lay blame upon the reprover, and so patch up the matter. It is not probed to the bottom, and is not healed, and they again fall into the same wrong, because they were not left to feel the extent of their wrong, and humble themselves before God, and let Him build them up. False sympathizers have worked in direct opposition to the mind of Christ and ministering angels.

Ministers of Christ should arise and engage in the work of God with all their energies. God's servants are not excused if they shun pointed testimony. They should reprove and rebuke wrong, and not suffer sin upon a brother. I must here introduce a portion of a letter addressed to Brother C:

"I was shown some things in regard to you. I saw that the living, pointed testimony had been crushed in the church. You have not been in harmony with the straight testimony. You have shunned to lay your hand decidedly upon wrong, and you have been tried with those who felt compelled to do so. Disaffected ones have had your sympathy. This has had a tendency to make you a weak man. You have not been in union with pointed, cutting testimony which has been sent home to the individual.

"God's servants are not excused if they shun pointed testimony. They must reprove and rebuke wrong, and not suffer sin upon a brother. You have often stretched out your hands to shield persons from the censure which they deserved, and the correction which the Lord designed they should have. If these persons fail to reform, their lack is set to your account. Instead of watching for their danger, and warning them of it, you have cast your influence against those who have followed the convictions of duty, and reproved and warned the erring.

"These are perilous times for the church of God, and the greatest danger now is that of self-deception. Individuals professing to believe the truth are blind to their own danger and wrongs. They reach the standard of piety which has been set up by their friends and themselves, they are fellowshiped by their brethren, and are satisfied, while they entirely fail to reach the gospel standard set up by our divine Lord. If they regard iniquity in their hearts, the Lord will not hear them. But with many it is not only regarded in the heart, but openly carried out in the life; yet in many cases the wrongdoers receive no rebuke.

"I was pointed back to ——. Your feelings were wrong there. You should have stood side by side with Elder D and made straight work, taken hold of and reproved individual wrongs. The burden you cast upon Elder D you deserved yourself, for your lack of moral courage to lay your hand upon wrong. You influenced others. The good work which God designed should be accomplished for certain ones was not accomplished, and they have been puffed up by Satan. If you had stood in the counsel of God at that time, an influence would have been cast which would have told upon the cause of God. The Spirit of the Lord was grieved. And this lack of union discourages those upon whom God lays the burden of reproof.

"I was shown that you had been wrong in sympathizing with E. The course you have taken in regard to him has injured your influence, and has greatly injured the cause of God. It is impossible for E to be fellowshiped by the church of God. He has placed himself where he cannot be helped by the church, where he can have no communion with nor voice in the church. He has placed himself there in the face of light and truth. He has stubbornly chosen his own course, and refused to listen to reproof. He has followed the inclinations of his corrupt heart, has violated the holy law of God, and has disgraced the cause of present truth. If he repents ever so heartily, the church must let his case alone. If he goes to heaven, it must be alone, without the fellowship of the church. A standing rebuke from God and the church must ever rest upon him, that the standard of morality be not lowered to the very dust. The Lord is displeased with your course in these things.

"You have injured the cause of God; your willful course has wounded the hearts of God's people. Your influence encourages a slack state of things in the church. You should bear a living, pointed testimony. Stand out of the way of the work of God, step not in between God and His people. You have too long wrapped up the sharp testimony, and stood opposed to the severe censure which God lays upon individual wrongs. God is correcting, and proving, and purifying His people. Stand out of the way that His work be not hindered. He will not accept a smooth testimony. Ministers must cry aloud, and spare not. The Lord has given you a powerful testimony, calculated to strengthen the church and arouse unbelievers. But these things wherein you lack must be corrected, or your testimony will become powerless, and your influence injure the cause of God. The people look to you for an example. Do not mislead them. Let your influence be to correct wrongs in your family and in the church."

I have been shown that the Lord is reviving the living, pointed testimony, which will develop character and purify the church. But while we are commanded to separate from the world, it is not necessary that we become coarse and rough, and descend to common expressions, and make our remarks as rude as possible. The truth is designed to elevate the receiver, to refine his taste and sanctify his judgment. There should be a continual effort to imitate the society we expect soon to join; namely, angels of God who have never fallen by sin. The character should be holy, the manners comely, the words without guile, and thus should we follow on step by step until we are fitted for translation.

DUTY TO CHILDREN

I have been shown that parents generally have not taken a proper course with their children. They have not restrained them as they should, but have left them to indulge in pride, and follow their own inclinations. Anciently, parental authority was regarded; children were then in subjection to their parents, and feared and reverenced them; but in these last days the order is reversed. Some parents are in subjection to their children. They fear to cross the will of their children, and therefore yield to them. But just as long as children are under the roof of the parents, dependent upon them, they should be subject to their control. Parents should move with decision, requiring that their views of right be followed out.

Eli might have restrained his wicked sons, but he feared their displeasure. He suffered them to go on in their rebellion, until they became a curse to Israel. Parents are required to restrain their children. The salvation of children depends very much upon the course pursued by the parents. In their mistaken love and fondness for their children, many parents indulge them to their hurt, nourish their pride, and put upon them trimmings and ornaments which make them vain, and lead them to think that dress makes the lady or gentleman. But a short acquaintance convinces those with whom they associate that an outside appearance is not sufficient to hide the deformity of a heart void of the Christian graces, but filled with self-love, haughtiness, and uncontrolled passions. Those who love meekness, humility, and virtue, should shun such society, even if it be Sabbathkeepers' children. Their company is poisonous; their influence leads to death. Parents realize not the destructive influence of the seed which they are sowing. It will spring up and bear fruit which will make their children despise parental authority.

Even after they are of age, children are required to respect their parents, and to look after their comfort. They should listen to the counsel of godly parents, and not feel that because a few more years are added to their life, they have grown out of their duty to them. There is a commandment with promise to those who honor their father and their mother. In these last days children are so noted for their disobedience and disrespect that God has especially noticed it, and it constitutes a sign that the end is near. It shows that Satan has almost complete control of the minds of the young. By many, age is no more respected. It is considered too old-fashioned to respect the aged: it dates back as far as the days of Abraham. Says God: "I know him, that he will command his children and his household after him."

Anciently, children were not permitted to marry without the consent of their parents. Parents chose for their children. It was considered a crime for children to contract marriage upon their own responsibility. The matter was first laid before the parents, and they were to consider whether the person to be brought into a close relation to them was worthy, and whether the parties could provide for a family. It was considered by them of the greatest importance that they, the worshipers of the true God, should not intermarry with an idolatrous people, lest their families be led away from God. Even after children were married, they were under the most solemn obligation to their parents. Their judgment was not then considered sufficient without the counsel of the parents, and they were required to respect and obey their wishes unless these should conflict with the requirements of God.

Again I was directed to the condition of the young in these last days. Children are not controlled. Parents, you should commence your first lesson of discipline when your children are babes in your arms. Teach them to yield their will to yours. This can be done by bearing an even hand, and manifesting firmness. Parents should have perfect control over their own spirits, and with mildness and yet firmness bend the will of the child until it shall expect nothing else but to yield to their wishes.

Parents do not commence in season. The first manifestation of temper is not subdued, and the children grow stubborn, which increases with their growth and strengthens with their strength. Some children, as they grow older, think it a matter of course that they must have their own way, and that their parents must submit to their wishes. They expect their parents to wait upon them. They are impatient of restraint, and when old enough to be a help to their parents, they do not bear the burdens they should. They have been released from responsibilities, and grow up worthless at home and worthless abroad. They have no power of endurance. The parents have borne the burden, and have suffered them to grow up in idleness, without habits of order, industry, or economy. They have not been taught habits of self-denial, but have been petted and indulged, their appetites gratified, and they come up with enfeebled health. Their manners and deportment are not agreeable. They are unhappy themselves, and make those around them unhappy. And while the children are but children still, while they need to be disciplined, they are allowed to go out in company and mingle with the society of the young, and one has a corrupting influence over another.

The curse of God will surely rest upon unfaithful parents. Not only are they planting thorns which will wound them here, but they must meet their own unfaithfulness when the judgment shall sit. Many children will rise up in judgment and condemn their parents for not restraining them, and charge upon them their destruction. The false sympathy and blind love of parents causes them to excuse the faults of their children and pass them by without correction, and their children are lost in consequence, and the blood of their souls will rest upon the unfaithful parents.

Children who are thus brought up undisciplined, have everything to learn when they profess to be Christ's followers. Their whole religious experience is affected by their bringing up in childhood. The same self-will often appears; there is the same lack of self-denial, the same impatience under reproof, the same love of self and unwillingness to seek counsel of others, or to be influenced by others' judgment, the same indolence, shunning of burdens, lack of bearing responsibilities. All this is seen in their relation to the church. It is possible for such to overcome; but how hard the battle! how severe the conflict! How hard to pass through the course of thorough discipline which is necessary for them to reach the elevation of Christian character! Yet if they overcome at last, they will be permitted to see, before they are translated, how near the precipice of eternal destruction they came, because of the lack of right training in youth, the failure to learn submission in childhood.

SYSTEMATIC BENEVOLENCE

I was pointed back to the children of Israel anciently. God required of them all, both poor and rich, a sacrifice according as He had prospered them. The poor were not excused because they had not the wealth of their rich brethren. They were required to exercise economy and self-denial. And if any were so poor that it was utterly impossible for them to bring an offering to the Lord, if sickness or misfortune had deprived them of the ability to bestow, those who were wealthy were required to help them to a humble mite that they come not before the Lord empty-handed. This arrangement preserved a mutual interest.

Some have not come up and united in the plan of systematic benevolence, excusing themselves because they were not free from debt. They plead that they must first "owe no man anything." But the fact that they are in debt does not excuse them. I saw that they should render to Caesar the things that are Caesar's, and to God the things that are God's. Some feel conscientious to "owe no man anything," and think that God can require nothing of them until their debts are all paid. Here they deceive themselves. They fail to render to God the things that are His. Everyone must bring to the Lord a suitable offering. Those who are in debt should take the amount of their debts from what they possess, and give a proportion of the remainder.

Some have felt under sacred obligations to their children.

They must give each a portion, but feel themselves unable to raise means to aid the cause of God. They make the excuse that they have a duty to their children. This may be right, but their first duty is to God. Render unto Caesar the things that are Caesar's, and to God the things that are God's. Rob not God by withholding from Him your tithes and offerings. It is the first sacred duty to render to God a suitable proportion. Let no one throw in his claims and lead you to rob God. Let not your children steal your offering from God's altar for their own benefit.

I saw that anciently the covetousness of some led them to withhold a suitable proportion; they made their offering stinted. This was recorded in heaven, and they were cursed in their harvest and their flocks just as they withheld. Some were visited with affliction in their families. God would not accept a lame offering. It must be without blemish, the best of their flocks, and the best fruits of their fields. And it must be a freewill offering, if they would have the blessing of the Lord rest upon their families and their possessions.

The case of Ananias and Sapphira was presented before me to illustrate the course of those who put down their property below its value. They pretended to make a freewill offering of their possessions to the Lord. Said Peter: "Tell me whether ye sold the land for so much?" The answer was "Yea, for so much." Some in this evil age would not consider that a lie. But the Lord regarded it thus. They had sold it for so much, and much more. They had professed to consecrate all to God. To Him they had dissembled, and their retribution lingered not.

I saw that in the arrangement of systematic benevolence, hearts will be tested and proved. It is a constant, living test. It brings one to understand his own heart, to see whether the truth or the love of the world predominates. Here is a test for the naturally selfish and covetous. They will put down their possessions at very low figures. Here they dissemble. Said the angel: "Cursed be he that doeth the work of the Lord deceitfully." Angels are watching the development of character, and the acts of such are carried to heaven by the heavenly messengers. Some will be visited of God for these things, and their increase will be brought down to their figures. "There is that scattereth, and yet increaseth; and there is that withholdeth more than is meet, but it tendeth to poverty. The liberal soul shall be made fat: and he that watereth shall be watered also himself." Proverbs 11:24, 25.

All are required to have an interest in this work. Those who use tobacco, tea, and coffee should lay aside those idols, and put their cost into the treasury of the Lord. Some have never made a sacrifice for the cause of God, and are asleep as to what God requires of them. Some of the very poorest will have the greatest struggle to deny themselves of these stimulants. This individual sacrifice is not required because the cause of God is suffering for means. But every heart will be tested, every character developed. It is principle that God's people must act upon. The living principle must be carried out in the life.

"Will a man rob God? Yet ye have robbed Me. But ye say, Wherein have we robbed Thee? In tithes and offerings. Ye are cursed with a curse: for ye have robbed Me, even this whole nation. Bring ye all the tithes into the storehouse, that there may be meat in Mine house, and prove Me now herewith, saith the Lord of hosts, if I will not open you the windows of heaven, and pour you out a blessing, that there shall not be room enough to receive it. And I will rebuke the devourer for your sakes, and he shall not destroy the fruits of your ground; neither shall your vine cast her fruit before the time in the field, saith the Lord of hosts." I saw that this scripture has been misapplied to speaking and praying in meeting. The prophecy has a special application to the last days, and teaches God's people their duty to bring a proportion of their substance as a freewill offering to the Lord.

OUR DENOMINATIONAL NAME

I was shown in regard to the remnant people of God taking a name. Two classes were presented before me. One class embraced the great bodies of professed Christians. They were trampling upon God's law and bowing to a papal institution. They were keeping the first day of the week as the Sabbath of the Lord. The other class, who were but few in number, were bowing to the great Lawgiver. They were keeping the fourth commandment. The peculiar and prominent features of their faith were the observance of the seventh day, and waiting for the appearing of our Lord from heaven.

The conflict is between the requirements of God and the requirements of the beast. The first day, a papal institution which directly contradicts the fourth commandment, is yet to be made a test by the two-horned beast. And then the fearful warning from God declares the penalty of bowing to the beast and his image. They shall drink the wine of the wrath of God, which is poured out without mixture into the cup of His indignation.

No name which we can take will be appropriate but that which accords with our profession and expresses our faith and marks us a peculiar people. The name Seventh-day Adventist is a standing rebuke to the Protestant world. Here is the line of distinction between the worshipers of God and those who worship the beast and receive his mark. The great conflict is between the commandments of God and the requirements of the beast. It is because the saints are keeping all ten of the commandments that the dragon makes war upon them. If they will lower the standard and yield the peculiarities of their faith, the dragon will be at peace; but they excite his ire because they have dared to raise the standard and unfurl their banner in opposition to the Protestant world, who are worshiping the institution of papacy.

The name Seventh-day Adventist carries the true features of our faith in front and will convict the inquiring mind. Like an arrow from the Lord's quiver, it will wound the transgressors of God's law, and will lead to repentance toward God and faith in our Lord Jesus Christ.

I was shown that almost every fanatic who has arisen, who wishes to hide his sentiments that he may lead away others, claims to belong to the church of God. Such a name would at once excite suspicion; for it is employed to conceal the most absurd errors. This name is too indefinite for the remnant people of God. It would lead to the supposition that we had a faith which we wished to cover up.

THE POOR

Some who are poor in this world's goods are apt to place all the straight testimony upon the shoulders of the men of property. But they do not realize that they also have a work to do. God requires them to make a sacrifice. He calls upon them to sacrifice their idols. They should lay aside such hurtful stimulants as tobacco, tea, and coffee. If they are brought into straitened circumstances while exerting themselves to do the best they can, it will be a pleasure for their wealthy brethren to help them out of trouble.

Many lack wise management and economy. They do not weigh matters well, and move cautiously. Such should not trust to their own poor judgment, but should counsel with their brethren who have experience. But those who lack economy and good judgment are often unwilling to seek counsel. They generally think that they understand how to conduct their temporal business, and are unwilling to follow advice. They make bad moves, and suffer in consequence.

Their brethren are grieved to see them suffer, and they help them out of difficulty. Their unwise management affects the church. It takes means from the treasury of God which should have been used to advance the cause of present truth. If these poor brethren take a humble course and are willing to be advised and counseled by their brethren, and are then brought into straitened places, the brethren should feel it a duty to cheerfully help them out of difficulty. But if they choose their own course, and rely upon their own judgment, they should be left to feel the full consequences of their unwise course, and learn by dear experience that "in multitude of counselors there is safety." God's people should be subject one to another. They should counsel with one another, that the lack of one may be supplied by the sufficiency of another. I saw that the stewards of the Lord have no duty to help those persons who persist in using tobacco, tea, and coffee.

SPECULATIONS

I saw that some have excused themselves from aiding the cause of God because they were in debt. Had they closely examined their own hearts, they would have discovered that selfishness was the true reason why they brought no freewill offering to God. Some will always remain in debt. Because of their covetousness, the prospering hand of God will not be with them to bless their undertakings. They love this world better than they love the truth. They are not being fitted up and made ready for the kingdom of God.

If a new patent passes through the country, men who profess to believe the truth find a way to raise means to invest in the enterprise. God is acquainted with every heart. Every selfish motive is known to Him, and He suffers circumstances to arise to try the hearts of His professed people, to prove them and develop character. In some instances the Lord will suffer men to go on, and meet with an entire failure. His hand is against them to disappoint their hopes and scatter what they possess. Those who really feel an interest in the cause of God, and are willing to venture something for its advancement, will find it a sure and safe investment. Some will have a hundredfold in this life, and in the world to come life everlasting. But all will not receive their hundredfold in this life, because they cannot bear it. If entrusted with much, they would become unwise stewards. The Lord withholds it for their good; but their treasure in heaven will be secure. How much better is such an investment as this!

The desire that some of our brethren possess to earn means fast, leads them to engage in a new enterprise and invest means, but often their expectations of making money are not realized. They sink that which they could have spent in God's cause. There is an infatuation in these new enterprises. And notwithstanding these things have been acted over so many times, and they have before them the example of others who have made investments and have met with an utter failure, yet many are slow to learn. Satan allures them on and makes them drunk with anticipated gains. When their hopes are blasted, they suffer many discouragements in consequence of their unwise adventures. If means is lost, the person looks upon it as a misfortune to himself—as his loss. But he must remember that it is the means of another which he is handling, that he is only a steward, and God is displeased with the unwise management of that means which could have been used to advance the cause of present truth. At the reckoning day the unfaithful steward must give an account of his stewardship.

A DISHONEST STEWARD

I was shown that the Spirit of God has had less and less influence upon F, until he has no strength from God to overcome. Self and self-interest have been prominent with him for some length of time. Pride of heart, a set, unsubdued will, and an unwillingness to confess and yield his wrongs, have brought him to the dreadful position he is in. Long has the cause been injured by his injudicious course.

He has been exacting, which has encouraged a spirit of faultfinding in the church. He has been severe where it was uncalled for and has lorded it over those upon whom he dared to exercise authority. His prayers and exhortations have led the brethren to think that he was a devoted Christian, which has prepared them to be affected by his wrong course. He has been notional, and his oddities have had a bad influence upon the minds of many. Some have been so weak as to imitate his example. I saw that he had done far greater injury than good to the cause.

Had he received the instruction given of God, and been corrected, he would have obtained the victory over these strong habits and besetments. But I saw that he had so long let these habits control him that the strong foe has bound him. His deal has not been correct. Dishonesty has been gaining upon him, and he has taken from the treasury means that he had no right to, and has used it to his own advantage. He has considered that he had better judgment in disposing of means than his brethren. When means was placed in his hands to be applied, and the giver named the individuals who were to receive it, he has acted from impulse, taken the liberty to apply it to suit himself, instead of carrying out the wishes of the giver, and has used what portion of it he saw fit for his own benefit. God has frowned upon these things. A dishonest course has been gaining upon him. He has considered that he was the Lord's steward, and could apply the means, even of another, as he saw fit. Every man is to be his own steward.

He has rejected the counsel and advice of his brethren, gone on in his own strength, followed his own will, and has rejected every means whereby he could be corrected. When he has been reproved, the manner or the person has not suited him, and the way for reform has been closed up. The Lord has not accepted his labors for some length of time. He has labored much more for his own interest than for the interest of the cause.

When he first goes to a place, his prayers and exhortations have effect, and brethren receive the idea that he is a perfect Christian. He is favored because he is considered a minister. But as they become acquainted, how they are disappointed to witness his selfishness, fretfulness, harshness, and oddities. Almost every day some peculiar notion is seen. His mind is almost constantly occupied in fixing up something for his own advantage. Then he will dispose of it to someone to good advantage to himself, and fix again. His fixing and planning have had a withering, blighting influence upon the cause of God. His course is calculated to tear to pieces, and it has wounded almost everywhere. What an example to the flock! He has been very selfish in his deal, and has taken advantage of those with whom he has dealt. God's frown is upon him. A good tree is known by its fruits.

FANATICISM IN WISCONSIN

I saw that the Lord especially directed my husband in going west last fall instead of going east as he at first decided. In Wisconsin there was a wrong to be corrected. The work of Satan was taking effect, and would destroy souls if not rebuked. The Lord saw fit to choose one who had had experience with fanaticism in the past, and had witnessed the working of Satan's power. Those who received this instrument of God's choosing were corrected, and souls were rescued from the snare which Satan had prepared for them.

I was shown that this device of Satan would not have taken so readily in Wisconsin if the minds and hearts of God's people had been united and in union with the work. The spirit of jealousy and suspicion still existed in the minds of some. The seed sown by the *Messenger* party had not been entirely rooted out. And while they professed to receive the third angel's message, their former feelings and prejudices had not been given up. Their faith was adulterated, and they were prepared for Satan's deception. Those who drank in the *Messenger* spirit must make clean work, and have every particle of it rooted out, and receive the spirit of the third angel's message, or it will cleave to them like the leprosy, making it easy for them to draw off from their brethren in present truth. It will be easy for them to think that they can go, an independent company, alone to heaven, and easy for them to fall into Satan's snare. He is very unwilling to let go his hold in Wisconsin. He has other deceptions prepared for those who are not united with the body.

I saw that persons who had been so enshrouded in darkness and deception that Satan had controlled not only the mind but the body, would have to take a most humble place in the church of God. He will not commit the care of His flock to unwise shepherds, who would mistake and feed them poison instead of wholesome food. God will have men care for the flock who can feed them with clean provender, thoroughly winnowed. Oh, what a blot, what a reproach, have these fanatical movements brought upon the cause of God! And those who held so fast to this spirit of dark fanaticism, notwithstanding the plain evidences that it was from Satan, are not to be relied upon; their judgment is not to be considered of any weight. God sent His servants to Brother and Sister G. They despised correction, and chose their own course. Brother G was jealous and stubborn, and his future course must be marked with great humility; for he has proved himself unworthy of the confidence of God's people. His heart is not right with God, neither has it been for a long time.

I saw that Satan's object has been to lead persons in Wisconsin into gross fanaticism. He has controlled their minds, and led them to act in accordance with the deception they were under. When his object was accomplished, and they had run the length of the course which he had marked out for them, he was willing that they should acknowledge that wrong, and then he would try to push them to an opposite extreme, to deny the gifts and operations of God's Spirit. Satan took advantage of Brother and Sister G's lack of union with the body. They desired to take an independent course, and to lead instead of yielding to be led. Brother G has a jealous disposition, which, together with his independence, has kept him to one side; for with this spirit he could not be a true yoke fellow with his ministering brethren. Sister G is of a jealous disposition, and possesses much firmness. She lacks experience, and has not been sound in the faith or united with the body. Her heart has risen up against the gifts of the church. There was a lack of meekness and humility in her articles sent to the *Review* for publication.

Everything seemed prepared for the work of Satan. He led many on to lay aside reason and judgment, and to be governed by impressions. The Lord requires His people to use their reason, and not lay it aside for impressions. His work will be intelligible to all His children. His teaching will be such as will commend itself to the understanding of intelligent minds. It is calculated to elevate the mind. God's power is not manifested upon every occasion. Man's necessity is God's opportunity.

I was shown companies in confusion exercised by a wrong

spirit, all making loud prayers together, some crying one thing and some another; and it was impossible to tell what was piped and what was harped. "God is not the author of confusion, but of peace." Satan stepped in and controlled matters as he pleased. Reason and health were sacrificed to this delusion.

God does not require His people to imitate Baal's prophets, to afflict their bodies and cry out and shout, and throw themselves into almost every attitude, having no regard for order, until their strength fails through sheer exhaustion. Religion does not consist in making a noise; yet when the soul is filled with the Spirit of the Lord, sweet, heartfelt praise to God glorifies Him. Some have professed to have great faith in God, and to have special gifts and special answers to their prayers, although the evidence was lacking. They mistook presumption for faith. The prayer of faith is never lost; but to claim that it will be always answered in the very way and for the particular thing we have expected, is presumption.

When the servants of God visited ——— and ———, this delusion was sifted. Evidence was given that this work was spurious. But the spirit of fanaticism was stubborn, and would not yield to the light there given. Oh, that those who were in error had been corrected by God's servants whom He sent to them! Then and there God wished them to acknowledge that they had been led by a wrong spirit. Then there would have been virtue in the confession of their wrongs. Then they would have been saved any further following out of Satan's plans, and would have made no further progress in this dreadful delusion. But they would not be convinced. Brother G had sufficient light to take his stand against that fanatical work; but he would not decide from the weight of evidence. His stubborn spirit refused to yield to the light brought him by the servants of God; for he had regarded them with suspicion, and watched them with a jealous eye.

I saw that the greater the light which the people reject, the greater will be the power of deception and darkness which will come upon them. The rejection of truth leaves men captives, the subjects of Satan's deception. After the Conferences at ——— and ———, the subjects of this delusion were left to still greater darkness, to enter deeper into this strong delusion, and bring upon the cause of God a stain which would not soon be wiped away. A fearful responsibility is resting upon Brother G. While professing to be a shepherd he suffered the devourer to enter the flock, and looked on while the sheep were torn and devoured. God's frown is upon him. He has not watched for souls as one who must give account.

I was pointed back, and saw that God had not blessed his labors for some time past. The Lord's hand has not been with him to build up the church, and convert souls to the truth. His heart is not right with God. He has not possessed the spirit of the third angel's message. He shut himself away from union and sympathy with God's people before this delusion arose, and this is one reason why he was left in such darkness. God does not leave His faithful, consecrated servants in darkness as to the character of such a fanatical spirit, to raise no cry to warn the people. When the servants of God brought the light, and raised their voices against this delusion, he knew not the voice of the True Shepherd speaking through them; his jealousy and stubbornness led him to regard it as the voice of a stranger. Shepherds of the flock, above all others, should understand the voice of the Chief Shepherd. God wants His people to be a holy and powerful people. When the spirit of holiness and perfect love abounds in the heart, working in those who profess the name of Christ, it will be like a refining fire, consuming the dross and scattering the darkness. Whatever is of the spirit of Satan takes the attitude of defense, and quickly works out its own destruction. But truth will triumph.

CONCEALING REPROOFS

I was shown the course of H and I. Although reproved, they have not corrected their wrongs. The people of God, espcially in the State of New York, have been affected by their wrong course. Their influence has been injurious to the cause of God. For the last ten years they have been often presented before me in vision, their wrongs have been shown me, and I have written to them concerning these things. But they were careful to conceal from their brethren the fact that they had been reproved, fearing it would have a tendency to destroy their influence. Those who were affected by their wrong course, should have been benefited by the reproofs which they received. I should have placed these messages in the hands of judicious brethren in the church, that if necessary, all might understand the instruction the Lord saw fit to give His people. But when I related the messages given me for these brethren to anyone but themselves, they censured me in the most unsparing manner. This caused me so much suffering of mind that I have been led to conceal what the Lord has given me in regard to the wrongs of individuals.

It was pride of heart which led these brethren to manifest so much fear lest others should know that they had been corrected. If they had humbly confessed their wrongs to the church, they would have acted out the faith they professed to have in the visions, and the church would have been strengthened to receive correction and confess their faults. These teachers stood in the way of the flock. They set them a wrong example, and the church have looked to them, and when reproved have inquired: "Why have not these ministers been reproved, when we are following their teachings?" A door has thus been opened for Satan to tempt them as to the truthfulness of the visions.

The brethren have been deceived and wronged. They believed that we were in union with these teachers, and followed their instructions, when they were all wrong; I have written to these ministers in anguish of spirit as I have seen the cause of God wounded by their injudicious course. How anxiously have I watched the effect of these messages. But they laid them aside, and the brethren were not permitted to know anything about them, therefore could not be benefited by the instructions which the Lord saw fit to give.

My labor has been most discouraging, as I have seen that what God designed has not been accomplished. Often I have inquired in distress: Of what account is all my labor? These brethren took this position: We believe the visions, but Sister White, in writing them, put in her own words, and we will believe that portion which we think is of God, and will not heed the other. This course they have pursued, and have not corrected their lives. They have professed to believe the visions, but have acted contrary to them. Their example and influence have raised doubts in the minds of others. It would have been better for the cause of present truth had they both opposed the gifts. Then the people would not have been deceived and would not have stumbled over these blind teachers. We have hoped and prayed that they might get right, and exert a good influence upon the flock, but hope has died, and we cannot, dare not, hold our peace longer. We have wronged the church of God, in that we have not spoken out before.

THE CAUSE IN OHIO

Since our visit to Ohio in the spring of 1858, H has done what he could to exert an influence against us; and where he thought he could affect individuals, he has done so by circulating reports to stir up wrong feelings. When we visited Ohio in the spring of 1858, a message was given me in regard to him and his family. This testimony was given to him. But very few persons knew that I had a message for him. He rose in rebellion against it, and, like some others who have been reproved, took the position that persons had prejudiced my mind against his family, when the vision pointed out the same faults in them that I had repeatedly seen for ten years. He said that he believed the visions, but that I was influenced by others in writing them.

What a conclusion! The Lord has a special work to perform through one of the acknowledged gifts but suffers the message given to be adulterated before it reaches the person whom He wishes to correct. Of what use are the visions if persons regard them in this light? They put their own construction upon them, and feel at liberty to reject that portion which does not agree with their feelings. H knows that every word of the vision given for him in Ohio was correct. And when he could keep the message from the church no longer (for it was called for, and read at the ______ Conference last fall), he acknowledged it all true. But he has kept up a blind warfare against that which he knew to be correct.

He has not ruled well his own house, and for the last ten years has been reproved for this. The frown of God has been upon him because he did not restrain his children. These children have been corrupt and a proverb of reproach, and have exerted a corrupting influence where they have lived. Every time they have been presented before me, I have been carried back to Eli, and shown the wickedness of his ungodly sons and the judgment which followed from God. I have been shown that the family of H has disgusted unbelievers, and brought a reproach upon the cause of present truth. The message given me in the spring of 1858 for Ohio, especially ______, was not received by many. It cut too close, and the hearts that were not deeply imbued with the spirit of the truth, rebelled against it.

The ministers who have labored in that State have not exerted a right influence. Hints and insinuations have been thrown out against Brother and Sister White, and the managers of the work at Battle Creek, which have found a ready reception in the hearts of many, especially the credulous and faultfinding. Satan knows how to make his attacks. He works upon minds to excite jealousy and dissatisfaction toward those at the head of the work. The gifts are next questioned; then, of course, they have but little weight, and instruction given through vision is disregarded.

Ministers who have labored in Ohio have done their share of causing dissatisfaction. H has condescended to move in a low sphere, breathing out a spirit of dissatisfaction, eagerly listening to false reports, gathering them up, and virtually saying: "Report, . . . and we will report it." He has worked in an underhand manner, carried false reports in regard to our dress, and our influence in Ohio, and has encouraged the idea that Brother White was speculating. He has not had the slightest union with us. He has felt very bitter toward us. And why? Simply because I have related to him what the Lord had shown me in regard to his family and his loose, slack manner of bringing them up, which has brought upon him the frown of God. He has regarded with jealous, unreconciled feelings the part we have acted in the cause of present truth.

The brethren in Ohio have been encouraged to look with distrust and suspicion at those who are in charge of the work at Battle Creek, and have stood prepared to rise against positions taken by them. Brother J has taken his position firmly, without regard to the body. He has imagined that evils would arise from headquarters that he must contend against. He placed himself in array for battle when there was no fighting to be done. He planted himself firmly to resist something which never arose. Many of the brethren in Ohio cherished the same feeling, placing themselves in opposition to something that never appeared. Their warfare has been unwise. They have been ready to cry out, Babylon, until they are a complete Babylon themselves.

Ministers have stood directly in the way of the work of God in Ohio. They should stand out of the way, that God may reach His people. They step in between God and His people, and turn aside His purposes. Brother J has exerted an influence in Ohio which he must labor to counteract. I saw that there were those in Ohio who would take the right position with right instructions. They have been willing to sustain the cause of present truth, but have seen so little accomplished that they have become discouraged. Their hands are feeble, and need staying up. I saw that the cause of God is not to be carried forward by pressed offerings. God does not accept such offerings. This matter is to be left wholly to the people. They are not to bring a yearly gift merely, but should also freely present a weekly and monthly offering before the Lord. This work is left to the people, for it is to be to them a weekly, monthly, living test. This tithing system, I saw, would develop character, and manifest the true state of the heart. If the brethren in Ohio have this matter presented before them in its true bearing, and are left to decide for themselves, they will see wisdom and order in the tithing system.

Ministers should not be severe, and draw upon any one man, and press means from him. If he does not give just as much as another thinks he should, they are not to denounce him, and throw him overboard. They should be as patient and forbearing as the angels are. They should work in union with Jesus. Christ and angels are watching the development of character, and weighing moral worth. The Lord bears long with His erring people. The truth will be brought to bear closer and closer, and will cut off one idol after another, until God reigns supreme in the hearts of His consecrated people. I saw that God's people must bring to Him a freewill offering; and the responsibility should be left wholly upon the individual, whether he will give much or little. It will be faithfully recorded. Give the people of God time to develop character.

Ministers of God should bear the pointed testimony. The living truths of His word should be brought to bear upon the heart. And when the people in Ohio have a worthy object placed before them, those whose hearts are in sympathy with the work will freely impart of their means to advance the cause of God. The Lord is testing and proving His people. If any have no heart in the work, and fail to bring their offerings to God, He will visit them; and if they continue to cling to their covetousness, He will separate them from His people. I saw that there must be a system which will draw upon all. Young men and young women who have health and strength, have felt but little burden of the work. They are accountable to God for their strength, and should bring a freewill offering to the Lord. And if they will not do this, His prospering hand will be removed from them.

I saw that the special hand of God has not been with the work in Ohio to prosper the cause there. There is a lack; there should be among preachers and people a close examination, a faithful searching of heart, to find the cause of so great a lack of the Spirit of God. Their sacrifices and offerings have nearly dried up. Why do not the truths of God's word warm the heart and lead to self-denial and sacrifice? Let the ministers search and see what kind of an influence they have exerted. There has been with Brother J an independent spirit that God does not approve. His influence has not told for the union of God's people or the advancement of the cause.

I have seen that those who have had but a few years' experience in the cause of present truth, are not the ones to lead out in the work. Such should manifest a delicacy in taking positions which will conflict with the judgment and opinion of those who witnessed the rise of the cause of present truth, and whose lives are interwoven with its progress. God will not select men of but little experience to lead out in this work. He will not choose those who have had no experience in the sufferings, trials, opposition, and privation endured to bring this work up to the platform on which it now rests. It is now easy, compared with what it once was, to preach the third angel's message. Those who now engage in this work, and teach the truth to others, have things made ready at their hand. They cannot experience such privations as laborers in present truth have endured before them. The truth is brought out for them. Arguments are all prepared. Such should be careful how they become exalted, lest they be overthrown. They should be very careful how they murmur against those who endured so much in the very commencement of the work.

Those experienced laborers who toiled under the burden when it was heavy and there were few to help bear it, God regards. Be careful how you reproach them, or murmur against them; for it will surely stand to your account, and the prospering hand of God will not be with you. Some brethren who have the least experience, who have felt no burden, and have done little or nothing to advance the cause of present truth, and who have no knowledge of matters at Battle Creek, are the first to find fault with the management of the work there. And those who do not observe order in their temporal concerns, and command their households after them, are the ones who oppose system, which will ensure order in the church of God. They exhibit no nice taste in worldly matters, and are opposed to anything of the kind in the church. Such persons should have no voice in matters of the church. Their influence should not have the least weight upon others.

ENTIRE CONSECRATION

Dear Brother and Sister K: In my last vision I was shown some things in regard to your family. The Lord has thoughts of mercy concerning you and will not forsake you unless you forsake Him. L and M are in a lukewarm condition. They must arouse and make efforts for salvation, or they will fail of everlasting life. They must feel an individual responsibility and have an experience for themselves. They need a work wrought in their hearts by the Holy Spirit of God, which will lead them to love and choose the society of God's people above any other, and to be separate from those who have no love for spiritual things. Jesus demands a whole sacrifice, an entire consecration. L and M, you have not realized that God requires your undivided affections. You have made a holy profession, yet have sunk down to the dead level of ordinary professors. You love the society of the young who have no regard for the sacred truths which you profess. You have appeared like your associates, and have been contented with as much religion as would render you agreeable to all, without incurring the censure of any.

Christ demands all. If He required less, His sacrifice was too dear, too great to make to bring us up to such a level. Our holy faith cries out, Separation. We should not be conformed to the world, or to dead, heartless professors. "Be ye transformed by the renewing of your mind." This is a self-denying way. And when you think that the way is too strait, that there is too much self-denial in this narrow path; when you say, How hard to give up all, ask yourselves the question, What did Christ give up for me? This question puts anything that we may call self-denial in the shade. Behold Him in the garden, sweating great drops of blood. A solitary angel is sent from heaven to strengthen the Son of God. Follow Him on His way to the judgment hall, while He is derided, mocked, and insulted by that infuriated mob. Behold Him clothed in that old purple kingly robe. Hear the coarse jest and cruel mocking. See them place upon that noble brow the crown of thorns, and then smite Him with a reed, causing the thorns to penetrate His temples, and the blood to flow from that holy brow. Hear that murderous throng eagerly crying for the blood of the Son of God. He is delivered into their hands, and they lead the noble sufferer away, pale, weak, and fainting, to His crucifixion. He is stretched upon the wooden cross, and the nails are driven through His tender hands and feet. Behold Him hanging upon the cross those dreadful hours of agony until the angels veil their faces from the horrid scene, and the sun hides its light, refusing to behold. Think of these things, and then ask, Is the way too strait? No, no.

In a divided, halfhearted life, you will find doubt and darkness. You cannot enjoy the consolations of religion, neither the peace which the world gives. Do not sit down in Satan's easy chair of do-little, but arise, and aim at the elevated standard which it is your privilege to attain. It is a blessed privilege to give up all for Christ. Look not at the lives of others and imitate them and rise no higher. You have only one true, unerring Pattern. It is safe to follow Jesus only. Determine that if others act on the principle of the spiritual sluggard you will leave them and march forward toward the elevation of Christian character. Form a character for heaven. Sleep not at your post. Deal faithfully and truly with your own soul.

You are indulging an evil which threatens to destroy your spirituality. It will eclipse all the beauty and interest of the sacred pages. It is love for storybooks, tales, and other reading which does not have an influence for good upon the mind that is in any way dedicated to the service of God. It produces a false, unhealthy excitement, fevers the imagination, unfits the mind for usefulness, and disqualifies it for any spiritual exercise. It weans the soul from prayer and love of spiritual things. Reading that will throw light upon the sacred volume, and quicken your desire and diligence to study it, is not dangerous, but beneficial. You were represented to me with your eyes turned from the Sacred Book and intently fixed upon exciting books, which are death to religion. The oftener and more diligently you peruse the Scriptures, the more beautiful will they appear, and the less relish will you have for light reading. The daily study of the Scriptures will have a sanctifying influence upon the mind. You will breathe a heavenly atmosphere. Bind this precious volume to your hearts. It will prove to you a friend and guide in perplexity.

You have had objects in view in your life, and how steadily and perseveringly have you labored to attain those objects! You have calculated and planned until your anticipations were realized. There is an object before you now worthy of a persevering, untiring, lifelong effort. It is the salvation of your soul—everlasting life. And this demands self-denial, sacrifice, and close study. You must be purified and refined. You lack the saving influence of the Spirit of God. You mingle with your associates and forget that you have named the name of Christ. You act and dress like them.

Sister K, I saw that you have a work to do. You must die to pride and let your whole interest be in the truth. Your eternal interest depends upon the course you now pursue. If you obtain eternal life, you must live for it and deny self. Come out from the world, and be separate. Your life must be marked with sobriety, watchfulness, and prayer. Angels are watching the development of character and weighing moral worth. All our words and acts are passing in review before God. It is a fearful, solemn time. The hope of eternal life is not to be taken up upon slight grounds; it must be settled between God and your own soul. Some will lean upon others' judgment and experience rather than be at the trouble of a close examination of their own hearts, and will pass along for months and years with no witness of the Spirit of God, or evidence of their acceptance. They deceive themselves. They have a supposed hope, but lack the essential qualifications of a Christian. First there must be a thorough heart work, then their manners will take that elevated, noble character which marks the true followers of Christ. It requires effort and moral courage to live out our faith.

God's people are peculiar. Their spirit cannot mingle with the spirit and influence of the world. You do not wish to bear the Christian name and yet be unworthy of it. You do not desire to meet Jesus with a profession only. You do not wish to be deceived in so important a matter. Thoroughly examine the grounds of your hope. Deal truly with your own soul. A supposed hope will never save you. Have you counted the cost? I fear not. Now decide whether you will follow Christ, cost what it will. You cannot do this and yet enjoy the society of those who pay no heed to divine things. Your spirits cannot mingle any more than oil and water.

It is a great thing to be a child of God, and a joint-heir with Christ. If this is your privilege, you will know the fellowship of Christ's sufferings. God looketh upon the heart. I saw that you must seek Him earnestly, and raise your standard of piety higher, or you will certainly fail of everlasting life. You may ask the question: Did Sister White see this? Yes; and I have tried to place it before you and give you the impressions which were given me. May the Lord help you to take heed.

Dear brother and sister, watch your children with jealous care. The spirit and influence of the world are destroying all desire in them to be true Christians. Let your influence be to draw them from young companions who have no interest in divine things. They must make a sacrifice if they win heaven at last.

September 20, 1860, my fourth child, John Herbert White, was born. When he was three weeks old, my husband felt it to be his duty to travel. It was decided at the Conference that Brother Loughborough should go west and he go east. A few days before they were to leave, my husband was greatly depressed in mind. At one time he thought he would give up the journey, yet he feared to do so. He felt that he had something to do, but was shut in by clouds of darkness. He could not rest or sleep. His mind was in continual agitation. He related the state of his mind to Brethren Loughborough and Cornell, and bowed before the Lord with them to seek counsel of Him. Then the clouds parted, and the clear light shone. My husband felt that the Spirit of the Lord was directing him west and Brother Loughborough east. After this they felt clear as to their duty and moved accordingly.

In my husband's absence we prayed that the Lord would sustain and strengthen him, and obtained the assurance that He would go with him. About one week before he was to visit Mauston, Wisconsin, we received letters for publication from Sister G purporting to be visions given her of the Lord. As we read these communications, we felt distressed; for we knew that they were not from the right source. And as my husband knew nothing of what he was about to meet at Mauston, we feared he would be unprepared to meet the fanaticism, and that it would have a discouraging influence upon his mind. We had passed through so many such scenes in our early experience, and had suffered so much from unruly, untamable spirits, that we dreaded to be brought in contact with them. I sent in a request for the church at Battle Creek to pray for my husband, and at our family altar we earnestly sought the Lord in his behalf. With brokenness of spirit, and many tears, we tried to fasten our trembling faith upon God's promises, and we had the evidence that He heard us pray and that He would stand by my husband and impart to him counsel and wisdom.

While looking in the Bible for a verse for Willie to commit to memory to repeat in the Sabbath school, this scripture arrested my attention: "The Lord is good, a stronghold in the day of trouble; and He knoweth them that trust in Him." I could but weep over these words, they seemed so appropriate. The whole burden upon my mind was for my husband and the church in Wisconsin. My husband did realize the blessing of God while in Wisconsin. The Lord was to him a stronghold in time of trouble and sustained him by His free Spirit while he bore a decided testimony against the wild fanaticism there.

While at Mackford, Wisconsin, my husband wrote me a letter in which he stated: " I fear that all is not well at home. I have had some impressions as to the babe." While praying for the family at home, he had a presentiment that the child was very sick. The babe seemed lying before him with face and head dreadfully swollen. When I received the letter, the child was as well as usual; but the next morning he was taken very sick. It was an extreme case of erysipelas in the face and head. When my husband reached Brother Wick's, near Round Grove, Illinois, he received a telegram informing him of the sickness of the child. After reading it, he stated to those present that he was not surprised at the news, for the Lord had prepared his mind for it, and that they would hear that the child's head and face were greatly affected.

My dear babe was a great sufferer. Twenty-four days and nights we anxiously watched over him, using all the means that we could for his recovery and earnestly presenting his case to the Lord. At times I could not control my feelings as I witnessed his sufferings. Much of my time was spent in tears and humble supplication to God. But our heavenly Father saw fit to remove the loved one.

December 14 he was taken worse, and I was called up. As I listened to his labored breathing and felt his pulseless wrist, I knew that he must die. The icy hand of death was already upon him. That was an hour of anguish for me. We watched his feeble, gasping breath until it ceased, and could but feel thankful that His sufferings were ended. When my child was dying, I could not weep. My heart ached as though it would break, but I could not shed a tear. At the funeral I fainted. We were disappointed in not having Brother Loughborough to conduct the funeral services, and my husband spoke upon the occasion to a crowded house. We then followed our child to Oak Hill Cemetery, there to rest until the Life-giver shall come, to break the fetters of the tomb and call him forth immortal.

After we returned from the funeral, my home seemed lonely. I felt reconciled to the will of God, yet despondency and gloom settled upon me. We could not rise above the discouragements of the past summer. From the state of God's people we knew not what to expect. Satan had gained control of the minds of some who were closely connected with us in the work, even of some who had been acquainted with our mission and seen the fruit of our labors, and who had not only witnessed the frequent manifestation of the power of God, but had felt its influence upon their own bodies. What could we hope for in the future? While my child lived, I thought I understood my duty. I pressed my dear babe to my heart and rejoiced that at least for one winter I should be released from any great responsibility, for it could not be my duty to travel in winter with my infant. But when he was taken from me, I was again thrown into great perplexity.

The condition of God's cause and people nearly crushed us. Our happiness ever depends upon the state of the cause of God. When His people are in a prosperous condition we feel free; but when they are backslidden and there is discord among them, nothing can make us joyful. Our whole interest and life have been interwoven with the rise and progress of the third angel's message. We are bound up in it, and when it does not prosper, we experience great suffering of mind.

About this time, my husband, as he reviewed the past, began to lose confidence in almost everyone. Many of those whom he had tried to befriend had acted the part of enemies, and some whom he had helped the most by his influence and from his own scanty purse, were continually trying to injure him and cast burdens upon him. One Sabbath morning as he was going to our place of worship, such an overpowering sense of injustice came over him that he turned aside and wept aloud, while the congregation waited for him.

From the commencement of our labors we have been called to bear a plain, pointed testimony, to reprove wrongs and spare not. And all the way there have been those who have stood in opposition to our testimony, and have followed after to speak smooth things, daub with untempered mortar, and destroy the influence of our labors. The Lord would rein us up to bear reproof, and then individuals would step right in between us and the people to make our testimony of no effect. Many visions have been given to the effect that we must not shun to declare the counsel of the Lord, but must occupy a position to stir up the people of God, for they are asleep in their sins. But few have sympathized with us, while many have sympathized with the wrong and with those who have been reproved. These things crushed us, and we felt that we had no testimony to bear in the church. We knew not in whom to confide. As all these things forced themselves upon us, hope died within us. We retired to rest about midnight, but I could not sleep. A severe pain was in my heart; I could find no relief and fainted a number of times.

My husband sent for Brethren Amadon, Kellogg, and

C. Smith. Their fervent prayers were heard, relief came, and I was taken off in vision. Then I was shown that we had a work to do, that we must still bear our testimony, straight and pointed. Individuals were presented before me who had shunned the pointed testimony. I saw the influence of their teachings upon God's people.

The condition of the people in ——— was also presented before me. They have the theory of truth, but are not sanctified through it. I saw that when the messengers enter a new place, their labor is worse than lost unless they bear a plain, pointed testimony. They should keep up the distinction between the church of Christ, and formal, dead professors. There was a failure in this respect in ———. Elder N was fearful of offending, fearful lest the peculiarities of our faith should appear; the standard was lowered to meet the people. It should have been urged upon them that we possess truths of vital importance, and that their eternal interest depended upon the decision they there made; that in order to be sanctified through the truth, their idols would have to be given up, their sins be confessed, and they bring forth fruit meet for repentance.

Those who engage in the solemn work of bearing the third angel's message must move out decidedly, and in the Spirit and power of God fearlessly preach the truth and let it cut. They should elevate the standard of truth and urge the people to come up to it. It has too frequently been lowered to meet the people in their condition of darkness and sin. It is the pointed testimony that will bring them up to decide. A peaceful testimony will not do this. The people have the privilege of listening to this kind of teaching from popular pulpits; but those servants to whom God has entrusted the solemn, fearful message which is to bring out and fit up a people for the coming of Christ should bear a plain, pointed testimony. Our truth is as much more solemn than that of nominal professors as the heavens are higher than the earth.

The people are asleep in their sins and need to be alarmed before they can shake off this lethargy. Their ministers have preached smooth things; but God's servants, who bear sacred, vital truths, should cry aloud and spare not, that the truth may tear off the garment of security and find its way to the heart. The straight testimony that should have been given to the people in ______ was shunned by the ministers; the seed of truth was sown among thorns and has been choked by them. With some, evil besetments have flourished, and the heavenly graces have died out.

God's servants must bear a pointed testimony, which will cut the natural heart and develop character. Brethren N and O moved with a perfect restraint upon them while in ______. Such preaching as was given there will never do the work that God designs should be accomplished. Ministers of the nominal churches do enough cringing, and wrapping up of the pointed truths which rebuke sin.

Unless persons embrace the message aright, and their hearts are prepared to receive it, they would better let it entirely alone. I was shown that the church in ______ have an experience to obtain; but it will be much harder for them to obtain it now than if the pointed testimony had been given them at the very commencement, when they first discovered that they were in error. Then the thorns could have been more easily rooted out. Yet I saw that there were men of moral worth in ______, some who will yet be tested upon present truth. If the church will arise and be converted, the Lord will return unto them and give them His Spirit. Then their influence will tell for the truth.

THE CAUSE IN THE WEST

I have seen that men of worth have embraced the truth West who will yet be pillars to the cause. When they can place their temporal affairs in a condition where they can use a portion of their means, they will do their part toward sustaining the cause. I also saw that some were willing to receive the truth, brought to them by the liberalities of their Eastern brethren, without its costing them anything. The brethren West should arouse and meet the expenses of their own states. God requires this at their hands, and they should feel it a privilege to do so. The Lord will prove them, He will try them to see if they will withdraw their affections from the world and make their faith perfect by works.

I saw that God's hand was stretched out to gather in souls in the West. He has been bringing out men who can teach the truth to others, whose duty it will be to bear the message into new fields. I saw that if the men who have moved from the East to the West and have endured the hardships of settling in a new country, receive present truth understandingly, they will manifest a perseverance and decision of character in regard to the truth, similar to that manifested in securing to themselves temporal possessions, and will engage as heartily in the work of advancing the truth. If this corresponding zeal is lacking, the truth has not yet had its saving, sanctifying influence upon them.

I was pointed back to a meeting in ______. Brother P felt the burden of the cause, but R had a spirit of opposition. His testimony was not in union with the work of God, and he brought grief and burden upon those who were laboring for its advancement. But it would have been better for the cause had he been suffered time longer, and the brethren borne the confusion he caused. I saw that Brother P moved unwisely in his case. It gave R and the enemies of our faith the advantage. Brother P should have waited until R's religious character was more fully developed. He would soon either have united with the remnant people of God or been left one side. But R obtained sympathy on account of his age. He had partaken of the spirit of the *Messenger* party, and his whole course was darkened by it. His wife has an excitable, bitter spirit, and has been zealous to spread false reports. She acts the part to her husband that Jezebel did to Ahab, and stirs him up to fight against the servants of God, who bear a pointed testimony.

Their influence East has been decidedly against the spirit of the truth and those who have devoted their lives to labor for its advancement. There is a class East who profess to believe the truth, but who cherish secret feelings of dissatisfaction against those who bear the burden in this work. The true sentiments of such do not appear until some influence opposed to the work of God arises, and then they manifest their true character. Such readily receive, cherish, and circulate reports which have no foundation in truth, to destroy the influence of those who are engaged in this work. All who wish to draw off from the body will have opportunity. Something will arise to test everyone. The great sifting time is just before us. The jealous and the faultfinding, who are watching for evil, will be shaken out. They hate reproof and despise correction. Those who love the spirit of the third angel's message can have no union with the spirit of R and his wife.

A QUESTION ANSWERED

The question is often asked by those who fall under the influence of my enemies: "Is Sister White getting proud? I have heard that she wore a bonnet filled with bows and ribbons."

I hope I am not getting proud. My manner of dress is the

same as it has been for several years. I am opposed to hoops and to wearing unnecessary bows and ribbons. I have worn one velvet bonnet two years without change of strings except to cleanse them with soap and water. I put the same velvet upon a new frame and am wearing it again this winter. I believe Sabbathkeepers should dress plainly and study economy in dress. Those who wish to talk will talk though we give them no occasion. I do not expect to suit every taste in regard to dress, but I believe it to be my duty to wear durable clothing, to dress neatly and orderly, and suit my own taste if it does not disagree with the word of God.

NUMBER SEVEN

TESTIMONY FOR THE CHURCH

THE NORTH AND THE SOUTH

January 4, 1862, I was shown some things in regard to our nation. My attention was called to the Southern rebellion. The South had prepared themselves for a fierce conflict, while the North were asleep as to their true feelings. Before President Lincoln's administration commenced, great advantage was taken by the South. The former administration planned and managed for the South to rob the North of their implements of war. They had two objects for so doing: 1. They were contemplating a determined rebellion, and must prepare for it; 2. When they should rebel, the North would be wholly unprepared. They would thus gain time, and by their violent threats and ruthless course they thought they could so intimidate the North that they would be obliged to yield to them and let them have everything their own way.

The North did not understand the bitter, dreadful hatred of the South toward them, and were unprepared for their deep-laid plots. The North had boasted of their strength and ridiculed the idea of the South leaving the Union. They considered it like the threats of a willful, stubborn child, and thought that the South would soon come to their senses, and, becoming sick of leaving the Union, would with humble apologies return to their allegiance. The North have had no just idea of the strength of the accursed system of slavery. It is this, and this alone, which lies at the foundation of the war. The South have been more and more exacting. They consider it perfectly right to engage in human traffic, to deal in slaves and the souls of men. They are annoyed and become perfectly exasperated if they cannot claim all the territory they desire. They would tear down the boundaries and bring their slaves to any spot they please, and curse the soil with slave labor. The language of the South has been imperious, and the North have not taken suitable measures to silence it.

The rebellion was handled so carefully, so slowly, that many who at first started with horror at the thought of rebellion were influenced by rebels to look upon it as right and just, and thousands joined the Southern Confederacy who would not had prompt and thorough measures been carried out by our Government at an early period of the rebellion, even as ill-prepared as it then was for war. The North have been preparing for war ever since, but the rebellion has been steadily increasing, and there is now no better prospect of its being subdued than there was months ago. Thousands have lost their lives, and many have returned to their homes, maimed and crippled for life, their health gone, their earthly prospects forever blighted; and yet how little has been gained! Thousands have been induced to enlist with the understanding that this war was to exterminate slavery; but now that they are fixed, they find that they have been deceived, that the object of this war is not to abolish slavery, but to preserve it as it is.

Those who have ventured to leave their homes and sacrifice their lives to exterminate slavery are dissatisfied. They see no good results from the war, only the preservation of the Union, and for this thousands of lives must be sacrificed and homes made desolate. Great numbers have wasted away and expired in hospitals; others have been taken prisoners by the rebels, a fate more to be dreaded than death. In view of all this, they inquire: If we succeed in quelling this rebellion, what has been gained? They can only answer discouragingly: Nothing. That which caused the rebellion is not removed. The system of slavery, which has ruined our nation, is left to live and stir up another rebellion. The feelings of thousands of our soldiers are bitter. They suffer the greatest privations; these they would willingly endure, but they find they have been deceived, and they are dispirited. Our leading men are perplexed, their hearts are failing them for fear. They fear to proclaim freedom to the slaves of the rebels, for by so doing they will exasperate that portion of the South who have not joined the rebellion but are strong slavery men. And again they have feared the influence of those strong antislavery men who were in command, holding responsible stations. They have feared the effects of a bold, decided tone, for it fanned to a flame the strong desire of thousands to wipe out the cause of this terrible rebellion, by letting the oppressed go free and breaking every yoke.

Many of those who are placed high in command to fill responsible stations have but little conscience or nobility of soul; they can exercise their power, even to the destruction of those under them, and it is winked at. These commanders could abuse the power given them and cause those subject to them to occupy dangerous positions where they would be exposed to terrible encounters with the rebels without the least hope of conquering them. In this way they could dispose of daring, thoroughgoing men, as David disposed of Uriah. 2 Samuel 11:14, 15.

Valuable men have thus been sacrificed to get rid of their strong antislavery influence. Some of the very men whom the North most need in this critical time, whose services would be of the highest value, *are not*. They have been wantonly sacrificed. The prospects before our nation are discouraging, for there are those filling responsible stations who are rebels at heart. There are commanding officers who are in sympathy with the rebels. While they are desirous of having the Union preserved, they despise those who are anti-slavery. Some of the armies also are composed largely of such material; they are so opposed to one another that no real union exists among many regiments.

As this war was shown to me, it looked like the most singular and uncertain that has ever occurred. A great share of the volunteers enlisted fully believing that the result of the war would be to abolish slavery. Others enlisted intending to be very careful to keep slavery just as it is, but to put down the rebellion and preserve the Union. And then to make the matter still more perplexing and uncertain, some of the officers in command are strong proslavery men whose sympathies are all with the South, yet who are opposed to a separate government. It seems impossible to have the war conducted successfully, for many in our own ranks are continually working to favor the South, and our armies have been repulsed and unmercifully slaughtered on account of the management of these proslavery men. Some of our leading men in Congress also are constantly working to favor the South. In this state of things, proclamations are issued for national fasts, for prayer that God will bring this war to a speedy and favorable termination. I was then directed to Isaiah 58:5-7: "Is it such a fast that I have chosen? a day for a man to afflict his soul? is it to bow down his head as a bulrush, and to spread sackcloth and ashes under him? wilt thou call this a fast, and an acceptable day to the Lord? Is not this the fast that I have chosen? to loose the bands of wickedness, to undo the heavy burdens, and to let the oppressed go free, and that ye break every yoke? Is it not to deal thy bread to the hungry, and that thou bring the poor that are cast out to thy house? when thou seest the naked, that thou cover him;

and that thou hide not thyself from thine own flesh?"

I saw that these national fasts were an insult to Jehovah. He accepts of no such fasts. The recording angel writes in regard to them: "Ye fast for strife and debate, and to smite with the fist of wickedness." I was shown how our leading men have treated the poor slaves who have come to them for protection. Angels have recorded it. Instead of breaking their yoke and letting the oppressed go free, these men have made the yoke more galling for them than when in the service of their tyrannical masters. Love of liberty leads the poor slaves to leave their masters and risk their lives to obtain liberty. They would never venture to leave their masters and expose themselves to the difficulties and horrors attending their recapture if they had not as strong a love for liberty as any of us. The escaped slaves have endured untold hardships and dangers to obtain their freedom, and as their last hope, with the love of liberty burning in their breasts, they apply to our Government for protection; but their confidence has been treated with the utmost contempt. Many of them have been cruelly treated because they committed so great a crime as to dare to make an effort to obtain their freedom. Great men, professing to have human hearts, have seen the slaves almost naked and starving, and have abused them, and sent them back to their cruel masters and hopeless bondage, to suffer inhuman cruelty for daring to seek their liberty. Some of this wretched class they thrust into unwholesome dungeons, to live or die, they cared not which. They have deprived them of the liberty and free air which heaven has never denied them, and then left them to suffer for food and clothing. In view of all this, a national fast is proclaimed! Oh, what an insult to Jehovah! The Lord saith by the mouth of Isaiah: "Yet they seek Me daily, and delight to know My ways, as a nation that did righteousness, and forsook not the ordinance of their God."

The escaped slaves have been told by their masters that the Northern men wanted to get possession of them that they might cruelly misuse them; that the abolitionists would treat them worse than they had been treated while in slavery. All manner of horrible stories have been repeated in their ears to make them detest the North, and yet they have had a confused idea that some hearts in the North felt for their grievances and would yet make an effort to help them. This has been the only star which has shed its glimmering light upon their distressed and gloomy bondage. The manner in which the poor slaves have been treated has led them to believe that their masters have told them the truth in these things. And yet a national fast is proclaimed! Saith the Lord: "Is not this the fast that I have chosen? to loose the bands of wickedness, to undo the heavy burdens, and to let the oppressed go free, and that ye break every yoke?" When our nation observes the fast which God has chosen, then will He accept their prayers as far as the war is concerned; but now they enter not into His ear. He turns from them, they are disgusting to Him. It is so managed that those who would undo the heavy burdens and break every yoke are placed under censure, or removed from responsible stations, or their lives are planned away by those who "fast for strife and debate, and to smite with the fist of wickedness."

I was shown that if the object of this war had been to exterminate slavery, then if desired, England would have helped the North. But England fully understands the existing feelings in the Government, and that the war is not to do away slavery, but merely to preserve the Union; and it is not for her interest to have it preserved. Our Government has been very proud and independent. The people of this nation have exalted themselves to heaven, and have looked down upon monarchical governments, and triumphed in their boasted liberty, while the institution of slavery, that was a thousand times worse than the tyranny exercised by monarchial governments was suffered to exist and was cherished. In this land of light a system is cherished which allows one portion of the human family to enslave another portion, degrading millions of human beings to the level of the brute creation. The equal of this sin is not to be found in the heathen lands.

Said the angel: "Hear, O heavens, the cry of the oppressed, and reward the oppressors double according to their deeds." This nation will yet be humbled into the dust. England is studying whether it is best to take advantage of the present weak condition of our nation, and venture to make war upon her. She is weighing the matter, and trying to sound other nations. She fears, if she should commence war abroad, that she would be weak at home, and that other nations would take advantage of her weakness. Other nations are making quiet yet active preparations for war, and are hoping that England will make war with our nation, for then they would improve the opportunity to be revenged on her for the advantage she has taken of them in the past and the injustice done them. A portion of the queen's subjects are waiting a favorable opportunity to break their yoke; but if England thinks it will pay, she will not hesitate a moment to improve her opportunities to exercise her power and humble our nation. When England does declare war, all nations will have an interest of their own to serve, and there will be general war, general confusion. England is acquainted with the diversity of feeling among those who are seeking to quell the rebellion. She well knows the perplexed condition of Government; she has looked with astonishment at the prosecution of this war—the slow, inefficient moves, the inactivity of our armies, and the ruinous expenses of our nation. The weakness of our Government is fully open before other nations, and they now conclude that it is because it was not a monarchial government, and they admire their own government, and look down, some with pity, others with contempt, upon our nation, which they have regarded as the most powerful upon the globe. Had our nation remained united it would have had strength, but divided it must fall.

GREAT DISTRESS COMING

I saw greater distress in the land than we have yet witnessed. I heard groans and cries of distress, and saw large companies in active battle. I heard the booming of the cannon, the clash of arms, the hand-to-hand fight, and the groans and prayers of the dying. The ground was covered with the wounded and the dead. I saw desolate, despairing families, and pinching want in many dwellings. Even now many families are suffering want, but this will increase. The faces of many looked haggard, pale, and pinched with hunger.

I was shown that the people of God should be closely united in the bonds of Christian fellowship and love. God alone can be our shield and strength in this time of our national calamities. The people of God should awake. Their opportunities to spread the truth should be improved, for they will not last long. I was shown distress and perplexity and famine in the land. Satan is now seeking to hold God's people in a state of inactivity, to keep them from acting their part in spreading the truth, that they may at last be weighed in the balance and found wanting.

God's people must take warning and discern the signs of the times. The signs of Christ's coming are too plain to be doubted, and in view of these things everyone who professes the truth should be a living preacher. God calls upon all, both preachers and people, to awake. All heaven is astir. The scenes of earth's history are fast closing. We are amid the perils of the last days. Greater perils are before us, and yet we are not awake. This lack of activity and earnestness in the cause of God is dreadful. This death stupor is from Satan. He controls the minds of unconsecrated Sabbathkeepers, and leads them to be jealous of one another, faultfinding, and censorious. It is his special work to divide hearts that the influence, strength, and labor of God's servants may be kept among unconsecrated Sabbathkeepers and their precious time be occupied in settling little differences when it should be spent in proclaiming the truth to unbelievers.

I was shown God's people waiting for some change to take place—a compelling power to take hold of them. But they will be disappointed, for they are wrong. They must act, they must take hold of the work themselves and earnestly cry to God for a true knowledge of themselves. The scenes which are passing before us are of sufficient magnitude to cause us to arouse and urge the truth home to the hearts of all who will listen. The harvest of the earth is nearly ripe.

I was shown how important it is that the ministers who engage in the solemn, responsible work of proclaiming the third angel's message be right. The Lord is not straitened for means or instruments with which to do His own work. He can speak at any time, by whom He will, and His word is powerful and will accomplish the thing whereunto it is sent. But if the truth has not sanctified, made pure and clean, the hands and heart of him who ministers in holy things, he is liable to speak according to his own imperfect experience, and when he speaks of himself, according to the decisions of his own unsanctified judgment, his counsel is not then of God, but of himself. As he that is called of God is called to be holy, so he that is approved and set apart of men must give evidence of his holy calling and show forth in his heavenly conversation and conduct that he is faithful to Him who hath called him.

There are fearful woes for those who preach the truth,

but are not sanctified by it, and also for those who consent to receive and maintain the unsanctified to minister to them in word and doctrine. I am alarmed for the people of God who profess to believe solemn, important truth, for I know that many of them are not converted nor sanctified through it. Men can hear and acknowledge the whole truth, and yet know nothing of the power of godliness. All who preach the truth will not themselves be saved by it. Said the angel: "Be ye clean, that bear the vessels of the Lord."

The time has come when those who choose the Lord for their present and future portion must trust in Him alone. Everyone professing godliness must have an experience of his own. The recording angel is making a faithful record of the words and acts of God's people. Angels are watching the development of character and weighing moral worth. Those who profess to believe the truth should be right themselves and exert all their influence to enlighten and win others to the truth. Their words and works are the channel through which the pure principles of truth and holiness are conveyed to the world. They are the salt of the earth and the light thereof. I saw that in looking heavenward we shall see light and peace, but in looking to the world we shall see that every refuge must soon fail us and every good soon pass away. There is no help for us but in God; in this state of earth's confusion we can be composed, strong, or safe, only in the strength of living faith; nor can we be at peace, only as we rest in God and wait for His salvation. Greater light shines upon us than shone upon our fathers. We cannot be accepted or honored of God in rendering the same service, or doing the same works, that our fathers did. In order to be accepted and blessed of God as they were, we must imitate their faithfulness and zeal, improve our light as they improved theirs, and do as they would have done had they lived in our day. We must walk in the light which shines upon us, otherwise that light will become darkness. God requires of us to exhibit to the world, in our character and works, that measure of the spirit of union and oneness which is in accordance with the sacred truths we profess and with the spirit of those prophecies that are fulfilling in these last days. The truth which has reached our understanding, and the light which has shone on the soul will judge and condemn us, if we turn away and refuse to be led by them.

What shall I say to arouse the remnant people of God? I was shown that dreadful scenes are before us; Satan and his angels are bringing all their powers to bear upon God's people. He knows that if they sleep a little longer he is sure of them, for their destruction is certain. I warn all who profess the name of Christ to closely examine themselves and make full and thorough confession of all their wrongs, that they may go beforehand to judgment, and that the recording angel may write pardon opposite their names. My brother, my sister, if these precious moments of mercy are not improved, you will be left without excuse. If you make no special effort to arouse, if you will not manifest zeal in repenting, these golden moments will soon pass, and you will be weighed in the balance and found wanting. Then your agonizing cries will be of no avail. Then will apply the words of the Lord: "Because I have called, and ye refused; I have stretched out My hand, and no man regarded; but ye have set at nought all My counsel, and would none of My reproof: I also will laugh at your calamity; I will mock when your fear cometh; when your fear cometh as desolation, and your destruction cometh as a whirlwind; when distress and anguish cometh upon you. Then shall they call upon Me, but I will not answer; they shall seek Me early, but they shall not find Me: for that they hated knowledge, and did not choose the fear of the Lord: they would none of My counsel: they despised all My reproof. Therefore shall they eat of the fruit of their own way, and be filled with their own devices. For the turning away of the simple shall slay them, and the prosperity of fools shall destroy them. But whoso hearkeneth unto Me shall dwell safely, and shall be quiet from fear of evil."

SLAVERY AND THE WAR

God is punishing this nation for the high crime of slavery. He has the destiny of the nation in His hands. He will punish the South for the sin of slavery, and the North for so long suffering its overreaching and overbearing influence.

At the Conference at Roosevelt, New York, August 3, 1861, when the brethren and sisters were assembled on the day set apart for humiliation, fasting, and prayer, the Spirit of the Lord rested upon us, and I was taken off in vision and shown the sin of slavery, which has so long been a curse to this nation. The fugitive slave law was calculated to crush out of man every noble, generous feeling of sympathy that should arise in his heart for the oppressed and suffering slave. It was in direct opposition to the teaching of Christ. God's scourge is now upon the North, because they have so long submitted to the advances of the slave power. The sin of Northern proslavery men is great. They have strengthened the South in their sin by sanctioning the extension of slavery; they have acted a prominent part in bringing the nation into its present distressed condition.

I was shown that many do not realize the extent of the evil which has come upon us. They have flattered themselves that the national difficulties would soon be settled and confusion and war end, but all will be convinced that there is more reality in the matter than was anticipated. Many have looked for the North to strike a blow and end the controversy.

I was pointed back to ancient Israel, held in bondage by the Egyptians. The Lord wrought by Moses and Aaron to deliver them. Miracles were performed before Pharaoh to convince him that these men were especially sent of God to bid him let Israel go. But Pharaoh's heart was hardened against the messengers of God, and he reasoned away the miracles performed by them. Then the Egyptians were made to feel God's judgments. They were visited with plagues, and while suffering under the effect of them, Pharaoh consented to let Israel go. But as soon as the cause of their suffering was removed, his heart was hardened. His counselors and mighty men strengthened themselves against God and endeavored to explain the plagues as the result of natural causes. Each visitation from God was more severe than the preceding one, yet they would not release the children of Israel until the angel of the Lord slew the firstborn of the Egyptians. From the king upon the throne down to the most humble and lowly, there was wailing and mourning. Then Pharaoh commanded to let Israel go; but after the Egyptians had buried their dead, he repented that he had let Israel go. His counselors and mighty men tried to account for their bereavement. They would not admit that the visitation or judgment was from God, and therefore they pursued after the children of Israel.

When the Israelites beheld the Egyptian host in pursuit, some upon horses and some in chariots, and equipped for war, their hearts failed them. The Red Sea was before, the Egyptian host behind. They could see no way of escape. A shout of triumph burst from the Egyptians to find Israel completely in their power. The Israelites were greatly terrified. But the Lord commanded Moses to bid them go forward, and to lift up the rod and stretch out his hand over the sea, and divide it. He did so, and lo, the sea parted, and the children of Israel passed over dry shod. Pharaoh had so long withstood God, and hardened his heart against His mighty, wondrous works, that he in blindness rushed into the path which God had miraculously prepared for His people. Again Moses was commanded to stretch forth his hand over the sea, "and the sea returned to his strength," and the waters covered the Egyptian host, and they were drowned.

This scene was presented before me to illustrate the selfish love of slavery, and the desperate measures which the South would adopt to cherish the institution and the dreadful lengths to which they would go before they would yield. The system of slavery has reduced and degraded human beings to the level of the brutes, and the majority of slave masters regard them as such. The consciences of these masters have become seared and hardened, as was Pharaoh's; and if compelled to release their slaves, their principles remain unchanged, and they would make the slave feel their oppressive power if possible. It looked to me like an impossibility now for slavery to be done away. God alone can wrench the slave from the hand of his desperate, relentless oppressor. All the abuse and cruelty exercised toward the slave is justly chargeable to the upholders of the slave system, whether they be Southern or Northern men.

The North and the South were presented before me. The North have been deceived in regard to the South. They are better prepared for war than has been represented. Most of their men are well skilled in the use of arms, some of them from experience in battle, others from habitual sporting. They have the advantage of the North in this respect, but have not, as a general thing, the valor and the power of endurance that Northern men have.

I had a view of the disastrous battle at Manassas, Virginia. It was a most exciting, distressing scene. The Southern army had everything in their favor and were prepared for a dreadful contest. The Northern army was moving on with triumph, not doubting but that they would be victorious. Many were reckless and marched forward boastingly, as though victory were already theirs. As they neared the battlefield, many were almost fainting through weariness and want of refreshment. They did not expect so fierce an encounter. They rushed into battle and fought bravely, desperately. The dead and dying were on every side. Both the North and the South suffered severely. The Southern men felt the battle, and in a little while would have been driven back still further. The Northern men were rushing on, although their destruction was very great. Just then an angel descended and waved his hand backward. Instantly there was confusion in the ranks. It appeared to the Northern men that their troops were retreating, when it was not so in reality, and a precipitate retreat commenced. This seemed wonderful to me.

Then it was explained that God had this nation in His own hand, and would not suffer victories to be gained faster than He ordained, and would permit no more losses to the North-ern men than in His wisdom He saw fit, to punish them for their sins. And had the Northern army at this time pushed the battle still further in their fainting, exhausted condition, the far greater struggle and destruction which awaited them would have caused great triumph in the South. God would not permit this, and sent an angel to interfere. The sudden falling back of the Northern troops is a mystery to all. They know not that God's hand was in the matter.

The destruction of the Southern army was so great that they had no heart to boast. The sight of the dead, the dying, and the wounded gave them but little courage to triumph. This destruction, occurring when they had every advantage, and the North great disadvantage, caused them much perplexity. They know that if the North have an equal chance with them, victory is certain for the North. Their only hope is to occupy positions difficult of approach, and then have formidable arrangements to hurl destruction on every hand.

The South have strengthened themselves greatly since their rebellion first commenced. If active measures had then been taken by the North this rebellion would have been speedily crushed out. But that which was small at first has increased in strength and numbers until it has become most powerful. Other nations are intently watching this nation, for what purpose I was not informed, and are making great preparations for some event. The greatest perplexity and anxiety now exists among our national men. Proslavery men and traitors are in the very midst of them; and while these are professedly in favor of the Union, they have an influence in making decisions, some of which even favor the South.

I was shown the inhabitants of the earth in the utmost confusion. War, bloodshed, privation, want, famine, and pestilence were abroad in the land. As these things surrounded God's people, they began to press together, and to cast aside their little difficulties. Self-dignity no longer controlled them; deep humility took its place. Suffering, perplexity, and privation caused reason to resume its throne, and the passionate and unreasonable man became sane, and acted with discretion and wisdom.

My attention was then called from the scene. There seemed to be a little time of peace. Once more the inhabitants of the earth were presented before me; and again everything was in the utmost confusion. Strife, war, and bloodshed, with famine and pestilence, raged everywhere. Other nations were engaged in this war and confusion. War caused famine. Want and bloodshed caused pestilence. And then men's hearts failed them for fear, "and for looking after those things which are coming on the earth."

PERILOUS TIMES

The unbelieving world will soon have something to think of besides their dress and appearance; and as their minds are torn from these things by distress and perplexity, they will have nothing to turn to. They are not prisoners of hope, and therefore do not turn to the Stronghold. Their hearts will fail them for repining and fear. They have not made God their refuge, and He will not be their consolation then, but will laugh at their calamity, and mock when their fear cometh. They have despised and trampled upon the truths of God's word. They have indulged in extravagant dress, and have spent their lives in hilarity and glee. They have sown to the wind; they must reap the whirlwind. In the time of distress and perplexity of nations there will be many who have not given themselves wholly to the corrupting influences of the world and the service of Satan, who will humble themselves before God and turn to Him with their whole heart and find acceptance and pardon.

Those among Sabbathkeepers who have been unwilling to make any sacrifice, but have yielded to the influence of the world, are to be tested and proved. The perils of the last days are upon us, and a trial is before the young which they have not anticipated. They are to be brought into most distressing perplexity. The genuineness of their faith will be proved. They profess to be looking for the coming of the Son of man, yet some of them have been a miserable example to unbelievers. They have not been willing to give up the world, but have united with them, have attended picnics and other gatherings of pleasure, flattering themselves that they were engaging in innocent amusement. Yet I was shown that it is just such indulgences that separate them from God and make them children of the world. God does not own the pleasure seeker as His follower. He has given us no such example. Those only who are self-denying, and who live a life of sobriety, humility, and holiness, are true followers of Jesus; and such cannot engage in and enjoy the frivolous, empty conversation of the lovers of the world.

A day of heart-rending anguish is before us. I was shown that pointed testimonies should be borne, and that those who will come up to the help of the Lord will receive His blessing. But Sabbathkeepers have a work to do. Hoops, I was shown, are an abomination, and every Sabbathkeeper's influence should be a rebuke to this ridiculous fashion, which has been a screen to iniquity and which arose from a house of ill fame in Paris. Individuals were shown me who will despise instruction, even if it comes from heaven; they will frame some excuse to avoid the most pointed testimony, and in defiance of all the light given will put on hoops because it is the fashion, and risk the consequences.

The prophecy of Isaiah 3 was presented before me as applying to these last days, and the reproofs are given to the daughters of Zion who have thought only of appearance and display. Read verse 25: "Thy men shall fall by the sword, and thy mighty in the war." I was shown that this scripture will be strictly fulfilled. Young men and women professing to be Christians, yet having no Christian experience, and having borne no burdens and felt no individual responsibility, are to be proved. They will be brought low in the dust and will long for an experience in the things of God, which they have failed to obtain.

War lifts his helmet to his brow;
O God, protect Thy people now.

ORGANIZATION

August 3, 1861, I was shown that some have feared that our churches would become Babylon if they should organize; but those in central New York have been perfect Babylon, confusion. And now unless the churches are so organized that they can carry out and enforce order, they have nothing to hope for in the future; they must scatter into fragments. Previous teachings have nourished the elements of disunion. A spirit has been cherished to watch and accuse, rather than to build up. If ministers of God would unitedly take their position, and maintain it with decision, there would be a uniting influence among the flock of God. Separating bars would be broken to fragments. Hearts would flow together and unite like drops of water. Then there would be a power and strength in the ranks of Sabbathkeepers far exceeding anything we have yet witnessed.

The hearts of God's servants are made sad as they journey from church to church, by meeting the opposing influence of other ministering brethren. There are those who have stood ready to oppose every advance step that God's people have taken. The hearts of those who have dared to venture out are saddened and distressed by the lack of union of action on the part of their fellow laborers. We are living in a solemn time. Satan and evil angels are working with mighty power, with the world on their side to help them. And professed Sabbathkeepers who claim to believe solemn, important truth unite their forces with the combined influence of the powers of darkness to distract and tear down that which God designs to build up. The influence of such is recorded as of those who retard the advancement of reform among God's people.

The agitation of the subject of organization has revealed a great lack of moral courage on the part of the ministers proclaiming present truth. Some who were convinced that organization was right have failed to stand up boldly and advocate it. They let some few understand that they favored it. Was this all that God required of them? No; He was displeased with their cowardly silence and lack of action. They feared blame and opposition. They watched the brethren generally to see how their pulse beat, before standing manfully for what they believed to be right. The people waited for the voice of their favorite ministers, and because they could hear no response in its favor from them, decided that organization was wrong.

Thus the influence of some of the ministers was against organization, while they professed to be in favor of it. They were afraid of losing their influence. But someone must move out and bear responsibility, and venture his influence; and as the one who has done this has become inured to censure and blame, he is suffered to bear it. His fellow laborers, who should stand by his side and take their share of the burden, are looking on to see how he succeeds in fighting the battle alone. But God marks his distress, his anguish, his tears, his discouragement and despair, while his mind is taxed almost beyond endurance; and when ready to sink, God lifts him up and points him to the rest for the weary, the reward for the faithful; and again he puts his shoulder under the heavy burden. I saw that all will be rewarded as their works shall be. Those who shun responsibility will meet with loss in the end. The time for ministers to stand together is when the battle goes hard.

DUTY TO THE POOR

Inquiries are often made in regard to our duty to the poor who embrace the third message; and we ourselves have long been anxious to know how to manage with discretion the cases of poor families who embrace the Sabbath. But while at Roosevelt, New York, August 3, 1861, I was shown some things in regard to the poor.

God does not require our brethren to take charge of every poor family that shall embrace this message. If they should do this, the ministers must cease to enter new fields, for the funds would be exhausted. Many are poor from their own lack of diligence and economy; they know not how to use means aright. If they should be helped, it would hurt them. Some will always be poor. If they should have the very best advantages, their cases would not be helped. They have not good calculation and would use all the means they could obtain, were it much or little. Some know nothing of denying self and economizing to keep out of debt and to get a little ahead for a time of need. If the church should help such individuals instead of leaving them to rely upon their own resources, it would injure them in the end, for they look to the church and expect to receive help from them and do not practice self-denial and economy when they are well provided for. And if they do not receive help every time, Satan tempts them, and they become jealous and very conscientious for their brethren, fearing they will fail to do all their duty to them. The mistake is on their own part. They are deceived. They are not the Lord's poor.

The instructions given in the word of God in regard to helping the poor do not touch such cases, but are for the unfortunate and afflicted. God in His providence has afflicted individuals to test and prove others. Widows and invalids are in the church to prove a blessing to the church. They are a part of the means which God has chosen to develop the true character of Christ's professed followers and to call into exercise the precious traits of character manifested by our compassionate Redeemer.

Many who can but barely live when they are single, choose to marry and raise a family when they know they have nothing with which to support them. And worse than this, they have no family government. Their whole course in their family is marked with their loose, slack habits. They have but little control over themselves, and are passionate, impatient, and fretful. When such embrace the message, they feel that they are entitled to assistance from their more wealthy brethren; and if their expectations are not met, they complain of the church and accuse them of not living out their faith. Who must be the sufferers in this case? Must the cause of God be sapped, and the treasury in different places exhausted, to take care of these large families of poor? No. The parents must be the sufferers. They will not, as a general thing, suffer any greater lack after they embrace the Sabbath than they did before.

There is an evil among some of the poor which will certainly prove their ruin unless they overcome it. They have embraced the truth with their coarse, rough, uncultivated habits, and it takes some time for them to see and realize their coarseness, and that it is not in accordance with the character of Christ. They look upon others who are more orderly and refined as being proud, and you may hear them say: "The truth brings us all down upon a level." But it is an entire mistake to think that the truth brings the receiver down. It brings him up, refines his taste, sanctifies his judgment, and, if lived out, is continually fitting him for the society of holy angels in the City of God. The truth is designed to bring us all up upon a level.

The more able should ever act a noble, generous part in their deal with their poorer brethren, and should also give them good advice, and then leave them to fight life's battles through. But I was shown that a most solemn duty rests upon the church to have an especial care for the destitute widows, orphans, and invalids.

POWER OF EXAMPLE

In the epistle of Paul to Titus, chapter 2:13, 14, we read: "Looking for that blessed hope, and the glorious appearing of the great God and our Saviour Jesus Christ; who gave Himself for us, that He might redeem us from all iniquity, and purify unto Himself a peculiar people, zealous of good works." This great work is to be performed for those only who are willing to be purified, willing to be peculiar, and who manifest a zeal in good works. How many shrink from the purifying process! They are unwilling to live out the truth, unwilling to appear singular in the eyes of the world. It is this mingling with the world that destroys our spirituality, pureness, and zeal. Satan's power is constantly exercised to stupefy the sensibilities of God's people, that their consciences may not be sensitive to wrong, and that the sign of distinction between them and the world may be destroyed.

I have frequently received letters of inquiry in regard to dress, and some have not rightly understood what I have written. The very class that have been presented before me as imitating the fashions of the world have been very slow, and the last, to be affected or reformed. Another class who lacked taste and order in dress have taken advantage of what I have written and have gone to the opposite extreme; considering that they were free from pride, they have looked upon those who dress neatly and orderly as being proud. Oddity and carelessness in dress have been considered a special virtue by some. Such take a course which destroys their influence over unbelievers. They disgust those whom they might benefit.

While the visions have reproved pride and imitating the fashions of the world, they have also reproved those who were careless in regard to their apparel and lacked cleanliness of person and dress. Especially have I been shown that those who profess present truth should have a special care to appear before God upon the Sabbath in a manner which would show that we respect the Creator who has sanctified and placed special honors upon that day. All who have any regard for the Sabbath should be cleanly in person, neat and orderly in dress; for they are to appear before the jealous God, who is offended at uncleanness and disorder, and who marks every token of disrespect. Some have thought it wrong to wear anything upon their heads but a sunbonnet. Such go to great extremes. It cannot be called pride to wear a neat, plain straw or silk bonnet. Our faith, if carried out, will lead us to be so plain in dress, and zealous of good works, that we shall be marked as peculiar. But when we lose taste for order and neatness in dress we virtually leave the truth, for the truth never degrades, but elevates. Unbelievers look upon Sabbathkeepers as degraded, and when persons are neglectful of their dress, and coarse and rough in their manners, their influence strengthens unbelievers in this conclusion.

Those who profess to be Christians amid the perils of the last days, and do not imitate the humble, self-denying Pattern, place themselves in the enemy's ranks. He considers them his subjects, and they serve as important a purpose for him as do any of his subjects, for they have a name to live, and are dead. Others take them as an example, and by following them lose heaven, when, had these not professed to be Christians, their example would have been shunned. These unconsecrated professors are not aware of the weight of their influence. They make the conflict much more severe for those who would be God's peculiar people. Paul, in Titus 2:15, refers to the people who are looking for the appearing of Christ. He says: "These things speak, and exhort, and rebuke with all authority. Let no man despise thee."

As we bear testimony against pride and following the fashions of the world, we are met with excuses and self-justification. Some urge the example of others. Such a sister wears hoops; if it is wrong for me to wear them, it is wrong for her. Children urge the example of other children, whose parents are Sabbathkeepers. Brother A is a deacon of the church. His children wear hoops, and why is it any worse for me to wear them than it is for them? Those who by their example furnish unconsecrated professors with arguments against those who would be peculiar, are laying a cause of stumbling in the way of the weak; they must render an account to God for their example. I am often asked: "What do you think of hoops?" I reply: I have given you the light which has been given me. I was shown that hoops are a shame, and that we should not give the least countenance to a fashion carried to such ridiculous lengths.

I am often surprised to hear that "Sister White says it is

not wrong to wear small hoops." No one has ever heard me say this. After seeing what I have in regard to hoops, nothing would induce me to give the least encouragement to any to wear them. Heavy quilts and hoops are alike unnecessary. He that framed us never designed that we should be deformed with hoops, or anything to look like them. But God's people have so long been led by the inventions and fashions of the world that they are unwilling to move out independent of them. When I study the Scriptures, I am alarmed for the Israel of God in these last days. They are exhorted to flee from idolatry. I fear that they are asleep and so conformed to the world that it would be difficult to discern between him that serveth God and him that serveth Him not. The distance is widening between Christ and His people, and lessening between them and the world. The marks of distinction between Christ's professed people and the world have almost disappeared. Like ancient Israel, they follow after the abominations of the nations around them.

From what has been shown me, hoops are an abomination. They are indecent; and God's people err if they in the least degree follow, or give countenance to, this fashion. Those who profess to be God's chosen, peculiar people, should discard hoops, and their practice should be a living rebuke to those who wear them. Some may plead convenience. I have traveled much, and have seen a great deal of inconvenience attending the wearing of hoops. Those who plead necessity on account of health, wear them in the winter, when they are a greater injury than quilted skirts. While traveling in the cars and stages, I have often been led to exclaim: O Modesty, where is thy blush! I have seen large companies crowding into the cars, and in order to make any headway, the hoops had to be raised and placed in a shape which was indecent. And the exposure of the form was tenfold more with those who wore hoops than with those who did not. Were it not for fashion, those who thus immodestly expose themselves would be hissed at; but modesty and decency must be sacrificed to the god of fashion. May the Lord deliver His people from this grievous sin! God will not pity those who will be slaves to fashion. But supposing there is some little convenience in wearing hoops, does this prove that it is right to wear them? Let the fashion change, and convenience would no longer be mentioned. It is the duty of every child of God to inquire: "Wherein am I separate from the world?" Let us suffer a little inconvenience, and be on the safe side. What crosses do God's people bear? They mingle with the world, partake of their spirit, dress, talk, and act like them.

Read 1 Timothy 2:9, 10: "In like manner also, that women adorn themselves in modest apparel, with shamefacedness and sobriety; not with broided hair, or gold, or pearls, or costly array; but (which becometh women professing godliness) with good works." Also 1 Peter 3:3-5: "Whose adorning let it not be that outward adorning of plaiting the hair, and of wearing of gold, or of putting on of apparel; but let it be the hidden man of the heart, in that which is not corruptible, even the ornament of a meek and quiet spirit, which is in the sight of God of great price. For after this manner in the old time the holy women also, who trusted in God, adorned themselves, being in subjection unto their own husbands."

The power of example is great. Sister A ventures to wear small hoops. Sister B says: It is no worse for me to wear hoops than for Sister A, and she wears them a little larger. Sister C imitates the example of Sisters A and B, and wears her hoops a little larger than A and B, but all contend that their hoops are small.

Parents who would teach their children the evil of following the fashions of the world, have a hard battle. They are met with: "Why, mother, Sisters A, B, and C wear hoops; if it is wicked for me, it is for them." What can the parents say? They should set a right example before their children and although the example of professed followers of Christ causes the children to think that their parents are too careful and severe in their restrictions, yet God will bless the efforts of these conscientious parents. If parents do not take a decided, firm course, their children will be borne down with the current, for Satan and his evil angels are working upon their minds, and the example of unconsecrated professors makes the work of overcoming far more laborious for them. Yet with faith in God and earnest prayer, believing parents should press on in the rugged path of duty. The way of the cross is an onward, upward way. And as we advance therein, seeking the things that are above, we must leave farther and farther in the distance the things which belong to the earth. While the world and carnal professors are rushing downward to death, those who climb the hill will have to put forth efforts or they will be carried down with them.

The children of the world are called the children of darkness. They are blinded by the god of this world, and are led by the spirit of the prince of darkness. They cannot enjoy heavenly things. The children of light have their affections set on things above. They leave behind them the things of this world. They fulfill the command: "Come out from among them, and be ye separate." Here is the conditional promise: "I will receive you." From the beginning, Christ has chosen His people out of world and required them to be separate, having no fellowship with the unfruitful works of darkness. If they love God and keep His commandments, they will be far from having the friendship, and loving the pleasures, of the world. There is no concord between Christ and Belial.

The prophet Ezra, and other faithful servants of the Jewish church, were astonished when the princes came to them saying: "The people of Israel and the priests and the Levites, have not separated themselves from the people of the lands, doing according to their abominations." "And after all that is come upon us for our evil deeds, and for our great trespass, seeing that Thou our God hast punished us less than our iniquities deserve, and hast given us such deliverance as this, should we again break Thy commandments, and join in affinity with the people of these abominations? wouldest not Thou be angry with us till Thou hadst consumed us, so that there should be no remnant nor escaping? O Lord God of Israel, Thou art righteous: for we remain yet escaped, as it is this day: behold, we are before Thee in our trespasses: for we cannot stand before Thee because of this." Ezra 9:1, 13-15.

2 Chronicles 36:14-16: "Moreover all the chief of the priests, and the people, transgressed very much after all the abominations of the heathen; and polluted the house of the Lord which He had hallowed in Jerusalem. And the Lord God of their fathers sent to them by His messengers, rising up betimes, and sending; because He had compassion on His people, and on His dwelling place: but they mocked the messengers of God, and despised His words, and misused His prophets, until the wrath of the Lord arose against His people, till there was no remedy."

Leviticus 18:26, 27: "Ye shall therefore keep My statutes and My judgments, and shall not commit any of these abominations; neither any of your own nation, nor any stranger that sojourneth among you: (for all these abominations have the men of the land done, which were before you, and the land is defiled)."

Deuteronomy 32:16-22: "They provoked Him to jealousy with strange gods, with abominations provoked they Him to anger. They sacrificed unto devils, not to God; to gods whom they knew not, to new gods that came newly up, whom your fathers feared not. Of the Rock that begat thee thou art unmindful, and hast forgotten God that formed thee. And when the Lord saw it, He abhorred them, because of the provoking of His sons, and of His daughters. And He said, I will hide My face from them, I will see what their end shall be: for they are a very froward generation, children in whom is no faith. They have moved Me to jealousy with that which is not God; they have provoked Me to anger with their vanities: and I will move them to jealousy with those which are not a people; I will provoke them to anger with a foolish nation. For a fire is kindled in Mine anger, and shall burn unto the lowest hell, and shall consume the earth with her increase, and set on fire the foundations of the mountains."

We here read the warnings which God gave to ancient Israel. It was not His good pleasure that they should wander so long in the wilderness; He would have brought them immediately to the Promised Land had they submitted and loved to be led by Him; but because they so often grieved Him in the desert, He sware in His wrath that they should not enter into His rest, save two who wholly followed Him. God required His people to trust in Him alone. He did not wish them to receive help from those who did not serve Him.

Please read Ezra 4:1-5: "Now when the adversaries of Judah and Benjamin heard that the children of the captivity builded the temple unto the Lord God of Israel; then they came to Zerubbabel, and to the chief of the fathers, and said unto them, Let us build with you: for we seek your God, as ye do; and we do sacrifice unto Him since the days of Esarhaddon king of Assur, which brought us up hither. But Zerubbabel, and Jeshua, and the rest of the chief of the fathers of Israel, said unto them, Ye have nothing to do with us to build an house unto our God; but we ourselves together will build unto the Lord God of Israel, as King Cyrus the king of Persia hath commanded us. Then the people of the land weakened the hands of the people of Judah, and troubled them in building and hired counselors against them, to frustrate their purpose."

Ezra 8:21-23: "Then I proclaimed a fast there, at the river of Ahava, that we might afflict ourselves before our God, to seek of Him a right way for us, and for our little ones, and for all our substance. For I was ashamed to require of the king a band of soldiers and horsemen to help us against the enemy in the way: because we had spoken unto the king, saying, The hand of our God is upon all them for good that seek Him; but His power and His wrath is against all them that forsake Him. So we fasted and besought our God for this: and He was entreated of us."

The prophet and these fathers did not regard the people of the land as worshipers of the true God, and though these professed friendship and wished to help them, they dared not unite with them in anything relating to His worship. When going up to Jerusalem to build the temple of God and to restore His worship, they would not ask help of the king to assist them in the way, but by fasting and prayer sought the Lord for help. They believed that God would defend and prosper His servants in their efforts to serve Him. The Creator of all things needs not the help of His enemies to establish His worship. He asks not the sacrifice of wickedness, nor accepts the offerings of those who have other gods before the Lord.

We often hear the remark: "You are too exclusive." As a people we would make any sacrifice to save souls, or lead them to the truth. But to unite with them, to love the things that they love, and have friendship with the world, we dare not, for we should then be at enmity with God.

By reading the following scriptures we shall see how God regarded ancient Israel:

Psalm 135:4: "For the Lord hath chosen Jacob unto Himself, and Israel for His peculiar treasure."

Deuteronomy 14:2: "For thou art an holy people unto the Lord thy God, and the Lord hath chosen thee to be a peculiar people unto Himself, above all the nations that are upon the earth."

Deuteronomy 7:6, 7: "For thou art an holy people unto the Lord thy God: the Lord thy God hath chosen thee to be a special people unto Himself, above all people that are upon the face of the earth. The Lord did not set His love upon you, nor choose you, because ye were more in number than any people; for ye were the fewest of all people."

Exodus 33:16: "For wherein shall it be known here that I and Thy people have found grace in Thy sight? is it not in that Thou goest with us? so shall we be separated, I and Thy people, from all the people that are upon the face of the earth."

How frequently ancient Israel rebelled, and how often they were visited with judgments, and thousands slain, because they would not heed the commands of God who had chosen them! The Israel of God in these last days are in constant danger of mingling with the world and losing all signs of being the chosen people of God. Read again Titus 2:13-15. We are here brought down to the last days, when God is purifying unto Himself a peculiar people. Shall we provoke Him as did ancient Israel? Shall we bring His wrath upon us by departing from Him and mingling with the world, and following the abominations of the nations around us?

The Lord hath set apart him that is godly for Himself; this consecration to God and separation from the world is plainly and positively enjoined in both the Old and the New Testament. There is a wall of separation which the Lord Himself has established between the things of the world and the things He has chosen out of the world and sanctified unto Himself. The calling and character of God's people are peculiar, their prospects are peculiar, and these peculiarities distinguish them from all other people. All of God's people upon the earth are one body, from the beginning to the end of time. They have one Head that directs and governs the body. The same injunctions that rested upon ancient Israel, rest upon God's people now, to be separate from the world. The great Head of the church has not changed. The experience of Christians in these days is much like the travels of ancient Israel. Please read 1 Corinthians 10, especially from the 6th to the 15th verse:

"Now these things were our examples, to the intent we should not lust after evil things, as they also lusted. Neither be ye idolaters, as were some of them; as it is written, The people sat down to eat and drink, and rose up to play. . . . Neither let us tempt Christ, as some of them also tempted, and were destroyed of serpents. Neither murmur ye, as some of them also murmured, and were destroyed of the destroyer. Now all these things happened unto them for ensamples: and they are written for our admonition, upon whom the ends of the world are come. Wherefore let him that thinketh he standeth take heed lest he fall. There hath no temptation taken you but such as is common to man: but God is faithful, who will not suffer you to be tempted above that ye are able; but will with the temptation also make a way to escape, that ye may be able to bear it. Wherefore, my dearly beloved, flee from idolatry. I speak as to wise men; judge ye what I say."

1 John 3:1: "Behold, what manner of love the Father hath bestowed upon us, that we should be called the sons of God: therefore the world knoweth us not, because it knew Him not."

1 John 2:15-17: "Love not the world, neither the things that are in the world. If any man love the world, the love of the Father is not in him. For all that is in the world, the lust of the flesh, and the lust of the eyes, and the pride of life, is not of the Father, but is of the world. And the world passeth away, and the lust thereof; but he that doeth the will of God abideth forever."

2 Peter 2:20: "For if after they have escaped the pollutions of the world through the knowledge of the Lord and Saviour Jesus Christ, they are again entangled therein, and overcome, the latter end is worse with them than the beginning."

James 4:4: "Know ye not that the friendship of the world is enmity with God? whosoever therefore will be a friend of the world is the enemy of God."

James 1:27: "Pure religion and undefiled before God and the Father is this, To visit the fatherless and widows in their affliction, and to keep himself unspotted from the world."

Titus 2:12: "Teaching us that, denying ungodliness and worldly lusts, we should live soberly, righteously, and godly, in this present world."

Romans 12:2: "And be not conformed to this world: but be ye transformed by the renewing of your mind, that ye may prove what is that good, and acceptable, and perfect, will of God."

John 17:14, 15, 17: "I have given them Thy word; and the world hath hated them, because they are not of the world, even as I am not of the world. I pray not that Thou shouldest take them out of the world, but that Thou shouldest keep them from the evil." "Sanctify them through Thy truth: Thy word is truth."

Luke 6:22, 23: "Blessed are ye, when men shall hate you, and when they shall separate you from their company, and shall reproach you, and cast out your name as evil, for the Son of man's sake. Rejoice ye in that day, and leap for joy: for, behold, your reward is great in heaven: for in the like manner did their fathers unto the prophets."

John 15:16-19: "Ye have not chosen Me, but I have chosen you, and ordained you, that ye should go and bring forth fruit, and that your fruit should remain: that whatsoever ye shall ask of the Father in My name, He may give it you. These things I command you, that ye love one another. If the world hate you, ye know that it hated Me before it hated you. If ye were of the world, the world would love his own: but because ye are not of the world, but I have chosen you out of the world, therefore the world hateth you."

1 John 4:4, 5: "Ye are of God, little children, and have

overcome them: because greater is He that is in you, than he that is in the world. They are of the world: therefore speak they of the world, and the world heareth them."

1 John 2:5, 6: "But whoso keepeth His word, in him verily is the love of God perfected: hereby know we that we are in Him. He that saith he abideth in Him ought himself also so to walk, even as He walked."

1 Peter 2:9: "But ye are a chosen generation, a royal priesthood, an holy nation, a peculiar people; that ye should show forth the praises of Him who hath called you out of darkness into His marvelous light."

As we read the word of God, how plain it appears that His people are to be peculiar and distinct from the unbelieving world around them. Our position is interesting and fearful; living in the last days, how important that we imitate the example of Christ, and walk even as He walked. "If any man will come after Me, let him deny himself, and take up his cross, and follow Me." The opinions and wisdom of men must not guide or govern us. They always lead away from the cross. The servants of Christ have neither their home nor their treasure here. Would that all of them could understand that it is only because the Lord reigns that we are even permitted to dwell in peace and safety among our enemies. It is not our privilege to claim special favors of the world. We must consent to be poor and despised among men, until the warfare is finished and the victory won. The members of Christ are called to come out and be separate from the friendship and spirit of the world; their strength and power consists in being chosen and accepted of God.

The Son of God was the heir of all things, and the dominion and glory of the kingdoms of this world were promised to Him. Yet when He appeared in this world, it was without riches or splendor. The world understood not His union with the Father; the excellency and glory of His divine character were hid from them. He was therefore "despised and rejected of men," and "we did esteem Him stricken, smitten of God, and afflicted." Even as Christ was in the world, so are His followers. They are the sons of God, and joint heirs with Christ; and the kingdom and dominion belong to them. The world understand not their character and holy calling; they perceive not their adoption into the family of God. Their union and fellowship with the Father and Son is not manifest, and while the world behold their humiliation and reproach, it does not appear what they are, or what they shall be. They are strangers. The world know them not, and appreciate not the motives which actuate them.

The world is ripening for its destruction. God can bear with sinners but a little longer. They must drink the dregs of the cup of His wrath unmixed with mercy. Those who will be heirs of God, and joint heirs with Christ to the immortal inheritance, will be peculiar. Yes, so peculiar that God places a mark upon them as His, wholly His. Think ye that God will receive, honor, and acknowledge a people so mixed up with the world that they differ from them only in name? Read again Titus 2:13-15. It is soon to be known who is on the Lord's side, who will not be ashamed of Jesus. Those who have not moral courage to conscientiously take their position in the face of unbelievers, leave the fashions of the world, and imitate the self-denying life of Christ, are ashamed of Him, and do not love His example.

CONSECRATION

The people of God will be tested and proved. A close and searching work must go on among Sabbathkeepers. Like ancient Israel, how soon we forget God and His wondrous works, and rebel against Him. Some look to the world and desire to follow its fashions and participate in its pleasure, just as the children of Israel looked back to Egypt and lusted for the good things which they had enjoyed there, and which God chose to withhold from them to prove them and thereby test their fidelity to Him. He wished to see if His people valued His service, and the freedom He had so miraculously given them, more highly than the indulgences they enjoyed in Egypt while in servitude to a tyrannical, idolatrous people.

All true followers of Jesus will have sacrifices to make. God will prove them and test the genuineness of their faith. I have been shown that the true followers of Jesus will discard picnics, donations, shows, and other gatherings for pleasure. They can find no Jesus there, and no influence which will make them heavenly minded and increase their growth in grace. The word of God obeyed leads us to come out from all these things and be separate. The things of the world are sought for, and considered worthy to be admired and enjoyed, by all those who are not devoted lovers of the cross and spiritual worshipers of a crucified Jesus.

There is chaff among us, and this is why we are so weak. Some are constantly leaning to the world. Their views and feelings harmonize much better with the spirit of the world than with that of Christ's self-denying followers. It is perfectly natural for them to prefer the company of those whose spirit will best agree with their own. And such have quite too much influence among God's people. They take part with them, and have a name among them, and are a text for unbelievers and the weak and unconsecrated ones in the church. These persons of two minds will ever have objections to the plain, pointed testimony which reproves individual wrongs. In this refining time these persons will either be wholly converted, and sanctified by obeying the truth, or they will be left with the world, where they belong, to receive their reward with them.

"By their fruits ye shall know them." All the followers of Christ bear fruit to His glory. Their lives testify that a good work has been wrought in them by the Spirit of God, and their fruit is unto holiness. Their lives are elevated and pure. Those who bear no fruit have no experience in the things of God. They are not in the Vine. Read John 15:4, 5: "Abide in Me, and I in you. As the branch cannot bear fruit of itself, except it abide in the vine; no more can ye, except ye abide in Me. I am the Vine, ye are the branches: He that abideth in Me, and I in him, the same bringeth forth much fruit: for without Me ye can do nothing."

If we would be spiritual worshipers of Jesus Christ, we must sacrifice every idol and fully obey the first four commandments. Matthew 22:37, 38: "Jesus said unto him, Thou shalt love the Lord thy God with all thy heart, and with all thy soul, and with all thy mind. This is the first and great commandment." The first four commandments allow no separation of the affections from God. Nor is anything allowed to divide, or share, our supreme delight in Him. Whatever divides the affections, and takes away from the soul supreme love to God, assumes the form of an idol. Our carnal hearts would cling to our idols and seek to carry them along; but we cannot advance until we put them away, for they separate us from God. The great Head of the church has chosen His people out of the world and requires them to be separate. He designs that the spirit of His commandments shall draw them to Himself and separate them from the elements of the world. To love God and keep His commandments is far from loving the world's pleasures and friendship. There is no concord between Christ and Belial. The people of God may safely trust in Him alone and without fear press on in the way of obedience.

PHILOSOPHY AND VAIN DECEIT

I have been shown that we must be guarded on every side and perseveringly resist the insinuations and devices of Satan. He has transformed himself into an angel of light and is deceiving thousands and leading them captive. The advantage he takes of the science of the human mind, is tremendous. Here, serpent-like, he imperceptibly creeps in to corrupt the work of God. The miracles and works of Christ he would make appear as the result of human skill and power. If he should make an open, bold attack upon Christianity, it would bring the Christian in distress and agony to the feet of his Redeemer, and his strong and mighty Deliverer would put the bold adversary to flight. He therefore transforms himself into an angel of light and works upon the mind to allure from the only safe and right path. The sciences of phrenology, psychology, and mesmerism are the channel through which he comes more directly to this generation and works with that power which is to characterize his efforts near the close of probation.

Read 2 Thessalonians 2:8-12: "And then shall that wicked be revealed, whom the Lord shall consume with the spirit of His mouth, and shall destroy with the brightness of His coming: even him, whose coming is after the working of Satan with all power and signs and lying wonders, and with all deceivableness of unrighteousness in them that perish; because they received not the love of the truth, that they might be saved. And for this cause God shall send them strong delusion, that they should believe a lie: that they all might be damned who believed not the truth, but had pleasure in unrighteousness."

Satan has come unperceived through these sciences and has poisoned the minds of thousands and led them to infidelity. He is well pleased to have the knowledge of these sciences widespread. It is a plan which he himself has laid that he may gain access to minds and influence them as he pleases. While it is believed that one human mind so wonderfully affects another, Satan, ready at hand, insinuates himself and works on the right hand and on the left. And while those devoted to these sciences laud them to the heavens because of the great and good works they affirm are wrought by them, they are cherishing and glorifying Satan himself, who steps in and works with all power and signs and lying wonders—with all deceivableness of unrighteousness. Said the angel: "Mark its influence. The controversy between Christ and Satan is not yet ended." This entering in of Satan through the sciences is well devised by his satanic majesty, and in the minds of thousands will eventually destroy true faith in Christ's being the Messiah, the Son of God.

I was directed to the power of God manifested through Moses when the Lord sent him in before Pharaoh. Satan understood his business and was upon the ground. He well knew that Moses was chosen of God to break the yoke of bondage upon the children of Israel, and that in his work he prefigured Christ's first advent to break Satan's power over the human family and deliver those who were made captives by his power. Satan knew that when Christ should appear, mighty works and miracles would be wrought by Him, that the world might know that the Father had sent Him. He trembled for his power. He consulted with his angels how to accomplish a work which should answer a twofold purpose: 1. To destroy the influence of the work wrought by God through His servant Moses, by working through his agents, and thus counterfeiting the true work of God; 2. To exert an influence by his work through the magicians which would reach down through all ages and destroy in the minds of many true faith in the mighty miracles and works to be performed by Christ when He should come to this world. He knew that his kingdom would suffer, for the power which he held over mankind would be subject to Christ. It was no human influence or power possessed by Moses that produced those miracles wrought before Pharaoh. It was the power of God. Those signs and wonders were wrought through Moses to convince Pharaoh that the great "I AM" sent him to command Pharaoh to let Israel go that they might serve Him.

Pharaoh called for the magicians to work with their enchantments. They also showed signs and wonders, for Satan came to their aid to work through them. Yet even here the work of God was shown to be superior to the power of Satan, for the magicians could not perform all those miracles which God wrought through Moses. Only a few of them could they do. The magicians' rods did become serpents,* but Aaron's rod swallowed them up. After the magicians sought to produce the lice, and could not, they were compelled by the power of God to acknowledge even to Pharaoh, saying: "This is the finger of God." Satan wrought through the magicians in a manner calculated to harden the heart of the tyrant Pharaoh against the miraculous manifestations of God's power. Satan thought to stagger the faith of Moses and Aaron in the divine origin of their mission, and then his instruments, the magicians, would prevail. Satan was unwilling to have the people of Israel released from Egyptian servitude that they might serve God. The magicians failed to produce the miracle of the lice, and could no more imitate Moses and Aaron. God would not suffer Satan to proceed further, and the magicians could not save themselves from the plagues. "And the magicians could not stand before Moses because of the boils; for the boil was upon the magicians, and upon all the Egyptians." Exodus 9:11.

God's controlling power here cut off the channel through which Satan worked, and caused even those through whom Satan had wrought so wonderfully to feel His wrath. Suffi-

---

*See Appendix.

cient evidence was given to Pharaoh to believe, if he would. Moses wrought by the power of God. The magicians wrought not by their own science alone, but by the power of their god, the devil, who ingeniously carried out his deceptive work of counterfeiting the work of God.

As we near the close of time, the human mind is more readily affected by Satan's devices. He leads deceived mortals to account for the works and miracles of Christ upon general principles. Satan has ever been ambitious to counterfeit the work of Christ and establish his own power and claims. He does not generally do this openly and boldly. He is artful and knows that the most effectual way for him to accomplish his work is to come to poor, fallen man in the form of an angel of light. Satan came to Christ in the wilderness in the form of a beautiful young man—more like a monarch than a fallen angel—with scripture in his mouth. Said he: "It is written." Our suffering Saviour met him with scripture, saying: "It is written." Satan took advantage of the weak, suffering condition of Christ, who had taken upon Him our human nature.

Read Matthew 4:8-11: "Again, the devil taketh Him up into an exceeding high mountain, and showeth Him all the kingdoms of the world, and the glory of them; and saith unto Him, All these things will I give Thee, if Thou wilt fall down and worship me. Then saith Jesus unto him, Get thee hence, Satan: for it is written, Thou shalt worship the Lord thy God, and Him only shalt thou serve. Then the devil leaveth Him, and, behold, angels came and ministered unto Him."

Here Satan spread the world before Christ in the most attractive light and intimated to Him that He need not endure so much suffering to obtain the kingdoms of the earth; Satan would yield all his claims if Christ would but worship him. Satan's dissatisfaction first commenced in heaven because he could not be first and highest in command

—equal with God, exalted above Christ. He rebelled and lost his estate; and he, and those who sympathized with him, were turned out of heaven. In the wilderness he hoped to gain advantage through the weak and suffering condition of Christ, and obtain from Him that homage which he could not obtain in heaven. But Jesus, even in His faint and exhausted condition, yielded not to the temptation of Satan for a moment, but showed His superiority and exercised His authority by bidding Satan: "Get thee hence"—or, Depart from Me. Satan was baffled. He then studied how he could accomplish his purpose and receive the honor from the human race which was refused him in heaven and by Jesus upon earth. Could he have succeeded in tempting Christ, then the plan of salvation would have failed, and he would have succeeded in bringing hopeless misery upon mankind. But that which Satan failed to effect in coming to Christ he has accomplished in coming to man.

If Satan can so befog and deceive the human mind as to lead mortals to think that there is an inherent power in themselves to accomplish great and good works, they cease to rely upon God to do for them that which they think there is power in themselves to do. They acknowledge not a superior power. They give not God the glory which He claims, and which is due to His great and excellent Majesty. Satan's object is thus accomplished, and he exults that fallen men presumptuously exalt themselves as he exalted himself in heaven and was thrust out. He knows that if man exalts himself, his ruin is just as certain as was his own.

Satan failed in his temptations to Christ in the wilderness. The plan of salvation has been carried out. The dear price has been paid for man's redemption. And now Satan seeks to tear away the foundation of the Christian's hope and turn the minds of men into such a channel that they may not be benefited or saved by the great sacrifice offered. He leads fallen man, through his "all deceivableness of unrighteousness," to believe that he can do very well without an atonement, that he need not depend upon a crucified and risen Saviour, that man's own merits will entitle him to God's favor. And then he destroys man's confidence in the Bible, well knowing that if he succeeds here, and faith in the detector which places a mark upon himself is destroyed, he is safe. He fastens upon minds the delusion that there is no personal devil, and those who believe this make no effort to resist and war against that which they think does not exist. Thus poor, blind mortals finally adopt the maxim, "Whatever is, is right." They acknowledge no rule to measure their course.

Satan leads many to believe that prayer to God is useless and but a form. He well knows how needful are meditation and prayer to keep Christ's followers aroused to resist his cunning and deception. By his devices he would divert the mind from these important exercises, that the soul may not lean for help upon the Mighty One and obtain strength from Him to resist his attacks. I was pointed to the fervent, effectual prayers of God's people anciently. "Elias was a man subject to like passions as we are, and he prayed earnestly." Daniel prayed unto his God three times a day. Satan is enraged at the sound of fervent prayer, for he knows that he will suffer loss. Daniel was preferred above the presidents and the princes because an excellent spirit was in him. Fallen angels feared that his influence would weaken their control over the rulers of the kingdom, for Daniel was high in command. The accusing host of evil angels stirred up the presidents and princes to envy and jealousy, and they watched Daniel closely to find some occasion against him that they might report him to the king; but they failed. Then these agents of Satan sought to make his faithfulness to God the cause of his destruction. Evil angels laid out the plan for them, and these agents readily carried it into effect.

The king was ignorant of the subtle mischief purposed

against Daniel. With full knowledge of the king's decree, Daniel still bows before his God, "his windows being open." He considers supplication to God of so great importance that he would rather sacrifice his life than relinquish it. On account of his praying to God, he is cast into the lions' den. Evil angels thus far accomplish their purpose. But Daniel continues to pray, even in the den of lions. Was he suffered to be consumed? Did God forget him there? Oh, no; Jesus, the mighty Commander of the hosts of heaven, sent His angel to close the mouths of those hungry lions that they should not hurt the praying man of God; and all was peace in that terrible den. The king witnessed his preservation and brought him out with honors. Satan and his angels were defeated and enraged. The agents he had employed were doomed to perish in the same terrible manner in which they had plotted to destroy Daniel.

The prayer of faith is the great strength of the Christian and will assuredly prevail against Satan. This is why he insinuates that we have no need of prayer. The name of Jesus, our Advocate, he detests; and when we earnestly come to Him for help, Satan's host is alarmed. It serves his purpose well if we neglect the exercise of prayer, for then his lying wonders are more readily received. That which he failed to accomplish in tempting Christ, he accomplishes by setting his deceitful temptations before man. He sometimes comes in the form of a lovely young person, or of a beautiful shadow. He works cures, and is worshiped by deceived mortals as a benefactor of our race. Phrenology and mesmerism are very much exalted. They are good in their place, but they are seized upon by Satan as his most powerful agents to deceive and destroy souls. His arts and devices are received as from heaven, and faith in the detector, the Bible, is destroyed in the minds of thousands. Satan here receives the worship which suits his satanic majesty. Thousands are conversing with, and receiving instructions from, this demon-god and acting according to his teachings. The world which is supposed to be benefited so much by phrenology and animal magnetism, never was so corrupt. Satan uses these very things to destroy virtue and lay the foundation of spiritualism.

I was directed to this scripture as especially applying to modern spiritualism: Colossians 2:8: "Beware lest any man spoil you through philosophy and vain deceit, after the tradition of men, after the rudiments of the world, and not after Christ." Thousands, I was shown, have been spoiled through the philosophy of phrenology and animal magnetism, and have been driven into infidelity. If the mind commences to run in this channel, it is almost sure to lose its balance and be controlled by a demon. "Vain deceit" fills the minds of poor mortals. They think there is such power in themselves to accomplish great works that they realize no necessity of a higher power. Their principles and faith are "after the tradition of men, after the rudiments of the world, and not after Christ." Jesus has not taught them this philosophy. Nothing of the kind can be found in His teachings. He did not direct the minds of poor mortals to themselves, to a power which they possessed. He was ever directing their minds to God, the Creator of the universe, as the source of their strength and wisdom. Special warning is given in verse 18: "Let no man beguile you of your reward in a voluntary humility and worshiping of angels, intruding into those things which he hath not seen, vainly puffed up by his fleshly mind."

The teachers of spiritualism come in a pleasing, bewitching manner to deceive you, and if you listen to their fables you are beguiled by the enemy of righteousness and will surely lose your reward. When once the fascinating influence of the archdeceiver overcomes you, you are poisoned, and its deadly influence adulterates and destroys your faith in Christ's being the Son of God, and you cease to rely on the merits of His blood. Those deceived by this philosophy are beguiled of their reward through the deceptions of Satan. They rely upon their own merits, exercise voluntary humility, are even willing to make sacrifices, and debase themselves, and yield their minds to the belief of supreme nonsense, receiving the most absurd ideas through those whom they believe to be their dead friends. Satan has so blinded their eyes and perverted their judgment that they perceive not the evil; and they follow out the instructions purporting to be from their dead friends now angels in a higher sphere.

Satan has chosen a most certain, fascinating delusion, one that is calculated to take hold of the sympathies of those who have laid their loved ones in the grave. Evil angels assume the form of these loved ones and relate incidents connected with their lives and perform acts which their friends performed while living. In this way they deceive and lead the relatives of the dead to believe that their deceased friends are angels hovering about them and communing with them. These they regard with a certain idolatry, and what they may say has greater influence over them than the word of God. These evil angels, who assume to be dead friends, will either utterly reject God's word as idle tales, or, if it suit their purpose best, will select the vital portions which testify of Christ and point out the way to heaven, and change the plain statements of the word of God to suit their own corrupt nature and ruin souls. With due attention to the word of God, all may be convinced if they will of this soul-destroying delusion. The word of God declares in positive terms that "the dead know not anything." Ecclesiastes 9:5, 6: "For the living know that they shall die: but the dead know not anything, neither have they any more a reward; for the memory of them is forgotten. Also their love, and their hatred, and their envy, is now perished; neither have they any more a portion forever in anything that is done under the sun."

Deceived mortals are worshiping evil angels, believing

them to be the spirits of their dead friends. The word of God expressly declares that the dead have no more a portion in anything done under the sun. Spiritualists say that the dead know everything that is done under the sun, that they communicate to their friends on earth, give valuable information, and perform wonders. Psalm 115:17: "The dead praise not the Lord, neither any that go down into silence." Satan, transformed into an angel of light works with all deceivableness of unrighteousness. He who could take up the Son of God, who was made a little lower than the angels, and place Him upon a pinnacle of the temple, and take Him up into an exceeding high mountain to present before Him the kingdoms of the world, can exercise his power upon the human family, who are far inferior in strength and wisdom to the Son of God, even after He had taken upon Himself man's nature.

In this degenerate age, Satan holds control over those who depart from the right and venture upon his ground. He exercises his power upon such in an alarming manner. I was directed to these words: "Intruding into those things which he hath not seen, vainly puffed up by his fleshly mind." Some, I was shown, gratify their curiosity and tamper with the devil. They have no real faith in spiritualism and would start back with horror at the idea of being mediums. Yet they venture and place themselves in a position where Satan can excercise his power upon them. Such do not mean to enter deep into this work, but they know not what they are doing. They are venturing on the devil's ground and are tempting him to control them. This powerful destroyer considers them his lawful prey and exercises his power upon them, and that against their will. When they wish to control themselves they cannot. They yielded their minds to Satan, and he will not release his claims, but holds them captive. No power can deliver the ensnared soul but the power of God in answer to the earnest prayers of His faithful followers.

The only safety now is to search for the truth as revealed in the word of God, as for hid treasure. The subjects of the Sabbath, the nature of man, and the testimony of Jesus are the great and important truths to be understood; these will prove as an anchor to hold God's people in these perilous times. But the mass of mankind despise the truths of God's word and prefer fables. 2 Thessalonians 2:10, 11: "Because they received not the love of the truth, that they might be saved. And for this cause God shall send them strong delusion, that they should believe a lie."

The most licentious and corrupt are highly flattered by these satanic spirits, which they believe to be the spirits of their dead friends, and they are vainly puffed up in their fleshly minds. Colossians 2:19: "And not holding the Head, from which all the body by joints and bands having nourishment ministered, and knit together, increaseth with the increase of God," they deny Him who ministers strength to the body, that every member may increase with the increase of God.

Vain philosophy. The members of the body are controlled by the head. Spiritualists lay aside the Head and believe that all the members of the body must act themselves and that fixed laws will lead them on in a state of progression to perfection without a head. John 15:1, 2, 4-6: "I am the True Vine, and My Father is the Husbandman. Every branch in Me that beareth not fruit, He taketh away: and every branch that beareth fruit, He purgeth it, that it may bring forth more fruit." "Abide in Me, and I in you. As the branch cannot bear fruit of itself, except it abide in the vine; no more can ye, except ye abide in Me. I am the Vine, ye are the branches: He that abideth in Me, and I in him, the same bringeth forth much fruit: for without Me ye can do nothing. If a man abide not in Me, he is cast forth as a branch, and is withered; and men gather them, and cast them into the fire, and they are burned."

Christ is the source of our strength. He is the Vine, we are the branches. We must receive nourishment from the living Vine. Deprived of the strength and nourishment of that Vine, we are as members of the body without a head and are in the very position which Satan wishes us to be in, that he may control us as pleases himself. He works "with all deceivableness of unrighteousness in them that perish; because they received not the love of the truth, that they might be saved. And for this cause God shall send them strong delusion, that they should believe a lie." Spiritualism is a lie. It is founded upon the great original lie, "Ye shall *not* surely die." Thousands cut off the Head, and the result is the members act without Jesus for their head, and another guides the body. Satan controls them.

I was shown that Satan cannot control minds unless they are yielded to his control. Those who depart from the right are in serious danger now. They separate themselves from God and from the watchcare of His angels, and Satan, ever upon the watch to destroy souls, begins to present to them his deceptions. Such are in the utmost peril; and if they see and try to resist the powers of darkness and to free themselves from Satan's snare, it is not an easy matter. They have ventured on Satan's ground, and he claims them. He will not hesitate to engage all his energies and call to his aid all his evil host to wrest a single human being from the hand of Christ. Those who have tempted the devil to tempt them will have to make desperate efforts to free themselves from his power. But when they begin to work for themselves, then angels of God whom they have grieved will come to their rescue. Satan and his angels are unwilling to lose their prey. They contend and battle with the holy angels, and the conflict is severe. But if those who have erred continue to plead, and in deep humility confess their wrongs, angels who excel in strength will prevail and wrench them from the power of the evil angels.

As the curtain was lifted and I was shown the corruption of this age, my heart sickened, my spirit nearly fainted within me. I saw that the inhabitants of the earth were filling up the measure of the cup of their iniquity. God's anger is kindled and will be no more appeased until the sinners are destroyed out of the earth. Satan is Christ's personal enemy. He is the originator and leader of every species of rebellion in heaven and earth. His rage increases; we do not realize his power. If our eyes could be opened to discern the fallen angels at work with those who feel at ease and consider themselves safe, we would not feel so secure. Evil angels are upon our track every moment. We expect a readiness on the part of bad men to act as Satan suggests; but while our minds are unguarded against his invisible agents, they assume new ground and work marvels and miracles in our sight. Are we prepared to resist them by the word of God, the only weapon we can use successfully?

Some will be tempted to receive these wonders as from God. The sick will be healed before us. Miracles will be performed in our sight. Are we prepared for the trial which awaits us when the lying wonders of Satan shall be more fully exhibited? Will not many souls be ensnared and taken? By departing from the plain precepts and commandments of God, and giving heed to fables, the minds of many are preparing to receive these lying wonders. We must all now seek to arm ourselves for the contest in which we must soon engage. Faith in God's word, prayerfully studied and practically applied, will be our shield from Satan's power and will bring us off conquerors through the blood of Christ.

NUMBER EIGHT

TESTIMONY FOR THE CHURCH

FAMILY RELIGION

I have been shown the high and responsible position which God's people should occupy. They are the salt of the earth and the light of the world, and they must walk even as Christ walked. They will come up through great tribulation. The present is a time of warfare and trial. Our Saviour says in Revelation 3:21: "To him that overcometh will I grant to sit with Me in My throne, even as I also overcame, and am set down with My Father in His throne." The reward is not given to all who profess to be followers of Christ, but to those who overcome even as He overcame. We must study the life of Christ and learn what it is to confess Him before the world.

In order to confess Christ, we must have Him to confess. No one can truly confess Christ unless the mind and spirit of Christ are in him. If a form of godliness, or an acknowledgment of the truth, were always a confession of Christ, we might say: Broad is the way that leadeth until life, and many there be that find it. We must understand what it is to confess Christ and wherein we deny Him. It is possible with our lips to confess Christ yet in our works deny Him. The fruits of the Spirit manifested in the life are a confession of Him. If we have forsaken all for Christ, our lives will be humble, our conversation heavenly, our conduct blameless. The powerful, purifying influence of truth in the soul, and the character of Christ exemplified in the life, are a confession of Him. If the words of eternal life are sown in our hearts, the fruit is righteousness and peace. We may deny Christ in our life by indulging love of ease or love of self, by jesting and joking, and by seeking the honor of the world. We may deny Him in our outward appearance by conformity to the world, by a proud look or costly apparel. Only by constant watchfulness and persevering and almost unceasing prayer shall we be able to exhibit in our life the character of Christ or the sanctifying influence of the truth. Many drive Christ from their families by an impatient, passionate spirit. Such have something to overcome in this respect.

The present enfeebled condition of the human family was presented before me. Every generation has been growing weaker, and disease of every form afflicts the race. Thousands of poor mortals with deformed, sickly bodies, shattered nerves, and gloomy minds are dragging out a miserable existence. Satan's power upon the human family increases. If the Lord should not soon come and destroy his power, the earth would erelong be depopulated.

I was shown that Satan's power is especially exercised upon the people of God. Many were presented before me in a doubting, despairing condition. The infirmities of the body affect the mind. A cunning and powerful enemy attends our steps and employs his strength and skill in trying to turn us out of the right way. And it is too often the case that the people of God are not on their watch, therefore are ignorant of his devices. He works by means which will best conceal himself from view, and he often gains his object.

Brethren have invested means in patent rights and other enterprises, and have induced others to interest themselves, who could not bear the perplexity and care of such business. Their anxious, overtaxed minds seriously affect their already diseased bodies, and they then yield to despondency, which increases to despair. They lose all confidence in themselves and think that God has forsaken them, and they dare not believe that He will be merciful to them. These poor souls will not be left to the control of Satan. They will make their way through the gloom and again fasten their trembling faith upon the promises of God: He will deliver them and turn their sorrow and mourning into peace and gladness. But such, I was shown, must learn by the things they suffer to let patent rights and these various enterprises alone. They should not allow even their brethren to flatter them to entangle themselves in such enterprises, for their anticipations will not be realized, and then they will be thrown upon the enemy's battlefield unarmed for the conflict. Means which should be put into the treasury of God to advance His cause is worse than lost by being invested in some of these modern improvements. If any who profess the truth feel at liberty to engage, and capable of engaging, in these patent rights and inventions, they should not go among their brethren and make that their field of operation, but go among unbelievers. Let not your name and profession as an Adventist decoy your brethren who wish to consecrate their means to God. But go out into the world, and let that class invest their means who care not for the advancement of the cause of God.

I was shown the necessity of opening the doors of our houses and hearts to the Lord. When we begin to work in earnest for ourselves and for our families, then we shall have help from God. I was shown that merely observing the Sabbath and praying morning and evening are not positive evidences that we are Christians. These outward forms may all be strictly observed, and yet true godliness be lacking. Titus 2:14: "Who gave Himself for us, that He might redeem us from all iniquity, and purify unto Himself a peculiar people, *zealous of good works*." All who profess to be

Christ's followers should have command of their own spirit, not allowing themselves to speak fretfully or impatiently. The husband and father should check that impatient word he is about to utter. He should study the effect of his words, lest they leave sadness and a blight.

Infirmities and disease especially affect women. The happiness of the family depends much upon the wife and mother. If she is weak and nervous, and is suffered to be overtaxed with labor, the mind becomes depressed, for it sympathizes with the weariness of the body; and then she too often meets with cold reserve from the husband. If everything does not move off just as pleasantly as he could wish, he blames the wife and mother. He is almost wholly unacquainted with her cares and burdens, and does not always know how to sympathize with her. He does not realize that he is aiding the great enemy in his work of tearing down. He should by faith in God lift up a standard against Satan; but he seems blinded to his own interest and hers. He treats her with indifference. He knows not what he is doing. He is working directly against his own happiness and is destroying the happiness of his family. The wife becomes desponding and discouraged. Hope and cheerfulness are gone. She goes her daily rounds mechanically because she sees that her work must be done. Her lack of cheerfulness and courage is felt throughout the family circle. There are many such miserable families all through the ranks of Sabbathkeepers. Angels bear the shameful tidings to heaven, and the recording angel makes a record of it all.

The husband should manifest great interest in his family. Especially should he be very tender of the feelings of a feeble wife. He can shut the door against much disease. Kind, cheerful, and encouraging words will prove more effective than the most healing medicines. These will bring courage to the heart of the desponding and discouraged, and the happiness and sunshine brought into the family by kind acts and encouraging words will repay the effort tenfold. The husband should remember that much of the burden of training his children rests upon the mother, that she has much to do with molding their minds. This should call into exercise his tenderest feelings, and with care should he lighten her burdens. He should encourage her to lean upon his large affections, and direct her mind to heaven, where there is strength and peace, and a final rest for the weary. He should not come to his home with a clouded brow, but should with his presence bring sunlight into the family, and should encourage his wife to look up and believe in God. Unitedly they can claim the promises of God and bring His rich blessing into the family. Unkindness, complaining, and anger shut Jesus from the dwelling. I saw that angels of God will flee from a house where there are unpleasant words, fretfulness, and strife.

I have also been shown that there is often a great failure on the part of the wife. She does not put forth strong efforts to control her own spirit and make home happy. There is often fretfulness and unnecessary complaining on her part. The husband comes home from his labor weary and perplexed, and meets a clouded brow instead of cheerful, encouraging words. He is but human, and his affections become weaned from his wife, he loses the love of his home, his pathway is darkened, and his courage destroyed. He yields his self-respect and that dignity which God requires him to maintain. The husband is the head of the family, as Christ is the head of the Church; and any course which the wife may pursue to lessen his influence and lead him to come down from that dignified, responsible position is displeasing to God. It is the duty of the wife to yield her wishes and will to her husband. Both should be yielding, but the word of God gives preference to the judgment of the husband. And it will not detract from the dignity of the wife to yield to him whom she has chosen to be her counselor, adviser, and protector. The husband should maintain his position in his family with all meekness, yet with decision. Some have asked the question, Must I be on my guard and feel a restraint upon me continually? I have been shown that we have a great work before us to search our own hearts, and watch ourselves with jealous care. We should learn wherein we fail, and then guard ourselves upon that point. We must have perfect control over our own spirit. "If any man offend not in word, the same is a perfect man, and able also to bridle the whole body." The light that shines upon our path, the truth that commends itself to our consciences, will condemn and destroy the soul, or sanctify and transform it. We are living too near the close of probation to be content with a superficial work. The same grace which we have hitherto considered sufficient will not sustain us now. Our faith must be increased, and we must become more like Christ in conduct and disposition in order to endure, and successfully resist, the temptations of Satan. The grace of God is sufficient for every follower of Christ.

Our efforts to resist the attacks of Satan must be earnest and persevering. He employs his strength and skill in trying to turn us out of the right way. He watches our going out and our coming in, that he may find opportunity to hurt or destroy us. He works most successfully in darkness, injuring those who are ignorant of his devices. He could not gain advantage if his method of attack were understood. The instruments he employs to effect his purposes, and transmit his fiery darts, are often the members of our own families.

Those we love may speak or act unguardedly, which may wound us deeply. It was not their intention to do this; but Satan magnifies their words and acts before the mind, and thus hurls a dart from his quiver to pierce us. We brace ourselves to resist the one whom we think has injured us, and by so doing we encourage Satan's temptations. Instead of praying to God for strength to resist Satan, we suffer our happiness to be marred by trying to stand for what we term "our rights." Thus we allow Satan a double advantage. We act out our aggrieved feelings, and Satan uses us as his agents to wound and distress those who did not intend to injure us. The requirements of the husband may sometimes seem unreasonable to the wife, when if she should calmly, candidly take the second view of the matter, in as favorable a light for him as possible, she would see that to yield her own way and submit to his judgment, even if it conflicted with her feelings, would save them both from unhappiness and would give them great victory over the temptations of Satan.

I saw that the enemy will contend either for the usefulness or the life of the godly, and will try to mar their peace as long as they live in this world. But his power is limited. He may cause the furnace to be heated, but Jesus and angels will watch the trusting Christian, that nothing may be consumed but the dross. The fire kindled by Satan can have no power to destroy or hurt the true metal. It is important to close every door possible, against the entrance of Satan. It is the privilege of every family so to live that Satan can take no advantage of anything they may say or do, to tear one another down. Every member of the family should bear in mind that all have just as much as they can do to resist our wily foe, and with earnest prayers and unyielding faith each must rely upon the merits of the blood of Christ and claim His saving strength.

The powers of darkness gather about the soul and shut Jesus from our sight, and at times we can only wait in sorrow and amazement until the cloud passes over. These seasons are sometimes terrible. Hope seems to fail, and despair seizes upon us. In these dreadful hours we must learn to trust, to depend solely upon the merits of the atonement, and in all our helpless unworthiness cast ourselves upon the merits of the crucified and risen Saviour. We shall never perish while we do this—*never!* When light shines on our pathway, it is no great thing to be strong in the strength of grace. But to wait patiently in hope when clouds envelop us and all is dark, requires faith and submission which causes our will to be swallowed up in the will of God. We are too quickly discouraged, and earnestly cry for the trial to be removed from us, when we should plead for patience to endure and grace to overcome.

Without faith it is impossible to please God. We can have the salvation of God in our families, but we must believe for it, live for it, and have a continual, abiding faith and trust in God. We must subdue a hasty temper and control our words, and in this we shall gain great victories. Unless we control our words and temper, we are slaves to Satan. We are in subjection to him. He leads us captive. All jangling and unpleasant, impatient, fretful words are an offering presented to his satanic majesty. And it is a costly offering, more costly than any sacrifice we can make for God, for it destroys the peace and happiness of whole families, destroys health, and is eventually the cause of forfeiting an eternal life of happiness. The restraint which God's word imposes upon us is for our own interest. It increases the happiness of our families and of all around us. It refines our taste, sanctifies our judgment, and brings peace of mind, and, in the end, everlasting life. Under this holy restraint we shall increase in grace and humility, and it will become easy to speak right. The natural, passionate temper will be held in subjection. An indwelling Saviour will strengthen us every hour. Ministering angels will linger in our dwellings and with joy carry heavenward the tidings of our advance in the divine life, and the recording angel will make a cheerful, happy record.

JEALOUSY AND FAULTFINDING

Brother G: At _____ you asked me some questions of which I have been thinking much. From my conversation with you, I am convinced that you do not realize the part you have acted and the wound you have brought upon the cause of God. That which had been shown me in regard to you, came vividly before me, and I have compared that which has been recently shown me with the testimony published in regard to you in *Testimony* No. 6, and I cannot see the least apology for your course. Before you were a partaker in, and lent your influence to, the late fanaticism in Wisconsin, you were not right in the sight of God.

Brother G, if you had honestly followed the light, you would never have pursued the course you have taken. You have willfully, stubbornly followed your own course, and relied on your own judgment, refusing to be led. The Lord sent you help, but you refused to accept it. What more could heaven have done for you than has been done? When you have thought that others were more highly esteemed than yourself, you have felt dissatisfied and irritated, and have been pettish and distant like a spoiled child. You have wished to be highly esteemed, but have taken a course to greatly lower yourself in the estimation of those whose approbation you desire.

Before your fanatical course you were jealous of those at Battle Creek, and have thrown out hints which would excite suspicion. You have been jealous of my husband and myself, and have surmised evil. Envy and suspicion have been united. Under an appearance of conscientiousness you have suggested doubts in regard to the movements of those who are bearing the burden of the work at Battle Creek, and have thrown out hints in regard to matters of which you were wholly ignorant, and utterly incapable of judging rightly. The burden of matters there was not laid upon you.

I was shown that God would not select a person with a mind constituted like yours, and lay heavy burdens upon him, and call him to fill the most responsible positions; for self-esteem would be so prominent that it would be ruinous to himself and to God's people. Had you esteemed yourself less, you would have had less jealousy and suspicion.

Brother G, had you fully united with the body, and stood in union and sympathy with those whom God has seen fit to place at the head of the work; had you accepted the gifts which God has placed in the church, and committed yourself fully in regard to them; had you established yourself decidedly upon all points of present truth, and drawn in even cords with those of experience in the cause, you and yours would have been perfectly free and safe from this delusion. You would have had an anchor which would have held you. But you have taken an indefinite position, fearing that you would gratify those whose whole soul was in the work and cause of God. God requires you to stand firmly, decidedly, upon the platform with your brethren. God and holy angels were displeased with your course, and would bear with your folly no longer. You were left to follow your own judgment which you had so highly esteemed, until you should wish to be taught, and without jealous, stubborn feelings, without complaining or censuring others, learn of those who have felt the burden and weight of the cause of God. You have been reaching out for an original position of your own, seeking to lead out independent of the body, where you would be approved and exalted, until I saw that God had given you up to manage and manifest that wisdom you thought superior to others, and you were left to your blind judgment to figure in the most unreasonable, foolish, wild fanaticism that ever cursed Wisconsin.

And yet I was shown that you did not realize the influence of your past course upon the cause, and your present position and duty in regard to that fanaticism. Instead of working with all your energy to free yourself and counteract the influence you exerted, you came up out of all this excusing yourself and censuring those whom God sent to you, and ready to dictate, and even to suggest a plan whereby the Lord might have arrested you by His servants pursuing some different course from that which they did pursue. Your judgment was perverted by Satan's power, and while enshrouded in darkness you were an incompetent judge of the best course to be pursued toward you. If you knew just what course the servants of God ought to pursue in order to help you, you knew enough to come out yourself. God gave you your choice, to be taught, to be instructed through His servants in His own appointed way, or to go on, maintain your willful course, and fall into bewildering fanaticism.

You chose to have *your* way. And now you have only yourself to blame. You profess to be a watchman on the walls of Zion, a shepherd to the flock, yet you saw the poor sheep torn and scattered and gave no warning. "Son of man, I have made thee a watchman unto the house of Israel: therefore hear the word at My mouth, and give them warning from Me. When I say unto the wicked, Thou shalt surely die; and thou givest him not warning, nor speakest to warn the wicked from his wicked way, to save his life; the same wicked man shall die in his iniquity; but his blood will I require at thine hand. Yet if thou warn the wicked, and he turn not from his wickedness, nor from his wicked way, he shall die in his iniquity, but thou hast delivered thy soul." "Nevertheless if thou warn the righteous man, that the righteous sin not, and he doth not sin, he shall surely live, because he is warned; also thou hast delivered thy soul." Ezekiel 3:17-19, 21.

The sin of those in Wisconsin who went into fanaticism rests more heavily upon you, Brother G, than upon any other one. You were an unfaithful watchman. You discerned not the evil, because you were unfaithful. God sent His faithful watchmen who stood in the light and could discern the evil to warn *you* and the erring flock. Had you then listened to the warning, a great amount of evil would have been saved. Your influence would have been preserved. You would have stood out of the way, that the testimony of the servants of God might reach the distracted flock. The erring would not hear the voice of God through His chosen servants. They made their spirit strong against the warning of the watchmen sent to them, and strengthened themselves in their unreasonable, self-deceived course. The shepherd would not hear. He was offended because this fanaticism was handled so decidedly. He perceived not the danger. He saw no haste in the matter. He had sufficient light to decide, but was too willful and too suspicious of God's servants to yield to their testimony.

Brother G wished to wait until the fanaticism should develop, and it went on just as Satan would have it, until it did develop with terrible results. There were not reasonable, sensible manifestations to characterize that work as being of God. The Lord's servants executed their mission, freed their garments from the blood of souls, and kept themselves clear of the cursed influence, while you bear the fearful weight of the sin of this woeful fanaticism. You have deeply regretted it, yet do not see your own wrongs in relation to it. You censure and blame the weak, erring sheep for leading you out of the way. What is a watchman for, unless it be to watch for evil and give the warning? What is a shepherd for, unless it be to watch for every danger lest the sheep be harmed and destroyed by wolves? What excuse could a shepherd plead for suffering the flock to stray from the true pasture, and be torn and scattered and devoured by wolves? How would an excuse stand made by the shepherd that the sheep led him astray? They left the true pasture, and led him out of the way? Such a plea would tell with force against that shepherd's ability to watch over the sheep. No more confidence could be placed in him as a faithful shepherd to care for the sheep, and bring them back as they might stray from the right path.

The reproach resting upon the cause in regard to Sister A rests heavily upon you. You made much of her exercises and experience. She was weak, yet could in a measure fill her place in her family and keep her children together; but she had been from her home but a short time before her reason was dethroned. The backslidden state of the professed Sabbathkeepers in ——— led you to influence Sister A to leave her family who needed her care, and come to ——— that her influence might help the Sabbathkeepers there. An unhealthy excitement marked her course. Some of the inexperienced were deluded. The weak mind of Sister A was overtaxed, and disease fastened upon the brain. And the cause of God is deeply wounded and reproached on account of this. Brother A has been wronged; he must now suffer under a living trouble, and his children must be scattered. Those whose influence led to these sad consequences, have a work to do to relieve the mind of Brother A, and by a faithful and full acknowledgment to him of the sin of the course pursued, and the wrong done him, counteract the evil as far as possible.

Had you been standing in the counsel of God, acknowledging the gifts of His Spirit as occupying their proper place in the church; had you been in heart and principle with the *Review,* established upon the strong truths applicable for this time; had you been giving meat in due season to the people of God, your influence in ——— and vicinity would have been very different. You would have had a pointed testimony to bear in harmony with those who are leading out in this great work. Individual wrongs would have been reproved. Faithful labor would have brought up the Sabbathkeepers there, so that they would not have been behind other churches. But they have almost everything to learn. You should have borne a pointed testimony, impressing upon them the necessity of sacrificing, and all doing a part to bear the burden of the cause. You should have brought them up upon systematic benevolence, leading all to act a part and exert themselves to do something to advance the cause of truth. Your indefinite position, and leaving matters so loose and slack in —— has had a bad influence upon the cause there. The opposition you felt and talked out in regard to organization and the advance of God's people, has borne fruit which can be seen in many places in northern Wisconsin.

If you had been a prompt, thorough laborer, keeping pace with God's opening providence, the fruit now manifested would be of an altogether different character. Souls would be decided somewhere, either wholly for or against the commandments of God and other truths connected with the third angel's message. They would not be hanging on the skirts of Zion to weigh down those who would be right. But there has not been faithfulness manifested by you. Straight and thorough work has not been made. You have not encouraged in the church, by a pointed application of truth, the necessity of everyone practically, harmoniously carrying out his profession; and many are not as willing to exert themselves to do something to advance the truth, as they are to be gratified with listening to the truth. They love the cause in word and profession, but not in *deed* and in *truth*.

Your position has led many in and about —— to think less highly of the *Review* than they otherwise would have done, and they have held very lightly the truths found in it. Thus the *Review* failed to have the influence upon them that God designed it should have. And everyone has followed his own course, and done that which seemed right in his own eyes; hence all are far upon the background, and unless there is a thorough work accomplished for them, they will be weighed in the balance and found wanting.

I was shown that you seek to throw the result of your wrongs upon others, but as a watchman God holds you responsible. You have most humble confessions to make in ——, ——, ——, and other places where your influence has been exerted in opposition to God's servants. Brother and Sister B have been greatly injured by this fanaticism. They have been embarrassed temporally as well as spiritually, and nearly ruined by this deception of Satan. Brother G, you have run to great lengths in this sad fanaticism; your body has been affected as well as your mind, and you now seek to charge it all upon others. You have not a true sense of your position and course in the past. You are free to confess that which others have done, and that which you did not do; but you have failed to confess that which you did do.

Your influence in —— has been injurious. You were opposed to organization, and preached against it in an indefinite manner, not so boldly as some might have done, but you went just as far as you dared to go. In this way you have many times gratified your envious feelings, and created distrust and uncertainty in the minds of many, when if you had come out openly, you would have been plainly understood and could have done but little mischief. When charged with advocating sentiments contrary to the faith of the body, you would not acknowledge it, but mystified your position, and made it appear that the brethren misunderstood you, when you know that the charge was correct. As you now are, the church cannot depend on you. When you manifest the fruits of an entire reform, and give evidence that you are converted, and have overcome your jealousy, then God will again trust His flock to your care. But until you make thorough restitution, you will exert the best influence by staying at home, and being "not slothful in business."

By your noncommittal position, and by your course in

this fanaticism you have done more injury to the cause of God in Wisconsin than you have done good in all your life. Our faith has been made disgusting to unbelievers; a wound, an incurable wound, has been given to the cause of God, and yet many, with yourself, seem astonished that so much is said and made of this fanaticism. One evil seed sown takes root, grows rank, and bears fruit, and there is an abundant harvest. Evil flourishes and needs no culture while the good seed sown needs to be watered, carefully tended, and continually nourished, or the precious plants will die. Satan, evil angels and wicked men are trying to root up and destroy the good, and it requires the greatest vigilance, and the most constant care, to have it live and flourish. An evil seed sown cannot be easily rooted out. It spreads, and springs up in every direction, to crush out the precious seed; and if left alone it will grow strong, and shut out the rays of the sun from the precious plants, until they grow sickly and die.

We met your influence at ——. The division existing there would not have been had you taken a right position, and received the word of the Lord through His servants. But this you would not do. God's servants had to deal plainly with your wrong course. Had they taken stronger ground, and been much more severe with the course you had pursued, God would have approved them. It would have been better had you remained entirely away from —— , for every time God's servants exposed that fanaticism, the reproof hit Brother G, and you shrank, felt abused, neglected, etc. You pursued your blind course among different families in ——; you labored for sympathy, and created opposition of feeling against Brethren C, D, and E. You felt wrong, felt slighted; you talked and acted out your feelings, and thus created jealousy and distrust in many minds in regard to God's servants whom He had especially sent to you. Your course destroyed the force of their testimony on some minds, but some felt thankful that light had come, and that Satan's snare was broken, and they had escaped. Others felt hard, and decided against the testimony borne, and there was a division in the body. You can take the responsibility of this. We have had to labor for the church in ______ with distress of spirit to do away the wrong influence and impressions you had created. You have a work to do there.

I saw that some have been very jealous for you, fearing that you would not be rightly dealt with, and not have justice done you by your ministering brethren. Such should stand out of the way, and be faithful to confess their own wrongs, and let all the censure and weight of your wrongs rest upon your own head. God designs that they shall rest there until you thoroughly remove them by repentance and hearty confession. Those who have a perverted sympathy for you cannot help you. Let them manifest zeal in repenting of their own backslidings, and leave you to stand for yourself. You have been altogether out of the way, and unless you make thorough work, confess your wrongs without censuring your brethren, and are willing to be instructed, you can have no part with God's people.

You have stood aloof from those upon whom God has laid the heavy burden of His work. While my husband already had the labor and burden which three men should have shared, you have injured him by remarks and hints, and have helped others to bring burdens upon him. You must see this. You have had no special burden laid upon you, but have had time for reflection and study, rest and sleep, while my husband has been obliged to labor day after day, and often long into the night, and sometimes when he did lie down to rest, he could not sleep, but could only weep and groan for the cause of truth, and the injustice of his brethren toward him, whose whole interest and life was devoted to the cause.

He has had the care and responsibility of the business in the office, the care of the paper, and much care of the churches in different states. And yet some of his ministering brethren have helped to perplex and distress by their unwise course. You with some others have looked upon Brother White as a business character, not enjoying much religion. Such do not know him. Satan deceives many in regard to him. God has seen fit to lay the burden of His work upon him, to choose him to lead out in different enterprises, and He has selected one who is sensitive, and can sympathize with the unfortunate; who is conscientious, and yet independent; who will not cover sin, but will be quick to see and feel wrong, and to reprove it and give no place to it, even if he has to stand alone in consequence. This is why he suffers so keenly. His brethren generally know nothing of his burdens, and some care nothing about them, but by their own unwise, crooked course add to his cares and perplexities. Heaven marks these things. Men who have no weight or burdens upon them, who can have hours of ease, with nothing in particular to do, who can reflect, and study, and improve their minds, can manifest great moderation. They see nothing to urge them to manifest any special zeal, and are ready to spend hours in private conversation. Some look upon such as being the best and holiest men on earth. But God sees not as man sees. God looks at the heart. Those who have such an easy position will be rewarded according to their works.

The position occupied by my husband is not an enviable one. It requires the closest attention, care, and mental labor. It requires the exercise of sound judgment and wisdom. It requires self-denial, a whole heart, and a firm will to push matters through. In that important position God will have a man to venture, to risk something, to move out firmly for the right, whatever may be the consequences; to battle against obstacles, and waver not, even though life be at stake.

The weight and responsibility of this work lead to great carefulness, cause sleepless nights, and call forth earnest, fervent, agonizing prayer to God. The Lord has led my husband forward to take one responsible position after another. Censure from his brethren wrings his soul with anguish, yet he must not falter in the work. Fellow laborers having an appearance of godliness oppose every advance which God leads him to make, and his precious time must be occupied in traveling from place to place, laboring with distress of mind among the churches to undo what these professed brethren have been doing. Poor mortals! They mistake matters; they have not a true sense of what constitutes a Christian. Those who have been thrust out to bear a plain, pointed testimony, in the fear of God to reprove wrong, to labor with all their energies to build up God's people, and to establish them upon important points of present truth, have too often received censure instead of sympathy and help, while those who, like yourself, have taken a noncommittal position, are thought to be devoted, and to have a mild spirit. God does not thus regard them. The forerunner of Christ's first advent was a very plain-spoken man. He rebuked sin, and called things by their right names. He laid the ax at the root of the tree. He thus addressed one class of professed converts who came to be baptized of him in Jordan: "O generation of vipers, who hath warned you to flee from the wrath to come? Bring forth therefore fruits meet for repentance. . . . And now also the ax is laid unto the root of the trees: therefore every tree which bringeth not forth good fruit is hewn down, and cast into the fire."

In this fearful time, just before Christ is to come the second time, God's faithful preachers will have to bear a still more pointed testimony than was borne by John the Baptist. A responsible, important work is before them; and those who speak smooth things, God will not acknowledge as His shepherds. A fearful woe is upon them.

This strange fanaticism in Wisconsin grew out of the false theory of holiness, advocated by Brother K—a holiness not dependent upon the third angel's message, but outside of present truth. Sister G received this false theory from him, carried it out herself, and zealously taught it to others. This nearly destroyed her love for the sacred, important truths for this time, which, if she had loved and obeyed, would have proved an anchor to hold her upon the right foundation. But she, with many others, made this theory of holiness or consecration the one great thing, and the important truths of God's word were of but little consequence, "if the heart was only right." And poor souls were left without an anchor, to be carried about by feeling, and Satan came in and controlled minds and gave impressions and feelings to suit himself. Reason and judgment were despised, and the cause of God was cruelly reproached.

The fanaticism into which you have fallen should lead you and others to investigated before deciding in regard to this appearance of consecration. *Appearance* is not positive evidence of Christian character. You and others are afraid of receiving a little more censure than is due you, and you look with earnestness upon a seeming error or wrong in others, or a neglect from them, and feel injured. You are too exacting. You have been wrong and have deceived yourself. If others have misjudged you in some things, it is no more than might be expected, considering the circumstances. You should, with the deepest sorrow and humility, mourn your sad departure from the right, which has given occasion for a variety of feelings and views and expressions in regard to you; and if in every particular you do not consider them correct, you must let them pass, and lay not censure upon others. You must confess your faults without censuring any other one, and cease complaining that your brethren have neglected you. They have given you more attention than you deserved, considering the position you have for years occupied. If you could see these things as God regards them, you would ever despise the complaints you make, and would humble yourself under the hand of God. "Behold, to obey is better than sacrifice, and to hearken than the fat of rams. For rebellion is as the sin of witchcraft, and stubbornness is as iniquity and idolatry."

UNITY OF FAITH

Professed believers in and about ——— do not come up to the work, and practice the truths which they profess. A blighting influence is upon the cause in northern Wisconsin. If all had felt that attachment for the *Review* which God designed they should, they would have been benefited and instructed by the truths it advocates. They would have had a correct faith, a settled position upon the truth applicable for this time, and would have been guarded and saved from this fanaticism. The sensibilities of many are blunted; false excitement has destroyed their discernment and spiritual eyesight. It is of the highest importance now for them to move understandingly, that Satan's object may not be fully accomplished in overthrowing those whom he has had power to deceive.

When those who have witnessed and experienced false exercises, are convinced of their mistake, then Satan takes advantage of their error, and holds it constantly before them, to make them afraid of any spiritual exercise, and in this way he seeks to destroy their faith in true godliness. Because they were once deceived, they fear to make any effort by earnest, fervent prayer to God for special aid and victory. Such must not let Satan gain his object, and drive them to cold formality and unbelief. They must remember that the foundation of God standeth sure. Let God be true, and every man a liar. Their only safety is to plant their feet upon a firm platform, to see and understand the third angel's message, to prize, love, and obey the truth.

Christ is leading out a people, and bringing them into the unity of the faith, that they may be one, as He is one with the Father. Differences of opinion must be yielded, that all may come into union with the body, that they may have one mind and one judgment. 1 Corinthians 1:10: "Now I beseech you, brethren, by the name of our Lord Jesus Christ, that ye all speak the same thing, and that there be no divisions among you; but that ye be perfectly joined together in the same mind and in the same judgment." Romans 15:5, 6: "Now the God of patience and consolation grant you to be like-minded one toward another according to Christ Jesus: that ye may with one mind and one mouth glorify God, even the Father of our Lord Jesus Christ." Philippians 2:2: "Fulfill ye my joy, that ye be like-minded, having the same love, being of one accord, of one mind."

All the people of God should have an interest in His cause. There has been a lack of this interest among the brethren in Wisconsin. There has also been a lack of energy. Some think it no sin to idle away their time, while others who love the precious cause of truth, economize their time, and in the strength of God exert themselves and labor hard that their families may be made neat and comfortable, and they have something besides to invest in the cause, that they may do their part to keep the work of God moving and lay up a treasure in heaven. One is not to be eased and others burdened. God requires those who have health and strength of body, to do what they can, and use their strength to His glory, for they are not their own. They are accountable to God for the use they make of their time and strength, which are granted them of Heaven.

The duty to help in the advancement of truth does not rest only upon the wealthy. All have a part to act. The man who has employed his time and strength to accumulate property is accountable for the disposition he makes of that property. If one has health and strength, that is his capital, and he must make a right use of it. If he spends hours in idleness and needless visiting and talking, he is slothful in business, which God's word forbids. Such have a work to do to provide for their own families, and then lay by them in store for charitable purposes as God has prospered them.

We are not placed in this world merely to care for ourselves, but we are required to aid in the great work of salvation, thus imitating the self-denying, self-sacrificing, useful life of Christ. Those who love their own ease better than they love the truth of God, will not be anxious to use their time and strength wisely and well, that they may act a part in spreading the truth. Many of the young in Wisconsin have not felt the weight of the cause or the necessity of their making any sacrifice to advance it. They can never gain strength until they change their course and make special efforts to advance the truth, that souls may be saved. Some deny themselves and manifest an interest and have double labor, because of their untiring efforts to sustain the cause they love. They make the cause of God a part of them; if it suffers, they suffer with it, when it prospers, they are happy.

Proverbs 3:9, 10: "Honor the Lord with thy substance, and with the first fruits of all thine increase: so shall thy barns be filled with plenty, and thy presses shall burst out with new wine." Those who are slothful may quiet themselves with the thought that God requires nothing of them because they have no increase. This will be no excuse for them; for if they had diligently employed their time, if they had not been slothful in business, they would have had increase. Had they resolutely exerted themselves to earn something to cast into the treasury of God, ways would be opened for them, and they would have some increase to devote to the cause of God, and thus to lay up a treasure in heaven.

NORTHERN WISCONSIN

While in Roosevelt, New York, August 3, 1861, different churches and families were presented before me. The different influences that have been exerted, and their discouraging results, were shown me. Satan has used as agents individuals professing to believe a part of present truth, while they were warring against a part. Such he can use more successfully than those who are at war with all our faith. His artful manner of bringing in error through partial believers in the truth, has deceived many, and distracted and scattered their faith. This is the cause of the divisions in northern Wisconsin. Some receive a part of the message, and reject another portion. Some accept the Sabbath and reject the third angel's message; yet because they have received the Sabbath they claim the fellowship of those who believe all the present truth. Then they labor to bring others into the same dark position with themselves. They are not responsible to anyone. They have an independent faith of their own. Such are allowed to have influence, when no place should be given to them, notwithstanding their pretensions to honesty.

Honest souls will see the straight chain of present truth. They will see its harmonious connections, link after link uniting into a great whole, and will lay hold upon it. The present truth is not difficult to be understood, and the people whom God is leading will be united upon this broad, firm platform. He will not use individuals of different faith, opinions, and views, to scatter and divide. Heaven and holy angels are working to unite, to bring into the unity of the faith, into the one body. Satan opposes this, and is determined to scatter, and divide, and bring in different sentiments, that the prayer of Christ may not be answered: "Neither pray I for these alone, but for them also which shall believe on Me through their word; that they all may be one; as Thou, Father, art in Me, and I in Thee, that they also may be one in Us: that the world may believe that Thou hast sent Me." John 17:20, 21. Jesus designed that the faith of His people should be one. If one goes forth preaching one thing, and another differing with him preaches something else, how can those who believe through their word be one? There will be difference of sentiments.

I saw that if God's people in Wisconsin would prosper, they must take a decided position in regard to these things, and thereby cut off the influence of those who are causing distraction and division by teaching sentiments contrary to the body. Such are wandering stars. They seem to emit a little light; they profess and carry along a little truth, and thus deceive the inexperienced. Satan endows them with his spirit, but God is not with them; His Spirit does not dwell in them. Jesus prayed that His disciples might be one, as He is one with the Father, "that the world may believe that Thou hast sent Me." The oneness and unity of God's truth-believing remnant people carries powerful conviction to the world that they have the truth, and are the peculiar, chosen people of God. This oneness and unity disconcerts the enemy, and he is determined that it shall not exist. The present truth, believed in the heart and exemplified in the life, makes God's people one, and gives them a powerful influence.

Had professed Sabbathkeepers in Wisconsin earnestly sought and labored to be in union with the prayer of Christ, to be one as He is one with the Father, Satan's work would have been defeated. If all had sought to be in union with the body, the fanaticism which has brought so deep a stain upon the cause of present truth in northern Wisconsin would not have arisen; for it is the result of drawing off from the body, and seeking to have an original, independent faith, regardless of the faith of the body.

In the last vision given at Battle Creek I was shown that

an unwise course was taken at _____ in regard to the visions at the time of the organization of the church there. There were some in _____ who were God's children, and yet doubted the visions. Others had no opposition, yet dared not take a decided stand in regard to them. Some were skeptical, and they had sufficient cause to make them so. The false visions and fanatical exercises, and the wretched fruits following, had an influence upon the cause in Wisconsin to make minds jealous of everything bearing the name of visions. All these things should have been taken into consideration, and wisdom exercised. There should be no trial or labor with those who have never seen the individual having visions, and who have had no personal knowledge of the influence of the visions. Such should not be deprived of the benefits and privileges of the church, if their Christian course is otherwise correct, and they have formed a good Christian character.

Some, I was shown, could receive the published visions, judging of the tree by its fruits. Others are like doubting Thomas; they cannot believe the published *Testimonies,* nor receive evidence through the testimony of others; but must see and have the evidence for themselves. Such must not be set aside, but long patience and brotherly love should be exercised toward them until they find their position and become established for or against. If they fight against the visions, of which they have no knowledge; if they carry their opposition so far as to oppose that in which they have had no experience, and feel annoyed when those who believe that the visions are of God speak of them in meeting, and comfort themselves with the instruction given through vision, the church may know that they are not right. God's people should not cringe and yield, and give up their liberty to such disaffected ones. God has placed the gifts in the church that the church may be benefited by them; and when professed believers in the truth oppose these gifts, and fight against the visions, souls are in danger through their influence, and it is time then to labor with them, that the weak may not be led astray by their influence.

It has been very hard for the servants of God to labor in ———, for there has been a class of self-righteous, talkative, unruly ones there, who have stood in the way of the work of God. If received into the church, they would tear it to pieces. They would not be subject to the body, and would never be satisfied unless the reins of church government were in their own hands.

Brother G sought to move with great caution. He knew that the class who opposed the visions were wrong, that they were not genuine believers in the truth; and therefore, to shake off these clogs, he proposed to receive none into the church who did not believe the third angel's message and the visions. This kept out some few precious souls who had not fought against the visions. They dared not unite with the church, fearing that they should commit themselves upon that which they did not understand and fully believe. And there were those at hand ready to prejudice these conscientious ones, and to place matters before them in the worst possible light. Some have felt grieved and offended because of the condition of membership, and since the organization their feelings of dissatisfaction have greatly increased. Strong prejudice has governed them.

I was shown the case of Sister H. She was presented before me in connection with a professed sister who was strongly prejudiced against my husband and myself, and opposed to the visions. This spirit had led her to love and cherish every lying report in regard to us and the visions, and she has communicated this to Sister H. She has had a bitter spirit of war against me, when she had no personal knowledge of me. She was unacquainted with my labors, yet has nourished the most wicked feelings of prejudice against me, and has influenced Sister H, and they have united together in their bitter remarks and speeches. The person shown me in connection with Sister H was a strong-minded woman, sanguine, and exalted in her own estimation. She has thought that her views were correct, and that others must rely upon her word, when she only darkened counsel by words, and manifested the spirit of the dragon host to war against those who would be united on the commandments of God and the testimony of Jesus.

Since Sister H has been at ——, she has despised the visions, and has related hearsay reports, as though she knew that they were true. She has resisted no influence calculated to injure me. She did not know but that the visions were of God; she had no personal acquaintance with the humble instrument; and yet she has united with unconsecrated ones in —— to exert a strong influence against me. They have strengthened one another by loving and reporting false stories coming from different sources, and in this way have nourished their prejudice. There can be no union between their spirit and the spirit of the messages which the Lord sees fit to give for the benefit of His humble people. The spirit which dwells in their hearts cannot harmonize with the light given of God.

Many poor souls do not know what they are doing. They unite their influence with Satan's forces, and aid him in his work. They manifest great zeal and earnestness in their blind opposition, as though they were verily doing God's service by fighting against the visions. All who desire to do so can acquaint themselves with the fruits of these visions. For seventeen years God has seen fit to let them survive and strengthen against the opposition of Satan's forces, and the influence of human agencies that have aided Satan in his work.

Other women were shown me in —— who were at war with the truth. One was presented before me who embraced a few points of truth, and then went no further with God's remnant people. She was exalted in her own eyes, and thought she understood it all. She was wise in her own opinion, and was shown me as constantly looking back and referring to an old experience, because she had received a degree of light in the past, she had become lifted up, and thought she had sufficient light and knowledge to instruct the whole body. Her faith is scattered and disconnected. Many of her ideas of truth are erroneous, yet she is egotistical, and righteous in her own estimation. She is forward to instruct, but will not be taught. She has despised instruction, and cast behind her the teachings of God through His servants. I saw her pointing to her righteousness, her devotion, her prayerful life. Like the Pharisee, she enumerates her good deeds. "God, I thank Thee, that I am not as other men are, extortioners, unjust, adulterers, or even as this publican. I fast twice in the week, I give tithes of all that I possess." The Pharisee's prayer was not regarded; but the poor publican who could only say, "God be merciful to me a sinner," moved the pity of the Lord. His prayer was accepted, while the prayer of the boasting Pharisee was rejected. "For everyone that exalteth himself shall be abased, and he that humbleth himself shall be exalted."

Revelation 3:17, 18: "Because thou sayest, I am rich, and increased with goods, and have need of nothing and knowest not that thou art wretched, and miserable, and poor, and blind, and naked; I counsel thee to buy of Me gold tried in the fire, that thou mayest be rich and white raiment, that thou mayest be clothed and that the shame of thy nakedness do not appear; and anoint thine eyes with eyesalve, that thou mayest see."

This person, whose countenance I recognized when I saw her, I was told was Mrs I. I saw that her life was not marked with that humility which should ever characterize the followers of Christ. When poor mortals, however high their profession, become just in their own eyes, then Jesus leaves them to be deceived in regard to themselves. I was shown that this woman has influenced others, and some have united with her to hold up the visions in a ridiculous light. To God they must answer for all this; for every word of derision against the light which God has seen fit to communicate in His own chosen way, is recorded.

I was shown still another woman who is not in union with the people whom God is leading out. The spirit of truth dwells not in her heart, and she has been busy doing the work which well pleases the enemy of all good, to distract and confuse minds. (I recognized this woman the last day of the meeting; she left before it closed.) She is a great talker, and is ever ready to hear and tell some new thing, dwelling upon what she calls others' wrongs, and she terms her evil surmisings discernment. She puts light for darkness, and darkness for light, and for a pretense makes long prayers. She loves to be approved and thought righteous, and has deceived some. She wishes to teach others, and thinks that God teaches her above others. But the truth has no place in her heart.

those I have mentioned, and together they do what they can to draw off from the body and cause confusion; and their influence brings the truth of God into disrepute. Jesus and holy angels are bringing up and uniting God's people into one faith, that they may all have one mind and one judgment. And while they are being brought into the unity of the faith, to see eye to eye upon the solemn, important truths for this time, Satan is at work to oppose their advancement. Jesus is at work through His instruments to gather and unite. Satan works through his instruments to scatter and divide. "For, lo, I will command, and I will sift the house of Israel among all nations, like as corn is sifted in a sieve, yet shall not the least grain fall upon the earth."

God is now testing and proving His people. Character is being developed. Angels are weighing moral worth, and keeping a faithful record of all the acts of the children of men. Among God's professed people are corrupt hearts; but they will be tested and proved. That God who reads the hearts of everyone, will bring to light hidden things of darkness where they are often least suspected, that stumbling blocks which have hindered the progress of truth may be removed, and God have a clean and holy people to declare His statutes and judgments.

The Captain of our salvation leads His people on step by step, purifying and fitting them for translation, and leaving in the rear those who are disposed to draw off from the body, who are not willing to be led, and are satisfied with their own righteousness. If therefore the light that is in thee be darkness, how great is that darkness! No greater delusion can deceive the human mind than that which leads men to indulge a self-confident spirit, to believe that they are right and in the light, when they are drawing away from God's people, and their cherished light is darkness.

The class in ______ who have been drawing off from the body have possessed a hard, bitter spirit against those whom God is using as His instruments to bring His people up united upon the only true platform. Their spirit is opposed to the work of God, and their influence has brought reproach upon the cause of God, and has made our faith disgusting to unbelievers, and caused Satan to exult. Those who are walking in church capacity and trying to serve God, may for a time be annoyed with those among them who are not right, and who have been shown me as self-righteous and pharisaical; but if they are patient, and walk humbly before God, earnestly praying for His power and Spirit, they will advance, and those who are unsound in the faith will be left behind.

Brother J was presented before me, and I was shown that his course has not been pleasing to God. He was unstable. He has been befogged with the Age-to-Come, and as there is not the least harmony between the Age-to-Come theory and the third angel's message, he lost his love for and faith in the message, and felt irritated because so much had been said in regard to it. The third angel is proclaiming a most solemn message to the inhabitants of the earth; and shall God's chosen people be indifferent to it, and not unite their voice to sound this solemn warning? Brother J is deceived, and is deceiving others. His theme has been consecration, when his heart was not right. His mind has been divided. He has had no anchor to hold him, and has been floating about without a settled faith. Much of his time has been occupied in relating to one and another reports and stories calculated to distract and unsettle minds. He has had much to say in regard to my husband and myself, and against the visions. He has stood in a position, "Report, . . . and we will report it." God sent him not on such a mission. He has not known whom he has been serving. Satan has been using him to throw minds into confusion. What little influence he had he has used to prejudice minds against the third angel's message. He has by false reports presented the visions in a wrong light, and weak souls who were not established in all the present truth have fed upon these things instead of clean provender thoroughly winnowed. He has been deceived in regard to sanctification. Unless he now changes his course, and is willing to be instructed, and cherishes the light given, he will be left of God to pursue his own course and follow his own imperfect judgment until he will make shipwreck of faith, and by his unwise course become a signal warning to those who choose to go independent of the body. God will open the eyes of honest souls to understand the cruel work of those who scatter and divide. He will mark those who cause divisions, that every honest one may escape from Satan's snare.

Brother J received from Elder K a false theory of sanctification, which is outside of the third angel's message, and wherever received destroys the love for the message. I was shown that Elder K was upon dangerous ground. He is not in union with the third angel. He once enjoyed the blessing of God, but does not now, for he has not prized and cherished the light of truth which has shone upon his pathway. He has brought along with him a theory of Methodist sanctification, and presents that in front, making it of the highest importance. And the sacred truths applicable to this time are by him made of little consequence. He has followed his own light, and been growing darker and darker, and going further and further from the truth, until it has but little influence upon him. Satan has controlled his mind, and he has done great injury to the cause of truth in northern Wisconsin.

It was this theory of sanctification which Sister G received of Elder K, and which she tried to follow out, that carried her into that dreadful fanaticism. Elder K has bewildered and confused many minds with this theory of sanctification. All who embrace it lose to a great extent their interest in and love for the third angel's message. This view of sanctification is a very pretty-looking theory. It whitewashes over poor souls who are in darkness, error, and pride. It gives them an appearance of being good Christians, and of possessing holiness, when their hearts are corrupt. It is a peace-and-safety-theory, which does not bring to light evil and reprove and rebuke wrong. It heals the hurt of the daughter of God's people slightly, crying: Peace, peace, when there is no peace. Men and women of corrupt hearts throw around them the garb of sanctification, and are looked upon as examples to the flock, when they are Satan's agents, used by him to allure and deceive honest souls into a bypath, that they may not feel the force and importance of the solemn truths proclaimed by the third angel.

Elder K has been looked up to as an example, while he has been an injury to the cause of God. His life has not been blameless. His ways have not been in accordance with the holy law of God, or with the spotless life of Christ. His corrupt nature is not subdued; and yet he dwells much upon sanctification, and thereby deceives many. I was directed to his past labors. He has failed to bring out souls into the truth, and to establish them upon the third angel's message. He presents a theory of sanctification as a matter of the utmost importance, while he makes of but little importance the channel through which God's blessing comes. "Sanctify them through Thy truth; Thy word is truth." The present truth, which is the channel, is not regarded, but is trampled underfoot. Men may cry, Holiness! holiness! sanctification! sanctification! consecration! consecration! and yet know no more by experience of what they talk than the sinner with his corrupt propensities. God will soon tear off this whitewashed garb of professed sanctification which some who are carnally minded have thrown around them to hide the deformity of the soul.

A faithful record is kept of the acts of the children of men. Nothing can be concealed from the eye of the high and holy One. Some take a course directly opposed to the law of God, and then, to cover up their sinful course, they profess to be consecrated to God. This profession of holiness does not make itself manifest in their daily lives. It does not have a tendency to elevate their minds, and lead them to "abstain from all appearance of evil." We are made a spectacle unto the world, to angels, and to men. Our faith is blasphemed in consequence of the crooked course of the carnally minded. They profess a part of the truth, which gives them influence, while they have no union with those who believe and are united upon the whole truth. What has been Elder K's influence? What have been the fruits of his labors? How many have been brought out and established upon present truth? How many has he brought into the unity of the faith? He has not gathered with Christ. His influence has been to scatter. There is a lack in his preaching, and his converts lack that which would prove their rock and defense in the day of God's anger. His preaching lacks the salt, the savor. He does not bring out souls thoroughly converted to the truth, separating them from the world, and uniting them with God's peculiar people. His converts have no anchor to hold them, and they drift here and there, until many of them are bewildered and lost in the world.

Elder K knows not of what spirit he is. He is uniting his influence with the dragon host to oppose those who keep the commandments of God, and who have the testimony of Jesus. He has a hard warfare before him. As far as the Sabbath is concerned, he occupies the same position as the Seventh Day Baptists. Separate the Sabbath from the messages, and it loses its power; but when connected with the message of the third angel, a power attends it which convicts unbelievers and infidels, and brings them out with strength to stand, to live, grow, and flourish in the Lord. It is time for God's people in Wisconsin to find their position. "Who will be on the Lord's side?" should be sounded by the faithful, experienced ones in every place. God requires them to come out and cut loose from the various influences which would separate them from one another and from the great platform of truth upon which God is bringing His people.

I was shown the case of Mr. L. He has much to say upon sanctification, but he is deceived in himself, and others are deceived in him. His sanctification may last him while he is in meeting, but it cannot bear the test. Bible holiness purifies the life, but L's heart is not cleansed. Evil exists in the heart, and is carried out in the life, and the enemies of our faith have had occasion to reproach Sabbathkeepers. They judge of the tree by its fruits.

2 Corinthians 4:2: "But have renounced the hidden things of dishonesty, not walking in craftiness, nor handling the

word of God deceitfully; but by manifestation of the truth commending ourselves to every man's conscience in the sight of God."

Many go directly contrary to the above scripture. They do walk in craftiness, and handle the word of God deceitfully. They do not exemplify the truth in their lives. They have special exercises upon sanctificaton, yet cast the word of God behind them. They pray sanctificaton, sing sanctification, and shout sanctification. Men with corrupt hearts put on the air of innocence, and profess to be consecrated, but this is no evidence that they are right. Their deeds testify of them. Their consciences are seared, but the day of God's visitation is coming, and every man's work shall be manifest, of what sort it is. And every man shall receive according to his deeds.

Said the angel, as he pointed to L: " What hast thou to do to declare My statutes, or that thou shouldest take My covenant in thy mouth? seeing thou hatest instruction, and castest My words behind thee. When thou sawest a thief, then thou consentedest with him, and hast been partaker with adulterers. Thou givest thy mouth to evil, and thy tongue frameth deceit." God will scatter and shake off these dividing influences, and will free His people, if those professing the whole truth will come up to the help of the Lord.

There is no Bible sanctification for those who cast a part of the truth behind them. There is light enough given in the word of God, so that none need err. The truth is so elevated as to be admired by the greatest minds, and yet it is so simple that the humblest, feeblest child of God can comprehend it, and be instructed by it. Those who see not the beauty that there is in the truth, who attach no importance to the third angel's message, will be without excuse; for the truth is plain.

2 Corinthians 4:3, 4: "But if our gospel be hid, it is hid to them that are lost: in whom the god of this world hath blinded the minds of them which believe not, lest the light

of the glorious gospel of Christ, who is the image of God, should shine unto them."

John 17:17, 19: "Sanctify them through Thy truth: Thy word is truth." "And for their sakes I sanctify Myself, that they also might be sanctified through the truth."

1 Peter 1:22: "Seeing ye have purified your souls in obeying the truth through the Spirit unto unfeigned love of the brethren, see that ye love one another with a pure heart fervently."

2 Corinthians 7:1: "Having therefore these promises, dearly beloved, let us cleanse ourselves from all filthiness of the flesh and spirit, perfecting holiness in the fear of God."

Philippians 2:12-15: "Wherefore, my beloved, as ye have always obeyed, not as in my presence only, but now much more in my absence, work out your own salvation with fear and trembling. For it is God which worketh in you both to will and to do of His good pleasure. Do all things without murmurings and disputings: that ye may be blameless and harmless, the sons of God, without rebuke, in the midst of a crooked and perverse nation, among whom ye shine as lights in the world."

John 15:3: "Now ye are clean through the word which I have spoken unto you."

Ephesians 5:25-27: "Husbands, love your wives, even as Christ also loved the church, and gave Himself for it; that He might sanctify and cleanse it with the washing of water by the word, that He might present it to Himself a glorious church, not having spot, or wrinkle, or any such thing; but that it should be holy and without blemish."

Here is Bible sanctification. It is not merely a show or outside work. It is sanctification received through the channel of truth. It is truth received in the heart, and practically carried out in the life.

Jesus, considered as a man, was perfect, yet He grew in grace. Luke 2:52: "And Jesus increased in wisdom and stature, and in favor with God and man." Even the most perfect Christian may increase continually in the knowledge and love of God.

2 Peter 3:14, 18: "Wherefore, beloved, seeing that ye look for such things, be diligent that ye may be found of Him in peace, without spot, and blameless." "But grow in grace, and in the knowledge of our Lord and Saviour Jesus Christ. To Him be glory both now and forever. Amen."

Sanctification is not the work of a moment, an hour, or a day. It is a continual growth in grace. We know not one day how strong will be our conflict the next. Satan lives, and is active, and every day we need to cry earnestly to God for help and strength to resist him. As long as Satan reigns we shall have self to subdue, besetments to overcome, and there is no stopping place, there is no point to which we can come and say we have fully attained.

Philippians 3:12: "Not as though I had already attained, either were already perfect: but I follow after, if that I may apprehend that for which also I am apprehended of Christ Jesus."

The Christian life is constantly an onward march. Jesus sits as a refiner and purifier of His people; and when His image is perfectly reflected in them, they are perfect and holy, and prepared for translation. A great work is required of the Christian. We are exhorted to cleanse ourselves from all filthiness of the flesh and spirit, perfecting holiness in the fear of God. Here we see where the great labor rests. There is a constant work for the Christian. Every branch in the parent vine must derive life and strength from that vine, in order to yield fruit.

THE POWER OF SATAN

Fallen man is Satan's lawful captive. The mission of Christ was to rescue him from the power of his great adversary. Man is naturally inclined to follow Satan's suggestions, and he cannot successfully resist so terrible a foe unless Christ, the mighty Conqueror, dwells in him, guiding his desires, and giving him strength. God alone can limit the power of Satan. He is going to and fro in the earth, and walking up and down in it. He is not off his watch for a single moment, through fear of losing an opportunity to destroy souls. It is important that God's people understand this, that they may escape his snares. Satan is preparing his deceptions, that in his last campaign against the people of God they may not understand that it is he. 2 Corinthians 11:14: "And no marvel; for Satan himself is transformed into an angel of light." While some deceived souls are advocating that he does not exist, he is taking them captive, and is working through them to a great extent. Satan knows better than God's people the power that they can have over him when their strength is in Christ. When they humbly entreat the mighty Conqueror for help, the weakest believer in the truth, relying firmly upon Christ, can successfully repulse Satan and all his host. He is too cunning to come openly, boldly, with his temptations, for then the drowsy energies of the Christian would arouse, and he would rely upon the strong and mighty Deliverer. But he comes in unperceived, and works in disguise through the children of disobedience who profess godliness.

Satan will go to the extent of his power to harass, tempt, and mislead God's people. He who dared to face, and tempt, and taunt our Lord, and who had power to take Him in his arms and carry Him to a pinnacle of the temple, and up into an exceedingly high mountain, will exercise his power to a wonderful degree upon the present generation, who are far inferior in wisdom to their Lord, and who are almost wholly ignorant of Satan's subtlety and strength. In a marvelous manner will he affect the bodies of those who are naturally inclined to do his bidding. Satan exults that he is regarded as a fiction. When he is made light of, and represented by some childish illustration, or as some animal, it suits him well. He is thought so inferior that the minds of men are wholly unprepared for his wisely laid plans, and he almost always succeeds well. If his power and subtlety were understood, many would be prepared to successfully resist him.

All should understand that Satan was once an exalted angel. His rebellion shut him out of heaven, but did not destroy his powers and make him a beast. Since his fall he has turned his mighty strength against the government of heaven. He has been growing more artful, and has learned the most successful manner in which to come to the children of men with his temptations.

Satan has originated fables with which to deceive. He commenced in heaven to war against the foundation of God's government, and since his fall he has carried on his rebellion against the law of God, and has brought the mass of professed Christians to trample under their feet the fourth commandment, which brings to view the living God. He has torn down the original Sabbath of the Decalogue, and substituted in its place one of the laboring days of the week.

The great original lie which he told to Eve in Eden, "Ye shall not surely die," was the first sermon ever preached on the immortality of the soul. That sermon was crowned with success, and terrible results followed. He has brought minds to receive that sermon as truth, and ministers preach it, sing it, and pray it.

No literal devil, and probation after the coming of Christ, are fast becoming popular fables. The Scriptures plainly declare that every person's destiny is forever fixed at the coming of the Lord. Revelation 22:11, 12: "He that is unjust, let him be unjust still; and he which is filthy, let him be filthy still: and he that is righteous, let him be righteous still; and he that is holy, let him be holy still. And, behold, I come quickly; and My reward is with Me, to give every man according as his work shall be."

Satan has taken advantage of these popular fables to hide himself. He comes to poor, deceived mortals through modern spiritualism, which places no bounds to the carnally minded, and, if carried out, separates families, creates jealousy and hatred, and gives liberty to the most degrading propensities. The world knows but little as yet of the corrupting influence of spiritualism. The curtain was lifted, and much of its dreadful work was revealed to me. I was shown some who have had an experience in spiritualism, and have since renounced it, who shudder as they reflect upon how near they came to utter ruin. They had lost control of themselves, and Satan made them do that which they detested. But even they have but a faint idea of spiritualism as it is. Ministers inspired of Satan can eloquently dress up this hideous monster, hide its deformity, and make it appear beautiful to many. But it comes so direct from his satanic majesty, that he claims the right to control all who have to do with it, for they have ventured upon forbidden ground, and have forfeited the protection of their Maker.

Some poor souls who have been fascinated with the eloquent words of the teachers of spiritualism, and have yielded to its influence, afterward find out its deadly character, and would renounce and flee from it, but cannot. Satan holds them by his power, and is not willing to let them go free. He knows that they are surely his while he has them under his special control, but that if they once free themselves from his power, he can never bring them again to believe in spiritualism, and to place themselves so directly under his control. The only way for such poor souls to overcome

Satan, is to discern between pure Bible truth and fables. As they acknowledge the claims of truth, they place themselves where they can be helped. They should entreat those who have had a religious experience and who have faith in the promises of God, to plead with the mighty Deliverer in their behalf. It will be a close conflict. Satan will reinforce his evil angels who have controlled these persons; but if the saints of God with deep humility fast and pray, their prayers will prevail. Jesus will commission holy angels to resist Satan, and he will be driven back and his power broken from off the afflicted ones. Mark 9:29: "And He said unto them, This kind can come forth by nothing, but by prayer and fasting."

The popular ministry cannot successfully resist spiritualism. They have nothing wherewith to shield their flocks from its baleful influence. Much of the sad result of spiritualism will rest upon ministers of this age; for they have trampled the truth under their feet, and in its stead have preferred fables. The sermon which Satan preached to Eve upon the immortality of the soul—"Ye shall not surely die"—they have reiterated from the pulpit; and the people receive it as pure Bible truth. It is the foundation of spiritualism. The word of God nowhere teaches that the soul of man is immortal. Immortality is an attribute of God only. 1 Timothy 6:16: "Who only hath immortality, dwelling in the light which no man can approach unto; whom no man hath seen, nor can see: to whom be honor and power everlasting. Amen."

God's word, rightly understood and applied, is a safeguard against spiritualism. An eternally burning hell preached from the pulpit, and kept before the people, does injustice to the benevolent character of God. It presents Him as the veriest tyrant in the universe. This widespread dogma has turned thousands to universalism, infidelity, and atheism. The word of God is plain. It is a straight chain of truth, and will prove an anchor to those who are willing to receive it, even if they have to sacrifice their cherished fables. It will save them from the terrible delusions of these perilous times. Satan has led the minds of the ministers of different churches to cling tenaciously to their popular errors, as he led the Jews in their blindness to cling to their sacrifices, and crucify Christ. The rejection of light and truth leaves men captives, the subjects of Satan's deception. The greater the light they reject, the greater will be the power of deception and darkness which will come upon them.

I was shown that God's true people are the salt of the earth and the light of the world. God requires of them continual advancement in the knowledge of the truth, and in the way of holiness. Then will they understand the coming in of Satan, and in the strength of Jesus will resist him. Satan will call to his aid legions of his angels to oppose the advance of even one soul, and, if possible, wrest it from the hand of Christ.

I saw evil angels contending for souls, and angels of God resisting them. The conflict was severe. Evil angels were corrupting the atmosphere with their poisonous influence, and crowding about these souls to stupefy their sensibilities. Holy angels were anxiously watching and waiting to drive back Satan's host. But it is not the work of good angels to control the minds of men against their will. If they yield to the enemy, and make no effort to resist him, then the angels of God can do but little more than hold in check the host of Satan, that they shall not destroy, until further light be given to those in peril, to move them to arouse and look to heaven for help. Jesus will not commission holy angels to extricate those who make no effort to help themselves.

If Satan sees that he is in danger of losing one soul, he will exert himself to the utmost to keep that one. And when the individual is aroused to his danger, and, with distress and fervor, looks to Jesus for strength, Satan fears that he will lose a captive, and he calls a reinforcement of his angels to hedge in the poor soul, and form a wall of darkness around him, that heaven's light may not reach him. But if the one in danger perseveres, and in his helplessness casts himself upon the merits of the blood of Christ, our Savior listens to the earnest prayer of faith, and sends a reinforcement of those angels that excel in strength to deliver him. Satan cannot endure to have his powerful rival appealed to, for he fears and trembles before His strength and majesty. At the sound of fervent prayer, Satan's whole host trembles. He continues to call legions of evil angels to accomplish his object. And when angels, all-powerful, clothed with the armory of heaven, come to the help of the fainting, pursued soul, Satan and his host fall back, well knowing that their battle is lost. The willing subjects of Satan are faithful, active, and united in one object. And although they hate and war with one another, yet they improve every opportunity to advance their common interest. But the great Commander in heaven and earth has limited Satan's power.

My experience has been singular, and for years I have suffered peculiar trials of mind. The condition of God's people, and my connection with the work of God have often brought upon me a weight of sadness and discouragement which cannot be expressed. For years I have looked to the grave as a sweet resting place. In my last vision I inquired of my attending angel why I was left to suffer such perplexity of mind, and was so often thrown upon Satan's battle ground. I entreated that if I must be so closely connected with the cause of truth, I might be delivered from these severe trials. There is power and strength with the angels of God, and I pleaded that I might be shielded.

Then our past life was presented before me, and I was shown that Satan had sought in various ways to destroy our usefulness; that many times he had laid his plans to remove us from the work of God; he had come in different ways, and through different agencies, to accomplish his purposes; but through the ministration of holy angels he had been defeated. I saw that in our journeying from place to place, he had frequently placed his evil angels in our path to cause accident which would destroy our lives; but holy angels were sent upon the ground to deliver. Several accidents have placed my husband and myself in great peril, and our preservation has been wonderful. I saw that we had been the special objects of Satan's attacks, because of our interest in and connection with the work of God. As I saw the great care which God has every moment for those who love and fear Him, I was inspired with confidence and trust in God, and felt reproved for my lack of faith.

THE TWO CROWNS

In the vision given me at Battle Creek, Michigan, October 25, 1861, I was shown this earth, dark and gloomy. Said the angel: "Look carefully!" Then I was shown the people upon the earth. Some were surrounded by angels of God, others were in total darkness, surrounded by evil angels. I saw an arm reached down from heaven, holding a golden scepter. On the top of the scepter was a crown studded with diamonds. Every diamond emitted light, bright, clear, and beautiful. Inscribed upon the crown were these words: "All who win me are happy, and shall have everlasting life."

Below this crown was another scepter, and upon this also was placed a crown, in the center of which were jewels, gold, and silver, reflecting some light. The inscription upon the crown was: "Earthly treasure. Riches is power. All who win me have honor and fame." I saw a vast multitude rushing forward to obtain this crown. They were clamorous. Some in their eagerness seemed bereft of reason. They would thrust one another, crowding back those who were weaker than they, and trampling upon those who in their haste fell. Many eagerly seized hold of the treasures within the crown, and held them fast. The heads of some were as white as silver, and their faces were furrowed with care and anxiety. Their own relatives, bone of their bone, and flesh of their flesh, they regarded not; but, as appealing looks were turned to them, they held their treasures more firmly, as though fearful that in an unguarded moment they should lose a little, or be induced to divide with them. Their eager eyes would often fasten upon the earthly crown, and count and recount its treasures. Images of want and wretchedness appeared in that multitude, and looked wishfully at the treasures there, and turned hopelessly away as the stronger overpowered and drove back the weaker. Yet they could not give it up thus, but with a multitude of deformed, sickly, and aged, they sought to press their way to the earthly crown. Some died in seeking to reach it. Others fell just in the act of taking hold of it. Many had but just laid hold of it when they fell. Dead bodies strewed the ground, yet on rushed the multitude, trampling over the fallen and dead bodies of their companions. Everyone who reached the crown possessed a share in it, and was loudly applauded by an interested company standing around it.

A large company of evil angels were very busy. Satan was in the midst of them, and all looked with the most exulting satisfaction upon the company struggling for the crown. He seemed to throw a peculiar charm upon those who eagerly sought it. Many who sought this earthly crown were professed Christians. Some of them seemed to have a little light. They would look wishfully upon the heavenly crown, and would often seem charmed with its beauty, yet they had no true sense of its value and glory. While with one hand they were reaching forth languidly for the heavenly, with the other they reached eagerly for the earthly, determined to possess that; and in their earnest pursuit for the earthly, they lost sight of the heavenly. They were left in darkness, yet were anxiously groping about to secure the earthly crown. Some became disgusted with the company who sought it so eagerly; they seemed to have a sense of their danger, and turned from it, and earnestly sought for the heavenly crown. The countenances of such soon changed from dark to light, from gloom to cheerfulness and holy joy.

I then saw a company pressing through the crowd with their eyes intently fixed upon the heavenly crown. As they earnestly urged their way through the disorderly crowd, angels attended them, and made room for them to advance. As they neared the heavenly crown, the light emanating from it shone upon them and around them, dispelling their darkness, and growing clearer and brighter, until they seemed to be transformed, and resembled the angels. They cast not one lingering look upon the earthly crown. Those who were in pursuit of the earthly, mocked them, and threw black balls after them. These did them no injury while their eyes were fixed upon the heavenly crown, but those who turned their attention to the black balls were stained with them. The following scripture was presented before me:

Matthew 6:19-24: "Lay not up for yourselves treasures upon earth, where moth and rust doth corrupt, and where thieves break through and steal: but lay up for yourselves treasures in heaven, where neither moth nor rust doth corrupt, and where thieves do not break through nor steal: for where your treasure is, there will your heart be also. The light of the body is the eye; if therefore thine eye be single, thy whole body shall be full of light. But if thine eye be evil, thy whole body shall be full of darkness. If therefore the light that is in thee be darkness, how great is that darkness! No man can serve two masters: for either he will hate the one, and love the other; or else he will hold to the one, and despise the other. Ye cannot serve God and mammon."

Then that which I had seen was explained to me as follows: The multitude who were so eagerly striving for the earthly crown, were those who love this world's treasure, and are deceived and flattered with its short-lived attractions. Some, I saw, who profess to be the followers of Jesus, are so ambitious to obtain earthly treasures that they lose their love for heaven, act like the world, and are accounted of God as of the world. They profess to be seeking an immortal crown, a treasure in the heavens; but their interest and principal study is to acquire earthly treasures. Those who have their treasures in this world, and love their riches, cannot love Jesus. They may think that they are right, and, although they cling to their possessions with a miser's grasp, they cannot be made to see it, or to feel that they love money more than the cause of truth or the heavenly treasure.

"If therefore the light that is in thee be darkness, how great is that darkness!" There was a point of time in the experience of such, when the light given them was not cherished, and it became darkness. Said the angel: "Ye cannot love and worship the treasures of earth, and have the true riches." When the young man came to Jesus and said to Him, "Good Master, what good thing shall I do, that I may have eternal life?" Jesus gave him his choice, to part with his possessions and have eternal life, or retain them and lose it. His riches were of greater value to him than the heavenly treasure. The condition that he must part with his treasures and give to the poor in order to become a follower of Christ and have eternal life, chilled his desire; and he went away sorrowful.

Those who were shown me as clamorous for the earthly crown, were those who will resort to any means to acquire property. They become insane upon that point. All their thoughts and energies are directed to the acquirement of earthly riches. They trample upon the rights of others, and oppress the poor, and the hireling in his wages. If they can take advantage of those who are poorer and less shrewd than they, and thus manage to increase their riches, they will not hesitate a moment to oppress them, and even see them brought to beggary.

The men whose heads were white with age, and whose faces were furrowed with care, yet who were eagerly grasping the treasures within the crown, were the aged, who have but a few years before them. Yet they were eager to secure their earthly treasures. The nearer they came to the grave, the more anxious they were to cling to them. Their own relatives were not benefited. The members of their own families were permitted to labor beyond their strength to save a little money. They did not use it for others' good, or for their own. It was enough for them to know that they had it. When their duty to relieve the wants of the poor, and to sustain God's cause are presented before them, they are sorrowful. They would gladly accept the gift of everlasting life, but are not willing that it should cost them anything. The conditions are too hard. But Abraham would not withhold his only son. In obedience to God he could sacrifice this child of promise more easily than many would sacrifice some of their earthly possessions.

It was painful to see those who should have been ripening for glory, and daily fitting for immortality, exerting all their strength to keep their earthly treasures. Such, I saw, could not value the heavenly treasure. Their strong affections for the earthly cause them to show by their works that they do not esteem the heavenly inheritance enough to make any sacrifice for it. The "young man" manifested a willingness to keep the commandments, yet our Lord told him that he lacked one thing. He desired eternal life, but loved his possessions more. Many are self-deceived. They have not sought for truth as for hid treasures. Their powers are not put to the best account. Their minds, which might be illuminated with heaven's light, are perplexed and troubled. "The cares of this world, and the deceitfulness of riches, and the lusts of other things entering in, choke the word, and it becometh unfruitful." "Such," said the angel, "are without excuse." I saw the light waning away from them. They did not desire to understand the solemn, important truths for this time, and thought they were well off without understanding them. Their light went out, and they were groping in darkness.

The multitude of deformed and sickly pressing for the earthly crown are those whose interests and treasures are in this world. Although they are disappointed on every side, they will not place their affections on heaven, and secure to themselves a treasure and home there. They fail of the earthly, yet while in pursuit of it, lose the heavenly. Notwithstanding the disappointment and unhappy life and death of those who were wholly bent upon obtaining earthly riches, others follow the same course. They rush madly on, disregarding the miserable end of those whose example they are following.

Those who reached the crown, and possessed a share in it, and were applauded, are those who obtain that which is the whole aim of their life—riches. They receive that honor which the world bestows upon those who are rich. They have influence in the world. Satan and his evil angels are satisfied. They know that such are surely theirs, that while they are living in rebellion against God, they are Satan's powerful agents.

The ones who became disgusted with the company clamoring for the earthly crown are those who have marked the life and end of all who strive for earthly riches. They see that such are never satisfied, but are unhappy, and they become alarmed, and separate themselves from that unhappy class, and seek the true and durable riches.

Those who are urging their way through the crowd for the heavenly crown, attended by holy angels, were shown me to be God's faithful people. Angels lead them on, and they are inspired with zeal to press forward for the heavenly treasure.

The black balls which were thrown after the saints were the reproachful falsehoods put in circulation concerning God's people by those who love and make a lie. We should take the greatest care to live a blameless life, and abstain from all appearance of evil, and then it is our duty to move boldly forward, and pay no regard to the reproachful falsehoods of the wicked. While the eyes of the righteous are fixed upon the heavenly priceless treasure, they will become more and more like Christ, and thus they will be transformed and fitted for translation.

THE FUTURE

At the transfiguration, Jesus was glorified by His Father. We hear Him say: "Now is the Son of man glorified, and God is glorified in Him." Thus before His betrayal and crucifixion He was strengthened for His last dreadful sufferings. As the members of the body of Christ approach the period of their last conflict, "the time of Jacob's trouble," they will grow up into Christ, and will partake largely of His spirit. As the third message swells to a loud cry, and as great power and glory attend the closing work, the faithful people of God will partake of that glory. It is the latter rain which revives and strengthens them to pass through the time of trouble. Their faces will shine with the glory of that light which attends the third angel.

I saw that God will in a wonderful manner preserve His people through the time of trouble. As Jesus poured out His soul in agony in the garden, they will earnestly cry and agonize day and night for deliverance. The decree will go forth that they must disregard the Sabbath of the fourth commandment, and honor the first day, or lose their lives; but they will not yield, and trample under their feet the Sabbath of the Lord, and honor an institution of papacy. Satan's host and wicked men will surround them, and exult over them, because there will seem to be no way of escape for them. But in the midst of their revelry and triumph, there is heard peal upon peal of the loudest thunder. The heavens have gathered blackness, and are only illuminated by the blazing light and terrible glory from heaven, as God utters His voice from His holy habitation.

The foundations of the earth shake; buildings totter and fall with a terrible crash. The sea boils like a pot, and the whole earth is in terrible commotion. The captivity of the righteous is turned, and with sweet and solemn whisperings they say to one another: "We are delivered. It is the voice of God." With solemn awe they listen to the words of the voice. The wicked hear, but understand not the words of the voice of God. They fear and tremble, while the saints rejoice. Satan and his angels, and wicked men, who had been exulting that the people of God were in their power, that they might destroy them from off the earth, witness the glory conferred upon those who have honored the holy law of God. They behold the faces of the righteous lighted up and reflecting the image of Jesus. Those who were so eager to destroy the saints cannot endure the glory resting upon the delivered ones, and they fall like dead men to the earth. Satan and evil angels flee from the presence of the saints glorified. Their power to annoy them is gone forever.

NUMBER NINE

TESTIMONY FOR THE CHURCH

THE REBELLION*

The dreadful state of our nation calls for deep humility on the part of God's people. The one all-important inquiry which should now engross the mind of everyone is: Am I prepared for the day of God? Can I stand the trying test before me?

I saw that God is purifying and proving His people. He will refine them as gold, until the dross is consumed and His image is reflected in them. All have not that spirit of self-denial and that willingness to endure hardness and to suffer for the truth's sake, which God requires. Their wills are not subdued, they have not consecrated themselves wholly to God, seeking no greater pleasure than to do His will. Ministers and people lack spirituality and true godliness. Everything is to be shaken that can be shaken. God's people will be brought into most trying positions, and all must be settled, rooted, and grounded in the truth, or their steps will surely slide. If God comforts and nourishes the soul with His inspiring presence, they can endure, though the way may be dark and thorny. For the darkness will soon pass away, and the true light shine forever. I was pointed to Isaiah 58; 59:1-15; Jeremiah 14:10-12, as a description of the present state of our nation. The people of this nation have forsaken and forgotten God. They have chosen other gods and fol-

---

*See Appendix.

lowed their own corrupt ways until God has turned from them. The inhabitants of the earth have trampled upon the law of God and broken His everlasting covenant.

I was shown the excitement created among our people by the article in the *Review* headed, "The Nation." Some understood it one way, and some another. The plain statements were distorted, and made to mean what the writer did not intend. He gave the best light that he then had. It was necessary that something be said. The attention of many was turned to Sabbathkeepers because they manifested no greater interest in the war and did not volunteer. In some places they were looked upon as sympathizing with the Rebellion. The time had come for our true sentiments in relation to slavery and the Rebellion to be made known. There was need of moving with wisdom to turn away the suspicions excited against Sabbathkeepers. We should act with great caution. "If it be possible, as much as lieth in you, live peaceably with all men." We can obey this admonition, and not sacrifice one principle of our faith. Satan and his host are at war with commandment keepers, and will work to bring them into trying positions. They should not by lack of discretion bring themselves there.

I was shown that some moved very indiscreetly in regard to the article mentioned. It did not in all respects accord with their views, and instead of calmly weighing the matter, and viewing it in all its bearings, they became agitated, excited, and some seized the pen and jumped hastily at conclusions which would not bear investigation. Some were inconsistent and unreasonable. They did that which Satan is ever hurrying them to do, namely, acted out their own rebellious feelings.

In Iowa they carried things to quite a length, and ran into fanaticism. They mistook zeal and fanaticism for conscientiousness. Instead of being guided by reason and sound judgment, they allowed their feelings to take the lead. They were ready to become martyrs for their faith. Did all this feeling lead them to God? to greater humility before Him? Did it lead them to trust in His power to deliver them from the trying position into which they might be brought? Oh, no! Instead of making their petitions to the God of heaven and relying solely upon His power, they petitioned the legislature and were refused. They showed their weakness and exposed their lack of faith. All this only served to bring that peculiar class, Sabbathkeepers, into special notice, and expose them to be crowded into difficult places by those who have no sympathy for them.

Some have been holding themselves ready to find fault and complain at any suggestion made. But few have had wisdom in this most trying time to think without prejudice and candidly tell what shall be done. I saw that those who have been forward to talk so decidedly about refusing to obey a draft do not understand what they are talking about. Should they really be drafted and, refusing to obey, be threatened with imprisonment, torture, or death, they would shrink and then find that they had not prepared themselves for such an emergency. They would not endure the trial of their faith. What they thought to be faith was only fanatical presumption.

Those who would be best prepared to sacrifice even life, if required, rather than place themselves in a position where they could not obey God, would have the least to say. They would make no boast. They would feel deeply and meditate much, and their earnest prayers would go up to heaven for wisdom to act and grace to endure. Those who feel that in the fear of God they cannot conscientiously engage in this war will be very quiet, and when interrogated will simply state what they are obliged to say in order to answer the inquirer, and then let it be understood that they have no sympathy with the Rebellion.

There are a few in the ranks of Sabbathkeepers who sympathize with the slaveholder. When they embraced the truth, they did not leave behind them all the errors they should have left. They need a more thorough draft from the cleansing fountain of truth. Some have brought along with them their old political prejudices, which are not in harmony with the principles of the truth. They maintain that the slave is the property of the master, and should not be taken from him. They rank these slaves as cattle and say that it is wronging the owner just as much to deprive him of his slaves as to take away his cattle. I was shown that it mattered not how much the master had paid for human flesh and the souls of men; God gives him no title to human souls, and he has no right to hold them as his property. Christ died for the whole human family, whether white or black. God has made man a free moral agent, whether white or black. The institution of slavery does away with this and permits man to exercise over his fellow man a power which God has never granted him, and which belongs alone to God. The slave master has dared assume the responsibility of God over his slave, and accordingly he will be accountable for the sins, ignorance, and vice of the slave. He will be called to an account for the power which he exercises over the slave. The colored race are God's property. Their Maker alone is their master, and those who have dared chain down the body and the soul of the slave, to keep him in degradation like the brutes, will have their retribution. The wrath of God has slumbered, but it will awake and be poured out without mixture of mercy.

Some have been so indiscreet as to talk out their proslavery principles—principles which are not heaven-born, but proceed from the dominion of Satan. These restless spirits talk and act in a manner to bring a reproach upon the cause of God. I will here give a copy of a letter written to Brother A, of Oswego County, New York:

"I was shown some things in regard to you. I saw that you were deceived in regard to yourself. You have given occasion for the enemies of our faith to blaspheme, and to reproach Sabbathkeepers. By your indiscreet course, you have closed the ears of some who would have listened to the truth. I saw that we should be as wise as serpents and as harmless as doves. You have manifested neither the wisdom of the serpent nor the harmlessness of the dove.

"Satan was the first great leader in rebellion. God is punishing the North, that they have so long suffered the accursed sin of slavery to exist; for in the sight of heaven it is a sin of the darkest dye. God is not with the South, and He will punish them dreadfully in the end. Satan is the instigator of all rebellion. I saw that you, Brother A, have permitted your political principles to destroy your judgment and your love for the truth. They are eating out true godliness from your heart. You have never looked upon slavery in the right light, and your views of this matter have thrown you on the side of the Rebellion, which was stirred up by Satan and his host. Your views of slavery cannot harmonize with the sacred, important truths for this time. You must yield your views or the truth. Both cannot be cherished in the same heart, for they are at war with each other.

"Satan has been stirring you up. He would not let you rest until you should express your sentiments upon the side of the powers of darkness, thus strengthening the hands of the wicked, whom God has cursed. You have cast your influence on the wrong side, with those whose course of life is to sow thorns and plant misery for others. I saw you casting your influence with a degraded company, a Godforsaken company; and angels of God fled from you in disgust. I saw that you were utterly deceived. Had you followed the light which God has given you, had you heeded the instructions of your brethren, had you listened to their advice, you would have saved yourself and saved the precious cause of truth from reproach. But notwithstanding all the light given, you have given publicity to your sentiments. Unless you undo what you have done, it will be the duty of God's people to publicly withdraw their sympathy and fellowship from you, in order to save the impression which must go out in regard to us as a people. We must let it be known that we have no such ones in our fellowship, that we will not walk with them in church capacity.

"You have lost the sanctifying influence of the truth. You have lost your connection with the heavenly host. You have allied yourself with the first great rebel, and God's wrath is upon you; for His sacred cause is reproached, and the truth is made disgusting to unbelievers. You have grieved God's people, and despised the counsel of His ambassadors upon earth, who labor together with Him, and are in Christ's stead beseeching souls to be reconciled to God.

"I was shown that as a people we cannot be too careful what influence we exert; we should watch every word. When we by word or act place ourselves upon the enemy's battle ground, we drive holy angels from us, and encourage and attract evil angels in crowds around us. This you have done, Brother A, and by your unguarded, willful course have caused unbelievers to look upon Sabbathkeepers all around you with suspicion. These words were presented before me as referring to the servants of God: 'He that heareth you heareth Me, and he that despiseth you despiseth Me; and he that despiseth Me despiseth Him that sent Me.' May God help you, my deceived brother, to see yourself as you are, and to have your sympathies with the body."

Our kingdom is not of this world. We are waiting for our Lord from heaven to come to earth to put down all authority and power, and set up His everlasting kingdom.

Earthly powers are shaken. We need not, and cannot, expect union among the nations of the earth. Our position in the image of Nebuchadnezzar is represented by the toes, in a divided state, and of a crumbling material, that will not hold together. Prophecy shows us that the great day of God is right upon us. It hasteth greatly.

I saw that it is our duty in every case to obey the laws of our land, unless they conflict with the higher law which God spoke with an audible voice from Sinai, and afterward engraved on stone with His own finger. "I will put My laws into their mind, and write them in their hearts: and I will be to them a God, and they shall be to Me a people." He who has God's law written in the heart will obey God rather than men, and will sooner disobey all men than deviate in the least from the commandment of God. God's people, taught by the inspiration of truth, and led by a good conscience to live by every word of God, will take His law, written in their hearts, as the only authority which they can acknowledge or consent to obey. The wisdom and authority of the divine law are supreme.

I was shown that God's people, who are His peculiar treasure, cannot engage in this perplexing war, for it is opposed to every principle of their faith. In the army they cannot obey the truth and at the same time obey the requirements of their officers. There would be a continual violation of conscience. Worldly men are governed by worldly principles. They can appreciate no other. Worldly policy and public opinion comprise the principle of action that governs them and leads them to practice the form of rightdoing. But God's people cannot be governed by these motives. The words and commands of God, written in the soul, are spirit and life, and there is power in them to bring into subjection and enforce obedience. The ten precepts of Jehovah are the foundation of all righteous and good laws. Those who love God's commandments will conform to every good law of the land. But if the requirements of the rulers are such as conflict with the laws of God, the only question to be settled is: Shall we obey God, or man?

In consequence of long-continued and progressive rebellion against the higher constitution and laws, a gloomy pall of darkness and death is spread over the earth. The earth groans under the burden of accumulated guilt, and everywhere dying mortals are compelled to experience the wretchedness included in the wages of unrighteousness. I was shown that men have carried out the purposes of Satan by craft and deceit, and a dreadful blow has recently been given. It can be truly said: "Justice standeth afar off: for truth is fallen in the street, and equity cannot enter," "and he that departeth from evil maketh himself a prey." In some of the free states the standard of morality is sinking lower and lower. Men with depraved appetites and corrupt lives have now an opportunity to triumph. They have chosen for their rulers those whose principles are debasing, who would not check evil, or repress the depraved appetites of men, but let them have full sway. If those who choose to become like the beasts, by drinking liquid poison, were the only sufferers; if they alone would reap the fruit of their own doings, then the evil would not be so great. But many, very many, must pass through incredible suffering on account of others' sins. Wives and children, although innocent, must drain the bitter cup to its dregs.

Without the grace of God, men love to do evil. They walk in darkness, and do not possess the power of self-control. They give loose rein to their passions and appetites until all the finer feelings are lost and only the animal passions are manifested. Such men need to feel a higher, controlling power, which will constrain them to obey. If rulers do not exercise a power to terrify the evildoer, he will sink to the level of the brute. The earth is growing more and more corrupt.

Many were blinded and grossly deceived in the last election, and their influence was used to place in authority men who would wink at evil, men who would witness a flood of woe and misery unmoved, whose principles are corrupt, who are Southern sympathizers, and would preserve slavery as it is.

In positions of trust in the Northern army there are men who are rebels at heart, who value the life of a soldier no more than they would the life of a dog. They can see them torn, and mangled, and dying, by thousands, unmoved. The officers of the Southern army are constantly receiving information in regard to the plans of the Northern army. Correct information has been given to Northern officers in regard to the movements and approach of rebels, which has been disregarded and despised because the informer was black. And by neglecting to prepare for an attack, the Union forces have been surprised and nearly cut to pieces, or what is as bad, many of the poor soldiers have been taken prisoners to suffer worse than death.

If there were union in the Northern army, this Rebellion would soon cease. Rebels know they have sympathizers all through the Northern army. The pages of history are growing darker and still darker. Loyal men, who have had no sympathy with the Rebellion, or with slavery which has caused it, have been imposed upon. Their influence has helped place in authority men to whose principles they were opposed.

Everything is preparing for the great day of God. Time will last a little longer until the inhabitants of the earth have filled up the cup of their iniquity, and then the wrath of God which has so long slumbered, will awake, and this land of light will drink the cup of His unmingled wrath. The desolating power of God is upon the earth to rend and destroy. The inhabitants of the earth are appointed to the sword, to famine, and to pestilence.

Very many men in authority, generals and officers, act in

conformity with instructions communicated by spirits. The spirits of devils, professing to be dead warriors and skillful generals, communicate with men in authority and control many of their movements. One general has directions from these spirits to make special moves and is flattered with the hope of success. Another receives directions which differ widely from those given to the first. Sometimes those who follow the directions given obtain a victory, but more frequently they meet with defeat.

The spirits sometimes give these leading men an account of events to transpire in battles in which they are about to engage, and of individuals who will fall in the battle. Sometimes it is found to be as these spirits foretold, and this strengthens the faith of the believers in spiritual manifestations. And again it is found that correct information has not been given, but the deceiving spirits make some explanation, which is received. The deception upon minds is so great that many fail to perceive the lying spirits which are leading them on to certain destruction.

The great leading rebel general, Satan, is acquainted with the transactions of this war, and he directs his angels to assume the form of dead generals, to imitate their manners, and exhibit their peculiar traits of character. And leaders in the army really believe that the spirits of their friends and of dead warriors, the fathers of the Revolutionary War, are guiding them. If they were not under the strongest fascinating deception, they would begin to think that the warriors in heaven (?) did not manifest good and successful generalship, or had forgotten their famed earthly skill.

Instead of the leading men in this war trusting in the God of Israel, and directing their armies to trust in the only One who can deliver them from their enemies, the majority inquire of the prince of devils and trust in him. Deuteronomy 32:16-22. Said the angel: "How can God prosper such a people? If they would look to and trust in Him; if they would only come where He could help them, according to His own glory, He would readily do it."

I saw that God would not give the Northern army wholly into the hands of a rebellious people, to be utterly destroyed by their enemies. I was referred to Deuteronomy 32:26-30: "I said, I would scatter them into corners, I would make the remembrance of them to cease from among men: were it not that I feared the wrath of the enemy, lest their adversaries should behave themselves strangely, and lest they should say, Our hand is high, and the Lord hath not done all this. For they are a nation void of counsel, neither is there any understanding in them. Oh, that they were wise, that they understood this, that they would consider their latter end! How should one chase a thousand, and two put ten thousand to flight, except their Rock had sold them, and the Lord had shut them up?"

There are generals in the army who are wholly devoted and seek to do all they can to stop this dreadful Rebellion and unnatural war. But most of the officers and leading men have a selfish purpose of their own to serve. Each is looking for gain from his own quarter, and many of the true, wholehearted soldiers are becoming fainthearted and discouraged. They nobly perform their part when in an engagement with the enemy, but the treatment which they receive from their own officers is brutal. Among the soldiers there are men that have fine feelings and independence of spirit. They have never been accustomed to mingling with so degraded a class of men as war brings together, and being tyrannized over and abused, and treated like brutes. It is very hard for them to endure all this. Many officers have brutal passions, and as they are placed in authority they have good opportunity to act out their brutal natures. They tyrannize over those under them as Southern masters tyrannize over their slaves.

These things will make it difficult to procure men for the army.

In some cases when generals have been in most terrible conflict, where their men have fallen like rain, a reinforcement at the right time would have given them a victory. But other generals cared nothing how many lives were lost, and rather than come to the help of those in an engagement, as though their interests were one, they withheld the necessary aid, fearing that their brother general would receive the honor of successfully repulsing the enemy. Through envy and jealousy they have even exulted to see the enemy gain the victory and repulse Union men. Southern men possess a hellish spirit in this Rebellion, but Northern men are not clear. Many of them possess a selfish jealousy, fearing that others will obtain honors and be exalted above themselves. Oh, how many thousands of lives have been sacrificed on this account! Those of other nations who have conducted war have had but one interest. With a disinterested zeal they have moved on to conquer or to die. Leading men in the Revolution acted unitedly, with zeal, and by that means they gained their independence. But men now act like demons instead of human beings.

Satan has, through his angels, communicated with officers who were cool, calculating men when left to themselves, and they have given up their own judgment and have been led by these lying spirits into very difficult places, where they have been repulsed with dreadful slaughter. It suits his satanic majesty well to see slaughter and carnage upon the earth. He loves to see the poor soldiers mowed down like grass. I saw that the rebels have often been in positions where they could have been subdued without much effort; but the communications from spirits have led the Northern generals and blinded their eyes until the rebels were beyond their reach. And some generals would rather allow the rebels to escape than to subdue them. They think more of the darling institution of slavery than of the prosperity of the nation. These are among the reasons why the war is so protracted.

Information sent by our generals to Washington concerning the movement of our armies might nearly as well be telegraphed directly to the rebel forces. There are rebel sympathizers right at the heart of the Union authorities. This war is unlike any other. The great lack of union of feeling and action makes it look dark and discouraging. Many of the soldiers have thrown off restraint and have sunk to an alarming state of degradation. How can God go forth with such a corrupt army? How can He, according to His honor, defeat their enemies and lead them on to victory? There is discord, and strife for honor, while the poor soldiers are dying by thousands on the battlefield or from their wounds and from exposure and hardships.

This war is a most singular and at the same time a most horrible and heartsickening conflict. Other nations are looking on with disgust at the transactions of the armies of both North and South. They see such a determined effort to protract the war at an enormous sacrifice of life and money, while at the same time nothing is really gained, that it looks to them like a strife to see which can kill the most men. They are indignant.

I saw that the Rebellion had been steadily increasing and that it had never been more determined than at the present moment. Many professed Union men, holding important positions, are disloyal at heart. Their only object in taking up arms was to preserve the Union as it was, and slavery with it. They would heartily chain down the slave to his life of galling bondage, had they the privilege. Such have a strong degree of sympathy with the South. Blood has been poured out like water, and for nought. In every town and village there is mourning. Wives are mourning for their husbands, mothers for their sons, and sisters for their brothers. But notwithstanding all this suffering, they do not turn to God.

I saw that both the South and the North were being punished. In regard to the South, I was referred to Deuteronomy 32:35-37: "To Me belongeth vengeance, and recompense; their foot shall slide in due time: for the day of their calamity is at hand, and the things that shall come upon them make haste. For the Lord shall judge His people, and repent Himself for His servants, when He seeth that their power is gone, and there is none shut up, or left. And He shall say, Where are their gods, their rock in whom they trusted?"

DANGERS AND DUTY OF MINISTERS

I have been shown that more can now be accomplished by laboring in places where a few have been raised up, than in entirely new fields, unless the opening is very good. A few in different towns who really believe the truth will exert an influence and excite inquiry in regard to their faith; and if their lives are exemplary, their light will shine, and they will have a gathering influence. And yet I was shown places where the truth has not been proclaimed, which should be visited soon. But the great work now to be accomplished is to bring up the people of God to engage in the work and exert a holy influence. They should act the part of laborers. With wisdom, caution, and love, they should labor for the salvation of neighbors and friends. There is too distant a feeling manifested. The cross is not laid right hold of and borne as it should be. All should feel that they are their brother's keeper, that they are in a great degree responsible for the souls of those around them. The brethren err when they leave this work all to the ministers. The harvest is great, and the laborers are few. Those who are of good repute, whose lives are in accordance with their faith, can be workmen. They can converse with others, and urge upon them the importance of the truth. They must not wait for the ministers and neglect a plain duty which God has left for them to perform.

Some of our ministers feel but little disposition to take upon them the burden of the work of God and labor with that disinterested benevolence which characterized the life of our divine Lord. The churches, as a general rule, are farther advanced than some of the ministers. They have had faith in the testimonies which God has been pleased to give, and have acted upon them, while some of the preachers are far behind. They profess to believe the testimony borne, and some do harm by making them an iron rule for those who have had no experience in reference to them, but they fail to carry them out themselves. They have had repeated testimonies which they have utterly disregarded. The course of such is not consistent.

The people of God generally feel a united interest in the spread of the truth. They cheerfully contribute toward a liberal support for those who labor in word and doctrine. And I saw that it is the duty of those who have the responsibility of distributing means, to see that the liberalities of the church are not squandered. Some of these liberal brethren have been laboring for years with shattered nerves and broken-down constitutions, caused by excessive labor in the past to obtain possessions here, and now as they freely give a portion of the substance which has cost them so much, it is the duty of those who labor in word and doctrine to manifest a zeal and self-sacrifice at least equal to that shown by these brethren.

God's servants must go out free. They must know in whom they trust. There is power in Christ and His salvation to make them free men, and unless they are free in Him, they cannot build up His church and gather in souls. Will God send out a man to rescue souls from the snare of Satan when his own feet are entangled in the net? God's servants must not be wavering. If their feet are sliding, how can they say to those of a fearful heart: "Be strong"? God would have His servants hold up the feeble hands, and strengthen the wavering. Those who are not prepared to do this would better first labor for themselves and pray until they are endowed with power from on high.

God is displeased with the lack of self-denial in some of His servants. They have not the burden of the work upon them. They seem to be in a deathlike stupor. Angels of God stand amazed and ashamed of this lack of self-denial and perseverance. While the Author of our salvation was laboring and suffering for us, He denied Himself, and His whole life was one continued scene of toil and privation. He could have passed His days on earth in ease and plenty, and appropriated to Himself the pleasures of this life; but He considered not His own convenience. He lived to do others good. He suffered to save others from suffering. He endured to the end and finished the work which was given Him to do. All this was to save us from ruin. And now, can it be that we, the unworthy objects of so great love, will seek a better position in this life than was given to our Lord? Every moment of our lives we have been partakers of the blessings of His great love, and for this very reason we cannot fully realize the depths of ignorance and misery from which we have been saved. Can we look upon Him whom our sins have pierced and not be willing to drink with Him the bitter cup of humiliation and sorrow? Can we look upon Christ crucified and wish to enter His kingdom in any other way than through much tribulation?

The preachers are not all given up to the work of God, as He requires them to be. Some have felt that the lot of a preacher was hard because they had to be separated from their families. They forget that once it was harder laboring than it is now. Once there were but few friends of the cause. They forget those upon whom God laid the burden of the work in the past. There were but a few then who received the truth as the result of much labor. God's chosen servants wept and prayed for a clear understanding of truth, and suffered privation and much self-denial in order to carry it to others. Step by step they followed as God's opening providence led the way. They did not study their own convenience or shrink at hardships. Through these men God prepared the way and made the truth plain to the understanding of every honest mind. Everything has been made ready to the hands of ministers who have since embraced the truth, yet some of them have failed to take upon them the burden of the work. They seek for an easier lot, a less self-denying position. This earth is not the resting place of Christians, much less for the chosen ministers of God. They forget that Christ left His riches and glory in heaven, and came to earth to die, and that He has commanded us to love one another even as He has loved us. They forget those of whom the world was not worthy, who wandered about in sheepskins and goatskins, and were afflicted and tormented.

I was shown the Waldenses, and what they suffered for their religion. They conscientiously studied the word of God, and lived up to the light which shone upon them. They were persecuted, and driven from their homes; their possessions, gained by hard labor, were taken from them, and their houses burned. They fled to the mountains and there suffered incredible hardships. They endured hunger, fatigue, cold, and nakedness. The only clothing which many of them could obtain was the skins of animals. And yet the scattered and homeless ones would assemble to unite their voices in singing, and praising God that they were accounted worthy to suffer for Christ's name. They encouraged and cheered one another, and were grateful for even their miserable retreat. Many of their children sickened and died from cold and hunger, yet the parents did not for a moment think of yielding their religion. They prized the love and favor of God far above earthly ease or worldly riches. They received consolation from God and with pleasing anticipations looked forward to the recompense of reward.

Again, I was shown Martin Luther, whom God raised up to do a special work. How precious to him was the knowledge of truth revealed in the word of God! His mind was starving for something sure upon which to build his hope that God would be his Father, and heaven his home. The new and precious light which dawned upon him from the word of God was of priceless value, and he thought that if he went forth with it, he could convince the world. He stood up against the ire of a fallen church and strengthened those who with him were feasting upon the rich truths contained in the word of God. Luther was God's chosen instrument to tear off the garb of hypocrisy from the papal church and expose her corruption. He raised his voice zealously and in the power of the Holy Spirit cried out against and rebuked the existing sins of the leaders of the people. Proclamations went forth to kill him wherever he might be found; he seemed left to the mercies of a superstitious people who were obedient to the head of the Roman Church. Yet he counted not his life dear unto himself. Luther knew that he was not safe anywhere, yet he trembled not. The light which he saw and feasted upon was life to him, and was of more value than all the treasures of earth. Earthly treasures he knew would fail; but the rich truths opened to his understanding, operating upon his heart, would live, and, if obeyed, would lead him to immortality.

When summoned to Augsburg to answer for his faith, he obeyed the summons. That one lone man who had stirred the rage of priests and people was arraigned before those who had caused the world to tremble—a meek lamb surrounded by angry lions; yet for the sake of Christ and the truth he stood up undaunted, and with holy eloquence, which the truth alone can inspire, he gave the reasons of his faith. His enemies tried by various means to silence the bold advocate for truth. At first they flattered him, and held out the promise that he should be exalted and honored. But life and honors were valueless to him if purchased at the sacrifice of the truth. Brighter and clearer shone the word of God upon his understanding, giving him a more vivid sense of the errors, corruptions, and hypocrisy of the papacy. His enemies then sought to intimidate him and cause him to renounce his faith, but he boldly stood in defense of the truth. He was ready to die for his faith, if God required; but to yield it—never. God preserved his life. He bade angels attend him and baffle the rage and purposes of his enemies, and bring him unharmed through the stormy conflict.

The calm, dignified power of Luther humbled his enemies, and dealt a most dreadful blow to the papacy. The great and proud men in power meant that his blood should atone for the mischief he had done their cause. Their plans were laid, but a mightier than they had charge of Luther. His work was not finished. The friends of Luther hastened his departure from Augsburg. He left the city by night, mounted upon a horse without bridle, himself unarmed and without boots or spurs. In great weariness he pursued his journey until he was among his friends.

Again the indignation of the papacy was aroused, and they resolved to stop the mouth of that fearless advocate of truth. They summoned him to Worms, fully determined to make him answer for his folly. He was in feeble health, yet he did not excuse himself. He well knew the dangers that were before him. He knew that his powerful enemies would take any measures to silence him. They were crying for his blood as eagerly as the Jews clamored for the blood of Christ. Yet he trusted in that God who preserved the three worthies in the burning fiery furnace. His anxiety and care were not for himself. He sought not his own ease; but his great anxiety was that the truth, to him so precious, should not be exposed to the insults of the ungodly. He was ready to die rather than allow its enemies to triumph. As he entered Worms, thousands of persons pressed around and followed him. Emperors and others in high authority were attended with no greater company. The excitement was intense; and one in that throng, with a shrill and plaintive voice, chanted a funeral dirge to warn Luther of what awaited him. But the Reformer had counted the cost and was ready to seal his testimony with his blood if God so ordained.

Luther was about to appear to answer for his faith before a most imposing assembly, and he looked to God in faith for strength. For a little time his courage and faith were tested. Perils in every form were presented before him. He became sad. Clouds gathered around him and hid from him the face of God. He longed to go forth with a confident assurance that God was with him. He could not be satisfied unless he was shut in with God. With broken cries he sent up his agonizing prayer to Heaven. His spirit at times seemed to faint, as his enemies, in his imagination, multiplied before him. He trembled at his danger. I saw that God in His wise providence prepared him in this way that he might not forget in whom to trust, and that he should not rush on presumptuously into danger. As His own instrument, God was fitting him for the great work before him.

Luther's prayer was heard. His courage and faith returned as he met his enemies. Meek as a lamb he stood, surrounded by the great men of the earth, who, like angry wolves, fastened their eyes upon him, hoping to awe him with their power and greatness. But he had taken hold of the strength of God and feared not. His words were spoken with such majesty and power that his enemies could do nothing against him. God was speaking through Luther, and He had brought together emperors and professed wise men that He might publicly bring to nought their wisdom, and that they all might see the strength and firmness of feeble man when leaning upon God, his eternal Rock.

The calm bearing of Luther was in striking contrast to the passion and rage exhibited by those so-called great men. They could not frighten him into a recantation of the truth. In noble simplicity and calm firmness he stood like a rock. The opposition of his enemies, their rage and threats, like a mighty wave, surged against him and broke harmless at his feet. He remained unmoved. They were chagrined that their power, which had caused kings and nobles to tremble, should be thus despised by a humble man, and they longed to make him feel their wrath by torturing his life away. But One who is mightier than the potentates of earth had charge of this fearless witness. God had a work for him to do. He must yet suffer for the truth. He must see it wade through bloody persecutions. He must see it clothed in sackcloth and covered with reproach by fanatics. He must live to justify it and to be its defender when the mighty powers of earth should seek to tear it down. He must live to see it triumph and tear away the errors and superstitions of the papacy. Luther gained a victory at Worms which weakened the papacy, the news of which spread to other kingdoms and nations. It was an effectual blow in favor of the Reformation.

Ministers who are preaching present truth were held up to me in contrast with the leading men of the Reformation; especially was Luther's devoted, zealous life placed beside the lives of some of our preachers. He proved his undying love for the truth by his courage, his calm firmness, his self-denial. He encountered trials and sacrifices, and at times suffered the deepest anguish of soul, while standing in defense of the truth; yet he murmured not. He was hunted like a wild beast of prey, yet for Christ's sake he endured all cheerfully.

The last merciful message is entrusted to God's humble, faithful servants of this time. God has led along those who would not shun responsibility, and has laid burdens upon them, and has through them presented to His people a plan of systematic benevolence in which all can engage and work in harmony. This system has been carried out and has worked like magic. It liberally sustains the preachers and the cause. As soon as the preachers ceased their opposition and stood out of the way, the people heartily responded to the call and prized the system. Everything is made convenient and easy for the preachers that they may work, free from embarrassment. Our people have taken hold with a will and an interest which is not to be found among any other class. And God is displeased with preachers who now complain and fail to throw their whole energies into this all-important work. They are without excuse, yet some are deceived and think that they are sacrificing much, and are having a hard time, when they really know nothing about suffering, self-denial, or want. They may often be weary; so would they be if they were dependent on manual labor for a support.

Some have thought it would be easier to labor with their hands and have often expressed their choice to do so. Such do not know what they are talking about. They are deceiving themselves. Some have very expensive families to provide for, and they lack management. They do not realize that they are indebted to the cause of God for their homes and all that they have. They have not realized how much it costs to live. Should they engage in manual labor, they would not be free from anxiety and weariness. They could not, while laboring to support their families, be sitting down at their own firesides. It is only a few weary hours that a laboring man with a family dependent upon him for support can spend with his family at home. Some ministers do not love industrious labor, and they have cherished a feeling of dissatisfaction which is very unreasonable. God has marked every murmuring thought and word and feeling. Heaven is insulted by such an exhibition of weakness and lack of devotion to the cause of God.

Some have given a willing ear to the tempter and have talked out their unbelief and wounded the cause. Satan has claims upon them, for they have not recovered themselves from his snare. They have conducted themselves like children who were wholly unacquainted with the wiles of the tempter. They have had sufficient experience and should have understood his workings. He has suggested doubts to their minds, and, instead of repelling them at once, they have reasoned and parleyed with the archdeceiver, and listened to his reasonings, as though charmed by the old serpent. A few texts which were not perfectly explainable to the satisfaction of their own minds have been sufficient to shake the whole structure of truth and to obscure the plainest facts of the word of God. These men are erring mortals. They have not perfect wisdom and knowledge in all the Scriptures. Some passages are placed beyond the reach of human minds until such a time as God chooses, in His own wisdom, to open them. Satan has been leading some on a trail which ends in certain infidelity. They have suffered their unbelief to becloud the harmonious, glorious chain of truth, and have acted as though it was their business to solve every difficult passage of Scripture, and if our faith did not enable them to do this, it was faulty.

I saw that those who have an evil heart of unbelief will doubt and will think it noble and a virtue to doubt the word of God. Those who think it a virtue to quibble can have plenty of room to disbelieve the inspiration and truth of God's word. God does not compel any to believe. They can choose to rely upon the evidences He has been pleased to give, or doubt, and cavil, and perish.

I was shown that those who are troubled with doubts and infidelity should not go out to labor for others. That which is in the mind must flow out, and they realize not the effect of a hint or the smallest doubt expressed. Satan makes it a barbed arrow. It acts like a slow poison, which, before the victim is made sensible of his danger, affects the whole system, undermines a good constitution, and finally causes death. It is just so with the poison of doubt and unbelief of Scripture facts. One who has influence suggests to others that which Satan has suggested to him, that one scripture contradicts another; and thus, in a very wise manner as though he had found out some wonderful mystery which had been hid from believers and the holy in every age of the world, he casts midnight darkness into other minds. They lose the relish they once had for the truth and become infidels. All this is the work of a few words spoken, which had a hidden power because they seemed involved in mystery.

This is the work of a cunning devil. Those who are troubled with doubts, and have difficulties which they cannot solve, should not throw other weak minds into the same perplexity. Some have hinted or talked their unbelief and have passed on, little dreaming of the effect produced. In some instances the seeds of unbelief have taken immediate effect, while in others they have lain buried quite a length of time, until the individual has taken a wrong course and given place to the enemy, and the light of God has been withdrawn from him, and he has fallen under the powerful temptations of Satan. Then the seeds of infidelity which were sown so long ago spring up. Satan nourishes them, and they bear fruit. Anything coming from ministers who should stand in the light has a powerful influence. And when they have not stood in the clear light of God, Satan has used them as agents and has through them transmitted his fiery darts to minds not prepared to resist what has come from their ministers.

I saw that ministers, as well as people, have a warfare before them to resist Satan. The professed minister of Christ is in a fearful position when serving the purposes of the tempter, by listening to his whisperings, and letting him captivate the mind and guide the thoughts. The minister's most grievous sin in the sight of God is talking out his unbelief and drawing other minds into the same dark channel, thus suffering Satan to carry out a twofold purpose in tempting him. He unsettles the mind of the one whose course has encouraged his temptations and then leads that one to unsettle the minds of many.

It is time that the watchmen upon the walls of Zion understood the responsibility and sacredness of their mission. They should feel that a woe is upon them if they do not perform the work which God has committed to them. If they become unfaithful, they are endangering the safety of the flock of God, endangering the cause of truth, and exposing it to the ridicule of our enemies. Oh, what a work is this! It will surely meet its reward. Some ministers, as well as people, need converting. They need to be torn to pieces and made over new. Their work among the churches is worse than lost, and in their present weak, tottering condition, it would be more pleasing to God for them to cease their efforts to help others, and labor with their hands until they are converted. Then they could strengthen their brethren.

Ministers must arouse. They profess to be generals in the army of the great King, and at the same time are sympathizers with the great rebel leader and his host. Some have exposed the cause of God, and the sacred truths of His word, to the reproaches of the rebel host. They have removed a portion of their armor, and Satan has hurled in his poisoned arrows. They have strengthened the hands of the rebel leaders, and weakened themselves, and caused Satan and his hellish clan to rear their heads in triumph, and exult on account of the victory they have let him gain. Oh, what a lack of wisdom! What blindness! What foolish generalship, to open their weakest points to their deadliest foes!

How unlike the course pursued by Luther! He was willing to sacrifice his life, if need be, but the truth, never. His words are: "Let us only take care that the gospel be not exposed to the insults of the ungodly, and let us shed our blood in its defense, rather than allow them to triumph. Who will say whether my life or my death would contribute most to the salvation of my brethren?"

God is not dependent upon any man for the advancement of His cause. He is raising up and qualifying men to bear the message to the world. He can make His strength perfect in the weakness of men. The power is of God. Ready speech, eloquence, great talents, will not convert a single soul. The efforts in the pulpit may stir up minds, the plain arguments may be convincing, but God giveth the increase. Godly men, faithful, holy men, who carry out in their everyday life that which they preach, will exert a saving influence. A powerful discourse delivered from the desk may affect minds; but a little imprudence upon the part of the minister out of the pulpit, a lack of gravity of speech and true godliness, will counteract his influence, and do away the good impressions made by him. The converts will be his; in many instances they will seek to rise no higher than their preacher. There will be in them no thorough heart work. They are not converted to God. The work is superficial, and their influence will be an injury to those who are really seeking the Lord.

The success of a minister depends much upon his deportment out of the desk. When he ceases preaching and leaves the desk, his work is not finished; it is only commenced. He must then carry out what he has preached. He should not move heedlessly, but set a watch over himself, lest something that he may do and say be taken advantage of by the enemy, and a reproach be brought upon the cause of Christ. Ministers cannot be too guarded, especially before the young. They should use no lightness of speech, jesting or joking, but should remember that they are in Christ's stead, that they must illustrate by example the life of Christ. "For we are laborers together with God." "We then, as workers together with Him, beseech you also that ye receive not the grace of God in vain."

I was shown that the usefulness of young ministers, married or unmarried, is often destroyed by the attachment shown to them by young women. Such do not realize that other eyes are upon them, and that the course pursued by them may have a tendency to very much injure the influence of the minister to whom they give so much attention. If they would strictly regard the rules of propriety, it would be much better for them and much better for their minister. It places him in a disagreeable position and causes others to look upon him in a wrong light. Yet I saw that the burden of the matter rests upon the ministers themselves. They should show a distaste for these things, and if they take the course which God would have them, they will not be troubled long. They should shun every appearance of evil, and when young women are very sociable, it is their duty to let them know that it is not pleasing. They must repulse this forwardness even if they are thought to be rude. Such things should be rebuked in order to save the cause from reproach. Young women who have been converted to the truth and to God will listen to reproof and will be reformed.

Ministers should follow up their public labors by private efforts, laboring personally for souls whenever there is an opportunity, conversing around the fireside, and entreating souls to seek for those things which make for their peace. Our work here is soon to close, and every man will receive his reward according to his own labor. I was shown the saints' reward, the immortal inheritance, and saw that those who had endured the most for the truth's sake will not think they have had a hard time, but will count heaven cheap enough.

WRONG USE OF THE VISIONS

I have been shown that some, especially in Iowa, make the visions a rule by which to measure all, and have taken a course which my husband and myself have never pursued. Some are unacquainted with me and my labors, and they are very skeptical of anything bearing the name of visions. This is all natural, and can be overcome only by experience. If persons are not settled in regard to the visions, they should not be crowded off. The course to pursue with such may be found in *Testimony* No. 8, pp. 328, 329, which I hope will be read by all. Ministers should have compassion of some, making a difference; others save with fear, pulling them out of the fire. God's ministers should have wisdom to give to everyone his portion of meat and to make that difference with different persons which their cases require. The course pursued with some in Iowa who are unacquainted with me has not been careful and consistent. Those who were, comparatively, strangers to the visions have been dealt with in the same manner as those who have had much light and experience in the visions. Some have been required to endorse the visions when they could not conscientiously do so, and in this way some honest souls have been driven to take positions against the visions and against the body which they never would have taken had their cases been managed with discretion and mercy.

Some of our brethren have had long experience in the truth and have for years been acquainted with me and with the influence of the visions. They have tested the truthfulness of these testimonies and asserted their belief in them. They have felt the powerful influence of the Spirit of God resting upon them to witness to the truthfulness of the visions. If such, when reproved through vision, rise up against them, and work secretly to injure our influence, they should be faithfully dealt with, for their influence is endangering those who lack experience.

Ministers of present truth, while they bear a pointed testimony, reproving individual wrongs and seeking to tear away the idols from the camp of Israel, should manifest forbearance. They should preach the truth in its solemnity and importance, and if this finds its way to the heart it will accomplish that for the receiver which nothing else can. But if the truth spoken in the demonstration of the Spirit does not cut away the idols, it will be of no avail to denounce and bear down upon the individual. It may appear that some are joined to their idols, yet I saw that we should be very reluctant to give up the poor, deceived ones. We should ever bear in mind that we are all erring mortals, and that Christ exercises much pity for our weakness, and loves us although we err. If God should deal with us as we often deal with one another, we should be consumed. While ministers preach the plain, cutting truth, they must let the truth do the cutting and hewing, not do it themselves. They should lay the ax, the truths of God's word, at the root of the tree, and something will be accomplished. Pour out the testimony just as straight as it is found in the word of God, with a heart full of the warming, quickening influence of His Spirit, all in tenderness, yearning for souls, and the work among God's people will be effectual. The reason why there is so little of the Spirit of God manifested is that ministers learn to do without it. They lack the grace of God, lack forbearance and patience, lack a spirit of consecration and sacrifice; and this is the only reason why some are doubting the evidences of God's word. The trouble is not at all in the word of God, but in themselves. They lack the grace of God, lack devotion, personal piety, and holiness. This leads them to be unstable, and throws them often on Satan's battlefield. I saw that however strongly men may have advocated the truth, however pious they may appear to be, when they begin to talk unbelief in regard to some scriptures, claiming that they cause them to doubt the inspiration of the Bible, we should be afraid of them, for God is at a great distance from them.

PARENTS AND CHILDREN

I have been shown that while parents who have the fear of God before them restrain their children, they should study their dispositions and temperaments, and seek to meet their wants. Some parents attend carefully to the temporal wants of their children; they kindly and faithfully nurse them in sickness, and then think their duty done. Here they mistake. Their work has but just begun. The wants of the mind should be cared for. It requires skill to apply the proper remedies to cure a wounded mind. Children have trials just as hard to bear, just as grievous in character, as those of older persons. Parents themselves do not feel the same at all times. Their minds are often perplexed. They labor under mistaken views and feelings. Satan buffets them, and they yield to his temptations. They speak irritably, and in a manner to excite wrath in their children, and are sometimes exacting and fretful. The poor children partake of the same spirit, and the parents are not prepared to help them, for they were the cause of the trouble. Sometimes everything seems to go wrong. There is fretfulness all around, and all have a very miserable, unhappy time. The parents lay the blame upon their poor children and think them very disobedient and unruly, the worst children in the world, when the cause of the disturbance is in themselves.

Some parents raise many a storm by their lack of self-control. Instead of kindly asking the children to do this or that, they order them in a scolding tone, and at the same time a censure or reproof is on their lips which the children have not merited. Parents, this course pursued toward your children destroys their cheerfulness and ambition. They do your bidding, not from love, but because they dare not do otherwise. Their heart is not in the matter. It is a drudgery, instead of a pleasure, and this often leads them to forget to follow out all your directions, which increases your irritation, and makes it still worse for the children. The faultfinding is repeated, their bad conduct arrayed before them in glowing colors, until discouragement comes over them, and they are not particular whether they please or not. A spirit of "I don't care" seizes them, and they seek that pleasure and enjoyment away from home, away from their parents, which they do not find at home. They mingle with street company and are soon as corrupt as the worst.

Upon whom rests this great sin? If home had been made attractive, if the parents had manifested affection for their children, and with kindness found employment for them, and in love instructed them how to obey their wishes, they would have touched an answering chord in their hearts, and willing feet and hands and hearts would all have readily obeyed them. By controlling themselves, and speaking kindly, and praising the children when they try to do right, parents may encourage their efforts, make them very happy, and throw over the family circle a charm which will chase away every dark shadow and bring cheerful sunlight in.

Parents sometimes excuse their own wrong course because they do not feel well. They are nervous, and think they cannot be patient and calm, and speak pleasantly. In this they deceive themselves and please Satan, who exults that the grace of God is not regarded by them as sufficient to overcome natural infirmities. They can and should at all times control themselves. God requires it of them. They should realize that when they yield to impatience and fretfulness they cause others to suffer. Those around them are affected by the spirit they manifest, and if they in their turn act out the same spirit, the evil is increased and everything goes wrong.

Parents, when you feel fretful, you should not commit so great a sin as to poison the whole family with this dangerous irritability. At such times set a double watch over yourselves, and resolve in your heart not to offend with your lips, that you will utter only pleasant, cheerful words. Say to yourselves: "I will not mar the happiness of my children by a fretful word." By thus controlling yourselves, you will grow stronger. Your nervous system will not be so sensitive. You will be strengthened by the principles of right. The consciousness that you are faithfully discharging your duty will strengthen you. Angels of God will smile upon your efforts and help you. When you feel impatient, you too often think the cause is in your children, and you blame them when they do not deserve it. At another time they might do the very same things and all would be acceptable and right. Children know, and mark, and feel these irregularities, and *they* are not always the same. At times they are somewhat prepared to meet changeable moods, and at other times they are nervous and fretful, and cannot bear censure. Their spirit rises up in rebellion against it. Parents want all due allowance made for their state of mind, yet do not always see the necessity of making the same allowance for their poor children. They excuse in themselves that which, if seen in their children who have not their years of experience and discipline, they would highly censure. Some parents are of a nervous temperament, and when fatigued with labor or oppressed with care, they do not preserve a calm state of mind, but manifest to those who should be dearest to them on earth, a fretfulness and lack of forbearance which displeases God and brings a cloud over the family. Children, in their troubles, should often be soothed with tender sympathy. Mutual kindness and forbearance will make home a paradise and attract holy angels into the family circle.

The mother can and should do much toward controlling her nerves and mind when depressed; even when she is sick, she can, if she only schools herself, be pleasant and cheerful, and can bear more noise than she would once have thought possible. She should not make the children feel her infirmities and cloud their young, sensitive minds by her depression of spirits, causing them to feel that the house is a tomb and the mother's room the most dismal place in the world. The mind and nerves gain tone and strength by the exercise of the will. The power of the will in many cases will prove a potent soother of the nerves.

Do not let your children see you with a clouded brow. If they yield to temptation, and afterward see and repent of their error, forgive them just as freely as you hope to be forgiven by your Father in heaven. Kindly instruct them, and bind them to your hearts. It is a critical time for children. Influences will be thrown around them to wean them from you, which you must counteract. Teach them to make you their confidant. Let them whisper in your ear their trials and joys. By encouraging this, you will save them from many a snare that Satan has prepared for their inexperienced feet. Do not treat your children only with sternness, forgetting your own childhood, and forgetting that they are but children. Do not expect them to be perfect or try to make them men and women in their acts at once. By so doing, you will close the door of access which you might otherwise have to them, and will drive them to open a door for injurious influences, for others to poison their young minds before you awake to their danger.

Satan and his host are making most powerful efforts to sway the minds of the children, and they must be treated with candor, Christian tenderness, and love. This will give you a strong influence over them, and they will feel that they can repose unlimited confidence in you. Throw around your children the charms of home and of your society. If you do this, they will not have so much desire for the society of young associates. Satan works through these, leading them to influence and corrupt the minds of one another. It is the most effectual way in which he can work. The young have a powerful influence over one another. Their conversation is not always choice and elevated. Evil communications are breathed into the ear, which, if not decidedly resisted, find a lodgment in the heart, take root, and spring up to bear fruit and corrupt good manners. Because of the evils now in the world, and the restriction necessary to be placed upon the children, parents should have double care to bind them to their hearts and let them see that they wish to make them happy.

Parents should not forget their childhood years, how much they yearned for sympathy and love, and how unhappy they felt when censured and fretfully chided. They should be young again in their feelings and bring their minds down to understand the wants of their children. Yet with firmness, mixed with love, they should require obedience from their children. The parents' word should be implicitly obeyed.

Angels of God are watching the children with the deepest interest to see what characters they develop. If Christ dealt with us as we often deal with one another and with our children, we would stumble and fall through utter discouragement. I saw that Jesus knows our infirmities, and has Himself shared our experience in all things but in sin; therefore He has prepared for us a path suited to our strength and capacity, and, like Jacob, has marched softly and in evenness with the children as they were able to endure, that He might entertain us by the comfort of His company, and be to us a perpetual guide. He does not despise, neglect, or leave behind the children of the flock. He has not bidden us move forward and leave them. He has not traveled so hastily as to leave us with our children behind. Oh, no; but He has evened the path to life, even for children. And parents are required in His name to lead them along the narrow way. God has appointed us a path suited to the strength and capacity of children.

LABOR IN THE EAST

I have been shown that the time has come for more effective labor in the East. The necessity of organization and order is at last felt there. Ministers will not now be obliged to labor under such discouragements as before. The angel of mercy is hovering over the East. Said the angel: "Strengthen the things that remain. Proclaim the message to those who have not heard it." There are some in the East who will be in danger of going to extremes when the Lord shall revive His work among them. They should remember that the Lord removed His work from them to the West to humble them, and to subdue an independent, rebellious spirit in them, and lead them to better prize the efforts of His faithful servants.

NUMBER TEN

TESTIMONY FOR THE CHURCH

DANGERS OF THE YOUNG

June 6, 1863, I was shown some of the dangers of the young. Satan is controlling the minds of the youth and leading their inexperienced feet astray. They are ignorant of his devices, and in these perilous times parents should be awake and work with perseverance and industry to shut out the first approach of the foe. They should instruct their children when they go out and when they come in, when they rise up, and when they sit down, giving line upon line, precept upon precept, here a little and there a little.

The mother's work commences with the infant. She should subdue the will and temper of her child, and bring it into subjection, teach it to obey. As the child grows older, relax not the hand. Every mother should take time to reason with her children, to correct their errors, and patiently teach them the right way. Christian parents should know that they are instructing and fitting their children to become children of God. The entire religious experience of the children is influenced by the instructions given, and the character formed, in childhood. If the will is not then subdued and made to yield to the will of the parents, it will be a difficult task to learn the lesson in after years. What a severe struggle, what a conflict, to yield that will which never was subdued, to the requirements of God! Parents who neglect this important work commit a great error, and sin against their poor children and against God.

Children who are under strict discipline will at times have dissatisfied feelings. They will become impatient under restraint, and will wish to have their own way, and go and come as they please. Especially from the age of ten to eighteen, they will often feel that there would be no harm in going to picnics and other gatherings of young associates; yet their experienced parents can see danger. They are acquainted with the peculiar temperaments of their children and know the influence of these things upon their minds, and from a desire for their salvation keep them back from these exciting amusements. When these children decide for themselves to leave the pleasures of the world and become Christ's disciples, what a burden is lifted from the hearts of careful, faithful parents! Yet even then the labor of the parents must not cease. The children should not be left to take their own course and always choose for themselves. They have but just commenced in earnest the warfare against sin, pride, passion, envy, jealousy, hatred, and all the evils of the natural heart. And parents need to watch and counsel their children, and decide for them, and show them that if they do not yield cheerful, willing obedience to their parents, they cannot yield willing obedience to God, and it is impossible for them to be Christians.

Parents should encourage their children to confide in *them,* and unburden to them their heart griefs, their little daily annoyances and trials. Thus the parents can learn to sympathize with their children, and can pray with and for them that God would shield and guide them. They should point them to their never-failing Friend and Counselor, who will be touched with the feeling of their infirmities, who was tempted in all points like as we are, yet without sin.

Satan tempts children to be reserved with their parents and to choose as their confidants their young and inexperienced companions, such as cannot help them, but will give them bad advice. Girls and boys get together and chat, and laugh, and joke, and drive Christ out of their hearts, and angels from their presence, by their foolish nonsense. Unprofitable conversation upon the acts of others, small talk about this young man or that girl, withers noble, devotional thoughts and feelings, and drives good and holy desires from the heart, leaving it cold and destitute of true love for God and His truth.

Children would be saved from many evils if they would be more familiar with their parents. Parents should encourage in their children a disposition to be open and frank with them, to come to them with their difficulties, and when they are perplexed as to what course is right, to lay the matter just as they view it before the parents and ask their advice. Who are so well calculated to see and point out their dangers as godly parents? Who can understand the peculiar temperaments of their own children as well as they? The mother who has watched every turn of the mind from infancy, and is thus acquainted with the natural disposition, is best prepared to counsel her children. Who can tell as well what traits of character to check and restrain, as the mother, aided by the father?

Children who are Christians will prefer the love and approbation of their God-fearing parents above every earthly blessing. They will love and honor their parents. It should be one of the principal studies of their lives, how to make their parents happy. In this rebellious age, children who have not received right instruction and discipline have but little sense of their obligations to their parents. It is often the case that the more their parents do for them, the more ungrateful they are, and the less they respect them. Children who have been petted and waited upon, always expect it; and if their expectations are not met, they are disappointed and discouraged. This same disposition will be seen through their whole lives; they will be helpless, leaning upon others for aid, expecting others to favor them and yield to them. And if they are opposed, even after they have grown to manhood and womanhood, they think themselves abused; and thus they worry their way through the world, hardly able to bear their own weight, often murmuring and fretting because everything does not suit them.

Mistaken parents are teaching their children lessons which will prove ruinous to them, and are also planting thorns for their own feet. They think that by gratifying the wishes of their children, and letting them follow their own inclinations, they can gain their love. What an error! Children thus indulged grow up unrestrained in their desires, unyielding in their dispositions, selfish, exacting, and overbearing, a curse to themselves and to all around them. To a great extent, parents hold in their own hands the future happiness of their children. Upon them rests the important work of forming the character of these children. The instructions given in childhood will follow them all through life. Parents sow the seed which will spring up and bear fruit either for good or evil. They can fit their sons and daughters for happiness or for misery.

Children should be taught very young to be useful, to help themselves, and to help others. Many daughters of this age can, without remorse of conscience, see their mothers toiling, cooking, washing, or ironing, while they sit in the parlor and read stories, knit edging, crochet, or embroider. Their hearts are as unfeeling as a stone. But where does this wrong originate? Who are the ones usually most to blame in this matter? The poor, deceived parents. They overlook the future good of their children, and in their mistaken fondness, let them sit in idleness, or do that which is of but little account, which requires no exercise of the mind or muscles, and then excuse their indolent daughters because they are weakly. What has made them weakly? In many cases it has been the wrong course of the parents. A proper amount of exercise about the house would improve both mind and body. But children are deprived of this through false ideas, until they are averse to work. It is disagreeable and does not accord with their ideas of gentility. It is thought to be unladylike and even coarse to wash dishes, iron, or stand over the washtub. This is the fashionable instruction which is given children in this unfortunate age.

God's people should be governed by higher principles than worldlings, who seek to gauge all their course of action according to fashion. God-fearing parents should train their children for a life of usefulness. They should not permit their principles of government to be tainted with the extravagant notions prevailing in this age, that they must conform to the fashions and be governed by the opinions of worldlings. They should not permit their children to choose their own associates. Teach them that it is your duty to choose for them. Prepare them to bear burdens while young. If your children have been unaccustomed to labor, they will soon become weary. They will complain of side ache, pain in the shoulders, and tired limbs; and you will be in danger, through sympathy, of doing the work yourselves, rather than have them suffer a little. Let the burden upon the children be very light at first, and then increase it a little every day, until they can do a proper amount of labor without becoming so weary. Inactivity is the greatest cause of side ache and shoulder ache among children.

There is a class of young ladies in this age who are merely useless creatures, only good to breathe, eat, wear, chat, and talk nonsense, while they hold in their fingers a bit of embroidery or crochet. But few of the youth show real sound judgment and good common sense. They lead a butterfly life with no special object in view. When this class of worldly associates get together, about all you can hear is a few silly remarks about dress, or some frivolous matter, and then they laugh at their own remarks which they consider very bright. This is frequently done in the presence of older persons, who can but feel saddened at such lack of reverence for their years. These youth seem to have lost all sense of modesty and good manners. Yet the manner in which they have been instructed leads them to think it the height of gentility.

This spirit is like a contagious disease. God's people should choose the society for their children and teach them to avoid the company of these vain worldlings. Mothers should take their daughters with them into the kitchen and patiently educate them. Their constitution will be better for such labor, their muscles will gain tone and strength, and their meditations will be more healthy and elevated at the close of the day. They may be weary, but how sweet is rest after a proper amount of labor. Sleep, nature's sweet restorer, invigorates the weary body, and prepares it for the next day's duties. Do not intimate to your children that it is no matter whether they labor or not. Teach them that their help is needed, that their time is of value, and that you depend on their labor.

I have been shown that much sin has resulted from idleness. Active hands and minds do not find time to heed every temptation which the enemy suggests, but idle hands and brains are all ready for Satan to control. The mind, when not properly occupied, dwells upon improper things. Parents should teach their children that idleness is sin. I was referred to Ezekiel 16:49: "Behold, this was the iniquity of thy sister Sodom, pride, fullness of bread, and abundance of idleness was in her and in her daughters, neither did she strengthen the hand of the poor and needy."

Children should feel that they are indebted to their parents, who have watched over them in infancy and nursed them in sickness. They should realize that their parents have suffered much anxiety on their account. Especially have conscientious, godly parents felt the deepest interest that their children should take a right course. As they have seen faults in their children, how heavy have been their hearts. If the children who caused those hearts to ache could see the effect of their course, they would certainly relent. If they could see their mother's tears and hear her prayers to God in their behalf, if they could listen to her suppressed and broken sighs, their hearts would feel, and they would speedily confess their wrongs and ask to be forgiven. There is a work to be accomplished for old and young. Parents should better qualify themselves to discharge their duty to their children. Some parents do not understand their children and are not really acquainted with them. There is often a great distance between parents and children. If the parents would enter more fully into the feelings of their children and draw out what is in their hearts, it would have a beneficial influence upon them.

Parents should deal faithfully with the souls committed to their trust. They should not encourage in their children pride, extravagance, or love of show. They should not teach them, or suffer them to learn, little pranks which appear cunning in small children, but which they will have to unlearn, and for which they must be corrected, when they are older. The habits first formed are not easily forgotten. Parents, you should commence to discipline the minds of your children while very young, to the end that they may be Christians. Let all your efforts be for their salvation. Act as though they were placed in your care to be fitted as precious jewels to shine in the kingdom of God. Beware how you lull them to sleep over the pit of destruction with the mistaken thought that they are not old enough to be accountable, not old enough to repent of their sins and profess Christ.

I was referred to the many precious promises on record for those who seek their Saviour early. Ecclesiastes 12:1: "Remember now thy Creator in the days of thy youth, while the evil days come not, nor the years draw nigh, when thou shalt say, I have no pleasure in them." Proverbs 8:17: "I love them that love Me; and those that seek Me early shall find Me." The Great Shepherd of Israel is still saying: "Suffer little children to come unto Me, and forbid them not: for of such is the kingdom of God." Teach your children that youth is the best time to seek the Lord. Then the burdens of life are not heavy upon them, and their young minds are not harassed with care, and while so free they should devote the best of their strength to God.

We are living in an unfortunate age for children. A heavy current is setting downward to perdition, and more than childhood's experence and strength is needed to press against this current and not be borne down by it. The youth generally seem to be Satan's captives, and he and his angels are leading them to certain destruction. Satan and his hosts are warring against the government of God, and all who have a desire to yield their hearts to him and obey his requirements, Satan will try to perplex and overcome with his temptations, that they may become discouraged and give up the warfare.

Parents, help your children. Arouse from the lethargy which has been upon you. Watch continually to cut off the current and roll back the weight of evil which Satan is pressing in upon your children. The children cannot do this of themselves, but parents can do much. By earnest prayer and living faith great victories will be gained. Some parents have not realized the responsibilities resting upon them and have neglected the religious education of their children. In the morning the Christian's first thoughts should be upon God. Worldly labor and self-interest should be secondary. Children should be taught to respect and reverence the hour of prayer. Before leaving the house for labor, all the family should be called together, and the father, or the mother in the father's absence, should plead fervently with God to keep them through the day. Come in humility with a heart full of tenderness and with a sense of the temptations and dangers before yourselves and your children; by faith bind them upon the altar, entreating for them the care of the Lord. Ministering angels will guard children who are thus dedicated to God. It is the duty of Christian parents, morning and evening, by earnest prayer and persevering faith, to make a hedge about their children. They should patiently instruct them, kindly and untiringly teach them how to live in order to please God.

Impatience in the parents excites impatience in the children. Passion manifested by the parents creates passion in the children and stirs up the evils of their nature. Some parents correct their children severely in a spirit of impatience, and often in passion. Such corrections produce no good result. In seeking to correct one evil, they create two. Continual censuring and whipping hardens children and weans them from their parents. Parents should first learn to control themselves, then they can more successfully control their children. Every time they lose self-control, and speak and act impatiently, they sin against God. They should first reason with their children, clearly point out their wrongs, show them their sin, and impress upon them that they have not only sinned against their parents, but against God. With your own heart subdued and full of pity and sorrow for your erring children, pray with them before correcting them. Then your correction will not cause your children to hate you. They will love you. They will see that you do not punish them because they have put you to inconvenience, or because you wish to vent your displeasure upon them; but from a sense of duty, for their good, that they may not be left to grow up in sin.

Some parents have failed to give their children a religious education and have also neglected their school education. Neither should have been neglected. Children's minds will be active, and if not engaged in physical labor, or occupied with study, they will be exposed to evil influences. It is a sin for parents to allow their children to grow up in ignorance. They should supply them with useful and interesting books, and should teach them to work, to have hours for physical labor, and hours to devote to study and reading. Parents should seek to elevate the minds of their children and to improve their mental faculties. The mind left to itself, uncultivated, is generally low, sensual, and corrupt. Satan improves his opportunity and educates idle minds.

Parents, the recording angel writes every impatient, fretful word you utter to your children. Every failure on your part to give them proper instruction, and show them the exceeding sinfulness of sin, and the final result of a sinful course, is marked against your name. Every unguarded word spoken before them, carelessly or in jest, every word that is not chaste and elevated, the recording angel marks as a spot against your Christian character. All your acts are recorded, whether they are good or bad.

Parents cannot succeed well in the government of their children until they first have perfect control of themselves. They must first learn to subdue themselves, to control their words, and the very expression of the countenance. They should not suffer the tones of their voice to be disturbed or agitated with excitement and passion. Then they can have a decided influence over their children. Children may wish to do right, they may purpose in their hearts to be obedient and kind to their parents or guardians; but they need help and encouragement from them. They may make good resolutions; but unless their principles are strengthened by religion and their lives influenced by the renewing grace of God, they will fail to come up to the mark.

Parents should redouble their efforts for the salvation of their children. They should faithfully instruct them, not leaving them to gather up their education as best they can. The young should not be suffered to learn good and evil indiscriminately, with the idea that at some future time the good will predominate and the evil lose its influence. The evil will increase faster than the good. It is possible that the evil they have learned may be eradicated after many years; but who will venture this? Time is short. It is easier and much safer to sow clean and good seed in the hearts of your children than to pluck up the weeds afterward. It is the duty of parents to watch lest surrounding influences have an injurious effect upon their children. It is their duty to select the society for them and not suffer them to choose for themselves. Who will attend to this work if the parents do not? Can others have that interest for your children which you should have? Can they have that constant care and deep love that parents have?

Sabbathkeeping children may become impatient of restraint, and think their parents too strict; hard feelings may even arise in their hearts, and discontented, unhappy thoughts may be cherished by them against those who are working for their present and their future and eternal good. But if life shall be spared a few years, they will bless their parents for that strict care and faithful watchfulness over them in their years of inexperience. Parents should explain and simplify the plan of salvation to their children that their young minds may comprehend it. Children of eight, ten, or twelve years are old enough to be addressed on the subject of personal religion. Do not teach your children with reference to some future period when they shall be old enough to repent and believe the truth. If properly instructed, very young children may have correct views of their state as sinners and of the way of salvation through Christ. Ministers are generally too indifferent to the salvation of children and are not as personal as they should be. Golden opportunities to impress the minds of children frequently pass unimproved.

The evil influence around our children is almost overpowering; it is corrupting their minds and leading them down to perdition. The minds of youth are naturally given to folly; and at an early age, before their characters are formed, and their judgment matured, they frequently manifest a preference for associates who will have an injurious influence over them. Some form attachments for the other sex, contrary to the wishes and entreaties of their parents, and break the fifth commandment by thus dishonoring them. It is the duty of parents to watch the going out and the coming in of their children. They should encourage them, and present inducements before them which will attract them at home, and lead them to see that their parents are interested for them. They should make home pleasant and cheerful.

Fathers and mothers, speak kindly to your children; remember how sensitive you are, how little you can bear to be blamed; reflect, and know that your children are like you. That which you cannot bear, do not lay upon them. If you cannot bear censure and blame, neither can your children, who are weaker than you and cannot endure as much. Let your pleasant, cheerful words ever be like sunbeams in your family. The fruits of self-control, thoughtfulness, and painstaking on your part will be a hundredfold. Parents have no right to bring a gloomy cloud over the happiness of their children by faultfinding or severe censure for trifling mistakes. Actual wrong and sin should be made to appear just as sinful as it is, and a firm, decided course should be pursued to prevent its recurrence. Children should be impressed with a sense of their wrongs, yet they should not be left in a hopeless state of mind, but with a degree of courage that they can improve and gain your confidence and approval.

Some parents mistake in giving their children too much liberty. They sometimes have so much confidence in them that they do not see their faults. It is wrong to allow children, at some expense, to visit at a distance, unaccompanied by their parents or guardians. It has a wrong influence upon the children. They come to feel that they are of considerable consequence and that certain privileges belong to them, and if these are not granted, they think themselves abused. They refer to children who go and come, and have many privileges, while they have so few.

And the mother, fearing that her children will think her unjust, gratifies their wishes, which in the end proves a great injury to them. Young visitors, who have not a parent's watchful eye over them to see and correct their faults often receive impressions which it will take months to remove. I was referred to cases of parents who had good, obedient children, and who, having the utmost confidence in certain families, trusted their children to go from them at a distance to visit these friends. From that time there was an entire change in the deportment and character of their children. Formerly they were contented and happy at home, and had no great desire to be much in the company of other young persons. When they return to their parents, restraint seems unjust, and home is like a prison to them. Such unwise movements of parents decide the character of their children.

By thus visiting, some children form attachments which prove their ruin in the end. Parents, keep your children with you if you can, and watch them with the deepest solicitude. When you let them visit at a distance from you, they feel that they are old enough to take care of and choose for themselves. When the young are thus left to themselves, their conversation is often upon subjects which will not refine or elevate them, or increase their love for the things of religion. The more they are permitted to visit, the greater will be their desire to go, and the less attractive will home seem to them.

Children, God has seen fit to entrust you to the care of your parents for them to instruct and discipline, and thus act their part in forming your character for heaven. And yet it rests with you to say whether you will develop a good Christian character by making the best of the advantages you have had from godly, faithful, praying parents. Notwithstanding all the anxiety and faithfulness of parents in behalf of their children, they alone cannot save them. There is a work for the children to do. Every child has an individual case to attend to. Believing parents, you have a responsible work before you to guide the footsteps of your children, even in their religious experience. When they truly love God, they will bless and reverence you for the care which you have manifested for them, and for your faithfulness in restraining their desires and subduing their wills.

The prevailing influence in the world is to suffer the youth to follow the natural turn of their own minds. And if very wild in youth, parents say they will come right after a while, and when sixteen or eighteen years of age, will reason for themselves, and leave off their wrong habits, and become at last useful men and women. What a mistake! For years they permit an enemy to sow the garden of the heart; they suffer wrong principles to grow, and in many cases all the labor afterward bestowed on that soil will avail nothing. Satan is an artful, persevering workman, a deadly foe. Whenever an incautious word is spoken to the injury of youth, whether in flattery or to cause them to look upon some sin with less abhorrence, Satan takes advantage of it and nourishes the evil seed that it may take root and yield a bountiful harvest. Some parents have suffered their children to form wrong habits, the marks of which may be seen all through life. Upon the parents lies this sin. These children may profess to be Christians, yet without a special work of grace upon the heart and a thorough reform in life their past habits will be seen in all their experience, and they will exhibit just the character which their parents allowed them to form.

The standard of piety is so low among professed Christians generally that those who wish to follow Christ in sincerity find the work much more laborious and trying than they otherwise would. The influence of worldly professors is injurious to the young. The mass of professed Christians have removed the line of distinction between Christians and the world, and while they profess to be living for Christ, they are living for the world. Their faith has but little restraining influence upon their pleasures; while they profess to be children of the light, they walk in darkness and are children of the night and of darkness. Those who walk in darkness cannot love God and sincerely desire to glorify Him. They are not enlightened to discern the excellence of heavenly things, and therefore cannot truly love them. They profess to be Christians because it is considered honorable, and there is no cross for them to bear. Their motives are often selfish. Some such professors can enter the ballroom and unite in all the amusements which it affords. Others cannot go to such a length as this, yet they can attend parties of pleasure, picnics, donation parties, and exhibitions. And the most discerning eye would fail to detect in such professed Christians one mark of Christianity. One would fail to see in their appearance any difference between them and the greatest unbeliever. The professed Christian, the profligate, the open scoffer at religion, and the openly profane all mingle together as one. And God regards them as one in spirit and practice.

A profession of Christianity without corresponding faith and works will avail nothing. No man can serve two masters. The children of the wicked one are their own master's servants; to whom they yield themselves servants to obey, his servants they are, and they cannot be the servants of God until they renounce the devil and all his works. It cannot be harmless for servants of the heavenly King to engage in the pleasures and amusements which Satan's servants engage in, even though they often repeat that such amusements are harmless. God has revealed sacred and holy truths to separate His people from the ungodly and purify them unto Himself. Seventh-day Adventists should live out their faith. Those who obey the Ten Commandments view the state of the world and religious things from a standpoint altogether different from that of professors who are lovers of pleasure, who shun the cross, and live in violation of the fourth commandment. In the present state of things in society it is no easy task for parents to restrain their children and instruct them according to the Bible rule of right. Professors of religion have so departed from the word of God that when His people return to His sacred word, and would train their children according to its precepts, and like Abraham of old command their households after them, the poor children with such an influence around them think their parents unnecessarily exacting and over careful in regard to their associates. They naturally desire to follow the example of worldly, pleasure-loving professors.

In these days, persecution and reproach for Christ's sake are scarcely known. Very little self-denial and sacrifice is necessary in order to put on a form of godliness and have the name upon the church book; but to live in such a manner that our ways will be pleasing to God, and our names registered in the book of life, will require watchfulness and prayer, self-denial and sacrifice on our part. Professed Christians are no example for the youth, only as far as they follow Christ. Right actions are unmistakable fruits of true godliness. The Judge of all the earth will give everyone according to his works. Children who follow Christ have a warfare before them; they have a daily cross to bear in coming out from the world and being separate, and imitating the life of Christ.

WALK IN THE LIGHT

I was shown that God's people dwell too much under a cloud. It is not His will that they should live in unbelief. Jesus is light, and in Him is no darkness at all. His children are the children of light. They are renewed in His image, and called out of darkness into His marvelous light. He is the light of the world, and so also are they that follow Him. They shall not walk in darkness, but shall have the light of life. The more closely the people of God strive to imitate Christ, the more perseveringly will they be pursued by the enemy; but their nearness to Christ strengthens them to resist the efforts of our wily foe to draw them from Christ.

I was shown that there was too much comparing ourselves among ourselves, taking fallible mortals for a pattern, when we have a sure, unerring pattern. We should not measure ourselves by the world, nor by the opinions of men, nor by what we were before we embraced the truth. But our faith and position in the world, as they now are, must be compared with what they would have been if our course had been continually onward and upward since we professed to be followers of Christ. This is the only safe comparison that can be made. In every other there will be self-deception. If the moral character and spiritual state of God's people do not correspond with the blessings, privileges, and light which have been conferred upon them, they are weighed in the balance, and angels make the report, WANTING.

With some the knowledge of their true state seems to be hidden from them. They see the truth, but perceive not its importance or its claims. They hear the truth, but do not fully understand it, because they do not conform their lives to it, and therefore are not sanctified through obeying it. And yet they rest as unconcerned and well satisfied as though the cloud by day and the pillar of fire by night, as token of God's favor, went before them. They profess to know God, but in works deny Him. They reckon themselves His chosen, peculiar people, yet His presence and power to save to the uttermost are seldom manifested among them. How great is the darkness of such! yet they know it not. The light shines, but they do not comprehend it. No stronger delusion can deceive the human mind than that which makes them believe that they are right, and that God accepts their works, when they are sinning against Him. They mistake the form of godliness for the spirit and power thereof. They suppose that they are rich, and have need of nothing, when they are poor, wretched, blind, and naked, and need all things.

There are some who profess to be Christ's followers, yet put forth no effort in spiritual things. In any worldly enterprise they put forth effort, and manifest ambition to accomplish their object, and bring about the desired end; but in the enterprise of everlasting life, where all is at stake, and their eternal happiness depends upon their success, they act as indifferent as though they were not moral agents, as though another were playing the game of life for them, and they had nothing to do but wait the result. Oh, what folly! what madness! If all will only manifest that degree of ambition, zeal, and earnestness for everlasting life that they manifest in their worldly pursuits, they will be victorious overcomers. Everyone, I saw, must obtain an experience for himself, each must act well and faithfully his part in the game of life. Satan watches his opportunity to seize the precious graces when we are unguarded, and we shall have a severe conflict with the powers of darkness to retain them, or to regain a heavenly grace if through lack of watchfulness we lose it.

But I was shown that it is the privilege of Christians to obtain strength from God to hold every precious gift. Fervent and effectual prayer will be regarded in heaven. When the servants of Christ take the shield of faith for their defense, and the sword of the Spirit for war, there is danger in the enemy's camp, and something must be done. Persecution and reproach only wait for those who are endowed with power from on high to call them into action. When the truth in its simplicity and strength prevails among believers, and is brought to bear against the spirit of the world, it will be evident that there is no concord between Christ and Belial. The disciples of Christ must be living examples of the life and spirit of their Master.

Young and old have a conflict, a warfare, before them. They should not sleep for a moment. A wily foe is constantly on the alert to lead them astray and overcome them. Believers in present truth must be as watchful as their enemy and manifest wisdom in resisting Satan. Will they do this? Will they persevere in this warfare? Will they be careful to depart from all iniquity? Christ is denied in many ways. We may deny Him by speaking contrary to truth, by speaking evil of others, by foolish talking or jesting, or by words that are idle. In these things we manifest but little shrewdness or wisdom. We make ourselves weak; our efforts are feeble to resist our great enemy, and we are conquered. "Out of the abundance of the heart the mouth speaketh," and through lack of watchfulness we confess that Christ is not in us. Those who hesitate to devote themselves unreservedly to God make poor work of following Christ. They follow Him at so great a distance that half the time they do not really know whether they are following His footprints or the footsteps of their great enemy. Why are we so slow to give up our interest in the things of this world and take Christ for our only portion? Why should we wish to keep the friendship of our Lord's enemies, and follow their customs, and be led by their opinions? There must be an entire, unreserved surrender to God, a forsaking and turning away from the love of the world and earthly things, or we cannot be Christ's disciples.

The life and spirit of Christ is the only standard of excellence and perfection, and our only safe course is to follow His example. If we do this He will guide us by His counsel and afterward receive us to glory. We must strive diligently and be willing to suffer much in order to walk in the footsteps of our Redeemer. God is willing to work for us, to give us of His free Spirit, if we will strive for it, live for it, believe for it; and then we can walk in the light as He is in the light. We can feast upon His love and drink in of His rich fullness.

THE CAUSE IN THE EAST

The fanaticism which raged in years past has left its desolating effects in the East. I saw that God tested His people upon time in 1844, but that no time which has since been set has borne the special marks of His hand. He has not tested His people upon any particular time since 1844. We have been, and still are, in the patient waiting time. Considerable excitement was created by the 1854 time, and many have settled it that that movement was in the order of God because it was quite extensive and some were apparently converted by it. But such conclusions are not necessary. There was much preached in connection with the time in 1854 that was reasonable and right. Some who were honest took truth and error together, and sacrificed much of what they possessed to carry out the error, and after their disappointment they gave up both truth and error, and are now where it is very difficult for the truth to reach them. Some who endured the disappointment have seen the evidences of present truth, and have embraced the third angel's message, and are striving to carry it out in their lives. But where there is one who has been benefited by believing the 1854 time, there are ten who have been injured by it; and many of these are placed where they will not be convinced of the truth, though it be presented before them ever so clearly.

The proclamation of the 1854 time was attended with a spirit which was not of God. It was a noisy, rough, careless, excitable spirit. Noise was considered by many the essential of true religion, and there was a tendency to bring all down upon a low level. Many regarded this as humility; but when opposed in their peculiar views, they would become excited in a moment, manifest an overbearing spirit, and accuse those who did not agree with them of being proud and of resisting the truth and the power of God.

Holy angels have been displeased and disgusted with the irreverent manner in which many have used the name of God, the great Jehovah. Angels mention that sacred name with the greatest awe, ever veiling their faces when they speak the name of God; and the name of Christ is so sacred to them that they speak it with the greatest reverence. But how opposite the spirit and influence attending the 1854 time movement. Some who are still under the same influence speak of God as they would of a horse or of any other commonplace thing. In their prayers they use the words God Almighty in a very common and irreverent manner. Those who do this have no sense of the exalted character of God, of Christ, or of heavenly things.

I was shown that when God sent His angels anciently to minister or communicate to individuals, and these persons learned that they had seen and talked with an angel, they were struck with awe and were afraid that they should die. They had so exalted views of the terrible majesty and power of God that they thought it would destroy them to be brought into close connection with one direct from His holy presence. I was referred to Judges 13:21, 22: "Then Manoah knew that he was an angel of the Lord. And Manoah said unto his wife, We shall surely die, because we have seen God." Judges 6:22, 23: "And when Gideon perceived that he was an angel of the Lord, Gideon said, Alas, O Lord God! for because I have seen an angel of the Lord face to face. And the Lord said unto him, Peace be unto thee; fear not: thou shalt not die." Joshua 5:13-15: "And it came to pass, when Joshua was by Jericho, that he lifted up his eyes and looked, and, behold, there stood a man over against him with his sword drawn in his hand: and Joshua went unto him, and said unto him: Art thou for us, or for our adversaries? And he said, Nay; but as captain of the host of the Lord am I now come. And Joshua fell on his face to the earth, and did worship, and said unto him, What saith my Lord unto his servant? And the captain of the Lord's host said unto Joshua, Loose thy shoe from off thy foot; for the place whereon thou standest is holy. And Joshua did so." If angels were thus feared and honored because they came from the presence of God, with how much greater reverence should God Himself be regarded.

Many who were converted through the influence of the 1854 movement need to be converted anew. And now tenfold more labor is required to correct the wrong, distracting views which they have received from their teachers, and to lead them to receive the truth unmixed with error, than would have been necessary to bring them out in the first place upon the third angel's message. This class must unlearn before they can learn aright, else the poisonous weeds of error would grow rank and root out the precious seeds of truth. Error must first be rooted up, then the soil is prepared for the good seed to spring up and bear fruit to the glory of God.

The only remedy for the East is thorough discipline and organization. A spirit of fanaticism has ruled a certain class of Sabbathkeepers there; they have sipped but lightly at the fountain of truth and are unacquainted with the spirit of the message of the third angel. Nothing can be done for this class until their fanatical views are corrected. Some who were in the 1854 movement have brought along with them erroneous views, such as the nonresurrection of the wicked, and the future age, and they are seeking to unite these views and their past experience with the message of the third angel. They cannot do this; there is no concord between Christ and

Belial. The nonresurrection of the wicked and their peculiar views of the age to come are gross errors which Satan has worked in among the last-day heresies to serve his own purpose to ruin souls. These errors can have no harmony with the message of heavenly origin.

Some of these persons have exercises which they call gifts and say that the Lord has placed them in the church. They have an unmeaning gibberish which they call the unknown tongue, which is unknown not only by man but by the Lord and all heaven. Such gifts are manufactured by men and women, aided by the great deceiver. Fanaticism, false excitement, false talking in tongues, and noisy exercises have been considered gifts which God has placed in the church. Some have been deceived here. The fruits of all this have not been good. "Ye shall know them by their fruits." Fanaticism and noise have been considered special evidences of faith. Some are not satisfied with a meeting unless they have a powerful and happy time. They work for this and get up an excitement of feeling. But the influence of such meetings is not beneficial. When the happy flight of feeling is gone, they sink lower than before the meeting because their happiness did not come from the right source. The most profitable meetings for spiritual advancement are those which are characterized with solemnity and deep searching of heart; each seeking to know himself, and earnestly, and in deep humility, seeking to learn of Christ.

Brother Lunt of Portland, Maine, has suffered much in his feelings. He has felt that the spirit which often ruled in their meetings was not in harmony with the message of the third angel. He has had an experience in the fanaticism which has left desolation in the East, and this leads him to look with suspicion upon everything which appears like fanaticism. He has the past before him as a warning and has felt like keeping aloof from, and speaking plainly with, those who had any degree of fanaticism, for he felt that both they and the cause of God were in danger. He has looked upon things in about the right light.

There are many restless spirits who will not submit to discipline, system, and order. They think that their liberties would be abridged were they to lay aside their own judgment and submit to the judgment of those of experience. The work of God will not progress unless there is a disposition to submit to order and expel the reckless, disorderly spirit of fanaticism from their meetings. Impressions and feelings are no sure evidence that a person is led by the Lord. Satan will, if he is unsuspected, give feelings and impressions. These are not safe guides. All should thoroughly acquaint themselves with the evidences of our faith, and the great study should be how they can adorn their profession and bear fruit to the glory of God. None should take a course to make themselves disgusting to unbelievers. We should be chaste, modest, and elevated in conversation, and blameless in life. A trifling, joking, reckless spirit should be rebuked. It is no evidence of the grace of God upon the heart for persons to talk and pray with talent in meeting, and then give up to a rough, careless manner of talking and acting when out of meeting. Such are miserable representatives of our faith; they are a reproach to the cause of God.

There is a strange mixture of views among professed Sabbathkeepers in ——. Some are not in harmony with the body, and while they continue to occupy the position they now do, they will be subject to the temptations of Satan and will be affected with fanaticism and the spirit of error. Some have fanciful views which blind their eyes to important, vital points of truth, leading them to place their own fanciful inferences upon a level with vital truth. The appearance of such, and the spirit which attends them, makes the Sabbath which they profess very objectionable to the sensible unbeliever. It would be far better for the progress and success of the third angel's message if such persons would leave the truth.

According to the light which God has given me, there will yet be a large company raised up in the East to consistently obey the truth. Those who follow in the distracted course they have chosen will be left to embrace errors which will finally cause their overthrow; but they will for a time be stumbling blocks to those who would receive the truth. Ministers who labor in word and doctrine should be thorough workmen, and should present the truth in its purity, yet with simplicity. They should feed the flock with clean provender, thoroughly winnowed. There are wandering stars professing to be ministers sent of God who are preaching the Sabbath from place to place, but who have truth mixed up with error and are throwing out their mass of discordant views to the people. Satan has pushed them in to disgust intelligent and sensible unbelievers. Some of these have much to say upon the gifts and are often especially exercised. They give themselves up to wild, excitable feelings and make unintelligible sounds which they call the gift of tongues, and a certain class seem to be charmed with these strange manifestations. A strange spirit rules with this class, which would bear down and run over anyone who would reprove them. God's Spirit is not in the work and does not attend such workmen. They have another spirit. Still, such preachers have success among a certain class. But this will greatly increase the labor of those servants whom God shall send, who are qualified to present before the people the Sabbath and the gifts in their proper light, and whose influence and example are worthy of imitation.

The truth should be presented in a manner which will make it attractive to the intelligent mind. We are not understood as a people, but are looked upon as poor, weak-minded, low, and degraded. Then how important for all who teach, and all who believe the truth, to be so affected by its sanctifying influence that their consistent, elevated lives shall show unbelievers that they have been deceived in this people. How important that the cause of truth be stripped of everything like a false and fanatical excitement, that the truth may stand upon its own merits, revealing its native purity and exalted character.

I saw that it is highly important for those who preach the truth to be refined in their manners, to shun oddities and eccentricities, and present the truth in its purity and clearness. I was referred to Titus 1:9: "Holding fast the faithful word as he hath been taught, that he may be able by sound doctrine both to exhort and to convince the gainsayers." In verse 16 Paul speaks of a class who profess that they know God, but in works deny him, being "unto every good work reprobate." He then exhorts Titus: "But speak thou the things which become sound doctrine: that the aged men be sober, grave, temperate, sound in faith, in charity, in patience. . . . Young men likewise exhort to be sober-minded. In all things showing thyself a pattern of good works: in doctrine showing uncorruptness, gravity, sincerity, sound speech, that cannot be condemned; that he that is of the contrary part may be ashamed, having no evil thing to say of you." This instruction is written for the benefit of all whom God has called to preach the word, and also for the benefit of His people who hear the word.

The truth of God will never degrade, but will elevate the receiver, refine his taste, sanctify his judgment, and perfect him for the company of the pure and holy angels in the kingdom of God. There are some whom the truth finds coarse, rough, odd, boastful, who take advantage of their neighbors if they can, in order to benefit themselves; they err in many ways, yet when the truth is believed by them from the heart, it will work an entire change in their lives. They will immediately commence the work of reformation. The pure influence of truth will elevate the whole man. In his business deal with his fellow men he will have the fear of God before him and will love his neighbor as himself, and will deal just as he would wish to be dealt by. His conversation will be truthful, chaste, and of so elevating a character that unbelievers cannot take advantage of it, or say evil of him justly, and are not disgusted with his uncourteous ways and unbecoming speech. He will carry the sanctifying influence of the truth into his family and let his light so shine before them that they by seeing his good works may glorify God. He will in all the walks of life exemplify the life of Christ.

The law of God will be satisfied with nothing short of perfection, of perfect and entire obedience to all its claims. To come halfway to its requirements, and not render perfect and thorough obedience, will avail nothing. The worldling and the infidel admire consistency and have ever been powerfully convicted that God was of a truth with His people when their works correspond with their faith. "By their fruits ye shall know them." Every tree is known by its own fruits. Our words, our actions, are the fruit we bear. There are many who hear the sayings of Christ, but do them not. They make a profession, but their fruits are such as to disgust unbelievers. They are boastful, and pray and talk in a selfrighteous manner, exalting themselves, recounting their good deeds, and, like the Pharisee, virtually thanking God that they are not as other men. Yet these very ones are crafty, and overreach in business deal. Their fruits are not good. Their words and acts are wrong, and yet they seem to be blinded to their destitute, wretched condition.

I was shown that the following scripture is applicable to those who are under such a deception: "Not everyone that saith unto Me, Lord, Lord, shall enter into the kingdom of heaven; but he that doeth the will of My Father which is in heaven. Many will say to Me in that day, Lord, Lord, have not we prophesied in Thy name? and in Thy name have cast out devils? and in Thy name done many wonderful works? And then will I profess unto them, I never knew you: depart from Me, ye that work iniquity."

Here is the greatest deception that can affect the human mind; these persons believe that they are right when they are wrong. They think that they are doing a great work in their religious life, but Jesus finally tears off their self-righteous covering and vividly presents before them the true picture of themselves in all their wrongs and deformity of religious character. They are found wanting when it is forever too late to have their wants supplied. God has provided means to correct the erring: yet if those who err, choose to follow their own judgment, and despise the means which He has ordained to correct them and unite them upon the truth, they will be brought into the position described by the words of our Lord quoted above.

God is bringing out a people and preparing them to stand as one, united, to speak the same things, and thus carry out the prayer of Christ for His disciples. "Neither pray I for these alone, but for them also which shall believe on Me through their word; that they all may be one; as Thou, Father, art in Me, and I in Thee, that they also may be one in Us: that the world may believe that Thou hast sent Me."

There are little companies continually rising who believe that God is only with the very few, the very scattered, and their influence is to tear down and scatter that which God's servants build up. Restless minds who want to be seeing and believing something new continually are constantly rising, some in one place and some in another, all doing a special work for the enemy, yet claiming to have the truth. They stand separate from the people whom God is leading out and prospering, and through whom He is to do His great work. They are continually expressing their fears that the body of Sabbathkeepers are becoming like the world, but there are scarcely two of these whose views are in harmony. They are scattered and confused, and yet deceive themselves so much as to think that God is especially with them. Some of these profess to have the gifts among them; but are led by the influence and teachings of these gifts to hold in doubt those upon whom God has laid the special burden of His work, and to lead off a class from the body. The people, who, in accordance with God's word, are putting forth every effort to be one, who are established in the message of the third angel, are looked upon with suspicion for the reason that they are extending their labor and are gathering souls into the truth. They are considered worldly because they have an influence in the world, and their acts testify that they expect God yet to do a special and great work upon the earth, to bring out a people and fit them for Christ's appearing.

This class do not know what they really believe, or the reasons for their belief. They are ever learning, and never able to come to the knowledge of the truth. One man arises with wild, erroneous views, and claims that God has sent him with new and glorious light, and all must believe what he brings. Some who have no established faith, who are not subject to the body, but are drifting about without an anchor to hold them, receive that wind of doctrine. His light shines in such a manner as to cause the world to turn from him in disgust and to hate him. Then he blasphemously places himself by the side of Christ and claims that the world hate him for the same reason that they hated Christ. Another rises, claiming to be led of God, and advocates the heresy of the nonresurrection of the wicked, which is one of Satan's great masterpieces of error. Another cherishes erroneous views in regard to the future age. Another zealously urges the American costume. They all want full religious liberty, and each acts independent of the others, and yet they claim that God is especially at work among them.

Some rejoice and exult that they have the gifts, which

others have not. May God deliver His people from such gifts. What do these gifts do for them? Are they through the exercise of these gifts, brought into the unity of the faith? And do they convince the unbeliever that God is with them of a truth? When these discordant ones, holding their different views, come together and there is considerable excitement and the unknown tongue, they let their light so shine that unbelievers would say: These people are not sane; they are carried away with a false excitement, and we know that they do not have the truth. Such stand directly in the way of sinners; their influence is effectual to keep others from accepting the Sabbath. Such will be rewarded according to their works. Would to God they would be reformed or give up the Sabbath! They would not then stand in the way of unbelievers.

God has led out men who have toiled for years, who have been willing to make any sacrifice, who have suffered privation, and endured trials to bring the truth before the world, and by their consistent course remove the reproach that fanatics have brought upon the cause of God. They have met opposition in every form. They have toiled night and day in searching the evidences of our faith that they might bring out the truth in its clearness, in a connected form, that it might withstand all opposition. Incessant labor and mental trials in connection with this great work have worn down more than one constitution and prematurely sprinkled heads with gray hairs. They have not worn out in vain. God has marked their earnest, tearful, agonizing prayers that they might have light and truth, and that the truth might shine in its clearness to others. He has marked their self-sacrificing efforts, and He will reward them as their works have been.

On the other hand, those who have not toiled to bring out these precious truths have come up and received some points, like the Sabbath truth, which are all prepared to their hand, and then all the gratitude they manifest for that which cost them nothing, but others so much, is to rise up like Korah, Dathan, and Abiram, and reproach those upon whom God has laid the burden of His work. They would say: "Ye take too much upon you, seeing all the congregation are holy, every one of them, and the Lord is among them." They are strangers to gratitude. They possess a strong spirit which will not yield to reason and which will lead them on to their own destruction.

God has blessed His people who have moved forward following His opening providence. He has brought out a people from every class upon the great platform of truth. Infidels have been convinced that God was with His people and have humbled their hearts to obey the truth. The work of God moves steadily on. Yet notwithstanding all the evidences that God has been leading the body, there are, and will continue to be, those who profess the Sabbath, who will move independent of the body, and believe and act as they choose. Their views are confused. Their scattered state is a standing testimony that God is not with them. By the world the Sabbath and their errors are placed upon a level and thrown away together. God is angry with those who pursue a course to make the world hate them. If a Christian is hated because of his good works and for following Christ, he will have a reward; but if he is hated because he does not take a course to be loved, hated because of his uncultivated manners and because he makes the truth a matter of quarrel with his neighbors, and takes a course to make the Sabbath as annoying as possible to them, he is a stumbling block to sinners, a reproach to the sacred truth, and unless he repents it were better for him that a millstone were hung about his neck and he were cast into the sea.

No occasion should be given to unbelievers to reproach our faith. We are considered odd and singular, and should not take a course to lead unbelievers to think us more so than our faith requires us to be.

Some who believe the truth may think that it would be more healthful for the sisters to adopt the American costume, yet if that mode of dress would cripple our influence among unbelievers so that we could not so readily gain access to them, we should by no means adopt it, though we suffered much in consequence. But some are deceived in thinking there is so much benefit to be received from this costume. While it may prove a benefit to some, it is an injury to others.*

I saw that God's order has been reversed, and His special directions disregarded, by those who adopt the American costume. I was referred to Deuteronomy 22:5: "The woman shall not wear that which pertaineth unto a man, neither shall a man put on a woman's garment: for all that do so are abomination unto the Lord thy God." God would not have His people adopt the so-called reform dress. It is immodest apparel, wholly unfitted for the modest, humble followers of Christ.

There is an increasing tendency to have women in their dress and appearance as near like the other sex as possible, and to fashion their dress very much like that of men, but God pronounces it abomination. "In like manner also, that women adorn themselves in modest apparel, with shamefacedness and sobriety." 1 Timothy 2:9.

Those who feel called out to join the movement in favor of woman's rights and the so-called dress reform might as well sever all connection with the third angel's message. The spirit which attends the one cannot be in harmony with the other. The Scriptures are plain upon the relations and rights of men and women. Spiritualists have, to quite an extent, adopted this singular mode of dress. Seventh-day Adventists, who believe in the restoration of the gifts, are often branded as spiritualists. Let them adopt this costume, and their influence is dead. The people would place them on a level with spiritualists and would refuse to listen to them.

---

*See Appendix.

With the so-called dress reform there goes a spirit of levity and boldness just in keeping with the dress. Modesty and reserve seem to depart from many as they adopt that style of dress. I was shown that God would have us take a course consistent and explainable. Let the sisters adopt the American costume and they would destroy their own influence and that of their husbands. They would become a byword and a derision. Our Saviour says: "Ye are the light of the world." "Let your light so shine before men, that they may see your good works, and glorify your Father which is in heaven." There is a great work for us to do in the world, and God would not have us take a course to lessen or destroy our influence with the world.

THE PRAYER OF DAVID

I was shown David entreating the Lord not to forsake him when he should be old, and what it was that called forth his earnest prayer. He saw that most of the aged around him were unhappy and that unhappy traits of character increased especially with age. If persons were naturally close and covetous, they were most disagreeably so in their old age. If they were jealous, fretful, and impatient, they were especially so when aged.

David was distressed as he saw that kings and nobles who seemed to have the fear of God before them while in the strength of manhood, became jealous of their best friends and relatives when aged. They were in continual fear that it was selfish motives which led their friends to manifest an interest for them. They would listen to the hints and the deceptive advice of strangers in regard to those in whom they should confide. Their unrestrained jealousy sometimes burned into a flame because all did not agree with their failing judgment.

Their covetousness was dreadful. They often thought that their own children and relatives were wishing them to die in order to take their place and possess their wealth, and receive the homage which had been bestowed upon them. And some were so controlled by their jealous, covetous feelings as to destroy their own children.

David marked that although the lives of some while in the strength of manhood had been righteous, as old age came upon them they seemed to lose their self-control. Satan stepped in and guided their minds, making them restless and dissatisfied. He saw that many of the aged seemed forsaken of God and exposed themselves to the ridicule and reproaches of his enemies. David was deeply moved; he was distressed as he looked forward to the time when he should be aged. He feared that God would leave him and that he would be as unhappy as other aged persons whose course he had noticed, and would be left to the reproach of the enemies of the Lord. With this burden upon him he earnestly prays: "Cast me not off in the time of old age; forsake me not when my strength faileth." "O God, Thou hast taught me from my youth: and hitherto have I declared Thy wondrous works. Now also when I am old and grayheaded, O God, forsake me not; until I have showed Thy strength unto this generation, and Thy power to everyone that is to come." Psalm 71:9, 17, 18. David felt the necessity of guarding against the evils which attend old age.

It is frequently the case that aged persons are unwilling to realize and acknowledge that their mental strength is failing. They shorten their days by taking care which belongs to their children. Satan often plays upon their imagination and leads them to feel a continual anxiety in regard to their money. It is their idol, and they hoard it with miserly care. They will sometimes deprive themselves of many of the comforts of life, and labor beyond their strength, rather than use the means which they have. In this way they place themselves in continual want, through fear that sometime in the future they shall want. All these fears originate with Satan. He excites the organs which lead to slavish fears and jealousies which corrupt nobleness of soul and destroy elevated thoughts and feelings. Such persons are insane upon the subject of money. If they would take the position which God would have them, their last days might be their best and happiest. Those who have children in whose honesty and judicious management they have reason to confide, should let their children make them happy. Unless they do this, Satan will take advantage of their lack of mental strength and will manage for them. They should lay aside anxiety and burdens, and occupy their time as happily as they can, and be ripening up for heaven.

EXTREMES IN DRESS

We do not think it in accordance with our faith to dress in the American costume, to wear hoops, or to go to an extreme in wearing long dresses which sweep the sidewalks and streets. If women would wear their dresses so as to clear the filth of the streets an inch or two, their dresses would be modest, and they could be kept clean much more easily, and would wear longer. Such a dress would be in accordance with our faith. I have received several letters from sisters inquiring my opinion in regard to wearing corded skirts. These questions were answered in a letter which I sent to a sister in Wisconsin. I will give the letter here for the benefit of others:

"We as a people do not believe it our duty to go out of the world to be out of the fashion. If we have a neat, plain, modest, and comfortable plan of dress, and worldlings choose to dress as we do, shall we change this mode of dress in order to be different from the world? No, we should not be odd or singular in our dress for the sake of differing from the world, lest they despise us for so doing. Christians are the light of the world, the salt of the earth. Their dress should be neat and modest, their conversation chaste and heavenly, and their deportment blameless.

"How shall we dress? If any wore heavy quilts before the introduction of hoops, merely for show and not for comfort, they sinned against themselves by injuring their health, which it is their duty to preserve. If any wear them now merely to look like hoops, they commit sin, for they are seeking to imitate a fashion which is disgraceful. Corded skirts were worn before hoops were introduced. I have worn a light corded skirt since I was fourteen years of age, not for show but for comfort and decency. Because hoops were introduced I did not lay off my corded skirt for them. Shall I now throw it aside because the fashion of hoops is introduced? No; that would be carrying the matter to an extreme.

"I should ever bear in mind that I must be an example and therefore must not run into this or that fashion, but pursue an even and independent course and not be driven to extremes in regard to dress. To throw off my corded skirt that was always modest and comfortable, and put on a thin cotton skirt, and thus appear ridiculous in the other extreme, would be wrong, for then I would not set a right example, but would put an argument into the mouths of hoop wearers. To justify themselves for wearing hoops they would point to me as one who does not wear them, and say that they would not disgrace themselves in that way. By going to such extremes we would destroy all the influence which we might otherwise have had, and lead the wearers of hoops to justify their course. We must dress modestly, without the least regard to the hoop fashion.

"There is a medium position in these things. Oh, that we all might wisely find that position and keep it. In this solemn time let us all search our own hearts, repent of our sins, and humble ourselves before God. The work is between God and our own souls. It is an individual work, and all will have enough to do without criticizing the dress, actions, and motives of their brethren and sisters. 'Seek ye the Lord, all ye meek of the earth, which have wrought His judgment; seek righteousness, seek meekness: it may be ye shall be hid in the day of the Lord's anger.' Here is our work. It is not sinners who are here addressed, but all the meek of the earth, who have wrought His judgments or kept His commandments. There is work for everyone, and if all will obey, we shall see sweet union in the ranks of Sabbathkeepers."

COMMUNICATIONS TO ELDER HULL*

November 5, 1862, I was shown the condition of Brother Hull. He was in an alarming state. His lack of consecration and vital piety left him subject to Satan's suggestions. He has relied upon his own strength instead of the strong arm of the Lord, and that mighty arm has been partially removed.

I was shown that the most alarming feature in the case of Brother Hull is that he is asleep to his danger. He feels no alarm, feels perfectly secure and at rest, while Satan and his

---

*The General Conference Committee would here express their approval of the publication of this *Testimony.* Especially do we recommend the publication of the letters addressed to Elder Hull and given to him at the time of their dates. We call the particular attention of the reader to the declaration on page 442. It is there stated that Elder Hull needed to be led as a blind man who depends on another for sight. At the General Conference in Battle Creek, May, 1863, Elder Hull acknowledged the justness of the statement, but has since protested against it. The Committee now maintain that his course in the short space of the past four months in abandoning every point of religious faith dear to us as a people, is a most palpable demonstration of the correctness of the above statement that he should follow the counsel of his brethren.

GEN. CONF. COM.

angels are exulting over their conquest. Just as long as Brother Hull maintained a conflict, his mind was reined up, and there was a collision of spirits. He has now ceased the conflict, and the collision ceases. His mind is at rest, and Satan lets him have peace. Oh how dangerous was the position in which he was shown me! His case is nearly hopeless, because he makes no effort to resist Satan and extricate himself from his dreadful snare.

Brother Hull has been dealt with faithfully. He has felt that he was too much restrained, that he could not act out his nature. While the power of the truth, in all its force influenced him, he was comparatively safe; but break the force and power of truth upon the mind, and there is no restraint, the natural propensities take the lead, and there is no stopping place. He has become tired of the conflict, and has for some time wished that he could more freely act himself, and has felt hurt at the reproofs of his brethren. He was presented to me as standing upon the brink of an awful gulf, ready to leap. If he takes the leap, it will be final; his eternal destiny will be fixed. He is doing work and making decisions for eternity. The work of God is not dependent upon Brother Hull. If he leaves the ranks of those who bear the bloodstained banner of Prince Immanuel, and joins the company who bear the black banner, it will be his own loss, his own eternal destruction.

I saw that those who wish can have plenty of room to doubt the inspiration and truth of God's word. God compels none to believe. They can choose to rely upon the evidences which He has been pleased to give, or doubt and perish. It is life or death with you, Brother Hull. Already I saw a cloud of evil angels surrounding you, and you at perfect ease among them. Satan has been telling you a pleasing story about an easier way than to be in constant warfare with conflicting spirits; but if you choose that way, you will find in the end that you will have a heavy and fearful toll to pay.

I saw that you have felt strong in yourself, felt that you had arguments which could not be gainsaid, and you have not relied upon the strength of the Lord. You have too often rushed upon Satan's ground to meet an opponent. You have not waited until you knew that the truth or the cause of God demanded a discussion, but have engaged with opponents where with a little forethought you would have decided that the truth could not be advanced or the cause of God benefited. Precious time has thus been spent.

Satan looked on and witnessed the heavy blow which Brother Hull dealt to spiritualism in Battle Creek. Spiritualists understood his organization, and felt assured it would not be in vain to make a determined effort to overthrow him who injured their cause so much. In discussing with spiritualists you have not merely to meet man and his arguments, but Satan and his angels. And never should one man be sent forth alone to combat with a spiritualist. If the cause of God really demands that we confront Satan and his host as represented by a spiritual medium, if enough is at stake to call for such a discussion, then several should go forth together that with prayer and faith the host of darkness may be driven back and the speaker shielded by angels that excel in strength.

Brother Hull, you were shown me under the soothing influence of a fascination which will prove fatal unless the spell is broken. You have parleyed with Satan, and reasoned with him, and tarried upon forbidden ground, and have exercised your mind in things which were too great for you, and by indulging in doubts and unbelief have attracted evil angels around you, and driven from you the pure and holy angels of God. If you had steadfastly resisted Satan's suggestions and sought strength from God with a determined effort, you would have broken every fetter, driven back your spiritual foe, come closer to God, and triumphed in His name. I saw that it was presumption in you to go forth to meet a spiritualist when you were yourself enshrouded and bewildered by clouds of unbelief. You went to battle with Satan and his host without an armor, and have been grievously wounded, and are insensible to your wound. I greatly fear that the thunders and lightnings of Sinai would fail to move you. You are in Satan's easy chair and do not see your fearful condition and make an effort to escape. If you do not arouse and recover yourself from the snare of the devil, you must perish. The brethren and sisters would save you, but I saw that they could not. You have something to do; you have a desperate effort to make, or you are lost. I saw that those who are under the bewitching influence of spiritualism know it not. You have been charmed and mesmerized, yet you do not know it, and therefore do not make the least effort to come to the light.

I saw that we are now in the shaking time. Satan is working with all his power to wrest souls from the hand of Christ and cause them to trample underfoot the Son of God. An angel slowly and emphatically repeated these words: "Of how much sorer punishment, suppose ye, shall he be thought worthy, who hath trodden underfoot the Son of God, and hath counted the blood of the covenant, wherewith he was sanctified, an unholy thing, and hath done despite unto the Spirit of grace?" Character is being developed. Angels of God are weighing moral worth. God is testing and proving His people. These words were presented to me by the angel: "Take heed, brethren, lest there be in any of you an evil heart of unbelief, in departing from the living God. But exhort one another daily, while it is called today; lest any of you be hardened through the deceitfulness of sin. For we are made partakers of Christ, if we hold the *beginning of our confidence steadfast unto the end*." God is displeased that any of His people who have known the power of His grace should talk their doubts, and by thus doing make themselves a channel for Satan to transmit his suggestions to other minds. A seed of unbelief and evil sown is not readily rooted up. Satan nourishes it every hour, and it flourishes and becomes strong. A good seed sown needs to be nourished, watered, and tenderly cared for; because every poisonous influence is thrown about it to hinder its growth and cause it to die.

Satan's efforts are more powerful now than ever before, for he knows that his time to deceive is short. Brother Hull, I saw that you had injured yourself greatly by exposing your weakness and telling your doubts to those who are Satan's agents. You have been deceived by soft words and fair speeches, and have exposed yourself in a most reckless manner to the attacks of Satan. How could you thus wound yourself and reproach God's word? You have recklessly rushed upon Satan's battleground, and it is no marvel that your mind is so stupid and unfeeling. Already has Satan through his agents poisoned the atmosphere you breathe; already have evil angels telegraphed to his agents upon earth in regard to the course to be pursued toward you. And this is one whom God has called to stand between the living and the dead; this is one of the watchmen stationed upon the walls of Zion to tell the people the time of night. A heavy responsibility rests upon you. If you go down, you will not go alone; for Satan will employ you as his agent to lead souls to death.

I saw that angels of God were looking sorrowfully toward you. They had left your side and were turning mournfully away, while Satan and his angels were grinning in exultation over you. If you had yourself battled with your doubts and not encouraged the devil to tempt you, by talking out your unbelief and loving to dwell upon it, you would not have attracted the fallen angels about you in such numbers. But you chose to talk your darkness, you chose to dwell upon it; and the more you talk and dwell upon it, the darker and darker you grow. You are shutting out from you every ray of heaven's light; and a great gulf is coming between you and the only ones who can help you. If you proceed in the way you have started, misery and woe are before you. God's hand will arrest you in a manner that will not suit you. His wrath will not slumber. But now He invites you. Now, just now, He calls upon you to return unto Him without delay, and He will graciously pardon and heal all your backslidings. God is leading out a people who are peculiar. He will cleanse and purify them, and fit them for translation. Every carnal thing will be separated from God's peculiar treasures until they shall be like gold seven times purified.

I saw that it was a cruel position for Brethren A and B to be in, to be serving the purposes of Satan by suffering their minds to run just as he would lead them in the channel of unbelief. Their greatest sin was in talking out these dark doubts, this midnight unbelief, and drawing other minds into the same dark channel.

God's people will be sifted, even as corn is sifted in a sieve, until all the chaff is separated from the pure kernels of grain. We are to look to Christ for an example and imitate the humble pattern. You do not feel reconciled to the discipline you need and do not exercise and practice that self-denial which Christ requires of those who are truly heirs of salvation. Those who are engaged in the work of saving souls are co-workers with Christ. His was a work of disinterested benevolence, of constant self-sacrifice. Those who have had so great a sacrifice made for them that they might become partakers of His heavenly grace should in their turn sacrifice and deny self to aid in the great work of bringing others to the knowledge of the truth. Self-interest should be laid aside; selfish desires and self-comfort should not now stand in the way of God's work in saving souls. God's ministers are laboring in Christ's stead; they are His ambassadors. They are not to study their ease, comfort, pleasure, desires, or convenience. They must suffer for Christ, be crucified with Him, and rejoice that they can in every sense of the word know the fellowship of the sufferings of Christ.

I saw that ministers who labor in word and doctrine have a great work before them; a heavy responsibility rests upon them. In their labor they do not come close enough to hearts. Their work is too general, and often too scattered. Their labor must be concentrated to the very ones for whom they are laboring. When they preach from the desk, they only commence their work. They must then live out their preaching, ever guarding themselves, that they bring not a reproach upon the cause of God. They should illustrate by example the life of Christ. 1 Corinthians 3:9: "For we are laborers together with God." 2 Corinthians 6:1: "We then, as workers together with Him, beseech you also that ye receive not the grace of God in vain." The minister's work is not done when he leaves the desk. He should not then throw off the burden and occupy his mind with reading or writing unless this is actually necessary. He should follow up his public labors by private efforts, laboring personally for souls whenever an opportunity presents, conversing around the fireside, beseeching and entreating souls in Christ's stead to be reconciled to God. Our work here is soon to close, "and every man shall receive his own reward according to his own labor."

I was shown the saints' reward, the immortal inheritance. Then I was shown how much God's people had endured for the truth's sake, and that they would count heaven cheap enough. They reckoned that the sufferings of this present time were not worthy to be compared with the glory which should be revealed in them. The people of God in these last days will be tried. But soon their last trial will come, and then they will receive the gift of eternal life.

Brother Hull, you have suffered reproach for the truth's sake. You have felt the power of the truth and of an endless life. You have had God's Spirit witness with yours that you were owned and accepted of Him. I saw that if you gird on the armor anew, and stand at your post, resisting the devil and fighting manfully the battles of the Lord, you will be victorious, and will soon lay off your armor and wear a conqueror's crown. Oh, is not the inheritance rich enough? Did it not cost a dear price, the agony and blood of the Son of God? I call upon you in the name of the Lord to awake. Break away from the awful deception which Satan has thrown over you. Lay hold on everlasting life. Resist the devil. Evil angels are around you, whispering in your ears, visiting you with lying dreams, and you listen to them and are pleased. Oh, for the sake of Christ, for your own soul's sake, tear away from this dreadful influence before you grieve God's Spirit entirely from you.

Sabbath, June 6, 1863, I was shown some things in regard to the work of God and the spread of the truth. Preachers and people have too little faith, too little devotion and true godliness. The people imitate the preacher, and thus he has a very great influence upon them. Brother Hull, God wants you to come nearer to Him, where you can take hold of His strength, and by living faith claim His salvation, and be a strong man. If you were a devotional, godly man, in the pulpit and out, a mighty influence would attend your preaching. You do not closely search your own heart. You have studied many works to make your discourses thorough, able, and pleasing; but you have neglected the greatest and most necessary study, the study of yourself. A thorough knowledge of yourself, meditation and prayer, have come in as secondary things. Your success as a minister depends upon your keeping your own heart. You will receive more strength by spending one hour each day in meditation, and in mourning over your failings and heart corruptions and pleading for God's pardoning love and the assurance of sins forgiven, than you would by spending many hours and days in studying the most able authors, and making yourself acquainted with every objection to our faith, and with the most powerful evidences in its favor.

The reason why our preachers accomplish so little is that they do not walk with God. He is a day's journey from most of them. The more closely you watch your own heart, the more watchful and guarded you will be, lest by your words or acts you dishonor the truth, give occasion for the tongue of slander to follow you and the truth, and cause souls to be lost through your neglect of self-examination, of heart study, and of vital godliness. The holy deportment of the minister of Christ should be a rebuke to vain, frothy professors. The beams of truth and holiness shining from your serious, heavenly conversation will convict others and lead them to the truth, and those around you will be compelled to say, God is with this man, of a truth. It is the carelessness and looseness of professed ministers of Christ that gives them so little influence. There are many professors, but there are few praying men. If our preachers were men who prayed more in secret, who carried their preaching into practice in their families, who ruled their houses with dignity and gravity, their light would indeed shine to those around them.

Brother Hull, I have been shown that if you would dedicate yourself to God, hold communion with Him, meditate much, watch your failings, mourn and lament before the Lord in the deepest humility on account of them, relying upon Him for strength, you would be in the most profitable business in which you were ever engaged; for you would be drinking at a living fountain, and could then give others to drink from that same fountain which revived and strengthened you.

Dear brother, unless there is a change in your Christian character, you will fail of everlasting life; for our busy foe will lay his snares for your feet, and if you are not near to God you will fall into the net. You feel restless and uneasy, and study is your element; but you sometimes fail in the subject. When you should be studying your own heart, you are engaged in reading books. When you should by faith be drawing near to Christ, you are studying books. I saw that all your study will be useless unless you faithfully study yourself. You are not acquainted with yourself, and your mind dwells but little upon God. You are self-confident, and pass along without knowing that self must die if you would be a successful minister of Christ. You lack sobriety and gravity out of the pulpit. These things counteract your pulpit labor.

Ever since your case was first presented to me in vision, I have seen a lack in you. Your mind is not elevated. You stand in the desk and handle the most holy, sacred, elevating truths in an able manner; but when treating upon the most solemn subjects, you often bring in something comical to create a smile, and this frequently destroys the force of your whole discourse. You handle solemn truths with ease, but do not live them, and that is the reason why the heavenly endorsement is lacking. Many whose ears you have pleased will talk of the smart discourse, the able preacher, but are no more impressed with the necessity of obeying the truth than before they listened to it. They go on transgressing God's law as before. It was the minister that pleased them, not the truths which he uttered. You remain at so great a distance from God that His power does not set home the truth. You should live religion at home, and it would have an influence to elevate your family, to elevate your wife. When at home you throw off restraint and act like a boy, the weight of the truth and the burden of the work do not rest upon you. You are not choice of your words or of your example.

Your only safety is in studying yourself, your weakness and failings. Do not cease to guard yourself. Watch yourself more closely when at home. Watch yourself when away from home. You neglect your closet duties, lay off your armor, and give up to a spirit of recklessness that drives angels from you and from your family. Do not neglect to search your own heart at home. Lavish not all your affections upon your family. Preserve your heart's best affections to devote to Jesus, who has redeemed you by His blood. When at home, be fitting up all the time for your Master's business when you shall be away from home. If you do this, you will have on the armor every moment. Your soul's highest desire will be to glorify God, to do His will upon earth, and you will have sweet confidence and trust in Him. You will not feel so restless, but will have a constant theme for meditation, devotion, and holiness. I was referred to 1 Corinthians 9:27: "But I keep under my body, and bring it into subjection: lest that by any means, when I have preached to others, I myself should be a castaway." You have a work to do to understand yourself. Be not flattered by remarks which unwise and foolish brethren may make concerning your efforts. If they praise your preaching, let it not elate you. If God's blessing attends your labors, fruits will be seen. Your preaching will not merely please, but will gather in souls.

Brother Hull, you must be guarded on every side. I saw that whatever divides the affections, or takes away from the heart supreme love for God, or prevents unlimited confidence and entire trust in Him, assumes the character and takes the form of an idol. I was pointed to the first great commandment: "Thou shalt love the Lord thy God with all thy heart, and with all thy soul, and with all thy mind." There is allowed no separation of our affections from God. Nothing is to divide our supreme love for Him or our delight in Him. Your will, wishes, plans, desires, and pleasures must all be in subjection. You have something to learn, to exalt the Lord God in your heart, in your conversation, in all your acts; and then Jesus can teach you, and help you, as you cast your net on the right side of the ship, to bring it to shore full of fishes. But without the help of Christ in casting your net, you may toil weeks, months, and years without seeing much fruit of your labor.

I saw that you would be tempted to feel that your brethren want to gauge you, that they want to put too much restraint upon you. But your brethren only want you to live according to the instructions of God's word, and God wishes to bring you there, and angels are watching you with the deepest solicitude. You must conform your life to the word of God, that you may be blessed and strengthened of Him, or you will fall out by the way, and while you preach to others, you yourself will be a castaway. But you may be an overcomer, and may win eternal life. You are recovering yourself from the snare of Satan, but he is preparing other snares for you. God will help and strengthen you if you seek Him earnestly. But study yourself. Try every motive; let it not be your aim to preach brilliant discourses to exhibit Moses Hull, but seek to exhibit Christ. Simplify the truth to your hearers so that small minds may comprehend it. Make your discourses plain, pointed, and solemn. Bring the people to a decision. Make them feel the vital force of truth. If any speak one word of flattery to you, rebuke them sharply. Tell them that Satan has troubled you with that for some time, and they need not help him in his work.

When among the sisters, be reserved. No matter if they think you lack courtesy. If sisters, married or unmarried, show any familiarity, repulse them. Be abrupt and decided, that they may ever understand that you give no countenance to such weakness. When before the young, and at all times, be grave, be solemn. I saw that if Brother Loughborough and yourself make God your strength, a work will be accomplished by you for His poor people, for two can be a host. Come close to each other, pray together and separately, be free with each other. Brother Hull should confide in Brother Loughborough's judgment, and listen to his counsel and advice.

UNCONSECRATED MINISTERS

Ministers who preach the third message should labor because they feel that God has laid upon them the burden of the work. Our ministers are placed above want, if they exercise any degree of economy. If they lack, they will be in want in any position in which they may be placed. Give them the most favorable chance and they would spend all they receive. This has been the case with Elder Hull. Such need an almost inexhaustible fund to draw from in order to be satisfied.

Those who fail to manage wisely in temporal matters, generally lack in spiritual things. They fail to build up the church. They may possess natural talents and be called smart speakers, and yet lack moral worth. They may draw large congregations and raise considerable excitement; but when the fruit is sought for, there is very little, if any, to be found. Such men frequently get above the work and lose their love for the simplicity of the gospel. They are not sanctified through the truths they preach. This has been the case with Elder Hull. He has lacked that grace which establishes the soul and elevates and ennobles the character of the man. It is a good thing that the heart be established with grace. This is the ground of our steadfastness.

In places where Elder Hull has given a course of lectures, the people have been pleased with his witticisms and his peculiar style of preaching, yet but few have embraced the truth as the result of his labors; and even of these quite a proportion soon renounce the faith. Many have been disappointed that there was so little fruit to be found after his labor. I was shown the reason. Humility, simplicity, purity, and holiness of life were lacking. He has thought that his smart labor was invaluable, and that the cause would hardly exist if he should be disconnected from it; but if he could have known the anxiety which the real laborers in the cause, who have tried to help him, have suffered on his account, he would not have had so high an estimate of his own labors. His course has been a continual burden to the cause, and it would have prospered better without his influence. The anxiety of his brethren to save him from falling has led them to do too much for him in point of means. They have been pleased with his preaching talent, and some have been so indiscreet as to extol him and show a decided preference for him above other preaching brethren whose influence would tell for the advancement of the cause anywhere. This has hurt him. He had not sufficient humility or enough of the grace of God to stand against the flattery of his brethren. May God help these brethren to feel over their mistake and never again to be guilty of injuring a young minister by flattery.

All who desire to draw away from God's remnant people in order to follow their own corrupt hearts would throw themselves willingly into Satan's hands, and should have the privilege. There are others among us who are in danger. They have an exalted opinion of their own ability, while their influence in many respects has been but little better than that of Elder Hull. Unless they thoroughly reform, the cause would be better off without them. Unsanctified ministers injure the cause and are a heavy tax upon their brethren. They need someone to follow after them to correct their mistakes and to straighten up and strengthen those who have been weakened and torn down through their influence. They are jealous of those who have borne burdens in the work, those who would sacrifice even their lives if necessary to advance the cause of truth. They judge their brethren to have no higher motives than they have had. Doing much for ministers who are thus subject to Satan's temptations injures them and is a waste of means. It gives them influence, and thus places them where they can wound their brethren and the cause of God most deeply.

I have been shown that the doubts expressed in regard to the truthfulness of our position and the inspiration of the word of God are not caused as many suppose them to be. These difficulties are not so much with the Bible or with the evidences of our faith as with their own hearts. The requirements of God's word are too close for their unsanctified natures. "The carnal mind is enmity against God: for it is not subject to the law of God, neither indeed can be." If the feelings of the natural heart are not restrained and brought into subjection by the sanctifying influence of the grace of God received through the channel of faith, the thoughts of the heart are not pure and holy. The conditions of salvation brought to view in the word of God are reasonable, plain, and positive, being nothing less than perfect conformity to the will of God and purity of heart and life. We must crucify self with the lusts thereof. We must cleanse ourselves from all filthiness of the flesh and spirit, perfecting holiness in the fear of God.

In almost every case where persons become unsettled in regard to the inspiration of the word of God, it is on account of their unsanctified lives, which that word condemns. They will not receive its reproofs and threatenings because these reflect upon their wrong course of action. They do not love those who would convert and restrain them. Difficulties and doubts which perplex the vicious heart will be cleared away before the one practicing the pure principles of truth.

Many possess talents which would accomplish much good if sanctified and used in the cause of Christ, or much harm if employed in the service of unbelief and Satan. The gratification of self and its various lusts will pervert the talents and make them a curse instead of a blessing. Satan, the archdeceiver, possesses wonderful talents. He was once an exalted angel, next to Christ. He fell through self-exaltation, and created a rebellion in heaven, and caused many to fall with him.

Then his talents and skill were employed against the government of God, to cause all whom he could control to despise the authority of heaven. Those who are charmed with his satanic majesty may choose to imitate this fallen general and share with him his fate at last.

Purity of life imparts refinement, which will lead those possessing it to shrink more and more from coarseness and indulgence in sin. Such will not be led away from the truth or be given up to doubt the inspiration of the word of God. On the contrary, they will engage in the daily study of the sacred word with ever-increasing interest, and the evidences of Christianity and inspiration will stamp their impress on the mind and life. Those who love sin will turn away from the Bible, will love to doubt, and will become reckless in principle. They will receive and advocate false theories. Such will ascribe man's sins to his circumstances, and when he commits some great sin they make him a subject of pity instead of looking upon him as a criminal to be punished. This will always suit a depraved heart, which in course of time will develop the principles of fallen nature. By some general process, men abolish sin at once to avoid the unpleasant necessity of individual reformation and exertion. In order to free themselves from the obligation of present effort, many are ready to declare of no account all the labor and effort of their lives while following the sacred principles of God's word. Elder Hull's philosophical necessity has its stronghold in the corruptions of the heart. God is raising up men to go forth to labor in the harvest field, and if they are humble, devoted, and godly, they will take the crowns which those ministers lose who concerning the faith are reprobate.

November 5, 1862, I was shown that some men mistake their calling. They think that if a man cannot labor with his hands, or if he is not a business character, he will make a minister. Many make a great mistake here. A man who has no business tact may make a minister, but he will lack qualifications that every minister must possess in order to deal wisely in the church and build up the cause. But when a minister is good in the pulpit, and, like Elder Hull, fails in management, he should never go out alone. Another should go with him to supply his lack and manage for him. And although it may be humiliating, he should give heed to the judgment and counsel of this companion, as a blind man follows one who has sight. By so doing he will escape many dangers that would prove fatal to him were he left alone.

The prosperity of the cause of God depends much upon the ministers who labor in the gospel field. Those who teach the truth should be devotional, self-sacrificing, godly men who understand their business and go about doing good because they know that God has called them to the work, men who feel the worth of souls and will bear burdens and responsibilities. A thorough workman is known by the perfection of his work.

There are but few preachers among us. And because the cause of God seemed to need help so much, some have been led to think that almost anyone claiming to be a minister would be acceptable. Some have thought that because persons could pray and exhort with a degree of freedom in meeting, they were qualified to go forth as laborers. And before they were proved, or could show any good fruit of their labors, men whom God has not sent have been encouraged and flattered by some brethren lacking experience. But their work shows the character of the workman. They scatter and confuse, but do not gather in and build up. A few may receive the truth as the fruit of their labors, but these generally rise no higher than those from whom they learned the truth. The same lack which marked their own course is seen in their converts.

The success of this cause does not depend upon our having

a large number of ministers, but it is of the highest importance that those who do labor in connection with the cause of God should be men who really feel the burden and sacredness of the work to which He has called them. A few self-sacrificing godly men, small in their own estimation, can do a greater amount of good than a much larger number if a part of these are unqualified for the work, yet self-confident and boastful of their own talents. A number of these in the field, who would better fill some calling at home, would make it necessary that nearly all the time of the faithful ministers be spent in following after them to correct their wrong influence. The future usefulness of young preachers depends much upon the manner in which they enter upon their labors. Brethren who have the cause of God at heart are so anxious to see the truth advance that they are in danger of doing too much for ministers who have not been proved, by helping them liberally to means and giving them influence. Those who enter the gospel field should be left to earn themselves a reputation, even if it must be through trials and privations. They should first give full proof of their ministry.

Brethren of experience should be guarded; and instead of expecting these young preachers to help and lead them, should feel a responsibility upon them to take charge of these young preachers, to instruct, advise, and lead them, to have a fatherly care for them. Young ministers should have system, a firm purpose, and a mind to work, that they may eat no man's bread for nought. They should not go from place to place, and introduce some points of our faith calculated to stir up prejudice, and leave before the evidences of present truth are half presented. Young men who think that they have a duty to do in connection with the work should not take the responsibility of teaching the truth until they have availed themselves of the privilege of being under the influence of some experienced preacher who is systematic in his work;

they should learn of him as a pupil at school would learn of his teacher. They should not go hither and thither, with no definite object or matured plans to carry out in their labor.

Some who have but little experience, and are least qualified to teach the truth are the last to ask advice and counsel of their experienced brethren. They put on the minister, and place themselves on a level with those of long and tried experience, and are not satisfied unless they can lead, thinking that because they are ministers, they know all that is worth knowing. Such preachers certainly lack a true knowledge of themselves. They do not possess becoming modesty and have altogether too high an opinion of their own abilities. Ministers of experience, who realize the sacredness of the work, and feel the weight of the cause upon them, are jealous of themselves. They consider it a privilege to advise with their brethren and are not offended if improvements are suggested in their plans of labor or in their manner of speaking.

Those ministers who have come out from the different denominations to embrace the third angel's message often wish to teach when they should be learners. Some have a great share of their former teaching to unlearn before they can fully learn the principles of present truth. Ministers will injure the cause of God by going forth to labor for others when there is as great a work to be done for them to fit them for their labors as they may wish to do for unbelievers. If they are unqualified for the work, it will require the labor of two or three faithful ministers to follow after and correct their wrong influence. In the end it would be cheaper for the cause of God to give such ministers a good support to remain at home and do no injury in the field.

Preachers have been regarded by some as especially inspired, as being only mediums for the Lord to speak through. If the aged and those of long experience see failings in a minister and suggest improvements in his manners, in the tone of his voice, or in his gestures, he has sometimes felt hurt, and has reasoned that God called him just as he was, that the power was of God and not of himself, and that God must do the work for him, that he did not preach according to man's wisdom, etc. It is a mistake to think that a man cannot preach unless he becomes wrought up to a high degree of excitement. Men who are thus dependent upon feeling may be of use in exhortation when they feel just like it; but they will never make good, burden-bearing laborers. When the work moves hard and everything assumes a discouraging aspect, the excitable and those dependent upon feeling are not prepared to bear their share of the burdens. In times of discouragement and darkness how important to have calm-thinking men, who are not dependent on circumstances, but who trust God and labor on in the darkness as well as in the light. Men who serve God from principle, although their faith may be severely tried, will be seen leaning securely upon the never-failing arm of Jehovah.

Young preachers, and men who have once been ministers, who have been coarse and rough in their manners, making expressions in their conversation which were not perfectly modest and chaste, are not fit to engage in this work until they give evidence of an entire reform. One word spoken unadvisedly may do more harm than a series of meetings held by them will do good. They leave the standard of truth, which should be ever exalted, lowered to the dust before the community. Their converts generally come up no higher than the standard raised for them by the ministers. Men who are standing between the living and the dead should be just right. The minister should not be off his guard for a single moment. He is laboring to elevate others by bringing them up upon the platform of truth. Let him show to others that the truth has done something for him. He should see the evil of these careless, rough, vulgar expressions, and should put away and despise everything of this character. Unless he does this, his converts will pattern after him. And when faithful ministers shall follow after and labor with these converts to correct their wrongs, they will excuse themselves by referring to the minister. If you condemn his course, they will turn to you and ask: Why do you uphold and give influence to men by sending them out to preach to sinners while they are sinners themselves?

The work in which we are engaged is a responsible and exalted work. Those who minister in word and doctrine should themselves be patterns of good works. They should be examples in holiness, cleanliness, and order. The appearance of the servant of God, out of the pulpit and in, should be that of a living preacher. He can accomplish far more by his godly example than by merely preaching in the desk, while his influence out of the desk is not worthy of imitation. Those who labor in this cause are bearing to the world the most elevated truth that was ever committed to mortals.

Men who are chosen of God to labor in this cause will give proof of their high calling and will consider it their highest duty to grow and improve until they shall become able workmen. Then, as they manifest an earnestness to improve upon the talent which God has entrusted to them, they should be helped judiciously. But the encouragement given them should not savor of flattery, for Satan himself will do enough of that kind of work. Men who think that they have a duty to preach should not be sustained in throwing themselves and their families at once upon the brethren for support. They are not entitled to this until they can show good fruits of their labor. There is now danger of injuring young preachers, and those who have but little experience, by flattery, and by relieving them of burdens in life. When not preaching they should be doing what they can for their own support. This is the best way to test the nature of their call to preach. If they desire to preach only that they may be supported as ministers, and the church pursue a judicious course, they will soon lose the burden and leave preaching for more profitable business. Paul, a most eloquent preacher, miraculously converted of God to do a special work, was not above labor. He says: "Even unto this present hour we both hunger, and thirst, and are naked, and are buffeted, and have no certain dwelling place; and labor, working with our own hands: being reviled, we bless; being persecuted, we suffer it." 1 Corinthians 4:11, 12. "Neither did we eat any man's bread for nought; but wrought with labor and travail night and day, that we might not be chargeable to any of you." 2 Thessalonians 3:8.

I have been shown that many do not rightly estimate the talents which are among them. Some brethren do not understand what preaching talent would be the best for the advancement of the cause of truth, but think only of the present gratification of their feelings. Without reflection they will show preference for a speaker who manifests considerable zeal in his preaching and relates anecdotes which please the ear and animate the mind for a moment, but leave no lasting impression. At the same time they will put a low estimate upon a preacher who has prayerfully studied that he may present before the people the arguments of our position in a calm manner and in a connected form. His labor is not appreciated, and he is often treated with indifference.

A man may preach in a spirited manner and please the ear, but convey no new idea or real intelligence to the mind. The impressions received through such preaching last no longer than while the speaker's voice is heard. When search is made for the fruit of such labor, there is little to be found. These flashy gifts are not as beneficial, and well calculated to advance the cause of truth, as a gift that can be trusted in hard, difficult places. In the work of teaching the truth it is necessary that the important points of our position be well fortified with

Scripture evidences. Assertions may silence the unbeliever, but will not convince him. Believers are not the only ones for whose benefit laborers are sent into the field. The salvation of souls is the great object.

Some brethren have erred in this respect. They have thought that Brother C was the right man to labor in Vermont and that he could accomplish more than any other minister in that state. Such do not view matters from a right standpoint. Brother C can speak in a manner to interest a congregation, and if this were all that is necessary to make a successful preacher, then a class of brethren and sisters would be right in their estimation of him. But he is not a thorough workman; he is not reliable. In church trials he is of no account. He has not experience, judgment, and discernment to be of any benefit to the church when in trial. He has not been a thoroughgoing man in temporal matters, and although he has but a small family, he has needed assistance more or less. The same lack is manifested in spiritual things as in temporal affairs. Had the right course been pursued toward him in the commencement of his preaching, he might now be of some use in this cause. His brethren injured him by making too much of him and by leaving him to bear but few of the burdens of life, until he has thought that his labors were of the greatest consequence. He has been willing that brethren in Vermont should bear his burdens while he was relieved from care. He has not had a suitable amount of exercise to give tone and strength to his muscles, and for the good of his health.

He is not capable of building up churches. When he feels the woe upon him if he preach not the gospel, as self-sacrificing preachers have felt it in the past, then like them he will be willing to labor with his hands a part of the time to earn means to support his family that they may not be burdensome to the church, and then he will go forth, not merely to preach, but to save souls. Efforts made with such a spirit will accomplish something. He has been exalted in his own estimation, has thought himself equal to any of the laborers in Vermont, and has felt that he should be ranked with them and should be consulted in business matters of the church, when he has not earned a reputation nor proved himself worthy. What self-sacrifice or devotion has he manifested for the church? What perils or hardships has he endured, that the brethren can have their confidence established in him as a laborer whom they can trust, whose influence will be good wherever he goes? Until he possesses an entirely different spirit and acts from unselfish principles, he would better give up the idea of preaching.

Brethren in Vermont have overlooked the moral worth of men like the Brethren Bourdeau, Pierce, and Stone, who have a depth of experience and whose influence has been such as to gain the confidence of the community. Their industrious and consistent lives have made them daily, living preachers, and their labors have removed a great amount of prejudice and have gathered and built up. Yet brethren have not appreciated the labor of these men, while they have been pleased with that of some who will not bear to be tested and proved, and who can show but little fruit of their labor.

THE MINISTER'S WIFE

June 5, 1863, I was shown that Satan is ever at work to dishearten and lead astray ministers whom God has chosen to preach the truth. The most effectual way in which he can work is through home influences, through unconsecrated companions. If he can control their minds, he can through them the more readily gain access to the husband, who is laboring in word and doctrine to save souls. I was referred to the warnings which God has repeatedly given, and to the duties which have been pointed out as belonging to the wife of a minister; yet these warnings have not had a lasting influence. The testimonies given have had effect but a short time. The light has been but partially followed. Obedience and devotion to God have been forgotten, many have disregarded the sacred obligation resting upon them to improve the light and privileges given, and walk as children of the light. If the veil could be parted and all could see just how their cases are regarded in heaven, there would be an awakening, and each would with fear inquire, What shall I do to be saved?

The minister's wife who is not devoted to God is no help to her husband. While he dwells upon the necessity of bearing the cross and urges the importance of self-denial, the daily example of his wife often contradicts his preaching and destroys its force. In this way she becomes a great hindrance and often leads her husband away from his duty and from God. She does not realize what a sin she is committing. Instead of seeking to be useful, seeking with true love for souls to help such as need help, she shrinks from the task and prefers a useless life. She is not constrained by the power of Christ's love and by unselfish, holy principles. She does not choose to do the will of God, to be a co-worker with her husband, with angels, and with God. When the wife of the minister accompanies her husband in his mission to save souls, it is a great sin for her to hinder him in his work by manifesting unhappy discontent. Yet instead of entering heartily into his labors, seeking every opportunity to unite her interest and labor with his, she often studies how she can make it more easy or pleasant for herself. If things around them are not as agreeable as she could wish (as they will not always be), she should not indulge homesick feelings, or by lack of cheerfulness and by spoken complaints harass the husband and make his task harder, and perhaps by her discontent draw him from the place where he could do good. She should not divert the interest of her husband from laboring for the salvation of souls, to sympathize with her ailments and gratify her whimsical, discontented feelings. If she would forget herself and labor to help others, talk and pray with poor souls, and act as if their salvation was of higher importance than any other consideration, she would have no time to be homesick. She would feel from day to day a sweet satisfaction as a reward for her unselfish labor; I cannot call it sacrifice, for some of our ministers' wives do not know what it is to sacrifice or suffer for the truth's sake.

In former years the wives of ministers endured want and persecution. When their husbands suffered imprisonment, and sometimes death, those noble, self-sacrificing women suffered with them, and their reward will be equal to that bestowed on the husband. Mrs. Boardman and the Mrs. Judsons suffered for the truth, suffered with their companions. They sacrificed home and friends in every sense of the word to aid their companions in the work of enlightening those who sat in darkness, to reveal to them the hidden mysteries of the word of God. Their lives were in constant peril. To save souls was their great object, and for this they could suffer cheerfully.

I was shown the life of Christ. When His self-denial and sacrifice is compared with the trials and sufferings of the wives of some of our ministers, it causes anything which they may call sacrifice to sink into insignificance. If the minister's wife speaks words of discontent and discouragement, the influence upon the husband is disheartening and tends to cripple him in his labor, especially if his success depends upon surrounding influences. Must the minister of God in such cases be crippled or torn from his field of labor to gratify the feelings of his wife, which arise from an unwillingness to yield inclination to duty? The wife should conform her wishes and pleasures to duty, and give up her selfish feelings for the sake of Christ and the truth. Satan has had much to do with controlling the labors of the ministers through the influence of selfish, ease-loving companions.

If a minister's wife accompanies her husband in his travels, she should not go for her own special enjoyment, to visit, and to be waited upon, but to labor with him. She should have a united interest with him to do good. She should be willing to accompany her husband, if home cares do not hinder, and she should aid him in his efforts to save souls. With meekness and humility, yet with a noble self-reliance, she should have a leading influence upon minds around her, and should act her part and bear her cross and burden in meeting, and around the family altar, and in conversation at the fireside. The people expect this, and they have a right to expect it. If these expectations are not realized, the husband's influence is more than half destroyed. The wife of a minister can do much if she will. If she possesses the spirit of self-sacrifice and has a love for souls, she can with him do almost an equal amount of good.

A sister laborer in the cause of truth can understand and reach some cases, especially among the sisters, that the minister cannot. A responsibility rests upon the minister's wife which she should not and cannot lightly throw off. God will require the talent lent her, with usury. She should work earnestly, faithfully, and unitedly with her husband to save souls. She should never urge her wishes and desires, or express a lack of interest in her husband's labor, or dwell upon homesick, discontented feelings. All these natural feelings must be overcome. She should have a purpose in life which should be unfalteringly carried out. What if this conflicts with the feelings, and pleasures, and natural tastes? These should be cheerfully and readily sacrificed in order to do good and save souls.

The wives of ministers should live devoted, prayerful lives. But some would enjoy a religion in which there are no crosses and which calls for no self-denial and exertion on their part. Instead of standing nobly for themselves, leaning upon God for strength and bearing their individual responsibility, they have much of the time been dependent upon others, deriving their spiritual life from them. If they would only lean confidingly, in childlike trust, upon God, and have their affections centered in Jesus, deriving their life from Christ, the living Vine, what an amount of good they might do, what a help they might be to others, what a support to their husbands, and what a reward would be theirs in the end. "Well done, good and faithful servants," would fall like sweetest music upon their ears. The words, "Enter thou into the joy of thy Lord," would repay them a thousand times for all suffering and trials endured to save precious souls.

Those who will not improve the talent which God has given them will fail of everlasting life. Those who have been of but little use in the world will be rewarded accordingly, as their works have been. When everything goes smoothly, they are borne along on the wave; but when they need earnestly and untiringly to apply the oar, and row against wind and tide, there seems to be no energy in their Christian character. They will not take the trouble to work, but lay down their oars and contentedly let the current carry them downstream. Thus they generally remain until someone takes the burden and labors earnestly and energetically to pull them upstream. Every time they yield to such indolence they lose strength and have less inclination to work in the cause of God. It is only the faithful conqueror who wins eternal glory.

A minister's wife should ever have a leading influence on the minds of those with whom she associates, and she will be a help or a great hindrance. She either gathers with Christ or scatters abroad. A self-sacrificing missionary spirit is lacking among the companions of our ministers. It is self first, and then Christ secondly, and even thirdly. Never should a minister take his wife with him unless he knows that she can be a spiritual help, that she is one who can bear, and endure, and suffer, to do good, and to benefit souls for Christ's sake. Those who accompany their husbands should go to labor unitedly with them. They must not expect to be free from trials and disappointments. They should not think too much of pleasant feelings. What have feelings to do with duty?

I was cited the case of Abraham. God said to him, "Take now thy son, thine only son Isaac, whom thou lovest, and get thee into the land of Moriah; and offer him there for a burnt offering upon one of the mountains which I will tell thee of." Abraham obeyed God. He did not consult his feelings, but with a noble faith and confidence in God he prepared for his journey. With a heart rent with anguish he beheld the proud and loving mother gazing with fond affection upon the son of promise. But he led that loved son away. Abraham suffered, yet he did not let his will rise in rebellion against the will of God. Duty, stern duty, controlled him. He dared not consult his feelings or yield to them for one moment. His only son walked by the side of the stern, loving, suffering father, talking engagedly, uttering over and over the fond name of father, and then inquiring: "Where is the sacrifice?" Oh, what a test for the faithful father! Angels looked with pleased wonder upon the scene. The faithful servant of God even bound his beloved son and laid him upon the wood. The knife was raised, when an angel cried out: "Abraham, Abraham. . . . Lay not thine hand upon the lad."

I saw that it is no light thing to be a Christian. It is a small matter to profess the Christian name; but it is a great and sacred thing to live a Christian life. There is but a little time now to secure the immortal crown, to have a record of good acts and fulfilled duties recorded in heaven. Every tree is judged by its fruit. Everyone will be judged according to his deeds, not his profession or his faith. The question will never be asked, How much did he profess? but, What fruit did he bear? If the tree is corrupt, the fruit is evil. If the tree is good, it cannot produce evil fruit.

PATENT RIGHTS

Many of our brethren involve themselves by engaging in new enterprises which look flattering; but in a short time they find themselves disappointed and their means gone, which should have been used to support their families and advance the cause of present truth. Then come remorse, regret, and self-reproach, and some conscientious ones cast away their confidence, and lose their spiritual enjoyment, and in consequence of mental distress their health also suffers.

Those who believe the truth should practice economy, live upon plain, wholesome food, always making it a rule to live within their means. Brethren should never engage in new enterprises without consulting those of experience who are good managers in temporal and spiritual matters. By doing this they would save themselves much perplexity.

Brethren would better be contented with a small income, and handle that little prudently, rather than run risks to better their condition, and suffer continual losses thereby. Some Sabbathkeepers who have engaged in the sale of patent rights, have traveled among their brethren to save expense, and have induced them to invest their means in patent rights. Such will not be clear before God until they have made up the loss which these brethren have sustained.

NUMBER ELEVEN

TESTIMONY FOR THE CHURCH

REFORM IN DRESS*

Dear Brethren and Sisters: My apology for calling your attention again to the subject of dress is that some do not seem to understand what I have before written; and an effort is made, perhaps by those who do not wish to believe what I have written, to make confusion in our churches upon this important subject. Many letters have been written to me, stating difficulties, which I have not had time to answer; and now, to answer the many inquiries, I give the following statements, which it is hoped will forever put the subject at rest, so far as my testimonies are concerned.

Some contend that what I wrote in *Testimony for the Church* No. 10 does not agree with my testimony in the work entitled, *How to Live*. They were written from the same view, hence are not two views, one contradicting the other, as some may imagine; if there is any difference, it is simply in the form of expression. In *Testimony for the Church* No.10 I stated as follows:

"No occasion should be given to unbelievers to reproach our faith. We are considered odd and singular, and should not take a course to lead unbelievers to think us more so than our faith requires us to be. Some who believe the truth may think that it would be more healthful for the sisters to adopt

---

*See Appendix.

the American costume, yet if that mode of dress would cripple our influence among unbelievers so that we could not so readily gain access to them, we should by no means adopt it, though we suffered much in consequence. But some are deceived in thinking there is so much benefit to be received from this costume. While it may prove a benefit to some, it is an injury to others.

"I saw that God's order has been reversed, and His special directions disregarded, by those who adopt the American costume. I was referred to Deuteronomy 22:5: 'The woman shall not wear that which pertaineth unto a man, neither shall a man put on a woman's garment: for all that do so are abomination unto the Lord thy God.' God would not have His people adopt the so-called reform dress. It is immodest apparel, wholly unfitted for the modest, humble followers of Christ.

"There is an increasing tendency to have women in their dress and appearance as near like the other sex as possible, and to fashion their dress very much like that of men, but God pronounces it abomination. 'In like manner also, that women adorn themselves in modest apparel, with shamefacedness and sobriety.' 1 Timothy 2:9.

"Those who feel called out to join the movement in favor of woman's rights and the so-called dress reform might as well sever all connection with the third angel's message. The spirit which attends the one cannot be in harmony with the other. The Scriptures are plain upon the relations and rights of men and women. Spiritualists have, to quite an extent, adopted this singular mode of dress. Seventh-day Adventists, who believe in the restoration of the gifts, are often branded as spiritualists. Let them adopt this costume, and their influence is dead. The people would place them on a level with spiritualists and would refuse to listen to them.

"With the so-called dress reform there goes a spirit of levity and boldness just in keeping with the dress. Modesty and reserve seem to depart from many as they adopt that style of dress. I was shown that God would have us take a course consistent and explainable. Let the sisters adopt the American costume and they would destroy their own influence and that of their husbands. They would become a byword and a derision. Our Saviour says: 'Ye are the light of the world.' 'Let your light so shine before men, that they may see your good works, and glorify your Father which is in heaven.' There is a great work for us to do in the world, and God would not have us take a course to lessen or destroy our influence with the world."

The foregoing was given me as a reproof to those who are inclined to adopt a style of dress resembling that worn by men; but at the same time I was shown the evils of the common style of woman's dress, and to correct these, also gave the following found in *Testimony for the Church,* No. 10:

"We do not think it in accordance with our faith to dress in the American costume, to wear hoops, or to go to an extreme in wearing long dresses which sweep the sidewalks and streets. If women would wear their dresses so as to clear the filth of the streets an inch or two, their dresses would be modest, and they could be kept clean much more easily, and would wear longer. Such a dress would be in accordance with our faith."

I will now give an extract from what I have elsewhere said upon this subject:

"Christians should not take pains to make themselves a gazing-stock by dressing differently from the world. But if when following out their convictions of duty in respect to dressing modestly and healthfully, they find themselves out of fashion, they should not change their dress in order to be like the world; but they should manifest a noble independence and moral courage to be right, if all the world differ from them. If the world introduce a modest, convenient, and healthful mode of dress, which is in accordance with the Bible, it will not change our relation to God or to the world to adopt such a style of dress. Christians should follow Christ and make their dress conform to God's word. They should shun extremes. They should humbly pursue a straightforward course, irrespective of applause or of censure, and should cling to the right because of its own merits.

"Women should clothe their limbs with regard to health and comfort. Their feet and limbs need to be clad as warmly as men's. The length of the fashionable dress is objectionable for several reasons:

"1. It is extravagant and unnecessary to have the dress of such a length that it will sweep the sidewalk and street.

"2. A dress thus long gathers dew from the grass, and mud from the streets, and is therefore unclean.

"3. In its bedraggled condition it comes in contact with the sensitive ankles, which are not sufficiently protected, quickly chilling them, and thus endangering health and life. This is one of the greatest causes of catarrh and of scrofulous swellings.

"4. The unnecessary length is an additional weight upon the hips and bowels.

"5. It hinders the walking, and is also often in other people's way.

"There is still another style of dress which is adopted by a class of so-called dress reformers. They imitate the opposite sex as nearly as possible. They wear the cap, pants, vest, coat, and boots, the last of which is the most sensible part of the costume. Those who adopt and advocate this style of dress carry the so-called dress reform to very objectionable lengths. Confusion will be the result. Some who adopt this costume may be correct in their general views upon the health question, but they would be instrumental in accomplishing vastly more good if they did not carry the matter of dress to such extremes.

"In this style of dress God's order has been reversed and His special directions disregarded. Deuteronomy 22:5: 'The woman shall not wear that which pertaineth unto a man, neither shall a man put on a woman's garment: for all that do so are abomination unto the Lord thy God. God would not have His people adopt this style of dress. It is not modest apparel, and is not at all fitting for modest, humble women who profess to be Christ's followers. God's prohibitions are lightly regarded by all who advocate doing away with the distinction of dress between males and females. The extreme position taken by some dress reformers upon this subject cripples their influence.

"God designed that there should be a plain distinction between the dress of men and women, and has considered the matter of sufficient importance to give explicit directions in regard to it; for the same dress worn by both sexes would cause confusion and great increase of crime. Were the apostle Paul alive, and should he behold women professing godliness with this style of dress, he would utter a rebuke. 'In like manner also, that women adorn themselves in modest apparel, with shamefacedness and sobriety; not with broided hair, or gold, or pearls, or costly array; but (which becometh women professing godliness) with good works.' The mass of professed Christians utterly disregard the teachings of the apostles, and wear gold, pearls, and costly array.

"God's loyal people are the light of the world and the salt of the earth, and they should ever remember that their influence is of value. Were they to exchange the extreme long dress for the extreme short one, they would, to a great extent, destroy their influence. Unbelievers, whom it is their duty to benefit and seek to bring to the Lamb of God, would be disgusted. Many improvements can be made in the dress of women in reference to health without making so great a change as to disgust the beholder.

"The form should not be compressed in the least with corsets and whalebones. The dress should be perfectly easy that the lungs and heart may have healthy action. The dress should reach somewhat below the top of the boot, but should be short enough to clear the filth of the sidewalk and street without being raised by the hand. A still shorter dress than this would be proper, convenient, and healthful for women when doing their housework, and especially for those who are obliged to perform more or less out-of-door labor. With this style of dress, one light skirt, or two at most, is all that is necessary, and this should be buttoned on to a waist, or suspended by straps. The hips were not formed to bear heavy weights. The heavy skirts worn by some, and allowed to drag down upon the hips, have been the cause of various diseases which are not easily cured. The sufferers seem to be ignorant of the cause of their sufferings, and continue to violate the laws of their being by girding their waists and wearing heavy skirts, until they are made lifelong invalids. When told of their mistake, many will immediately exclaim, 'Why, such a style of dress would be old-fashioned!' What if it is? I wish we could be old-fashioned in many respects. If we could have the old-fashioned strength that characterized the old-fashioned women of past generations, it would be very desirable. I do not speak unadvisedly when I say that the way in which women clothe themselves, together with their indulgence of appetite, is the greatest cause of their present feeble, diseased condition. There is but one woman in a thousand who clothes her limbs as she should. Whatever may be the length of the dress, their limbs should be clothed as thoroughly as are the men's. This may be done by wearing lined pants, gathered into a band and fastened about the ankle, or made full and tapering at the bottom; and these should come down long enough to meet the shoe. The limbs and ankles thus clothed are protected against a current of air. If the feet and limbs are kept comfortable with warm clothing, the circulation will be equalized, and the blood will remain pure and healthy because it is not chilled or hindered in its natural passage through the system."

The principal difficulty in the minds of many is in regard to the length of the dress. Some insist that "the top of the boot," has reference to the top of such boots as are usually worn by men, which reach nearly to the knee. If it were the custom of women to wear such boots, then these persons should not be blamed for professing to understand the matter as they have; but as women generally do not wear such boots, these persons have no right to understand me as they have pretended.

In order to show what I did mean, and that there is a harmony in my testimonies on this subject, I will here give an extract from my manuscripts written about two years ago:

"Since the article on dress appeared in *How to Live,* there has been with some a misunderstanding of the idea I wished to convey. They have taken the extreme meaning of that which I have written in regard to the length of the dress, and have evidently had a very hard time over the matter. With their distorted views of the matter they have discussed the question of shortening the dress until their spiritual vision has become so confused that they can only see men as trees walking. They have thought they could see a contradiction in my article on dress, recently published in *How to Live,* and that article on the same subject contained in *Testimony for the Church,* No. 10. I must contend that I am the best judge of the things which have been presented before me in vision; and none need fear that I shall by my life contradict my own testimony, or that I shall fail to notice any real contradiction in the views given me.

"In my article on dress in *How to Live* I tried to present a healthful, convenient, economical, yet modest and becoming style of dress for Christian women to wear, if they should choose so to do. I tried, perhaps imperfectly, to describe such a dress. 'The dress should reach somewhat below the top of the boot, but should be short enough to clear the filth of the sidewalk and street, without being raised by the hand.' Some have contended that by the top of the boot, I meant the top of such boots as men usually wear. But by 'the top of the boot,' I designed to be understood the top of a boot, or gaiter shoe, usually worn by women. Had I thought I should be misunderstood, I would have written more definitely. If it were the custom for women to wear high-topped boots like men, I could see sufficient excuse for this misunderstanding. I think the language is very plain as it now reads, and no one needs to be thrown into confusion. Please read again: 'The dress should reach somewhat below the top of the boot.' Now look at the qualification: 'But should be short enough to clear the filth of the sidewalk and street, without being raised by the hand. A still shorter dress than this would be proper, convenient, and healthful for women when doing their housework, and especially for those who are obliged to perform more or less out-of-door labor.'

"I can see no excuse for reasonable persons misunderstanding and perverting my meaning. In speaking of the length of the dress, had I referred to high-topped boots reaching nearly to the knee, why should I have added, 'but [the dress] should be short enough to clear the filth of the sidewalk and street, without being raised by the hand'? If high-topped boots were meant, the dress would most certainly be short enough to keep clear of the filth of the street without being raised, and would be sufficiently short for all working purposes. Reports have been circulated that 'Sister White wears the American costume,' and that this style of dress is generally adopted and worn by the sisters in Battle Creek. I am here reminded of the saying that 'a lie will go around the world while truth is putting on his boots.' One sister gravely told me that she had received the idea that the American costume was to be adopted by the Sabbathkeeping sisters, and that if such a style of dress should be enforced, she would not submit to it, for she never could bring her mind to wear such a dress.

"In regard to my wearing the short dress, I would say, I have but one short dress, which is not more than a finger's length shorter than the dresses I usually wear. I have worn this short dress occasionally. In the winter I rose early, and putting on my short dress, which did not require to be raised by my hands to keep it from draggling in the snow, I walked briskly from one to two miles before breakfast. I have worn it several times to the office, when obliged to walk through light snow, or when it was very wet or muddy. Four or five sisters of the Battle Creek church have prepared for themselves a short dress to wear while doing their washing and house cleaning. A short dress has not been worn in the streets of the city of Battle Creek, and has never been worn to meeting. My views were calculated to correct the present fashion, the extreme long dress, trailing upon the ground, and also to correct the extreme short dress, reaching about to the knees, which is worn by a certain class. I was shown that we should shun both extremes. By wearing the dress reaching about to the top of a woman's gaiter boot we shall escape the evils of the extreme long dress and shall also shun the evils and notoriety of the extreme short dress.

"I would advise those who prepare for themselves a short dress for working purposes to manifest taste and neatness in getting it up. Have it arranged in order, to fit the form nicely. Even if it is a working dress, it should be made becoming, and should be cut after a pattern. Sisters when about their work should not put on clothing which would make them look like images to frighten the crows from the corn. It is more gratifying to their husbands and children to see them in a becoming, well-fitting attire than it can be to mere visitors or strangers. Some wives and mothers seem to think it is no matter how they look when about their work and when they are seen only by their husbands and children, but they are very particular to dress in taste for the eyes of those who have no special claims upon them. Is not the esteem and love of husband and children more to be prized than that of strangers or common friends? The happiness of husband and children should be more sacred to every wife and mother than that of all others. Christian sisters should not at any time dress extravagantly, but should at all times dress as neatly, modestly, and healthfully as their work will allow."

The above-described dress we believe to be worthy of the name of the reform short dress. It is being adopted at the Western Health Reform Institute and by some of the sisters at Battle Creek and other places where the matter is properly set before the people. In wide contrast with this modest dress is the so-called American costume, resembling very nearly the dress worn by men. It consists of a vest, pants, and a dress resembling a coat and reaching about halfway from the hip to the knee. This dress I have opposed, from what has been shown me as in harmony with the word of God; while the other I have recommended as modest, comfortable, convenient, and healthful.

Another reason which I offer as an apology for calling attention again to the subject of dress is that not one in twenty of the sisters who profess to believe the *Testimonies* has taken the first step in the dress reform. It may be said that Sister White generally wears her dresses in public longer than the dress she recommends to others. To this I reply, When I visit a place to speak to the people where the subject is new and prejudice exists, I think it best to be careful and not close the ears of the people by wearing a dress which would be objectionable to them. But after bringing the subject before them and fully explaining my position, I then appear before them in the reform dress, illustrative of my teachings.

As to the matter of wearing hoops, the reform in dress is entirely in advance of them. It cannot use them. And it is altogether too late to talk about wearing hoops, large or small.

My position upon that question is precisely what it ever has been, and I hope not to be held responsible for what others may say on this subject, or for the course pursued by those who put on hoops. I protest against the perversion of my private conversations on this subject, and ask that what I have written and published be regarded as my settled position.

OUR MINISTERS

In the vision given me in Rochester, New York, December 25, 1865, I was shown that a most solemn work is before us. Its importance and magnitude are not realized. As I marked the indifference which was everywhere apparent, I was alarmed for ministers and people. There seemed to be a paralysis upon the cause of present truth. The work of God seemed stayed. Ministers and people are unprepared for the time in which they live, and nearly all who profess to believe present truth are unprepared to understand the work of preparation for this time. In their present state of worldly ambition, with their lack of consecration to God, their devotion to self, they are wholly unfitted to receive the latter rain and, having done all, to stand against the wrath of Satan, who by his inventions would cause them to make shipwreck of faith, fastening upon them some pleasing self-deception. They think they are all right when they are all wrong.

Ministers and people must make greater advancement in the work of reform. They should commence without delay to correct their wrong habits of eating, drinking, dressing, and working. I saw that quite a number of the ministers are not awake upon this important subject. They are not all where God would have them. The result is, some can show but little fruit of their labors. Ministers should be ensamples to the flock of God. But they are not safe from Satan's temptations. They are the very ones whom he will seek to ensnare. If he can succeed in lulling one minister to carnal security, and by so doing divert his mind from the work, or deceive him with regard to his own true condition before God, he has accomplished much.

I saw that the cause of God was not progressing as it might and as it should. Ministers fail to take hold of the work with that energy, devotion, and decided perseverance which the importance of the work demands. They have a vigilant adversary to contend with whose diligence and perseverance are untiring. The feeble effort of ministers and people can bear no comparison with those of their adversary, the devil. On one side are the ministers who battle for the right and have the help of God and holy angels. They should be strong and valiant, and wholly devoted to the cause in which they are engaged, having no separate interest. They should not be entangled with the things of this life, that they may please Him who hath chosen them to be soldiers.

On the other side are Satan and his angels, with all his agents on earth, who make every effort and use every device to advance error and wrong, and to cover up their hideousness and deformity with a pleasing garb. Selfishness, hypocrisy, and every species of deception, Satan clothes with a garment of apparent truth and righteousness, and triumphs in his success, even with ministers and people who profess to understand his wiles. The greater distance they keep from Christ their great Leader, the less they are like Him in character, the more close is their resemblance in life and character to the servants of their great adversary, and the more sure is he of them at last. While they profess to be servants of Christ, they are servants of sin. Some ministers have their minds too much on the wages they receive. They labor for wages and lose sight of the sacredness and importance of the work.

Some become slack and negligent in their labor; they pass over the ground, but are weak and unsuccessful in their efforts. Their hearts are not in the work. The theory of truth is clear. Many of them had no part in searching out this truth by hard study and earnest prayer, and they know nothing of its preciousness and value by being compelled to sustain their positions against the opposition of its enemies. They do not see the necessity of preserving a spirit of entire consecration to the work. Their interest is divided between themselves and the work.

I saw that before the work of God can make any decided progress, the ministers must be converted. When converted they will place less estimate upon wages and far more value upon the important, sacred, solemn work which they have accepted at the hand of God to perform, and which He requires them to do faithfully and well, as those who must render to Him a strict account. A faithful record of all their works is daily made by the recording angels. All their acts, and even the intents and purposes of the heart, stand faithfully revealed. Nothing is hid from the all-seeing eye of Him with whom we have to do. Those who have thrown all their energies into the cause of God, and who have ventured out and invested something, will feel that the work of God is a part of them, and will not labor merely for wages. They will not be eyeservants and seek to please themselves, but will consecrate themselves and all their interests to this solemn work.

Some in their public labors with the churches are in danger of making mistakes from a lack of thoroughness. It is for their own interest and that of the cause that they should search closely, try their motives, and be certain to divest themselves of selfishness. They should watch lest, while they preach straight truths to others, they fail to live by the same rule, and allow Satan to substitute something else for the deep heartwork. They should be thorough with themselves and with the cause of God lest they work for wages and lose sight of the important and exalted character of the work. They should not let self rule instead of Jesus, and they should be careful not to say to the sinner in Zion, It shall be well with thee, when God has pronounced a curse upon him.

Ministers must arouse and manifest a life, zeal, and devotion to which they have for quite a length of time been almost strangers because they have failed to walk with God. The cause of God in many places is not improving. Soul work is needed. The people are overcharged with surfeiting and drunkenness and the cares of this life. They are entering deeper and deeper into a spirit of worldly enterprise. They are ambitious to get gain. Spirituality and devotion are rare. The spirit that prevails is to work, to accumulate, and to add to that which they already possess. "What will be the end of these things?" was the burden of my inquiry.

Conference meetings have accomplished no lasting good. Those who attend the meetings carry a spirit of traffic with them. Ministers and people frequently bring their merchandise to these large gatherings, and the truths spoken from the desk fail to impress the heart. The sword of the Spirit, the word of God, fails to do its office work; it falls tamely upon the hearers. The exalted work of God is made to connect too closely with common things.

The ministers must be converted before they can strengthen their brethren. They should not preach themselves, but Christ and His righteousness. A reformation is needed among the people, but it should first begin its purifying work with the ministers. They are watchmen upon the walls of Zion, to sound the note of warning to the careless, the unsuspecting; also to portray the fate of the hypocrite in Zion. It seemed to me that some of the ministers had forgotten that Satan was yet alive, as persevering, earnest, and artful as ever; that he was still seeking to allure souls from the path of righteousness.

One important part of the work of the ministry is to faithfully present to the people the health reform as it stands connected with the third angel's message as part and parcel of the same work. They should not fail to adopt it themselves, and should urge it upon all who profess to believe the truth.

Ministers should have no separate interest aside from the great work of leading souls to the truth. Their energies are all needed here. They should not engage in merchandise, in peddling, or in any business aside from this one great work. The solemn charge given to Timothy rests with equal weight upon them, laying upon them the most solemn obligations and most fearful responsibilities. "I charge thee therefore before God, and the Lord Jesus Christ, who shall judge the quick and the dead at His appearing and His kingdom; preach the word; be instant in season, out of season; reprove, rebuke, exhort with all long-suffering and doctrine." "But watch thou in all things, endure afflictions, do the work of an evangelist, make full proof of thy ministry."

Wrong habits of life have lessened our mental and physical sensibilities, and all the strength we can acquire by right living and placing ourselves in the best relation to health and life should be devoted unreservedly to the work which God has assigned us. We cannot afford to use the few enfeebled, crippled energies which we possess to serve tables or to mingle merchandise with the work God has committed to us. Every faculty of mind and body is now needed. The work of God requires this, and no separate business can be engaged in aside from this great work without taking time and strength of mind and body, and thus lessening the vigor and force of our labor in the cause of God. Ministers who do this will not have all that time for meditation and prayer, and all that strength and clearness of mind that they should have to understand the cases of those who need help, and to be prepared to "be instant in season, out of season." A word fitly spoken at the right time may save some poor, erring, doubting, fainting soul. Paul exhorted Timothy: "Meditate upon these things;

give thyself wholly to them, that thy profiting may appear to all."

In Christ's commission to His disciples He tells them: "Whatsoever ye shall bind on earth shall be bound in heaven: and whatsoever ye shall loose on earth shall be loosed in heaven." If this is the fearfully responsible work of God's ministers, how important that they give themselves wholly to it and watch for souls as they that must give an account. Should any separate or selfish interest come in here and divide the heart from the work? Some ministers linger about their homes, and run out on the Sabbath, and then return and exhaust their energies in farming or in attending to home matters. They labor for themselves through the week, and then spend the remnant of their exhausted energies in laboring for God. But such feeble efforts are not acceptable to Him. They have no mental or physical strength to spare. At best their efforts are feeble enough. But after they have been engrossed and entangled all through the laboring days of the week with the cares and perplexities of this life, they are wholly unfitted for the high, the sacred, the important work of God. The destiny of souls hangs upon the course they pursue and the decisions they make. How important then that they should be temperate in *all* things, not only in their eating, but in their labor, that their strength may be unabated and devoted to their sacred calling.

A great mistake has been made by some who profess present truth, by introducing merchandise in the course of a series of meetings and by their traffic diverting minds from the object of the meetings. If Christ were now upon earth, He would drive out these peddlers and traffickers, whether they be ministers or people, with a scourge of small cords, as when He entered the temple anciently and "cast out all them that sold and bought in the temple, and overthrew the tables of the money-changers, and the seats of them that sold doves, and said unto them, It is written, My house shall be called the house of prayer; but ye have made it a den of thieves." These traffickers might have pleaded as an excuse that the articles they held for sale were for sacrificial offerings. But their object was to get gain, to obtain means, to accumulate.

I was shown that if the moral and intellectual faculties had not been clouded by wrong habits of living, ministers and people would have been quick to discern the evil results of mixing sacred and common things Ministers have stood in the desk and preached a most solemn discourse, and then by introducing merchandise, and acting the part of a salesman, even in the house of God, they have diverted the minds of their hearers from the impressions received, and destroyed the fruit of their labor. If the sensibilities had not been blunted, they would have had discernment to know that they were bringing sacred things down upon a level with common. The burden of selling our publications should not rest upon ministers who labor in word and doctrine. Their time and strength should be held in reserve, that their efforts may be thorough in a series of meetings. Their time and strength should not be drawn upon to sell our books when they can be properly brought before the public by those who have not the burden of preaching the word. In entering new fields it may be necessary for the minister to take publications with him to offer for sale to the people, and it may be necessary in some other circumstances also to sell books and transact business for the office of publication. But such work should be avoided whenever it can be done by others.

Ministers have all that they ought to do to preach the word, and after they have urged solemn truth upon the people they should maintain a humble dignity as the preachers of exalted truth and as representatives of the truth presented to the people. After their labored effort they need rest. Even selling books upon present truth is a care, a tax to the mind, and a weariness to the body. If there are those who still have a reserve force and can be taxed without injury to themselves, there is important work for them to do, and it has but just commenced when they have spoken the truth to the people. Then come the exemplary preaching, the watchful care, the seeking to do good to others, the conversation, and visiting at the fireside from house to house, entering into the condition of mind and the spiritual state of those who listened to the discourse from their lips; exhorting this one, reproving that one, rebuking another, and comforting the afflicted, suffering, and desponding. The mind should be as free from weariness as possible that they may be minutemen, "instant in season, out of season." They should obey the injunction given by Paul to Timothy: "Meditate upon these things; give thyself wholly to them."

The responsibility of the work rests very lightly upon some. They feel that after they leave the desk their work is done. It is a burden to visit, a burden to talk; and the people who are really desirous of getting all the good there is for them, and who wish to hear and learn that they may see all things clearly, are not benefited and satisfied. Ministers excuse themselves because they are weary, and yet some exhaust their precious strength and spend their time in work which another could do just as well as they. They should preserve moral and physical vigor that as faithful workmen of God they may give full proof of their ministry.

In every important place there should be a depository for publications. And someone who really appreciates the truth should manifest an interest to get these books into the hands of all who will read. The harvest is great, but the laborers are few, and the few experienced laborers now in the field have all they should do to labor in word and doctrine. Men will arise who claim that God has laid upon them the burden of teaching the truth to others. All such should be proved and tried. They should not be relieved from all care, neither should they be lifted into responsible positions at once; but they should be encouraged if they deserve encouragement, to give full proof of their ministry. It would not be the best course for such ones to pursue, to enter into other men's labors. Let them first labor in connection with one of experience and wisdom, and he can soon see whether they are capable of exerting an influence that will be saving. Young preachers who have never had wearing labor, nor felt the draft upon their mental and physical strength, should not be encouraged to hope for a support independent of their own physical labor, for this will only injure them and will be a bait to entice men to engage in the work who realize nothing of the burden of it or the responsibility resting upon God's chosen ministers. Such will feel competent to teach others when they have scarcely learned the first principles themselves.

Many who profess the truth are not sanctified by it and are not endowed with wisdom; they are not led and taught of God. God's people, as a general thing, are worldly-minded and have departed from the simplicity of the gospel. This is the cause of the great lack of spiritual discernment in the course they have pursued toward ministers. If a minister preaches with freedom, some will praise him to his face. Instead of dwelling upon the truths he uttered, and improving upon them, thus showing themselves to be not forgetful hearers, but doers of the work, they exalt him by referring to what he has done. They dwell upon the virtues of the poor instrument, but forget Christ who employed the instrument. Ever since the fall of Satan, who was once an exalted angel in glory, ministers have fallen through exaltation. Unwise Sabbathkeepers have pleased the devil well by praising their ministers. Were they aware that they were aiding Satan in his work? They would have been alarmed had they realized what they were doing. They were blinded, they were not standing in the counsel of God. I lift my voice of warning against praising or flattering the ministers. I have seen the evil, the dreadful evil, of this. Never, never speak a word in praise of ministers to their faces. Exalt God. Ever respect a faithful minister, realize his burdens and lighten them if you can; but do not flatter him, for Satan stands ready at his watchtower to do that kind of work himself.

Ministers should not use flattery or be respecters of persons. There ever has been, and still is, great danger of erring here, of making a little difference with the wealthy, or flattering them by special attention, if not by words. There is danger of "having men's persons in admiration" for the sake of gain, but in doing this their eternal interests are endangered. The minister may be the special favorite of some wealthy man, and he may be very liberal with him; this gratifies the minister, and he in turn lavishes praise upon the benevolence of his donor. His name may be exalted by appearing in print, and yet that liberal donor may be entirely unworthy of the credit given him. His liberality did not arise from a deep, living principle to do good with his means, to advance the cause of God because he appreciated it, but from some selfish motive, a desire to be thought liberal. He may have given from impulse and his liberality have no depth of principle. He may have been moved upon by listening to stirring truth which for the time being loosed his purse strings; yet, after all, his liberality has no deeper motive. He gives by spasms; his purse opens spasmodically and closes just as securely spasmodically. He deserves no commendation, for he is in every sense of the word a stingy man, and unless thoroughly converted, purse and all, will hear the withering denunciation: "Go to now, ye rich men, weep and howl for your miseries that shall come upon you. Your riches are corrupted, and your garments are moth-eaten." Such will awake at last from a horrible self-deception. Those who praised their spasmodic liberalities helped Satan to deceive them and make them think that they were very liberal, very sacrificing, when they knew not the first principles of liberality or self-sacrifice.

Some men and women make themselves believe that they do not consider the things of this world of much value, but prize the truth and its advancement higher than any worldly gain. Many will awake at last to find that they have been deceived. They may have once appreciated the truth, and earthly treasures in comparison with truth may have appeared to them valueless; but after a time, as their worldly treasure increased, they became less devotional. Although they have enough for a comfortable sustenance, yet all their acts show that they are in nowise satisfied. Their works testify that their hearts are bound up in their earthly treasure. Gain, gain, is their watchword. To this end every member of the family participates in their labor. They give themselves scarcely any time for devotion or for prayer. They work early and late. Sickly, diseased women and feeble children whip up their flagging ambition and use up the vitality and strength they have to reach an object, to gain a little, make a little more money. They flatter themselves that they are doing this that they may help the cause of God. Terrible deception! Satan looks on and laughs for he knows that they are selling soul and body through their lust for gain. They are continually making flimsy excuses for thus selling themselves for gain. They are blinded by the god of this world. Christ has bought them by His own blood; but they rob Christ, rob God, tear themselves to pieces, and are almost useless in society.

They devote but little time to the improvement of the mind, and but little time to social or domestic enjoyment. They are of but little benefit to anyone. Their lives are a terrible mistake. Those who thus abuse themselves feel that their course of unremitting labor is praiseworthy. They are destroying themselves by their presumptuous labor. They are marring the temple of God by continually violating the laws of their being through excessive labor, and yet they think it a virtue. When God calls them to account, when He requires of them the talents He has lent them, with usury, what can they say? What excuse can they make? Were they heathen who know nothing of the living God, and in their blind idolatrous zeal throw themselves under the car of Juggernaut, their cases would be more tolerable. But they had the light, they had warning upon warning to preserve their bodies, which God calls His temple, in as healthy a condition as possible that they might glorify Him in their bodies and spirits, which are His. The teachings of Christ they disregarded: "Lay not up for yourselves treasures upon earth, where moth and rust doth corrupt, and where thieves break through and steal: but lay up for yourselves treasures in heaven, where neither moth nor rust doth corrupt, and where thieves do not break through nor steal. For where your treasure is, there will your heart be also." They let worldly cares entangle them. But they that will be rich fall into temptation and a snare, and into many foolish and hurtful lusts, which drown men in destruction and perdition." They worship their earthly treasure, as the ignorant heathen does his idols.

Many flatter themselves that their desire for gain is that they may help the cause of God. Some promise that when they have gained such an amount then they will do good with it and advance the cause of present truth. But when they have realized their expectations; they are no more ready to help the cause than before. They again pledge themselves that after they purchase that desirable house or piece of land, and pay for it, then they will do a great deal with their means to advance the work of God. But as the desire of their heart is attained, they have far less disposition than in the days of their poverty to aid in the advancement of the work of God. "He also that received seed among the thorns is he that heareth the word; and the care of this world, and the deceitfulness of riches, choke the word, and he becometh unfruitful." The deceitfulness of riches leads them on, step by step, until they lose all love for the truth, and yet they flatter themselves that they believe it. They love the world and the things of the world, but the love of God or of the truth is not in them.

In order to gain a little money, many deliberately arrange their business matters so that it necessarily brings a great amount of hard work upon those laboring out of doors, and upon their families in the house. The bone, muscle, and brain of all are taxed to the utmost, a great amount of work is before them to be done, and the excuse is, they must accomplish just all that they possibly can or there will be a loss, something will be wasted. Everything *must* be saved, let the result be what it may. What have such gained? Perhaps they have been able to keep the principal good and add to it. But, on the other hand, what have they lost? Their capital of health, which is invaluable to the poor as well as the rich, has been steadily diminishing. The mother and the children have made repeated drafts upon their fund of health and strength, thinking that such an extravagant expenditure would never exhaust their capital, until they are surprised at last to find their vigor of life exhausted. They have nothing left to draw upon in case of emergency. The sweetness and happiness of life is embittered by racking pains and sleepless nights. Both physical and mental vigor are gone. The husband and father, who for the sake of gain, made the unwise arrangement of his business, it may be with the full sanction of the wife and mother, may, as the result, bury the mother and one or more of the children. Health and life were sacrificed for the love of money. "For the love of money is the root of all evil: which while some coveted after, they have erred from the faith, and pierced themselves through with many sorrows."

There is a great work to be accomplished for Sabbathkeepers. Their eyes must be opened and they see their true condition, and be zealous and repent, or they will fail of everlasting life. The spirit of the world has taken possession of them, and they are brought into captivity by the powers of darkness. They do not heed the exhortation of the apostle Paul: "And be not conformed to this world: but be ye transformed by the renewing of your mind, that ye may prove what is that good, and acceptable, and perfect, will of God." With many, a worldly spirit, with covetousness and selfishness, predominates. Those who possess it are looking out for their own special interest. The selfish rich man does not interest himself in the things of his neighbors, unless it be to study how he can advantage himself at their disadvantage. The noble and godlike in man is parted with, sacrificed for selfish interests. The love of money is the root of all evil. It blinds the vision and prevents people from discerning their obligations to God or to their neighbors.

Some flatter themselves that they are liberal because they at times donate freely to ministers and for the advancement of the truth. Yet these so-called liberal men are close in their deal and ready to overreach. They have abundance of this world, and this binds upon them great responsibilities as God's stewards. Yet, when dealing with a poor, hard-laboring brother, they are exacting to the last farthing. The poor side to a bargain is the poor man's legacy. Instead of favoring his poor brother, the sharp, exacting rich man takes all the advantage and adds to his already accumulated wealth by the misfortune of the other. He prides himself because of his shrewdness, but with his wealth he is heaping up to himself a heavy curse and laying a stumbling block in the way of his brother. By his meanness and close calculation he is cutting off his ability to benefit him with his religious influence. All this lives in the memory of that poor brother, and the most earnest prayers and apparently zealous testimonies from his rich brother's lips will only have an influence to grieve and disgust. He looks upon him as a hypocrite; a root of bitterness springs up whereby many are defiled. The poor man cannot forget the advantages taken of him; neither can he forget how he has been crowded into difficult places because he was willing to bear burdens, while the wealthy brother ever had some excuse ready for not putting his shoulder under the load. Yet the poor man may be so imbued with the spirit of Christ as to forgive the abuses of his rich brother.

True, noble, disinterested benevolence is too rarely found among the wealthy. In their ambition for wealth they overlook the claims of humanity. They cannot see and feel the cramped, disagreeable position of their brethren in poverty, who perhaps have labored as hard as themselves. Like Cain they say: "Am I my brother's keeper?" "I have worked hard for what I have; I must hold on to it." Instead of praying, "Help me to feel my brother's woe," their constant study is to forget that he has any woes, any claims upon their sympathy or liberalities.

Many Sabbathkeepers who are wealthy are guilty of grinding the face of the poor. Do such think that God takes no notice of their little acts of meanness? If their eyes could be opened they would see an angel following them wherever they go, making a faithful record of all their acts in their families and at their places of business. The True Witness is on their track, declaring: *"I know thy works."* As I saw this spirit of defrauding, of overreaching, of meanness, even among some professed Sabbathkeepers, I cried out in anguish of spirit. This great evil, this terrible curse, is folding around some of the Israel of God in these last days, making them a detestation to even noble-spirited unbelievers. This is the people professedly waiting for the coming of the Lord.

There is a class of poor brethren who are not free from temptation. They are poor managers, they have not wise judgment, they wish to obtain means without waiting the slow process of persevering toil. Some are in such haste to better their condition that they engage in various enterprises without consulting men of good judgment and experience. Their expectations are seldom realized; instead of gaining, they lose, and then come temptation and a disposition to envy the rich. They really want to be benefited by the wealth of their brethren, and feel tried because they are not. But they are not worthy of receiving special help. They have evidence that their efforts have been scattered. They have been changeable in business, and full of anxiety and cares which bring but small returns. Such persons should listen to the counsel of those of experience. But frequently they are the last ones to seek advice. They think they have superior judgment and will not be taught.

These are often the very ones who are deceived by those sharp, shrewd peddlers of patent rights whose success depends upon the art of deception. These should learn that no confidence whatever can be put in such peddlers. But the brethren are credulous in regard to the very things they should suspect and shun. They do not take home the instruction of Paul to Timothy: "But godliness with contentment is great gain." "And having food and raiment let us be therewith content." Let not the poor think that the rich are the only covetous ones. While the rich hold what they have with a covetous grasp, and seek to obtain still more, the poor are in great danger of coveting the rich man's wealth. There are very few in our land of plenty who are really so poor as to need help. If they would pursue a right course, they could in almost every case be above want. My appeal to the rich is, Deal liberally with your poor brethren, and use your means to advance the cause of God. The worthy poor, those who are made poor by misfortune and sickness, deserve your special care and help. "Finally, be ye all of one mind, having compassion one of another, love as brethren, be pitiful, be courteous."

Men and women professing godliness and expecting translation to heaven without seeing death, I warn you to be less greedy of gain, less self-caring. Redeem your godlike manhood, your noble womanhood, by noble acts of disinterested benevolence. Heartily despise your former avaricious spirit and regain true nobility of soul. From what God has shown me, unless you zealously repent, Christ will spew you out of His mouth. Sabbathkeeping Adventists profess to be followers of Christ, but the works of many of them belie their profession. "Ye shall know them by their fruits." "Not everyone that saith unto Me, Lord, Lord, shall enter into the kingdom of heaven; but he that doeth the will of My Father which is in heaven."

I appeal to all who profess to believe the truth, to consider the character and life of the Son of God. He is our example. His life was marked with disinterested benevolence. He was ever touched with human woe. He went about doing good. There was not one selfish act in all His life. His love for the fallen race, His desire to save them, was so great that He took upon Himself the wrath of His Father, and consented to suffer the penalty of that transgression which plunged guilty man in degradation. He bore the sins of man in His own body. "He hath made Him to be sin for us, who knew no sin; that we might be made the righteousness of God in Him."

True generosity is too frequently destroyed by prosperity and riches. Men and women in adversity or in humble poverty will sometimes express very great love for the truth and special interest for the prosperity of the cause of God and for the salvation of their fellow men, and will tell what they would do if they only had the means. God frequently proves these; He prospers them, blesses them in basket and in store, far beyond their expectations. But their hearts are deceitful. Their good intentions and promises are like the rolling sand. The more they have the more they desire. The more they are prospered the more eager are they for gain. Some of these, who in their poverty were once even benevolent, become penurious and exacting. Money becomes their god. They delight in the power which money gives them, in the honor they receive because of it. Said the angel: "Mark ye how they stand the test. Watch the development of character under the influence of riches." Some were oppressing the needy poor and would obtain their services for the lowest figure. They were overbearing; money was power to them. God's eye, I saw, was upon them. They were deceived. "And, behold, I come quickly; and My reward is with Me, to give every man according as his work shall be."

Some who are wealthy do not withhold from ministers. They keep up their systematic benevolence exactly and pride themselves upon their punctuality and generosity, and think their duty ends here. This is well as far as it goes, but their duty does not cease here. God has claims upon them that they do not realize. Society has claims upon them; their fellow men have claims upon them. Every member of their family has claims upon them. All these claims should be regarded; not one should be overlooked or neglected. Some men give to ministers and put into the treasury with as much satisfaction as though it would entitle them to heaven. Some think that they can do nothing to aid the cause of God unless they constantly have a large increase. They feel that they can in nowise touch the principal. Should our Saviour speak the same words to them that He did to the certain ruler, "Go and sell that thou hast, and give to the poor, and thou shalt have treasure in heaven: and come and follow Me," they would go away sorrowful, choosing like him to run the risk of retaining their idols, riches, rather than to part with them to secure treasure in heaven. This ruler claimed that he had kept all the commandments of God from his youth up, and confident in his fidelity and righteousness, and thinking that he was perfect, he asks: "What lack I yet?" Jesus immediately tears off his sense of security by referring to his idols, his possessions. He had other gods before the Lord, which were of greater value to him than eternal life. Supreme love to God was lacking. Thus it is with some who profess to believe the truth. They think they are perfect, think that there is no lack, when they are far from perfection and are cherishing idols which will shut them out of heaven.

Many pity the Southern slaves because they are bound down to labor, while slavery exists in their own families. Mothers and children are allowed to toil from morning till night; they have no recreation. A ceaseless round of labor is before them and crowded upon them. They profess to be Christ's followers, but where is the time for them to meditate and pray, and obtain food for the intellect, that the mind, with which we serve God, may not be dwarfed in its growth? God calls upon every individual to use the talents He has committed to them to His glory, and by thus improving them to gain others also. God has laid obligations upon us to benefit others. Our work in this world for the good of others is not done until Christ shall say in heaven: "It is done." "He that is unjust, let him be unjust still: and he which is filthy, let him be filthy still: and he that is righteous, let him be righteous still: and he that is holy, let him be holy still."

Many seem to have no true sense of their responsibility before God. They are required to strive to enter in at the strait gate, because many shall seek to enter in and shall not be able. Heaven requires them to try to induce others also to strive to enter in at the strait gate. A work is before young and old to labor earnestly to save not only their own souls, but the souls of others. There are none who have reasoning faculties who have not some influence. By their indifference they use that influence to hinder souls from striving to enter in at the strait gate, or by their earnest, persevering, untiring efforts they urge upon them the necessity of striving diligently to enter there. No one occupies a neutral position, doing nothing to encourage others and doing nothing to hinder them. Says Christ: They that gather not with Me scatter abroad. Take heed, old and young; you are either doing the work of Christ, to save souls, or the work of Satan, to lead them to perdition. "Let your light so shine before men, that they may see your good works, and glorify your Father which is in heaven."

The young can exert a powerful influence if they will give up their pride and selfishness, and devote themselves to God, but as a general thing they will not bear burdens for others. They have to be carried themselves. The time has come when God requires a change in this respect. He calls upon young and old to be zealous and repent. If they continue in their state of lukewarmness, He will spew them out of His mouth. Says the True Witness: "I know thy works." Young man, young woman, your works are known, whether they be good or whether they be evil. Are you rich in good works? Jesus comes to you as a counselor: "I counsel thee to buy of Me gold tried in the fire, that thou mayest be rich; and white raiment, that thou mayest be clothed, and that the shame of thy nakedness do not appear; and anoint thine eyes with eyesalve, that thou mayest see."

THE HEALTH REFORM

In the vision given me in Rochester, New York, December 25, 1865, I was shown that our Sabbathkeeping people have been negligent in acting upon the light which God has given in regard to the health reform, that there is yet a great work before us, and that as a people we have been too backward to follow in God's opening providence as He has chosen to lead us.

I was shown that the work of health reform has scarcely been entered upon yet. While some feel deeply and act out their faith in the work, others remain indifferent and have scarcely taken the first step in reform. There seems to be in them a heart of unbelief, and, as this reform restricts the lustful appetite, many shrink back. They have other gods before the Lord. Their taste, their appetite, is their god; and when the ax is laid at the root of the tree and those who have indulged their depraved appetites at the expense of health are touched, their sin pointed out, their idols shown them, they do not wish to be convinced, and although God's voice should speak directly to them to put away those health-destroying indulgences, some would still cling to the hurtful things which they love. They seem joined to their idols, and God will soon say to His angels: Let them alone.

The health reform, I was shown, is a part of the third angel's message and is just as closely connected with it as are the arm and hand with the human body. I saw that we as a people must make an advance move in this great work. Ministers and people must act in concert. God's people are not prepared for the loud cry of the third angel. They have a work to do for themselves which they should not leave for God to do for them. He has left this work for them to do. It is an individual work; one cannot do it for another. "Having therefore these promises, dearly beloved, let us cleanse ourselves from all filthiness of the flesh and spirit, perfecting holiness in the fear of God." Gluttony is the prevailing sin of this age. Lustful appetite makes slaves of men and women, and beclouds their intellects and stupefies their moral sensibilities to such a degree that the sacred, elevated truths of God's word are not appreciated. The lower propensities have ruled men and women.

In order to be fitted for translation, the people of God must know themselves. They must understand in regard to their own physical frames that they may be able with the psalmist to exclaim: "I will praise Thee; for I am fearfully and wonderfully made." They should ever have the appetite in subjection to the moral and intellectual organs. The body should be servant to the mind, and not the mind to the body.

I was shown that there is a much greater work before us than we as yet have any idea of, if we would ensure health by placing ourselves in the right relation to life. Dr. A has been doing a great and good work in the treatment of disease and in enlightening those who have all their lives been in ignorance in regard to the relation that eating, drinking, and working sustain to health. God in His mercy has given His people light through His humble instrument that in order to overcome disease they must deny a depraved appetite and practice temperance in all things. He has caused great light to shine upon their pathway. Shall those who are "looking for that blessed hope, and the glorious appearing of the great God and our Saviour Jesus Christ; who gave Himself for us, that He might redeem us from all iniquity, and purify unto Himself a peculiar people, zealous of good works," be behind the religionists of the day who have no faith in the soon appearing of our Saviour? The peculiar people whom He is purifying unto Himself to be translated to heaven without seeing death, should not be behind others in good works. In their efforts to cleanse themselves from all filthiness of the flesh and spirit, perfecting holiness in the fear of God, they should be as far ahead of any other class of people on the earth as their profession is more exalted than that of others.

Some have sneered at this work of reform and have said it was all unnecessary, that it was an excitement to divert minds from present truth They have said that matters were being carried to extremes. Such do not know what they are talking about. While men and women professing godliness are diseased from the crown of their head to the soles of their feet, while their physical, mental, and moral energies are enfeebled through gratification of depraved appetite and excessive labor, how can they weigh the evidences of truth and comprehend the requirements of God? If their moral and intellectual faculties are beclouded, they cannot appreciate the value of the atonement or the exalted character of the work of God, nor delight in the study of His word. How can a nervous dyspeptic be ready always to give an answer to every man that asketh him a reason of the hope that is in him, with meekness and fear? How soon would such a one become confused and agitated, and by his diseased imagination be led to view matters in altogether a wrong light, and by a lack of that meekness and calmness which characterized the life of Christ be caused to dishonor his profession while contending with unreasonable men? Viewing matters from a high religious standpoint, we must be thorough reformers in order to be Christlike.

I saw that our heavenly Father has bestowed upon us the great blessing of light upon the health reform that we may obey the claims which He has upon us and glorify Him in our bodies and spirits which are His and finally stand without fault before the throne of God. Our faith requires us to elevate the standard and take advance steps. While many question the course pursued by other health reformers, they as reasonable men should do something themselves. Our race is in a deplorable condition, suffering from disease of every description. Many have inherited disease and are great sufferers because of the wrong habits of their parents, and yet they pursue the same wrong course in regard to themselves and their children which was pursued toward them. They are ignorant in regard to themselves. They are sick and do not know that their own wrong habits are causing them immense suffering.

There are but few as yet who are aroused sufficiently to

understand how much their habits of diet have to do with their health, their characters, their usefulness in this world, and their eternal destiny. I saw that it is the duty of those who have received the light from heaven and have realized the benefit of walking in it, to manifest a greater interest for those who are still suffering for want of knowledge. Sabbathkeepers who are looking for the soon appearing of their Saviour should be the last to manifest a lack of interest in this great work of reform. Men and women must be instructed, and ministers and people should feel that the burden of the work rests upon them to agitate the subject and urge it home upon others.

I was shown that we should provide a home for the afflicted and those who wish to learn how to take care of their bodies that they may prevent sickness. We should not remain indifferent and compel those who are sick and desirous of living out the truth to go to popular water cure institutions for the recovery of health, where there is no sympathy for our faith. If they recover health it may be at the expense of their religious faith. Those who have suffered greatly from bodily infirmities are weak both mentally and morally. As they realize the benefit derived from the correct application of water, the right use of air, and a proper diet, they are led to believe that the physicians who understood how to treat them so successfully cannot be greatly at fault in their religious faith; that as they are engaged in the great and good work of benefiting suffering humanity, they must be nearly or quite right. And thus our people are in danger of being ensnared through their efforts to recover health at these establishments.

Again I was shown that those who are strongly fortified with religious principles and are firm to obey all God's requirements cannot receive that benefit from the popular health institutions of the day that others of a different faith can. Sabbathkeepers are singular in their faith. To keep all God's commandments as He requires them to do in order to be owned and approved of Him is exceedingly difficult in a popular water cure. They have to carry along with them at all times the gospel sieve and sift everything they hear, that they may choose the good and refuse the bad.

The water cure establishment at _____ has been the best institution in the United States. Its managers have been doing a great and good work as far as the treatment of disease is concerned. Yet we cannot have confidence in their religious principles. While they professed to be Christians, they recommend to their patients card playing, dancing, and attending theaters, all of which have a tendency to evil, or, to say the very least, have the appearance of evil, and are directly contrary to the teachings of Christ and His apostles. Conscientous Sabbathkeepers who visit these institutions for the purpose of regaining health cannot receive the benefit they would if they were not obliged to keep themselves constantly guarded lest they compromise their faith, dishonor the cause of their Redeemer, and bring their own souls into bondage.

I was shown that Sabbathkeepers should open a way for those of like precious faith to be benefited without their being under the necessity of expending their means at institutions where their faith and religious principles are endangered, and where they can find no sympathy or union in religious matters. God in His providence directed the course of Dr. B to _____ that he might there obtain an experience he would not otherwise have gained, for He had a work for him to do in the health reform. As a practicing physician he had for years been obtaining a knowledge of the human system, and God would now have him by precept and practice learn how to apply the blessings placed within the reach of man. He would have him become prepared to benefit the sick and instruct those who do not understand how to preserve the strength and health they already have, and how to prevent disease by a wise use of heaven's remedies—pure water, air, and diet.

I was shown that Dr. B was a cautious and strictly conscientious man, a man whom God loves. He has passed through many trials which have worked for his good, although while passing through them he could not at all times see how he was to be benefited by them. Dr. B is not a man who will become exalted while he believes the truth and follows in its path. He is not a man who will be arbitrary or overbearing. He is too fearful of putting on that dignity which his position would allow him to maintain. He will counsel with others and is easy to be entreated; his great danger will be a willingness to take on burdens which he ought not to bear. He sees and feels what ought to be done, and will be in danger of doing too much. He is extremely sensitive and sympathetic, and will feel to the very depth for all his patients; and if he is permitted, will carry so heavy a load of responsibility as to be crushed under its weight.

Men and women of influence should help Brother B by their prayers, their sympathy, their hearty cooperation, their cheering, hopeful words, and their councel and advice—all of which will be appreciated by him. His position cannot be an enviable one. If he assumes so great responsibilities it will not be from choice or to obtain a livelihood, for he can procure this in a much easier way and avoid the care, anxiey, and perplexity which such a position would bring upon him. Duty alone will lead him; and when once convinced where the path of duty lies, he will follow it and stand at his post, let the consequences be what they may. He should have the sympathy and co-operation of those who have influence, those whom God would have stand by his side and sustain him in his laborous work.

Dr. B could, so far as this world is concerned, do better than in the position he now occupies. I was shown that this position would be most difficult. Many who have no experience would have no idea of the magnitude of the enterprise and would want things to go according to their ideas. Some would wonder why the poor could not come and be treated for nothing, and would be tempted to think that it was a money-making enterprise after all; and this one and that one would wish to have something to say, and would have just about so much fault to find, let matters go as they might; for I was shown that some would consider it a virtue to be jealous and stand out and oppose. They pride themselves on not receiving everything just as soon as it comes. Like Thomas, they boast of their unbelief. But did Jesus commend unbelieving Thomas? While granting him the evidence he had declared that he would have before believing, Jesus said unto him: "Thomas because thou hast seen Me, thou hast believed: blessed are they that have not seen, and yet have believed."

I was shown that there is no lack of means among Sabbathkeeping Adventists. At present their greatest danger is in their accumulations of property. Some are continually increasing their cares and labors; they are overcharged. The result is, God and the wants of His cause are nearly forgotten by them; they are spiritually dead. They are required to make a sacrifice to God, an offering. A sacrifice does not increase, but decreases and consumes. Here, I was shown, was a worthy enterprise for God's people to engage in, one in which they can invest means to His glory and the advancement of His cause. Much of the means among our people is only proving an injury to those who are holding on to it.

Our people should have an institution of their own, under their own control, for the benefit of the diseased and suffering among us who wish to have health and strength that they may glorify God in their bodies and spirits, which are His. Such an institution, rightly conducted, would be the means of bringing our views before many whom it would be impossible for us to reach by the common course of advocating the truth. As unbelievers shall resort to an institution devoted to the successful treatment of disease and conducted by Sabbathkeeping physicians, they will be brought directly under the influence of the truth. By becoming acquainted with our people and our real faith, their prejudice will be overcome and they will be favorably impressed. By thus being placed under the influence of truth, some will not only obtain relief from bodily infirmities, but will find a healing balm for their sin-sick souls.

As the health of invalids improves under judicious treatment, and they begin to enjoy life, they have confidence in those who have been instrumental in their restoration to health. Their hearts are filled with gratitude, and the good seed of truth will the more readily find a lodgment there and in some cases will be nourished, spring up, and bear fruit to the glory of God. One such precious soul saved will be worth more than all the means needed to establish such an institution. Some will not have enough moral courage to yield to their convictions. They may be convinced that Sabbathkeepers have the truth, but the world and unbelieving relatives stand in the way of their receiving it. They cannot bring their minds to the point to sacrifice all for Christ. Yet some of this last-mentioned class will go away with their prejudice removed and will stand as defenders of the faith of Seventh-day Adventists. Some who go away restored or greatly benefited will be the means of introducing our faith in new places and raising the standard of truth where it would have been impossible to gain access had not prejudice been first removed from minds by a tarry among our people for the object of gaining health.

Others will prove a source of trial as they go to their homes. Yet this should not discourage any or hinder them in their efforts in this good work. Satan and his agents will do all they can to hinder, to perplex, and to bring burdens upon those who heartily engage in the work of advancing this reform.

There is a liberal supply of means among our people, and if all felt the importance of the work, this great enterprise could be carried forward without embarrassment. All should feel a special interest in sustaining it. Especially should those who have means invest in this enterprise. A suitable home should be fitted up for the reception of invalids that they may, by the use of proper means and the blessing of God, be relieved of their infirmities and learn how to take care of themselves and thus prevent sickness.

Many who profess the truth are growing close and covetous. They need to be alarmed for themselves. They have so much of their treasure upon the earth that their hearts are on their treasure. Much the larger share of their treasure is in this world and but little in heaven; therefore their affections are placed on earthly possessions instead of on the heavenly inheritance. There is now a good opportunity for them to use their means for the benefit of suffering humanity and also for the advancement of the truth. This enterprise should never be left to struggle in poverty. These stewards to whom God has entrusted means should now come up to the work and use their means to His glory. To those who through covetousness withhold their means, it will prove a curse rather than a blessing.

Those to whom God has entrusted means should provide a fund to be used for the benefit of the worthy poor who are sick and not able to defray the expenses of receiving treatment at the institution. There are some precious, worthy poor whose influence has been a benefit to the cause of God. A fund should be raised to be used for the express purpose of treating such of the poor as the church where they reside shall decide are worthy to be benefited. Unless those who have an abundance give for this object, without calling for returns, the poor will be unable to avail themselves of the benefits derived from the treatment of disease at such an institution, where so much means is required for labor bestowed. Such an institution should not in its infancy, while struggling to live, become embarrassed by a constant expenditure of means without realizing any returns.

NUMBER TWELVE

TESTIMONY FOR THE CHURCH

ADDRESS TO THE YOUNG

Young Sabbathkeepers are given to pleasure seeking. I saw that there is not one in twenty who knows what experimental religion is. They are constantly grasping after something to satisfy their desire for change, for amusement; and unless they are undeceived and their sensibilities aroused so that they can say from the heart, "I count all things but loss for the excellency of the knowledge of Christ Jesus my Lord," they are not worthy of Him and will come short of everlasting life. The young, generally, are in a terrible deception, and yet they profess godliness. Their unconsecrated lives are a reproach to the Christian name; their example is a snare to others. They hinder the sinner, for in nearly every respect they are no better than unbelievers. They have the word of God, but its warnings, admonitions, reproofs, and corrections are unheeded, as are also the encouragements and promises to the obedient and faithful. God's promises are all on condition of humble obedience. One pattern only is given to the young, but how do their lives compare with the life of Christ? I feel alarmed as I witness everywhere the frivolity of young men and young women who profess to believe the truth. God does not seem to be in their thoughts. Their minds are filled with nonsense. Their conversation is only empty, vain talk.

They have a keen ear for music, and Satan knows what organs to excite to animate, engross, and charm the mind so that Christ is not desired. The spiritual longings of the soul for divine knowledge, for a growth in grace, are wanting.

I was shown that the youth must take a higher stand and make the word of God the man of their counsel and their guide. Solemn responsibilities rest upon the young, which they lightly regard. The introduction of music into their homes, instead of inciting to holiness and spirituality, has been the means of diverting their minds from the truth. Frivolous songs and the popular sheet music of the day seem congenial to their taste. The instruments of music have taken time which should have been devoted to prayer. Music, when not abused, is a great blessing; but when put to a wrong use, it is a terrible curse. It excites, but does not impart that strength and courage which the Christian can find only at the throne of grace while humbly making known his wants and with strong cries and tears pleading for heavenly strength to be fortified against the powerful temptations of the evil one. Satan is leading the young captive. Oh, what can I say to lead them to break his power of infatuation! He is a skillful charmer, luring them on to perdition. Listen to the instructions from the Inspired Book of God. I saw that Satan had blinded the minds of the youth that they could not comprehend the truths of God's word. Their sensibilities are so blunted that they regard not the injunctions of the holy apostle:

"Children, obey your parents in the Lord: for this is right. Honor thy father and mother; which is the first commandment with promise; that it may be well with thee, and thou mayest live long on the [new] earth." "Children, obey your parents in all things: for this is well pleasing unto the Lord." Children who dishonor and disobey their parents, and disregard their advice and instructions, can have no part in the earth made new. The purified new earth will be no place for the rebellious, the disobedient, the ungrateful, son or daughter. Unless such learn obedience and submission here, they will never learn it; the peace of the ransomed will not be marred by disobedient, unruly, unsubmissive children. No commandment breaker can inherit the kingdom of heaven. Will all the youth please read the fifth commandment of the law spoken by Jehovah from Sinai and engraven with His own finger upon tables of stone? "Honor thy father and thy mother: that thy days may be long upon the land which the Lord thy God giveth thee."

I was referred to many passages of Scripture that clearly show the young the will of God concerning them. These plain teachings they must meet in the judgment. Yet there is not one young man or young woman in twenty professing the present truth who heeds these Bible teachings. The youth do not read the word of God enough to know its claims upon them; and yet these truths will judge them in the great day of God, when young and old will be rewarded according to the deeds done in the body.

Says John: "I have written unto you, young men, because ye are strong, and the word of God abideth in you, and ye have overcome the wicked one. Love not the world, neither the things that are in the world. If any man love the world, the love of the Father is not in him. For all that is in the world, the lust of the flesh, and the lust of the eyes, and the pride of life, is not of the Father, but is of the world. And the world passeth away, and the lust thereof: but he that doeth the will of God abideth forever."

This exhortation to young men extends to young women also. Their youth does not excuse them from the responsibilities resting upon them. They are strong and are not worn down with cares and the weight of years; their affections are ardent, and if they withdraw these from the world and place them upon Christ and heaven, doing the will of God, they will have a hope of the better life that is enduring, and they will abide forever, being crowned with glory, honor, immortality, eternal life. If the youth live to gratify the lust of the flesh, the lust of the eyes, and the pride of life, they are seeking for the things of the world, pleasing their great adversary, and separating themselves from the Father. And when these things that are sought after pass away, their hopes are blasted and their expectations perish. Separated from God they will then bitterly repent their folly in serving their own pleasure, gratifying their own desires, and for a few frivolous enjoyments selling a life of bliss that they might have enjoyed forever.

"Love not the world, neither the things that are in the world," says the inspired apostle. Then he adds the warning: "If any man love the world, the love of the Father is not in him." It is an alarming fact that the love of the world predominates in the minds of the young. They decidedly love the world and the things that are in the world, and for this very reason the love of God finds no room in their hearts. They find their pleasures in the world and in the things of the world, and are strangers to the Father and the graces of His Spirit. God is dishonored by the frivolity and fashion, and empty, vain talking and laughing that characterize the life of the youth generally. Paul exhorts the youth to sobriety: "Young men likewise exhort to be sober-minded. In all things showing thyself a pattern of good works: in doctrine showing uncorruptness, gravity, sincerity, sound speech, that cannot be condemned; that he that is of the contrary part may be ashamed, having no evil thing to say of you."

I entreat the youth for their souls' sake to heed the exhortation of the inspired apostle. All these gracious instructions, warnings, and reproofs will be either a savor of life unto life or of death unto death. Many of the young are reckless in their conversation. They choose to forget that by their words they are to be justified or condemned. All should take heed to the words of our Saviour: "A good man out of the good treasure of the heart bringeth forth good things: and an evil man out of the evil treasure bringeth forth evil things. But I say unto you, That every idle word that men shall speak, they shall give account thereof in the day of judgment. For by thy words thou shalt be justified, and by thy words thou shalt be condemned." How little regard is paid even to the instructions of the heavenly Teacher. Many either do not study the word of God or do not heed its solemn truths, and these plain truths will rise up in judgment and condemn them.

Words and acts testify plainly what is in the heart. If vanity and pride, love of self and love of dress, fill the heart, the conversation will be upon the fashions, the dress, and the appearance, but not on Christ or the kingdom of heaven. If envious feelings dwell in the heart, they will be manifested in words and acts. Those who measure themselves by others, do as others do, and make no higher attainments, excusing themselves because of the faults and wrongs of others, are feeding on husks and will remain spiriual dwarfs as long as they gratify Satan by thus indulging their own unconsecrated feelings. Some dwell upon what they shall eat and drink, and wherewithal they shall be clothed. These thoughts flow out from the abundance of the heart, as though temporal things were the grand aim in life, the highest attainment. These persons forget the words of Christ: "Seek ye first the kingdom of God, and His righteousness; and all these things shall be added unto you."

The youth have their hearts filled with the love of self. This is manifested in their desire to see their faces daguerreotyped by the artist; and they are not satisfied with being once represented, but sit again and again for their picture, each time hoping that the last will excel all their previous efforts and appear really more beautiful than the original. Their Lord's money is squandered in this way, and what is gained? Merely their poor shadow upon paper. The hours that should have been devoted to prayer are occupied upon their own poor selves; precious hours of probation are thus wasted.

Satan is gratified to have the attention of youth attracted by anything to divert their minds from God so that the deceiver can steal a march upon them and they, unprepared for his attacks, be ensnared. They are not aware that the great heavenly Artist is taking cognizance of every act, every word, and that their deportment, and even the thoughts and intents of the heart, stand faithfully delineated. Every defect in their moral character stands revealed to the gaze of angels, and they will have the faithful picture presented to them in all its deformity at the execution of the judgment. Those vain, frivolous words are all written in the book. Those false words are written. Those deceptive acts, whose motives were concealed from human eyes, but discerned by the all-seeing eye of Jehovah, are all written in living characters. Every selfish act is exposed.

The young generally conduct themselves as though the precious hours of probation, while mercy lingers, were one grand holiday, and they were placed in this world merely for their own amusement, to be gratified with a continued round of excitement. Satan has been making special efforts to lead them to find happiness in worldly amusements and to justify themselves by endeavoring to show that these amusements are harmless, innocent, and even important for health. The impression has been given by some physicians that spirituality and devotion to God are detrimental to health. This suits the adversary of souls. There are persons with diseased imaginations who do not rightly represent the religion of Christ; such have not the pure religion of the Bible. Some are scourging themselves all through life because of their sins; all they can see is an offended God of justice. Christ and His redeeming power through the merits of His blood they fail to see. Such have not faith. This class are generally those who have not well-balanced minds. Through disease transmitted to them from their parents, and an erroneous education in youth, they have contracted wrong habits which injure the constitution and the brain, causing the moral organs to become diseased and making it impossible for them to think and act rationally upon all points. They have not well-balanced minds. Godliness and righteousness are not destructive to health, but are health to the body and strength to the soul. Says Peter: "He that will love life, and see good days, . . . let him eschew evil, and do good; let him seek peace, and ensue it: for the eyes of the Lord are over the righteous, and His ears are open unto their prayers: but the face of the Lord is against them that do evil." "But and if ye suffer for righteousness' sake, happy are ye: and be not afraid of their terror, neither be troubled."

The consciousness of rightdoing is the best medicine for diseased bodies and minds. The special blessing of God resting upon the receiver is health and strength. A person whose mind is quiet and satisfied in God is in the pathway to health. To have a consciousness that the eyes of the Lord are upon us and His ears open to our prayers is a satisfaction indeed. To know that we have a never-failing Friend in whom we can confide all the secrets of the soul is a privilege which words can never express. Those whose moral faculties are beclouded by disease are not the ones to rightly represent the Christian life or the beauties of holiness. They are too often in the fire of fanaticism or the water of cold indifference or stolid gloom. The words of Christ are of more worth than the opinions of all the physicians in the universe: "Seek ye first the kingdom of God, and His righteousness; and all these things shall be added unto you." This is the first great object—the kingdom of heaven, the righteousness of Christ. Other objects to be attained should be secondary to these.

Satan will present the path of holiness as difficult while the paths of worldly pleasure are strewed with flowers. In false and flattering colors will the tempter array the world with its pleasures before you. Vanity is one of the strongest traits of our depraved natures, and he knows that he can appeal to it successfully. He will flatter you through his agents. You may receive praise which will gratify your vanity and foster in you pride and self-esteem, and you may think that with such advantages and attractions it really is a great pity for you to come out from the world and be separate, and become a Christian, to forsake your companions, and be alike dead to their praise or censure. Satan tells you that with the advantages which you possess you could to a high degree enjoy the pleasures of the world. But consider that the pleasures of earth will have an end, and that which you sow you must also reap. Are personal attractions, ability, or talents too valuable to devote to God, the Author of your being, He who watches over you every moment? Are your qualifications too precious to devote to God?

The young urge that they need something to enliven and divert the mind. I saw that there is pleasure in industry, a satisfaction in pursuing a life of usefulness. Some still urge that they must have something to interest the mind when business ceases, some mental occupation or amusement to which the mind can turn for relief and refreshment amid cares and wearing labor. The Christian's hope is just what is needed. Religion will prove to the believer a comforter, a sure guide to the Fountain of true happiness. The young should study the word of God and give themselves to meditation and prayer, and they will find that their spare moments cannot be better employed. Young friends, you should take time to prove your own selves, whether you are in the love of God. Be diligent to make your calling and election sure. It depends upon your own course of action whether you secure to yourselves the better life.

Wisdom's "ways are ways of pleasantness, and all her paths

are peace." The future abode of the righteous and their everlasting reward are high and ennobling themes for the young to contemplate. Dwell upon the marvelous plan of salvation, the great sacrifice made by the King of glory that you might be elevated through the merits of His blood and by obedience finally be exalted to the throne of Christ. This subject should engage the noblest contemplation of the mind. To be brought into favor with God—what a privilege! To commune with Him—what can more elevate, refine, and exalt us above the frivolous pleasures of earth? To have our corrupt natures renovated by grace, our lustful appetites and animal propensities in subjection, to stand forth with noble, moral independence, achieving victories every day, will give peace of conscience which can arise alone from rightdoing.

Young friends, I saw that with such employment and diversion as this you might be happy. But the reason why you are restless is, you do not seek to the only true source for happiness. You are ever trying to find *out* of Christ that enjoyment which is found only *in* Him. In Him are no disappointed hopes. Prayer, oh, how is this precious privilege neglected! The reading of the word of God prepares the mind for prayer. One of the greatest reasons why you have so little disposition to draw nearer to God by prayer is, you have unfitted yourselves for this sacred work by reading fascinating stories which have excited the imagination and aroused unholy passions. The word of God becomes distasteful, the hour of prayer is forgotten. Prayer is the strength of the Christian. When alone he is not alone; he feels the presence of One who has said: "Lo, I am with you alway."

The young want just what they have not; namely, *religion*. Nothing can take the place of this. Profession alone is nothing. Names are registered upon the church books upon earth, but not in the book of life. I saw that there is not one in twenty of the youth who knows what experimental religion is.

They serve themselves and yet profess to be servants of Christ; but unless the spell which is upon them be broken, they will soon realize that the portion of the transgressor is theirs. As for self-denial or sacrifice for the truth's sake, they have found an easier way above it all. As for the earnest pleading with tears and strong cries to God for His pardoning grace and for strength from Him to resist the temptations of Satan, they have found it unnecessary to be so earnest and zealous; they can get along well without it. Christ, the King of glory, went often alone to the mountains and desert places to pour out His soul's request to His Father; but sinful man, in whom is no strength, thinks he can live without so much prayer.

Christ is our pattern; His life was an example of good works. He was a man of sorrows and acquainted with grief. He wept over Jerusalem because they would not be saved by accepting the redemption which He offered them. They would not come to Him that they might have life. Compare your course of life with that of your Master, who made so great a sacrifice that you might be saved. He frequently spent the entire night upon the damp ground in agonizing prayer. You are seeking your own pleasure. Listen to the vain, frivolous conversation; hear the laugh, the jesting, the joking. Is this imitating the pattern? Still listen—is Jesus mentioned? Is the truth the theme of conversation? Are the speakers glorying in the cross of Christ? It is this fashion, that bonnet, that dress, what that young man said, or that young lady said, or the amusements they are planning. What glee! Are angels attracted and pressing close around them to ward off the darkness which Satan is pressing upon and around them? Oh, no. See, they turn away in sorrow. I see tears upon the faces of these angels. Can it be that angels of God are made to weep? It is even so.

Eternal things have little weight with the youth. Angels

of God are in tears as they write in the roll the words and acts of professed Christians. Angels are hovering around yonder dwelling. The young are there assembled; there is the sound of vocal and instrumental music. Christians are gathered there, but what is that you hear? It is a song, a frivolous ditty, fit for the dance hall. Behold the pure angels gather their light closer around them, and darkness envelops those in that dwelling. The angels are moving from the scene. Sadness is upon their countenances. Behold, they are weeping. This I saw repeated a number of times all through the ranks of Sabbathkeepers, and especially in _____. Music has occupied the hours which should have been devoted to prayer. Music is the idol which many professed Sabbathkeeping Christians worship. Satan has no objection to music if he can make that a channel through which to gain access to the minds of the youth. Anything will suit his purpose that will divert the mind from God and engage the time which should be devoted to His service. He works through the means which will exert the strongest influence to hold the largest numbers in a pleasing infatuation, while they are paralyzed by his power. When turned to good account, music is a blessing; but it is often made one of Satan's most attractive agencies to ensnare souls. When abused, it leads the unconsecrated to pride, vanity, and folly. When allowed to take the place of devotion and prayer, it is a terrible curse. Young persons assemble to sing, and, although professed Christians, frequently dishonor God and their faith by their frivolous conversation and their choice of music. Sacred music is not congenial to their taste. I was directed to the plain teachings of God's word, which have been passed by unnoticed. In the judgment all these words of inspiration will condemn those who have not heeded them.

The apostle Paul exhorts Timothy "by the commandments of God our Saviour, and Lord Jesus Christ": "I will therefore that men pray everywhere, lifting up holy hands, without wrath and doubting. In like manner also, that women adorn themselves in modest apparel, with shamefacedness and sobriety; not with broided hair, or gold, or pearls, or costly array; but (which becometh women professing godliness) with good works."

Peter writes to the church: "Wherefore gird up the loins of your mind, be sober, and hope to the end for the grace that is to be brought unto you at the revelation of Jesus Christ; as obedient children, not fashioning yourselves according to the former lusts in your ignorance: but as He which hath called you is holy, so be ye holy in all manner of conversation; because it is written, Be ye holy; for I am holy."

The inspired Paul directs Titus to give special instructions to the church of Christ, "that they may adorn the doctrine of God our Saviour in all things." He says: "Teaching us that, denying ungodliness and worldly lusts, we should live soberly, righteously, and godly, in this present world; looking for that blessed hope, and the glorious appearing of the great God and our Saviour Jesus Christ; who gave Himself for us, that He might redeem us from all iniquity, and purify unto Himself a peculiar people, zealous of good works."

Peter exhorts the churches to "be sober, be vigilant; because your adversary the devil, as a roaring lion, walketh about, seeking whom he may devour." "The end of all things is at hand: be ye therefore sober, and watch unto prayer." Again he says: "But sanctify the Lord God in your hearts: and be ready always to give an answer to every man that asketh you a reason of the hope that is in you with meekness and fear: having a good conscience; that, whereas they speak evil of you, as of evildoers, they may be ashamed that falsely accuse your good conversation in Christ. For it is better, if the will of God be so, that ye suffer for well-doing, than for evil-doing."

Are the youth in a position where they can with meekness

and fear give an answer to every man that asketh a reason of their hope? I saw that the youth greatly fail of understanding our position. Terrible scenes are just before them, a time of trouble which will test the value of character. Those who have the truth abiding in them will then be developed. Those who have shunned the cross, neglected the word of life, and paid adoration to their own poor selves will be found wanting. They are ensnared by Satan, and will learn too late that they have made a terrible mistake. The pleasures they have sought after prove bitter in the end. Said the angel: "Sacrifice all for God. Self must die. The natural desires and propensities of the unrenewed heart must be subdued." Flee to the neglected Bible; the words of inspiration are spoken to you; pass them not lightly by. You will meet every word again, to render an account whether you have been a doer of the work, shaping your life according to the holy teachings of God's word. Holiness of heart and life are necessary. All who have taken the name of Christ and have enlisted in His service should be good soldiers of the cross. They should show that they are dead to the world, and that their life is hid with Christ in God.

Paul writes to his Colossian brethren as follows: "If ye then be risen with Christ, seek those things which are above, where Christ sitteth on the right hand of God. Set your affection on things above, not on things on the earth. For ye are dead, and your life is hid with Christ in God. When Christ, who is our life, shall appear, then shall ye also appear with Him in glory." "And above all these things put on charity, which is the bond of perfectness. And let the peace of God rule in your hearts, to the which also ye are called in one body; and be ye thankful. Let the word of Christ dwell in you richly in all wisdom; teaching and admonishing one another in psalms and hymns and spiritual songs, singing with grace in your hearts to the Lord. And whatsoever ye do in word or deed, do all in the name of the Lord Jesus, giving thanks to God and the Father by Him."

To the Ephesians he writes: "See then that ye walk circumspectly, not as fools, but as wise, redeeming the time, because the days are evil. Wherefore be ye not unwise, but understanding what the will of the Lord is. And be not drunk with wine, wherein is excess; but be filled with the Spirit; speaking to yourselves in psalms and hymns and spiritual songs, singing and making melody in your heart to the Lord; giving thanks always for all things unto God and the Father in the name of our Lord Jesus Christ."

God is glorified by songs of praise from a pure heart filled with love and devotion to Him. When consecrated believers assemble, their conversation will not be upon the imperfections of others or savor of murmuring or complaint; charity, or love, the bond of perfectness, will encircle them. Love to God and their fellow men flows out naturally in words of affection, sympathy, and esteem for their brethren. The peace of God rules in their hearts; their words are not vain, empty, and frivolous, but to the comfort and edification of one another. If Christians will obey the instructions given to them by Christ and His inspired apostles, they will adorn the religion of the Bible and save themselves severe trials and much perplexity which they attribute to their afflictions in consequence of believing unpopular truth. This is a sad mistake. Very many of their trials are of their own creating because they depart from the word of God. They yield to the world, place themselves upon the enemy's battlefield, and tempt the devil to tempt them. Those who adhere strictly to the admonitions and instructions of God's word, prayerfully seeking to know and do His righteous will, feel not the petty grievances daily occurring. The gratitude which they feel, and the peace of God ruling within, cause them to make melody in their hearts unto the Lord and by words to make mention of the debt of love and thankfulness due the dear Saviour, who so loved them as to die that they might have life. No one who has an indwelling Saviour will dishonor Him before others by producing strains from a musical instrument which call the mind from God and heaven to light and trifling things.

The young are required in whatsoever they do, in word or deed, to do all in the name of the Lord Jesus, giving thanks to God and the Father by Him. I saw that but few of the youth understand what it is to be Christians, to be Christlike. They will have to learn the truths of God's word before they can conform their lives to the pattern. There is not one young person in twenty who has experienced in his life that separation from the world which the Lord requires of all who would become members of His family, children of the heavenly King. "Wherefore come out from among them, and be ye separate, saith the Lord, and touch not the unclean thing; and I will receive you, and will be a father unto you, and ye shall be My sons and daughters, saith the Lord Almighty."

What a promise is here made upon condition of obedience! Do you have to cut loose from friends and relatives in deciding to obey the elevated truths of God's word? Take courage, God has made provision for you, His arms are open to receive you. Come out from among them and be separate, and touch not the unclean, and He will receive you. He promises to be a Father unto you. Oh, what a relationship is this! higher and holier than any earthly tie. If you make the sacrifice, if you have to forsake father, mother, sisters, brothers, wife, and children for Christ's sake, you will not be friendless. God adopts you into His family; you become members of the royal household, sons and daughters of the King who rules in the heaven of heavens. Can you desire a more exalted position than is here promised? Is not this enough? Said the angel: "What could God do for the children of men more than He has already done? If such love, such exalted promises are not appreciated, could He devise anything higher, anything richer and more lofty? All that God could do has been done for the salvation of man, and yet the hearts of the children of men have become hardened. Because of the multiplicity of the blessings with which God has surrounded them, they receive them as common things and forget their gracious Benefactor."

I saw that Satan is a vigilant foe intent upon his purpose of leading the youth to a course of action entirely contrary to that which God would approve. He well knows that there is no other class that can do as much good as young men and young women who are consecrated to God. The youth, if right, could sway a mighty influence. Preachers, or laymen advanced in years, cannot have one half the influence upon the young that the youth, devoted to God, can have upon their associates. They ought to feel that a responsibility rests upon them to do all they can to save their fellow mortals, even at a sacrifice of their pleasure and natural desires. Time, and even means, if required, should be consecrated to God. All who profess godliness should feel the danger of those who are out of Christ. Soon their probation will close. Those who might have exerted an influence to save souls had they stood in the counsel of God, yet failed to do their duty through selfishness, indolence, or because they were ashamed of the cross of Christ, will not only lose their own souls, but will have the blood of poor sinners upon their garments. Such will be required to render an account for the good that they could have done had they been consecrated to God, but did not do because of their unfaithfulness. Those who have really tasted the sweets of redeeming love will not, cannot, rest until all with whom they associate are made acquainted with the plan of salvation. The young should inquire: " 'Lord, what wilt Thou have me to do?' How can I honor and glorify Thy name upon the earth?" Souls are perishing all around us, and yet what burden do the youth bear to win souls to Christ? Those who attend school could have an influence for the Saviour; but who name the name of Christ? and who are seen pleading with tender earnestness with their companions to forsake the ways of sin and choose the path of holiness?

I was shown that this is the course which the believing young should take, but they do not; it is more congenial to their feelings to unite with the sinner in sport and pleasure. The young have a wide sphere of usefulness, but they see it not. Oh, that they would now exert their powers of mind in seeking ways to approach perishing sinners, that they might make known to them the path of holiness, and by prayer and entreaty win even one soul to Christ! What a noble enterprise! One soul to praise God through eternity! One soul to enjoy happiness and everlasting life! One gem in their crown to shine as a star forever and ever! But even more than one can be brought to turn from error to truth, from sin to holiness. Says the Lord by the prophet: "And they that turn many to righteousness [shall shine] as the stars for ever and ever." Then those who engage with Christ and angels in the work of saving perishing souls are richly rewarded in the kingdom of heaven.

I saw that many souls might be saved if the young were where they ought to be, devoted to God and to the truth; but they generally occupy a position where constant labor must be bestowed upon *them*, or they will become of the world themselves. They are a source of constant anxiety and heartache. Tears flow on their account, and agonizing prayers are wrung from the hearts of parents in their behalf. Yet they move on, reckless of the pain which their course of action causes. They plant thorns in the breasts of those who would die to save them and have them become what Christ designed they should through the merits of the blood of Christ.

The youth exercise their ability to execute this or that nice piece of art, but do not feel that God requires them to turn their talents to a better account, that of adorning their profession and seeking to save souls for whom Christ died. One such soul saved is of more value than worlds. Gold and earthly treasure can bear no comparison to the salvation of even one poor soul.

Young men and young women, I saw that God has a work for you to do; take up your cross and follow Christ, or you are unworthy of Him. While you remain in listless indifference, how can you tell what is the will of God concerning you? and how do you expect to be saved, unless as faithful servants you do your Lord's will? Those who possess eternal life will all have *done well*. The King of glory will exalt them to His right hand while He says to them: "Well done, good and faithful servants." How can you tell how many souls you might save from ruin if, instead of studying your own pleasure, you were seeking what work you could do in the vineyard of your Master? How many souls have these gatherings for conversation and the practice of music been the means of saving? If you cannot point to one soul thus saved, turn, oh, turn to a new course of action. Begin to pray for souls; come near to Christ, close to His bleeding side. Let a meek and quiet spirit adorn your lives, and let your earnest, broken, humble petitions ascend to Him for wisdom that you may have success in saving not only your own soul, but the souls of others. *Pray more than you sing*. Do you not stand in greater need of prayer than of singing? Young men and women, God calls upon you to work, work for Him. Make an entire change in your course of action. You can do work that those who minister in word and doctrine cannot do. You can reach a class whom the minister cannot affect.

RECREATION FOR CHRISTIANS

I was shown that Sabbathkeepers as a people labor too hard without allowing themselves change or periods of rest. Recreation is needful to those who are engaged in physical labor and is still more essential for those whose labor is principally mental. It is not essential to our salvation, nor for the glory of God, to keep the mind laboring constantly and excessively, even upon religious themes. There are amusements, such as dancing, card playing, chess, checkers, etc., which we cannot approve, because Heaven condemns them. These amusements open the door for great evil. They are not beneficial in their tendency, but have an exciting influence, producing in some minds a passion for those plays which lead to gambling and dissipation. All such plays should be condemned by Christians, and something perfectly harmless should be substituted in their place.

I saw that our holidays should not be spent in patterning after the world, yet they should not be passed by unnoticed, for this will bring dissatisfaction to our children. On these days when there is danger that our children will be exposed to evil influences, and become corrupted by the pleasures and excitement of the world, let the parents study to get up something to take the place of more dangerous amusements. Give your children to understand that you have their good and happiness in view.

Let several families living in a city or village unite and leave the occupations which have taxed them physically and mentally, and make an excursion into the country to the side of a fine lake or to a nice grove where the scenery of nature is beautiful. They should provide themselves with plain, hygenic food, the very best fruits and grains, and spread their table under the shade of some tree or under the canopy of heaven. The ride, the exercise, and the scenery will quicken the appetite, and they can enjoy a repast which kings might envy.

On such occasions parents and children should feel free from care, labor, and perplexity. Parents should become children with their children, making everything as pleasant for them as possible. Let the whole day be given to recreation. Exercise in the open air for those whose employment has been withindoors and sedentary will be beneficial to health. All who can, should feel it a duty to pursue this course. Nothing will be lost, but much gained. They can return to their occupations with new life and new courage to engage in their labor with zeal, and they are better prepared to resist disease.

I saw that but few realize the constant, wearing labor of those who are bearing the responsibilities of the work in the office. They are confined withindoors day after day and week after week, while a constant strain upon the mental powers is surely undermining their constitutions and lessening their hold on life. These brethren are in danger of breaking suddenly. They are not immortal, and without a change they must wear out and be lost to the work.

We have precious gifts in Brethren A, B, and C. We cannot afford to have them ruin their health through close confinement and incessant toil. Where can we find men with their experience to supply their places? Two of these brethren have been fourteen years connected with the work in the office, laboring earnestly, conscientiously, and unselfishly for the advancement of the cause of God. They have had scarcely any variation except what fevers and other sickness have given them. They should have a change frequently, should often devote a day wholly to recreation with their families, who are almost entirely deprived of their society. All may not be able to leave the work at the same time; but they should so arrange their work that one or two may go, leaving others to supply their places, and then let these in their turn have the same opportunity.

I saw that these brethren, A, B, and C, should as a religious duty take care of the health and strength which God has given them. The Lord does not require them just now to become martyrs to His cause. They will obtain no reward for making this sacrifice, for God wants them to live. They can serve the cause of present truth far better by their lives than by their death. If any one of these brethren should be suddenly prostrated by disease, no one should regard it as a direct judgment from the Lord. It will be only the sure result of the violation of nature's laws. They should take heed to the warning given, lest they transgress and have to suffer the heavy penalty.

I saw that these brethren could benefit the cause of God by attending, as often as practicable, convocation meetings at a distance from their place of labor. The work committed to them is important, and they need healthy nerves and brains; but it is impossible for their minds to be enlivened and invigorated as God would have them, while they are incessantly confined at the office. I was shown that it would be a benefit to the cause at large for these men, standing at the head of the work at Battle Creek, to become acquainted with their brethren abroad by associating with them in meeting. It will give the brethren abroad confidence in those who are bearing the responsibiltities of the work, and will relieve these brethren of the taxation upon the brain, and will make them better acquainted with the progress of the work and the wants of the cause. It will enliven their hope, renew their faith, and increase their courage. Time thus taken will not be lost, but will be spent to the very best advantage. These brethren have qualities which render them in the highest degree capable of enjoying social life. They would enjoy their stay at the homes of brethren abroad, and would benefit and be benefited by interchange of thought and views.

Especially do I appeal to Brother C to change his course of life. He cannot exercise as others in the office can. Indoor, sedentary employment is preparing him for a sudden breakdown. He cannot always do as he has done. He must spend more time in the open air, having periods of light labor of some special nature, or exercise of a pleasant, recreative character. Such confinement as he has imposed upon himself would break down the constitution of the strongest animal. It is cruel, it is wicked, a sin against himself, against which I raise my voice in warning. Brother C, more of your time must be spent in the open air, in riding or in pleasant exercise, or you must die, your wife become a widow, and your children, who love you so much, become orphans. Brother C is qualified to edify others in the exposition of the word. He can serve the cause of God and benefit himself by going out to the large gatherings of Sabbathkeepers and bearing his testimony for the edification of those who are privileged to hear him. This change would bring him more out of doors, into the open air. His blood flows sluggishly through his veins for want of the vivifying air of heaven. He has done well his part in the work at the office, but still he has needed the electrifying influence of pure air and sunlight out of doors to make his work still more spiritual and enlivening.

June 5, 1863, I was shown that my husband should preserve his strength and health, for God had yet a great work for us to do. In His providence we had obtained an experience in this work from its very commencement, and thus our labors would be of greater account to His cause. I saw that my husband's constant and excessive labor was exhausting his fund of strength, which God would have him preserve; that if he continued to overtask his physical and mental energies as he had been doing, he would be using up his future resources of strength and exhausting the capital, and would break down prematurely, and the cause of God would be deprived of his labor. Much of the time he was performing labor connected with the office which others might do, or was engaged in business transactions which he should avoid. God would have us both reserve our strength to be used when specially required to do that work which others could not do, and for which He has raised us up, preserved our lives, and given us a valuable experience; in this way we could be a benefit to His people.

I did not make this public, because it was given specially to us. If this caution had been fully heeded, the affliction under which my husband has been so great a sufferer would have been saved. The work of God was urgent and seemed to allow of no relaxation or separation from it. My husband seemed compelled to constant, wearing labor. Anxiety for his brethren liable to the draft, and also concerning the rebellion in Iowa, kept his mind continually strained, and the physical energies were utterly exhausted. Instead of his having relief, burdens never pressed heavier; and care, instead of lessening, was trebled. But there certainly was a way of escape, or God would not have given the caution He did and would not have permitted him to break down under the taxation. I saw that had he not been specially sustained by God he would have realized the prostration of his physical and mental powers much sooner than he did.

When God speaks, He means what He says. When He cautions, it becomes those noticed to take heed. The reason why I now speak publicly is that the same caution which was given to my husband has been given to others connected with the office. I saw that unless they change their course of action, they are just as liable to be stricken down as was my husband. I am not willing that others should suffer as he has done. But that which is most to be dreaded is, they would be lost for a time to the cause and work of God, when the help and influence of all are so much needed.

Those connected with the office cannot endure the amount of care and labor that my husband has borne for years. They have not the constitution, the capital to draw upon, which my husband had. They can never endure the perplexities and the constant, wearing labor which have come upon him and which he has borne for twenty years. I cannot endure the thought that any in the office should sacrifice strength and health through excessive labor, so that their usefulness should prematurely end and they be unable to work in the vineyard of the Lord. It is not merely the gatherers of the fruit that are the essential laborers; all who assist in digging about the plants, watering, pruning, and lifting up the drooping, trailing vines, and leading their tendrils to entwine about the true trellis, the sure support, are workmen who cannot be spared.

The brethren in the office feel that they cannot leave the work for a few days for a change, for recreation; but this is a mistake. They can and should do so. Even if there were not as much accomplished, it would be better to leave for a few days than to be prostrated by disease and be separated from the work for months, and perhaps never be able to engage in it again.

My husband thought it wrong for him to spend time in social enjoyment. He could not afford to rest. He thought that the work in the office would suffer if he should. But after the blow fell upon him, causing physical and mental prostration, the work had to be carried on without him. I saw that the brethren engaged in the responsible labor in the office should work upon a different plan and make their arrangements to have change. If more help is needed, obtain it, and let relief come to those who are suffering from constant confinement and brain labor. They should attend convocation meetings. They need to throw off care, share the hospitality of the brethren, and enjoy their society and the blessings of the meetings. They will thus receive fresh thoughts, and their wearied energies will be awakened to new life, and they will return to the work far better qualified to perform their part, for they will better understand the wants of the cause.

Brethren abroad, are you asleep to this matter? Must your hearts be made faint by the fall of another of God's workmen, whom you love? These men are the property of the church. Will you suffer them to die under the burdens? I appeal to you to advise a different order of things. I pray God that the bitter experience that has come upon us may never be allowed to come to any one of the brethren in the office. Especially do I commend Brother C to your care. Shall he die for want of air, the vitalizing air of heaven? The course he is pursuing is really shortening his life. Through his confinement indoors his blood is becoming foul and sluggish, the liver is deranged, the action of the heart is not right. Unless he works a change for himself, nature will take the work into her own hands. She will make a grand attempt to relieve the system by expelling the impurities from the blood. She will summon all the vital powers to work, and the whole organism will be deranged, and all this may end in paralysis or apoplexy. If he should ever recover from this crisis, his loss of time would be great; but the probabilities of recovery are very small. If Brother C cannot be aroused, I advise you, brethren, who have an interest in the cause of present truth, to take him, as Luther was taken by his friends, and carry him away from his work.

Since writing the above, I learn that most of *Thoughts on the Revelation,* was written in the night, after the author's day's work was done. This was the course which my husband pursued; I protest against such suicide. The brethren whom I have mentioned, who are so closely confined in the office, would be serving the cause of God by attending meetings and taking periods of recreation. They would be preserving physical health and mental strength in the best condition to devote to the work. They should not be left to feel crippled because they are not earning wages. Their wages should go on and they be free. They are doing a great work.

THE REFORM DRESS

In answer to letters of inquiry from many sisters relative to the proper length of the reform dress, I would say that in our part of the State of Michigan we have adopted the uniform length of about nine inches from the floor. I take this opportunity to answer these inquiries in order to save the time required to answer so many letters. I should have spoken before, but have waited to see something definite on this point in the *Health Reformer.* I would earnestly recommend uniformity in length, and would say that nine inches as nearly accords with my views of the matter as I am able to express it in inches.

As I travel from place to place I find that the reform dress is not rightly represented, and am made to feel that something more definite should be said that there may be uniform action in this matter. This style of dress is unpopular, and for this reason neatness and taste should be exercised by those who adopt it. I have spoken once upon this point, yet some fail to follow the advice given. There should be uniformity as to the length of the reform dress among Sabbathkeepers. Those who make themselves peculiar by adopting this dress should not think for a moment that it is unnecessary to show order, taste, and neatness. Before putting on the reform dress, our sisters should obtain patterns of the pants and sack worn with it. It is a great injury to the dress reform to have persons introduce into a community a style which in every particular needs reforming before it can rightly represent the reform dress. Wait, sisters, till you can put the dress on right.

In some places there is great opposition to the short dress. But when I see some dresses worn by the sisters, I do not wonder that people are disgusted and condemn the dress. Where the dress is represented as it should be, all candid persons are constrained to admit that it is modest and convenient. In some of our churches I have seen all kinds of reform dresses, and yet not one answering the description presented before me. Some appear with white muslin pants, white sleeves, dark delaine dress, and a sleeveless sack of the same description as the dress. Some have a calico dress with pants cut after their own fashioning, not after "the pattern," without starch or stiffening to give them form, and clinging close to the limbs. There is certainly nothing in *these* dresses manifesting taste or order. Such a dress would not recommend itself to the good judgment of sensible-minded persons. In every sense of the word it is a deformed dress.

Sisters who have opposing husbands have asked my advice in regard to their adopting the short dress contrary to the wishes of the husband. I advise them to wait. I do not consider the dress question of so vital importance as the Sabbath. Concerning the latter there can be no hesitation. But the opposition which many might receive should they adopt the dress reform would be more injurious to health than the dress would be beneficial. Several of these sisters have said to me: "My husband likes your dress; he says he has not one word of fault to find with it." This has led me to see the necessity of our sisters' representing the dress reform aright, by manifesting neatness, order, and uniformity in dress. I shall have patterns prepared to take with me as we travel, ready to hand to our sisters whom we shall meet, or to send by mail to all who may order them. Our address will be given in the *Review.*

Those who adopt the short dress should manifest taste in the selection of colors. Those who are unable to buy new cloth must do the best they can to exercise taste and ingenuity in fixing over old garments, making them new again. Be particular to have the pants and dress of the same color and material, or you will appear fantastic. Old garments may be cut after a correct pattern and arranged tastefully, and appear like new. I beg of you, sisters, not to form your patterns after your own particular ideas. While there are correct patterns and good tastes, there are also incorrect patterns and bad tastes.

This dress does not require hoops, and I hope that it will never be disgraced by them. Our sisters need not wear many skirts to distend the dress. It appears much more becoming falling about the form naturally over one or two light skirts. Moreen is excellent material for outside skirts; it retains its stiffness and is durable. If anything is worn in skirts, let it be very small. Quilts are unnecessary. Yet I frequently see them worn, and sometimes hanging a trifle *below* the dress. This gives it an immodest, untidy appearance. White skirts, worn with dark dresses, do not become the short dress. Be particular to have your skirts clean, neat, and nice; make them of good material and in all cases at least three inches shorter than the dress. If anything is worn to distend the skirt, let is be small and at least one quarter or one half a yard from the bottom of the dress or outside skirt. If a cord, or anything answering the place of cords, is placed directly around the bottom of the skirt, it distends the dress merely at the bottom, making it appear very unbecoming when the wearer is sitting or stooping.

None need fear that I shall make dress reform one of my principal subjects as we travel from place to place. Those who have heard me upon this matter will have to act upon the light that has already been given. I have done my duty; I have borne my testimony, and those who have heard me and read that which I have written must now bear the responsibility of receiving or rejecting the light given. If they choose to venture to be forgetful hearers, and not doers of the work, they run their own risk and will be accountable to God for the course they pursue. I am clear. I shall urge none and condemn none. This is not the work assigned me. God knows His humble, willing, obedient children and will reward them according to their faithful performance of His will. To many the dress reform is too simple and humbling to be adopted.

They cannot lift the cross. God works by simple means to separate and distinguish His children from the world; but some have so departed from the simplicity of the work and ways of God that they are above the work, not in it.

I was referred to Numbers 15:38-41: "Speak unto the children of Israel, and bid them that they make them fringes in the borders of their garments throughout their generations, and that they put upon the fringe of the borders a ribband of blue: and it shall be unto you for a fringe, that ye may look upon it, and remember all the commandments of the Lord, and do them; and that ye seek not after your own heart and your own eyes, after which ye use to go a whoring: that ye may remember, and do all My commandments, and be holy unto your God. I am the Lord your God, which brought you out of the land of Egypt, to be your God: I am the Lord your God." Here God expressly commanded a very simple arrangement of dress for the children of Israel for the purpose of distinguishing them from the idolatrous nations around them. As they looked upon their peculiarity of dress, they were to remember that they were God's commandment-keeping people, and that He had wrought in a miraculous manner to bring them from Egyptian bondage to serve Him, to be a holy people unto Him. They were not to serve their own desires, or to imitate the idolatrous nations around them, but to remain a distinct, separate people, that all who looked upon them might say: These are they whom God brought out of the land of Egypt, who keep the law of Ten Commandments. An Israelite was known to be such as soon as seen, for God through simple means distinguished him as His.

The order given by God to the children of Israel to place a ribbon of blue in their garments was to have no direct influence on their health, only as God would bless them by obedience, and the ribbon would keep in their memory the high claims of Jehovah and prevent them from mingling with other nations, uniting in their drunken feasts, and eating swine's flesh and luxurious food detrimental to health. God would now have His people adopt the reform dress not only to distinguish them from the world as His "peculiar people," but because a reform in dress is essential to physical and mental health. God's people have, to a great extent, lost their peculiarity, and have been gradually patterning after the world, and mingling with them, until they have in many respects become like them. This is displeasing to God. He directs them, as He directed the children of Israel anciently, to come out from the world and forsake their idolatrous practices, not following their own hearts (for their hearts are unsanctified) or their own eyes, which have led them to depart from God and to unite with the world.

Something must arise to lessen the hold of God's people upon the world. The reform dress is simple and healthful, yet there is a cross in it. I thank God for the cross and cheerfully bow to lift it. We have been so united with the world that we have lost sight of the cross and do not suffer for Christ's sake.

We should not wish to invent something to make a cross; but if God presents to us a cross, we should cheerfully bear it. In the acceptance of the cross we are distinguished from the world, who love us not and ridicule our peculiarity. Christ was hated by the world because He was not of the world. Can His followers expect to fare better than their Master? If we pass along without receiving censure or frowns from the world we may be alarmed, for it is our conformity to the world which makes us so much like them that there is nothing to arouse their envy or malice; there is no collision of spirits. The world despises the cross. "For the preaching of the cross is to them that perish foolishness; but unto us which are saved it is the power of God." 1 Corinthians 1:18. "But God forbid that I should glory, save in the cross of our Lord Jesus Christ, by whom the world is crucified unto me, and I unto the world." Galatians 6:14.*

* See Appendix.

SURMISINGS ABOUT BATTLE CREEK

In 1865 I saw that some have felt at liberty, through envious feelings, to speak lightly of the church at Battle Creek. Some look suspiciously on all that is going on there and seem to exult if they can get hold of anything to take advantage of to the discredit of Battle Creek. God is displeased with such a spirit and course of action. From what source do our churches abroad obtain their light and knowledge of the truth? It has been from the means which God has ordained, which center at Battle Creek. Who have the burdens of the cause? It is those who are zealously laboring at Battle Creek. Burdens and heavy trials necessarily come upon those who stand in the forefront of the hottest battle, and perplexities and wearing thought are attendant upon all who engage in making highly important decisions in connection with the work of God. Our brethren abroad, who are relieved from all this, should feel thankful and praise God that they are thus favored and should be the last to be jealous, envious, and faultfinding, occupying a position, "Report, and we will report it."

The church at Battle Creek have borne the burdens of the Conferences, which have been a severe tax upon nearly all. In consequence of the extra labor many have brought upon themselves debility which has lasted for many months. They have borne the burden cheerfully, but have felt saddened and disheartened by the heartless indifference of some and the cruel jealousy of others after they returned to the several churches whence they came. Remarks are thoughtlessly made—by some designedly, by others carelessly—concerning the burden bearers there and concerning those who stand at the head of the work. God has marked all these speeches and the jealousy and envy which prompted them; a faithful record is kept. Many thank God for the truth and then turn around and question and find fault with the very means which Heaven has ordained to make them what they are or what they ought to be. How much more pleasing to God it would be for them to act the part of Aaron and Hur and help hold up the hands of those who are bearing the great and heavy burdens of the work in connection with the cause of God. Murmurers and complainers should remain at home, where they will be out of the way of temptation, where they cannot find food for their jealousies, evil surmisings, and faultfindings, for the presence of such is only a burden to the meetings; they are clouds without water.

Those who feel at liberty to find fault with and censure those whom God has chosen to act an important part in this last great work would better seek to be converted and to obtain the mind of Christ. Let them remember the children of Israel who were so ready to find fault with Moses, whom God had ordained to lead His people to Canaan, and to murmur against even God Himself. All these murmurers fell in the wilderness. It is easy to rebel, easy to give battle before considering matters rationally, calmly, and settling whether there is anything to war against. The children of Israel are an example to us upon whom the ends of the world are come.

It is easier for many to question and find fault in regard to matters at Battle Creek than to tell what should be done. Some would even venture to take this responsibility, but they would soon find themselves deficient in experience and would run the work into the ground. If these talkers and faultfinders would themselves become burden bearers and pray for the laborers, they would be blessed themselves and would bless others with their godly example, with their holy influence and lives. It is easier for many to talk than to pray; such lack spirituality and holiness, and their influence is an injury to the cause of God. Instead of feeling that the work at Battle Creek is their work, and that they have an interest in its prosperity, they stand aside more as spectators, to question and find fault. Those who do this are the very ones who lack experience in this work and who have suffered but little for the truth's sake.

SHIFTING RESPONSIBILITIES

Those Sabbathkeeping brethren who shift the responsibility of their stewardship into the hands of their wives, while they themselves are capable of managing the same, are unwise and in the transfer displease God. The stewardship of the husband cannot be transferred to the wife. Yet this is sometimes attempted, to the great injury of both. A believing husband has sometimes transferred his property to his unbelieving companion, hoping thereby to gratify her, disarm her opposition, and finally induce her to believe the truth. But this is no more nor less than an attempt to purchase peace, or to hire the wife to believe the truth. The means which God has lent to advance His cause the husband transfers to one who has no sympathy for the truth; what account will such a steward render when the great Master requires His own with usury?

Believing parents have frequently transferred their property to their unbelieving children, thus putting it out of their power to render to God the things that are His. By so doing they lay off that responsibility which God has laid upon them, and place in the enemy's ranks means which God has entrusted to them to be returned to Him by being invested in His cause when He shall require it of them. It is not in God's order that parents who are capable of managing their own business should give up the control of their property, even to children who are of the same faith. These seldom possess as much devotion to the cause as they should, and they have not been schooled in adversity and affliction so as to place a high estimate upon the eternal treasure and less upon the earthly. The means placed in the hands of such is the greatest evil. It is a temptation to them to place their affections upon the earthly and trust to property and feel that they need but little besides. When means which they have not acquired by their own exertion comes into their possession, they seldom use it wisely.

The husband who transfers his property to his wife opens for her a wide door of temptation, whether she is a believer or an unbeliever. If she is a believer and naturally penurious, or inclined to selfishness and acquisitiveness, the battle will be much harder for her with her husband's stewardship and her own to manage. In order to be saved, she must overcome all these peculiar, evil traits and imitate the character of her divine Lord, seeking opportunity to do others good, loving others as Christ has loved us. She should cultivate the precious gift of love possessed so largely by our Saviour. His life was characterized by noble, disinterested benevolence. His whole life was not marred by one selfish act.

Whatever the motives of the husband, he has placed a terrible stumbling block in his wife's way to hinder her in the work of overcoming. And if the transfer be made to the children, the same evil results may follow. God reads his motives. If he is selfish and has made the transfer to conceal his covetousness and excuse himself from doing anything to advance the cause, the curse of Heaven will surely follow. God reads the purposes and intents of the heart, and tries the motives of the children of men. His signal, visible displeasure may not be manifested as in the case of Ananias and Sapphira, yet in the end the punishment will in no case be lighter than that which was inflicted upon them. In trying to deceive men, they were lying to God. "The soul that sinneth, it shall die."

Such can stand the test of the judgment no better than the man who received the one talent and hid it in the earth. When called to account, he accused God of injustice: "I knew Thee that Thou art an hard man, reaping where Thou hast not sown, and gathering where Thou hast not strewed: and I was afraid, and went and hid Thy talent in the earth [where the cause of God could not be benefited with it]: lo, there Thou hast that is Thine." Saith God: "Take therefore the talent from him, and give it unto him which hath ten talents. . . . And cast ye the unprofitable servant into outer darkness: there shall be weeping and gnashing of teeth." This man was afraid that his Lord would be benefited by the improvement of his talent.

I saw that there are many who have wrapped their talent in a napkin and hid it in the earth. They seem to think that every penny which is invested in the cause of God is lost to them beyond redemption. To those who feel thus, it is even so. They will receive no reward. They give grudgingly only because they feel obliged to do something. God loveth the cheerful giver. Those who flatter themselves that they can shift their responsibility upon the wife or children are deceived by the enemy. A transfer of property will not lessen their responsibility. They are accountable for the means which Heaven has entrusted to their care, and in no way can they excuse themselves from this responsibility until they are released by rendering back to God that which He has committed to them.

The love of the world separates from God. "If any man love the world, the love of the Father is not in him." It is impossible for any to discern the truth while the world has their affections. The world comes between them and God, beclouding the vision and benumbing the sensibilities to such a degree that it is impossible for them to discern sacred things. God calls upon such: "Cleanse your hands, ye sinners; and purify your hearts, ye double-minded. Be afflicted, and mourn, and weep: let your laughter be turned to mourning, and your joy to heaviness." Those who have stained their hands with the pollution of the world are required to cleanse themselves from its stains. Those who think they can serve the world and yet love God are double-minded. But they cannot serve God and mammon. They are men of two minds, loving the world and losing all sense of their obligation to God, and yet professing to be Christ's followers. They are neither the one thing nor the other. They will lose both worlds unless they cleanse their hands and purify their hearts through obedience to the pure principles of truth. "He that saith he abideth in Him ought himself also so to walk, even as He walked." "Herein is our love made perfect, that we may have boldness in the day of judgment: because as He is, so are we in this world." "Whereby are given unto us exceeding great and precious promises: that by these ye might be partakers of the divine nature, having escaped the corruption that is in the world through lust."

It is worldly lust that is destroying true godliness. Love of the world and the things that are in the world is separating from the Father. The passion for earthly gain is increasing among those who profess to be looking for the soon appearing of our Saviour. The lust of the flesh, the lust of the eye, and the pride of life control even professed Christians. They are seeking for the things of the world with avaricious lust, and many will sell eternal life for unholy gain.

PROPER OBSERVANCE OF THE SABBATH

December 25, 1865, I was shown that there has been too much slackness in regard to the observance of the Sabbath. There has not been promptness to fulfill the secular duties within the six working days which God has given to man and carefulness not to infringe upon one hour of the holy, sacred time which He has reserved to Himself. There is no business of man's that should be considered of sufficient importance to cause him to transgress the fourth precept of Jehovah. There are cases in which Christ has given permission to labor even on the Sabbath in saving the life of men or of animals. But if we violate the letter of the fourth commandment for our own advantage from a pecuniary point of view we become Sabbathbreakers and are guilty of transgressing all the commandments, for if we offend in one point we are guilty of all. If in order to save property we break over the express command of Jehovah, where is the stopping place? Where shall we set the bounds? Transgress in a small matter, and look upon it as no particular sin on our part, and the conscience becomes hardened, the sensibilities blunted, until we can go still further and perform quite an amount of labor and still flatter ourselves that we are Sabbathkeepers, when, according to Christ's standard, we are breaking every one of God's holy precepts. There is a fault with Sabbathkeepers in this respect; but God is very particular, and all who think that they are saving a little time, or advantaging themselves by infringing a little on the Lord's time, will meet with loss sooner or later. He cannot bless them as it would be His pleasure to do, for His name is dishonored by them, His precepts lightly esteemed. God's curse will rest upon them, and they will lose ten or twentyfold more than they gain. "Will a man rob God? Yet ye have robbed Me, . . . even this whole nation."

God has given man six days in which to work for himself, but He has reserved one day in which He is to be specially honored. He is to be glorified, His authority respected. And yet man will rob God by stealing a little of the time which the Creator has reserved for Himself. God reserved the seventh day as a period of rest for man, for the good of man as well as for His own glory. He saw that the wants of man required a day of rest from toil and care, that his health and life would be endangered without a period of relaxation from the labor and anxiety of the six days.

The Sabbath was made for the benefit of man; and to knowingly transgress the holy commandment forbidding labor upon the seventh day is a crime in the sight of heaven which was of such magnitude under the Mosaic law as to require the death of the offender. But this was not all that the offender was to suffer, for God would not take a transgressor of His law to heaven. He must suffer the second death, which is the full and final penalty for the transgressor of the law of God.

POLITICAL SENTIMENTS

At Rochester, New York, December 25, 1865, I was shown many things concerning the people of God in connection with His work for these last days. I saw that many professed Sabbathkeepers will come short of everlasting life. They fail to take warning from the course pursued by the children of Israel and fall into some of their evil ways. If they continue in these sins they will fall like the Israelites and never enter the heavenly Canaan. "Now all these things happened unto them for ensamples: and they are written for our admonition, upon whom the ends of the world are come."

I saw that many would fall this side of the kingdom. God is testing and proving His people, and many will not endure the test of character, the measurement of God. Many will have close work to overcome their peculiar traits of character and be without spot or wrinkle or any such thing, unrebukable before God and man. Many professed Sabbathkeepers will be no special benefit to the cause of God or the church without a thorough reformation on their part. Many Sabbathkeepers are not right before God in their political views. They are not in harmony with God's word or in union with the body of Sabbathkeeping believers. Their views do not accord with the principles of our faith. Sufficient light has been given to correct all who wish to be corrected. All who still retain political sentiments which are not in accordance with the spirit of truth are living in violation of the principles of heaven. Therefore as long as they thus remain they cannot possess the spirit of freedom and holiness.

Their principles and positions in political matters are a great hindrance to their spiritual advancement. These are a constant snare to them and a reproach to our faith, and those who retain these principles will eventually be brought just where the enemy would be glad to have them, where they will be finally separated from Sabbathkeeping Christians. These brethren cannot receive the approval of God while they lack sympathy for the oppressed colored race and are at variance with the pure, republican principles of our Government. God has no more sympathy with rebellion upon earth than with the rebellion in heaven, when the great rebel questioned the foundation of God's government and was thrust out with all who sympathized with him in his rebellion.

USURY

In the view given me in Rochester, New York, December 25, 1865, I was shown that the subject of taking usury should be considered by Sabbathkeepers. Wealthy men have no right to take interest from their poor brethren, but they may receive usury from unbelievers. "And if thy brother be waxen poor, and fallen in decay with thee; then thou shalt relieve him. . . . Take thou no usury of him, or increase: but fear thy God; that thy brother may live with thee. Thou shalt not give him thy money upon usury, nor lend him thy victuals for increase."

"Thou shalt not lend upon usury to thy brother; usury of money, usury of victuals, usury of anything that is lent upon usury: unto a stranger thou mayest lend upon usury; but unto thy brother thou shalt not lend upon usury: that the Lord thy God may bless thee in all that thou settest thine hand to in the land whither thou goest to possess it."

God has been displeased with Sabbathkeepers for their avaricious spirit. Their desire to get gain is so strong that they have taken advantage of poor, unfortunate brethren in their distress and have added to their own already abundant means, while these poorer brethren have suffered for the same means. "Am I my brother's keeper?" is the language of their hearts.

A few years ago some of the poorer brethren were in danger of losing their souls through wrong impressions. Everywhere Satan was tempting them in regard to the wealthy. These poor brethren were constantly expecting to be favored, when it was their duty to rely upon their own energies; and had they been favored, it would have been the worst thing that could have been done for them. All through the ranks of Sabbathkeepers, Satan was seeking to overthrow the poorer class by his temptations. Some who have lacked judgment and wisdom have taken their own course, being unwilling to ask advice or follow it. Such have had to suffer as the result of their miserable calculation, and yet these same ones would feel that they should be favored by their brethren who have property. These things needed to be corrected. The first-mentioned class did not realize the responsibilities resting upon the wealthy, nor the perplexity and cares they were compelled to have because of their means. All they could see was that these had means to use, while they themselves were cramped for the same. But as a general thing the wealthy have regarded all the poor in the same light, when there is a class of poor who are doing the best in their power to glorify God, to do good, to live for the truth. These persons are of solid worth. Their judgment is good, their spirit precious in the sight of God; and the amount of good which they accomplish in their unpretending way is tenfold greater than that accomplished by the wealthy, although the latter may give large sums on certain occasions. The rich fail to see and realize the necessity of doing good, of being rich in good works, ready to distribute, willing to communicate.

DECEITFULNESS OF RICHES

Some who profess to believe the truth are lacking in discernment and fail to appreciate moral worth. Persons who boast much of their fidelity to the cause and talk as though they think they know all that is worth knowing, are not humble in heart. They may have money and property, and this is sufficient to give them influence with some; but it will not raise them one jot in favor with God. Money has power and sways a mighty influence. Excellence of character and moral worth are often overlooked if possessed by the poor man. But what does God care for money, for property? The cattle upon a thousand hills are His. The world and all that is therein are His. The inhabitants of the earth are as grasshoppers before Him. Men and property are but as the small dust of the balance. He is no respecter of persons.

Men of property often look upon their wealth and say: By my wisdom have I gotten me this wealth. But who gave them power to get wealth? God has bestowed upon them the ability which they possess, but instead of giving Him the glory they take it to themselves. He will prove them and try them, and will bring their glorying to the dust; He will remove their strength and scatter their possessions. Instead of a blessing they will realize a curse. An act of wrong or oppression, a deviation from the right way, should no sooner be tolerated in a man who possesses property than in a man who has none. All the riches that the most wealthy ever possessed are not of sufficient value to cover the smallest sin before God; they will not be accepted as a ransom for transgression. Repentance, true humility, a broken heart, and a contrite spirit alone will be accepted of God. And no man can have true humility before God unless the same is exemplified before others. Nothing less than repentance, confession, and forsaking of sin is acceptable to God.

Many rich men have obtained their wealth by close deal, by advantaging themselves and disadvantaging their poorer fellow men or their brethren; and these very men glory in their shrewdness and keenness in a bargain. But the curse of God will rest upon every dollar thus obtained, and upon the increase of it in their hands. As these things were shown me, I could see the force of our Saviour's words: "It is easier for a camel to go through the eye of a needle, than for a rich man to enter into the kingdom of God." Those who possess the ability to acquire property need to be constantly on the watch or they will turn their acquisitiveness to bad account and not maintain strict honesty. Thus many fall into temptation, overreach, receive more for a thing than it is worth, and sacrifice the generous, benevolent, noble principles of their manhood for sordid gain.

I was shown that many who profess to be Sabbathkeepers so love the world and the things that are in the world that they have been corrupted by its spirit and influence; the divine has disappeared from their characters and the satanic has crept in, transforming them to serve the purposes of Satan, to be instruments of unrighteousness. Then in contrast with these men I was shown the industrious, honest, poor men who stand ready to help those who need help, who would rather suffer themselves to be disadvantaged by their wealthy brethren than to manifest so close and acquisitive a spirit as they manifest;

men who esteem a clear conscience and right, even in little things, of greater value than riches. They are so ready to help others, so willing to do all the good in their power, that they do not amass wealth; their earthly possessions do not increase. If there is a benevolent object to call forth means or labor, they are the first to be interested in and respond to it, and frequently do far beyond their real ability, and thus deny themselves some needed good, to carry out their benevolent purposes.

Because these men can boast of but little earthly treasure, they may be looked upon as deficient in ability, in judgment, and in wisdom. They may be counted of no special worth, and their influence may not be esteemed by men; yet how does God regard these poor wise men? They are regarded precious in His sight, and, although not increasing their treasure upon earth, they are laying up for themselves an incorruptible treasure in the heavens, and in doing this they manifest a wisdom as far superior to that of the wise, calculating, acquisitive professed Christian as the divine and godlike is superior to the earthly, carnal, and satanic. It is moral worth that God values. A Christian character unblotted with avarice, possessing quietness, meekness, and humility, is more precious in His sight than the most fine gold, even the golden wedge of Ophir.

Wealthy men are to be tested more closely than they ever yet have been. If they stand the test and overcome the blemishes upon their character, and as faithful stewards of Christ render to God the things that are His, it will be said to them: "Well done, good and faithful servant; thou has been faithful over a few things, I will make thee ruler over many things: enter thou into the joy of thy Lord."

I was then directed to the parable of the unjust steward: "And I say unto you, Make to yourselves friends of the mammon of unrighteousness; that, when ye fail, they may receive you into everlasting habitations. He that is faithful in that which is least is faithful also in much: and he that is unjust in the least is unjust also in much. If therefore ye have not been faithful in the unrighteous mammon, who will commit to your trust the true riches? And if ye have not been faithful in that which is another man's, who shall give you that which is your own?"

If men fail to render to God that which He has lent them to use to His glory, and thus rob Him, they will make an entire failure. He has lent them means which they can improve upon by losing no opportunity to do good, and thus they may be constantly laying up treasure in heaven. But if, like the man who had one talent, they hide it, fearing that God will get that which their talent gains, they will not only lose the increase which will finally be awarded the faithful steward, but also the principal which God gave them to work upon. Because they have robbed God, they will not have laid up treasure in heaven, and they lose their earthly treasure also. They have no habitation on earth, and no Friend in heaven to receive them into the everlasting habitation of the righteous.

Christ declares: "No man can serve two masters: for either he will hate the one, and love the other; or else he will hold to the one, and despise the other. Ye cannot serve God and mammon"—cannot serve God and your riches, too. "The Pharisees also, who were covetous, heard all these things: and they derided Him." Mark the words of Christ to them: "Ye are they which justify yourselves before men; but God knoweth your hearts: for that which is highly esteemed among men [which is riches acquired by oppression, by deception, by overreaching, by fraud, or in any other dishonest manner] is abomination in the sight of God." Then Christ presents the two characters, the rich man who was clothed with purple and fine linen, and who fared sumptuously every day, and Lazarus, who was in abject poverty and loathsome to the sight, and who begged the few crumbs which the rich man despised. Our Saviour shows His estimate of the two. Although Lazarus was in so deplorable and mean a condition, he had true faith, true moral worth, which God saw, and which He considered of so great value that He took this poor, despised sufferer and placed him in the most exalted position, while the honored and ease-loving man of wealth was thrust out from the presence of God and plunged into misery and woe unutterable. God did not value the riches of this wealthy man, because he had not true moral worth. His character was worthless. His riches did not recommend him to God nor have any influence to secure His favor.

By this parable Christ would teach His disciples not to judge or value men by their wealth or by the honors which they received of others. Such was the course pursued by the Pharisees, who, while possessing both riches and worldly honor, were valueless in the sight of God and, more than this, were despised and rejected of Him, cast out from His sight as disgusting to Him because there was no moral worth or soundness in them. They were corrupt, sinful, and abominable in His sight. The poor man, despised by his fellow mortals and disgusting to their sight, was valuable in the sight of God because he possessed moral soundness and worth, thus qualifying him to be introduced into the society of refined, holy angels and to be an heir of God and a joint heir with Christ.

In Paul's charge to Timothy he warns him of a class who will not consent to wholesome words and who place a wrong estimate on riches. He says: "If any man teach otherwise, and consent not to wholesome words, even the words of our Lord Jesus Christ, and to the doctrine which is according to godliness; he is proud, knowing nothing, but doting about questions and strifes of words, whereof cometh envy, strife, railings, evil surmisings, perverse disputings of men of corrupt minds, and destitute of the truth, supposing that gain is godliness: from such withdraw thyself. But godliness with contentment is great gain. For we brought nothing into this world, and it is certain we can carry nothing out. And having food and raiment let us be therewith content. But they that will be rich fall into temptation and a snare, and into many foolish and hurtful lusts, which drown men in destruction and perdition. For the love of money is the root of all evil: which while some coveted after, they have erred from the faith, and pierced themselves through with many sorrows. But thou, O man of God, flee these things; and follow after righteousness, godliness, faith, love, patience, meekness. Fight the good fight of faith, lay hold on eternal life, whereunto thou art also called, and hast professed a good profession before many witnesses." "Charge them that are rich in this world, that they be not high-minded, nor trust in uncertain riches, but in the living God, who giveth us richly all things to enjoy; that they do good, that they be rich in good works, ready to distribute, willing to communicate; laying up in store for themselves a good foundation against the time to come, that they may lay hold on eternal life."

Paul in this letter to Timothy would impress upon his mind the necessity of giving such instruction as should remove the deception which so easily steals upon the rich, that because of their riches they are superior to those who are in poverty, that because of their ability to acquire they are superior in wisdom and judgment—in short, that gain is godliness. Here is a fearful deception. How few heed the charge which Paul commissioned Timothy to make to the rich! How many flatter themselves that their acquisitiveness is godliness! Paul declares, "Godliness with contentment is great gain." Although rich persons may devote their whole lives to the one object of getting riches, yet as they brought nothing into the world, they can carry nothing out. They must die and leave that which cost them so much labor to obtain. They staked their all, their eternal interest, to obtain this property, and have lost both worlds.

Paul shows what risks men will run to become rich. But

many are determined to be rich; this is their study, and in their zeal eternal considerations are overlooked. They are blinded by Satan and make themselves believe that it is for good purposes they desire this gain; they strain their consciences, deceive themselves, and are constantly coveting riches. Such have erred from the faith and pierced themselves through with many sorrows. They have sacrificed their noble, elevated principles, given up their faith for riches, and, if not disappointed in their object, they are disappointed in the happiness which they supposed riches would bring. They are entangled, perplexed with care; they have made themselves slaves to their avarice and compelled their families to the same slavery, and the advantages they reap are "many sorrows." "Charge them that are rich in this world, that they be not high-minded, nor trust in uncertain riches, but in the living God, who giveth us richly all things to enjoy." Men are not to hoard up their riches and take no good of them, depriving themselves of the comforts of life and virtually becoming slaves in order to retain or increase their earthly treasure.

The apostle Paul shows the only true use for riches, and bids Timothy charge the rich to do good, that they be rich in good works, ready to distribute, willing to communicate; for in so doing they are laying up in store for themselves a good foundation against the time to come,—referring to the close of time,—that they may lay hold on eternal life. The teachings of Paul harmonize perfectly with the words of Christ: "Make to yourselves friends of the mammon of unrighteousness; that, when ye fail, they may receive you into everlasting habitations." Godliness with contentment is great gain. Here is the true secret of happiness, and real prosperity of soul and body.

OBEDIENCE TO THE TRUTH

Dear Brother D: I recollect your countenance among several others that were shown me in vision in Rochester, New York, December 25, 1865. I was shown that you were upon the background. Your judgment is convinced that we have the truth, but you have not as yet experienced its sanctifying influence. You have not followed closely the footsteps of our Redeemer, therefore you are unprepared to walk even as He walked. As you listen to the words of truth, your judgment says that it is correct, it cannot be gainsaid; but immediately the unsanctified heart says: "These are hard sayings, who can hear them? you would better give up your efforts to keep pace with the people of God, for new and strange and trying things will be continually arising; you will have to stop sometime, and you may just as well stop now, and better than to go further."

You cannot consent to profess the truth and not live it; you have ever admired a life consistent with profession. I was shown a book in which was written your name with many others. Against your name was a black blot. You were looking upon this and saying: "It can never be effaced." Jesus held His wounded hand above it and said: "My blood alone can efface it. If thou wilt from henceforth choose the path of humble obedience, and rely solely upon the merits of My blood to cover thy past transgressions, I will blot out thy transgressions, and cover thy sins. But if you choose the path of transgressors you must reap the transgressor's reward. The wages of sin is death."

I saw evil angels surrounding you seeking to divert your mind from Christ, causing you to look upon God as a God of justice and to lose sight of the love, compassion, and mercy of a crucified Saviour who will save to the uttermost all that come unto Him. Said the angel: "If any man sin, we have an advocate with the Father, Jesus Christ the righteous."

When you are under the pressure of mental anxieties, when you are hearkening to the suggestions of Satan and murmuring and complaining, a ministering angel is commissioned to bear you the succor you need and put to shame the language of your unbelieving mind. You distrust God; you disbelieve in His power to save to the uttermost. You dishonor God by this cruel unbelief and cause yourself much needless suffering. I saw heavenly angels surrounding you, driving back the evil angels, and looking with pity and sorrow upon you, and pointing you to heaven, the crown of immortality, saying: "He that would win must fight."

Although you have been in doubt and perplexity, you have not dared to entirely sever the connecting link between yourself and God's commandment-keeping people. Yet you have not yielded all for the truth's sake; you have not yielded yourself, your own will. You fear to lay yourself and all that you have upon the altar of God, lest you may be required to yield back to Him some portion of that which He has lent you. Heavenly angels are acquainted with our words and actions, and even with the thoughts and intents of the heart. You, dear brother, fear that the truth will cost you too much, but this is one of Satan's suggestions. Let it take all that you possess, and it does not cost too much; the value received, if rightly estimated, is an eternal weight of glory. How little is required of us! How small the sacrifice that we can make in comparison with that which our divine Lord made for us! And yet a spirit of murmuring comes over you because of the cost of everlasting life. You, as well as others of your brethren at ______, have had severe conflicts with the great adversary of souls. You have several times nearly yielded the conflict, but the influence of your wife and eldest daughter has prevailed.

These members of your family would obey the truth with the whole heart could they have your influence to sustain them.

Your daughters look to you for an example, for they think their father must be right. Their salvation depends much upon the course which you pursue. If you cease striving for everlasting life, you will exert a powerful influence to carry your children with you, you will bow down the spirit of your faithful wife, crush her hopes, and lessen her hold on life. How can you in the judgment meet these to testify that your unfaithfulness proved their ruin?

I saw that you had several times yielded to the suggestions of Satan to cease striving to live out the truth, for the tempter told you that you would fail with the best endeavors you might make, that with all your weakness and failings it was impossible for you to maintain a life of devotion. I was shown that your wife and eldest daughter have been your good angels, to grieve over you, to encourage you to resist in a measure the powerful suggestions of Satan; and through your love for them you have been induced to try again to fix your trembling faith upon the promises of God. Satan is waiting to overthrow you that he may exult over your downfall. Those who are trampling underfoot the law of God are strengthened by you in their rebellion. It is impossible for you to be strong until you take a decided stand for the truth.

Systematic benevolence looks to you as needless; you overlook the fact that it originated with God, whose wisdom is unerring. This plan He ordained to save confusion, to correct covetousness, avarice, selfishness, and idolatry. This system was to cause the burden to rest lightly, yet with due weight, upon all. The salvation of man cost a dear price, even the life of the Lord of glory, which He freely gave to lift man from degradation and to exalt him to become heir of the world. God has so ordained that man shall aid his fellow man in the great work of redemption. He who excuses himself from this, who is unwilling to deny himself that others may become partakers with him of the heavenly benefit, proves himself unworthy of the life to come, unworthy of the heavenly treasure which cost so great a sacrifice. God wants no unwilling offering, no pressed sacrifice. Those who are thoroughly converted and who appreciate the work of God will give cheerfully the little required of them, considering it a privilege to bestow.

Said the angel: "Abstain from fleshly lusts which war against the soul." You have stumbled at the health reform. It appears to you to be a needless appendix to the truth. It is not so; it is a part of the truth. Here is a work before you which will come closer and be more trying than anything which has yet been brought to bear upon you. While you hesitate and stand back, failing to lay hold upon the blessing which it is your privilege to receive, you suffer loss. You are stumbling over the very blessing which Heaven has placed in your path to make your progress less difficult. Satan presents this before you in the most objectionable light, that you may combat that which would prove the greatest benefit to you, which would be for your physical and spiritual health. Of all men you are one to be benefited by health reform; the truth received on every point in this matter of reform will be of the greatest advantage. You are a man whom a spare diet will benefit. You *were* in danger of being stricken down in a moment of paralysis, one half of you becoming dead. A denial of appetite is salvation to you, yet you view it as a great privation.

The reason why the youth of the present age are not more religiously inclined is because of the defect in their education. It is not true love exercised toward children which permits in them the indulgence of passion, or allows disobedience of parental laws to go unpunished. "Just as the twig is bent the tree is inclined." The mother should ever have the co-operation of the father in her efforts to lay the foundation of a good Christian character in her children. A doting father should not close his eyes to the faults of his children because it is not pleasant to administer correction. You both need to arouse and with firmness, not in a harsh manner, but with determined purpose, let your children know they must obey you.

A father must not be as a child, moved merely by impulse. He is bound to his family by sacred, holy ties. Every member of the family centers in the father. His name, "house-band," is the true definition of husband. He is the lawmaker, illustrating in his own manly bearing the sterner virtues, energy, integrity, honesty, and practical usefulness. The father is in one sense the priest of the household, laying upon the altar of God the morning and evening sacrifice, while the wife and children unite in prayer and praise. With such a household Jesus will tarry, and through His quickening influence the parents' joyful exclamations shall yet be heard amid more exalted scenes, saying: "Behold, I and the children whom the Lord hath given me." Saved, saved, eternally saved! freed from the corruption that is in the world through lust, and through the merits of Christ made heirs of immortality! I saw that but few fathers realize their responsibility. They have not learned to control themselves, and until this lesson is learned they will make poor work in governing their children. Perfect self-control will act as a charm upon the family. When this is attained, a great victory is gained. Then they can educate their children to self-control.

My heart yearns over the church at ———, for there is a work to be accomplished there. It is God's design to have a people in that place. There is material there for a good church, but there is considerable work to be done to remove the rough edges and prepare them for working order, that all may labor unitedly and draw in even cords. It has hitherto been the case that when one or two felt the necessity of arousing and standing unitedly and more firmly upon the elevated platform of truth, others would make no effort to arise. Satan puts in them a spirit to rebel, to discourage those who would advance. They brace themselves when urged to take hold of the work, a stubborn spirit comes upon some, and when they should help they hinder. Some will not submit to the planing knife of God. As it passes over them, and the uneven surface is disturbed, they complain of too close and severe work. They wish to get out of God's workshop, where their defects may remain undisturbed. They seem to be asleep as to their condition; but their only hope is to remain where the defects in their Christian character will be seen and remedied.

Some are indulging lustful appetite which wars against the soul and is a constant hindrance to their spiritual advancement. They constantly bear an accusing conscience, and if straight truths are talked they are prepared to be offended. They are self-condemned and feel that subjects have been purposely selected to touch their case. They feel grieved and injured, and withdraw themselves from the assemblies of the saints. They forsake the assembling of themselves together, for then their consciences are not so disturbed. They soon lose their interest in the meetings and their love for the truth, and unless they entirely reform, will go back and take their position with the rebel host who stand under the black banner of Satan. If these will crucify fleshly lusts which war against the soul, they will get out of the way, where the arrows of truth will pass harmlessly by them. But while they indulge lustful appetite, and thus cherish their idols, they make themselves a mark for the arrows of truth to hit, and if truth is spoken at all, they must be wounded. Some think that they cannot reform, that health would be sacrificed should they attempt to leave the use of tea, tobacco, and flesh meats. This is the suggestion of Satan. It is these hurtful stimulants that are surely undermining the constitution and preparing the system for acute diseases by impairing Nature's fine machinery and battering down her fortifications erected against disease and premature decay.

Those who make a change and leave off these unnatural stimulants will for a time feel their loss and suffer considerably without them, as does the drunkard who is wedded to his liquor. Take away intoxicating drinks and he suffers terribly. But if he persists he will soon overcome the dreadful lack. Nature will come to his aid and remain at her post until he again substitutes the false prop in her place. Some have so benumbed the fine sensibilities of Nature that it may require a little time for her to recover from the abuse she has been made to suffer through the sinful habits of man, the indulgence of an acquired, depraved appetite, which has depressed and weakened her powers. Give Nature a chance, and she will rally and again perform her part nobly and well. The use of unnatural stimulants is destructive to health and has a benumbing influence upon the brain, making it impossible to appreciate eternal things. Those who cherish these idols cannot rightly value the salvation which Christ has wrought out for them by a life of self-denial, continual suffering and reproach, and by finally yielding His own sinless life to save perishing man from death.

LIFE INSURANCE

I was shown that Sabbathkeeping Adventists should not engage in life insurance. This is a commerce with the world which God does not approve. Those who engage in this enterprise are uniting with the world, while God calls His people to come out from among them and to be separate. Said the angel: "Christ has purchased you by the sacrifice of His life.

'What? know ye not that your body is the temple of the Holy Ghost which is in you, which ye have of God, and ye are not your own? For ye are bought with a price: therefore, glorify God in your body, and in your spirit, which are God's.' 'For ye are dead, and your life is hid with Christ in God. When Christ, who is your life, shall appear, then shall ye also appear with Him in glory.' " Here is the only life insurance which heaven sanctions.

Life insurance is a worldly policy which leads our brethren who engage in it to depart from the simplicity and purity of the gospel. Every such departure weakens our faith and lessens our spirituality. Said the angel: "But ye are a chosen generation, a royal priesthood, an holy nation, a peculiar people; that ye should show forth the praises of Him who hath called you out of darkness into His marvelous light." As a people we are in a special sense the Lord's. Christ has bought us. Angels that excel in strength surround us. Not a sparrow falls to the ground without the notice of our heavenly Father. Even the hairs of our head are numbered. God has made provision for His people. He has a special care for them, and they should not distrust His providence by engaging in a policy with the world.

God designs that we should preserve in simplicity and holiness our peculiarity as a people. Those who engage in this worldly policy invest means which belong to God, which He has entrusted to them to use in His cause, to advance His work. But few will realize any returns from life insurance, and without God's blessing even these will prove an injury instead of a benefit. Those whom God has made His stewards have no right to place in the enemy's ranks the means which He has entrusted to them to use in His cause.

Satan is constantly presenting inducements to God's chosen people to attract their minds from the solemn work of preparation for the scenes just in the future. He is in every sense of the word a deceiver, a skillful charmer. He clothes his plans and snares with coverings of light borrowed from heaven. He tempted Eve to eat of the forbidden fruit by making her believe that she would be greatly advantaged thereby. Satan leads his agents to introduce various inventions and patent rights and other enterprises, that Sabbathkeeping Adventists who are in haste to be rich may fall into temptation, become ensnared, and pierce themselves through with many sorrows. He is wide awake, busily engaged in leading the world captive, and through the agency of worldlings he keeps up a continual pleasing excitement to draw the unwary who profess to believe the truth to unite with worldlings. The lust of the eye, the desire for excitement and pleasing entertainment, is a temptation and snare to God's people. Satan has many finely woven, dangerous nets which are made to appear innocent, but with which he is skillfully preparing to infatuate God's people. There are pleasing shows, entertainments, phrenological lectures, and an endless variety of enterprises constantly arising calculated to lead the people of God to love the world and the things that are in the world. Through this union with the world, faith becomes weakened, and means which should be invested in the cause of present truth are transferred to the enemy's ranks. Through these different channels Satan is skillfully draining the purses of God's people, and for it the displeasure of the Lord is upon them.

CIRCULATE THE PUBLICATIONS

I have been shown that we are not doing our duty in the gratuitous circulation of small publications. There are many honest souls who might be brought to embrace the truth by this means alone. Should there be on each copy of these small tracts an advertisement of our publications and the place where they can be obtained, it would extend the circulation of the larger publications and the *Review, Instructor,* and *Reformer.*

These small tracts of four, eight, or sixteen pages can be furnished for a trifle from a fund raised by the donations of those who have the cause at heart. When you write to a friend you can enclose one or more without increasing postage. When you meet persons in the cars, on the boat, or in the stage who seem to have an ear to hear, you can hand them a tract. These tracts should not at present be scattered promiscuously like the autumn leaves, but should be judiciously and freely handed to those who would be likely to prize them. Thus our publications and the Publishing Association will be advertised in a manner that will result in much good.

THE "HEALTH REFORMER"

The people are perishing for want of knowledge. Says the apostle: "Add to your faith virtue; and to virtue knowledge." After receiving the faith of the gospel, our first work is to seek to add virtuous and pure principles, and thus cleanse the mind and heart for the reception of true knowledge. Disease of almost every description is pressing upon the people, yet they seem willing to remain in ignorance of the means of relief and the course to pursue to avoid disease.

In the establishment of the Health Institute it was the design of God not only that knowledge might be imparted to the comparatively few who should visit it, but that the many might be instructed as to home treatment. The *Health Reformer* is the medium through which rays of light are to shine upon the people. It should be the very best health journal in our country. It must be adapted to the wants of the common people, ready to answer all proper questions and fully explain the first principles of the laws of life and how to obey them and preserve health. The great object to be kept in view by the publication of such a journal should be the good of the suffering people of God. The common people, especially those too poor to attend the Institute, must be reached and instructed by the *Health Reformer.*

THE HEALTH INSTITUTE

In the vision given me December 25, 1865, I saw that the health reform was a great enterprise, closely connected with the present truth, and that Seventh-day Adventists should have a home for the sick where they could be treated for their diseases and also learn how to take care of themselves so as to prevent sickness. I saw that our people should not remain indifferent upon this subject and leave the rich among us to go to the popular water cure institutions of the country for the recovery of health, where they would find opposition to, rather than sympathy with, their views of religious faith. Those who are reduced by disease suffer not only for want of physical but also of mental and moral strength; and afflicted, conscientious Sabbathkeepers cannot receive as much benefit where they feel that they must be constantly guarded lest they compromise their faith and dishonor their profession, as at an institution whose physicians and conductors are in sympathy with the truths connected with the third angel's message.

When persons who have suffered much from disease are relieved by an intelligent system of treatment, consisting of baths, healthful diet, proper periods of rest and exercise, and the beneficial effects of pure air, they are often led to conclude that those who successfully treat them are right in matters of religious faith, or, at least, cannot greatly err from the truth. Thus if our people are left to go to those institutions whose physicians are corrupt in religious faith, they are in danger of being ensnared. The institution at ——, I then saw (in 1865), was the best in the United States. So far as the treatment of the sick is concerned, they have been doing a great and good work; but they urge upon their patients dancing and card playing, and recommend attendance at theaters and such places of worldly amusement, which is in direct opposition to the teachings of Christ and the apostles.

Those connected with the Health Institute now located at Battle Creek should feel that they are engaged in an important and solemn work, and in no way should they pattern after the physicians at the institution at —— in matters of religion and amusements. Yet I saw that there would be danger of imitating them in many things and losing sight of the exalted character of this great work. And should those connected with this enterprise cease to look at their work from a high religious standpoint, and descend from the exalted principles of present truth to imitate in theory and practice those at the head of institutions where the sick are treated only for the recovery of health, the special blessing of God would not rest upon our institution more than upon those where corrupt theories are taught and practiced.

I saw that a very extensive work could not be accomplished in a short time, as it would not be an easy matter to find physicians whom God could approve and who would work together harmoniously, disinterestedly, and zealously for the good of suffering humanity. It should ever be kept prominent that the great object to be attained through this channel is not only health, but perfection, and the spirit of holiness, which cannot be attained with diseased bodies and minds. This object cannot be secured by working merely from the worldling's standpoint. God will raise up men and qualify them to engage in the work, not only as physicians of the body, but of the sin-sick soul, as spiritual fathers to the young and inexperienced.

I was shown that the position of Dr. E in regard to amusements was wrong, and that his views of physical exercise were not all correct. The amusements which he recommends hinder the recovery of health in many cases to one that is helped by them. He has to a great degree condemned physical labor for the sick, and his teaching in many cases has proved a great injury to them. Such mental exercise as playing cards, chess, and checkers excites and wearies the brain and hinders recovery, while light and pleasant physical labor will occupy the time, improve the circulation, relieve and restore the brain, and prove a decided benefit to the health. But take from the invalid all such employment, and he becomes restless, and, with a diseased imagination, views his case as much worse than it really is, which tends to imbecility.

For years I have from time to time been shown that the sick should be taught that it is wrong to suspend all physical labor in order to regain health. In thus doing the will becomes dormant, the blood moves sluggishly through the system and constantly grows more impure. Where the patient is in danger of imagining his case worse than it really is, indolence will be sure to produce the most unhappy results. Well-regulated labor gives the invalid the idea that he is not totally useless in the world, that he is, at least, of some benefit. This will afford him satisfaction, give him courage, and impart to him vigor, which vain mental amusements can never do.

The view that those who have abused both their physical and mental powers, or who have broken down in either mind or body, must suspend activity in order to regain health, is a great error. In a very few cases entire rest for a short period may be necessary, but these instances are very rare. In most cases the change would be too great. Those who have broken down by intense mental labor should have rest from wearing thought, yet to teach them that it is wrong and even dangerous for them to exercise their mental powers to a degree leads them to view their condition as worse than it really is. They become still more nervous and are a great trouble and annoyance to those who have the care of them. In this state of mind their recovery is doubtful indeed.

Those who have broken down by physical exertion must have less labor, and that which is light and pleasant. But to shut them away from all labor and exercise would in many cases prove their ruin. The will goes with the labor of their hands, and those accustomed to labor would feel that they were only machines to be acted upon by physicians and attendants, and the imagination would become diseased. Inactivity is the greatest curse that could come upon such. Their powers become so dormant that it is impossible for them to resist disease and languor, as they must do in order to regain health.

Dr. E has made a great mistake in regard to exercise and amusements, and a still greater in his teaching concerning religious experience and religious excitement. The religion of the Bible is not detrimental to the health of body or mind. The exalting influence of the Spirit of God is the best restorative for the sick. Heaven is all health, and the more fully the heavenly influences are felt the more sure the recovery of the believing invalid. The influence of such views as are advanced by Dr. E has reached us as a people in some degree. Sabbathkeeping health reformers must be free from all these. Every true and real reform will bring us nearer to God and heaven, closer to the side of Jesus, and increase our knowledge of spiritual things and deepen in us the holiness of Christian experience.

It is true that there are unbalanced minds that impose upon themselves fasting which the Scriptures do not teach, and prayers and privation of rest and sleep which God has never required. Such are not prospered and sustained in their voluntary acts of righteousness. They have a pharisaical religion which is not of Christ, but of themselves. They trust in their good works for salvation, vainly hoping to earn heaven by their meritorious works instead of relying, as every sinner should, upon the merits of a crucified, risen, and exalted Saviour. These are almost sure to become sickly. But Christ and true godliness are health to the body and strength to the soul.

Let invalids do something instead of occupying their minds with a simple play, which lowers them in their own estimation and leads them to think their lives useless. Keep the power of the will awake, for the will aroused and rightly directed is a potent soother of the nerves. Invalids are far happier to be employed, and their recovery is more easily effected.

I saw that the greatest curse that ever came upon my husband and Sister F was the instructions they received at ——— in regard to remaining inactive in order to recover. The imagination of both was diseased, and their inactivity resulted in the thought and feeling that it would be dangerous to health and life to exercise, especially if in doing so they became weary. The machinery of the system, so seldom put in motion, lost its elasticity and strength, so that when they did exercise, their joints were stiff and their muscles feeble, and every move required great effort and of course caused pain. Yet this very weariness would have proved a blessing to them had they, irrespective of feeling or unpleasant symptoms, perseveringly resisted their inclinations to inactivity.

I saw that it would be far better for Sister F to be with her family by herself and feel the responsibilities resting upon her. This would awaken into life her dormant energies. I was shown that the broken-up condition of this dear family while at ——— was unfavorable to the education and training of their children. For their own good these children should be learning to take responsibilities in household labor and should feel that some burdens in life rest upon them. The mother, engaged in the education and training of her children, is employed in the very work which God has assigned to her and for the sake of which He has in mercy heard the prayers offered for her recovery. While she should shun wearing labor, she should above all avoid a life of inactivity.

When the vision was given me at Rochester, New York, I saw that it would be far better for these parents and children to form a family by themselves. The children should each do a part of the family labor and thus obtain a valuable education which could not be obtained in any other way. Life at _____ or in any other place, surrounded by waiters and helpers, is the greatest possible injury to mothers and children. Jesus invites Sister F to find rest in Him and to let her mind receive a healthy tone by dwelling upon heavenly things and earnestly seeking to bring up her little flock in the nurture and admonition of the Lord. In this way she can best assist her husband by relieving him of the feeling that she must be the object of so much of his attention, care, and sympathy.

As to the extent of the accommodations of the Health Institute at Battle Creek, I was shown, as I have before stated, that we should have such an institution, small at its commencement, and cautiously increased, as good physicians and helpers could be procured and means raised, and as the wants of invalids should demand; and all should be conducted in strict accordance with the principles and humble spirit of the third angel's message. And as I have seen the large calculations hastily urged by those who have taken a leading part in the work, I have felt alarmed, and in many private conversations and in letters I have warned these brethren to move cautiously. My reasons for this are that without the special blessing of God there are several ways in which this enterprise might be hindered, for a time at least, any one of which would be detrimental to the institution and an injury to the cause. Should the physicians fail, through sickness, death, or any other cause, to fill their places, the work would be hindered till others were raised up; or should means fail to come in when extensive buildings were in process of erection, and the work stop, capital would be sunk, and a general discouragement would come over all interested; also there might be a lack of patients to occupy present accommodations, consequently a lack of means to meet present expenses. With all the efforts in every department put forth in a correct and judicious manner, and with the blessing of God, the institution will prove a glorious success, while a single failure in any one direction might sooner or later prove a great injury. It should not be forgotten that out of many hygienic institutions started in the United States within the last twenty-five years but few maintain even a visible existence at the present time.

I have publicly appealed to our brethren in behalf of an institution to be established among us, and have spoken in the highest terms of Dr. F as the man who has in the providence of God obtained an experience to act a part as physician. This I have said upon the authority of what God has shown me. If necessary, I would unhesitatingly repeat all that I have said. I have no desire to withdraw one sentence that I have written or spoken. The work is of God and must be prosecuted with a firm yet cautious hand.

The health reform is closely connected with the work of the third message, yet it is not the measage. Our preachers should teach the health reform, yet they should not make this the leading theme in the place of the message. Its place is among those subjects which set forth the preparatory work to meet the events brought to view by the message; among these it is prominent. We should take hold of every reform with zeal, yet should avoid giving the impression that we are vacillating and subject to fanaticism. Our people should furnish means to meet the wants of a growing Health Institute among us, as they are able to do without giving less for the other wants of the cause. Let the health reform and the Health Institute grow up among us as other worthy enterprises have grown, taking into the account our feeble strength in the past and our greater ability to do much in a short period of time now. Let the Health Institute grow, as other interests among us have grown, as fast as it can safely and not cripple other branches of the great work which are of equal or greater importance at this time. For a brother to put a large share of his property, whether he has much or little into the Institute, so as to be unable to do as much in other directions as he otherwise should, would be wrong. And for him to do nothing would be as great a wrong. With every stirring appeal to our people for means to put into the Institute there should have been a caution not to rob other branches of the work; especially should the liberal poor have been cautioned. Some feeble poor men with families, without a home of their own, and too poor to go to the Institute to be treated, have put from one fifth to one third of all they possess into the Institute. This is wrong. Some brethren and sisters have several shares when they should not have one, and should for a short time attend the Institute, having their expenses paid, wholly or in part, from the charity fund. I do not see the wisdom of making great calculations for the future and letting those suffer who need help now. Move no faster, brethren, than the unmistakable providence of God opens the way before you.

The health reform is a branch of the special work of God for the benefit of His people. I saw that in an institution established among us *the greatest danger would be of its managers' departing from the spirit of the present truth and from that simplicity which should ever characterize the disciples of Christ*. A warning was given me against lowering the standard of truth in any way in such an institution in order to help the feelings of unbelievers and thus secure their patronage. The great object of receiving unbelievers into the institution is to lead them to embrace the truth. If the standard be lowered, they will get the impression that the truth is of little importance, and they will go away in a state of mind harder of access than before.

But the greatest evil resulting from such a course would be

its influence upon the poor, afflicted, believing patients, which would affect the cause generally. They have been taught to trust in the prayer of faith, and many of them are bowed down in spirit because prayer is not now more fully answered. I saw that the reason why God did not hear the prayers of His servants for the sick among us more fully was that He could not be glorified in so doing while they were violating the laws of health. And I also saw that He designed the health reform and Health Institute to prepare the way for the prayer of faith to be fully answered. Faith and good works should go hand in hand in relieving the afflicted among us, and in fitting them to glorify God here and to be saved at the coming of Christ. God forbid that these afflicted ones should ever be disappointed and grieved in finding the managers of the Institute working only from a worldly standpoint instead of adding to the hygienic practice the blessings and virtues of nursing fathers and mothers in Israel.

Let no one obtain the idea that the Institute is the place for them to come to be raised up by the prayer of faith. That is the place to find relief from disease by treatment and right habits of living, and to learn how to avoid sickness. But if there is one place under the heavens more than another where soothing, sympathizing prayer should be offered by men and women of devotion and faith it is at such an institute. Those who treat the sick should move forward in their important work with strong reliance upon God for His blessing to attend the means which He has graciously provided, and to which He has in mercy called our attention as a people, such as pure air, cleanliness, healthful diet, proper periods of labor and repose, and the use of water. They should have no selfish interest outside of this important and solemn work. To care properly for the physical and spiritual interests of the afflicted people of God who have reposed almost unlimited confidence in them and have at great expense placed themselves under their care will require their undivided attention. No one has so great a mind, or is so skillful, but that the work will be imperfect after he has done his very best.

Let those to whom are committed the physical and also to a great extent the spiritual interests of the afflicted people of God, beware how they, through worldly policy or personal interest or a desire to be engaged in a great and popular work, call down upon themselves and this branch of the cause the frown of God. They should not depend upon their skill alone. If the blessing, instead of the frown, of God be upon the institution, angels will attend patients, helpers, and physicians to assist in the work of restoration, so that in the end the glory will be given to God and not to feeble, shortsighted man. Should these men work from a worldly policy, and should their hearts be lifted up and they feel to say, "My power, and the might of my hand hath done this," God would leave them to work under the great disadvantages of their inferiority to other institutions in knowledge, experience, and facilities. They could not then accomplish half as much as other institutions do.

I saw the beneficial influence of outdoor labor upon those of feeble vitality and depressed circulation, especially upon women who have induced these conditions by too much confinement indoors. Their blood has become impure for want of fresh air and exercise. Instead of amusements to keep these persons indoors, care should be taken to provide outdoor attractions. I saw there should be connected with the Institute ample grounds, beautified with flowers and planted with vegetables and fruits. Here the feeble could find work, appropriate to their sex and condition, at suitable hours. These grounds should be under the care of an experienced gardener to direct all in a tasteful, orderly manner.

The relation which I sustain to this work demands of me an unfettered expression of my views. I speak freely and choose this medium to speak to all interested. What appeared in *Testimony* No. 11 concerning the Health Institute should not have been given until I was able to write out all I had seen in regard to it. I intended to say nothing upon the subject in No. 11, and sent all the manuscript that I designed for that *Testimony* from Ottawa County, where I was then laboring, to the office at Battle Creek, stating that I wished them to hasten out that little work, as it was much needed, and as soon as possible I would write No. 12, in which I designed to speak freely and fully concerning the Institute. The brethren at Battle Creek who were especially interested in the Institute knew I had seen that our people should contribute of their means to establish such an institution. They therefore wrote to me that the influence of my testimony in regard to the Institute was needed immediately to move the brethren upon the subject, and that the publication of No. 11 would be delayed till I could write.

This was a great trial to me, as I knew I could not write out all I had seen, for I was then speaking to the people six or eight times a week, visiting from house to house, and writing hundreds of pages of personal testimonies and private letters. This amount of labor, with unnecessary burdens and trials thrown upon me, unfitted me for labor of any kind. My health was poor, and my mental sufferings were beyond description. Under these circumstances I yielded my judgment to that of others and wrote what appeared in No. 11 in regard to the Health Institute, being unable then to give all I had seen. In this I did wrong. I must be allowed to know my own duty better than others can know it for me, especially concerning matters which God has revealed to me. I shall be blamed by some for speaking as I now speak. Others will blame me for not speaking before. The disposition manifested to crowd the matter of the Institute so fast has been one of the heaviest trials I have ever borne. If all who have used my testimony to move the brethren had been equally moved by it themselves, I should be better satisfied. Should I delay longer to speak my views and feelings, I should be blamed the more both by those who think I should have spoken sooner and by those also who may think I should not give any cautions. For the good of those at the head of the work, for the good of the cause and the brethren, and to save myself great trials, I have freely spoken

---

HEALTH AND RELIGION*

God would have a health institution established which will in its influence be closely connected with the closing work for mortals fitting for immortality, one that will have no tendency to weaken the religious principles of old or young and which will not improve the health of the body to the detriment of spiritual growth. The great object of this institution should be to improve the health of the body, that the afflicted may more highly appreciate eternal things. If this object is not continually set before the mind and efforts are not made to this end, it will prove a curse instead of a blessing, spirituality will be regarded as a secondary thing, and the health of the body and diversion will be made primary.

I saw that the high standard should not be lowered in the least in order that the institution may be patronized by unbelievers. If unbelievers choose to come while its conductors occupy the exalted spiritual position which God designs they should, there will be a power that will affect their hearts. With God and angels on their side, His commandment-keeping people can but prosper. This institution is not to be established for the object of gain, but to aid in bringing God's peo-

---

*This and the following article are extracts from letters which I addressed to those at the head of the Health Institute, the first one the first of May, 1867, and the second, in June following. E. G. W.

ple into such a condition of physical and mental health as will enable them to rightly appreciate eternal things and to correctly value the redemption so dearly purchased by the sufferings of our Saviour. This institution is not to be made a place for diversion or amusement. Those who cannot live unless they have excitement and diversion will be of no use to the world; none are made better for their living. They might just as well be out of the world as to be in it.

I saw that the view that spirituality is a detriment to health, which Dr. E sought to instill into the minds of others, is but the sophistry of the devil. Satan found his way into Eden and made Eve believe that she needed something more than that which God had given for her happiness, that the forbidden fruit would have a special exhilarating influence upon her body and mind, and would exalt her even to be equal with God in knowledge. But the knowledge and benefit she thought to gain proved to her a terrible curse.

There are persons with a diseased imagination to whom religion is a tyrant, ruling them as with a rod of iron. Such are constantly mourning over their depravity and groaning over supposed evil. Love does not exist in their hearts; a frown is ever upon their countenances. They are chilled by the innocent laugh from the youth or from anyone. They consider all recreation or amusement a sin and think that the mind must be constantly wrought up to just such a stern, severe pitch. This is one extreme. Others think that the mind must be ever on the stretch to invent new amusements and diversions in order to gain health. They learn to depend on excitement, and are uneasy without it. Such are not true Christians. They go to another extreme. The true principles of Christianity open before all a source of happiness, the height and depth, the length and breadth of which are immeasurable. It is Christ in us a well of water springing up into everlasting life. It is a continual wellspring from which the Christian can drink at will and never exhaust the fountain.

That which brings sickness of body and mind to nearly all is dissatisfied feelings and discontented repinings. They have not God, they have not the hope which reaches to that within the veil, which is as an anchor to the soul both sure and steadfast. All who possess this hope will purify themselves even as He is pure. Such are free from restless longings, repinings, and discontent; they are not continually looking for evil and brooding over borrowed trouble. But we see many who are having a time of trouble beforehand; anxiety is stamped upon every feature; they seem to find no consolation, but have a continual fearful looking for of some dreadful evil.

Such dishonor God, and bring the religion of Christ into disrepute. They have not true love for God, nor for their companions and children. Their affections have become morbid. But vain amusements will never correct the minds of such. They need the transforming influence of the Spirit of God in order to be happy. They need to be benefited by the mediation of Christ, in order to realize consolation, divine and substantial. "For he that will love life, and see good days, let him refrain his tongue from evil, and his lips that they speak no guile: let him eschew evil, and do good; let him seek peace, and ensue it. For the eyes of the Lord are over the righteous, and His ears are open unto their prayers; but the face of the Lord is against them that do evil." Those who have an experimental knowledge of this scripture are truly happy. They consider the approbation of Heaven of more worth than any earthly amusement; Christ in them the hope of glory will be health to the body and strength to the soul.

The simplicity of the gospel is fast disappearing from professed Sabbathkeepers. I inquire a hundred times a day, How can God prosper us? There is but little praying. In fact, prayer is almost obsolete. Few are willing to bear the cross of Christ, who bore the shameful cross for us. I cannot feel that things are moving at the Institute as God would have them move. I fear that He will turn His face from it. I was shown that physicians and helpers should be of the highest order, those who have an experimental knowledge of the truth, who will command respect, and whose word can be relied on. They should be persons who have not a diseased imagination, persons who have perfect self-control, who are not fitful or changeable, who are free from jealousy and evil surmising, persons who have a power of will that will not yield to slight indispositions, who are unprejudiced, who will think no evil, who think and move calmly, considerately, having the glory of God and the good of others ever before them. Never should one be exalted to a responsible position merely because he desires it. Those only should be chosen who are qualified for the position. Those who are to bear responsibilities should first be proved and give evidence that they are free from jealousy, that they will not take a dislike to this or that one, while they have a few favored friends and take no notice of others. God grant that all may move just right in that institution.

WORK AND AMUSEMENTS

Dear Brother F: My mind has been considerably exercised upon one or two points. When I get where I am writing letters to you night after night in my sleep, I then think it time to carry out my convictions of duty. When I was shown that Dr. E erred in some things in regard to the instructions he gave his patients, I saw that you had received the same ideas in many things and that the time would come when you would see correctly in regard to the matter. These are concerning work and amusements. I was shown that it would prove more beneficial to most patients to allow light work, and even to urge it upon them, than to urge them to remain inactive and idle. If the power of the will be kept active to arouse the dormant faculties, it will be the greatest help to recover health. Remove all labor from those who have been overtaxed all their lives and in nine cases out of ten the change will be an injury. This has proved true in the case of my husband. I was shown that physical, outdoor exercise is far preferable to indoor; but if this cannot be secured, light indoor employment would occupy and divert the mind, and prevent it from dwelling upon symptoms and little ailments, and would also prevent homesickness.

This do-nothing system, I saw, had been the greatest curse to your wife and my husband. God gave employment to the first pair in Eden because He knew they would be happier when employed. From what has been shown me, this do-nothing system is a curse to soul and body. Light employment will not excite or tax the mind or strength any more than amusements. The sick often get where they look at their poor feelings and think themselves utterly unable to do anything, when, if they would arouse the will and compel themselves to do an amount of physical labor every day, they would be far happier and improve much faster. I shall write more fully upon this point hereafter.

I understand from a recent Rochester paper that card playing is no longer practiced as an amusement at the institution in ——.

E. G. W., *note to first edition*

NUMBER THIRTEEN

TESTIMONY FOR THE CHURCH

INTRODUCTION

Again I feel it my duty to speak to the Lord's people in great plainness. It is humiliating to me to point out the errors and rebellion of those who have long been acquainted with us and our work. I do it to correct wrong statements that have gone abroad concerning my husband and myself calculated to injure the cause, and as a warning to others. If we only were to suffer, I would be silent; but when the cause is in danger of reproach and suffering, I must speak, however humiliating. Proud hypocrites will triumph over our brethren because they are humble enough to confess their sins. God loves His people who keep His commandments, and reproves them, not because they are the worst, but because they are the best people in the world. "As many as I love," says Jesus, "I rebuke and chasten."

I would call especial attention to the remarkable dreams given in this little work, all with harmony and distinctness illustrating the same things. The multitude of dreams arise from the common things of life, with which the Spirit of God has nothing to do. There are also false dreams, as well as false visions, which are inspired by the spirit of Satan. But dreams from the Lord are classed in the word of God with visions and are as truly the fruits of the spirit of prophecy as visions. Such dreams, taking into the account the persons who have them and the circumstances under which they are given, contain their own proofs of their genuineness.

May the blessing of God attend this little work.

SKETCH OF EXPERIENCE

From December 19, 1866 to April 25, 1867

Having become fully satisfied that my husband would not recover from his protracted sickness while remaining inactive, and that the time had fully come for me to go forth and bear my testimony to the people, I decided, contrary to the judgment and advice of the church at Battle Creek, of which we were members at that time, to venture a tour in northern Michigan, with my husband in his extremely feeble condition, in the severest cold of winter. It required no small degree of moral courage and faith in God to bring my mind to the decision to risk so much, especially as I stood alone, with the influence of the church, including those at the head of the work at Battle Creek, against me.

But I knew that I had a work to do, and it seemed to me that Satan was determined to keep me from it. I had waited long for our captivity to be turned and feared that precious souls would be lost if I remained longer from the work. To remain longer from the field seemed to me worse than death, and should we move out we could but perish. So, on the 19th of December, 1866, we left Battle Creek in a snowstorm for Wright, Ottawa County, Michigan. My husband stood the long and severe journey of ninety miles much better than I feared, and seemed quite as well when we reached our old home at Brother Root's as when we left Battle Creek. We were kindly received by this dear family and as tenderly cared for as Christian parents can care for invalid children.

We found this church in a very low condition. With a large portion of its members the seeds of disunion and dissatisfaction with one another were taking deep root, and a worldly spirit was taking possession of them. And notwithstanding their low state they had enjoyed the labors of our preachers so seldom that they were hungry for spiritual food. Here commenced our first effective labors since the sickness of my husband. Here he commenced to labor as in former years, though in much weakness. He would speak thirty or forty minutes in the forenoon of both Sabbath and first day, and I would fill up the rest of the time, and then speak about an hour and a half in the afternoon of each day. We were listened to with the greatest attention. I saw that my husband was growing stronger, clearer, and more connected in his subjects. And when on one occasion he spoke one hour with clearness and power, with the burden of the work upon him as when he used to speak, my feelings of gratitude were beyond expression. I arose in the congregation and for nearly half an hour tried with weeping to give utterance to them. The congregation felt deeply. I felt assured that this was the dawn of better days for us.

We remained with this people six weeks. I spoke to them twenty-five times, and my husband twelve times. As our labors with this church progressed, individual cases began to open before me, and I commenced to write out testimonies for them, amounting in all to one hundred pages. Then commenced labor for these persons as they came to Brother Root's, where we were stopping, and with some of them at their homes, but more especially in meetings at the house of worship. In this kind of labor I found that my husband was a great help. His long experience in this kind of work, as he had labored with me in the past, had qualified him for it. And now that he entered upon it again he seemed to manifest all that clearness of thought, good judgment, and faithfulness in dealing with the erring, of former days. In fact, no other two of our ministers could have rendered me the assistance that he did.

A great and good work was done for this dear people.

Wrongs were freely and fully confessed, union was restored, and the blessing of God rested down upon the work. My husband labored to bring up the systematic benevolence of the church to the figures which should be adopted in all our churches, and his efforts resulted in raising the amount to be paid into the treasury annually by that church about three hundred dollars. Those in the church who had been in trial about some of my testimonies, especially respecting the dress question, became fully settled on hearing the matter explained. The health and the dress reform were adopted, and a large amount was raised for the Health Institute.

Here I think it my duty to state that as this work was in progress, unfortunately a wealthy brother from the State of New York visited Wright after calling at Battle Creek and there learning that we had started out contrary to the opinion and advice of the church and those standing at the head of the work at Battle Creek. He chose to represent my husband, even before those for whom we had the greatest labor, as being partially insane and his testimony consequently as of no weight. His influence in this matter, as stated to me by Brother Root, the elder of the church, set the work back at least two weeks. I state this that unconsecrated persons may beware how they in their blind, unfeeling state cast an influence in an hour which may take the worn servants of the Lord weeks to counteract. We were laboring for persons of wealth, and Satan saw that this wealthy brother was just the man for him to use. May the Lord bring him where he can see, and in humility of mind confess, his wrong. By two weeks more of the most wearing labor, with the blessing of God, we were able to remove this wrong influence and give that dear people full proof that God had sent us to them. As a further result of our labors, seven were soon after baptized by Brother Waggoner, and two in July by my husband at the time of our second visit to that church.

The brother from New York returned with his wife and daughter to Battle Creek, not in a state of mind to give a correct report of the good work at Wright or to help the feelings of the church at Battle Creek. As facts have since come to light, it appears that he injured the church, and the church injured him, in their mutual enjoyment from house to house in taking the most unfavorable views of our course and making it the theme of conversation. About the time this cruel work was going on, I had the following dream:

I was visiting Battle Creek in company with a person of commanding manner and dignified deportment. In my dream I was passing around to the houses of our brethren. As we were about to enter, we heard voices engaged in earnest conversation. The name of my husband was frequently mentioned, and I was grieved and astonished to hear those who had professed to be our firmest friends relating scenes and incidents which had occurred during the severe affliction of my husband, when his mental and physical powers were palsied to a great degree. I was grieved to hear the voice of the professed brother from New York before mentioned, relating in an earnest manner, and in an exaggerated light, incidents of which those at Battle Creek were ignorant, while our friends in Battle Creek, in their turn, related that which they knew. I became faint and sick at heart, and in my dream came near falling, when the hand of my attendant supported me, and he said: "You must listen. You must know this even if it is hard to bear."

At the several houses we approached, the same subject was the theme of conversation. It was their *present truth*. Said I: "Oh, I did not know this! I was ignorant that such feelings existed in the hearts of those whom we have regarded as our friends in prosperity, and our fast friends in suffering, affliction, and adversity. Would I had never known this! We have accounted these our very best and truest friends."

The person with me repeated these words: "If they would only engage as readily and with as much earnestness and zeal in conversation upon their Redeemer, dwelling upon His matchless charms, His disinterested benevolence, and His merciful forgiveness, His pitiful tenderness to the suffering, His forbearance and inexpressible love, how much more precious and valuable would be the fruits."

I then said: "I am grieved. My husband has not spared himself to save souls. He stood under the burdens until they crushed him; he was prostrated, broken physically and mentally; and now to gather up words and acts and use them to destroy his influence, after God has put His hand under him to raise him up that his voice may again be heard, is cruel and wicked."

Said the person who accompanied me: "The conversation where Christ and the characteristics of His life are the themes dwelt upon will refresh the spirit and the fruit will be unto holiness and everlasting life." He then quoted these words: "Whatsoever things are true, whatsoever things are honest, whatsoever things are just, whatsoever things are pure, whatsoever things are lovely, whatsoever things are of good report; if there be any virtue, and if there be any praise, think on these things." These words so impressed me that I spoke upon them the next Sabbath.

My labors in Wright were very wearing. I had much care of my husband by day, and sometimes in the night. I gave him baths, and took him out to ride, and twice a day, cold, stormy, or pleasant, walked out with him. I used the pen while he dictated his reports for the *Review,* and also wrote many letters, in addition to the many pages of personal testimonies, and most of No. 11, besides visiting and speaking as often and as long and earnestly as I did. Brother and Sister Root fully sympathized with me in my trials and labors, and watched with the tenderest care to supply all our wants. Our prayers were frequent that the Lord would bless them in basket and in store, in health as well as in grace and spiritual strength. And I felt that a special blessing would follow them. Though sickness has since come into their dwelling, yet I learn by Brother Root that they now enjoy better health than before. And among the items of temporal prosperity he reports that his wheat fields have produced twenty-seven bushels to the acre, and some forty, while the average yield of his neighbors' fields has been only seven bushels per acre.

January 29, 1867, we left Wright, and rode to Greenville, Montcalm County, a distance of forty miles. It was the most severely cold day of the winter, and we were glad to find a shelter from the cold and storm at Brother Maynard's. This dear family welcomed us to their hearts and to their home. We remained in this vicinity six weeks, laboring with the churches at Greenville and Orleans, and making Brother Maynard's hospitable home our headquarters.

The Lord gave me freedom in speaking to the people; in every effort made I realized His sustaining power. And as I became fully convinced that I had a testimony for the people, which I could bear to them in connection with the labors of my husband, my faith was strengthened that he would yet be raised to health to labor with acceptance in the cause and work of God. His labors were received by the people, and he was a great help to me in the work. Without him I could accomplish but little, but with his help, in the strength of God, I could do the work assigned me. The Lord sustained him in every effort which he put forth. As he ventured, trusting in God, regardless of his feebleness, he gained in strength and improved with every effort. As I realized that my husband was regaining physical and mental vigor, my gratitude was unbounded in view of the prospect that I should again be unfettered to engage anew and more earnestly in the work of God, standing by the side of my husband, we laboring unitedly in the closing work for God's people. Previous to his being stricken down, the position he occupied in the office confined him there the greater part of the time. And as I could not travel without him I was necessarily kept at home much of the time. I felt that God would now prosper him while he labored in word and doctrine, and devoted himself more especially to the work of preaching. Others could do the labor in the office, and we were settled in our convictions that he would never again be confined, but be free to travel with me that we both might bear the solemn testimony which God had given us for His remnant people.

I sensibly felt the low state of God's people, and every day I was aware that I had gone to the extent of my strength. While in Wright we had sent my manuscript for No. 11 to the office of publication, and I was improving almost every moment when out of meeting in writing out matter for No. 12. My energies, both physical and mental, had been severely taxed while laboring for the church in Wright. I felt that I should have rest, but could see no opportunity for relief. I was speaking to the people several times a week, and writing many pages of personal testimonies. The burden of souls was upon me, and the responsibilities I felt were so great that I could obtain but a few hours of sleep each night.

While thus laboring in speaking and writing, I received letters of a discouraging character from Battle Creek. As I read them I felt an inexpressible depression of spirits, amounting to agony of mind, which seemed for a short period to palsy my vital energies. For three nights I scarcely slept at all. My thoughts were troubled and perplexed. I concealed my feelings as well as I could from my husband and the sympathizing family with whom we were. None knew my labor or burden of mind as I united with the family in morning and evening devotion, and sought to lay my burden upon the great Burden Bearer. But my petitions came from a heart wrung with anguish, and my prayers were broken and disconnected because of uncontrollable grief. The blood rushed to my brain, frequently causing me to reel and nearly fall. I had the nosebleed often, especially after making an effort to write. I was compelled to lay aside my writing, but could not throw off the burden of anxiety and responsibility upon me, as I realized that I had testimonies for others which I was unable to present to them.

I received still another letter, informing me that it was thought best to defer the publication of No. 11 until I could write out that which I had been shown in regard to the Health Institute, as those in charge of that enterprise stood in great want of means and needed the influence of my testimony to move the brethren. I then wrote out a portion of that which was shown me in regard to the Institute, but could not get out the entire subject because of pressure of blood to the brain. Had I thought that No. 12 would be so long delayed, I should not in any case have sent that portion of the matter contained in No. 11. I supposed that after resting a few days I could again resume my writing. But to my great grief I found that the condition of my brain made it impossible for me to write. The idea of writing testimonies, either general or personal, was given up, and I was in continual distress because I could not write them.

In this state of things it was decided that we would return to Battle Creek and there remain while the roads were in a muddy, broken-up condition, and that I would there complete No. 12. My husband was very anxious to see his brethren at Battle Creek and speak to them and rejoice with them in the work which God was doing for him. I gathered up my writings, and we started on our journey. On the way we held two meetings in Orange and had evidence that the church was profited and encouraged. We were ourselves refreshed by the Spirit of the Lord. That night I dreamed that I was in Battle Creek looking out from the side glass at the door and saw a company marching up to the house, two and two. They looked stern and determined. I knew them well and turned to open the parlor door to receive them, but thought I would look again. The scene was changed. The company now presented the appearance of a Catholic procession. One bore in his hand a cross, another a reed. And as they approached, the one carrying a reed made a circle around the house, saying three times: "This house is proscribed. The goods must be confiscated. They have spoken against our holy order." Terror seized me, and I ran through the house, out of the north door, and found myself in the midst of a company, some of whom I knew, but I dared not speak a word to them for fear of being betrayed. I tried to seek a retired spot where I might weep and pray without meeting eager, inquisitive eyes wherever I turned. I repeated frequently: "If I could only understand this! If they will tell me what I have said or what I have done!"

I wept and prayed much as I saw our goods confiscated. I tried to read sympathy or pity for me in the looks of those around me, and marked the countenances of several whom I thought would speak to me and comfort me if they did not fear that they would be observed by others. I made one attempt to escape from the crowd, but seeing that I was watched, I concealed my intentions. I commenced weeping aloud, and saying: "If they would only tell me what I have done or what I have said!" My husband, who was sleeping in a bed in the same room, heard me weeping aloud and awoke me. My pillow was wet with tears, and a sad depression of spirits was upon me.

Brother and Sister Howe accompanied us to West Windsor, where we were received and welcomed by Brother and Sister

Carman. Sabbath and first day we met the brethren and sisters from the churches in the vicinity and had freedom in bearing our testimony to them. The refreshing Spirit of the Lord rested upon those who felt a special interest in the work of God. Our conference meetings were good, and nearly all bore testimony that they were strengthened and greatly encouraged.

In a few days we found ourselves again at Battle Creek after an absence of about three months. On the Sabbath, March 16, my husband delivered before the church the sermon on "Sanctification" phonographically reported by the editor of the *Review* and published in Volume 29, No. 18. He also spoke with clearness in the afternoon and on first-day forenoon. I bore my testimony with usual freedom. Sabbath, the 23d, we spoke with freedom to the church in Newton and labored with the church at Convis the following Sabbath and first day. We designed to return north and went thirty miles, but were obliged to turn back on account of the condition of the roads. My husband was terribly disappointed at the cold reception which he met at Battle Creek, and I also was grieved. We decided that we could not bear our testimony to this church till they gave better evidence that they wished our services, and concluded to labor in Convis and Monterey till the roads should improve. The two following Sabbaths we spent at Convis and have proof that a good work was done, as the best of fruits are now seen.

I came home to Battle Creek like a weary child who needed comforting words and encouragement. It is painful for me here to state that we were received with great coldness by our brethren, from whom, three months before, I had parted in perfect union, excepting on the point of our leaving home. The first night spent in Battle Creek, I dreamed that I had been laboring very hard and had been traveling for the purpose of attending a large meeting, and that I was very weary.

Sisters were arranging my hair and adjusting my dress, and I fell asleep. When I awoke I was astonished and indignant to find that my garments had been removed, and there had been placed upon me old rags, pieces of bedquilts knotted and sewed together. Said I: "What have you done to me? Who has done this shameful work of removing my garments and replacing them with beggars' rags?" I tore off the rags and threw them from me. I was grieved, and with anguish cried out: "Bring me back my garments which I have worn for twenty-three years and have not disgraced in a single instance. Unless you give me back my garments I shall appeal to the people, who will contribute and return me my own garments which I have worn twenty-three years."

I have seen the fulfillment of this dream. At Battle Creek we met reports which had been put in circulation to injure us, but which had no foundation in truth. Letters had been written by some making a temporary stay at the Health Institute, and by others living in Battle Creek, to churches in Michigan and other states, expressing fears, doubts, and insinuations in regard to us. I was filled with grief as I listened to a charge from a fellow laborer whom I had respected, that they were hearing from every quarter things which I had spoken against the church at Battle Creek. I was so grieved that I knew not what to say. We found a strong, accusing spirit against us. As we became fully convinced of the existing feelings we felt homesick. We were so disappointed and distressed that I told two of our leading brethren that I did not feel at home, as we met distrust and positive coldness instead of welcome and encouragement, and that I had yet to learn that this was the course to pursue toward those who had broken down among them by overexertion and devotion to the work of God. I then said that we thought we should move from Battle Creek and seek a more retired home.

Grieved in spirit beyond measure, I remained at home,

dreading to go anywhere among the church for fear of being wounded. Finally, as no one made an effort to relieve my feelings, I felt it to be my duty to call together a number of experienced brethren and sisters, and meet the reports which were circulating in regard to us. Weighed down and depressed, even to anguish, I met the charges against me, giving a recital of my journey east, one year since, and the painful circumstances attending that journey.

I appealed to those present to judge whether my connection with the work and cause of God would lead me to speak lightly of the church at Battle Creek, from whom I had not the slightest alienation of feeling. Was not my interest in the cause and work of God as great as it was possible for theirs to be? My whole experience and life were interwoven with it. I had no separate interest aside from the work. I had invested everything in this cause, and had considered no sacrifice too great for me to make in order to advance it. I had not allowed affection for my loved babes to hold me back from performing my duty as God required it in His cause. Maternal love throbbed just as strongly in my heart as in the heart of any mother that lived, yet I had separated from my nursing children and allowed another to act the part of mother to them. I had given unmistakable evidences of my interest in, and devotion to, the cause of God. I have shown by my works how dear it was to me. Could any produce stronger proof than myself? Were they zealous in the cause of truth? I more. Were they devoted to it? I could prove greater devotion than anyone living engaged in the work. Had they suffered for the truth's sake? I more. I had not counted my life dear unto me. I had not shunned reproach, suffering, or hardships. When friends and relatives had despaired of my life, because disease was preying upon me, I had been borne in my husband's arms to the boat or cars. At one time, after traveling until midnight, we found ourselves in the city of Boston without means. On two or three occasions we walked by faith seven miles. We traveled as far as my strength would allow and then knelt on the ground and prayed for strength to proceed. Strength was given, and we were enabled to labor earnestly for the good of souls. We allowed no obstacle to deter us from duty or separate us from the work.

The spirit manifested in this meeting distressed me greatly. I returned home still burdened, as those present made no effort to relieve me by acknowledging that they were convinced that they had misjudged me and that their suspicions and accusations against me were unjust. They could not condemn me, neither did they make any effort to relieve me.

For fifteen months my husband had been so feeble that he had not carried his watch or purse, or driven his own team when riding out. But with the present year he had taken his watch and purse, the latter empty in consequence of our great expenses, and had driven his own team. He had, during his sickness, refused at different times to accept money from his brethren to the amount of nearly one thousand dollars, telling them that when he was in want he would let them know it. We were at last brought to want. My husband felt it his duty, before becoming dependent, to first sell what we could spare. He had some few things at the office, and scattered among the brethren in Battle Creek, of little value, which he collected and sold. We disposed of nearly one hundred and fifty dollars worth of furniture. My husband tried to sell our sofa for the meetinghouse, offering to give ten dollars of its value, but could not. At this time our only and very valuable cow died. My husband then for the first time felt that he could receive help, and addressed a note to a brother, stating that if the church would esteem it a pleasure to make up the loss of the cow they might do so. But nothing was done about it only to charge my husband with being insane on the subject of money. The brethren knew him well enough to know that he would never ask for help unless driven to it by stern necessity. And now that he had done it, judge of his feelings and mine when no notice was taken of the matter only to use it to wound us in our want and deep affliction.

At this meeting my husband humbly confessed that he was wrong in several things of this nature, which he never should have done and never would have done but for fear of his brethren and a desire to be just right and in union with the church. This led those who were injuring him to apparently despise him. We were humbled into the very dust and distressed beyond expression. In this state of things we started to fill an appointment at Monterey. On the journey I suffered the keenest anguish of spirit. I tried to explain to myself why it was that our brethren did not understand in regard to our work. I had felt quite sure that when we should meet them they would know what spirit we were of, and that the Spirit of God in them would answer to the same in us, His humble servants, and there would be union of feeling and sentiment. Instead of this we were distrusted and suspiciously watched, which was a cause of the greatest perplexity I ever experienced. As I was thus thinking, a portion of the vision given me at Rochester, December 25, 1865, came like a flash of lightning to my mind, and I immediately related it to my husband:

I was shown a cluster of trees standing near together, forming a circle. Running up over these trees was a vine which covered them at the top and rested upon them, forming an arbor. Soon I saw the trees swaying to and fro, as though moved by a powerful wind. One branch after another of the vine was shaken from its support until the vine was shaken loose from the trees except a few tendrils which were left clinging to the lower branches. A person then came up and severed the remaining clinging tendrils of the vine, and it lay prostrated upon the earth.

The distress and anguish of my mind as I saw the vine

lying upon the ground was beyond description. Many passed and looked pityingly upon it, and I waited anxiously for a friendly hand to raise it; but no help was offered. I inquired why no hand raised the vine. Presently I saw an angel come to the apparently deserted vine. He spread out his arms and placed them beneath the vine and raised it so that it stood upright, saying: "Stand toward heaven, and let thy tendrils entwine about God. Thou art shaken from human support. Thou canst stand, in the strength of God, and flourish without it. Lean upon God alone, and thou shalt never lean in vain, or be shaken therefrom." I felt inexpressible relief, amounting to joy, as I saw the neglected vine cared for. I turned to the angel and inquired what these things meant. Said he: "Thou art this vine. All this thou wilt experience, and then, when these things occur, thou shalt fully understand the figure of the vine. God will be to thee a present help in time of trouble." From this time I was settled as to my duty and never more free in bearing my testimony to the people. If I ever felt the arm of the Lord holding me up, it was at that meeting. My husband was also free and clear in his preaching, and the testimony of all was: We have had an excellent meeting.

After we returned from Monterey, I felt it my duty to call another meeting, as my brethren made no effort to relieve my feelings. I decided to move forward in the strength of God and again express my feelings and free myself from the suspicions and reports circulated to our injury. I bore my testimony and related things which had been shown me in the past history of some present, warning them of their dangers and reproving their wrong course of action. I stated that I had been placed in most disagreeable positions. When families and individuals were brought before me in vision, it was frequently the case that what was shown me in relation to them was of a private nature, reproving secret sins. I have labored with some for months in regard to wrongs of which others knew nothing. As my brethren see these persons sad, and hear them express doubts in regard to their acceptance with God, also feelings of despondency, they have cast censure upon me, as though I were to blame for their being in trial. Those who thus censured me were entirely ignorant of what they were talking about. I protested against persons' sitting as inquisitors upon my course of action. It has been the disagreeable work assigned me to reprove private sins. Were I, in order to prevent suspicions and jealousy, to give a full explanation of my course, and make public that which should be kept private, I should sin against God and wrong the individuals. I have to keep private reproofs of private wrongs to myself, locked in my own breast. Let others judge as they may, I will never betray the confidence reposed in me by the erring and repentant, or reveal to others that which should only be brought before the ones that are guilty. I told those assembled that they must take their hands off and leave me free to act in the fear of God. I left the meeting relieved of a heavy burden.

LABORERS IN THE OFFICE

Here I will give two testimonies, one of them written March, 1867, addressed to all engaged in the work at the Review office, the other addressed to the young who labor in the office. I am sorry to say that all those warned have more or less disregarded these testimonies and now have to confess that they pursued a course contrary to that pointed out by the testimonies. The first is as follows:

While in Rochester, New York, December 25, 1865, I was shown some things concerning those who are engaged in the work at the office, also in regard to ministers whom God has called to labor in word and doctrine. Neither of these should engage in merchandise or traffic. They are called to a more sacred, elevated work, and it would be impossible for them to do justice to the work and still carry on their traffic. Those engaged at the office should have no separate interest. When they have given to the work that attention and care which it demands, they have done all they are able to do, and should not be further taxed. If trafficking which has no connection with the work of God engages the mind and occupies time, the work will not be done thoroughly and well. At the best, those engaged in the work have no physical or mental energy to spare. All are to a greater or less degree enfeebled. Such a cause, such a sacred work, as that in which they are employed should engage the powers of the mind; they should not labor mechanically, but be sanctified to the work and act as though the cause was a part of them, as though they had invested something in this great and solemn work. Unless they thus take hold of this matter with interest, their efforts will not be acceptable to God.

Satan is very artful, busy, and active. His special power is brought to bear upon those who are now engaged in the work of preaching or publishing the present truth. All in connection with this work need to keep on the whole armor, for they are the special marks for Satan to attack. I saw that there is danger of becoming unguarded so that Satan will obtain an entrance and imperceptibly divert the mind from the great work. Those who fill responsible positions in the office are in danger of getting above the work and losing humbleness of mind and the simplicity which has hitherto characterized the work.

Satan had a special object in striking down one at the head of the work who had a thorough experience in the rise and progress of present truth. He designed to get him out of the way, that he himself might come in and imperceptibly affect minds that were not experienced and thoroughly consecrated to the work. God designed to raise my husband to health after others had become acquainted with the burdens he had borne and had felt some of the weariness attending these burdens. At the same time they will never throw their whole soul, all the energies of mind and body, into the work and venture what he has ventured. It would never be their duty to do as he has done, for they could not stand at their post should they pass through a twentieth part of what he has endured.

Satan designs to obtain a foothold in that office, and unless there is a united effort and thorough watchfulness, he will accomplish his object. Some will get above the simplicity of the work and will feel that they are sufficient when their strength is perfect weakness. God will be glorified in this great work. And unless they cherish deep and constant humility and a firm trust in God, they will trust in self, indulge self-sufficiency, and one or more will drink the bitter cup of affliction. As the work increases, there is greater necessity for thorough trust in God and dependence upon Him and a thorough interest in, and devotion to, the work. Selfish interests should be laid aside. There should be much prayer, much meditation, for this is highly necessary for the success and prosperity of the work. A spirit of traffic should not be allowed in anyone who is connected with the office. If it is permitted, the work will be neglected and marred. Common things will be placed too much upon a level with sacred things.

There is great danger that some connected with the work will labor merely for wages. They manifest no special interest in the work, their heart is not in it, and they have no special sense of its sacred, exalted character. There is also special danger that those at the head of the work will become lifted up, exalted, and that the work of God will thus be marred, bearing the impress of the human instead of the divine. Satan is wide awake and persevering, yet Jesus lives, and all who make Him their righteousness, their defense, will be especially sustained.

I was shown that Brethren A, B, and C were in danger of injuring their health by remaining a considerable part of their time in heated rooms not sufficiently ventilated. These brethren need more physical exercise. Their employment is sedentary, and too much of the time they breathe heated, impure air. Their lack of exercise causes a depressed circulation, and they are in danger of injuring their health permanently by neglecting to heed the laws of their being. If they violate these laws they will at some future period just as surely suffer the penalty in some form as my husband has suffered it. They will be sustained no more than was he. No one of them is capable of enduring even a small part of the physical and mental taxation which he endured.

These brethren take the work with the heaviest battles fought, the sorest trials passed through, to establish the cause in its present standing. And yet a great and solemn work is before us, and it calls for devotedness from them and also from Brother D, who is in danger of exaltation. God will prove him and try him, and he must be girded about with truth and have on the armor of righteousness, or he will fall by the hand of the enemy. All these brethren need to adhere most strictly and perseveringly to a healthful, spare diet, for all are in danger of congested brains, and paralysis may fell one or more or all of them, if they continue living carelessly or recklessly.

I saw that God had specially selected Brother B to engage in a great and exalted work. He would have cares and burdens, and yet all these could be so much more easily borne with true devotion and consecration to the work. Brother B, you need a deeper draft from salvation's fountain, a more thorough draft from the fountain of sanctification. Your will has not yet been fully submitted to the will of God. You move on because you think you cannot do otherwise; but to walk in cheerful light because you can see that Christ Jesus leads the way before you, you have failed to do. Standing in the responsible place which you occupy, you have in all this hurt your own soul and influenced others. If you walk contrary to God, He will walk contrary to you. God wants to use you, but you must die to self and sacrifice your pride. The Lord designs to use you in His cause if you will follow His opening providence and heartily and fully sanctify yourself and cleanse yourself from all filthiness of the flesh and spirit, perfecting holiness in the fear of God.

The following is the second testimony, written in May, 1867, and addressed to the young who were laboring in the office:

Dear Young Friends who are employed in the office of publication at Battle Creek: A burden is resting upon me in regard to you. I have been repeatedly shown that all who are connected with the work of God in publishing the present truth to be scattered to every part of the field should be Christians, not only in name, but in deed and in truth. Their object should not be merely to work for wages, but all engaged in this great and solemn work should feel that their interest is in the work, and that it is a part of them. Their motives and influence in connecting themselves with this great and solemn work must bear the test of the judgment. None should be allowed to become connected with the office of publication who manifest selfishness and pride.

I was shown that lightness and folly, joking and laughing, should not be indulged by the workers in the office. Those engaged in the solemn work of preparing truth to go to every part of the field should realize that their deportment has its influence. If they are careless, jesting, joking, and laughing while reading and preparing solemn truth for publication, they show that their hearts are not in the work or sanctified through the truth. They do not discern sacred things, but handle truth that is to test character, truth which is of heavenly origin, as a common tale, as a story, merely to come before the mind and be readily effaced.

While in Rochester I saw that we had everything to fear in regard to the office from a health standpoint; that not one connected with it realized the necessity of thorough ventilation. Their rooms were overheated, and the atmosphere was poisoned by impurities resulting from exhalations from the lungs, and other causes. It is impossible for their minds to be in a healthy condition so as to be rightly impressed by the pure and holy truths with which they have so much to do, unless they place the proper value upon the pure, vitalizing air of heaven.

I was shown that if those who are so closely connected with revealed truth give no special evidence in their lives that they are made better by the truth which is kept so constantly before them, if their lives do not testify to the fact that they are loving the truth and its sacred requirements more and more fervently, they are growing harder, and will be less and less affected by the truth and work of God, until they find themselves destitute of the emotions of the Spirit of God, dead to the heavenly impress of truth. Eternal things will not be discerned by them, but will be placed upon a low level with common things. This, I saw, had been the case with some connected with the office, and all have been remiss in this respect to a greater or lesser degree.

I saw that the work of present truth should engage the interest of all. The publication of truth is God's ordained plan as a means of warning, comforting, reproving, exhorting, or convicting all to whose notice the silent, voiceless messengers may be brought. Angels of God have a part to act in preparing hearts to be sanctified by the truths published, that they may be prepared for the solemn scenes before them. None in that office are sufficient of themselves for the important work of discreetly managing matters connected with the publication of the truth. Angels must be near them to guide, to counsel, and to restrain, or the wisdom and folly of human agencies will be apparent.

I saw that angels were frequently in the office, in the folding room, and in the room where the type is set. I was made to hear the laughing, the jesting, the idle, foolish talking. Again, I saw the vanity, the pride and selfishness exhibited. Angels looked sad and turned away grieved. The words I had heard, the vanity, pride, and selfishness exhibited, caused me to groan with anguish of spirit as angels left the room in disgust. Said an angel: "The heavenly messengers came to bless, that the truth carried by the voiceless preachers might have a sanctifying, holy power to attend its mission; but those engaged in this work were so distant from God, they possessed so little of the divine, and were so conformed to the spirit of the world, that the powers of darkness controlled them, and they could not be made susceptible of divine impressions." At the same time these youth were deceived and thought they were rich and increased in goods and had need of nothing, and knew not that they were poor and miserable, blind and naked. Those who handle precious truth as they would sand know not how many times their heartless indifference to eternal things, their vanity, self-love, and pride, their laughing and senseless chatting, have driven the messengers of heaven away from the office.

In deportment, words, and acts all in that office should be reserved, modest, humble, and disinterested, as was their Pattern, Jesus, the dear Saviour. They should seek God and obtain righteousness. The office is not the place for sport, for visiting, for idlers, for laughing or useless words. All should feel that they are doing a work for their Master. These truths which they read, which they act their part to prepare to send out to the people, are invitations of mercy, are reproofs, threatenings, warnings, or encouragements. These are doing their work as a savor of life unto life, or of death unto death. If rejected, the judgment must decide the matter. The prayer of all in the office should be: "O God, make these truths, which are of such vital importance, clear to the comprehension of the humblest minds! May angels accompany these silent preachers and bless their influence, that souls may be saved by this humble means!"

The heart should go out in fervent prayer while the hands are busy, and Satan will not find such ready access, and the soul, instead of being lifted up unto vanity, will be constantly refreshed, will be like a watered garden. Angels will delight to be near such workers, for their presence will be continually encouraged by them. A power will attend the truths published. Divine rays of light from the heavenly sanctuary will attend the precious truths sent forth, so that those who read will be refreshed and strengthened, and souls that are opposed to the truth will be convicted and compelled to say: These things are so; they cannot be gainsaid.

All should feel that the office is a holy place, as sacred as the house of God. But God has been dishonored by the frivolity and lightness indulged by some connected with the work. I saw that strangers from abroad often went away from the office disappointed. They had associated it with everything sacred; but when they saw the youth, or others connected with the office, possessing but little gravity, careless in words and acts, it caused them to doubt whether, after all, this is really the work of God to prepare a people for translation to heaven.

May God bless this to all concerned.

CONFLICTS AND VICTORY

Experiences from April 26, 1867 to October 20, 1867

We returned north, and on our way held a good meeting at West Windsor, and after reaching home held meetings at Fairplains and Orleans, and also gave some attention to the matter of building, planted our garden, and set out grapes, blackberries, raspberries, and strawberries. Then in company with a good delegation we returned to the General Conference at Battle Creek.

The first Sabbath on our way we spent at Orleans and observed the fast. It was a day of great solemnity with us; we sought to humble ourselves before God, and with brokenness of spirit and much weeping we all prayed fervently that God would bless and strengthen us to do His will at the Conference. We had some faith and hope that our captivity would be turned at that meeting.

When we came to Battle Creek we found that our previous efforts had not accomplished what we had hoped. Reports and jealousy still existed. My soul was filled with intense anguish, and I wept aloud for some hours, unable to restrain my grief. In conversation a friend with whom I had been acquainted for twenty-two years related to me reports which he heard, that we were extravagant in expending means. I inquired wherein we had been extravagant. He mentioned the purchase of an expensive chair. I then related the circumstances. My husband was greatly emaciated, and it was exceedingly wearisome and even painful for him to sit long in a common rocking chair, and for this reason he would lie down upon the bed or lounge a great share of the time. I knew that this was no way for him to obtain strength and begged him to sit up more, but the chair was an objection.

On my way east to attend the bedside of my dying father, I left my husband at Brookfield, New York, and while at Utica looked for a spring, sofa-seat chair. The dealers had none made at the price which I wished to pay, which was about fifteen dollars, but they offered me a very excellent chair, with rollers instead of rockers, price thirty dollars, for seventeen. I knew that this was the chair in every respect. But the brother with me urged me to wait to have a chair made, which would cost only three dollars less. The chair offered for seventeen dollars possessed the real value in itself; but I yielded to the judgment of another, waited to see the cheaper chair put together, paid for it myself, and had it carried to my husband. The report concerning our extravagance in purchasing the chair I met in Wisconsin and Iowa. But who can condemn me? Had I the same to do over again, I would do as I did, with this exception: I would rely upon my own judgment, and purchase a chair costing a few dollars more, and worth double the one I got. Satan sometimes so influences minds as to destroy all feelings of mercy or compassion. The iron seems to enter the heart, and both the human and the divine disappear.

Reports also reached me that a sister had stated in Memphis and Lapeer that the Battle Creek church had not the slightest confidence in Sister White's testimony. The question was asked if this referred to the written testimony. The answer was, No, not to her published visions, but to the testimonies borne in meeting to the church, because her life contradicts them. I again requested an interview with a few select, experienced brethren and sisters, including the persons who had circulated these things. I there requested that they would now show me wherein my life had not been in accordance with my teachings. If my life had been so inconsistent as to warrant the statement that the church at Battle Creek had not the slightest confidence in my testimony, it could not be a difficult matter to present the proofs of my unchristian course. They could produce nothing to justify the statements made, and they confessed that they were all wrong in the reports circulated, and that their suspicions and jealousies were unfounded. I freely forgave those who had injured us, and told them that all I would ask on their part was to counteract the influence they had exerted against us, and I would be satisfied. They promised to do this, but have not done it.

Many other reports against us, all either utterly false or greatly exaggerated, were freely talked over in different families at the time of the Conference, and most looked upon us, especially my husband, with suspicion. Some persons of influence manifested a disposition to crush us. We were in want, and my husband had tried to sell loose property, and he was thought to be wrong for this. He had stated his willingness to have his brethren make up the loss of our cow, and this was looked upon as a grievous sin. Supposing that our property at Battle Creek was as good as sold, we bought and began to build in Greenville. But we could not sell the Battle Creek property, and in our cramped position my husband wrote to different brethren to hire money. For this they condemned him and charged him with the sin of grasping for money. And the brother minister most active in this work was heard to say: "We do not want Brother E to buy Brother White's place, for we want his money for the Health Institute." What could we do? No way could we turn but we were blamed.

Only sixty-five hours before my husband was stricken down, he stood until midnight in a house of worship calling for three hundred dollars to finish paying for that house; and to give his call force he headed the subscription with ten dollars for himself and the same for me. Before midnight the sum was nearly raised. The elder of that church was an old friend, and in our extreme want and friendless condition my husband wrote to him, stating that we were in want, and if that church now wished to return the twenty dollars we would receive it. At the time of the Conference this brother called on us and made the matter a serious wrong. But before he came to our house he had taken some stock at least in the general infection. We felt these things most keenly, and if we had not been especially sustained by the Lord we could not have borne our testimony at the Conference with any degree of freedom.

Before we returned from the Conference, Brethren Andrews, Pierce, and Bourdeau had a special season of prayer at our house, in which we were all greatly blessed, especially my husband. This gave him courage to return to our new home. And then commenced his keen sufferings from his teeth, also our labors reported in the *Review.* He stopped preaching only one week in his toothless condition, but labored at Orange and Wright, with the church at home, at Greenbush and Bushnell, preaching and baptizing as before.

After returning from the Conference, a great uncertainty came upon me in relation to the prosperity of the cause of God. Doubts existed in my mind where none had been six months before. I viewed God's people as partaking of the spirit of the world, imitating its fashions, and getting above the simplicity of our faith. It seemed that the church at Battle Creek were backsliding from God, and it was impossible to arouse their sensibilities. The testimonies given me of God had the least influence and were the least heeded in Battle Creek of any part of the field. I trembled for the cause of God. I knew that the Lord had not forsaken His people, but that their sins and iniquities had separated them from God. At Battle Creek is the great heart of the work. Every pulsation is felt by the members of the body all over the field. If this great heart is in health, a vital circulation will be felt all through the body of Sabbathkeepers. If the heart is diseased, the languishing condition of every branch of the work will attest the fact.

My interest is in this work; my life is interwoven with it. When Zion prospers, I am happy; if she languishes, I am sad, desponding, discouraged. I saw that God's people were in an alarming condition, and His favor was being removed from them. I pondered upon this sad picture day and night, and pleaded in bitter anguish: "O Lord, give not Thine heritage to reproach. Let not the heathen say, Where is their God?" I felt that I was cut loose from everyone at the head of the work and was virtually standing alone. I dared not trust anyone. In the night I have awakened my husband, saying: "I am afraid that I shall become an infidel." Then I would cry for the Lord to save me by His own powerful arm. I could not see that my testimonies were regarded, and I entertained the thought that perhaps my work in the cause was done. We had appointments at Bushnell, but I told my husband that I could not go. He soon returned from the post office with a letter from Brother Matteson, containing the following dream:

Dear Brother White: May the blessing of God be with you, and these lines find you still prospering and improving in health and spiritual strength. I feel very thankful to the Lord for His goodness to you, and trust that you may yet enjoy perfect health and freedom in the proclamation of the last message.

"I have had a remarkable dream about you and Sister White, and feel it my duty to relate the same to you as far as I can remember. I dreamed that I related it to Sister White, as well as the interpretation thereof, which also was given me in the dream. When I awoke, something urged me to get up and write down all the particulars, lest I should forget them; but I neglected to do so, partly because I was tired, and partly because I thought it was nothing but a dream. But seeing that I never dreamed of you before, and that this dream was so intelligent, and so intimately connected with you, I have come to the conclusion that I ought to tell you. The following is all I can remember of it:

"I was in a large house where there was a pulpit somewhat like those we use in our meetinghouses. On it stood many lamps which were burning. These lamps needed a constant supply of oil, and quite a number of us were engaged in carrying oil and filling them. Brother White and his companion were busily engaged, and I noticed that Sister White poured in more oil than any other. Then Brother White went to a door which opened into a warehouse, where there were many barrels of oil. He opened the door and went in, and Sister White followed. Just then a company of men came along, with a great quantity of black stuff that looked like soot, and heaped it all upon Brother and Sister White, completely covering them with it. I felt much grieved, and looked anxiously to see the end of these things. I could see Brother and Sister W. both working hard to get out from under the soot, and after a long struggle they came out as bright as ever, and the evil men and the soot disappeared. Then Brother and Sister White engaged again more heartily than ever in supplying the lamps with oil, but Sister W. still had the precedence.

"I dreamed that the following was the interpretation: The lamps represented the remnant people. The oil was the truth and heavenly love, of which God's people need a constant supply. The people engaged in supplying the lamps were the servants of God laboring in the harvest. Who the evil company were in particular I could not tell, but they were men moved upon by the devil, who directed their evil influence specially against Brother and Sister White. The latter were in great distress for a season, but were at last delivered by the grace of God and their own earnest efforts. Then finally the power of God rested upon them, and they acted a prominent part in the proclamation of the last message of mercy. But Sister White had a richer supply of heavenly wisdom and love than the rest.

"This dream has rather strengthened my confidence that the Lord will lead you out and finish the work of restoration that is begun, and that you will once more enjoy the Spirit of God as you did in times past, yea, more abundantly. Forget not that humility is the door that leads to the rich supplies of the grace of God. May the Lord bless you and your companion and children, and grant us to meet in the heavenly kingdom. Yours in bonds of Christian love.

"John Matteson.

"Oakland, Wisconsin, July 15, 1867."

This dream gave me some encouragement. I had confidence in Brother Matteson. Before I saw him with my natural eyes, his case was shown me in vision, in contrast with that of F of Wisconsin. The latter was utterly unworthy to bear the name of Christian, much more to be a messenger; but Brother Matteson was shown me as one who possessed humility, and who, if he maintained his consecration, would be qualified to point souls to the Lamb of God. Brother Matteson had no knowledge of my trials of mind. Not a line had ever passed between us, and the dream coming when and from whom it did, looked to me like the hand of God reached forth to help me.

We had the care of building with hired money, which caused perplexity. We kept up our appointments and labored extremely hard all through the hot weather. For want of means we went into the field together, hoeing, and cutting and raking hay. I took the fork and built the stack, while my husband, with his feeble arms, pitched the hay to me. I took the brush and painted the inside of much of our house. In these things we both wearied ourselves too much. Finally I suddenly failed and could do no more. For several mornings I fainted, and my husband had to attend the Greenbush grove meeting without me.

Our old, hard-riding carriage had been well-nigh killing us and our team. Long journeyings with it, the labor of meetings, home cares and labors, were too much for us, and I feared that my work was done. My husband tried to encourage me and urged me to start out again to fill our appointments at Orange, Greenbush, and Ithaca. Finally I resolved to start, and, if I was no worse, continue the journey. I rode ten miles kneeling in the carriage on a cushion and leaning my head upon another in my husband's lap. He drove and supported me. The next morning I was some better and decided to go on. God helped us to speak in power to the people at Orange, and a glorious work was done for backsliders and sinners. At Greenbush I had freedom and strength given me.

At Ithaca the Lord helped us to speak to a large congregation whom we had never met before.

In our absence, Brethren King, Fargo, and Maynard decided that in mercy to ourselves and team we should have a light, comfortable carriage; so on our return they took my husband to Ionia and purchased the one we now have. This was just what we needed and would have saved me much weariness in traveling in the heat of summer.

At this time we received earnest requests to attend the convocation meetings in the West. As we read these touching appeals we wept over them. My husband would say to me, "Ellen, we cannot attend these meetings. At best I could hardly take care of myself on such a journey, and should you faint, what could I do? But, Ellen, we must go;" and as he would thus speak, his tearful emotions would choke his utterance. In return, while pondering on our feeble condition, and the state of the cause in the West, and feeling that the brethren needed our labors, I would say: "James, we cannot attend these meetings in the West—but we must go." At this point, several of our faithful brethren, seeing our condition, offered to go with us. This was enough to decide the matter. In our new carriage we left Greenville August 29 to attend the general gathering at Wright. Four teams followed us. The journey was a comfortable one and very pleasant in company with sympathizing brethren. The meeting was one of victory.

September 7 and 8 we enjoyed a precious season at Monterey with the brethren of Allegan County. Here we met Brother Loughborough, who had begun to feel the wrongs existing in Battle Creek and was mourning over the part he had acted in connection with these wrongs, which had injured the cause and brought cruel burdens upon us. By our request he accompanied us to Battle Creek. But before we left Monterey, he related to us the following dream:

"When Brother and Sister White came to Monterey, September 7, they requested me to accompany them to Battle Creek. I hesitated about going, thinking that it might be duty to still follow up the interest in Monterey and thinking, as I expressed to them, that there was but little opposition to them in Battle Creek. After praying over the matter several days, I retired one evening anxiously soliciting the Lord for light in the matter.

"I dreamed that I, with a number of others, members of the Battle Creek church, was on board a train of cars. The cars were low—I could hardly stand erect in them. They were ill-ventilated, having an odor as though they had not been ventilated for months. The road over which they were passing was very rough, and the cars shook about at a furious rate, sometimes causing our baggage to fall off, and sometimes throwing off some of the passengers. We had to keep stopping to get on our passengers and baggage, or repair the track. We seemed to work some time and to make little or no headway. We were indeed a sorry-looking set of travelers.

"All at once we came to a turntable, large enough to take on the whole train. Brother and Sister White were standing there and, as I stepped off the train, they said: 'This train is going all wrong. It must be turned square about.' They both laid hold of cranks that moved the machinery turning the table and tugged with all their might. Never did men work harder propelling a handcar than they did at the cranks of the turntable. I stood and watched till I saw the train beginning to turn, when I spoke out and said, 'It moves,' and laid hold to help them. I paid but little attention to the train, we were so intent upon performing our labor of turning the table.

"When we had accomplished this task, we looked up, and the whole train was transformed. Instead of the low, ill-ventilated cars on which we had been riding, there were broad, high, well-ventilated cars, with large, clear windows, the whole trimmed and gilded in a most splendid manner, more elegant than any palace or hotel car I ever saw. The track was level, smooth, and firm. The train was filling up with passengers whose countenances were cheerful and happy, yet wore an expression of assurance and solemnity. All seemed to express the greatest satisfaction at the change which had been wrought, and the greatest confidence in the successful passage of the train. Brother and Sister White were on board this time, their countenances lit up with holy joy. As the train was starting, I was so overjoyed that I awoke, with the impression on my mind that that dream referred to the church at Battle Creek and matters connected with the cause there. My mind was perfectly clear in regard to my duty to go to Battle Creek and lend a helping hand in the work there. Glad am I now that I have been here to see the blessing of the Lord accompanying the arduous labors of Brother and Sister White in setting things in order.

"J. N. Loughborough."

Before we left Monterey, Brother Loughborough handed me the following account of another dream which he had about the time of the death of his wife. This was also a matter of encouragement to me.

" 'The prophet that hath a dream, let him tell a dream.' Jeremiah 23:28.

"One evening, after meditating upon the afflictions of Brother and Sister White, their connection with the work of the third angel's message, and my own failure to stand by them in their affliction; and after trying to confess my wrongs to the Lord, and imploring His blessing upon Brother and Sister White, I retired to rest.

"I thought in my dream that I was in my native town, at the foot of a long sidehill. I spoke with considerable earnestness and said: 'Oh, that I might find that all-healing fountain!' I thought a beautiful, well-dressed young man came along and said very pleasantly: 'I will conduct you to the spring.' He led the way, and I tried to follow. We went along the hillside, passing with much difficulty three wet boggy places, through which small streams of muddy water were flowing. There was no way to cross these only by wading. Having accomplished this, we came to nice, hard ground and a place where there was a jog in the bank, and a large spring of the purest sparkling water was boiling up. A large vat was placed there, very much like the plunge tub at the Health Institute at Battle Creek. A pipe was running from the spring into one end of the vat, and the water was overflowing at the other. The sun was shining brightly, and the water sparkled in its rays.

"As we approached the spring, the young man said nothing, but looked toward me and smiled with an expression of satisfaction, and waved one hand toward the spring, as much as to say: 'Don't you think that is an all-healing spring?' Quite a large company of persons, with Brother and Sister White at their head, came up to the spring on the opposite side from us. They all looked pleasant and cheerful, yet a holy solemnity seemed to be on their countenances.

"Brother White seemed greatly improved in health, and was cheerful and happy, but looked tired as though he had been walking some distance. Sister White had a large cup in her hand, which she dipped into the spring, drinking of the water, and then passing it to the others. I thought that Brother White was addressing the company and saying to them: 'Now you will have a chance to see the effects of this water.' He then drank, and it instantly revived him, as it did all others who drank of it, causing a look of vigor and strength in their countenances. I thought that while Brother White was talking and taking now and then a draft of water, he placed his hands on the side of the vat and plunged in three times. Every time he came up he was stronger than before, but he kept talking all the while and exhorting others to come and bathe in 'the fountain,' as he then called it, and drink of its healing stream. His voice, as well as that of Sister White, seemed melodious. I felt a spirit of rejoicing that I had found the spring. Sister

White was coming toward me with a cup of the water for me to drink, but I was so rejoiced that I awoke before I drank of the water.

"The Lord grant that I may drink largely of that water, for I believe that it is none other than that of which Christ spoke, which will 'spring up unto everlasting life.'

"John Loughborough.

"Monterey, Michigan, Sept. 8, 1867."

September 14 and 15 we held profitable meetings at Battle Creek. Here my husband with freedom struck a bold blow at some sins of those who stand in high places in the cause, and for the first time in twenty months he attended evening meetings and preached evenings. A good work was begun, and the church, as published in the *Review,* gave us the pledge to stand by us, if on our return from the West we would continue our labors with them.

In company with Brother and Sister Maynard, and Brethren Smith and Olmstead, we attended the large Western meetings, the principal victories of which have been fully given in the *Review.* While attending the meetings in Wisconsin, I was quite feeble. I had labored far beyond my strength at Battle Creek and nearly fainted in the cars on the journey. I had for four weeks suffered much with my lungs, and it was with difficulty that I spoke to the people. Sabbath evening a fomentation was applied over my throat and lungs; but the head cap was forgotten, and the difficulty of the lungs was driven to the brain. As I arose in the morning, I felt a singular sensation upon the brain. Voices seemed to vibrate, and everything appeared to be swinging before me. As I walked, I reeled and came near falling to the floor. I took my breakfast, hoping to be relieved by so doing; but the difficulty only increased. I grew very sick and could not sit up.

My husband came to the house after the forenoon meeting, saying that he had given an appointment for me to speak in the afternoon. It seemed impossible for me to stand before the people. When my husband asked what subject I would speak upon, I could not gather or retain a sentence in my mind. But I thought: If God will have me speak, He will surely strengthen me; I will venture by faith; I can but fail. I staggered to the tent with a strangely confused brain, but told the preaching brethren on the stand that if they would sustain me by their prayers, I would speak. I stood before the people in faith, and in about five minutes my head and lungs were relieved, and without difficulty I spoke more than one hour to fifteen hundred eager listeners. After I ceased speaking, a sense of the goodness and mercy of God came over me, and I could not forbear rising again and relating my sickness and the blessing of God which had sustained me while speaking. Since that meeting my lungs have been greatly relieved, and I have been improving in health.

In the West we met reports amounting to little less than slander against my husband. These were current at the time of the General Conference, and were carried to all parts of the field. I will state one as a sample. It was said that my husband was so crazy for money that he had engaged in selling old bottles. The facts are these: When we were about to move, I asked my husband what we should do with a lot of old bottles on hand. Said he: "Throw them away." Just then our Willie came in and offered to clean and sell them. I told him to do so, and he should have what he could get for them. And when my husband rode to the post office, he took Willie and the bottles into the carriage. He could do no less for his own faithful little son. Willie sold the bottles and took the money. On their way to the post office my husband took a brother connected with the Review office into the carriage, who conversed pleasantly with him as they rode to and from town, and because he saw Willie come out to the carriage and ask his father a question relative to the value of the bottles, and then saw the druggist in conversation with my husband relative to that which so much interested Willie, this brother, without saying one word to my husband about the matter, immediately reported that Brother White had been downtown selling old bottles and therefore must be crazy. The first we heard about the bottles was in Iowa, five months after.

These things have been kept from us so that we could not correct them, and have been carried, as on the wings of the wind, by our professed friends. And we have been astonished to find, by investigation and by recent confessions from nearly all the members of this church, that some one or more of the false reports have been fully credited by nearly all and that those professed Christians have cherished feelings of censure, bitterness, and cruelty against us, especially against my feeble husband who is struggling for life and liberty. Some have had a wicked, crushing spirit and have represented him as wealthy yet grasping for money.

Upon returning to Battle Creek, my husband called for a council of brethren to meet with the church that matters might be investigated before them and false reports met. Brethren came from different parts of the state, and my husband fearlessly called on all to bring what they could against him that he might meet it openly and thus put an end to this private slander. The wrongs which he had before confessed in the *Review* he now fully confessed in a public meeting and to individuals, and also explained many matters upon which false and foolish charges were based, and convinced all of the falsity of those charges.

And while looking up matters relative to the real value of our property, we found to his astonishment, and that of all present, that it amounted to only $1,500, besides his horses and carriage, and remnants of editions of books and charts, the sale of which for the past year, as stated by the secretary, has not been equal to the interest on the money he owes to the Publishing Association. These books and charts cannot at present be regarded of much value, and certainly not to us in our present condition.

When in health, my husband had no time to keep accounts, and during his sickness his matters were in the hands of others. The inquiry arose: What had become of his property? Had he been defrauded? Had mistakes been made in his accounts? Or had he, in the unsettled condition of his affairs, given to this and that good object, not knowing his real ability to give and not knowing how much he gave?

As one good result of the investigation, confidence in those who have had charge of accounts relative to our affairs is unshaken, and we have no good reason to conclude that our limited means can be attributed to errors in the accounts. Therefore in looking over my husband's business matters for ten years, and his liberal manner of handing out means to help the work in all its branches, the best and most charitable conclusion is that our property has been used in the cause of present truth. My husband has kept no accounts, and what he has given can be traced only from memory and from what has been receipted in the *Review.* The fact that we are worth so little, appearing at this time when my husband has been represented as wealthy and still grasping for more, has been a matter of rejoicing to us, as it is the best refutation to the false charges which threatened our influence and Christian character.

Our property may go, and we will still rejoice in God if it be used for the advancement of His cause. We have cheerfully spent the best of our days, the best of our strength, and have nearly worn out in the same cause, and feel the infirmities of premature age, and yet we will rejoice. But when our professed brethren attack our character and influence by representing us as wealthy, worldly, and grasping for more, it is then that we feel keenly. Let us enjoy the character and influence we have dearly earned during the past twenty years, with even poverty and a slight hold on health and this mortal life, and we will rejoice and cheerfully give to the cause the little there is left of us.

The investigation was a thorough one and resulted in freeing us from the charges brought against us, and restoring feelings of perfect union. Hearty and heart-rending confessions of the cruel course pursued toward us here have been made, and the signal blessing of God has come upon us all. Backsliders have been reclaimed, sinners have been converted, and forty-four have been buried in baptism, my husband baptizing sixteen, and Brethren Andrews and Loughborough, twenty-eight. We are encouraged, yet much worn. My husband and myself have had the burden of the work, which has been very laborious and exciting. How we have, in our feeble state, gone through with the investigation, with the feelings of nearly all against us, endured the preaching, the exhortations, and the late evening meetings, and at the same time prepared this work, my husband working with me, copying and preparing it for the printers, and reading proof, God only knows. Yet we have passed through it and hope in God that He will sustain us in our future labors.

We now believe that much in the foregoing dreams was given to illustrate our trials arising from wrongs existing at Battle Creek, our labors in clearing ourselves from cruel charges, and also our labors, with the blessing of God, in setting things right. If this view of the dreams be correct, may we not hope, from other portions of them not yet fulfilled, that our future will be more favorable than the past?

In concluding this narrative, I would say that we are living in a most solemn time. In the last vision given me, I was shown the startling fact that but a small portion of those who now profess the truth will be sanctified by it and be saved. Many will get above the simplicity of the work. They will conform to the world, cherish idols, and become spiritually dead. The humble, self-sacrificing followers of Jesus will pass on to perfection, leaving behind the indifferent and lovers of the world.

I was pointed back to ancient Israel. But two of the adults of the vast army that left Egypt entered the land of Canaan. Their dead bodies were strewn in the wilderness because of their transgressions. Modern Israel are in greater danger of forgetting God and being led into idolatry than were His ancient people. Many idols are worshiped, even by professed Sabbathkeepers. God especially charged His ancient people to guard against idolatry, for if they should be led away from serving the living God, His curse would rest upon them, while if they would love Him with all their heart, with all their soul, and with all their might, He would abundantly bless them in basket and in store, and would remove sickness from the midst of them.

A blessing or a curse is now before the people of God—a blessing if they come out from the world and are separate, and walk in the path of humble obedience; and a curse if they unite with the idolatrous, who trample upon the high claims of heaven. The sins and iniquities of rebellious Israel are recorded and the picture presented before us as a warning that if we imitate their example of transgression and depart from God we shall fall as surely as did they. "Now all these things happened unto them for ensamples: and they are written for our admonition, upon whom the ends of the world are come."

RESPONSE FROM BATTLE CREEK CHURCH

We esteem it a privilege as well as a duty to respond to the foregoing statements of Sister White. We have been favored with an acquaintance of many years with the labors of these servants of the Lord [Brother and Sister White]. We have known something of their sacrifices in the past, and have been witnesses of the blessing of God that has attended their plain, searching, faithful testimony. We have long been convinced that the teachings of the Holy Spirit in these visions were indispensable to the welfare of the people who are preparing for translation into the kingdom of God. In no other way can secret sins be rebuked and base men who creep "in unawares" into the flock of God be exposed and baffled in their evil designs. Long experience has taught us that such a gift is of inestimable value to the people of God. We believe also that God has called Brother White to bear a plain testimony in reproving wrongs thus made manifest, and that in this work he should have the support of those who truly fear God.

We have learned by painful experience, also, that when these testimonies are silent, or their warning lightly regarded, coldness, backsliding, worldly-mindedness, and spiritual darkness take possession of the church. We would not give glory to man, but we should be recreant to our sense of duty not to speak in strong and pointed language our views of the importance of these testimonies. The fearful apostasy of those who have slighted and despised them has furnished many sad proofs of the dangerous business of doing despite to the Spirit of grace.

We have been witnesses of the great affliction through which Brother and Sister White have passed in the severe and dangerous sickness of Brother White. The hand of God in his restoration is to us most apparent. Probably no other one upon whom such a blow has fallen ever recovered. Yet a severe shock of paralysis, seriously affecting the brain, has, by the good hand of God, been removed from His servant, and new strength granted him both in body and mind.

We think that the action of Sister White in taking her sick husband on her northern tour, in December last, was dictated by the Spirit of God; and that we, in standing opposed to such action, did not move in the counsel of God. We lacked heavenly wisdom in this matter and thus erred from the right path. We acknowledge ourselves to have been, at this time, lacking in that deep Christian sympathy that was called for by such great affliction, and that we have been too slow to see the hand of God in the recovery of Brother White. His labors and sufferings in our behalf entitled him to our warmest sympathy and support. But we have been blinded by Satan in respect to our own spiritual condition.

A spirit of prejudice respecting means came over us during the past winter, causing us to feel that Brother W. was asking for means when he did not need it. We now ascertain that at this very time he was really in want, and we were wrong in that we did not inquire into the case as we should. We acknowledge that this feeling was unfounded and cruel, though it was caused by misapprehension of the facts in the case.

We now accept with deep sorrow of heart the reproof given us in this testimony, and we ask that wherein we have erred from the right, through our lack of spiritual discernment, we may find forgiveness of God and of His people.

The labors of Brother and Sister White with us for a few days past have been attended with the signal blessing of God. Not only have deep and heartfelt confessions of backsliding and wrong been made, but solemn vows of repentance and of returning to God have accompanied them. The Spirit of God has set its seal to this work in such a manner that we cannot doubt. Many of the young have been brought to Christ, and nearly every person connected with this church has received a share of this heavenly blessing.

Let our brethren abroad understand that our hearts are in sympathy with Brother and Sister White, and that we believe them called of God to the responsible work in which they are engaged, and that we pledge ourselves to stand by them in this work.

In behalf of the church,

J. N. Andrews,
J. N. Loughborough,
Joseph Bates,
D. T. Bourdeau,
A. S.Hutchins,
John Byington,
Committee.

At a meeting of the church, Monday evening, October 21, the foregoing report was unanimously adopted.

Uriah Smith,
G. W. Amadon,
Elders.

"CUTTING AND SLASHING"

This expression is often used to represent the manners and words of persons who reprove those who are wrong or are supposed to be wrong. It is properly applied to those who have no duty to reprove their brethren, yet are ready to engage in this work in a rash and unsparing manner. It is improperly applied to those who have a special duty to do in reproving wrongs in the church. Such have the burden of the work and feel compelled, from a love of precious souls, to deal faithfully.

From time to time for the past twenty years I have been shown that the Lord had qualified my husband for the work of faithfully dealing with the erring, and had laid the burden upon him, and that if he should fail to do his duty in this respect he would incur the displeasure of the Lord. I have never regarded his judgment infallible, nor his words inspired; but I have ever believed him better qualified for this work than any other one of our preachers, because of his long experience, and because I have seen that he was especially called and adapted to the work; and also because in many cases where persons have risen up against his reproofs, I have been shown that he was right in his judgment of matters and in his manner of reproving.

For the past twenty years those who have been reproved, and their sympathizers, have indulged an accusing spirit toward my husband, which has worn upon him more than any other one of the cruel burdens he has unjustly borne. And when he fell beneath his burdens, many of those who had been reproved rejoiced, and from a mistaken idea of my view of his case, December 25, 1865, were much comforted with the thought that the Lord at that time reproved him for "cutting and slashing." This is all a mistake. I saw no such thing. That my brethren may know what I did see in the case of my husband, I give the following, which I wrote and handed to him the next day after I had the vision:

I was shown in vision, December 25, 1865, the case of the servant of the Lord, my husband, Elder James White. I was shown that God had accepted his humiliation, and the afflicting of his soul before Him, and his confessions of his lack of consecration to God, and his repentance for the errors and mistakes in his course which have caused him such sorrow and despondency of mind, during his protracted illness.

I was shown that his greatest wrong in the past has been an unforgiving spirit toward those brethren who have injured his influence in the cause of God and brought upon him extreme suffering of mind by their wrong course. He was not as pitiful and compassionate as our heavenly Father has been toward His erring, sinning, repenting children. When those who have caused him the greatest suffering acknowledged their wrongs heartily and fully, he could and did forgive them, and fellowship them as brethren. But although the wrong was healed in the sight of God, yet he sometimes in his own mind probed that wound, and by referring to the past he suffered it to fester and make him unhappy. The fact that he had in his past course suffered so much which in his opinion might have been avoided, led him to indulge a murmuring spirit against his brethren and against the Lord. In this way he lived over the past and revived trials which should have passed into oblivion instead of embittering his life with unprofitable remembrances. He has not always realized the pity and love that should be exercised toward those who have been so unfortunate as to fall under the temptations of Satan. They were the real sufferers, the losers, not he, as long as he was steadfast, possessing the spirit of Christ. When these souls began to see their errors, they had a hard battle to work their way to the light by humble confessions. They had Satan to contend with, and their own proud spirit to overcome, and they needed help from those who were in the light to bring them from their blind, discouraging condition, where they could begin to hope and obtain strength to bruise Satan under their feet.

I saw that my husband had been too exacting toward those who were wrong and had injured him. He indulged dissatisfied feelings, which could be of no benefit to the erring and could but make his own heart very unhappy, unfitting it for the peace of God to dwell there, which would lead him in everything to give thanks. The Lord permitted his mind to be desponding in regard to his own errors and mistakes, and to nearly despair of forgiveness, not because his sins were of such magnitude, but that he might know by experience how painful and agonizing it would be to be without the forgiveness of God, and that he might understand the scripture, "If ye forgive not men their trespasses, neither will your Father forgive your trespasses." I saw that if God should be as exacting as we are, and should deal with us as we deal with one another, we might all be thrown into a state of hopeless despair.

I was shown that God had suffered this affliction to come upon us to teach us much that we could not otherwise have learned in so short a time. It was His will that we should go to ——, for our experience could not have been thorough without it. He would have us see, and more fully understand, that it is impossible for those who obey the truth and are keeping His commandments, to live up to their convictions of duty and unite with the leaders at ——; so far as serving God is concerned, their principles can unite no better than oil and water. It is only those of the purest principles and the greatest independence of mind, who think and act for themselves, having the fear of God before them and trusting in Him, who can safely remain any length of time in ——. Those who are not thus qualified should not be advised to go to that institution, for their minds will become bewildered by the smooth words of its conductors and poisoned by their sophistry, which originates with Satan.

Their influence and teachings in regard to the service of God and a religious life are in direct opposition to the teachings of our Saviour and His disciples. By precept and example they lower the standard of piety and say that they need not sorrow for their sins or separate from the world in order to be followers of Christ, but can mingle with the world and participate in its pleasures. These leaders would not encourage their adherents to imitate the life of Christ in prayerfulness, sobriety, and dependence upon God. Persons of conscientious minds and firm trust in God cannot receive one half as much benefit at —— as those can who have confidence in the religious principles of the leaders of that institution. The former have to stand braced against much of their teachings, so far as religious principles are concerned, sifting everything they hear lest they should be deceived and Satan obtain advantage over them.

I saw that, as far as disease and its treatment is concerned, —— is the best health institution in the United States. Yet the leaders there are but men, and their judgment is not always correct. The leading physician there would have his patients believe that his judgment is perfect, even as the judgment of God. Yet he often fails. He exalts himself as God and fails to exalt the Lord as the only dependence. Those who have no trust or confidence in God, and who can see no beauty in holiness or in the cross-bearing life of the Christian, can receive more benefit at _____ than at any other health institution in the United States. The great secret of the success at this place is in the control which the managers have over the minds of their patients.

I saw that my husband and myself could not receive as much benefit there as could those of different experience and faith. Said the angel: "God has not designed that the mind of His servant, whom He has chosen for a special purpose, to do a special work, should be controlled by any living man, for that is His prerogative alone." Angels of God kept us while we were at _____. They were round about us, sustaining us every hour. But the time came when we could not benefit nor be benefited, and then the cloud of light, which had rested with us there, moved away, and we could find rest only in leaving there and going among the brethren in Rochester, where the cloud of light rested.

I saw that God would have us go to _____ for several reasons. Our position while there, the earnest prayers we offered, our manifest trust in God, the cheerfulness, courage, hope, and faith with which He inspired us amidst our afflictions, had an influence and were a testimony to all that the Christian has a source of strength and happiness to which the lovers of pleasure are strangers. God gave us a place in the hearts of all of influence at _____, and in the future as the patients now there shall be scattered to their different homes, our labors will bring us again to their notice, and when we are assailed, some at least will be our defenders. Again, in going to _____, the Lord would have us benefited by an experience which we would not obtain while at Battle Creek, surrounded by sympathizing brethren and sisters. We must be separated from them, lest we lean upon them instead of leaning upon the Lord and trusting in Him alone. Separated almost entirely from God's people, we were shaken from every earthly help and led to look to God alone. In so doing we obtained an experience which we could not have had if we had not gone to ——.

When my husband's courage and hope began to waver, we could not benefit anyone at that place and could not be benefited by a further experience there. It was the will of God that my husband should not remain there shorn of his strength, but that in his state of weakness he should go among his brethren who could help him bear his afflictions. While separated from God's people in our affliction, we had an opportunity to reflect, to carefully review our past life, and see our mistakes and wrongs, and to humble ourselves before God and seek His face by confession, humility, and frequent, earnest prayer. While engaged in active labor, bearing the burdens of others, and pressed with many cares, it was impossible for us to find time to reflect and carefully review the past, and learn the lessons which God saw that it was necessary for us to learn. I was then shown that God could not glorify His name by answering the supplications of His people and raising my husband to health in answer to their prayers, while we were at ——. It would be like uniting His power with the power of darkness. Had He been pleased to manifest His power in restoring my husband, the physicians there would have taken the glory which should be given to God.

Said the angel: "God will be glorified in the restoration of His servant to health. God has heard the prayers of His servants. His arms are beneath His afflicted servant. God has the case, and he must, although afflicted, dismiss his fears, his anxiety, his doubts and unbelief, and calmly trust in the great yet merciful God, who pities, loves, and cares for him. He will have conflicts with the enemy, but should ever be comforted with the remembrance that stronger than the enemy has charge of him, and he need not fear. By faith rely on the evidences which God has been pleased to give, and he will gloriously triumph in God."

I saw that the Lord was giving us an experience which would be of the highest value to us in the future in connection with His work. We are living in a solemn time amid the closing scenes of this earth's history, and God's people are not awake. They must arouse and make greater progress in reforming their habits of living, in eating, in dressing, in laboring and resting. In all these they should glorify God and be prepared to give battle to our great foe and to enjoy the precious victories which God has in reserve for those who are exercising temperance in all things while striving for an incorruptible crown.

I saw that God was fitting up my husband to engage in the solemn, sacred work of reform which He designs shall progress among His people. It is important that instructions should be given by ministers in regard to living temperately. They should show the relation which eating, working, resting, and dressing sustain to health. All who believe the truth for these last days have something to do in this matter. It concerns them, and God requires them to arouse and interest themselves in this reform. He will not be pleased with their course if they regard this question with indifference.

The abuses of the stomach by the gratification of appetite are the fruitful source of most church trials. Those who eat and work intemperately and irrationally, talk and act irrationally. An intemperate man cannot be a patient man. It is not necessary to drink alcoholic liquors in order to be intemperate. The sin of intemperate eating, eating too frequently, too much, and of rich, unwholesome food, destroys the healthy action of the digestive organs, affects the brain, and perverts the judgment, preventing rational, calm, healthy thinking and acting. And this is a fruitful source of church trials. Therefore in order for the people of God to be in an acceptable state with Him, where they can glorify Him in their bodies and spirits which are His, they must with interest and zeal deny the gratification of their appetites, and exercise temperance in all things. Then may they comprehend the truth in its beauty and clearness, and carry it out in their lives, and by a judicious, wise, straightforward course give the enemies of our faith no occasion to reproach the cause of truth. God requires all who believe the truth to make special, persevering efforts to place themselves in the best possbile condition of bodily health, for a solemn and important work is before us. Health of body and mind is required for this work; it is as essential to a healthy religious experience, to advancement in the Christian life and progress in holiness, as is the hand or foot to the human body. God requires His people to cleanse themselves from all filthiness of the flesh and spirit, perfecting holiness in the fear of the Lord. All those who are indifferent and excuse themselves from this work, waiting for the Lord to do for them that which He requires them to do for themselves, will be found wanting when the meek of the earth, who have wrought His judgments, are hid in the day of the Lord's anger.

I was shown that if God's people make no efforts on their part, but wait for the refreshing to come upon them and remove their wrongs and correct their errors; if they depend upon that to cleanse them from filthiness of the flesh and spirit, and fit them to engage in the loud cry of the third angel, they will be found wanting. The refreshing or power of God comes only on those who have prepared themselves for it by doing the work which God bids them, namely, cleansing themselves from all filthiness of the flesh and spirit, perfecting holiness in the fear of God.

I was shown that in some respects my husband's case is similar to that of those waiting for the refreshing. If he should wait for the power of God to come upon his body, to feel that he was made whole before he made efforts in accordance with his faith, saying, When the Lord heals me I will believe and do this or that, he might continue to wait and would realize no change, for the fulfillment of God's promise is only realized by those who believe and then work in accordance with their faith. I saw that he must believe God's word, that His promises are for him to claim, and they will never, no, never, fail. He should walk out by faith, relying upon the evidences that God has been pleased to give, and work, as much as possible, to the point of becoming a well man. Said the angel: "God will sustain him. His faith must be made perfect by works, for faith alone is dead. It must be sustained by works. A living faith is always manifested by works."

I saw that my husband would be inclined to shrink from making efforts in accordance with his faith. Fear and anxiety in regard to his own case have made him timid. He looks at appearances, at disagreeable feelings of the body. Said the angel: "Feeling is not faith. Faith is simply to take God at His word." I saw that in the name and strength of God my husband must resist disease and, by the power of his will, rise above his poor feelings. He must assert his liberty, in the name and strength of Israel's God. He must cease thinking and talking about himself as much as possible. He should be cheerful and happy.

I did see, December 25, 1865, as I have many times before seen, that Elder F had often erred and had done much harm by a rash, unfeeling course toward those whom he supposed to be in fault. I had often seen that his work was in new fields, and that when he should bring out a company upon the present truth he should leave the work of disciplining them to others, as his style of dealing, arising from his rash spirit, his lack of patience and of judgment, disqualified him for this work. I will here give the testimony which I had for Brother F, written December 26, 1865, to show what I did see in his case and because of the general application of much of the testimony and also because he has made no response whatever, only in stating to others that the Lord in that view reproved my husband for cutting and slashing. I would here state that another object in giving the following testimony is that our brethren may more fully understand that Brother F's work is in new fields, and that they may not place temptations in his way to leave his work, by urging him to labor here and there among the churches, or to settle here or there.

DANGER OF SELF-CONFIDENCE

Brother F: December 25, 1865, I was shown that a good work had commenced in Maine. Especially was the field of labor shown me where a company have been raised up as fruits of the labors of Brother Andrews and yourself, where they have manifested their interest and love for the truth by erecting a house of worship. There is yet a great work to be done for this company. Quite a number have been converted to the theory of the truth, some have decided from the weight of evidence; they see a beauty in the connected chain of truth, all uniting in a harmonious, perfect whole; they love the principles of the truth, yet they have not realized its sanctifying influence. These souls are exposed to the perils of the last days. Satan has prepared his deceptions and snares for the inexperienced. He is working through his agents, even ministers who despise the truth and trample upon the law of God themselves and teach all who will listen to them to do the same.

This company who have received unpopular truth can be safe only as they make God their trust and are sanctified by the truth which they profess. They have taken an important step and now need a religious experience which will make them sons and daughters of the most high God and heirs to the immortal inheritance purchased for them by His dear Son. Those who have been instrumental in presenting the truth to them should not withdraw their labors at this important period, but should still persevere in their efforts until these souls are gathered into the fold of Christ. Sufficient instruction should be given for them to understandingly obtain for themselves the evidence that the truth is to them salvation.

I saw that God would do a still greater work in Maine if all who labor in the cause there are consecrated to Him and trust not to their own strength, but to the Strength of Israel. I was shown that Brother Andrews and yourself have labored hard and have not had the rest which you should have given yourselves in order to preserve health. You should labor with care and observe periods of rest. By so doing you will retain your physical and mental vigor, and render your labor much more efficient. Brother F, you are a nervous man and move much from impulse. Mental depression influences your labor very much. At times you feel a want of freedom and think it is because others are in darkness or wrong, or that something is the matter, you can hardly tell what, and you make a drive somewhere and upon somebody, which is liable to do great harm. If you would quiet yourself when in this restless, nervous condition, and rest and calmly wait on God and inquire if the trouble is not in yourself, you would save wounding your own soul and wounding the precious cause of God.

I saw that Brother F was in danger of becoming lifted up if he was enabled in his discourses to strongly move the feelings of the congregation. He would often think himself the most effectual preacher on that account. Here he sometimes deceives himself. Although he may be for the time the most acceptable preacher, yet he may fail to accomplish the most good. The preacher who can affect the feelings to the greatest degree does not thereby give evidence that he is the most useful.

When Brother F is humble and makes God his trust, he can do much good. Angels come to his help, and he is blessed with clearness and freedom. But after a time of special victory he has too often been lifted up and thought himself equal to anything, thought that he was something, when he was only an instrument in the hands of God. After such seasons angels of God have left him to his own weak strength, and then, though he himself was the one at fault, he would too frequently charge upon his brethren and the people the darkness and weakness he felt. While in this unhappy state of mind he frequently bears down upon this one and that one, and, even when his work is not half done, feels that he must remove and commence labor elsewhere.

I saw that Brother F was in danger of going into battle in his own strength, but he will find that strength but weakness in the conflict. While he made God his trust, he has often been successful in combats with opposers of our faith. But he has sometimes felt elated with the victory which God has given truth over error, and has taken the glory to himself in these conflicts. Self has been magnified in his eyes.

I was shown that in his last two discussions he did not have the right spirit. Previous to the first he became exalted by the flattery of men who love not the truth. As he listened to, and acted some part in, a discussion carried on between two who were not in the faith, he became lifted up and thought himself sufficient to enter the battle with anyone. And while he was so confident, he was, in the very act, shorn of his strength. God was displeased with his disregard of the counsel of Brother Andrews. His self-sufficient spirit came near making that discussion an utter failure. Unless there is a decided gain in these combats, there is always a loss. They should never be rushed into heedlessly, but every move should be made cautiously, with the greatest wisdom, for far more is pending than in a national battle. Satan and his host are all astir at these conflicts between truth and error, and if the advocates of truth do not go into battle in the strength of God, Satan will manage to outgeneral them every time.

In the second combat there was much, very much at stake. Yet here again Brother F failed. He did not engage in that conflict feeling his weakness and in humility and simplicity relying upon the strength of God. He again felt a sufficiency in himself. His past successes had lifted him up. He thought that the victories he had gained were very much due to his aptness in using the powerful arguments furnished in the word of God.

I was shown that the advocates of truth should not seek discussions. And whenever it is necessary for the advancement of the cause of truth and the glory of God that an opponent be met, how carefully and with what humility should they go into the conflict. With heart-searching, confession of sin, and earnest prayer, and often fasting for a time, they should entreat that God would especially help them and give His saving, precious truth a glorious victory, that error might appear in its true deformity and its advocates be completely discomfited. Those who battle for the truth, against its opposers, should realize that they are not meeting merely men, but that they are contending with Satan and his angels, who are determined that error and darkness shall retain the field and the truth be covered up with error. As error is most in accordance with the natural heart, it is taken for granted to be clear. Men who are at ease love error and darkness and are unwilling to be reformed by the truth. They do not love to come to the light, lest their deeds should be reproved.

If those who stand in vindication of the truth, trust to the weight of argument, with but a feeble reliance upon God, and thus meet their opponents, nothing will be gained on the side of truth, but there will be a decided loss. Unless there is an evident victory in favor of truth, the matter is left worse than before the conflict. Those who might formerly have had convictions in regard to the truth set their minds at rest and decide in favor of error, because in their darkened state they cannot perceive that the truth had the advantage. These last two discussions did but little to advance the cause of God, and it would have been better had they not occurred. Brother F did not engage in them with a spirit of self-abasement and a firm reliance upon God. He was puffed up by the enemy and had a spirit of self-sufficiency and confidence not becoming a humble servant of Christ. He had on his own armor, not the armor of God.

Brother F, God had provided you with a laborer of deep experience, the ablest in the field. He was one who had been acquainted in his own experience with the wiles of Satan, and who had passed through most intense mental anguish. He had been permitted in the all-wise providence of God to feel the heat of the refining furnace and had there learned that every refuge but God would fail and every prop upon which he could lean for support would prove but a broken reed. You should have realized that Brother Andrews had as deep an interest in the discussion as yourself, and you should have listened in the spirit of humility to his counsel and profited by his instructions. But Satan had an object to gain here, to defeat the purpose of God, and he stepped in to take possession of your mind and thereby thwart the work of God. You rushed into battle in your own strength, and angels left you to carry it on. But God in mercy to His cause would not suffer the enemies of His truth to obtain a decided victory, and in answer to the earnest, agonizing prayers of His servant, angels came to the rescue. Instead of an utter failure there was a partial victory, that the enemies of truth might not exult over the believers. But nothing was gained by that effort, when there might have been a glorious triumph of truth over error. There were two of the ablest advocates of truth by your side; three men, with the strength of truth, to stand against one man who was seeking to cover up truth with error. In God you could have been a host, had you entered the conflict right. Your self-sufficiency caused it to be almost an entire failure.

Never should you enter a discussion where so much is at stake, relying upon your aptness to handle strong arguments. If it cannot be well avoided, enter the conflict, but enter upon it with firm trust in God and in the spirit of humility, in the spirit of Jesus, who has bidden you learn of Him, who is meek and lowly in heart. And then in order to glorify God and exemplify the character of Christ, you should never take unlawful advantage of your opponent. Lay aside sarcasm and playing upon words. Remember that you are in a combat with Satan and his angels, as well as with the man. He who overcame Satan in heaven and vanquished the fallen foe and expelled him from heaven, and who died to redeem fallen man from his power, when at the grave of Moses, disputing about his body, durst not bring against Satan a railing accusation, but said: "The Lord rebuke thee."

In your last two discussions you despised counsel and would not listen to God's servant, whose whole soul was devoted to the work. God in His providence provided you an adviser whose talents and influence entitled him to your respect and confidence, and it could in no way have injured your dignity to be guided by his experienced judgment. God's angels marked your self-sufficiency and with grief turned from you. He could not safely display His power in your behalf, for you would have taken the glory to yourself, and your future labors would have been of but little value. I saw, Brother F, that you should not, in your labors, lean upon your own judgment, which has so often led you astray. You should yield to the judgment of those of experience. Do not stand upon your own dignity and feel so self-sufficient that you cannot take the advice and counsel of experienced fellow laborers.

Your wife has been no special help to you, but rather a hindrance. Had she received and heeded the testimonies given her more than two years ago she would now be a strong helper with you in the gospel. But she has not received and really acted upon that testimony. Had she done this, her course would have been entirely different. She has not been consecrated to God. She loves her ease, shuns burdens, and does not deny herself. She indulges in indolence, and her example is not worthy of imitation, but is an injury to the cause of God. At times she exerts a strong influence over you, especially if she feels homesick or discontented. Again, in church affairs she has an influence over you. She forms her opinion of this brother or that sister, and expresses dislike or strong attachment, while it has frequently been the case that the very ones she takes into her heart have been a source of great trial to the church. Her unconsecrated state leads her to feel very strong attachments to those who manifest great confidence and love for her, while precious souls whom God loves may be passed coldly by because no fervent expressions of attachment are heard from them toward herself and Brother F. And yet the love of these very souls is true and is to be more highly prized than that of those who make such protestations of their regard. The opinion your wife forms has a great influence on your mind. You often take it for granted that she is correct and think as she thinks and act in church matters accordingly.

You must exemplify the life of Christ, for solemn responsibilities rest upon you. Your wife is responsible to God for her course. If she is a hindrance to you she must render an account to God. Sometimes she arouses and humbles herself before God and is a real help, but she soon falls back into the same inactive state, shunning responsibilities, and excusing herself from mental and physical labor. Her health would be far better if she were more active, if she would engage more cheerfully and heartily in physical and mental labor. She does not lack the ability, but the disposition to act; she will not persevere in cultivating a love for activity. God can do nothing for her in her present condition. She has something to do to arouse herself and devote to God her physical and mental energies. God requires this of her, and in the day of God she will be found an unprofitable servant unless there is a thorough reformation on her part and she lives up to the light given. Until this reformation takes place, she should not be at all united with her husband in his labors.

God will bless and sustain Brother F if he moves forward in humility, leaning upon the judgment of experienced fellow laborers.

BE NOT DECEIVED

It is the work of Satan to deceive God's people and lead them from the right course. He will leave no means untried; he will come upon them where they are least guarded; hence the importance of fortifying every point. The Battle Creek church did not mean to turn against us, they are as good a church as lives; but there is much at stake at Battle Creek, and Satan will bring all his artillery against them if by so doing he can hinder the work. We deeply sympathize with this church in their present humbled condition and would say: Let not a spirit of triumph arise in any heart. God will heal all the wrongs of this dear people and yet make them a mighty defense of His truth if they walk humbly and watch and guard every point against the attacks of Satan. This people are kept continually under the fire of the enemy. No other church would probably stand it as well, therefore look with a pitying eye toward your brethren at Battle Creek and pray God to help them in keeping the fort.

When my husband was inactive, and I was kept at home on his account, Satan was pleased, and no one was pressed by him to cast upon us such trials as are mentioned in the foregoing pages. But when we started out, December 19, 1866, he saw that there was a prospect of our doing something in the cause of Christ to the injury of his cause and that some of his deceptions upon the flock of God would be exposed. He therefore felt called upon to do something to hinder us. And in no way could he so effectually do this as to lead our old friends at Battle Creek to withdraw their sympathy and cast burdens upon us. He took advantage of every unfavorable circumstance and drove matters as by steam power.

But, thank God, he did not stop us nor fully crush us. Thank God that we still live and that He has returned graciously to bless His erring, but now repenting, confessing people. Brethren, let us love them the more and pray for them the more now that God manifests His great love to them.

NUMBER FOURTEEN

TESTIMONY FOR THE CHURCH

PUBLISHING PERSONAL TESTIMONIES

In *Testimony* No. 13 I gave a brief sketch of our labors and trials from December 19, 1866, to October 21, 1867. In these pages I will notice the less painful experience of the past five months.

During this time I have written many personal testimonies. And for many persons whom I have met in our field of labor during the past five months I have testimonies still to write as I find time and have strength, but just what my duty is in relation to these personal testimonies has long been a matter of no small anxiety to me. With a few exceptions I have sent them to the ones to whom they related and have left these persons to dispose of them as they chose. The results have been various:

1. Some have thankfully received the testimonies and have responded to them in a good spirit and have profited by them. These have been willing that their brethren should see the testimonies and have freely and fully confessed their faults.

2. Others have acknowledged that the testimonies to them were true, but after reading them have laid them away to remain in silence, while they have made but little change in their lives. These testimonies related more or less to the churches to which these persons belonged, who could also have been bene-

fited by them. But all this was lost in consequence of these testimonies' being held private.

3. Still others have rebelled against the testimonies. Some of these have responded in a faultfinding spirit. Some have shown bitterness, anger, and wrath, and in return for my toil and pains in writing the testimonies they have turned upon us to injure us all they could; while others have held me for hours in personal interviews to pour into my ears and my aching heart their complaints, murmurings, and self-justifications, perhaps appealing to their own sympathies with weeping, and losing sight of their own faults and sins. The influence of these things has been terrible upon me and has sometimes driven me nearly to distraction. That which has followed from the conduct of these unconsecrated, unthankful persons has cost me more suffering and has worn upon my courage and health ten times more than all the toil of writing the testimonies.

And all this has been suffered by me, and my brethren and sisters generally have known nothing about it. They have had no just idea of the amount of wearing labor of this kind which I have had to perform, nor of the burdens and sufferings unjustly thrown upon me. I have given some personal communications in several numbers of my testimonies, and in some cases persons have been offended because I did not publish all such communications. On account of their number this would be hardly possible, and it would be improper from the fact that some of them relate to sins which need not, and should not, be made public.

But I have finally decided that many of these personal testimonies should be published, as they all contain more or less reproof and instruction which apply to hundreds or thousands of others in similar condition. These should have the light which God has seen fit to give which meets their cases. It is a wrong to shut it away from them by sending it to one person or to one place, where it is kept as a light under a bushel. My convictions of duty on this point have been greatly strengthened by the following dream:

A grove of evergreens was presented before me. Several, including myself, were laboring among them. I was bidden to closely inspect the trees and see if they were in a flourishing condition. I observed that some were being bent and deformed by the wind, and needed to be supported by stakes. I was carefully removing the dirt from the feeble and dying trees to ascertain the cause of their condition. I discovered worms at the roots of some. Others had not been watered properly and were dying from drought. The roots of others had been crowded together to their injury. My work was to explain to the workmen the different reasons why these trees did not prosper. This was necessary from the fact that trees in other grounds were liable to be affected as these had been, and the cause of their not flourishing and how they should be cultivated and treated must be made known.

In this testimony I speak freely of the case of Sister Hannah More, not from a willingness to grieve the Battle Creek church, but from a sense of duty. I love that church notwithstanding their faults. I know of no church that in acts of benevolence and general duty do so well. I present the frightful facts in this case to arouse our people everywhere to a sense of their duty. Not one in twenty of those who have a good standing with Seventh-day Adventists is living out the self-sacrificing principles of the word of God. But let not their enemies, who are destitute of the first principles of the doctrine of Christ, take advantage of the fact that they are reproved. This is evidence that they are the children of the Lord. Those who are without chastisement, says the apostle, are bastards and not sons. Then let not these illegitimate children boast over the lawful sons and daughters of the Almighty.

THE HEALTH INSTITUTE

In former numbers of *Testimonies for the Church* I have spoken of the importance of Seventh-day Adventists' establishing an institution for the benefit of the sick, especially for the suffering and sick among us. I have spoken of the ability of our people, in point of means, to do this and have urged that, in view of the importance of this branch of the great work of preparation to meet the Lord with gladness of heart, our people should feel themselves called upon, according to their ability, to put a portion of their means into such an institution. I have also pointed out, as they were shown to me, some of the dangers to which physicians, managers, and others would be exposed in the prosecution of such an enterprise; and I did hope that the dangers shown me would be avoided. In this, however, I enjoyed hope for a time, only to suffer disappointment and grief.

I had taken great interest in the health reform and had high hopes of the prosperity of the Health Institute. I felt, as no other one could feel, the responsibility of speaking to my brethren and sisters in the name of the Lord concerning this institution and their duty to furnish necessary means, and I watched the progress of the work with intense interest and anxiety. When I saw those who managed and directed, running into the dangers shown me, of which I had warned them in public and also in private conversation and letters, a terrible burden came upon me. That which had been shown me as a place where the suffering sick among us could be helped was one where sacrifice, hospitality, faith, and piety should be the ruling principles. But when unqualified calls were made for large sums of money, with the statement that stock taken would pay large per cent; when the brethren who occupied positions in the institution seemed more than willing to take larger wages than those were satisfied with who filled other and equally important stations in the great cause of truth and reform; when I learned, with pain, that, in order to make the institution popular with those not of our faith and to secure their patronage, a spirit of compromise was rapidly gaining ground at the Institute, manifested in the use of Mr., Miss, and Mrs., instead of Brother and Sister, and in popular amusements, in which all could engage in a sort of comparatively innocent frolic—when I saw these things, I said: This is not that which was shown me as an institution for the sick which would share the signal blessing of God. This is another thing.

And yet calculations for more extensive buildings were made, and calls for large sums of money were urged. As it was then managed, I could but regard the Institute, on the whole, as a curse. Although some were benefited healthwise, the influence on the church at Battle Creek and upon brethren and sisters who visited the Institute was so bad as to overbalance all the good that was done; and this influence was reaching churches in this and other states, and was terribly destructive to faith in God and in the present truth. Several who came to Battle Creek humble, devoted, confiding Christians, went away almost infidels. The general influence of these things was creating prejudice against the health reform in very many of the most humble, the most devoted, and the best of our brethren, and was destroying faith in my *Testimonies* and in the present truth.

It was this state of matters relative to the health reform and the Health Institute, with which other things were brought to bear, that made it my duty to speak as I did in *Testimony* No. 13. I well knew that that would produce a reaction and trial in many minds. I also knew that a reaction must come sooner or later, and, for the good of the Institute and the cause generally, the sooner the better. Had matters been moving in a wrong direction, to the injury of precious souls and the cause generally, the sooner this could be checked, and they be properly directed the better. The further the advance, the greater the ruin, the greater the reaction, and the greater the general discouragement. The misdirected work must have such a check; there must be time to correct errors and start again in the right direction.

The good work wrought for the church at Battle Creek last fall, the thorough reform and turning to the Lord by physicians, helpers, and managers at the Health Institute, and the general agreement of our brethren and sisters in all parts of the field relative to the great object of the Health Institute and the manner it should be conducted, to which is added the varied experience of more than one year, not only in the wrong course, but also in a right direction, give me more confidence that the health reform and the Health Institute will prove a success than I ever had before. I still fondly hope to see the Health Institute at Battle Creek prospering and in every respect the institute shown me. But it will take time to fully correct and outgrow the errors of the past. With the blessing of God this can and will be done.

The brethren who have stood at the head of this work have appealed to our people for means, on the ground that the health reform is a part of the great work connected with the third angel's message. In this they have been right. It is a branch of the great, charitable, liberal, sacrificing, benevolent work of God. Then why should these brethren say: "Stock in the Health Institute will pay a large per cent," "it is a good investment," "a paying thing"? Why not as well talk of stock in the Publishing Association paying a large per cent? If these are two branches of the same great, closing work of preparation for the coming of the Son of man, why not? Or why not make them both matters of liberality? The pen and the voice that appealed to the friends of the cause in behalf of the publishing fund held out no such inducements. Why, then, represent to wealthy, covetous Sabbathkeepers that they may do great good by investing their means in the Health Institute, and at the same time retain the principal, and also receive large per cent for the simple use of it? The brethren were called upon to donate for the Publishing Association, and they nobly and cheerfully sacrificed unto the Lord, following the example of the one who made the call, and the blessing of God has been upon that branch of the great work. But it is to be feared that His displeasure is upon the manner in which funds have been raised for the Health Institute, and that His blessing will not be upon that institution to the full, till this wrong shall be corrected. In my appeal to the brethren in behalf of such an institution, in *Testimony* No. 11, page 492, I said:

"I was shown that there is no lack of means among Sabbathkeeping Adventists. At present their greatest danger is in their accumulations of property. Some are continually increasing their cares and labors; they are overcharged. The result is, God and the wants of His cause are nearly forgotten by them; they are spiritually dead. They are required to make a sacrifice to God, an offering. A sacrifice does not increase, but decreases and consumes."

My view of this matter of means was that there should be "a sacrifice to God, an offering;" and I never received any other idea. But if the principal is to be held good by stockholders, and they are to draw a certain per cent, where is the decrease, or the consuming sacrifice? And how are the dangers of those Sabbathkeepers who are accumulating property decreased by the present plan of holding stock in the Institute? Their dangers are only increased. And here is an additional excuse for their covetousness. In investing in stock in the Institute, held as a matter of sale and purchase like any other property, they do not sacrifice. As a large per cent is held out as an inducement, the spirit of gain, not sacrifice, leads them to invest so largely in the stock of the Institute that they have but little if anything to give to sustain other and still more important branches of the work. God requires of these close, covetous, worldly persons a sacrifice for suffering humanity. He calls on them to let their worldly possessions decrease for the sake of the afflicted ones who believe in Jesus and the present truth. They should have a chance to act in full view of the decisions of the final judgment, as described in the following burning words of the King of kings:

Matthew 25:34-46: "Then shall the King say unto them on His right hand, Come, ye blessed of My Father, inherit the kingdom prepared for you from the foundation of the world: for I was anhungered, and ye gave Me meat: I was thirsty, and ye gave Me drink: I was a stranger, and ye took Me in: naked, and ye clothed Me: I was sick, and ye visited Me: I was in prison, and ye came unto Me. Then shall the righteous answer Him, saying, Lord, when saw we Thee anhungered, and fed Thee? or thirsty, and gave Thee drink? When saw we Thee a stranger, and took Thee in? or naked, and clothed Thee? Or when saw we Thee sick, or in prison, and came unto Thee? And the King shall answer and say unto them, Verily I say unto you, Inasmuch as ye have done it unto one of the least of these My brethren, ye have done it unto Me.

"Then shall He say also unto them on the left hand, Depart from Me, ye cursed, into everlasting fire, prepared for the devil and his angels: for I was anhungered, and ye gave Me no meat: I was thirsty, and ye gave Me no drink: I was a stranger, and ye took Me not in: naked, and ye clothed Me not: sick, and in prison, and ye visited Me not. Then shall they also answer Him, saying, Lord, when saw we Thee anhungered, or athirst, or a stranger, or naked, or sick, or in prison, and did not minister unto Thee? Then shall He answer them, saying, Verily I say unto you, Inasmuch as ye did it not to one of the least of these, ye did it not to Me. And these shall go away into everlasting punishment; but the righteous into life eternal."

Again on page 494 of *Testimony* No. 11, I said: "There is a liberal supply of means among our people, and if all felt the importance of the work, this great enterprise could be carried forward without embarrassment. All should feel a special interest in sustaining it. Especially should those who have means invest in this enterprise. A suitable home should be fitted up for the reception of invalids that they may, by the use of proper means and the blessing of God, be relieved of their infirmities and learn how to take care of themselves and thus prevent sickness.

"Many who profess the truth are growing close and covetous. They need to be alarmed for themselves. They have so much of their treasure upon the earth that their hearts are on their treasure. Much the larger share of their treasure is in this world, and but little in heaven; therefore their affections are placed on earthly possessions instead of on the heavenly inheritance. There is now a good opportunity for them to use their means for the benefit of suffering humanity and also for the advancement of the truth. This enterprise should never be left to struggle in poverty. These stewards to whom God has entrusted means should now come up to the work and use their means to His glory. To those who through covetousness withhold their means, it will prove a curse rather than a blessing."

In what I have been shown and what I have said, I received no other idea, and designed to give no other, than that the raising of funds for this branch of the work was to be a matter of liberality, the same as for the support of other branches of the great work. And although the change from the present plan to one that can be fully approved of the Lord may be attended with difficulties and require time and labor, yet I think that it can be made with little loss of stock already taken, and that it will result in a decided increase of capital donated to be used in a proper manner to relieve suffering humanity.

Many who have taken stock are not able to donate it. Some of these persons are suffering for the very money which they have invested in stock. As I travel from state to state, I find afflicted ones standing on the very verge of the grave, who should go to the Institute for a while, but cannot for want of the means they have in Institute stock. These should not have a dollar invested there. One case in Vermont I will mention. As early as 1850 this brother became a Sabbathkeeper, and from that date he contributed liberally to the several enterprises that have been undertaken to advance the cause, till he became reduced in property. Yet when the urgent, unqualified call came for the Institute, he took stock to the amount of one hundred dollars. At the meeting at ——— he introduced the case of his wife, who is very feeble, and who can be helped, but must be helped soon, if ever. He also stated his circumstances, and said that if he could command the one hundred dollars then in the Institute, he could send his wife there to be treated; but as it was, he could not. We replied that he should never have invested a dollar in the Institute, that there was a wrong in the matter which we could not help, and there the matter dropped. I do not hesitate to say that this sister should be treated, a few weeks at least, at the Institute free of charge. Her husband is able to do but little more than to pay her fare to and from Battle Creek.

The friends of humanity, of truth and holiness, should act in reference to the Institute on the plan of sacrifice and liberality. I have five hundred dollars in stock in the Institute, which I wish to donate, and if my husband succeeds with his anticipated book, he will give five hundred dollars more. Will those who approve this plan please address us at Greenville,

Montcalm County, Michigan, and state the sums they wish to donate, or to invest in stock to be held as the stock in the Publishing Association is held. When this is done, then let the donations come in as needed; let the sums, small and large, come in. Let means be expended judiciously. Let charges for patients be as reasonable as possible. Let brethren donate to partly pay the expenses at the Institute of the suffering, worthy poor among them. Let the feeble ones be led out, as they can bear it, to cultivate the beautifully situated acres owned by the Institute. Let them not do this with the narrow idea of pay, but with the liberal idea that the expense of the purchase of them was a matter of benevolence for their good. Let their labor be a part of their prescription, as much as the taking of baths. Let benevolence, charity, humanity, sacrifice for others' good, be the ruling idea with physicians, managers, helpers, patients, and with all the friends of Jesus, far and near, instead of wages, good investment, a paying thing, stock that will pay. Let the love of Christ, love for souls, sympathy for suffering humanity, govern all we say and do relative to the Health Institute.

Why should the Christian physician, who is believing, expecting, looking, waiting, and longing for the coming and kingdom of Christ, when sickness and death will no longer have power over the saints, expect more pay for his services than the Christian editor or the Christian minister? He may say that his work is more wearing. That is yet to be proved. Let him work as he can endure it, and not violate the laws of life which he teaches to his patients. There are no good reasons why he should overwork and receive large pay for it, more than the minister or the editor. Let all who act a part in the Institute and receive pay for their services, act on the same liberal principle. No one should be suffered to remain as helper in the Institute who does it simply for pay. There are those of ability who, for the love of Christ, His cause, and the suffering followers of their Master, will fill stations in that Institute faithfully and cheerfully, and with a spirit of sacrifice. Those who have not this spirit should remove and give place to those who have it.

As nearly as I am able to judge, one half of the afflicted among our people who should spend weeks or months at the Institute are not able to pay the entire expense of the journey and a tarry there. Shall poverty keep these friends of our Lord from the blessings which He has so bountifully provided? Shall they be left to struggle on with the double burden of feebleness and poverty? The wealthy feeble ones, who have all the comforts and conveniences of life, and are able to hire their hard work done, may, with care and rest, by informing themselves and taking home treatment, enjoy a very comfortable state of health without going to the Institute. But what can our poor, feeble brethren or sisters do to recover health? They may do something, but poverty drives them to labor beyond what they are really able. They have not even all the comforts of life; and as for conveniences in houseroom, furniture, means of taking baths, and arrangements for good ventilation, they do not have them. Perhaps their only room is occupied by a cookstove, winter and summer; and it may be that all the books they have in the house, excepting the Bible, could be held between the thumb and finger. They have no money to buy books that they may read and learn how to live. These dear brethren are the very ones who need help. Many of them are humble Christians. They may have faults, and some of these may reach far back and be the cause of their present poverty and misery. And yet they may be living up to duty better than we who have the means to improve our own condition and that of others. These must be patiently taught and cheerfully helped.

But they must be willing and anxious to be taught. They must cherish a spirit of gratitude to God and their brethren for the help they receive. Such persons generally have no just ideas of the real expense of treatment, board, room, fuel, etc., at a Health Institute. They do not realize the magnitude of the great work of present truth and reform, and the many calls for the liberalities of our people. They may not be aware that the numbers of our poor are many times larger than the numbers of our rich. And they may not also feel the force of the frightful fact that a majority of these wealthy ones are holding on to their riches and are in the sure road to perdition.

These poor afflicted persons should be taught that when they murmur at their lot and against the wealthy on account of their covetousness, they commit a great sin in the sight of heaven. They should first understand that their sickness and poverty are misfortunes most generally caused by their own sins, follies, and wrongs; and if the Lord puts it into the hearts and minds of His people to help them, it should inspire in them feelings of humble gratitude to God and His people. They should do all in their power to help themselves. If they have relatives who can and will defray their expenses at the Institute, these should have the privilege.

And in view of the many poor and afflicted ones who must, to a greater or less extent, be objects of the charity of the Institute, and because of the lack of funds and the want of accommodations at the present time, the stay of such at the Institute must be brief. They should go there with the idea of obtaining as fast and as far as possible, a practical knowledge of what they must do, and what they must not do, to recover health and to live healthfully. The lectures which they hear while at the Institute, and good books from which to learn how to live at home, must be the main reliance of such. They may find some relief during a few weeks spent at the Institute, but will realize more at home in carrying out the same principles. They must not rely on the physicians to cure them in a few weeks, but must learn so to live as to give nature a chance to work the cure. This may commence during a few weeks' stay at the Institute, and yet it may require years to complete the work by correct habits at home.

A man may spend all that he has in this world at a Health Institute, and find great relief, and may then return to his family and to his old habits of life, and in a few weeks or months be in a worse condition of health than ever before. He has gained nothing; he has spent his limited means for nothing. The object of the health reform and the Health Institute is not, like a dose of "Painkiller" or "Instant Relief," to quiet the pains of today. No, indeed! Its great object is to teach the people how to live so as to give nature a chance to remove and resist disease.

To the afflicted among our people I wish to say, Be not discouraged. God has not forsaken His people and His cause. Make known your state of health and your ability to meet the expenses of a stay at the Institute to the physicians, addressing Health Institute, Battle Creek, Michigan. Are you diseased, running down, feeble, then do not delay till your case is hopeless. Write immediately. But I must say again to the poor: At present but little can be done to help you, on account of capital already raised being invested in material and buildings. Do all you possibly can for yourselves, and others will help you some.

SKETCH OF EXPERIENCE

From October 21, 1867 to December 22, 1867

Our labor with the Battle Creek church had just closed, and, notwithstanding we were much worn, we had been so refreshed in spirit as we witnessed the good result that we cheerfully joined Brother J. N. Andrews in the long journey to Maine. On the way we held a meeting at Roosevelt, New York. *Testimony* No. 13 was doing its work, and those brethren who had taken part in the general disaffection were beginning to see things in their true light. This meeting was one of hard labor, in which pointed testimonies were given. Confessions were made, followed by a general turning to the Lord on the part of backsliders and sinners.

Our labors in Maine commenced with the Conference at Norridgewock the first of November. The meeting was large. As usual, my husband and myself bore a plain and pointed testimony in favor of truth and proper discipline, and against the different forms of error, confusion, fanaticism, and disorder naturally growing out of a want of such discipline. This testimony was especially applicable to the condition of things in Maine. Disorderly spirits who professed to observe the Sabbath were in rebellion and labored to diffuse the disaffection through the Conference. Satan helped them, and they succeeded to some extent. The details are too painful and of too little general importance to be given here.

It may be enough to say at this time that in consequence of this spirit of rebellion, faultfinding, and, with some, a sort of babyish jealousy, murmuring, and complaining, our work in Maine, which might have been done in two weeks, required seven weeks of the most trying, laborious, and disagreeable toil. Five weeks were lost, yes, worse than lost, to the cause in Maine; and our people in other portions of New England, New York, and Ohio were deprived of five general meetings in consequence of our being held in Maine. But as we left that state we were comforted with the fact that all had confessed their rebellion, and that a few had been led to seek the Lord and embrace the truth. The following, relative to ministers, order, and organization, has a special application to the condition of things in Maine.

MINISTERS, ORDER, AND ORGANIZATION

Some ministers have fallen into the error that they cannot have liberty in speaking unless they raise their voices to a high pitch and talk loud and fast. Such should understand that noise and loud, hurried speaking are not evidence of the presence of the power of God. It is not the power of the voice that makes the lasting impression. Ministers should be Bible students, and should thoroughly furnish themselves with the reasons of our faith and hope, and then, with full control of the voice and feelings, they should present these in such a manner that the people can calmly weigh them and decide upon the evidences given. And as ministers feel the force of the arguments which they present in the form of solemn, testing truth, they will have zeal and earnestness according to knowledge. The Spirit of God will sanctify to their own souls the truths which they present to others, and they will be watered themselves while they water others.

I saw that some of our ministers do not understand how to preserve their strength so as to be able to perform the greatest amount of labor without exhaustion. Ministers should not pray so loud and long as to exhaust their strength. It is not necessary to weary the throat and lungs in prayer. God's ear is ever open to hear the heartfelt petitions of His humble servants, and He does not require them to wear out the organs of speech in addressing Him. It is the perfect trust, the firm reliance, the steady claiming of the promises of God, the simple faith that He is and that He is a rewarder of all those who diligently seek Him, that prevails with God.

Ministers should discipline themselves and learn how to perform the greatest amount of labor in the brief period allotted them, and yet preserve a good degree of strength, so that if an extra effort should be required, they may have a reserve of vital force sufficient for the occasion, which they can employ without injuring themselves. Sometimes all the strength they have is needed to put forth effort at a given point, and if they have previously exhausted their fund of strength and cannot command the power to make this effort, all they have done is lost. At times all the mental and physical energies may be drawn upon to make the very strongest stand, to array evidences in the clearest light, and set them before the people in the most pointed manner, and urge them home by the strongest appeals. As souls are on the point of leaving the enemy's ranks and coming up on the Lord's side, the contest is most severe and close. Satan and his angels are unwilling that any who have served under the banner of darkness should take their position under the bloodstained banner of Prince Immanuel.

I was shown opposing armies who had endured a painful struggle in battle. The victory was gained by neither, and at length the loyal realize that their strength and force is wearing away, and that they will be unable to silence their enemies unless they make a charge upon them and obtain their instruments of warfare. It is then, at the risk of their lives, that they summon all their powers and rush upon the foe. It is a fearful struggle; but victory is gained, the strongholds are taken. If at the critical period the army is so weak through exhaustion that it is impossible to make the last charge and batter down the enemy's fortifications, the whole struggle of days, weeks, and even months is lost; and many lives are sacrificed and nothing gained.

A similar work is before us. Many are convinced that we have the truth, and yet they are held as with iron bands; they dare not risk the consequences of taking their position on the side of truth. Many are in the valley of decision, where special, close, and pointed appeals are necessary to move them to lay down the weapons of their warfare and take their position on the Lord's side. Just at this critical period Satan throws the strongest bands around these souls. If the servants of God are all exhausted, having expended their fund of physical and mental strength, they think they can do no more, and frequently leave the field entirely, to commence operations elsewhere. And all, or nearly all, the time, means, and labor have been spent for nought. Yes, it is worse than if they had never commenced the work in that place, for after the people have been deeply convicted by the Spirit of God, and brought to the point of decision, and are left to lose their interest, and decide against these evidences, they cannot as easily be brought where their minds will again be agitated upon the subject. They have in many cases made their final decision.

If ministers would preserve a reserve force, and at the very point where everything seems to move the hardest, then make the most earnest efforts, the strongest appeals, the closest applications, and, like valiant soldiers, at the critical moment make the charge upon the enemy, they would gain the victory. Souls would have strength to break the bands of Satan and make their decisions for everlasting life. Well-directed labor at the right time will make a long-tried effort successful, when to leave the labor even for a few days will in many cases cause an entire failure. Ministers must give themselves as missionaries to the work and learn how to make their efforts to the very best advantage.

Some ministers at the very commencement of a series of meetings become very zealous, take on burdens which God does not require them to bear, exhaust their strength in singing and in long, loud praying and talking, and then are worn out and must go home to rest. What was accomplished in that effort? Literally nothing. The laborers had spirit and zeal, but lacked understanding. They manifested no wise generalship. They rode upon the chariot of feeling, but there was not one victory gained against the enemy. His stronghold was not taken.

I was shown that ministers of Christ should discipline themselves for the warfare. Greater wisdom is required in generalship in the work of God than is required of the generals engaged in national battles. Ministers of God's choosing are engaged in a great work. They are warring not merely against men, but against Satan and his angels. Wise generalship is required here. They must become Bible students and give themselves wholly to the work. When they commence labor in a place, they should be able to give the reasons of our faith, not in a boisterous manner, not with a perfect storm, but with meekness and fear. The power which will convince is strong arguments presented in meekness and in the fear of God.

Able ministers of Christ are required for the work in these last days of peril, able in word and doctrine, acquainted with the Scriptures, and understanding the reasons of our faith. I was directed to these scriptures, the meaning of which has not been realized by some ministers: "But sanctify the Lord God in your hearts: and be ready always to give an answer to every man that asketh you a reason of the hope that is in you with meekness and fear." "Let your speech be always with grace, seasoned with salt, that ye may know how ye ought to answer every man." "And the servant of the Lord must not strive; but be gentle unto all men, apt to teach, patient, in meekness instructing those that oppose themselves; if God peradventure will give them repentance to the acknowledging of the truth; and that they may recover themselves out of the snare of the devil, who are taken captive by him at his will."

The man of God, the minister of Christ, is required to be thoroughly furnished unto all good works. A pompous minister, all dignity, is not needed for this good work. But decorum is necessary in the desk. A minister of the gospel should not be regardless of his attitude. If he is the representative of Christ, his deportment, his attitude, his gestures, should be of such a character as will not strike the beholder with disgust. Ministers should possess refinement. They should discard all uncouth manners, attitudes, and gestures, and should encourage in themselves humble dignity of bearing. They should be clothed in a manner befitting the dignity of their position. Their speech should be in every respect solemn and well chosen. I was shown that it is wrong to make coarse, irreverent expressions, relate anecdotes to amuse, or present comic illustrations to create a laugh. Sarcasm and playing upon the words of an opponent are all out of God's order. Ministers should not feel that they can make no improvement in voice or manners; much can be done. The voice can be cultivated so that quite lengthy speaking will not injure the vocal organs.

Ministers should love order and should discipline themselves, and then they can successfully discipline the church of God and teach them to work harmoniously like a well-drilled company of soldiers. If discipline and order are necessary for successful action on the battlefield, the same are as much more needful in the warfare in which we are engaged as the object to be gained is of greater value and more elevated in character than those for which opposing forces contend upon the field of battle. In the conflict in which we are engaged, eternal interests are at stake.

Angels work harmoniously. Perfect order characterizes all their movements. The more closely we imitate the harmony and order of the angelic host, the more successful will be the efforts of these heavenly agents in our behalf. If we see no necessity for harmonious action, and are disorderly, undisciplined, and disorganized in our course of action, angels, who are thoroughly organized and move in perfect order, cannot work for us successfully. They turn away in grief, for they are not authorized to bless confusion, distraction, and disorganization. All who desire the co-operation of the heavenly messengers must work in unison with them. Those who have the unction from on high will in all their efforts encourage order, discipline, and union of action, and then the angels of God can co-operate with them. But never, never will these heavenly messengers place their endorsement upon irregularity, disorganization, and disorder. All these evils are the result of Satan's efforts to weaken our forces, to destroy courage, and prevent successful action.

Satan well knows that success can only attend order and harmonious action. He well knows that everything connected with heaven is in perfect order, that subjection and thorough discipline mark the movements of the angelic host. It is his studied effort to lead professed Christians just as far from heaven's arrangement as he can; therefore he deceives even the professed people of God and makes them believe that order and discipline are enemies to spirituality, that the only safety for them is to let each pursue his own course, and to remain especially distinct from bodies of Christians who are united and are laboring to establish discipline and harmony of action. All the efforts made to establish order are considered dangerous, a restriction of rightful liberty, and hence are feared as popery. These deceived souls consider it a virtue to boast of their freedom to think and act independently. They will not take any man's say-so. They are amenable to no man. I was shown that it is Satan's special work to lead men to feel that it is in God's order for them to strike out for themselves and choose their own course, independent of their brethren.

I was pointed back to the children of Israel. Very soon after leaving Egypt they were organized and most thoroughly disciplined. God had in His special providence qualified Moses to stand at the head of the armies of Israel. He had been a mighty warrior to lead the armies of the Egyptians, and in generalship he could not be surpassed by any man. The Lord did not leave His holy tabernacle to be borne indiscriminately by any tribe that might choose. He was so particular as to specify the order He would have observed in bearing the sacred ark and to designate a special family of the tribe of the Levites to bear it. When it was for the good of the people and for the glory of God that they should pitch their tents in a certain place, God signified His will to them by causing the pillar of cloud to rest directly over the tabernacle, where it remained until He would have them journey again. In all their journeyings they were required to observe perfect order. Every tribe bore a standard with the sign of their father's house upon it, and each tribe was required to pitch under its own standard. When the ark moved, the armies journeyed, the different tribes marching in order, under their own standards. The Levites were designated by the Lord as the tribe in the midst of whom the sacred ark was to be borne, Moses and Aaron marching just in front of the ark, and the sons of Aaron following near them, each bearing trumpets. They were to receive directions from Moses, which they were to signify to the people by speaking through the trumpets. These trumpets gave special sounds which the people understood, and directed their movements accordingly.

A special signal was first given by the trumpeters to call the attention of the people; then all were to be attentive and obey the certain sound of the trumpets. There was no confusion of sound in the voices of the trumpets, therefore there was no excuse for confusion in movements. The head officer of each company gave definite directions in regard to the movements they were required to make, and none who gave attention were left in ignorance of what they were to do. If any failed to comply with the requirements given by the Lord to Moses, and by Moses to the people, they were punished with death. It would be no excuse to plead that they knew not the nature of these requirements, for they would only prove themselves willingly ignorant, and would receive the just punishment for their transgression. If they did not know the will of God concerning them, it was their own fault. They had the same opportunities to obtain the knowledge imparted as others of the people had, therefore their sin of not knowing, not understanding, was as great in the sight of God as if they had heard and then transgressed.

The Lord designated a special family of the tribe of Levi to bear the ark; and others of the Levites were specially appointed of God to bear the tabernacle and all its furniture, and to perform the work of getting up and taking down the tabernacle. And if any man from curiosity or from lack of order got out of his place and touched any part of the sanctuary or furniture, or even came near any of the workmen, he was to be put to death. God did not leave His holy tabernacle to be borne, erected, and taken down, indiscriminately, by any tribe who might choose the office; but persons were chosen who could appreciate the sacredness of the work in which they were engaged. These men appointed of God were directed to impress upon the people the special sacredness of the ark and all that appertained thereunto, lest they should look upon these things without realizing their holiness and should be cut off from Israel. All things pertaining to the most holy place were to be looked upon with reverence.

The travels of the children of Israel are faithfully described; the deliverance which the Lord wrought for them, their perfect organization and special order, their sin in murmuring against Moses and thus against God, their transgressions, their rebellions, their punishments, their carcasses strewn in the wilderness because of their unwillingness to submit to God's wise arrangements—this faithful picture is hung up before us as a warning lest we follow their example of disobedience and fall like them.

"But with many of them God was not well pleased: for they were overthrown in the wilderness. Now these things were our examples, to the intent we should not lust after evil things, as they also lusted. Neither be ye idolaters, as were some of them; as it is written, The people sat down to eat and drink, and rose up to play. Neither let us commit fornication, as some of them committed, and fell in one day three and twenty thousand. Neither let us tempt Christ, as some of them also tempted, and were destroyed of serpents. Neither murmur ye, as some of them also murmured, and were destroyed of the destroyer. Now all these things happened unto them for ensamples: and they are written for our admonition, upon whom the ends of the world are come. Wherefore let him that thinketh he standeth take heed lest he fall." Has God changed from a God of order? No; He is the same in the present dispensation as in the former. Paul says: "God is not the author of confusion, but of peace." He is as particular now as then. And He designs that we should learn lessons of order and organization from the perfect order instituted in the days of Moses for the benefit of the children of Israel.

FURTHER LABORS

Experiences from December 23, 1867 to February 1, 1868

I will now resume the sketch of incidents, and perhaps I cannot better give an idea of our labors up to the time of the Vermont meeting than by copying a letter which I wrote to our son at Battle Creek, December 27, 1867:

"My dear son Edson: I am now seated at the desk of Brother D. T. Bourdeau, at West Enosburgh, Vermont. After our meeting closed at Topsham, Maine, I was exceedingly weary. While packing my trunk, I nearly fainted from weariness. The last work I did there was to call Brother A's family together and have a special interview with them. I spoke to this dear family, giving words of exhortation and comfort, also of correction and counsel to one connected with them. All I said was fully received and was followed by confession, weeping, and great relief to Brother and Sister A. This is crossing work for me and wears me much.

"After we were seated in the cars, I lay down and rested about one hour. We had an appointment that evening at Westbrook, Maine, to meet the brethren from Portland and vicinity.

We made our home with the kind family of Brother Martin. I was not able to sit up during the afternoon; but, being urged to attend the meeting in the evening, I went to the schoolhouse, feeling that I had not strength to stand and address the people. The house was filled with deeply interested listeners. Brother Andrews opened the meeting, and spoke a short time; your father followed with remarks. I then arose, and had spoken but a few words, when I felt my strength renewed; all my feebleness seemed to leave me, and I spoke about one hour with perfect freedom. I felt inexpressible gratitude for this help from God at the very time when I so much needed it. On Wednesday evening I spoke with freedom nearly two hours upon the health and dress reforms. To have my strength so unexpectedly renewed, when I had felt completely exhausted before these two meetings, has been a source of great encouragement to me.

"We enjoyed our visit with the family of Brother Martin, and hope to see their dear children give their hearts to Christ, and with their parents war the Christian warfare, and wear the crown of immortality when the victory shall be gained.

"Thursday we went into Portland again and took dinner with the family of Brother Gowell. We had a special interview with them, which we hope will result in their good. We feel a deep interest for the wife of Brother Gowell. This mother's heart has been torn by seeing her children in affliction and in death, and laid in the silent grave. It is well with the sleepers. May the mother yet seek all the truth, and lay up a treasure in heaven, that when the Life-giver shall come to bring the captives from the great prison house of death, father, mother, and children may meet, and the broken links of the family chain be reunited, no more to be severed.

"Brother Gowell took us to the cars in his carriage. We had just time to get on the train before it started. We rode five hours, and found Brother A.W. Smith at the Manchester depot, waiting to take us to his home in that city. Here we expected to find rest one night; but, lo, quite a number were waiting to receive us. They had come nine miles from Amherst to spend the evening with us. We had a very pleasant interview, profitable, we hope, to all. Retired about ten. Early next morning we left the comfortable, hospitable home of Brother Smith, to pursue our journey to Washington. It was a slow, tedious route. We left the cars at Hillsborough, and found a team waiting to take us twelve miles to Washington. Brother Colby had a sleigh and blankets, and we rode quite comfortably until we were within a few miles of our destination. There was not snow enough to make good sleighing; the wind arose, and during the last two miles blew the falling sleet into our faces and eyes, producing pain and chilling us almost to freezing. We found shelter at last at the good home of Brother C. K. Farnsworth. They did all they could for our comfort, and everything was arranged so that we could rest as much as possible. That was but little, I can assure you.

"Sabbath your father spoke in the forenoon, and after an intermission of about twenty minutes I spoke, bearing a testimony of reproof for several who were using tobacco, also for Brother Ball, who had been strengthening the hands of our enemies by holding the visions up to ridicule, and publishing bitter things against us in the *Crisis*, of Boston, and in the *Hope of Israel,* a paper issued in Iowa. The meeting for the evening was appointed at Brother Farnsworth's. The church was present, and your father there requested Brother Ball to state his objections to the visions and give an opportunity to answer them. Thus the evening was spent. Brother Ball manifested much stiffness and opposition; he admitted himself satisfied upon some points, but held his position quite firmly. Brother Andrews and your father talked plainly, explaining matters which he had misunderstood, and condemning his unrighteous course toward the Sabbathkeeping Adventists. We all felt that we had done the best we could that day to weaken the forces of the enemy. Our meeting held until past ten.

"The next morning we attended meetings again in the meetinghouse. Your father spoke in the morning. But just before he spoke, the enemy made a poor, weak brother feel that he had a most astonishing burden for the church. He walked the slip, talked, and groaned, and cried, and had a terrible something upon him, which nobody seemed to understand. We were trying to bring those who professed the truth to see their state of dreadful darkness and backsliding before God, and to make humble confessions of the same, thus returning unto the Lord with sincere repentance, that He might return unto them, and heal their backslidings. Satan sought to hinder the work by pushing in this poor, distracted soul to disgust those who wished to move understandingly. I arose and bore a plain testimony to this man. He had taken no food for two days, and Satan had deceived him, and pushed him over the mark.

"Then your father preached. We had a few moments' intermission, and then I tried to speak upon the health and dress reforms, and bore a plain testimony to those who had been standing in the way of the young and of unbelievers. God helped me to say plain things to Brother Ball, and to tell him in the name of the Lord what he had been doing. He was considerably affected.

"Again we held an evening meeting at Brother Farnsworth's. The weather was stormy during the meetings, yet Brother Ball did not remain away from one of them. The same subject was resumed, the investigation of the course he had pursued. If ever the Lord helped a man talk, He helped Brother Andrews that night, as he dwelt upon the subject of suffering for Christ's sake. The case of Moses was mentioned, who refused to be called the son of Pharaoh's daughter, choosing rather to suffer affliction with the people of God than to enjoy the pleasures of sin for a season, esteeming the reproach of Christ greater riches than the treasures of Egypt; for he had respect unto the recompense of reward. He showed that this is one of many instances where the reproach of Christ was esteemed above worldly riches and honor, high-sounding titles, a prospective crown, and the glory of a kingdom. The eye of faith was fixed upon the glorious future, and the recompense of the reward was regarded of such value as to cause the richest things which earth can offer to appear valueless. The children of God endured mockings, scourgings, bonds, and imprisonments; they were stoned, sawn asunder, tempted, wandering about in sheepskins and goatskins, destitute, afflicted, tormented, and, sustained by hope and faith, they could call these light afflictions; the future, the eternal life, appeared of so great value that they accounted their sufferings small in comparison with the recompense of the reward.

"Brother Andrews related an instance of a faithful Christian about to suffer martyrdom for his faith. A brother Christian had been conversing with him in regard to the power of the Christian hope—if it would be strong enough to sustain him while his flesh should be consuming with fire. He asked this Christian, about to suffer, to give him a signal if the Christian faith and hope were stronger than the raging, consuming fire. He expected his turn to come next, and this would fortify him for the fire. The former promised that the signal should be given. He was brought to the stake amid the taunts and jeers of the idle and curious crowd assembled to witness the burning of this Christian. The fagots were brought and the fire kindled, and the brother Christian fixed his eyes upon the suffering, dying martyr, feeling that much depended upon the signal. The fire burned, and burned. The flesh was blackened, but the signal came not. His eye was not taken for a moment from the painful sight. The arms were already crisped. There was no appearance of life. All thought that the fire had done its work, and that no life remained; when, lo! amid the flames, up went both arms toward heaven. The brother Christian, whose heart was becoming faint, caught sight of the joyful signal; it sent a thrill through his whole being, and renewed his faith, his hope, his courage. He wept tears of joy.

"As Brother Andrews spoke of the blackened, burned arms raised aloft amid the flames, he, too, wept like a child. Nearly the whole congregation were affected to tears. This meeting closed about ten. There had been quite a breaking away of the clouds of darkness. Brother Hemingway arose and said he had been completely backslidden, using tobacco, opposing the visions, and persecuting his wife for believing them, but said he would do so no more. He asked her forgiveness, and the forgiveness of us all. His wife spoke with feeling. His daughter and several others rose for prayers. He stated that the testimony which Sister White had borne seemed to come direct from the throne, and he would never dare to oppose it again.

"Brother Ball then said that if matters were as we viewed them, his case was very bad. He said he knew he had been backslidden for years and had stood in the way of the young. We thanked God for that admission. We designed to leave early Monday morning, and had an appointment at Braintree, Vermont, to meet about thirty Sabbathkeepers. But it was very cold, rough, blustering weather to ride twenty-five miles after such constant labor, and we finally decided to hold on, and continue the work in Washington until Brother Ball decided either for or against the truth, that the church might be relieved in his case.

"Meeting commenced Monday at 10 a.m. Brethren Rodman and Howard were present. Brother Newell Mead, who was very feeble and nervous, almost exactly like your father in his past sickness, was sent for to attend the meeting. Again the condition of the church was dwelt upon, and the severest censure was passed upon those who had stood in the way of its prosperity. With the most earnest entreaties we pleaded with them to be converted to God and face rightabout. The Lord aided us in the work; Brother Ball felt, but moved slowly. His wife felt deeply for him. Our morning meeting closed at three or four in the afternoon. All these hours we had been engaged, first one of us, then another, earnestly laboring for the unconverted youth. We appointed another meeting for the evening, to commence at six.

"Just before going into the meeting, I had a revival of some interesting scenes which had passed before me in vision, and I spoke to Brethren Andrews, Rodman, Howard, Mead, and several others who were present. It seemed to me that the angels were making a rift in the cloud and letting in the beams of light from heaven. The subject that was presented so strikingly was the case of Moses. I exclaimed: "Oh, that I had the skill of an artist, that I might picture the scene of Moses upon the mount!" His strength was firm. "Unabated," is the language of the Scripture. His eye was not dimmed through age, yet he was upon that mount to die. The angels buried him, but the Son of God soon came down and raised him from the dead and took him to heaven. But God first gave him a view of the land of promise, with His blessing upon it. It was as it were a second Eden. As a panorama this passed before his vision. He was shown the appearing of Christ at His first advent, His rejection by the Jewish nation, and His death upon the cross. Moses then saw Christ's second advent and the resurrection of the just. I also spoke of the meeting of the two Adams—Adam the first, and Christ the second Adam—when Eden shall bloom on earth again. The particulars of these interesting points I design to write out for *Testimony* No. 14. The brethren wished me to repeat the same in the evening meeting.

"Our meeting through the day had been most solemn. I had such a burden upon me Sunday evening that I wept aloud for about half an hour. Monday, solemn appeals had been made, and the Lord was sending them home. I went into meeting Tuesday evening a little lighter. I spoke an hour with great freedom upon subjects I had seen in vision, which I have referred to. Our meeting was very free. Brother Howard wept like a child, as did also Brother Rodman. Brother Andrews talked in an earnest, touching manner, and with weeping. Brother Ball arose and said that there seemed to be two spirits about him that evening, one saying to him: Can you doubt that this testimony from Sister White is of heaven? Another spirit would present before his mind the objections he had opened before the enemies of our faith. 'Oh, if I could feel satisfied,' said he, 'in regard to all these objections, if they could be removed, I would feel that I had done Sister White a great injury. I have recently sent a piece to the *Hope of Israel*. If I had that piece, what would I not give!' He felt deeply, and wept much. The Spirit of the Lord was in the meeting. Angels of God seemed drawing very near, driving back the evil angels. Minister and people wept like children. We felt that we had gained ground, and that the powers of darkness had given back. Our meeting closed well.

"We appointed still another meeting for the next day, commencing at 10 a.m. I spoke upon the humiliation and glorification of Christ. Brother Ball sat near me and wept all the time I was talking. I spoke about an hour, then we commenced our labors for the youth. Parents had come to the meeting bringing their children with them to receive the blessing. Brother Ball arose and made humble confession that he had not lived as he should before his family. He confessed to his children and to his wife that he had been in a backslidden state, and had been no help to them, but rather a hindrance. Tears flowed freely; his strong frame shook, and sobs choked his utterance.

"Brother James Farnsworth had been influenced by Brother Ball, and had not been in full union with the Sabbathkeeping

Adventists. He confessed with tears. Then we pleaded earnestly with the children, until thirteen arose and expressed a desire to be Christians. Brother Ball's children were among the number. One or two had left the meeting, being obliged to return home. One young man, about twenty years old, walked forty miles to see us and hear the truth. He had never professed religion, but took his stand on the Lord's side before he left. This was one of the very best of meetings. At its close, Brother Ball came to your father and confessed with tears that he had wronged him, and entreated his forgiveness. He next came to me and confessed that he had done me a great injury. 'Can you forgive me and pray God to forgive me?' We assured him we would forgive him as freely as we hoped to be forgiven. We parted with all with many tears, feeling the blessing of heaven resting upon us. We had no meeting in the evening.

"Thursday we arose at 4 a.m. It had rained in the night and was still raining, yet we ventured to start to ride to Bellows Falls, a distance of twenty-five miles. The first four miles was exceedingly rough, as we took a private track through the fields to escape steep hills. We rode over stones and plowed ground, nearly throwing us out of the sleigh. About sunrise the storm cleared away, and we had very good sleighing when we reached the public road. The weather was very mild; we never had a more beautiful day to travel. On arriving at Bellows Falls, we found that we were one hour too late for the express train, and one hour too early for the accommodation train. We could not get to St. Albans until nine in the evening. We took seats in a nice car, then took our dinner, and enjoyed our simple fare. We then prepared to sleep if we could.

"While I was sleeping, someone shook my shoulder quite vigorously. I looked up, and saw a pleasant-looking lady bending over me. Said she: 'Don't you know me? I am Sister Chase. The cars are at White River. Stop only a few moments. I live just by here, and have come down every day this week and been through the cars to meet you.' I then remembered that I took dinner at her house at Newport. She was so glad to see us. Her mother and she keep the Sabbath alone. Her husband is conductor on the cars. She talked fast. Said she prized the *Review* much, as she had no meeting to attend. She wanted books to distribute to her neighbors, but had to earn all the money herself which she expended for books or for the paper. We had a profitable interview, although short, for the cars started, and we had to separate.

"At St. Albans we found Brethren Gould and A. C. Bourdeau. Brother B. had a convenient covered carriage and two horses, but he drove very slowly, and we did not reach Enosburgh until past one in the morning. We were weary and chilled. We lay down to rest a little after two o'clock and slept until after seven.

"Sabbath morning. There is quite a large gathering here although the roads are bad, neither sleighing nor good wagoning. I have just been in meeting and occupied a little time in conference. Your father speaks this morning, I in the afternoon. May the Lord help us, is our prayer. You see how long a letter I have written you. Read this to those who are interested, especially to father and mother White. You see, Edson, that we have work enough to do. I hope you do not neglect to pray for us. Your father works hard, too hard for his good. He sometimes realizes the special blessing of God, and this renews him and cheers him in the work. We have allowed ourselves no rest since coming East; we have labored with all our strength. May our feeble efforts be blessed to the good of God's dear people.

"Edson, I hope that you will adorn your profession by a well-ordered life and godly conversation. Oh, be earnest! be zealous and persevering in the work. Watch unto prayer. Cultivate humility and meekness. This will meet the approval of God. Hide yourself in Jesus; let self-love and self-pride be sacrificed, and you, my son, be fitting with a rich Christian experience, to be of use in any position that God may require you to occupy. Seek for thorough heartwork. A surface work will not stand the test of the judgment. Seek for thorough transformation from the world. Let not your hands be stained, your heart spotted, your character sullied, by its corruptions. Keep distinct. God calls: 'Come out from among them, and be ye separate, saith the Lord, and touch not the unclean thing; and I will receive you, and will be a Father unto you, and ye shall be My sons and daughters, saith the Lord Almighty.' 'Having therefore these promises, dearly beloved, let us cleanse ourselves from all filthiness of the flesh and spirit, perfecting holiness in the fear of God.'

"The work rests upon us to perfect holiness. When God sees us doing all we can on our part, then He will help us. Angels will aid us, and we shall be strong through Christ strengthening us. Do not neglect secret prayer. Pray for yourself. Grow in grace. Advance. Don't stand still, don't go back. Onward to victory. Courage in the Lord, my dear boy. Battle with the great adversary only a little longer, and then release will come, and the armor will be laid off at the feet of our dear Redeemer. Press through every obstacle. If the future looks somewhat clouded, hope on, believe on. The clouds will disappear, and light again shine. Praise God, my heart says, praise God for what He has done for you, for your father, and for myself. Commence the new year right. Your mother, E. G. W."

The meeting at West Enosburgh, Vermont, was one of deep interest. It seemed good to again meet with, and speak to, our old, tried friends in this state. A great and good work was done in a short time. These friends were generally poor and toiling for the comforts of life where one dollar is earned with more labor than two in the West, yet they were liberal with us. Many particulars of this meeting have been given in the *Review,* and want of room in these pages alone seems to forbid their repetition. In no state have the brethren been truer to the cause than in old Vermont.

On our way from Enosburgh, we stopped for the night with the family of Brother William White. Brother C. A. White, his son, introduced to us the matter of his Combined Patent Washer and Wringer, and wished counsel. As I had written against our people engaging in patent rights, he wished to know just how I viewed his patent. I freely told him what I did not mean in what I had written, and also what I did mean. I did not mean that it was wrong to have anything to do with patent rights, for this is almost impossible, as very many things with which we have to do daily are patented. Neither did I wish to convey the idea that it was wrong to patent, manufacture, and sell any article worthy of being patented. I did mean to be understood that it is wrong for our people to suffer themselves to be so imposed upon, deceived, and cheated by those men who go about the country selling the right of territory for this or that machine or article. Many of these are of no value, as they are no real improvement. And those who are engaged in their sale, are, with few exceptions, a class of deceivers.

And, again, some of our own people have engaged in the sale of patented wares which they had reason to believe were not what they represented them to be. That so many of our people, some of them after being fully warned, will still suffer themselves to be deceived by the false statements of these vendors of patent rights, seems astonishing. Some patents are really valuable, and a few have made well on them. But it is my opinion that where one dollar has been gained, one hundred dollars have been lost. No reliance whatever can be placed on these patent-right pledges. And the fact that those engaged in them are, with few exceptions, downright deceivers and liars, makes it hard for an honest man, who has a worthy article, to obtain the credit and patronage due him.

Brother White exhibited his Combined Washer and Wringer before the company, including the Brethren Bourdeau, Brother Andrews, my husband, and myself, and we could but look with favor upon it. He has since made us a present of one, which Brother Corliss from Maine, our hired man, in a few moments put together in running order. Sister Burgess, from Gratiot County, our hired girl, is very much pleased with it. It does the work well, and very fast. A feeble woman who has a son or husband to work this machine, can have a large washing done in a few hours, and she do but little more than oversee the work. Brother White sent circulars, which any can have by addressing us, enclosing postage.

Our next meeting was at Adams Center, New York. It was a large gathering. There were several persons in and around this place whose cases had been shown me, for whom I felt the deepest interest. They were men of moral worth. Some were in positions in life which made the cross of present truth heavy to bear, or, at least, they thought so. Others, who had reached the middle age of life, had been brought up from childhood to keep the Sabbath, but had not borne the cross of Christ. These were in a position where it seemed hard to move them. They needed to be shaken from relying on their good works and to be brought to feel their lost condition without Christ. We could not give up these souls, and labored with our might to help them. They were at last moved, and I have since been made glad to hear from some of them, and good news respecting all of them. We hope that the love of this world will not shut the love of God out of their hearts. God is converting strong men of wealth and bringing them into the ranks. If they would prosper in the Christian life, grow in grace, and at last reap a rich reward, they will have to use of their abundance to advance the cause of truth.

After leaving Adams Center, we stayed a few days at Rochester, and from that place came to Battle Creek, where we remained over Sabbath and first day. Thence we returned to our home, where we spent the next Sabbath and first day with the brethren who assembled from different places.

My husband had taken hold of the book matter at Battle Creek, and a noble example had been set by that church. At the meeting at Fairplains he presented the matter of placing in the hands of all who were not able to purchase, such works as *Spiritual Gifts, Appeal to Mothers, How to Live, Appeal to Youth, Sabbath Readings,* and the charts, with *Key of Explanation*. The plan met with general approval. But of this important work I will speak in another place.

THE CASE OF HANNAH MORE

The next Sabbath we met with the Orleans church, where my husband introduced the case of our much-lamented sister, Hannah More. When Brother Amadon visited us last summer, he stated that Sister More had been at Battle Creek, and not finding employment there, had gone to Leelenaw County to find a home with an old friend who had been a fellow laborer in missionary fields in Central Africa. My husband and myself felt grieved that this dear servant of Christ found it necessary to deprive herself of the society of those of like faith, and we decided to send for her to come and find a home with us. We wrote inviting her to meet us at our appointment at Wright, and come home with us. She did not meet us at Wright. I here give her response to our letter, dated August 29, 1867, which we received at Battle Creek:

Brother White: Your kind communication reached me by this week's mail. As the mail comes here only once a week, and is to leave tomorrow, I hasten to reply. We are here in the bush, as it were, and an Indian carries the mail Fridays on foot, and returns Tuesdays. I have consulted Brother Thompson as to the route, and he says my best and surest way will be to take a boat from here and go to Milwaukee, and thence to Grand Haven.

"As I spent all my money in coming here, and was invited to have a home in Brother Thompson's family, I have been assisting Sister Thompson in her domestic affairs and sewing, at one dollar and fifty cents per week of five days each, as they do not wish me to work for them on Sunday, and I do not work on the Sabbath of the Lord, the only one the Bible recognizes. They are not at all anxious to have me leave them, notwithstanding our difference of belief; and he says I may have a home with them, only I must not make my belief prominent among his people. He has even invited me to fill his appointments when on his preaching tour, and I have done so. Sister Thompson needs a governess for her children, as the influences are so very pernicious outside, and the schools so vicious that she is not willing to send her dear ones among them until they are Christians, as she says. Their eldest son, today sixteen years of age, is a pious and devoted young man. They have partially adopted the health reform, and I think will fully come into it erelong, and like it. He has ordered the *Health Reformer.* I showed him some copies which I brought.

"I hope and pray that he may yet embrace the holy Sabbath. Sister Thompson does believe in it already. He is wonderfully set in his own ways, and of course thinks he is right. Could I only get him to read the books I brought, the *History of the Sabbath,* etc., but he looks at them and calls them infidel, and says they seem to him to carry error in their front, when, if they would only read carefully each sentiment of our tenets, I can but think they would embrace them as Bible truths and see their beauty and consistency. I doubt not but that Sister T. would be glad to immediately become a Seventh-day Adventist were it not that her husband is so bitterly opposed to any such thing. It was impressed upon my mind that I had a work to do here before I came here; but the truth is present in the family, and if I can carry it no farther, it would seem that my work is done, or nearly so. I do not feel like being ashamed of Christ, or His, in this wicked generation, and would much rather cast in my lot with Sabbathkeepers and God's chosen people.

"I shall need ten dollars at least to get to Greenville. That, with the little I have earned, might be sufficient. But now I will wait for you to write me, and do what you think best about forwarding me the money. In the spring I would have enough to go, myself, and think I should like to do so. May the Lord guide and bless us in our every undertaking, is the ardent desire of my heart. And may I fill that very position my God allots for me in His moral vineyard, performing with alacrity every duty, however onerous it may seem, according to His good pleasure, is my sincere desire and heartfelt prayer.

"Hannah More."

On receiving this letter, we decided to send the needed sum to Sister More as soon as we could find time. But before we found the spare moments we decided to go to Maine, to return in a few weeks, when we could send for her before navigation should close. And when we decided to stay and labor in Maine, New Hampshire, Vermont, and New York, we wrote to a brother in this county to see leading brethren in the vicinity and consult with them concerning sending for Sister More and making her a home until we should return. But the matter was neglected until navigation closed, and we returned and found that no one had taken interest to help Sister More to this vicinity, where she could come to us when we should reach our home. We felt grieved and distressed, and at a meeting at Orleans the second Sabbath after we came home, my husband introduced her case to the brethren. A brief report of what was said and done in relation to Sister More was given by my husband in the *Review* for February 18, 1868, as follows:

"At this meeting we introduced the case of Sister Hannah More, now sojourning in northwestern Michigan with friends who do not observe the Bible Sabbath. We stated that this servant of Christ embraced the Sabbath while performing missionary labor in Central Africa. When this was known, her services in that direction were no longer wanted, and she returned to America to seek a home and employment with those of like faith. We judge, from her present location, that in this she has been disappointed. No one in particular may be worthy of blame in her case; but it appears to us that there is either a lack of suitable provisions connected with our system of organization, for the encouragement of such persons and to assist them to a field of useful labor, or that those brethren and sisters who have had the pleasure of seeing Sister More have not done their duty. A unanimous vote was then given to invite her to find a home with the brethren in this vicinity until General Conference, when her case should be presented to our people. Brother Andrews, being present, fully endorsed the action of the brethren."

From what we have since learned of the cold, indifferent treatment which Sister More met with at Battle Creek, it is evident that in stating that no one in particular was worthy of censure in her case, my husband took altogether a too charitable view of the matter. When all the facts are known, no Christian could but blame all members of that church who knew her circumstances and did not individually interest themselves in her behalf. It certainly was the duty of the officers to do this and report to the church, if others did not take up the matter before them. But individual members of that or any other church should not feel excused from taking an interest in such persons. After what has been said in the

Review of this self-sacrificing servant of Christ, every reader of the *Review* in Battle Creek, on learning that she had come to the city, would have been excused for giving her a personal call and inquiring into her wants.

Sister Strong, the wife of Elder P. Strong, Jr., was in Battle Creek at the same time as Sister More. They both reached that city the same day, and left at the same time. Sister Strong, who is by my side, says that Sister More wished her to intercede for her, that she might get employment, so as to remain with Sabbathkeepers. Sister More said she was willing to do anything, but teaching was her choice. She also requested Elder A. S. Hutchins to introduce her case to leading brethren at the Review office and try to get a school for her. This, Brother Hutchins cheerfully did. But no encouragement was given, as there appeared to be no opening. She also stated to Sister Strong that she was destitute of means and must go to Leelenaw County unless she could get employment at Battle Creek. She frequently spoke in words of touching lamentation that she was obliged to leave the brethren.

Sister More wrote to Mr. Thompson relative to accepting his offer to make it her home with his family, and she wished to wait until she should hear from him. Sister Strong went with her to find a place for her to stay until she should hear from Mr. T. At one place she was told that she could stay from Wednesday until Friday morning, when they were to leave home. This sister made Sister More's case known to her natural sister, living near, who was also a Sabbathkeeper. When she returned she told Sister More that she could stay with her until Friday morning; that her sister said it was not convenient to take her. Sister Strong has since learned that the real excuse was that she was not acquainted with Sister More. She could have taken her, but did not want her.

Sister More then asked Sister Strong what she should do. Sister Strong was almost a stranger in Battle Creek, but thought she could get her in with the family of a poor brother of her acquaintance who had recently moved from Montcalm County. Here she succeeded. Sister More remained until Tuesday, when she left for Leelenaw County by the way of Chicago. There she borrowed money to complete her journey. Her wants were known to some, at least, in Battle Creek, for as the result of their being made known, she was charged nothing for her brief stay at the Institute.

Immediately after our return from the East, my husband, learning that nothing had been done, as we had requested, to get Sister More where she could at once come to us on our return, wrote to her to come to us as soon as possible, to which she responded as follows:

"Leland, Leelenaw County, Michigan,
February 20, 1868.

"My Dear Brother White: Yours of February 3 is received. It found me in poor health, not being accustomed to these cold northern winters, with the snow three or four feet deep on a level. Our mails are brought on snowshoes.

"It does not seem possible for me to get to you till spring opens. The roads are bad enough without snow. They tell me my best way is to wait till navigation opens, then go to Milwaukee, and thence to Grand Haven, to take the railroad to the point nearest your place. I had hoped to get among our dear people last fall, but was not permitted the privilege.

"The truths which we believe seem more and more important, and our work of making ready a people prepared for the Lord's coming is not to be delayed. We must not only have on the wedding garment ourselves, but be faithful in recommending the preparation to others. I wish I could get to you, but it seems impossible, or at least impracticable, in my delicate state of health to set out alone on such a journey in the depth of winter. When is the General Conference to which you allude? and where? I suppose the *Review* will eventually inform me.

"I think my health has suffered from keeping the Sabbath alone in my chamber, in the cold; but I did not think I could keep it where all manner of work and worldly conversation was the order of the day, as with Sundaykeepers. I think it is the most laborious working day with those who keep first day. Indeed, it does not seem to me that the best of Sundaykeepers observe any day as they should. Oh, how I long to be again with Sabbathkeepers! Sister White will want to see me in the reform dress. Will she be so kind as to send me a pattern, and I will pay her when I get there. I suppose I shall need to be fitted out when I get among you. I like it much. Sister Thompson thinks she would like to wear the reform dress.

"I have had a difficulty in breathing, so that I have not been able to sleep for more than a week, occasioned, I suppose, by the stovepipe's parting and completely filling my room with smoke and gas at bedtime, and my sleeping there without proper ventilation. I did not, at the time, suppose smoke was so unwholesome, nor consider that the impure gas which generated from the wood and coal was mingled with it. I awoke with such a sense of suffocation that I could not breathe lying down, and spent the remainder of the night sitting up. I never before knew the dreadful feeling of stifling sensations. I began to fear I should never sleep again. I therefore resigned myself into the hands of God for life or death, entreating Him to spare me if He had any further need of me in His vineyard; otherwise I had no wish to live. I felt entirely reconciled to the hand of God upon me. But I also felt that satanic influences must be resisted. I therefore bade Satan get behind me and away from me, and told the Lord that I would not turn my hand over to choose either life or death, but that I would refer it implicitly to Him who knew me altogether. My future was unknown to myself, therefore said

I, Thy will is best. Life is of no account to me, so far as its pleasures are concerned. All its riches, its honors, are nothing compared with usefulness. I do not crave them; they cannot satisfy or fill the aching void which unperformed duty leaves to me. I would not live uselessly, to be a mere blot or blank in life. And though it seems a martyr's death to die thus, I am resigned, if that is God's will.

"I had said to Sister Thompson the day previous, 'Were I at Brother White's, I might be prayed for, and healed.' She inquired if we could send for you and Brother Andrews, but that seemed impracticable, as I could not, in all probability, live till you arrived. I knew that the Lord by His mighty power and with His potent arm could heal me here, were it best. To Him I felt safe in referring it. I knew He could send an angel to resist him that hath the power of death, that is, the devil, and felt sure He would, if best. I knew, also, that He could suggest measures, were they necessary, for my recovery, and I felt sure He would. I soon was better, and able to sleep some.

"Thus you see I am still a spared monument of God's mercy and faithfulness in afflicting His children. He doth not willingly afflict nor grieve the children of men; but sometimes trials are needed as a discipline, to wean us from earth—

> And bid us seek substantial bliss
> Beyond a fleeting world like this.

"Now I can say with the poet:

> Lord, it belongs not to my care,
> Whether I die or live.
> If life be long, I will be glad
> That I may long obey;
> If short, yet why should I be sad?
> This world must pass away.
> Christ leads me through no darker rooms,
> Than He went through before.
> Whoever into His kingdom comes,
> Must enter by His door.

Come, Lord when grace has made me meet
Thy blessed face to see;
For if, Thy work on earth be sweet,
What must Thy glory be?
I'll gladly end my sad complaints,
And weary, sinful days,
To join with the triumphant saints
That sing Jehovah's praise.
My knowledge of that state is small,
My eye of faith is dim;
But, 'tis enough that Christ knows all,
And I shall be with Him.

—*Baxter.*

"I had another wakeful season last night, and feel poorly today. Pray that whatever is God's will may be accomplished in and through me, whether it be by my life or death.

"Yours in hope of eternal life,

"Hannah More.

"If you know of any way by which I can reach you sooner, please inform me. H. M."

She being dead yet speaketh. Her letters, which I have given, will be read with deep interest by those who have read her obituary in a recent number of the *Review*. She might have been a blessing to any Sabbathkeeping family who could appreciate her worth, but she sleeps. Our brethren at Battle Creek and in this vicinity could have made more than a welcome home for Jesus, in the person of this godly woman. But that opportunity is past. It was not convenient. They were not acquainted with her. She was advanced in years and might be a burden. Feelings of this kind barred her from the homes of the professed friends of Jesus, who are looking for His near advent, and drove her away from those she loved, to those who opposed her faith, to northern Michigan, in the cold of winter, to be chilled to death. She died a martyr to the selfishness and covetousness of professed commandment keepers.

Providence has administered, in this case, a terrible rebuke for the conduct of those who did not take this stranger in. She was not really a stranger. By reputation she was known, and yet she was not taken in. Many will feel sad as they think of Sister More as she stood in Battle Creek, begging a home there with the people of her choice. And as they, in imagination, follow her to Chicago, to borrow money to meet the expenses of the journey to her final resting place,—and when they think of that grave in Leelenaw County, where rests this precious outcast,—God pity those who are guilty in her case.

Poor Sister More! She sleeps, but we did what we could. When we were at Battle Creek, the last of August, we received the first of the two letters I have given, but we had no money to send her. My husband sent to Wisconsin and Iowa for means, and received seventy dollars to bear our expenses to those western convocations, held last September. We hoped to have means to send to her immediately on our return from the West, to pay her expenses to our new home in Montcalm County.

The liberal friends West had given us the needed means; but when we decided to accompany Brother Andrews to Maine, the matter was deferred until we should return. We did not expect to be in the East more than four weeks, which would have given ample time to send for Sister More after our return, and to get her to our house before navigation should close. And when we decided to remain in the East several weeks longer than we first designed, we lost no time in addressing several brethren in this vincinity, recommending that they send for Sister More and give her a home till we should return. I say: We did what we could.

But why should we feel interested in this sister, more than others? What did we want of this worn-out missionary? She could not do our housework, and we had but one child at home for her to teach. And, certainly, much could not be expected of one worn as she was, who had nearly reached threescore years. We had no use for her, in particular, only to bring the blessing of God into our house. There are many reasons why our brethren should have taken greater interest in the case of Sister More than we. We had never seen her, and had no other means of knowing her history, her devotion to the cause of Christ and humanity, than all the readers of the *Review.* Our brethren at Battle Creek had seen this noble woman, and some of them knew more or less of her wishes and wants. We had no money with which to help her; they had. We were already overburdened with care and needed those persons in our house who possessed the strength and buoyancy of youth. We needed to be helped, instead of helping others. But most of our brethren in Battle Creek are so situated that Sister More would not have been the least care and burden. They have time, strength, and comparative freedom from care.

Yet no one took the interest in her case that we did. I even spoke to the large congregation before we went East last fall, of their neglect of Sister More. I spoke of the duty of giving honor to whom it is due; it appeared to me that wisdom had so far departed from the prudent that they were not capable of appreciating moral worth. I told that church that there were many among them who could find time to meet, and sing, and play their instruments of music; they could give their money to the artist to multiply their likenesses, or could spend it to attend public amusements; but they had nothing to give to a worn-out missionary who had heartily embraced the present truth and had come to live with those of like precious faith. I advised them to stop and consider what we were doing, and proposed that they shut up their instruments of music for three months and take time to humble themselves before God in self-examination, repentance, and prayer until they learned the claims which the Lord had upon them as His professed children. My soul was stirred with a sense of the wrong that had been done Jesus, in the person of Sister More, and I talked personally with several about it.

This thing was not done in a corner. And yet, notwithstanding the matter was made public, followed by the great and good work in the church at Battle Creek, no effort was made by that church to redeem the past by bringing Sister More back. And one, a wife of one of our ministers, stated afterward: "I do not see the need of Brother and Sister White's making such a fuss about Sister More. I think they do not understand the case." True, we did not understand the case. It is much worse than we then supposed. If we had understood it, we would never have left Battle Creek till we had fully set before that church the sin of suffering her to leave them as she did, and measures had been taken to call her back.

A member of that church in conversation about Sister More's leaving as she did, has since said in substance: "No one feels like taking the responsibility of such cases now. Brother White always took the charge of them." Yes, he did. He would take them to his own house till every chair and bed was full, then he would go to his brethren and have them take those whom he could not. If they needed means, he would give to them and invite others to follow his example. There must be men in Battle Creek to do as he has done, or the curse of God will follow that church. Not one man only, there are fifty there who can do, more or less, as he has done.

We are told that we must come back to Battle Creek. This we are not ready to do. Probably this will never be our duty. We stood under heavy burdens there till we could stand no longer. God will have strong men and women there to divide these burdens among them. Those who move to Battle Creek, who accept positions there, who are not ready to put their hands to this kind of work, would a thousand times better be somewhere else. There are those who can see and feel, and gladly do good to Jesus in the person of His saints. Let them have room to work. Let those who cannot do this go where they will not stand in the way of the work of God.

Especially is this applicable to those who stand at the head of the work. If they go wrong, all is wrong. The greater the responsibility, the greater the ruin in the case of unfaithfulness. If leading brethren do not faithfully perform their duty, those who are led will not do theirs. Those at the head of the work at Battle Creek must be ensamples to the flock everywhere. If they do this, they will have a great reward. If they fail to do this, and yet accept such positions, they will have a fearful account to give.

We did what we could. If we could have had means at our command last summer and fall, Sister More would now be with us. When we learned our real circumstances, as set forth in *Testimony* No. 13, we both took the matter joyfully and said we did not want the responsibility of means. This was wrong. God wants that we should have means that we may, as in time past, help where help is needed. Satan wants to tie our hands in this respect and lead others to be careless, unfeeling, and covetous, that such cruel work may go on as in the case of Sister More.

We see outcasts, widows, orphans, worthy poor, and ministers in want, and many chances to use means to the glory of God, the advancement of His cause, and the relief of suffering saints, and I want means to use for God. The experience of nearly a quarter of a century in extensive traveling, feeling the condition of those who need help, qualifies us to make a judicious use of our Lord's money. I have bought my own stationery, paid my own postage, and spent much of my life writing for the good of others, and all I have received for this work, which has wearied and worn me terribly, would not pay a tithe of my postage. When means has been pressed upon me, I have refused it, or appropriated it to such charitable objects as the Publishing Association. I shall do so no more. I shall do my duty in labor as ever, but my fears of receiving means to use for the Lord are gone. This case of Sister

More has fully aroused me to see the work of Satan in depriving us of means.

Poor Sister More! When we heard that she was dead, my husband felt terrible. We both felt as though a dear mother, for whose society our very hearts yearned, was no more. Some may say, If we had stood in the place of those who knew something of this sister's wishes and wants, we would not have done as they did. I hope you will never have to suffer the stings of conscience which some must feel who were so interested in their own affairs as to be unwilling to bear any responsibility in her case. May God pity those who are so afraid of deception as to neglect a worthy, self-sacrificing servant of Christ. The remark was made as an excuse for this neglect: We have been bitten so many times that we are afraid of strangers. Did our Lord and His disciples instruct us to be very cautious and not entertain strangers, lest we should possibly make some mistake and get bitten by having the trouble of caring for an unworthy person?

Paul exhorts the Hebrews: "Let brotherly love continue." Do not flatter yourselves that there is a time when this exhortation will not be needed; when brotherly love may cease. He continues: "Be not forgetful to entertain strangers: for thereby some have entertained angels unawares." Please read Matthew 25:31 and onward. Read it, brethren, the next time you take the Bible at your morning or evening family devotions. The good works performed by those who are to be welcomed to the kingdom were done to Christ in the person of His suffering people. Those who had done these good works did not see that they had done anything for Christ. They had done no more than their duty to suffering humanity. Those on the left hand could not see that they had abused Christ in neglecting the wants of His people. But they had neglected to do for Jesus in the person of His saints, and for this neglect they were to go away into everlasting punishment. And one definite point of their neglect is thus stated: "I was a stranger, and ye took Me not in."

These things do not belong alone to Battle Creek. I am grieved at the selfishness among professed Sabbathkeepers everywhere. Christ has gone to prepare eternal mansions for us, and shall we refuse Him a home for only a few days, in the person of His saints who are cast out? He left His home in glory, His majesty and high command, to save lost man. He became poor that we through His poverty might become rich. He submitted to insult, that man might be exalted, and provided a home that would be matchless for loveliness, and enduring as the throne of God. Those who finally overcome and sit down with Christ upon His throne will follow the example of Jesus, and from a willing, happy choice will sacrifice for Him in the person of His saints. Those who cannot do this from choice will go away into everlasting punishment.

HEALTHFUL COOKERY

During the last seven months we have been at home but about four weeks. In our travels we have sat at many different tables, from Iowa to Maine. Some whom we have visited live up to the best light they have. Others, who have the same opportunities of learning to live healthfully and well, have hardly taken the first steps in reform. They will tell you that they do not know how to cook in this new way. But they are without excuse in this matter of cooking; for in the work, *How to Live,* are many excellent recipes, and this work is within the reach of all. I do not say that the system of cookery taught in that book is perfect. I may soon furnish a small work more to my mind in some respects. But *How to Live* teaches cookery almost infinitely in advance of what the traveler will often meet, even among some Seventh-day Adventists.

Many do not feel that this is a matter of duty, hence they do not try to prepare food properly. This can be done in a simple, healthful, and easy manner, without the use of lard, butter, or flesh meats. Skill must be united with simplicity. To do this, women must read, and then patiently reduce what they read to practice. Many are suffering because they will not take the trouble to do this. I say to such: It is time for you to rouse your dormant energies and read up. Learn how to cook with simplicity, and yet in a manner to secure the most palatable and healthful food.

Because it is wrong to cook merely to please the taste, or to suit the appetite, no one should entertain the idea that an impoverished diet is right. Many are debilitated with disease, and need a nourishing, plentiful, well-cooked diet. We frequently find graham bread heavy, sour, and but partially baked. This is for want of interest to learn, and care to perform, the important duty of cook. Sometimes we find gem cakes, or soft biscuit, dried, not baked, and other things after the same order. And then cooks will tell you they can do very well in the old style of cooking, but, to tell the truth, their families do not like graham bread; that they would starve to live in this way.

I have said to myself: I do not wonder at it. It is your manner of preparing food that makes it so unpalatable. To eat such food would certainly give one the dyspepsia. These poor cooks, and those who have to eat their food, will gravely tell you that the health reform does not agree with them. The stomach has not power to convert poor, heavy, sour bread into good; but this poor bread will convert a healthy stomach into a diseased one. Those who eat such food know that they are failing in strength. Is there not a cause? Some of these persons call themselves health reformers, but they are not. They do not know how to cook. They prepare cakes, potatoes, and graham bread, but there is the same round, with scarcely a variation, and the system is not strengthened. They seem to think the time wasted which is devoted to obtaining a thorough experience in the preparation of healthful, palatable food. Some act as though that which they eat were lost, and anything they could toss into the stomach to fill it would do as well as food prepared with so much painstaking. It is important that we relish the food we eat. If we cannot do this, but eat mechanically, we fail to be nourished and built up as we would be if we could enjoy the food we take into the stomach. We are composed of what we eat. In order to make a good quality of blood, we must have the right kind of food, prepared in a right manner.

It is a religious duty for those who cook to learn how to prepare healthful food in different ways, so that it may be eaten with enjoyment. Mothers should teach their children how to cook. What branch of the education of a young lady can be so important as this? The eating has to do with the life. Scanty, impoverished, ill-cooked food is constantly depraving the blood by weakening the blood-making organs. It is highly essential that the art of cookery be considered one of the most important branches of education. There are but few good cooks. Young ladies consider that it is stooping to a menial office to become a cook. This is not the case. They do not view the subject from a right standpoint. Knowledge of how to prepare food healthfully, especially bread, is no mean science.

In many families we find dyspeptics, and frequently the reason of this is the poor bread. The mistress of the house decides that it must not be thrown away, and they eat it. Is this the way to dispose of poor bread? Will you put it into the stomach to be converted into blood? Has the stomach power to make sour bread sweet? heavy bread light? moldy bread fresh?

Mothers neglect this branch in the education of their daughters. They take the burden of care and labor, and are fast wearing out, while the daughter is excused, to visit, to crochet, or study her own pleasure. This is mistaken love, mistaken kindness. The mother is doing an injury to her child, which frequently lasts her lifetime. At the age when she should be capable of bearing some of life's burdens, she is unqualified to do so. Such will not take care and burdens. They go light-loaded, excusing themselves from responsibilities, while the mother is pressed down under her burden of care, as a cart beneath sheaves. The daughter does not mean to be unkind; but she is careless and heedless, or she would notice the tired look and mark the expression of pain upon the countenance of the mother, and would seek to do her part to bear the heavier part of the burden and relieve the mother, who must have freedom from care or be brought upon a bed of suffering and, it may be, of death.

Why will mothers be so blind and negligent in the education of their daughters? I have been distressed, as I have visited different families, to see the mother bearing the heavy burden, while the daughter, who manifested buoyancy of spirit and had a good degree of health and vigor, felt no care, no burden. When there are large gatherings, and families are burdened with company, I have seen the mother bearing the burden, with the care of everything upon her, while the daughters are sitting down chatting with young friends, having a social visit. These things seem so wrong to me that I can hardly forbear speaking to the thoughtless youth and telling them to go to work. Release your tired mother. Lead her to a seat in the parlor and urge her to rest and enjoy the society of her friends.

But the daughters are not the ones to be blamed wholly in this matter. The mother is at fault. She has not patiently taught her daughters how to cook. She knows that they lack knowledge in the cooking department, and therefore feels no release from the labor. She must attend to everything that requires care, thought, and attention. Young ladies should be thoroughly instructed in cooking. Whatever be their circumstances in life, here is knowledge which may be put to a practical use. It is a branch of education which has the most direct influence upon human life, especially the lives of those held most dear. Many a wife and mother who has not had the right education and lacks skill in the cooking department is daily presenting her family with ill-prepared food which is steadily and surely destroying the digestive organs, making a poor quality of blood, and frequently bringing on acute attacks of inflammatory disease and causing premature death. Many have been brought to their death by eating heavy, sour bread. An instance was related to me of a hired girl who made a batch of sour, heavy bread. In order to get rid of it and conceal the matter, she threw it to a couple of very large hogs Next morning the man of the house found his swine dead, and, upon examining the trough, found pieces of this heavy bread. He made inquiries, and the girl acknowledged what she had done. She had not a thought of the effect of such bread upon the swine. If heavy, sour bread will kill swine, which can devour rattlesnakes and almost every detestable thing, what effect will it have upon that tender organ, the human stomach?

It is a religious duty for every Christian girl and woman to learn at once to make good, sweet, light bread from unbolted wheat flour. Mothers should take their daughters into the kitchen with them when very young and teach them the art of cooking. The mother cannot expect her daughters to understand the mysteries of housekeeping without education. She should instruct them patiently, lovingly, and make the work as agreeable as she can by her cheerful countenance and encouraging words of approval. If they fail once, twice, or thrice, censure not. Already discouragement is doing its work and tempting them to say: "It is of no use; I can't do it." This is not the time for censure. The will is becoming weakened. It needs the spur of encouraging, cheerful, hopeful words, as:

"Never mind the mistakes you have made. You are but a learner and must expect to make blunders. Try again. Put your mind on what you are doing. Be very careful, and you will certainly succeed."

Many mothers do not realize the importance of this branch of knowledge, and rather than have the trouble and care of instructing their children and bearing with their failings and errors while learning, they prefer to do all themselves. And when their daughters make a failure in their efforts, they send them away with: "It is no use; you can't do this or that. You perplex and trouble me more than you help me."

Thus the first efforts of the learners are repulsed, and the first failure so cools their interest and ardor to learn that they dread another trial, and will propose to sew, knit, clean house—anything but cook. Here the mother was greatly at fault. She should have patiently instructed them that they might by practice obtain an experience which would remove the awkwardness and remedy the unskillful movements of the inexperienced worker. Here I will add extracts from *Testimony* No. 10, published in 1864:

"Children who have been petted and waited upon, always expect it; and if their expectations are not met, they are disappointed and discouraged. This same disposition will be seen through their whole lives; they will be helpless, leaning upon others for aid, expecting others to favor them and yield to them. And if they are opposed, even after they have grown to manhood and womanhood, they think themselves abused; and thus they worry their way through the world, hardly able to bear their own weight, often murmuring and fretting because everything does not suit them.

"Mistaken parents are teaching their children lessons which will prove ruinous to them, and are also planting thorns for their own feet. They think that by gratifying the wishes of their children, and letting them follow their own inclinations, they can gain their love. What an error! Children thus indulged grow up unrestrained in their desires, unyielding in their dispositions, selfish, exacting, and overbearing, a curse to themselves and to all around them. To a great extent, parents hold in their own hands the future happiness of their children. Upon them rests the important work of forming the character of these children. The instructions given in childhood will follow them all through life. Parents sow the seed which will spring up and bear fruit either for good or evil. They can fit their sons and daughters for happiness or for misery.

"Children should be taught very young to be useful, to help themselves, and to help others. Many daughters of this age can, without remorse of conscience, see their mothers toiling, cooking, washing, or ironing, while they sit in the parlor and read stories, knit edging, crochet, or embroider. Their hearts are as unfeeling as a stone. But where does this wrong originate? Who are the ones usually most to blame in this matter? The poor, deceived parents. They overlook the future good of their children, and in their mistaken fondness, let them sit in idleness, or do that which is of but little account, which requires no exercise of the mind or muscles, and then excuse their indolent daughters because they are weakly. What has made them weakly? In many cases it has been the wrong course of the parents. A proper amount of exercise about the house would improve both mind and body. But children are deprived of this through false ideas, until they are averse to work. It is disagreeable and does not accord with their ideas of gentility. It is thought to be unladylike and even coarse to wash dishes, iron, or stand over the washtub. This is the fashionable instruction which is given children in this unfortunate age.

"God's people should be governed by higher principles than worldlings, who seek to gauge all their course of action according to fashion. God-fearing parents should train their children for a life of usefulness. . . . Prepare them to bear burdens while young. If your children have been unaccustomed to labor, they will soon become weary. They will complain of side ache, pain in the shoulders, and tired limbs; and you will be in danger, through sympathy, of doing the work yourselves, rather than have them suffer a little. Let the burden upon the children be very light at first, and then increase it a little every day, until they can do a proper amount of labor without becoming so weary. Inactivity is the greatest cause of side ache and shoulder ache among children. . . .

"Mothers should take their daughters with them into the kitchen and patiently educate them. Their constitution will be better for such labor, their muscles will gain tone and strength, and their meditations will be more healthy and elevated at the close of the day. They may be weary, but how sweet is rest after a proper amount of labor. Sleep, nature's sweet restorer, invigorates the weary body, and prepares it for the next day's duties. Do not intimate to your children that it is no matter whether they labor or not. Teach them that their help is needed, that their time is of value, and that you depend on their labor."

BOOKS AND TRACTS

The proper circulation and distribution of our publications is one of the most important branches of the present work. But little can be done without this. And our ministers can do more in this work than any other class of persons. It is true that a few years ago many of our preachers were carrying the matter of the sale of books too far. Some of them added to the stock which they held for sale, not only publications of little real value, but also articles of merchandise equally valueless.

But some of our ministers now take an extreme view of

what I said in *Testimony* No. 11 upon the sale of our publications. One in the State of New York, upon whom the burdens of labor do not rest heavily, who had acted as agent, holding a good assortment of publications, decided to sell no more, and wrote to the office, stating that the publications were subject to their order. This is wrong. Here I will give an extract from *Testimony* No. 11:

"The burden of selling our publications should not rest upon ministers who labor in word and doctrine. Their time and strength should be held in reserve, that their efforts may be thorough in a series of meetings. Their time and strength should not be drawn upon to sell our books when they can be properly brought before the public by those who have not the burden of preaching the word. In entering new fields it may be necessary for the minister to take publications with him to offer for sale to the people, and it may be necessary in some other circumstances also to sell books and transact business for the office of publication. But such work should be avoided whenever it can be done by others."

The first portion of this extract is qualified by the last part. To be a little more definite, my views of this matter are, that such ministers as Elders Andrews, Waggoner, White, and Loughborough, who have the oversight of the work, and consequently have an extra amount of care, burden, and labor, should not add to their burdens by the sale of our publications, especially at tent meetings and at General Conferences. The view was given to correct those who at such meetings so far came down from the dignity of their work as to spread out before the crowd merchandise which had no connection with the work.

Our ministers who enjoy a comfortable state of health may, with the greatest propriety, engage at proper times in the sale of our important publications. Especially do the sale and circulation of such works as have recently been urged upon the attention of our people, claim vigorous efforts for them at this time. In four weeks, on our tour in the counties of Gratiot, Saginaw, and Tuscola, my husband sold, and gave to the poor, four hundred dollars' worth. He first set the importance of the books before the people; then they were ready to take them as fast as he, with several to help him, could wait upon them.

Why do not our brethren send in their pledges on the book and tract fund more liberally? And why do not our ministers take hold of this work in earnest? Our people should see that these works are just what is needed to help those who need help. Here is a chance to invest means according to the blessed plan of liberality. We can sometimes read men nearly as plainly as we read books. There are those among us who put from one hundred to one thousand dollars or more into the Health Institute, who have pledged only from five to twenty-five dollars in the great enterprise of publishing books, pamphlets, and tracts, setting forth truths which have to do with eternal life. One was supposed to be a paying investment. The other, as we might judge from the littleness of the pledges, is supposed to be a dead loss.

We shall not hold our peace upon this subject. Our people will come up to the work. The means will come. And we would say to those who are poor and want books. Send in your orders, with a statement of your condition as to this world's goods. We will send you a package of books containing four volumes of *Spiritual Gifts, How to Live, Appeal to Youth, Appeal to Mothers, Sabbath Readings,* and the two large charts, with *Key of Explanation.* If you have a part of these, state what you have, and we will send other books in their places, or send only such of these as you have not. Send fifty cents to pay the postage, and we will send you the five-dollar package and charge the fund four dollars.*

In this charitable book matter, all must act upon the great plan of liberality, such as is carried out in the publication and

*See Appendix.

sale of the American Bibles and tracts. In many respects the course of these mammoth societies is worthy of imitation. Liberality is seen in wills and donations, and it is carried out in sales and donations of Bibles and tracts. Seventh-day Adventists should be as far ahead of these in the book matter as in other things. May God help us. Our tracts should be offered by the hundred at what they cost, leaving a little margin to pay for packing, or wrapping for the mail, and directing. And ministers and people should engage in the circulation of books, pamphlets, and tracts, as never before. Sell where people are able and willing to purchase, and where they are not, give them the books.

THE CHRISTIAN'S WATCHWORD

Dear Brother B: I was shown that you move much from feeling instead of from firm principle. You lack a deep and thorough experience in the things of God. You need to be wholly converted to the truth. When a man's heart is fully converted, all that he possesses is consecrated to the Lord. This consecration you have not yet experienced. You love the truth in word, but do not manifest that love in your deeds and by your fruits. Your acts, your deeds, are evidences of the sincerity of your love, or of your indifference to God, His cause, and your fellow men.

How did Christ manifest His love for poor mortals? By the sacrifice of His own glory, His own riches, and even His most precious life. Christ consented to a life of humiliation and great suffering. He submitted to the cruel mockings of an infuriated, murderous multitude, and to the most agonizing death upon the cross. Said Christ: "This is My commandment, That ye love one another, as I have loved you. Greater love hath no man than this, that a man lay down his life for his friends. Ye are My friends, if ye do whatsoever I command you." We give evidence of being the friends of Christ when we manifest implicit obedience to His will. It is no evidence to say, and do not; but in doing, in obeying, is the evidence. Who are obeying the commandment to love one another as Christ has loved them? Brother B, you must have a firmer, deeper, and more unselfish love than you have ever yet possessed, if you obey the commandment of Christ.

You lack benevolence. You labor to save yourself from care, trouble, or expense for the cause of God. You have invested but little in the cause. The enterprise which man values the most will be seen by his investments. If he places a higher estimate upon eternal things than upon temporal things, he will show this by his works; he will invest the most, and venture the most, in that which he values the highest and which in the end brings him the greatest profit.

Men who profess the truth will engage in worldly enterprises, and invest much, and run great risks. If they lose nearly all they possess, they are deeply aggrieved, because they feel the inconvenience of the losses they have sustained; yet they do not feel that their unwise course has deprived the cause of God of means, and that as His stewards they must render an account for this squandering of the Lord's money. Should they be required to venture something for the cause of God, to invest a quarter even of that which they have lost by their investment in earthly things, they would feel that heaven costs too much.

Eternal things are not appreciated. You are not a rich man, yet your heart may be just as much placed upon the little you have, and you may cling to it just as closely as the millionaire to his treasures. Small, very small, will be the profits realized by you in your investments in worldly enterprises; while, on the other hand, if you invest in the cause of God, make that cause a part of you, and love it as you love yourself, and are willing to sacrifice for its advancement, showing your confidence and faith in its ultimate triumph, you will reap a precious harvest, if not in this life, in the better life than this. You will reap an eternal reward which is of as much higher value than any common, earthly gains as the immortal is higher than the perishable.

Brother B, you seemed anxious to find out what had been said in regard to your position in the church and what was our mind in regard to it. It was just this that I have written. I feared for you because of what I have been shown of your peculiarities. You moved by impulse. You would pray if you felt like it, and speak if you felt like it. You would go to meeting if so disposed, or stay at home if not. You greatly lacked the spirit of self-sacrifice. You have consulted your own wishes and ease, and pleased yourself, instead of feeling that you should please God. Duty, duty at your post every time. Have you enlisted as a soldier of the cross of Christ? If so, your feelings do not excuse you from duty. You must be willing to endure hardness as a good soldier. Go without the camp, bearing the reproach, for thus did the Captain of your salvation. The qualifications of a bishop, or of an elder or deacon, are, to be "blameless, as the steward of God; not self-willed, not soon angry, not given to wine, no striker, not given to filthy lucre; but a lover of hospitality, a lover of good men, sober, just, holy, temperate; holding fast the faithful word as he hath been taught, that he may be able by sound doctrine both to exhort and to convince the gainsayers."

Paul enumerates the precious gifts to be desired, and exhorts the brethren: "He that giveth, let him do it with simplicity; he that ruleth, with diligence; he that showeth mercy, with cheerfulness. Let love be without dissimulation. Abhor that which is evil; cleave to that which is good. Be kindly affectioned one to another with brotherly love; in honor preferring one another; not slothful in business; fervent in spirit;

serving the Lord; rejoicing in hope; *patient* in tribulation; continuing instant in prayer; distributing to the necessity of *saints;* given to hospitality." "Charge them that are rich in this world, that they be not high-minded, nor trust in uncertain riches, but in the living God, who giveth us richly all things to enjoy; that they do good, that they be rich in good works, ready to distribute, willing to communicate; laying up in store for themselves a good foundation against the time to come, that they may lay hold on eternal life." Here is a wise and perfectly safe investment; good works are here specified and recommended for our practice, for your practice. Here are profits that are valuable. There will be no danger of a failure here. A treasure may be secured in heaven, a constant accumulation which will give to the investor a title to eternal life. And when his life here shall close, and probation end, he may lay hold on eternal life.

Brother B, you are not a lover of hospitality, you shun burdens. You feel that it is a task to feed the saints and look after their wants, and that all you do in this direction is lost. Please read the above scriptures, and may God give you understanding and discernment, is my earnest prayer. As a family you need to cultivate liberality and to be less self-caring. Love to invite God's people to your house, and, as occasion may require, share with them cheerfully, gladly, that of which the Lord has made you stewards. Do not give grudgingly these little favors. As you do these things to Christ's disciples, you do it unto Him; just so, as you grudge the saints of God your hospitality, you grudge Jesus the same.

The health reform is essential for you both. Sister B has been backward in this good work and has suffered opposition to arise when she knew not what she was opposing. She has resisted the counsel of God against her own soul. Intemperate appetite has brought debility and disease, weakening the moral powers, and unfitting her to appreciate the sacred truth, the value of the atonement, which is essential to salvation. Sister B loves this world. She has not separated, in her affections, from the world, and given herself unreservedly to God, as He requires. He will not accept half a sacrifice. *All, all, all,* is God's, and we are required to render perfect service. Says Paul: "I beseech you therefore, brethren, by the mercies of God, that ye present your bodies a living [not dying] sacrifice, holy, acceptable unto God, which is your reasonable service. And be not conformed to this world but be ye transformed by the renewing of your mind, that ye may prove what is that good, and acceptable, and perfect, will of God." What a privilege is thus allowed us, to prove for ourselves, experimentally, the mind of the Lord and His will toward us. Praise His dear name for this precious gift! I have been shown that Sister B's grasp must be broken from this world before she can have a true, safe hold of the better world.

Brother B, you should move carefully and keep self under; be patient, meek, and lowly. A meek and quiet spirit is in the sight of God of great price. You should cherish that which God esteems of worth. A work must be accomplished for you both before you can meet the measurement of God. Work while the day lasts, for the night cometh in which no man can work. Stand in the clear light yourselves, then can you let your light so shine that others by seeing your good works will be led to glorify your heavenly Father.

Greenville, Michigan, Jan. 23, 1868.

SYMPATHY AT HOME

Dear Brother and Sister C: Your cases have been brought before me in vision. As I viewed your lives, they appeared to be a terrible mistake. Brother C, you have not a happy temperament. And not being happy yourself, you fail to make others happy. You have not cultivated affection, tenderness, and love. Your wife has suffered all through her married life for sympathy. Your married life has been very much like a desert—but very few green spots to look back upon with grateful remembrance. It need not have been thus.

Love can no more exist without revealing itself in outward acts than fire can be kept alive without fuel. You, Brother C, have felt that it was beneath your dignity to manifest tenderness by kindly acts, and to watch for an opportunity to evince affection for your wife by words of tenderness and kind regard. You are changeable in your feelings, and are very much affected by surrounding circumstances. You have not felt that it was wrong, displeasing to God, to allow your mind to be fully engrossed with the world, and then bring your worldly perplexities into your family, thus letting the adversary into your home. It is very easy for you thus to open the door, but you will find it not so easy to close; it will be very difficult to turn out the enemy when once you have brought him in. Leave your business cares and perplexities and annoyances when you leave your business. Come to your family with a cheerful countenance, with sympathy, tenderness, and love. This will be better than expending money for medicines or physicians for your wife. It will be health to the body and strength to the soul. Your lives have been very wretched. You have both acted a part in making them so. God is not pleased with your misery; you have brought it upon yourselves by want of self-control.

You let feelings bear sway. You think it beneath your dignity, Brother C, to manifest love, to speak kindly and affectionately. All these tender words, you think, savor of softness and weakness, and are unnecessary. But in their place come fretful words, words of discord, strife, and censure. Do you account these as manly and noble? as an exhibition of the sterner virtues of your sex? However you may consider them, God looks upon them with displeasure and marks them in His book. Angels flee from the dwelling where words of discord are exchanged, where gratitude is almost a stranger to the heart, and censure leaps like black balls to the lips, spotting the garments, defiling the Christian character.

When you married your wife, she loved you. She was extremely sensitive, yet with painstaking on your part, and fortitude on hers, her health need not have been what it is. But your stern coldness made you like an iceberg, freezing up the channel of love and affection. Your censure and faultfinding has been like desolating hail to a sensitive plant. It has chilled and nearly destroyed the life of the plant. Your love of the world is eating out the good traits of your character. Your wife is of a different turn and more generous. But when she has, even in small matters, exercised her generous instincts, you have felt a drawback in your feelings and have censured her. You indulge a close and grudging spirit. You make your wife feel that she is a tax, a burden, and that she has no right to exercise her generosity at your expense. All these things are of such a discouraging nature that she feels hopeless and helpless, and has not stamina to bear up against it, but bends to the force of the blast. Her disease is pain of the nerves. Were her married life agreeable, she would possess a good degree of health. But all through your married life the demon has been a guest in your family to exult over your misery.

Disappointed hopes have made you both completely wretched. You will have no reward for your suffering, for you have caused it yourselves. Your own words have been like deadly poison upon nerve and brain, upon bone and muscle. You reap that which you sow. You do not appreciate the feelings and sufferings of each other. God is displeased with the hard, unfeeling, world-loving spirit you possess. Brother C, the love of money is the root of all evil. You have loved money, loved the world; you have looked at the illness of your wife as a severe, a terrible, tax, not realizing that it is your fault in a great measure that she is sick. You have not the elements of a contented spirit. You dwell upon your troubles; imaginary want and poverty far ahead stare you in the face; you feel afflicted, distressed, agonized; your brain seems on fire, your spirits depressed. You do not cherish love to God and gratitude of heart for all the blessings which your kind heavenly Father has bestowed upon you. You see only the discomforts of life. A worldly insanity shuts you in like heavy clouds of thick darkness. Satan exults over you because you will have misery when peace and happiness are at your command.

You listen to a discourse, the truth affects you, and the nobler powers of your mind arouse to control your actions. You see how little you have sacrificed for God, how closely self has been cherished, and you are swayed to the right by the influence of the truth; but when you pass from under this sacred, sanctifying, soothing influence, you do not possess it in *your own* heart, and you soon fall into the same barren, ungenial state of feeling. Work, work, you must work; brain, bone, and muscle are taxed to the utmost to get means which your imagination tells you must be obtained, or want and starvation will be your lot. This is a delusion of Satan, one of his wily snares to lead you to perdition. "Sufficient unto the day is the evil thereof." But you make for yourself a time of trouble beforehand.

You have not faith and love and confidence in God. If you had, you would trust in Him. You worry yourself out of the arms of Christ, fearing that He will not care for you. Health is sacrificed. God is not glorified in your body and spirit, which are His. There is not a sweet, cheering home influence to soothe and counteract the evil which is predominant in your nature. The high, noble powers of your mind are overpowered by the lower organs; the evil traits of your character are developed.

You are selfish, exacting, and overbearing. This ought not to be. Your salvation depends on your acting from principle—serving God from principle, not from feeling, not from impulse. God will help you when you feel your need of help and set about the work with resolution, trusting in Him with all your heart. You are often discouraged without sufficient reason. You indulge feelings akin to hatred. Your likes and dislikes are strong. These you must restrain. Control the tongue. "If any man offend not in word, the same is a perfect man, and able also to bridle the whole body." Help has been laid upon One that is mighty. He will be your strength and support, your front guard and rearward.

What preparation are you making for the better life? It is Satan who makes you think that all your powers must be exercised to get along in this world. You are fearing and trembling for the future of this life, while you are neglecting the future, eternal life. Where is the anxiety, the earnestness, the zeal, lest you make a failure there and sustain an immense loss? To lose a little of this world seems to you a terrible calamity which would cost your life. But the thought of losing heaven does not cause half the fears to be manifested. Through your careful efforts to save this life, you are in danger of losing eternal life. You cannot afford to lose heaven, lose eternal life, lose the eternal weight of glory. You cannot afford to lose all these riches, this exceedingly precious, immeasurable happiness. Why do you not act like a sane man, and be as earnest, as zealous, and as persevering in your efforts for the better life, the immortal crown, the eternal, imperishable treasure, as you are for this poor, miserable life and these poor perishable, earthly treasures?

Your heart is on your earthly treasures, therefore you have no heart for the heavenly. These poor things which are seen —the earthly—eclipse the glory of the heavenly. Where your treasure is, there will your heart be also. Your words will declare, your acts will show, where your treasure is. If it is in this world, the little gain of earth, your anxieties will be manifested in that direction. If you are striving for the immortal inheritance with an earnestness, energy, and zeal proportionate to its value, then can you be a fair candidate for everlasting life, and heir of glory. You need a fresh conversion every day. Die daily to self, keep your tongue as with a bridle, control your words, cease your murmurings and complaints, let not one word of censure escape your lips. If this requires a great effort, make it; you will be repaid in so doing.

Your life is now miserable, full of evil forebodings. Gloomy pictures loom up before you; dark unbelief has enclosed you. By talking on the side of unbelief you have grown darker and darker; you take satisfaction in dwelling upon unpleasant themes. If others try to talk hopefully, you crush out in them every hopeful feeling by talking all the more earnestly and severely. Your trials and afflictions are ever keeping before your wife the soul-harrowing thought that you consider her a burden because of her illness. If you love darkness and despair, talk of them, dwell upon them, and harrow up your soul by conjuring up in your imagination everything you can to cause you to murmur against your family and against God, and make your own heart like a field which the fire has passed over, destroying all verdure, and leaving it dry, blackened, and crisped.

You have a diseased imagination and deserve pity. Yet no one can help you as well as yourself. If you want faith, talk faith; talk hopefully, cheerfully. May God help you to see the sinfulness of your course. You need help in this matter, the help of your daughter and your wife. If you suffer Satan to control your thoughts as you have done, you will become a special subject for him to use and will ruin your own soul and the happiness of your family. What a terrible influence has your daughter had! The mother, not receiving love and sympathy from you, has centered her affections upon the daughter and has idolized her. She has been a petted, indulged, and nearly spoiled child through the exercise of injudicious affection. Her education has been sadly neglected. Had she been instructed in household duties, taught to bear her share of the family burdens, she would now be more healthy and happy. It is the duty of every mother to teach her children to act their part in life, to share her burdens, and not be useless machines.

Your daughter's health would have been better had she been educated to physical labor. Her muscles and nerves are weak, lax, and feeble. How can they be otherwise when they have so little use? This child has but little power of endurance. A small amount of physical exercise wearies her and endangers health. There is not elasticity in muscles and nerves. Her physical powers have so long lain dormant that her life is nearly useless. Mistaken mother! know you not that in giving your daughter so many privileges of learning the sciences, and not educating her to usefulness and household labor, you do her a great injury? This exercise would have hardened, or confirmed, her constitution and improved her health. Instead of this tenderness proving a blessing, it will prove a terrible curse. Had the family burdens been shared with the daughter, the mother would not have overdone, and might have saved herself much suffering and benefited the daughter all the time. She should not now commence to labor all at once and bear the burdens which one at her age could bear, but she can educate herself to perform physical labor to a much greater extent than she has ever done in her life.

Sister C has a diseased imagination. She has secluded herself from the air until she cannot endure it without inconvenience. The heat of her room is very injurious to health. Her circulation is depressed. She has lived in the hot air so much that she cannot endure the exposure of a ride out of doors without realizing a change. Her poor health is owing somewhat to the exclusion of air, and she has become so tender that she cannot have air without making her sick. If she continues to indulge this diseased imagination, she will be able to bear scarcely a breath of air. She ought to have the windows lowered in her room all through the day, that there may be a circulation of air. God is not pleased with her for thus murdering herself. It is unnecessary. She has become thus sensitive through indulging a diseased mind. Air she needs, air she must have. She is destroying not only her own vitality, but that of her husband and daughter, and of all who visit her. The air in her room is decidedly impure and dead; none can have health who accustom themselves to such an atmosphere. She has petted herself in this matter until she cannot visit the houses of her brethren without taking cold. For her own sake and for the sake of those around her, she must change this; she should accustom herself to the air, increasing it a little every day, until she can breathe the pure, vitalizing air without injury. The surface of the skin is nearly dead, because it has no air to breathe. Its million little mouths are closed, because they are clogged by the impurities of the system, and for want of air. It would be presumption to let in a free draft of air at once from out of doors, all through the day. Let it in by degrees; change gradually. In a week she can have the windows down two or three inches day and night.

Lungs and liver are diseased because she deprives herself of vital air. Air is the free blessing of heaven, calculated to electrify the whole system. Without it the system will be filled with disease and become dormant, languid, feeble. Yet you have all been for years living with a very limited amount of air. In thus doing, your wife drags others into the same poisonous atmosphere with herself. None of you can possess clear, unclouded brains while breathing a poisonous atmosphere. Sister C dreads to stir out to go anywhere because she must feel the change in the atmosphere and take cold. She can yet be brought into a much better condition of health if she rightly treats herself. Twice a week she should take a general bath, as cool as will be agreeable, a little cooler every time, until the skin is toned up.

She need not linger along as she does, always sick, if you will all as a family heed the instructions given of the Lord. "He that will love life, and see good days, let him refrain his tongue from evil, and his lips that they speak no guile: let him eschew evil, and do good, let him seek peace, and ensue it. For the eyes of the Lord are over the righteous, and His ears are open unto their prayers: but the face of the Lord is against them that do evil." A contented mind, a cheerful spirit, is health to the body and strength to the soul. Nothing is so fruitful a cause of disease as depression, gloominess, and sadness. Mental depression is terrible. You all suffer from it. The daughter is fretful, partaking of the spirit of the father; and then the heated, oppressed atmosphere, deprived of vitality, benumbs the sensitive brain. The lungs contract, the liver is inactive.

Air, air, the precious boon of heaven which all may have, will bless you with its invigorating influence if you will not refuse it entrance. Welcome it, cultivate a love for it, and it will prove a precious soother of the nerves. Air must be in constant circulation to be kept pure. The influence of pure, fresh air is to cause the blood to circulate healthfully through the system. It refreshes the body and tends to render it strong and healthy, while at the same time its influence is decidedly felt upon the mind, imparting a degree of composure and serenity. It excites the appetite, and renders the digestion of food more perfect, and induces sound and sweet sleep.

The effects produced by living in close, ill-ventilated rooms are these: The system becomes weak and unhealthy, the circulation is depressed, the blood moves sluggishly through the system because it is not purified and vitalized by the pure, invigorating air of heaven. The mind becomes depressed and gloomy, while the whole system is enervated; and fevers and other acute diseases are liable to be generated. Your careful exclusion of external air and fear of free ventilation leave you to breathe the corrupt, unwholesome air which is exhaled from the lungs of those staying in these rooms, and which is poisonous, unfit for the support of life. The body becomes relaxed, the skin becomes sallow, digestion is retarded, and the system is peculiarly sensitive to the influence of cold. A slight exposure produces serious diseases. Great care should be exercised not to sit in a draft or in a cold room when weary, or when in a perspiration. You should so accustom yourself to the air that you will not be under the necessity of having the mercury higher than sixty-five degrees.

You can be a happy family if you will do what God has given you to do and has enjoined upon you as a duty. But the Lord will not do for you that which He has left for you to do. Brother C deserves pity. He has so long felt unhappy that life has become a burden to him. It need not be thus. His imagination is diseased, and he has so long kept his eyes on the dark picture that if he meets with adversity or disappointment, he imagines that everything is going to ruin, that he will come to want, that everything is against him, that he has the hardest time of anyone; and thus his life is made wretched. The more he thinks thus, the more miserable he makes his life and the lives of all around him. He has no reason to feel as he does; it is all the work of Satan. He must not suffer the enemy thus to control his mind. He should turn away from the dark and gloomy picture to that of the loving Saviour, the glory of heaven, and the rich inheritance prepared for all who are humble and obedient, and who possess grateful hearts and abiding faith in the promises of God. This will cost him an effort, a struggle; but it must be done.

Your present happiness and your future, eternal happiness depend upon your fixing your mind upon cheerful things, looking away from the dark picture, which is imaginary, to the benefits which God has strewn in your pathway, and beyond these, to the unseen and eternal.

You belong to a family who possess minds not well balanced, gloomy and depressed, affected by surroundings, and susceptible to influences. Unless you cultivate a cheerful, happy, grateful frame of mind, Satan will eventually lead you captive at his will. You can be a help, a strength to the church where you reside, if you will obey the instructions of the Lord and not move by feeling, but be controlled by principle. Never allow censure to escape your lips, for it is like desolating hail to those around you. Let cheerful, happy, loving words fall from your lips.

Brother C, your organism is not the best for your spiritual advancement, yet the grace of God can do much to correct the defects in your character and strengthen and more perfectly develop those powers of mind which are now weak and need force. In so doing you will bring into control those lower qualities which have overpowered the higher. You are like a man whose sensibilities are benumbed. You need to have the truth take hold of you and work a thorough reformation in your life. "Be not conformed to this world: but be ye transformed by the renewing of your mind, that ye may prove what is that good, and acceptable, and perfect, will of God." This is what you need, and what you must experience—the transformation which a sanctification through the truth will effect for you.

Do you believe that the end of all things is at hand, that the scenes of this earth's history are fast closing? If so, show your faith by your works. A man will show all the faith he has. Some think they have a good degree of faith, when if they have any, it is dead, for it is not sustained by works.

"Faith if it hath not works, is dead, being alone." Few have that genuine faith which works by love and purifies the soul. But all who are accounted worthy of everlasting life must obtain a moral fitness for the same. "Beloved, now are we the sons of God, and it doth not yet appear what we shall be: but we know that, when He shall appear, we shall be like Him; for we shall see Him as He is. And every man that hath this hope in Him purifieth himself, even as He is pure." This is the work before you, and you have none too much time if you engage in the work with all your soul.

You must experience a death to self, and must live unto God. "If ye then be risen with Christ, seek those things which are above, where Christ sitteth on the right hand of God." Self is not to be consulted. Pride, self-love, selfishness, avarice, covetousness, love of the world, hatred, suspicion, jealousy, evil surmisings, must all be subdued and sacrificed forever. When Christ shall appear, it will not be to correct these evils and then give a moral fitness for His coming. This preparation must all be made before He comes. It should be a subject of thought, of study, and earnest inquiry, What shall we do to be saved? What shall be our conduct that we may show ourselves approved unto God?

When tempted to murmur, censure, and indulge in fretfulness, wounding those around you, and in so doing wounding your own soul, oh! let the deep, earnest, anxious inquiry come from your soul, Shall I stand without fault before the throne of God? Only the faultless will be there. None will be translated to heaven while their hearts are filled with the rubbish of earth. Every defect in the moral character must first be remedied, every stain removed by the cleansing blood of Christ, and all the unlovely, unlovable traits of character overcome.

How long a time are you designing to take to prepare to

be introduced into the society of heavenly angels in glory? In the state which you and your family are in at present, all heaven would be marred should you be introduced therein. The work for you must be done here. This earth is the fitting-up place. You have not one moment to lose. All is harmony, peace, and love in heaven. No discord, no strife, no censuring, no unloving words, no clouded brows, no jars there; and no one will be introduced there who possesses any of these elements so destructive to peace and happiness. Study to be rich in good works, ready to distribute, willing to communicate, laying up for yourselves a good foundation against the time to come, that you may lay hold on everlasting life.

Forever cease your murmurings in regard to this poor life, but let your soul's burden be, how to secure the better life than this, a title to the mansions prepared for those who are true and faithful to the end. If you make a mistake here, everything is lost. If you devote your lifetime to securing earthly treasures, and lose the heavenly, you will find that you have made a terrible mistake. You cannot have both worlds. "What shall it profit a man, if he shall gain the whole world, and lose his own soul? Or what shall a man give in exchange for his soul?" Says the inspired Paul: "For our light affliction, which is but for a moment, worketh for us a far more exceeding and eternal weight of glory; while we look not at the things which are seen, but at the things which are not seen: for the things which are seen are temporal; but the things which are not seen are eternal."

These trials of life are God's workmen to remove the impurities, infirmities, and roughness from our characters, and fit us for the society of pure, heavenly angels in glory. But as we pass through these trials, as the fires of affliction kindle upon us, we must not keep the eye on the fire which is seen, but let the eye of faith fasten upon the things unseen, the eternal inheritance, the immortal life, the eternal weight of glory; and while we do this the fire will not consume us, but only remove the dross, and we shall come forth seven times purified, bearing the impress of the Divine.

Greenville, Michigan, March 7, 1868.

THE HUSBAND'S POSITION

Dear Brother and Sister D: While speaking in meeting Sunday afternoon, I could scarcely refrain from calling your names and relating some things which had been shown me. I saw that Brother D did not occupy that position in his family which God would have him. Sister D takes the lead; she possesses a strong will, which has not been subdued as God requires; and in order to please his wife and keep her from despondency, Brother D has yielded to her. Her judgment has swayed him, and he has not been a free man for years.

When Brother D first engaged in the work of teaching the truth, he was little in his own eyes, and God used him as His instrument. But I saw that for some time in the past he has not humbled himself under the hand of God. He has trusted to his own wisdom and weak judgment, and Satan has been obtaining an advantage over him. Instead of relying solely upon God, and staying himself upon His strength, he has had his judgment perverted by the influence of his wife. She has stood in a position to see, to hear, to understand, all that was going on around her. Did she possess a sanctified judgment and heavenly wisdom, then would she see through sanctified eyes, and hear through sanctified ears. She would make a right use of her eyes and ears. She has not done this. "Who is blind, but My servant? or deaf, as My messenger that I sent?" God does not wish us to hear all that is to be heard, or to see all that is to be seen. It is a great blessing to close the ears, that we hear not, and the eyes, that we see not. The greatest anxiety should be to have clear eyesight to discern our own shortcomings, and a quick ear to catch all needed reproof and instruction, lest by our inattention and carelessness we let them slip and become forgetful hearers and not doers of the work.

Brother D, for some time in the past your labors have not been as wisely and successfully directed as formerly. Your course of action has not borne the impress of God. Your wife has managed your temporal matters and borne burdens which were too heavy for her to bear, while you have been absent. This has excited your sympathy, and had a tendency to pervert your judgment, so that you have placed too high an estimate upon her qualifications because of her capability in managing your temporal matters. Satan has been watching his opportunity to make as much as possible to his own advantage of your confidence in your wife. He has purposed to trammel you and destroy you both. You have to a great degree thrown off your stewardship upon your wife. This is wrong; she will have all she can do to bear her share of the responsibility, without bearing that which comes upon you and for which God will hold you accountable.

Sister D has been deceived in some things. She has thought that God instructed her in a special sense, and you both have believed and acted accordingly. The discernment which she has thought she possessed in a *special* sense, is a deception of the enemy. She is naturally quick to see, quick to understand, quick to anticipate, and is of an extremely sensitive nature. Satan has taken advantage of these traits of character and has led you both astray. Brother D, you have been a bondman for quite a length of time. Much of that which Sister D has thought was discernment has been jealousy. She has been disposed to regard everything with a jealous eye, to be suspicious, surmising evil, distrustful of almost everything. This causes unhappiness of mind, despondency, and doubt, where faith and confidence should exist. These unhappy traits of character turn her thoughts into a gloomy channel, where she indulges a foreboding of evil, while a highly sensitive temperament leads her to imagine neglect, slight, and injury, when it does not exist. All these things stand in the way of the spiritual advancement of you both, and affect others to just that extent that you are connected with the cause and work of God. There is a work for you to do: Humble yourselves under the mighty hand of God, that you may be exalted in due time. These unhappy traits of character, with a strong, set will, must be corrected and reformed, or they will eventually cause you both to make shipwreck of your faith.

Brother D, you have a duty to do. Assume the stewardship you have resigned, and in the fear of God take your place at the head of your family. You must be shaken from the influence of your wife, and rely more fully upon God, and look to Him to lead you and guide you. God has not specially instructed Sister D, or given her light to teach others their duty. Neither you nor your wife can occupy the position God would have you, while things remain as they now are. You will never be established, strengthened, and settled until you allow your wife to take the position a wife should. While she occupies her proper place, respect her judgment, consult with her in regard to your plans, but be very cautious about taking it for granted that her judgment is as the judgment of God. Consult with your brethren upon whom God has seen fit to lay the burden of the work. Had you thus advised with those whose counsel you should have sought, you would not have committed so great an error, so sad a blunder, as you did in the case of E. God's cause was wounded and reproached in this case. Your wife thought she had light in this case; but her impressions were not of God, but of the enemy, because he saw that you could be affected in this direction. Your trusting so completely to your wife's judgment is contrary to heaven's arrangement. Satan has designed in this way to cut you off, in a great measure, from the influence of your fellow laborers and your brethren in general.

You have had trials that you would not have had if you had not considered your wife in a position where God has not placed her. You have too implicit confidence in her judgment and wisdom. She has not been consecrated to God, therefore her judgment has not been consecrated. She is not a happy woman, and the unhappy train her mind has taken has greatly injured her physical and mental health. Satan has designed to unsettle you and cause your brethren to lose confidence in your judgment. Satan is seeking to overthrow you. When God specially calls your wife to the work of teaching the truth, then should you lean to her counsel and advice, and confide in her instructions. God may give you both, as possessing an equal interest in and devotion to the work, equal qualifications to act a prominent part in the most solemn work of saving souls. The great work before her is to be diligent in making her calling and election sure, to cease watching others, and now begin the work to be very jealous of herself. She should seek to bless others by her godly example, her cheerfulness, fortitude, courage, faith, hopefulness, joy, in that perfect trust, that confidence in God, which will be the result of sanctification through the truth. An entire conformity to the will of God she must have. Christ says to her: "Thou shalt love the Lord thy God with all thy heart, and with all thy soul, and with all thy mind. This is the first and great commandment. And the second is like unto it, Thou shalt love thy neighbor as thyself. On these two commandments hang all the law and the prophets."

The above was written at Mount Pleasant, Iowa, October 4, 1867. I could not find time to finish the testimony and copy it, so laid it by, and did not have time to finish it until I returned from the East to Greenville, Michigan, when I took it in hand, January 30, 1868.

Dear Brother and Sister D: You should have had this long ago, but our labors have been so hard that I could not possibly get the time to write. Every place that we visited brought before my mind much that I had been shown of individual cases, and I have written in meeting, even while my husband was preaching.

The vision was given me about two years ago. The enemy has hindered me in every way he could to keep souls from having the light which God had given me for them. First, my husband's case was so perplexing, so distressing, that I could not write. Then the discouragements brought upon me by my brethren kept me in a condition of sadness and distress, unfitting me for labor of any description. When we started to travel last summer, I commenced to write, but we have traveled from place to place so rapidly that all we could do was to attend the meetings. There was much work to be done. I practice rising at four o'clock in the morning, to take hold of my writing. Yet constant, exciting labor in meeting so taxes the brain that I am unprepared for writing, my head is so weary.

I regret that you could not have had this before, but even now may God make it a blessing to you, is my sincere prayer. You, my dear brother, may have seen these things and corrected them ere this. I hope so, at least. You and also your wife have our sympathy and prayers. We have an interest for her as well as for yourself. Her soul is precious. We beseech her in Christ's stead to seek for a meek and quiet spirit, which in the sight of God is of great price. An angel pointed me to Sister D and repeated these words: "Whatsoever things are true, whatsoever things are honest, whatsoever things are just, whatsoever things are pure, whatsoever things are lovely, whatsoever things are of good report; if there be any virtue, and if there be any praise, think on THESE THINGS." Here is the healthful train of thought for the mind to follow. When it would go in a different channel, bring it back. Control the mind. Educate it to dwell only on those things which bring peace and love.

I commit this to you, hoping and praying that God may bless it to you, and that you both may obtain a fitness to be counted worthy of eternal life.

DATES OF FIRST PUBLICATION

All the *Testimonies for the Church* in this volume were first published in Battle Creek appearing in the following years: No. 1, 1855; No. 2, 1856; No. 3, 1857; No. 4, 1857; No. 5, 1859; No.6, 1861; No. 7, 1862; No. 8, 1862; No. 9, 1863; No. 10, 1864; No. 11, 1867; No. 12, 1867; No. 13, 1867; No. 14, 1868.

APPENDIX

As an aid to an understanding of the circumstances which led to the giving of certain testimonies, the following notes have been prepared by the Trustees of the Ellen G. White Publications.

Page 116, "Time to Begin the Sabbath"—For a period of about ten years Sabbathkeeping Adventists observed the Sabbath from 6 p. m. Friday to 6 p. m. Saturday. Elder Joseph Bates in his first pamphlet on the perpetuity of the Sabbath of the fourth commandment, published in 1846, had given reasons for the supposed Scriptural support for the observance of the Sabbath in this way. He cited the parable of the laborers in the vineyard, the last group of which had been called at "the eleventh hour" of the day and had wrought but one hour. The reckoning was made with them "when *even* was come." Matthew 20:6, 8, 12. Comparing this with Christ's question, "Are there not twelve hours in the day?" he argued that the "even" began with the twelfth hour, or six o'clock, reckoning with equatorial time or the beginning of the sacred year. Respect for his years and experience and his godly life may have been the main reasons for accepting his conclusions without further investigation.

As time passed and the message spread, an increasing number of Sabbathkeepers questioned the practice and advocated the sunset time for reckoning the beginning of the Sabbath. A thorough Bible investigation of the question was made by Elder J. N. Andrews, who wrote a paper setting forth the Biblical reasons in favor of the sunset time. This paper was introduced and discussed on Sabbath, November 17, 1855, at the Conference in Battle Creek, Michigan, with the result that nearly, but not quite, all present were convinced that Elder Andrew' s conclusion was correct. The presentation of the subject to Mrs. White in this vision, given two days later, answered the questions lingering in some minds and effected unity among the believers. Commenting on this experience, as illustrating the office of the visions to confirm conclusions based on Biblical study rather than to introduce new teachings, Elder James White wrote later:

"The question naturally arises, If the visions are given to correct the erring, why did she not sooner see the error of the six o'clock time? I have ever been thankful that God corrected the error in His own good time, and did not suffer an unhappy division to exist among us upon the point. But, dear reader, the work of the Lord upon this point is in perfect harmony with His manifestations to us on others, and in harmony with the correct position upon spiritual gifts. It does not appear to be the desire of the Lord to teach His people by the gifts of the Spirit on the Bible questions until His servants have diligently searched His word. When this was done upon the subject of the time to commence the Sabbath, and most were established, and some were in danger of being out of harmony with the body on this subject, then, yes, *then,* was the very time for God to magnify His goodness in the manifestation of the gift of His Spirit in the accomplishment of its proper work."—*Review and Herald,* Feb. 25, 1868.

Pages 116, 117, 122, 123, "The *Messenger* Party"—In the summer of 1854 there appeared among the Sabbathkeeping Adventists the first disaffection, or apostasy. Two men who had been preaching the message were reproved through the spirit of prophecy for a harsh, censorious spirit, for avarice, and for extravagance in the use of means placed in their hands. Becoming embittered instead of repentant, they joined with a few others in unjust recrimination against Elder and Mrs. White and other leaders, making false charges against them. Although continuing to advocate the Sabbath truth, they began the publication of a slanderous sheet which they called the *Messenger of Truth*.

They were joined by Elders Stephenson and Hall of Wisconsin. These men had been first-day Adventist preachers, who professed to accept the truths of the third angel's message, but who continued to hold doctrines regarding the Age-to-Come. According to this theory there was to be, during the millennium, a "second chance" for salvation. They agreed, however, to preach the message, without advocating this question, if the *Review* would not publish articles against it. However, as indicated in the text, they did not keep their promise and were soon opposing the *Review* and its supporters.

The course of these "opposers of the truth" was soon run. Both Stephenson and Hall lost their reason. The *Messenger of Truth* ceased publication in 1857, and early in 1858 Elder White reported regarding the party: "Not one of the eighteen messengers of which they once boasted as being with them is now bearing a public testimony, and not one place of regular meeting of our knowledge among them." —*Review and Herald,* Jan. 14, 1858.

Page 190, Systematic Benevolence—In the early days of the message, men impelled by the urge of conviction went forth to preach the new-found truths. They were dependent for their support upon their own labors or the freewill offerings of the believers. Such an uncertain method was more or less spasmodic and fluctuating. Early in 1859 the need for a more certain plan was felt, and earnest study was given to the matter. There grew out of this study the plan called Systematic Benevolence. In harmony with 1 Corinthians 16:2 giving regularly on the first day of the week was recommended, and, as suggested by 2 Corinthians 8:12-14, an equitable distribution of financial responsibility. The plan called for brethren to lay by in store weekly from five to twenty-five cents; the sisters, from two to ten cents; and for property owners to give weekly from one to five cents on each hundred dollars worth of assets.

The plan was generally received with favor, and here received the endorsement of the spirit of prophecy. The greatest sin in the church was pointed out to be covetousness. (Page 194.) Systematic Benevolence was not presented as a perfected plan, for it was also stated that "God *is leading* His people" in the matter, and *"is bringing"* them up. (Page 191.) As plans for support of the work and the ministry broadened, the spirit of liberality was encouraged more and more until at length light from the Scriptures revealed the system of tithes and offerings as they are known in the church today.

Page 210, Organization—Up to the year 1860 there had been no legal or church organization among the Sabbathkeeping Adventists. They had not even adopted a name. They spoke of themselves as the "Scattered Flock," the "Little Remnant," or some variation of such expressions. Now Elder White had announced through the *Review* that he must refuse to continue to assume *personal* responsibility for money lent to the Review and Herald office. He further expressed the hope that the time might soon come when "this people will be in that position necessary to be able to get church property insured, hold their meeting houses in a proper manner, that those persons making their wills, and wishing to do so, can appropriate a portion to the publishing department." He called upon his brethren to make suggestions as to how this desire might be effected so that "we as a people" might act to secure the above advantages.

Among the first responses to this request was one from the Brother B referred to in this connection, in which he expressed his conviction that it would be wrong to incorporate as a religious body according to law. This he held would be "making us a name," as was the purpose of the builders of the tower of Babel, and would "lie at the foundation of Babylon." As for insuring the meeting houses, were they not the Lord's property, and could He not take care of His own without the aid of insurance companies? Further, said he, those who lend money to the office should not insist on having a note signed by a legal corporation, for "they lend it to the Lord, and they must trust the Lord for it." —*Review and Herald,* Feb. 23, Mar. 22, 1860.

After much discussion the misgivings regarding the propriety of legally organizing the publishing office were largely overcome, and at a conference held in September, 1860, the Advent Review Publishing Association was formed. A few months later the name was changed to the Seventh-day Adventist Publishing Association. Even after this step there still remained with some a reluctance to enter into church organization, and the subject continued to be discussed. However, with the large majority favoring organization, the movement proceeded, first by the organization of churches, then of state conferences, and, finally in 1863, of the General Conference.

The testimony on "Organization" (pages 270-272) speaks of the opposition that was encountered in New York State to this move and of the vision given regarding it.

Page 292—The magicians did not really cause their rods to become serpents; but by magic, aided by the great deceiver, they were able to produce this appearance. It was beyond the power of Satan to change the rods to living serpents. The prince of evil, though possessing all the wisdom and might of an angel fallen, has not power to create or to give life; this is the prerogative of God alone. But all that was in Satan's power to do he did; he produced a counterfeit. To human sight the rods were changed to serpents. Such they were believed to be by Pharaoh and his court. There was nothing in their appearance to distinguish them from the serpent produced by Moses and Aaron. Thus the testimony speaks of it in the language of the Scriptures; while the same Spirit explains that the Scriptures speak of it as the case appeared. See *Testimony* No. 33, vol. 5, pp. 696-698.

Page 355, "The Rebellion" —At the time that this testimony was written, early in 1863, Seventh-day Adventists were faced with a serious problem. The nation was at war. Although at heart noncombatants, the sympathies of the church members were, almost without exception, entirely with the Government in its opposition to slavery. As the conflict progressed, more and more men were called to the army. At each call every district was under obligation to furnish a certain number of recruits, and when the voluntary enlistments fell below that number, names were drawn to make up the lack. For a time it was possible by the payment of money to buy a substitute and thus release one whose name had been drawn. As there was no provision made for assigning Seventh-day Adventists to noncombatant service, and no allowance for Sabbath observance, Sabbathkeepers, when drafted, usually in this way purchased their exemption. If the individual was unable to raise the money himself, he was helped by a fund raised for that purpose.

Now, as more men were needed, and a national conscription law without such exemption privileges was impending, our brethren were in perplexity regarding their response to such a draft, where they might be compelled to take up arms or to work on the Sabbath.

A few months prior to the appearance of this testimony, Elder White had published an editorial in the *Review and Herald* entitled "The Nation," to which reference is made on page 356. He believed the Government to be the best on earth and fighting for a righteous cause. His best counsel at that time was that in the event of drafting "it would be madness to resist," and added:

"He who would resist until, in the administration of military law, he was shot down, goes too far, we think, in taking the responsibility of suicide."—*Review and Herald,* Aug. 12, 1862.

The nature of some of the correspondence that followed this article, as pointed out by Mrs. White, had been such as to lead Elder White to protest against a virtual charge of "Sabbathbreaking and murder" which had been brought against him. Such extremists were reproved by Mrs. White on the one hand, and on the other hand a note of warning was sounded to those who were inclined to enlist.

In July, 1864, the national conscription law was so amended as to revoke the $300 exemption clause. Steps were immediately taken to secure for the Seventh-day Adventist young men the privileges granted to members of religious denominations who were conscientiously opposed to bearing arms—of being assigned to noncombatant service in hospital duty or in caring for freed men. Before a serious crisis was reached, these efforts were successful. In a few cases Seventh-day Adventist young men were drafted into the army and were assigned to hospital work or other noncombatant service. Whatever their assignment, they tried to let their light shine. Regularly for several months there ran through the columns of the *Review and Herald* a listing of receipts for a Soldier's Tract Fund to furnish literature for distribution among the men.

The experiences of Seventh-day Adventists in connection with the Civil War led them to take steps that secured for them a recognized status as noncombatants, which at the same time enabled them to follow the Scriptural injunctions regarding their relationships to "the powers that be," which are "ordained of God."

Pages 421, 456, Dress Reform—The dresses generally worn by women in America at the time this was written (1863, 1867), were very deleterious to health. They were especially objectionable because of their extreme length, the constriction of the waist by the corset, and the weight of the heavy skirts which were suspended from the hips. About a decade earlier a few women of national prominence initiated a movement to adopt a new style of dress that would be free from these serious objections. The new mode of dress was somewhat like the Turkish costume worn by men and women alike. The movement became so popular that for a time "dress reform" conventions were held annually.

"The American costume," here referred to by Mrs. White, was a modification of the earlier style and was sponsored by Dr. Harriet Austin of Dansville, New York. It combined the short skirt, "reaching about halfway from the hip to the knee," with mannish-looking trousers, coat, and vest. See description on page 465. This "so-called reformed dress" was in 1864 shown to Mrs. White to be unsuitable for adoption by God's people.

In 1865 Mrs. White, through *How to Live,* No. 6, appealed to our sisters to adopt a style of dress which was both modest and healthful. The next year the newly opened Health Reform Institute in Battle Creek took steps to design a pattern of dress that would correct the extremes of the short American costume or the ultra-long heavy dresses as commonly worn.

In 1867 *Testimony* No. 11 appeared with its first article, "Reform in Dress." See pages 456-466. In this the dress question was fully reviewed and further counsel given. A general pattern was recommended as embodying the principles revealed to Mrs. White, and was referred to as "worthy of the name of the reform short dress." No particular pattern was revealed to her in vision, and, when discussing the matter at a later date, Mrs. White stated:

"Some have supposed that the very pattern given was the pattern that all were to adopt. This is not so. But something as simple as this would be the best we could adopt under the circumstances. No one precise style has been given me as the exact rule to guide all in their dress."—E. G. White Letter 19, 1897. Quoted in *The Story of Our Health Message*, page 145.

As the years passed, the prevailing styles of women's dress changed for the better, becoming more sensible and healthful. The old health reform dress in its exact pattern was no longer urged, but there was ever a uniform testimony borne by Mrs. White regarding the fundamental principles that should guide the Christian in this matter. Thus in 1897 she wrote:

"Let our sisters dress plainly, as many do, having the dress of good material, durable, modest, appropriate for this age, and let not the dress question fill the mind."—*Ibid.*, page 146.

Page 525—For further explanation of the subject of dress the reader is referred to *Testimonies for the Church*, vol. 4, No. 30, article, "Simplicity in Dress."

Page 689—Since the organization of tract societies in many states, the furnishing of books and tracts to the worthy poor has been assumed by them. Some of the works here mentioned are now out of print.

THE TRUSTEES OF THE
ELLEN G. WHITE PUBLICATIONS

SCRIPTURAL INDEX

Malachi

Matthew

Mark

Luke

John

Acts

Romans

1 Corinthians

2 Corinthians

Galatians

Ephesians

Philippians

Colossians

1 Thessalonians

2 Thessalonians

1 Timothy

2 Timothy

Titus

Hebrews

James

1 Peter

2 Peter

1 John

Jude

Revelation

GENERAL INDEX